Assessment and Instruction of Reading and Writing Disability

Assessment and Instruction of Reading and Writing Disability

AN INTERACTIVE APPROACH
Second Edition

Marjorie Y. Lipson
The University of Vermont, Burlington

Karen K. Wixson
The University of Michigan, Ann Arbor

 LONGMAN

An imprint of Addison Wesley Longman, Inc.

New York • Reading, Massachusetts • Menlo Park, California • Harlow, England
Don Mills, Ontario • Sydney • Mexico City • Madrid • Amsterdam

Editor in Chief: Priscilla McGeehon
Cover Designer: Mary McDonnell
Electronic Production Manager: Angel Gonzalez Jr.
Project Coordination and Text Design: Ruttle Graphics, Inc.
Manufacturing Manager: Willie Lane
Electronic Page Makeup: Ruttle Graphics, Inc.
Printer and Binder: R. R. Donnelley & Sons Company
Cover Printer: Phoenix Color Corp.

Library of Congress Cataloging-in-Publication Data

Lipson, Marjorie Y.
    Assessment and instruction of reading and writing disability : an interactive
approach / Marjorie Y. Lipson, Karen K. Wixson. — 2nd ed.
        p.   cm.
    Includes bibliographical references (p.) and index.
    ISBN 0–673–99057–5
    1. Reading disability. 2. Reading—Ability testing. 3. Reading
comprehension. 4. Reading—Remedial teaching. I. Wixson, Karen K.
II. Title.
LB1050.5.L54 1996
428'.42—dc20
                                                                        96–19727
                                                                        CIP

ISBN 0–673–99057–5

2345678910—DOC—999897

To Vernon Youmans, who taught me to be inquisitive and to work hard.
Without these gifts, I could not have finished this book.
                                        –M.Y.L

and

To the memory of Susanne Baker, who was both my student and my teacher.
                                        –K.K.W.

Brief Table
of Contents

Table of Contents

SECTION IV Instruction   473

CHAPTER 12 Getting Started in Instruction   475

CHAPTER 13 Adapting Instruction to Focus on Word Recognition and Spelling   514

Preface

This text, like the earlier edition, is based on an interactive view of ability and disability. In the first edition of this text, we focused primarily on reading and dealt with writing as a means of enhancing reading performance. Since we first planned and wrote this text, the field has changed rapidly in its treatment of reading and writing. The cognitive movement of the 1980s made it easier for us to see the obvious relations between reading and writing processes that had been obscured by the previous emphasis on discrete skills. Now, the social movement of the 1990s has allowed us to understand the necessity of considering reading and writing together as integral dimensions of literacy.

There are still many obstacles to considering reading and writing together in a variety of educational contexts. For example, the primary professional organizations concerned with reading and writing education are still divided predominantly along elementary/reading versus secondary/writing lines. Although both the International Reading Association (IRA) and the National Council of Teachers of English (NCTE) deal with both reading and writing across the full spectrum of developmental levels, the primary areas of emphasis within each of these organizations remain clear.

These differences are further reinforced by the way we prepare teachers. Rarely is there any coordination between programs designed to prepare elementary teachers with a language arts emphasis and secondary English Education majors. Neither is it uncommon for districts to have separate coordinators for Reading/Language Arts and English/Composition. In addition, these two areas are often treated separately at national and state levels for the purposes of developing curriculum frameworks and assessments (for example, National Assessment of Educational Progress). Although there is a current effort to develop national standards in English language arts, this process has been fraught with many problems precisely because of the separatist tradition that has dominated educational practice for so long.

All of this is the long way of describing the difficulties of dealing with reading and writing in a text of this nature. Nevertheless, we have attempted in this edition to deal with reading and writing on a more equal plane than was intended in the first edition. The result is a reflection of the state of these efforts in the field — uneven. In some places we have succeeded in dealing with reading and writing equally within a given context. In others, there are still separations that reflect the current status of thinking in this area.

We continue to feel that the interactive view of reading and writing offers a productive alternative to the deficit view that continues to predominate in textbooks on reading and writing disability. Deficit models suggest that the cause of reading or writing difficulties lies entirely within the reader. Instructional programs based on a deficit model focus primarily on what Sarason and Doris (1979) call the "search for pathology" within the reader. In contrast, an interactive view suggests that reading or writing disability is a relative concept — not a static state — and that the problem often lies in the match between the learner and the conditions of the learning situation.

Consistent with an interactive perspective, this text focuses on the process of evaluating the existing match and identifying an optimal match between the learner and the instructional context. The content of this text also reflects our belief that the most important factor in effective assessment and instruction is the knowledge base of the teacher. Features of this text include both understanding and application sections devoted to each topic of discussion, a section on using relevant information to build a diagnostic portfolio, detailed chapter summaries, an extensive bibliography, detailed case studies, and numerous examples of how to implement informal assessment and instructional procedures.

Section I, Theory into Practice, contains three chapters that provide the knowledge base for using the remainder of the text. In Chapter 1, Perspectives on Reading and Writing Ability, we describe a historical and several theoretical views of reading and writing. We also discuss the legal and political perspectives on reading and writing disability. Chapter 2, An Interactive View of Reading and Writing, details an interactive view of reading and writing, providing a detailed picture of the various elements of skilled performance and the factors that influence it. In Chapter 3, Reading and Writing Disability and the Assessment-Instruction Process, we provide an overview of the assessment-instruction process that is used to guide the remainder of the text and provide a case study example.

The remaining chapters are organized in a manner that parallels the assessment-instruction process described in Chapter 3. Section II, Evaluating the Instructional Context, contains three sections, one on Getting Started with Assessment (Chapter 4); one on Evaluating the Reading/Writing Context (Chapters 5 and 6); and one on Evaluating the Learner (Chapters 7, 8, 9, and 10). Chapter 4, Getting Started with Assessment, provides guidelines for gathering initial information. Chapter 5, Instructional Settings and Resources, is the first of the two chapters related to evaluating context factors. It considers how the overall classroom setting and instructional resources (including texts) may influence reading and writing performance and provides tools for evaluating these aspects of the context. Chapter 6, Instructional Approaches and Tasks, describes how reading and writing performance can be affected by these factors and provides additional tools and strategies for assessing the context.

The next four chapters are focused on assessing the learner. Chapter 7, The Foundations of Literacy, is devoted to an understanding of emergent literacy concepts and the assessment of young learners. Chapter 8, Informal Classroom-Based Assessment, focuses on informal, continuous methods of assessing word recognition, comprehension, and writing. Chapter 9, Structured Inventories and Assessments, provides an in-depth discussion of issues and practices in using informal reading inventories (IRIs) and other more systematic assessment tools. Finally, Chapter 10, Formal Assessment, addresses the understanding of important statistical concepts and provides a detailed description of the characteristics and types of tests commonly associated with assessment in reading and writing .

Section III, Interactions, consists of single chapter, Chapter 11, Interactive Decision Making, emphasizing the juncture where assessment and instruction come together. The steps in the assessment-instruction process that involve evaluating the match between the learner and the context, reflecting and generating hypotheses about the source of interference with learning, and identifying an optimal instructional match are all described.

Section IV, Instruction, contains two sections. The first, Getting Started in Instruction (Chapter 12), describes "high utility" instructional strategies and provides a rationale for making decisions about the instructional issues and techniques. The other section, Adaptations (Chapters 13, 14, and 15), provides support to teachers as they plan and refine their instructional program to focus on the specific areas of word recognition and spelling (Chapter 13), vocabulary (Chapter 14), and comprehension and composition (Chapter 15).

The final section and chapter of the text, Section V and Chapter 16, both entitled Professional Roles and Responsibilities, place teachers and students in a broader context. This chapter provides techniques and frameworks for reporting information to others and addresses many of the ethical and legal responsibilities of reading professionals.

In closing, we would like to acknowledge our appreciation to the many people who provided advice, encouragement, and assistance in the development of this text. We gratefully acknowledge the special assistance provided us by Kathy Hric and Susan Sortino. Special thanks are extended to Molly McClasky for providing an inspiring teaching model and the entire teaching staff at Essex Elementary School for their professional commitment to literacy development. We also thank Kyle and his parents for allowing us to share in the excitement of learning to read. Thanks are also due to Chris Jennison, whose patience and bad poetry provided both the support and the impetus to complete this revision. Finally, we would like to acknowledge the special contribution of the students in our graduate and undergraduate courses who offered us feedback and ideas based on the original text.

We have been grateful to the many individuals who have communicated with us about the original text and hope that this revision keeps the dialogue alive. We look forward to our readers' response to the challenges presented in this text.

Marjorie Y. Lipson
Karen K. Wixson

Theory into Practice

PERSPECTIVES

IN THE FIRST SECTION of this book we provide a theoretical foundation and rationale for the remainder of the text. The section contains three chapters. In the first we describe various views of reading and writing. We use available theory and research to advance an interactive perspective on reading and writing that lays the foundation for the remainder of the text. In the final part of Chapter 1 we describe the legal and political aspects of special education and disability.

In the second chapter of this section, we discuss the component skills and strategies required to succeed in reading and writing tasks. This chapter may be a review for some students taking a graduate course in assessment and instruction, but the information is essential for teachers and clinicians to make sound decisions during assessment and to plan appropriate instruction. In addition, we discuss in detail how learner factors, text factors, and contextual factors influence student performance in reading and writing.

In Chapter 3 we show how an interactive model of reading and writing ability can and should be applied to reading and writing disability. This chapter also provides an overview of the assessment and instruction process. The overview simultaneously describes the way literacy assessment and instruction typically progress, and also provides a guided tour of the sequence of this text. The steps of the assessment-instruction process detailed in Chapter 3 are used throughout the remainder of the book. In introductory materials for subsequent sections, we highlight the particular step(s) to be considered in that section.

CHAPTER 1

Perspectives on Reading and Writing Ability

INTRODUCTION

Day in and day out, teachers must be prepared to engage students in some sort of activity. How do teachers decide what to do in the name of reading and writing instruction? Virtually all teachers in the United States have received instruction in planning, and all have been advised to place their statements of instructional objectives at the very beginning of the plan. Despite this training, many teachers start their planning not with desired learning outcomes, but with desirable activities (Clark 1984). These desirable activities often involve following other people's "good advice," such as the directives contained in teacher's manuals of basal readers.

Even under the best of circumstances, mechanical execution of such directives is not good practice, because good teaching always involves adapting instruction to the needs of specific individuals or groups of students. The pitfalls of such practice become painfully evident when we are concerned, as we are in this text, with students who are not learning to read and write easily and well. These students require thoughtfully planned and executed instruction, fitted to their particular needs. What is needed for one "disabled" learner may be quite different from what is required for another.

How can we make decisions about what to change, how to adapt existing practice, and what to do with these students who have failed to learn when given exposure to the usual and customary instruction? In order to make decisions, teachers need to consider theory. Theory sounds frightening and abstract but, in reality, all teachers have some sort of theory whether they realize it or not. Teachers' theories about reading and writing are extremely important because the particular theory held determines, at least in part, what is done in the name of reading and writing instruction. Theories help us simplify educational decisions. Theories give us explanations for things, but more importantly, they tell us how to behave.

In this chapter we describe the ways existing views of reading and writing have influenced both assessment and instruction over the years and provide information that will help you refine your own theories of reading and writing. In addition, we trace the legal and political roots of programs designed to address the needs of students with reading and writing difficulties. These various perspectives will help teachers to reflect on their existing knowledge and beliefs, setting the stage for an extensive discussion, in Chapter 2, of an interactive view of reading and writing.

UNDERSTANDING READING AND WRITING

In this section we describe the historical contexts in which reading and writing came to be viewed separately in education. This is followed by a discussion of more recent cognitive and social perspectives that have resulted in more integration of reading and writing in educational theory and practice.

Historical Perspectives on Reading and Writing

The field of literacy education as we know it today began as reading instruction in the public school at the primary grade levels. Public schooling was seen as a way to provide a growing population with the foundations of good citizenship, and reading was the way for students to acquire common moral and political principles. The first public schools gave instruction in reading brief Biblical passages and other moralistic texts; later, primers offered secular, patriotic readings with questions and answers for students to copy and recite (Clifford 1984; Squire 1991).

Writing was considered less important than oral communication, since most citizens of the new nation had no need to write except to sign their names. Like reading, writing was thought to be a simple matter, a way to put words that would otherwise be spoken into print; all students needed to know for that simple translation was handwriting and spelling (Clifford 1984; Russell 1991).

After the Civil War, the growing commercial and professional class was divided into many separate communities. These communities were linked more by written texts, such as memos, reports, professional literature, and administrative records, than by geography or social class (Russell 1991). The new professionals demanded that schools provide their children an education that would prepare them for roles in government, commerce, and the growing professions. The purposes for school literacy instruction expanded to serve the general population as well as the college-bound elite (Katz 1987; Russell 1991).

In 1894 a committee composed of university professors, professionals, and businessmen issued the Report of the Committee of Ten on public high schools. The report called for greater emphasis on English literature, since literature was seen as a vehicle for transmitting common values and "uplifting" ordinary citizens (Applebee 1974). Following this report, a National Conference on College Entrance Requirements produced a list of core readings—a literary canon, that dominated the entire high school English curriculum for decades (Applebee 1974).

The Committee of Ten also set standards for written expression that were accepted throughout the society (Heath 1991; Russell 1991). As a result, schools and other public institutions began emphasizing standard English in writing as well as speaking; correct spelling and grammar became a focus of instruction. Classroom writing activities typically consisted of copying texts, underlining, circling, and supplying one-word responses (Clifford 1989; North 1987). Graded reading books that matched children's age and ability level, first printed in 1836, became a standard by the late 1800s and established the pattern for the basal reading series still used today (Squire 1991).

From the mid–1800s through the first decades of the twentieth century, a progressive philosophy of education gained influence among educators. The foremost progressive philosopher, John Dewey, advocated a public school system that functioned neither to preserve privileged traditions nor to prepare students for prevailing social conditions, but to improve students' lives and create a society whose benefits accrued to all citizens (Applebee 1974; Cremin 1989). Dewey rejected the literary canon and recommended curriculum materials that had relevance to students. He promoted cooperation and group work in the classroom to encourage a free exchange of ideas and saw schools as learning communities (Hendley 1986; Applebee 1974; Russell 1991).

The scientific movement arose as a counterinfluence on schools during the progressive era. One of the early educational psychologists, Edward Thorndike, developed scientific theories that led to the development of objective measures of student achievement. These measures were used to sort students into ability groups so that teachers could provide instruction suited to particular needs. This movement came to exert the same control that the literary canon once had on curriculum and instruction in the form of skills instruction.

In the last thirty years, our understanding of how students learn and our approach to studying reading and writing has been changed rather dramatically by two new ways of thinking about teaching and learning: the cognitive revolution and the "social turn" (Geertz 1983). These two perspectives, described more fully in the next section, are important because they prompted researchers and educators to consider reading and writing together, rather than separately. In addition, they are the basis for the interactive view described in this text. In describing these perspectives, we are greatly indebted to the thinking of McCarthey and Raphael (1992) and Englert and Palincsar (1991).

Cognitive Information Processing Perspectives on Reading and Writing

During the World War II period, computer technology suggested new ways to model mental processes which influenced our views of learning. The new cognitive scientists viewed computers and the mind as similar: active, self-monitoring systems for processing information. Information processing theories have been used to develop several models of both reading and writing processes (For example, Gough 1972; Hayes and Flower 1980; Kintsch and vanDijk 1978; LaBerge and Samuels 1974).

When an information processing perspective is applied to reading and writing, three assumptions seem to operate: (1) reading and writing consist of a number of subprocesses used to perform specialized tasks; (2) readers and writers have limited capacity for attention so that trade-offs occur across the subprocesses, and (3) competence in reading and writing is determined by the degree of attention needed to operate subprocesses; the less memory needed, the more efficient the operation (McCarthey and Raphael 1992).

Subprocesses in reading and writing. Like the computer whose components perform specialized functions that interact to complete a task, information processing models divide reading and writing processes into subprocesses, each with a different function. For example, Gough (1972) proposed a model of reading as a linear, hierarchical process. The reader works from the smallest units of analysis (letters) to the largest (text meaning), and each level of analysis triggers the next, with the sum of these analyses adding up to meaning. The subprocesses identified in this model include a visual or iconic image, moving toward letter identification, searching one's lexicon, and accessing memory for meaning.

In contrast, LaBerge and Samuels (1974) described reading in terms of the component processes that relate to the functions of different types of memory: visual, phonological, semantic, and episodic. At the heart of their model is attention, the process that allocates the reader's efforts to the subprocess or memory type needed for the task at hand. In this view, progress through the subprocesses may not be linear, since attention may be allocated to different memories in different patterns.

These "bottom-up" models of text processing have given way to interactive models (Rumelhart 1977). Interactive models suggest that the processing of text is a flexible interaction of the different information sources available to the reader, and that the information contained in "higher" stages of processing can influence, as well as be influenced by, the analysis that occurs at lower stages of analysis.

Information processing models of writing are similar to those of reading. For example, Flower and Hayes (1981) described writing as consisting of three recursive phases: planning, in which writers set goals and make plans; translating, in which writers put ideas into written form; and reviewing, in which writers test the plans and translations. Similarly, Scardamalia, Bereiter, and Goelman (1982) distinguish between metacomponents, used to identify choices and make decisions, and performance components that allow writers to carry out their plans. Although these models differ in the division of tasks and specific definitions of the writing process, they share an emphasis on dividing the process into smaller components for analysis and description.

Limited capacity processors. Information processing theorists also use the computer metaphor to describe the limited capacity of readers and writers who must often juggle several subprocesses at once (accessing background knowledge, organizing ideas, making decisions about relevant and redundant information, and monitoring). Just as the computer cannot attend to everything at once, humans also have limitations on their processing capacities. The juggling required for successful reading and writing performance is explained in terms of how much attention is actually necessary to engage in a given activity and how effectively individuals switch their attention to the process most useful for a particular task.

Speed of processing. The term "automaticity" has been used to describe the way skilled readers' subprocesses operate as instinctive routines (LaBerge and Samuels 1974). Initially, subprocesses such as decoding in reading and handwriting in composition are so demanding of attentional resources that higher-level processes cannot be employed. Eventually, however, lower-level subprocesses are mastered to the point of automaticity and new routines can be learned. Although not all subprocesses become automatic (comprehension and planning always involve some conscious attention), the more that do become automatic, the better able the reader or writer is to attend to more cognitively demanding activities.

Implications. Information processing models and research have provided us with an increased understanding of reading and writing processes in terms of their components. As well, we have a better understanding of the knowledge base of skilled readers and writers. However, current information processing models do not account for the variability that occurs in reading and writing as a result of a host of contextual factors such as the nature of the task, goals, purposes, and instruction. Information processing models also tend to overlook or dismiss larger social and cultural factors that influence an individual's reading and writing performance.

There has been little effort to detail the specific links between reading and writing from within the information processing perspective. Although there is some research dealing with how reading and writing may be related (for example, Ehri 1989; Shanahan and Lomax 1986), information processing theory sheds little light on how to encourage their development or on how less successful or novice readers and writers become more skilled.

Social Perspectives on Reading and Writing

At about the same time as the cognitive revolution, social scientists were developing an orientation that brings into focus the social and cultural contexts that shape language and thought. Social theories of language and learning suggest that meaning is not an individual construction, but a social negotiation that depends on supportive interaction and shared use of language.

The assumptions underlying various social perspectives on reading and writing are quite different from those described above: (1) reading and writing are social and cultural phenomena; (2) knowledge is constructed through the individual's interaction with the sociocultural environment; and (3) cognitive processes related to reading and writing are acquired through contextualized activity and assisted learning (Englert and Palincsar 1991; McCarthey and Raphael 1992).

Sociocultural nature of reading and writing.   The societies or cultures within which we live, learn, and work determine how reading and writing are defined, instructed, and evaluated. For example, at the district level, curriculum decisions such as the choice of literature-based versus traditional basal reading materials influence the instructional and assessment practices of teachers.

At the school level, the principal's and teachers' beliefs about learning and teaching have an effect on practices that determine, for example, the extent to which diverse groups of students are accorded equal opportunities to learn. Culture also manifests itself in classrooms in the form of patterns of social interactions and the sets of rules or routines that guide teachers' and students' social exchanges. These routines develop, in the participants, shared understandings about what it means to read and write, about "what counts" as reading and writing, and about appropriate uses of reading and writing (Rogoff 1990).

According to sociocultural theorists, the oral and written texts that students produce don't stand alone. Instead, they must be seen as related to all the activity and experience that has gone before for that teacher and classroom. Books have been read, ideas have been exchanged, and social interactions have occurred; all of which influence the types of oral and written exchanges that happen today (Cole 1990).

Viewing reading and writing in terms of cultural practices means that we must understand the political and social, as well as cognitive dimensions, of literacy. When the classroom is viewed as a culture, we must be concerned with teachers' and students' beliefs about reading, writing, and the patterns of interactions occurring among students and between teachers and students rather than discrete activities. We must consider factors such as the ways in which reading and writing are represented to students and the occasions students have to participate as readers and writers within the classroom culture.

Knowledge construction through interaction.   The social perspective on learning asserts that learning to think, read, and write are not individual, independent activities. Instead, the acquisition of such functions begins with the interactions of parent and child, among siblings, or between teacher and students. The role of language and dialogue is critical since it is through speech and social interaction that the learner acquires abilities such as reading and writing (Vygotsky 1986).

Vygotsky (1978) proposed that in the early stages of development processes first appear between people on the social plane; they are jointly performed and constructed by teachers and students as they cooperatively engage in dialogue. Processes that begin as social and shared become internalized in a second phase. In this phase, students' performance is assisted by their own self-talk; social speech becomes internalized as egocentric speech and collaborative dialogue with oneself.

Finally, in a third phase, the self-directing speech of the learner goes underground as it becomes "inner speech." At this point, learners do not overtly vocalize or self-instruct, although self-talk may surface as the difficulty of the task increases. Learners do not simply take in information, they continually construct new, more complex meanings as they transform knowledge for application across a broad range of activities.

Contextualized activity and assisted learning.   Vygotsky (1978) suggested that mental processes are context specific and are best situated and learned through practical activity. This implies that reading and writing instruction must engage students at all ability levels as participants in contextualized, authentic, and holistic activities. Vygotsky (1978) proposed that the difference between what a child can do alone and what he or she can do with the assistance of a more-capable other represents the "zone of proximal development" (ZPD) in which instruction should occur. The concept of the ZPD assumes that a deliberate transfer of control from the more knowledgeable to the less knowledgeable person takes place.

How the adult, or more knowledgeable person, assists the student in taking control of a process is integral to social views of learning. Assisted learning and instruction have been compared to a scaffold in that it provides support, but is also temporary and adjustable (Palincsar 1984; Wood, Bruner, and Ross 1976). This educational scaffolding involves structuring tasks through modeling, explaining, questioning, and feedback until the learner can operate independently and is essential to learning in a social view of reading and writing (see Chapter 6).

Implications.   Social perspectives on reading and writing address a number of the weaknesses identified in information processing models. Specifically, they account for variations among cultures in literacy practices and in the ways students learn to read and write in different settings. They highlight the role of social context and bring our attention to the need to be sensitive to the values and practices of different cultural groups in schools. In addition, the focus on language as a cultural tool helps us understand how new learning is acquired and how important it is in developing new instructional strategies (McCarthey and Raphael 1992).

Social perspectives emphasize that reading and writing are connected through their uses within the culture and through the role dialogue plays in the development of literacy. Although there is research on issues related to the role of culture in literacy practices and in cognition, little has been done on the connections between reading and writing from this perspective.

An Interactive Perspective on Reading and Writing

The interactive perspective on reading and writing described in this book is an amalgam of the cognitive information processing and social views. It rests on several assumptions: (1) reading and writing are processes of constructing meaning; (2) the construction of meaning results from an interaction between the reader/writer and the context of the reading/writing situation; and (3) the interaction is dynamic, or variable, as a function of numerous reader/writer and contextual factors (see Figure 1.1). Meaning, in the form of skilled reading and writing performance, is generated from the interaction between the learner and the reading/writing context, and there are many factors that influence learners' ability to comprehend and compose. A general discussion of this perspective is provided below.

FIGURE 1.1
An Interactive View of Reading and Writing

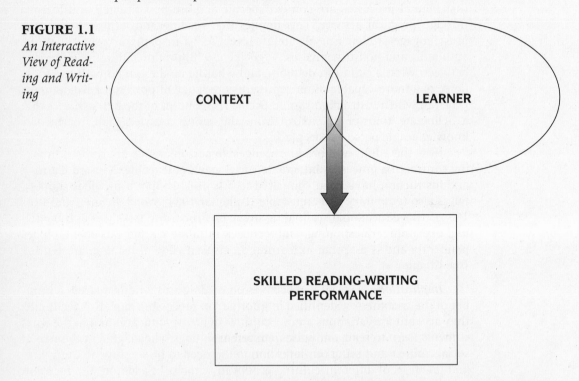

Construction of meaning in reading and writing.   An interactive perspective suggests that readers construct meaning when they comprehend in much the same way writers construct meaning when they compose. Meaning is created in the mind of the reader/writer as a function of the interplay between the cognitive information processing abilities of individuals and the context of the reading and/or writing event. As with the sociocultural perspective, skilled performance is viewed as the ability to use reading and writing for personal, recreational, academic, and civic purposes.

Interactions. The interactive view argues that *both* cognitive information processing structures and sociocultural aspects of context influence reading and writing processes and performance. Reader/writer factors that affect reading and writing performance and processes include prior knowledge of content, knowledge about reading and writing processes, and attitudes and motivation. Context factors include the setting for learning, the reading and writing curriculum, and the instructional methods, materials, and tasks employed. Each of these factors has been shown to affect how people approach reading and writing tasks and also how well they perform.

Dynamic interactions. The term "dynamic" is used to indicate that reading and writing are variable processes, adapting to the specific demands of each particular reading/writing experience. Reading and writing ability are relative properties, not stable, static constructs. Each person may have several reading abilities and several writing abilities, depending on texts, tasks, and contexts. For example, we may be very good at writing friendly letters but do poorly at writing research papers. Or, we may devour romance novels with good comprehension but shudder at the thought of reading a book about the latest breakthroughs in physics.

Implications. The variability within and across individuals means that reading and writing performance are a function of what learners *can* and *will* do at any given moment. Appropriate instruction requires that we understand the variability that exists within individual learners. Issues of linguistic background, motivation, and/or cultural understanding and values are each as relevant as whether the learner can read sight words or understands punctuation. Instruction that takes these issues into account focuses on providing students with a rich and diverse selection of reading materials and opportunities for ample self-selection during both reading and writing. In addition, students have opportunities to read and write for many different purposes.

Integrating Reading and Writing

Figure 1.2 (page 12) describes some of the shifts in views and practices related to reading and writing that have occurred since the 1970s. The shifts highlighted in this figure have been fueled by developments related to both the information processing and social perspectives described above. Tierney (1992) summarizes these and other developments as follows:

> —In conjunction with the process-based descriptions of writing as a problem-solving experience and composing activity, reading researchers developed models of the reader as writer, which complemented and extended the information processing views of meaning making.
> —Developments in linguistics prompted reading and writing researchers to describe meaning making in terms of author-reader interactions and the social dynamics of interpretive communities.

FIGURE 1.2
Reading and
Writing:
Shifts in
Perspective
and Practice

Shifts in Viewpoints	
1970s	**1990s**
Reading is receiving; writing is producing.	Reading and writing are composing, constructing, problem-solving activities.
Reading and writing are means of translating or transmitting ideas.	Reading and writing are vehicles for thinking.
Reading involves understanding the author's message; writing involves making your message clear for others.	Reading and writing involve interaction among participants as communicators, as well as the pursuit of self-discovery.
Reading and writing occur in a social context.	Reading and writing involve social processes.
Reading is a precursor to writing development.	Reading and writing development go hand in hand. Early writing is an avenue for reading development.
Writing development requires mastery of spelling conventions; reading development begins with mastery of skills and subskills.	Writing development involves invention as students pursue temporary spellings, negotiate conventions, etc. Reading development occurs naturally as students explore meaningful literacy experiences.

Shifts in Practice	
1970s	**1990s**
Reading and writing are taught separately.	Reading and writing are taught together.
Reading and writing skills are listed separately.	Reading and writing programs are developed from a list of skills and behaviors that apply to both processes.
Writing is excluded from reading; reading is excluded from writing.	Writing and reading occur together in collaboration.
Single texts are used to read or write.	Multiple texts are used to write, synthesize, pursue projects, develop reports, or analyze.
Beginning reading involves reading readiness activities.	Beginning reading involves shared reading and opportunities to write.
Early writing involves dictated stories and activities focused on mastering conventions.	Early writing involves allowing students to approximate and pursue conventions based on emerging hypotheses about language and how it works.

From "Ongoing research and new directions" by R. J. Tierney, in *Reading/writing connections: Learning from research,* 1992, pp. 247–259, edited by J. W. Irwin and M. A. Doyle. International Reading Association. Reprinted by permission.

—Studies of preschool literacy development challenged age-old notions of how literacy was acquired, and brought to the fore the extent to which reading and writing are intertwined and work together from a very early age.

—Studies of the relationship of reading and writing to thinking and learning indicated that when writing and reading were tied to one another, both thinking and learning were enhanced.

Tierney (1992) also notes that these developments did not occur in isolation, but that research was being shaped and spurred on by what was happening in schools. The result of these developments is the recognition that writing and reading have a synergistic relationship.

UNDERSTANDING THE LEGAL AND POLITICAL ASPECTS OF SPECIAL NEEDS STUDENTS

In this section, we turn away from theoretical perspectives and toward legal and political perspectives on the acquisition of literacy among students who are struggling. Until recently there were relatively few systematic identification or treatment procedures for students with severe physical, linguistic, cognitive, or emotional problems. Judicial and legislative actions over the past twenty-five years, however, have changed that situation. Because they influence literacy instruction so strongly, we consider the legal and social basis for present-day special education programs and describe the specific provisions for meeting existing legal requirements.

Legal and Social Roots of Special Education

The medical field exhibited early interest in reading-disabled individuals. This interest continued throughout the 1930s and 1940s, resulting in a variety of special treatments to be used in cases of severe reading disability (for example, Fernald 1943). These treatments resided outside the "normal" school environment, however, and children with moderate to severe physical, emotional, or cognitive problems were not typically included in regular classrooms or schools. In areas where placement facilities for these children were scarce, many teachers struggled to address extraordinary problems as best they could. In other areas, in the face of limited facilities, the students were simply excluded from any formal schooling.

During the 1950s and 1960s, a combination of social and political factors combined to create an environment in which unusual and extensive attention was focused on those students who were failing to learn easily and well in the public schools of the United States. National attention was captured by a series of legal battles initiated by a group of advocates who wanted to see that all students received appropriate public education.

Bricker (1986) relates the history of one such legal battle, *PARC v. Commonwealth of Pennsylvania* (1971), in which the court concluded that students had been excluded or excused from attendance in public schools simply because they were retarded and ordered the state to support public education for such students. As a result, "for the first time, any school-age child, no matter how impaired, was eligible to receive a free, appropriate public education" (Bricker 1986, 106).

Access to public education was only one of the problems confronting the field at that time, however. The practices surrounding testing and labeling students were suspect for many reasons. For minority students, the problems of abuses and inadequate protections were particularly apparent. Two other cases were directly related to practices in these areas. The decisions handed down by the court in *Diana v. Board of Education* (1970) and *Larry P. v. Riles* (which started in 1971 and concluded in 1979) required that the state of California test students in their primary language; reevaluate students from minority groups (African-Americans, Latinos, and Asians) currently in classes for the mentally retarded; and develop and standardize IQ tests appropriate for minority groups.

A final concern among advocates in the area of special education involved the treatment and instruction provided to handicapped individuals once they were placed in specialized institutional settings. In two cases, *Wyatt v. Stickney* and *New York ARC v. Rockefeller* (Willowbrook), judges ruled that residents of such placements had the right to appropriate treatment, and, in the *Wyatt* case, the judge specified that this treatment should occur in the least restrictive environment (Bricker 1986).

The active round of legal rulings prompted both attention and concern and provided the basis for the legislative initiatives to follow. Beginning in the early 1960s, laws were passed that established federal programs related to service, training, and research designed specifically for the handicapped. These legislative actions culminated with the passage of the 1975 Education for All Handicapped Act (PL 94–142), which mandates:

- the right to education—all handicapped children are to be provided with free, appropriate, public education
- the right to nondiscriminatory evaluation
- the right to an IEP (Individual Educational Plan)—a clear statement of objectives for each child along with documentation of the child's current and expected performance
- the right to education in the least restrictive environment
- the right to due process
- the right of parental participation (Gallagher 1984)

Special Education Identification: Provisions of PL 94–142

The actual procedures for implementing the mandates of PL 94–142 vary somewhat from community to community, but the process must include provisions for meeting each mandate. Practically speaking, a teacher, administrator, or parent may make an initial referral in order to determine whether a student is entitled to special education services. Following this referral, the child's parents must be fully informed about the prospective assessment process and permission to proceed must be received from them. Only after these stages have been completed are assessment procedures initiated to determine whether the student meets federal and local guidelines for exceptionality. In addition, the assessment is usually designed to determine the category of handicap that will be used for purposes of classification.

PL 94–142 clearly specifies procedures for the assessment phase. The procedures designed to address the mandate that students have "the right to nondiscriminatory evaluation" are as follows:

- tests must be selected and administered so as to ensure that results "accurately reflect the child's aptitude and achievement ... rather than reflecting the child's impaired sensory, manual, or speaking skills"
- no single testing procedure may be used for determining an appropriate educational program for the child
- the evaluation must be conducted by a multidisciplinary team
- the child must be assessed in all areas related to health, vision, hearing, social and emotional status, academic performance, communicative status, and motor abilities *(Federal Register* 1977, cited in Morgan 1981).

In addition, the law provides guidelines for the types of assessment instruments that may be used, stating that tests and other evaluation materials should:

- be provided and administered in the child's native language
- have been validated for the specific purpose for which they are used
- be administered by trained personnel
- include materials tailored to assess specific areas of educational need and not merely those which are designed to provide a single general intelligence quotient *(Federal Register* 1977, cited in Morgan 1981)

When the assessment phase is completed, PL 94–142 states clearly that there will be a meeting to develop the child's Individualized Education Plan (IEP). As previously noted, the IEP is mandated by the federal government and requires a clear statement of objectives for each child along with documentation of the child's current and expected performance. In addition, the IEP must contain a statement that specifies who will be responsible for each component of the plan and ensures periodic reevaluation of the child's status.

The planning group is often referred to as the Committee on the Handicapped and, according to PL 94–142, the following individuals shall be involved in the meeting at which the IEP is developed: a public education representative who is qualified to provide, or supervise the provision of, special education; the child's teacher; one or both of the child's parents; the child, where applicable; and other individuals at the discretion of the parent(s) or agency (Bricker 1986).

The parent(s) must agree to the designation of the child under a particular handicapping condition and to the information provided in the IEP. If the parents do not agree with the recommendations of the committee, a series of legal procedures are set in motion to settle the disagreement.

Students with Disabilities

A student's eligibility for special education services is determined by the type and degree of deficit in a particular area, following the guidelines developed through legal and judicial channels. There are presently nine categories of special needs students:

1. mental impairment
2. hearing impairment
3. visual impairment
4. speech impairment
5. orthopedic impairment
6. other health impairments (limited vitality, strength, or alertness due to chronic or acute health problems)
7. multiply handicapped
8. serious emotional impairment
9. specific learning disability

Congress has subsequently reaffirmed and extended the mandate; focusing on secondary education and preschool children in 1984 and adding a focus on infant and toddlers in 1986. Amendments to the law (PL 101–476) changed the name of the mandate to the Individuals with Disabilities (versus handicap) Education Act and included children with autism and traumatic brain injury to the categories of disability and also designates attention deficit disorder (ADD) as a category to be studied for possible inclusion (Palloway and Patton 1993).

Eligibility for children in many categories is established early and unequivocally because many handicapping conditions are apparent prior to a student's entrance into school. However, learning disability and the less-severe cases of mental and emotional impairment are often identified after a student has entered school and failed to meet certain academic expectations.

Reading and writing personnel are often involved with students who have been identified as having special needs in the area of learning disability because the referral is frequently made on the basis of a student's academic performance in the area of reading and writing. Although it is the newest classification, learning disability is presently the largest special education category and continues to grow at an alarming rate (Zins, Curtis, Graden, and Ponti 1988). Learning-disabled students currently account for well over half of the children served through special education programs (Allington 1994).

Learning disability is defined by the federal government in the following manner:

"Specific learning disability" means a disorder in one or more of the basic psychological processes involved in understanding or in using language, spoken or written, which may manifest itself in an imperfect ability to listen, think, speak, read, write, spell, or to do mathematical calculations. The term includes such conditions as perceptual handicaps, brain injury, minimal brain dysfunction, dyslexia, and developmental aphasia. The term does not include children who have learning problems which are primarily the result of visual, hearing, or motor handicaps, of mental retardation, of emotional disturbance, or of environmental, cultural, or economic disadvantage. *(Federal Register* Dec. 29, 1977, 65083)

It is important to understand how learning disability is related to other controversial issues surrounding reading and writing disability. For example, the similarity between the definition of learning disability and the definition of dyslexia offered by the World Federation of Neurology has not been lost on most educators:

> [Dyslexia] is a disorder manifested by difficulty in learning to read despite conventional instruction, adequate intelligence, and sociocultural opportunity. It is dependent upon fundamental cognitive disabilities which are frequently of constitutional origin. (Critchley 1975)

These definitions suggest that, for all practical purposes, learning disability and dyslexia are synonymous. What is most important is that both definitions clearly imply either a medical or nonspecified etiology within the learner.

Although it may appear that special education determinations are straightforward, they are generally far from clear-cut. In addition, schools throughout the country are struggling to decide what programs to offer, who should deliver instruction, and who is eligible for various special programs. For reading and writing professionals and for students who need help in reading and writing, these issues can be troublesome. In the next section we will describe the extent to which politics may play a part in disability determinations and services.

The Politics of Disability

It appears that the judicial and legislative actions in the area of special education have been most advantageous for individuals with clearly identifiable physical and/or mental impairments. Unfortunately, the situation in the area of learning disabilities is less clear. Indeed, more than any other classification of handicap, learning disabilities has revived discussion about the source of disability. In the process, troubling sociological issues have been raised as well.

The political issues arise at least in part from definitions of learning disability. As we have seen, both learning disability and dyslexia definitions are exclusionary. Many researchers have made the point that existing classification schemes work differently for different socioeconomic groups. The requirements of an exclusionary definition effectively "mean that children diagnosed as dyslexic tend to be the bright offspring of 'good' homes attending 'good' schools. There is no reason to suppose that dyslexia is in any real sense a 'middle-class disease,' only that those tend to be the children where psychologists feel most confident they can exclude other obvious causes of reading failure" (Ellis 1984, 106). Indeed, it is the case that minorities are underrepresented in the learning disabilities category (Sleeter 1985).

Students who are poor achievers and who are also less affluent normally receive reading and writing support from a different source, if at all. These students are generally assumed to experience reading and writing difficulties because of one of the other possibilities specified in the government's exclusionary definition of learning disability. They are classified into one of the other handicapping conditions (for example, mental retardation or emotional impairment). In fact, figures for the 1986–87 school year indicate that, while minority students constituted 30 percent of all public school students, they accounted for 42 percent of all students classified as educable mentally retarded and 40 percent of those classified as trainable mentally retarded (Hume 1988). Alternatively, students may be assumed to need compensatory education rather than special education. Title 1/Chapter 1 of the Elementary and Secondary Education Act of 1965 was passed in order to provide such programs for educationally disadvantaged students:

> In recognition of the special educational needs of children of low-income families and the impact that concentration of low-income families have on the ability of local educational programs, the Congress hereby declares it to be the policy of the United States to provide financial assistance to local educational agencies serving areas with concentrations of children from low-income families in order to expand and improve their educational programs by various means. (NIE 1977, 8, cited in Calfee and Drum 1979, 172)

Similarly, the Bilingual Education Act (BEA) of 1968 initiated demonstration projects for educating language minority students from low-income families. The reauthorization of the BEA in 1974 eliminated the requirement that students must be poor to qualify for services, and the 1978 reauthorization expanded services to include students with limited academic proficiency as well as those with limited English proficiency. Subsequent reauthorizations (1984 and 1988) do not ensure that students receive appropriate instructional support. Again, the lack of entitlement "has meant that 85 percent of the students identified as needing second-language services are not being attended to" (Garcia, Pearson, and Jimenez 1994).

The practical consequence of these developments is noted by Johnston, Allington, and Franzen (1985): "Two broad notions of reading [and writing] failure evolved, one linked to environmental deficits and the other to constitutional neurological dysfunction" (8). These authors discuss a number of potential concerns that arise from this situation. First, they note that learning-disabled students constitute a protected group under the law, whereas "educationally disadvantaged" students do not. In times of tight fiscal accounting, the special education student will, nevertheless, be "entitled" to appropriate educational provisions. The "educationally disadvantaged" disabled learner is "eligible" for such services but not entitled to them.

Second, the existence of two distinct federal systems for handling reading and writing difficulties implies that there really are two distinct and identifiably different groups of reading and writing disabled students, that the source of their reading and writing problems results in different disabilities, and that appropriate instructional programs are also identifiably different (Johnston,

Allington, and Franzen 1985). In many schools today there are both special education and reading and writing professionals serving students with reading and writing problems. In the vast majority of these situations, there is little qualitative difference between the programs offered.

Coles (1978) has argued that the learning disabled label is an example of "biologizing social problems." By positing biological bases for learning problems, the responsibility for failure is put "within the head of the child" rather than placed on the shoulders of schools, communities, and other institutions. "The classification plays its political role, moving the focus away from the general educational process, away from the need to change institutions, away from the need to appropriate more resources for social use toward the remedy of a purely medical problem" (333).

Similarly, Allington (1994) suggests:

> As schools have been expected to educate a greater proportion of children to increasingly higher standards of literacy, the regular education bureaucracy has put in place an increasing array of special programs and employed an expanding bevy of special personnel in attempts to minimize the roles and responsibilities of the regular education system in educating all children. (104–5)

He further argues that it is this sense of regular education's retreat from responsibility that has led the U.S. Department of Education to call for reducing exclusionary programs and set the stage for the current "inclusionary education" initiative for educating handicapped children (Will 1986). This concern has also led to a shift in federal program guidelines indicating that the academic success of disadvantaged students is the responsibility of the whole school not just the Title 1/Chapter 1 program (LeTendre 1991).

Integration/Inclusion

It is clear that there are stronger and more frequent calls for addressing the instructional needs of students with special needs within the mainstream classroom setting. Although the pace and the effort vary considerably, movements for *full inclusion* mean that many special education students now often receive their education in the mainstream setting (Smith, Polloway, Patton, and Dowdy 1995, Villa and Thousand 1995). In addition, criticisms of "pullout" programs in Title 1/Chapter 1 have also intensified (Allington and McGill-Franzen 1989; Slavin 1989). Although the majority of students in those programs still receive instruction in small-group settings out of the classroom, there is no doubt that this has and continues to change. Finally, there is no doubt that schools are serving an increasingly diverse student population (Day 1992).

All this means that all teachers, whether "special" or "regular" or "remedial," need to consider individual differences among students. In addition, they need the skills and knowledge to work in multiple settings with other professionals. For many, this means new roles and responsibilities.

Summarizing Reading and Writing for Special Needs Students

Judicial and legislative actions over the past twenty years have resulted in specific procedures for identifying and educating students with a range of physical, cognitive, linguistic, and/or social-emotional problems. Specific provisions and procedures were described for the special education programs legislated for students with handicapping conditions and for the compensatory education programs legislated for low achievers who are educationally disadvantaged. The establishment of two separate programs for low achievers suggests the existence of two distinct sources of learning problems and differentiated instructional programs for each. However, there are often few differences in practice between these two types of programs.

Although there is little doubt that neurological or constitutional dysfunction plays a role in certain cases of reading and writing disability, the percentage of cases accounted for by identifiable neurological problems appears to be extremely small. The majority of difficulties in reading and writing are more likely to result from a complex interaction between the learner and the reading and writing situation. It is this complex interaction to which we turn our attention for the remainder of the text.

CHAPTER SUMMARY

This chapter began with the idea that theories of reading and writing are important because they help us make decisions about assessment and instruction. We then suggested how reading and writing came to be treated separately in education and how the recent "cognitive revolution" and "social turn" have led to more integrated views of reading and writing.

Cognitive information processing perspectives on reading and writing were described as emphasizing subprocesses in reading and writing, readers and writers as limited capacity processors, and speed of processing. This view has increased our understanding of reading and writing processes in terms of their components and the knowledge base of skilled readers and writers, but cannot account for the variability in performance that occurs as a result of a host of social and cultural factors.

Social perspectives on reading and writing were described as emphasizing reading and writing as social and cultural phenomena, knowledge as constructed through the individual's interaction with the sociocultural environment, and the acquisition of cognitive processes related to reading and writing through contextualized activity and assisted learning. Social perspectives were seen as addressing some of the weaknesses observed in information processing views and as helpful in formulating pedagogical goals and strategies for reading and writing.

The interactive view of reading and writing which serves as the basis for this text was characterized as an amalgam of the information processing and social views. This perspective suggests that reading and writing are processes of constructing meaning through a dynamic interaction between the reader/writer and the context of the reading/writing situation. This means that reading and writing are not static but vary as a function of *contextual factors* such as setting, curriculum, and instructional conditions and *reader/writer factors* such as background knowledge, motivation, and interests. These interactions are described more fully in Chapter 2.

The second section of this chapter described the legal and social basis for present-day special education programs. The provisions of Public Law 94–142 for the rights of all handicapped children were noted and the procedures for implementing these provisions were discussed. We also noted the existence of two distinct programs for low achievers—one for those with handicapping conditions presumed to be internal to the learner and one for those whose problems result from educational disadvantage. Criticisms were presented of both special education and compensatory education programs as mechanisms for minimizing the roles and responsibilities of regular education in educating all children. Responses to these criticisms have led to the inclusionary education movement in special education and the movement to school-wide programs in compensatory education.

CHAPTER 2

An Interactive View of Reading and Writing

INTRODUCTION

The interactive view of reading and writing described in the first chapter provides the framework for thinking about the nature of reading and writing. We now turn our attention to a discussion of skilled reading and writing and the factors that interact and influence performance in these areas. Throughout this chapter we describe evidence that even the most mechanical aspects of reading and writing (for example, understanding and using punctuation) are influenced by both contextual (for example, text factors) and learner (for example, prior knowledge) factors. Consideration of the conventional aspects of reading and writing performance must be constrained by concerns for the ways in which learner and contextual factors interact to influence performance. Unless this complex and dynamic view of reading and writing is employed during assessment, we run the risk of developing a distorted picture of reading and writing processes. This poses serious problems for assessment, but even more serious concerns about the quality of instruction.

UNDERSTANDING THE ELEMENTS OF SKILLED PERFORMANCE

It is easy to lose sight of the "target" of skilled reading and writing when we are working with less able readers and writers. In the past, both assessment and instruction have too often focused on isolated aspects of students' knowledge and skill. Although we consider component aspects of reading and writing in the chapters that follow, we should always start with, and return to, questions of how these relate to skilled and motivated comprehension and composition.

So, what is desirable performance in reading and writing? First and foremost, readers and writers read and write. They *use* their knowledge and skill to accomplish personal, recreational, academic, and civic purposes (MRA 1993). This also means that reading and writing are not defined by classroom practices and texts, but move out into authentic, real-world materials and tasks. Readers and writers can and do apply their knowledge and skill in flexible ways to accomplish meaningful tasks, suggesting that both reading and writing are adaptive and intentional activities (Dole, Duffy, Roehler, and Pearson 1991). In addition, readers and writers from diverse backgrounds need to be able to perform appropriately in a wide range of contexts.

> People generally associate literacy with the ability to read and write. This is the common dictionary definition, the mark of literacy in society at large, and the one generally thought of in regard to schooling. However, literacy can be viewed in a broader and educationally more productive way, as the ability to think and reason like a literate person, *within a particular society*. As Vygotsky (1979) suggested, because the practices of literacy and ways of understanding them depend upon the social conditions in which they are learned, the skills, concepts, and ways of thinking that an individual develops reflect the uses and approaches to literacy that permeate the particular society in which that person is a participant (Langer 1991, 11).

Over the past three decades, we have come to know a great deal about the nature of skilled and motivated reading and writing performance and the learner and contextual factors that influence performance (see Figure 2.1). These are the elements and factors that we must examine in the assessment and instruction of students experiencing problems in reading and writing. Below we discuss first the elements of skilled performance and then the factors that influence it.

There is some risk in pulling out elements of skilled performance for discussion. In doing so we may lead some to believe that these are isolated or entirely separable components of reading and writing. However, as we have already discussed, and we will demonstrate again a bit later, each of these elements interact with others and are influenced by contextual and learner factors. In short, the whole of skilled performance is variable and dynamic. As educators and clinicians, though, we need to have some idea of the component elements so that we can consider which of these are targets for assessment and instruction. Skilled reading and writing performance is comprised of the following elements.

Comprehension

Comprehension is the ability to use previously acquired information to construct meaning for a given text. The two aspects of comprehension considered here are reading for understanding and reading to learn and/or remember.

Reading for understanding. This area focuses primarily on readers' ability to reason their way through a text by integrating existing knowledge with

FIGURE 2.1
An Elaborated Interactive View of Reading and Writing

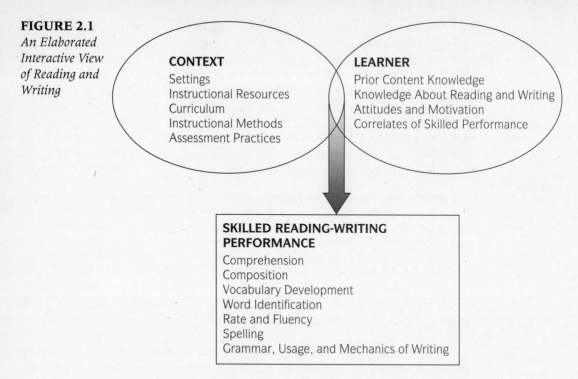

new information, drawing inferences, and forming and testing hypotheses. The goal of comprehension is the construction of an integrated representation of the information suggested by a text that is appropriate for the reading purpose. Other activities that are critical to good comprehension include establishing purposes for reading, identifying important elements of information and their relations within text, monitoring one's comprehension, and dealing with failures to comprehend (Baker and Brown 1984).

The successful accomplishment of the activities that comprise good comprehension requires the use of a variety of strategies (Dole, Duffy, Roehler, and Pearson 1991). Although there is no comprehensive list of such strategies, we can identify a range of possible strategies that are appropriate for different activities. As in the case of word analysis strategies, no one strategy is necessarily more or less important than the others. Rather, the appropriateness of a given strategy is determined by its utility in the interaction between a reader and a specific reading situation (Duffy 1993). What matters most is how effective and efficient a strategy is for accomplishing a specific purpose.

Rather than focus on the mastery of prerequisite skills, the interactive approach focuses assessment and instruction on the behaviors or activities that characterize good comprehension. Skills and strategies are the means to achieving the goal of good comprehension, not the end itself. It is important to keep this in mind, lest our old lists of skills be replaced by new lists of strategies, and our assessment and comprehension instruction remain unchanged from past practices.

Reading to remember/learn. Reading to learn and/or remember what has been comprehended or understood from text is often referred to as studying. There are three primary activities involved in effective studying. First, students must be able to preview text to familiarize themselves with its form and content and to make plans for reading. Second, students must be able to locate specific information within the text. Third, students must be able to identify the organization of information within the text.

As with comprehension, the successful accomplishment of studying activities requires the use of a variety of strategies. These strategies may include outlining, note-taking, summarizing, self-questioning, diagramming or mapping text, and underlining, as well as many of the strategies that are used in comprehending. What is most important is students' ability to select and apply these strategies in a manner that is appropriate to the study task at hand. It is not a question of which study strategies are best, but of how effective a selected strategy is in a given study situation.

Composition

Writing is essentially idea making. Drawing on their own knowledge of language and the conventions of various written genres, writers create texts for readers to use. The writing process refers to a series of nonlinear activities in which students engage to produce a finished piece of writing. These include prewriting, drafting, revising, editing, and publishing. To counteract the idea that these activities are not discrete steps or stages of a single composing process, Pappas, Levstik, and Keifer (1995) refer to them as experiences of writing for constructing texts and provide descriptions of each of these writing experiences as follows.

Prewriting experiences. Prewriting is generating and exploring ideas, recalling and rehearsing ideas, relating and probing ideas, planning, thinking, and deciding. Prewriting experiences occur when we talk, listen, read, research, observe, and so forth. They often include writing itself in forms such as notes, brainstorming, and outlines. Prewriting is an ongoing experience rather than a distinct period of writing that can interact with other writing experiences.

Drafting experiences. Drafting involves attempts to get the ideas down and create a whole text. Writers try not to worry too much about spelling and punctuation during drafting, because they know that the text will be reconsidered, rearranged, and revised. Drafting can be interrupted by prewriting and can occur simultaneously with revising.

Revising experiences. Revising has to do with attempts to rethink, review, remake, reconstruct, and reexamine the text. Revising is an ongoing activity that can occur during prewriting, or during and after drafting. The writer becomes a reader when the text is reread and revised. This is also when other readers such as teachers and peers may interact with the text and provide feedback. Readers' responses to draft text may lead to more drafting as well as more prewriting.

Editing experiences. Editing is intended to "clean up" text so that its message is communicated using the most appropriate language. It involves changing words and sentences, changing, deleting, or rearranging them to make the message more clear. The tone or style of the text, as well as the spelling, punctuation, and grammar are also checked during editing.

Publishing experiences. Classroom publishing emphasizes sharing. The publishing of final drafts takes various forms in terms of the nature of the final product and how it is shared. Because publishing has to do with sharing in general, it can apply to any writing, not just final drafts. Publishing can also occur with a range of audiences within the classroom or beyond in the school, community, or even state and national newspapers and magazines.

In summary, writing is a social, constructive, meaning-making process that consists of a variety of writing experiences in the production of texts representing a variety of genres. Both the text product and the process of constructing text are important.

Vocabulary Development

Skilled reading and writing require knowledge of the meanings of words and the ability to infer and learn the meanings of new words. Words are the labels for concepts and ideas and provide an index of readers' and writers' prior knowledge. Readers and writers who do not have adequate knowledge of important words and concepts and/or are unable to determine word meanings will have difficulty successfully comprehending or composing texts.

Vocabulary development is not simply the number of dictionary definitions of words that students have acquired. The primary focus of this area is the depth, breadth, and organization of students' vocabulary knowledge. The most sophisticated type of vocabulary knowledge involves precise definitions, analogies using the target word, and links among related concepts (Langer 1981). The least sophisticated form of vocabulary knowledge involves associated experiences that provide few, if any, meaning relations.

In addition to knowledge of specific vocabulary, we must consider the reader's ability to infer and to learn the meanings of new words and concepts. Students are frequently confronted in their reading with new words for which they may or may not already have a concept. Students need to develop strategies, such as different types of contextual and morphemic analysis as described in the next section, for inferring the meanings of unfamiliar vocabulary and independently increasing their vocabulary learning.

Word Identification

Rapid word identification is an essential component of skilled reading. Students must be able to recognize familiar words quickly and to decode unfamiliar words rapidly enough that the process of meaning construction is not unduly interrupted. As they read, people use a repertoire of word identification strategies and recruit a wide array of knowledge and skill. This information and these skills are related to each other but also make separate contributions to performance. That is, although readers and writers who are strong in one component area are generally strong in others, these can and do vary among individuals and may produce difficulties in some readers or writers.

Sight Word Recognition

The most efficient form of word identification occurs when students recognize words immediately upon sight, without sounding them out or using any other strategy to help identify them. Words that can be recognized instantly are called *sight words* and are considered part of a student's *sight vocabulary.*

Sight words fall into several categories, especially in early reading. The first words that children can recognize in print are generally *"high-potency"* words (Hunt n.d.), such as their own and other family members' names and words with heavy contextual support such as *McDonald's* (Hiebert 1981). These words are relatively easy to remember because of their visual distinctiveness and/or because of the strong affect attached to them (Ashton-Warner 1963).

A second type of sight words is the *high-frequency function* words (*the, of, but)* that appear over and over in written texts. These words are difficult to decode or figure out using word analysis strategies because they are irregular and may not follow basic decoding rules. They are often more difficult to remember than other words because many are similar in appearance (*where, there, here, when, then).* These words are usually learned as sight words when children are first learning how to read; however, many poor readers have not mastered these words even by seventh or eighth grade. Limited recognition of these high-frequency sight words affects fluency and comprehension.

The last type of sight words includes all of the other words that students have learned to recognize instantly. Many of these words are *content* words (*meal, bake, animal)* that are already part of a child's speaking or listening vocabularies. These words are often read initially through the application of various word analysis strategies and become sight words after repeated exposure through reading. Many poor readers simply do not read enough to acquire a sufficient number of these sight words. Others may rely too heavily on one or another of the word analysis strategies that are discussed in the next section. Either way, children who do not develop an adequate sight vocabulary are likely to have difficulty in all aspects of reading.

Word Analysis Strategies

These strategies are used to identify printed words that we do not recognize immediately upon sight. Unfortunately, word analysis has often been perceived as consisting only of (grapho)phonic analysis. There are a variety of word analysis strategies that students may employ, and no one strategy is necessarily any better or worse than another. Children who rely too heavily on only one strategy often produce distorted reading and have limited comprehension.

Although it may seem that skilled readers move through text so quickly that they must be recognizing every word at sight, it is clear that they actually do speed their word recognition by using graphophonic (letter/sound correspondence) cue systems within our language and by making predictions about words based on the context (meaning and sentence structure). For example, it is the contextual cue system that enables us to predict that the missing word in the sentence "The window in the kitchen of our new _____ is beautiful" could be either *house, home,* or *apartment.* However, it is the graphophonic cue system that assists you in determining that the missing word in the sentence "Our new h _ r _ _ is beautiful" is *horse* instead of *house* or *home.*

The utility of a given strategy depends on its effectiveness in the situation in which it is being applied. Therefore, children need to have a repertoire of word analysis strategies that are available for use in a variety of reading situations. *Contextual analysis* and *morphemic analysis* are both meaning-based word identification strategies. *Phonic analysis* is a strategy based on sound-symbol correspondence that results in approximate pronunciation of individual words.

Contextual analysis.   Probably the most common method of word analysis is to use the context of the sentence in which the unknown word appears and/or the context that surrounds the sentence to determine what the word is most likely to be. Mature readers make use of two sorts of context during reading: general and local context (Durkin 1983). General context is provided by the central topic and general organization of a text. For example, one would expect a story about the circus to include words such as *ringmaster, clown, acrobat, elephant,* and *trapeze,* or a chapter on heredity to include words such as *gene, meiosis,* and *chromosome.* Obviously, the use of general context requires prior knowledge about the topic of the text. Clues provided by the graphic aids in a text such as charts, maps, illustrations, titles, and subtitles are also likely to contribute to the general context of a text.

Readers who use local context take their cue from the phrases and sentences that surround an unknown word. For example, if you read "Nora wished she had a _____ so _____ could listen to her favorite station," you would expect the first word to be *radio* or possibly *Walkman,* because these are what we use to listen to a station. You would expect the second word to be the pronoun *she,* because of the other references to a girl's name, and *she* and *her* within the sentence. The possible choices are constrained by the syntactic and semantic cues provided by the local context.

Morphemic analysis.   Morphemic analysis is a strategy in which the reader breaks down words into smaller meaning-bearing units as an aid to word identification and understanding. *Morpheme* is a linguistic term for the smallest unit of meaning in our language.

The meaning-bearing units used in morphemic analysis are root words, affixes, and inflections. For example, the word *returnables* can be divided into four meaningful parts, *re-, turn, -able,* and *-s.* The prefix *re-* and the suffix *-able* are affixes that change the function of the root word. The inflectional ending

-s modulates the meaning of the root word without changing its function. Other common inflections signal possession *(-'s)*, verb tense *(-ed, -ing)*, or comparison *(-er, -est)*. Finally, morphemic analysis can be used as an aid in the identification and understanding of compound words *(*for example *fireman, breadbox)* and contractions *(*for example *don't, he'll)*.

   Phonic analysis.   When students use phonic analysis they decode unfamiliar words by identifying the sounds of each letter or group of letters in an unknown word and then saying the sounds together until the word is recognized. The ability to isolate *phonemes*, the linguistic term for the smallest unit of sound in our language, is central to successful application of phonic analysis. Words can be sounded out letter-by-letter or by using spelling patterns, letter clusters, or syllables that have predictable sounds. However, skilled readers most often use analogy with known words or word parts to pronounce unknown words (Cunningham 1975–76). Thus, *graphophonic analysis* proceeds by comparing the new, unknown display with known letter-sound combinations.

   The specific graphophonic patterns that are useful in phonic analysis are suggested by a framework for phonics instruction provided by Mason and Au (1990). These are: consonant-sound relations in the initial, medial, and final positions in words; blends of two or three consonants where each consonant retains its own sound *(spr, fl)*; consonant digraphs, or combinations of two consonants that are pronounced as one sound *(ch, th)*; vowel-sound patterns represented by vowels followed by *r* or *l* *(ar)*, and consonant-vowel-consonant *(sit)*, consonant-vowel-consonant-silent *e* *(lake)*, and consonant vowel-vowel *(meal)*; and, we would add, letter clusters or syllables that have consistent sounds *(-ot, -and)*.

   The use of graphophonic information in longer words often requires *structural analysis*. In structural analysis, readers must recognize and segment by syllable boundaries (either through "rules" or by identifying recurrent spelling patterns) and then apply known graphophonic patterns to decode the segments *(seg/ment)*. This phonological knowledge is critical to skilled reading. As Barker, Torgeson, and Wagner (1992) note,

> Skill at identifying words based on phonological information requires at least awareness of the phonological structure of words, knowledge of specific grapheme-phoneme correspondences, and skill in synthesizing the phonemes to produce a recognizable word. In many cases, phonological knowledge and skill can be used to identify words that have never before been encountered in print (335).

Orthographic Processes

Most experts today agree that word identification in skilled readers involves two types of knowledge and skill: phonological and orthographic. Orthographic processes are linked to the appearance of specific words. "Orthographic knowledge involves memory for specific visual/spelling patterns that identify individual words, or word parts, on the printed page. Orthographic knowledge

… would seem to be acquired by repeated exposure to printed words until a stable visual representation of the whole word, or meaningful subword units, has been acquired" (Barker, Torgeson, and Wagner 1992, 336).

Although there are relatively strong relationships between orthographic and phonologic skills in most individuals, it is also quite clear that these two abilities make unique and separate contributions to reading and writing performance (Juel, Griffith, and Gough 1986; Olson, Wise, Conners, Rack, and Fulker 1989). For example, orthographic skills appear to make a bigger difference in the reading of connected text (versus isolated word recognition) and also seem more highly related to fluency in reading (see below). It also appears that the relationships between phonological and orthographic skill are developmental, with orthographic skill making a stronger contribution to word reading after first grade (that is, after the initial stages of reading acquisition).

In summary, rapid and accurate word recognition is important to effective and efficient reading. A combination of strategies and abilities is useful, especially in the earliest stages of reading acquisition. However, as quickly as possible, students need to acquire accurate and rapid word identification skills that appear dependent on good phonologic and orthographic skills.

Rate and Fluency

Fluency and rate are not the same, although they are related in that fluent readers can enhance rate of reading. *Rate* of reading refers to the speed of oral and/or silent reading as measured in words per minute. Proficient reading requires *automaticity*, or the ability to identify words rapidly enough that sufficient resources are available for attention to comprehension. Research suggests that beginning readers who develop automatic word identification skills are better able to comprehend text (Perfetti and Hogaboam 1975). How fast is fast enough, and how slow is too slow, are questions that are still open for debate, however. Norms for reading rate vary widely, and research designed to improve comprehension by teaching rapid word identification has produced equivocal results. It appears that reading rate may be a necessary but insufficient condition for proficient reading, and that decisions about the adequacy of a student's reading rate may need to be made on an individual basis.

The important point here is that it is not enough to know the level of accuracy with which a reader identifies words or applies various word analysis strategies. It is also important to know how efficient the reader is in these areas. For example, a student may be able to recognize successfully many words, but may require so much time and effort that few resources remain available for use in comprehending what was read.

Oral fluency refers to readers' ability to group words into meaningful phrase units and use expression as they read. It is regarded by many as a necessary feature of good reading, and a lack of fluency, or word-by-word reading, is often noted as a characteristic of poor readers. Allington (1983b) notes that fluency is often overlooked in assessment and instruction because it is mistakenly assumed that it is merely a symptom of poor word identification skills. Unfortunately, he argues further, this interpretation often leads to additional instruction in letters, sounds, or words in isolation in the mistaken belief that more attention to these areas will result in improved reading.

Recent evidence from a special study conducted along the 1992 National Assessment of Educational Progress (NAEP) reading assessement suggests a strong relationship between oral fluency and silent reading comprehension (Pinnell et al. 1995). There is also evidence that high levels of fluency are related to ample opportunities to practice (Lipson and Lang 1990; Pinnell et al. 1995). This, in turn, is likely related to the fact that the development of good orthographic knowledge and skill seem to make a strong contribution to both rate and fluency. Perhaps, as Barker, Torgeson, and Wagner (1992) note, orthographic skills allow readers to recognize words as wholes automatically, circumventing the need for more discrete levels of phonological analysis. This, in turn, allows readers to focus more attention on the other aspects of reading text, most notably, meaning.

Spelling

English does not have a one-to-one correspondence between graphemes (letters) and phonemes (sounds). The twenty-six letters of the alphabet represent approximately forty-four phonemes. To further complicate the situation, three letters—c, q, and x—do not represent unique phonemes, and there are anywhere between 500 and 2,000 spellings to represent the forty-four phonemes in English. The sheer number of spellings and the lack of fit between phonemes and graphemes suggest that children are unlikely to learn to spell simply through memorization or sounding out words. Like learning to read and write, learning to spell is a developmental process.

Charles Read (1971, 1975, 1986) studied preschoolers' efforts to spell words and found that they used their knowledge of English phonology to invent spellings for words. Not all children invent spellings in exactly the same way or at the same pace, but they do develop spelling strategies in roughly the same sequence (Henderson 1980) and move through roughly the same stages to become conventional spellers (Gentry 1982). These five stages are described more fully in Chapter 7 (Emergent Literacy). Generally, children move from early scribbles and letter-like forms to representing sounds without reference to conventional spelling combinations. Eventually, children stop relying only on phonological information and begin to use morphological (word parts) and visual information to spell many words correctly.

Researchers continue to study children's spelling development in later years. For example, Firth (1980) found that older students who are good readers and spellers make spelling errors that are characteristic of the transitional stage, while students who are poor readers and spellers make errors that are characteristic of the semiphonetic and phonetic stages. Other studies indicate a developmental shift among better spellers from a reliance upon the phoneme-grapheme strategies used in the early school years toward a strategy of spelling words by analogy to other known words.

Although research on spelling ability is still emerging, the evidence to date indicates that the ability to spell is a consequence of knowing about words in many ways—their visual or graphic characteristics, their phonological and structural properties, and their meanings. These types of knowledge are clearly enhanced through immersion in a literate environment with daily opportunities to read and write.

Grammar, Usage, and the Mechanics of Writing

Grammar is the description of the structure of a language based on principles of word and sentence formation. In the case of oral language, students will need to learn about the appropriate use of language in different social situations and contexts and the reasons for paying attention to appropriateness. In the case of written language, students will learn that most grammar and usage issues come into play during the revision and editing phases of the writing process. Through practice, students gradually become more and more familiar with the conventions of grammar and usage, but at some point the "rules" of grammar and usage may need to be addressed directly. However, they must be viewed as part of a real social context or as part of the revising and editing phases of writing to be helpful.

Grammar

Grammar can be defined as a system of rules by which words are arranged into meaningful units. Everyone who speaks and understands English knows the rules, even if they can't articulate them. For example, we know that *The dog chased the cat up the tree* is a grammatical sentence, while *Tree up cat dog the the chased the* is not, because it violates rules of English grammar. Since we are aware of the violations, we must, on some level, know the rules that have been violated, even if we can't state them clearly. Rules such as these are best characterized as *subconscious abstract concepts*.

In contrast, *explicit* rules have been created by individuals trying to describe English grammar as it is used. A perfect set of explicit rules would be one that described all of the sentences that most people would consider grammatical and excluded any that would not be considered grammatical. No one has ever developed a perfect set of rules, but linguists continue to try and in the process have developed different types of grammars. Elements of two kinds of grammar—structural and transformational—are most relevant to our concerns with grammar instruction and learning. These elements are: form classes or parts of speech; structures of common sentences; and transformation of sentences.

Structural grammar focuses on sentence patterns and the functions of words in sentences. It identifies four form classes resembling nouns, verbs, adjectives, and adverbs. All the words that can fill a particular slot in a sentence belong to the same class. Advocates of structural grammars describe patterns or basic sentence types. For example, Roberts (1962) developed a sequence of ten patterns that are frequently used in textbooks that use a structural approach (Determiner—Noun—Verb [Intransitive]—Adverb).

Transformational grammar focuses on the process used to generate sentences and ideas. Using four or five basic sentence types (or kernels) as the starting point for making sentences, we add transformations to change our basic sentences into more complex ones. Three kinds of sentence transformations are those that: (1) change one type of sentence into another, such as questions, negatives, and passive sentences; (2) conjoin elements of several sentences into compounds; and (3) reduce some sentences into fragments and insert them into other sentences (Malmstrom 1968).

It appears that nearly all children can use the basic sentence types and, as well, that instruction in sentence combining is beneficial to a broad range of students, especially those who are less-skilled (Hillocks 1986). On the other hand, Applebee and his colleagues (Applebee et al. 1990), using data from the National Assessment of Educational Progress (NAEP), concluded that student writing among nine, thirteen, and seventeen year-olds across the country revealed that very few have any significant difficulty with sentences or fragments.

Usage
Language usage concerns the various language standards considered appropriate for different occasions, audiences, and purposes. Everyone's language varies, depending on the formality of the occasion. The number of usage levels available differs according to different grammarians. One scheme suggests three possible levels of usage—nonstandard English, general English, and formal English (Lodge and Trett 1968). However, it is important to recognize that language standards change from one group to another and with time. "In the final analysis, the appropriateness of usage must be determined within the social context in which the language is used" (Savage 1977, 369).

Mechanics of Writing
The mechanics of writing include punctuation and capitalization. Punctuation and capitalization are important because they clarify meaning. During oral exchanges, listeners hear pauses, speech stops, and rising and falling intonation that help them construct meaning. Readers and writers replace these verbal signals with punctuation and capitalization.

Studies show that punctuation—particularly with commas and periods—is frequently a problem for elementary-age students (Porter 1974). Most children seem to have fewer problems applying capitalization rules than applying punctuation rules. A recent NAEP report concluded that the writing of about 10 percent of the students reflected relatively serious problems with punctuation (Applebee et al. l990). Thus, attention to punctuation will be an issue for some students or for many students in some settings.

UNDERSTANDING CONTEXTUAL FACTORS THAT INFLUENCE PERFORMANCE

Contextual factors are the least likely to be considered in any discussion of reading and writing performance. Indeed, the importance of context has only recently been realized. In the following sections, we describe briefly several aspects of context that have been shown to influence reading and writing: the setting in which the reading and writing event occurs, the reading and writing curriculum, the instructional methods employed, and the instructional materials and tasks associated with reading and writing. This brief discussion serves only to introduce ideas that will be discussed at greater length in Chapters 5 and 6.

Settings

The community and culture of students exert central, often critical, influence on achievement in reading and writing. It also appears that the willingness and ability of the school to respond to local and/or cultural characteristics has a powerful impact on reading and writing acquisition and performance and can determine the effectiveness of instruction and achievement (Gallego and Hollingsworth 1992; Goldenberg and Gallimore 1991). For example, home environments different from the dominant culture are not pathological. Students can be hopelessly handicapped, however, if the school expects and accepts only one type of entry experience from its students.

The setting in which reading and writing and their instruction take place affects reading and writing performance. Meaning making depends on the broader context in which a text is being written or read. For example, imagine that you are reading or writing a text on common antidotes to poisoning. Now imagine the effect that context would have in the following situations: the evening newspaper; a test of reading comprehension; at home after you believe your child has ingested some poisonous substance; and a first aid course.

Similarly, researchers have found differences in students' performance on the same task, depending on subtle changes in the classroom context; that is, whether students were asked to do the task as part of an informal lesson or as part of a formal testing situation (Mosenthal and Na 1980). Indeed, there are several aspects of classroom settings that have been examined and found to contribute to students' reading and writing achievement. For example, grouping patterns influence both teachers and students. Reviews of ability grouping for reading instruction suggest that instructional and social reading experiences differ for students in high- and low-ability reading groups and that these differences influence students' learning (Allington 1983a; Hiebert 1983). Grouping practices may also communicate information to students about their relative ability that eventually influences their learning (Weinstein 1976).

Instructional Resources

Students are presented with an enormous array of materials and tasks during their development as readers and writers. Prominent among these are textual materials, commercial instructional programs and, most recently, technological resources.

Textual Materials

Students come in contact with a wide variety of textual materials in their daily lives as readers and writers—comic books, cereal boxes, instructions for constructing models, notes from friends, letters from relatives, and so forth. It is possible, and perhaps even desirable, to consider any or all of these materials as having instructional potential. However the range of materials used for instruction in most classrooms is more constrained than this, and the materials students are exposed to during instruction often differ from the materials they may encounter in other contexts.

In almost every classroom students are asked to read various types of prose, or written texts. Prose selections used for instructional purposes come from a variety of sources, including basal readers, trade books (children's literature), subject area textbooks, magazines, reference materials, weekly readers, and the students' own writing. Research consistently demonstrates that the printed materials students encounter in instructional contexts influence reading and writing. In the past, one of the only text features that was given much attention was its difficulty or readability, as measured by factors such as the number of syllables in the words and the number of words in the sentences. Current research has demonstrated that there are a number of other factors that have a significant impact on both how much and what students understand and learn from a text. The presence or absence of these factors determines the extent to which a given text can be considered "considerate" or "inconsiderate" (Armbruster 1984).

Considerate texts are designed to enable the learner to gather appropriate information with minimal effort; inconsiderate texts require the learner to put forth extra effort in order to compensate for the inadequacies of the text. Inconsiderate texts are not necessarily incomprehensible, but they do require more effort, skill, and prior knowledge to comprehend. Two factors that determine the "considerateness" of a given text are its type and organization. For example, under certain circumstances, students' oral reading and writing errors have been observed to vary according to the type of text they were reading and writing (stories versus informational articles; subject area texts versus basal materials). Stories are more easily comprehended than informational texts for many students, and well-constructed stories are more easily comprehended than less well-organized stories (Brennan, Bridge, and Winograd 1986; Olson 1985).

The linguistic properties of texts including word usage, sentence structure, and sentence connectives are another factor influencing its comprehensibility.

Each of these surface features influences performance on a variety of reading tasks. For example, texts that include a large proportion of words that occur with high frequency in our language are more easily comprehended than texts with a large proportion of low-frequency words (Ruddell 1965; Wittrock, Marks, and Doctorow 1975).

The comprehensibility or considerateness of a text is also influenced by its structural characteristics, including all the features of texts that authors and editors use to aid organization and understanding such as headings, boldface type, illustrations, diagrams, and end-of-chapter questions and activities. For example, there is evidence that comprehension is enhanced when main idea statements are highlighted through the use of italics or headings (Baumann 1986). It also appears that students are actually led to attend to unimportant ideas when structural features focus on trivial information. For example, if questions that follow reading focus on insignificant details, children are more likely to learn this information than the more important ideas in the text (Wixson 1984).

Commercial Programs

In many classrooms, students still work primarily from commercial programs and teachers rely heavily on the published plans that accompany these materials. These materials inevitably become a part of a teacher's instructional set and often determine both what is read and written and what instructional activity is employed. Analyses of the lesson frames, materials, and instructional activities provided in most basal reading programs indicates that publishers have been responsive to earlier criticisms, but that problems remain, especially when these materials are used nonselectively (Durkin 1981; Wepner and Feeley 1993). Too often, these materials still create an environment that involves mechanical completion of unconnected activities. Although there is variability, there is still too little reading in many programs and too little coherence in the skill work.

The *instructional tasks* and *practice activities* that students perform define reading and writing for them. For example, in some classrooms students spend more time doing seatwork activities than they do reading and writing. It should be noted that these materials generally provide practice of separate component areas, not practice in the holistic act of reading or writing. This is especially true for students who are experiencing reading and writing difficulties (Allington 1984; Allington et al. 1986).

Alternatively, many classrooms contain other types of materials and tasks, including extensive quantities of specially created small paperback books which are accompanied by instructional frameworks. These materials include reading levels and suggestions for assessment. These program materials are often used by teachers who identify themselves as "whole language" teachers and are exerting an influence on practice that is as substantial as basal programs. Similarly for writing, some programs are still defined by grammar books and teacher-assigned "creative writing" activities, while others involve writers' workshops, conferences, and self-selected topics. The students in these classrooms will think about reading and writing differently than students in classrooms where reading and writing are extensive and pervasive and where tasks are linked in authentic ways to the reading and writing products. These different tasks produce different types of writers.

Multimedia and Microcomputer Activities

Although access to them varies considerably by school and district, multimedia and microcomputer activities are an important additional type of material. Careful examination of these programs is especially important for teachers who work with less-able readers and writers. There is continuing pressure to operate remedial settings through the use of diagnostic-prescriptive management systems that involve microcomputer testing, computer-generated profiles of skill needs, and computer programs for remedial instruction. There are also many other types of computer programs intended for assessment and instruction in reading, and their role in instruction may have an important affect on students' reading and writing performance.

Curriculum

The curriculum in a particular setting can have a critical influence on student performance because it may influence access to instruction, dictate the type of instruction offered, and even determine what is counted as reading and writing performance. Over the past fifty years, writing and reading curriculum have had overlapping but separate histories (Langer and Allington 1992). Although the two areas were not conceptualized as being related or integrated, each area was faced with similar internal tensions; that is, the call for grammar exercises versus a student-centered curriculum in writing, and the call for reading basics versus a meaning-based curriculum in reading. During the 1980s these tensions became even more obvious as the emphasis on social perspectives focused attention on the importance of communication, context, and culture in learning.

Curriculum focuses instructional attention, helping teachers and schools decide what and how to teach. Although instructional methods and approaches have responded to researach over the past three decades, curriculum often has not. Studies of writing curriculum, for example, reveal little attention to writing extended texts for a wide variety of purposes accompanied by a heavy emphasis on mechanics — as recently as the 1980s at both the elementary and secondary levels (Graves 1983; Bridge and Hiebert 1985; Applebee 1981).

In reading, the curriculum has often been defined by commercially produced materials, typically basal reader series. A recent review of basal reading programs suggests that the curriculum presented by these programs has changed in the past decade (Hoffman et al. 1994). For example, the literature is drawn from children's literature rather than contrived or commissioned pieces; the vocabulary is less stringently controlled; and there is a decreased focus on phonics and isolated skills instruction. However, reading and writing are still more likely to be taught as separate areas than integrated with each other and the other language arts.

For students experiencing problems with reading and writing, the curriculum issue is even more complicated. When more children began attending school in the early part of the twentieth century, it was observed that not every student learned what they were supposed to learn at each grade level. In response to this observation, American education adopted the position that it was not fair to hold all students to the same standards and searched for the most appropriate techniques for differentiating instruction and for setting differential educational goals (Allington 1991).

Not until the 1970s and 1980s did people begin to suggest that what had been considered differentiation might actually be a form of discrimination (Carew and Lightfoot 1979). It was observed that students with the least adaptive capacity were asked to make the greatest adjustments across the school day (Good 1983), including exposure to multiple literacy curricula often representing divergent theories of reading and writing processes. Increasing evidence of the lack of efficacy of the "second system" programs that have evolved since the turn of the century (Allington 1994) has resulted in the current movement toward establishing a common set of high-level curriculum standards for ALL students. Many believe that this is the only way to ensure that all students are provided equal opportunities to achieve.

The important point for this discussion is that the reading and writing curriculum has a tremendous impact on student performance. Many local school districts have their own curriculum as do many states. Curricula that reflect a more skills-based perspective are likely to promote very different procedures for instruction and assessment than curricula that reflect a more interactive or sociocultural perspective. Current efforts to develop national standards in English language arts are likely to result in greater integration of the language arts, especially reading and writing, in both instruction and assessment (Pearson 1993). The nature of the curriculum cannot be underestimated as a factor in students' reading and writing performance.

Instructional Methods

Two major components of instruction are the content of instruction (what is being taught) and the methods that are used (how content is being taught). In addition to the curriculum issues discussed above, different emphases in content that influence performance can be characterized by the three types of instructional outcomes described by Duffy and Roehler (1989): *attitude* goals, *content* goals, and *process* goals. For example, there is evidence that instructional programs that focus on the processes of reading and writing have a powerful impact on students' awareness of what has been taught, awareness of comprehension and composing strategies, and performance on tasks that require strategic reading and writing (Duffy et al. 1986; Paris, Cross, and Lipson 1984).

Differences in instructional methods that influence performance vary along a continuum from direct, or explicit, instruction to discovery, or implicit, learning. Direct instruction involves explaining or telling students the procedures involved in engaging in a particular reading or writing activity. Indirect methods instruct through repeated practice with activities that are examples of the desired reading behavior. Discovery methods emphasize placing students in a literate environment in which reading and writing will develop naturally. These different types of instruction are likely to have a major impact on reading and writing performance.

Other aspects of instructional method that influence student performance include features such as "wait time" and the purposes and tasks associated with reading and writing activities. Teachers often provide very little "wait time" or "think time" to students after a question has been posed (Rowe 1974). This limited wait time results in student responses that tend to be low-level and closed. When teachers extend the wait time by even a small amount, however, student responses tend to be both longer and more thoughtful. In addition, more students respond, the responses tend to be more open-minded, and there are fewer occasions in which students fail to respond at all.

The purposes for which students' read or write and/or the tasks they must complete in association with their reading and writing can also make a difference in performance. For example, questioning is probably the most frequently used task in reading instruction. The evidence suggests that the type of questions children are asked can influence their comprehension. It appears that implicit or inferential questions are more difficult for many children than explicit or literal questions (Pearson, Hansen, and Gordon 1979). Furthermore, there is evidence that the type of questions asked influences the numbers and types of inferences students make. Specifically, questions with answers stated explicitly in the text result in fewer inferences, questions that require the integration of information in the text result in a larger number of text-based inferences, and questions that require students to draw heavily on their prior knowledge result in more knowledge-based inferences (Wixson 1983a).

Assessment Practices

There are at least two dimensions of assessment practices within specific instructional contexts that can influence reading and writing performance. The first dimension involves those assessments, often standardized tests, that are required for external accountability purposes. The second dimension involves the tests and alternative assessments that are selected and/or created by the teacher for evaluation and to inform instruction.

Measures used for external accountability purposes can include anything from standardized tests, to basal tests, to teacher-made examinations and questioning. These measures can influence student reading and writing performance in several ways. For example, when students are aware that their performance is being evaluated for the purpose of reporting to parents, the school, or beyond, they are likely to perform differently than they do on the "everyday" work of the classroom and beyond. Some are motivated by these circumstances to put forth additional effort and perform beyond the levels displayed on a daily basis. Others experience increased anxiety in these situations resulting in a loss in their performance.

The form and content of external accountability measures can also influence students' reading and writing performance. Specifically, students' performance is likely to suffer when the form and content of an external accountability measure is inconsistent with the form and content of classroom tasks. These types of inconsistencies can also confuse students about their learning goals. For example, many accountability measures consist of multiple-choice and short answer tasks focused on decontextualized skills. Students who have little experience with these types of tasks are likely to do less well than students who experience them on a regular basis. Furthermore, students who are evaluated in this manner are likely to evaluate their own competence in terms of their ability to perform a series of isolated skills tasks.

Concerns about the form and content of standardized tests have led many educators and researchers to develop alternative assessment procedures. These alternative assessments focus directly on students' work as a means of evaluating student performance and take a variety of forms including portfolios, observation, and performance tasks. Alternative assessments are characterized by features such as—contextualized, complex tasks that are truly representative of performance in the field, well-articulated criteria to guide evaluation, opportunities for student self-assessment and reflection, and students' public presentation of their work (Wiggins 1989).

When designed properly, alternative assessments can impact student performance in more positive ways than traditional accountability measures. For example, when students are involved in developing, exhibiting, and evaluating their own work, they are more likely to develop a sense of responsibility and ownership of their work. They are also more likely to analyze and reflect on their progress regularly. These are both important factors in developing motivated, strategic, and reflective readers and writers.

It is important to be aware of what types of assessments are being used and for what purposes within specific instructional contexts. If the only form of assessment is testing focused on isolated skills, then students are likely to be attending to skill mastery at the expense of integrated skill performances. In contrast, if the only form of assessment is student self-reflection, then students are likely to become more responsible for their own learning, but may miss some important skills and not progress as rapidly as needed to perform at desirable levels. As can be seen, assessment practices can have a significant impact on students' reading and writing performance.

UNDERSTANDING LEARNER FACTORS THAT INFLUENCE PERFORMANCE

An interactive view of reading and writing suggests that a variety of learner factors influence reading and writing performance. These include prior knowledge, knowledge about reading and writing, attitudes and motivation, and the physical, cognitive, linguistic, and social-emotional correlates of reading and writing disability.

Prior Content Knowledge

Put simply, what learners already know about the events, ideas, and objects described in a text influences the meaning they construct from that text (Lipson 1982, 1983). Current research supports the view that this background, or prior, knowledge is organized in long-term memory as knowledge structures. Each individual structured network is referred to as a *schema*.

Schema theory has had a strong influence on our understanding of how learners comprehend and compose. A schema-theoretic view of reading and writing suggests that meaning making occurs as learners construct relationships between an existing schema and the information suggested by a text they are reading or writing. The learner's schema provides a framework of expectations that includes slots for different elements of information.

For example, a restaurant schema contains slots for menus, waitpersons, food prices, and so forth, and these slots are further refined by additional information about the type of restaurant, such as fast food, diner, or gourmet. It is also clear that different people with different experiential backgrounds will have somewhat different restaurant schemas.

Comprehension proceeds so smoothly under ordinary circumstances that most adults are unaware of the process of constructing a model or interpretation of a text that fits with their knowledge of the world. It is instructive to try to understand material for which meaning is not immediately apparent. For example, take a moment to read and try to understand the paragraph in the following exercise, which was used in a classic study by Bransford and Johnson (1972):

> The procedure is actually quite simple. First you arrange things into different groups. Of course, one pile may be sufficient depending on how much there is to do. If you have to go somewhere else due to lack of facilities that is the next step, otherwise you are pretty well set. It is important not to overdo things. That is, it is better to do too few things at once than too many. In the short run this may not seem important, but complications can easily arise. A mistake can be expensive as well. At first the whole procedure will seem complicated. Soon, however, it will become just another facet of life. It is difficult to foresee any end to the necessity for this task in the immediate future, but then one never can tell. After the procedure is completed one arranges the materials into different groups again. Then they can be put into their appropriate places. Eventually they will be used once more and the whole cycle will then have to be repeated. However, that is part of life. (722)

Were there any words you could not pronounce, or for which you do not have some meaning? Is syntax too complex? You probably did not have problems in either of these areas. Yet, for most people, this passage does not make much sense. However, it does become meaningful as soon as we use the title

"Washing Clothes." Then the slots for procedures and sorting that are referred to in the passage can be filled with specific knowledge we have about the procedures and sorting that occur as part of washing clothes.

Learners also need to understand a great deal about social interactions and human relationships in order to connect ideas in texts. This type of prior knowledge seems to be especially important in inferential understanding (Trabasso 1981). Fragmented information and/or misconceptions can impede comprehension (Hynd and Alvermann 1986; Lipson 1982, 1983; Maria 1986). This is especially troublesome when students attempt to learn from informational texts. Misconceptions and limited information influence comprehension in a number of ways. People read unfamilar text more slowly, they remember less, they construct meanings that are inconsistent with the authors, and they sometimes reject the text information outright.

There are many times when a text written for an audience with certain background knowledge is given to an audience with different or limited knowledge of the topic. For example, note the difficulties certain learners will have trying to understand the materials in Figure 2.3 that were taken from newspapers in Vermont and Australia. Now suppose you were asked to identify the main ideas of these texts. If you failed to complete this task successfully, would it mean that you do not know how to "get" a main idea? Obviously not; it simply means that you do not have sufficient background knowledge about the game of cricket, or about dairy cows, to be able to understand the most important points in these texts. Yet we rarely consider our students' prior knowledge in evaluating their performance on comprehension tasks.

Although there is little direct evidence regarding the role of prior knowledge as a factor in writing, common sense suggests that it would influence performance in analogous ways. Almost all views of the writing process, for example, involve a prewriting stage in which writers either activate existing topic knowledge or engage in experiences or information-gathering activities to expand knowledge. Authors can only use the voice they have or convey the knowledge and experience they possess.

A basic fallacy of skills-based views of reading and writing is that skills are static across all reading and writing situations, and that students' skill performance under one set of reading and writing conditions is indicative of their performance under all reading and writing conditions. Clearly, this is not the case for us or for our students. Children do not have the same experiential background as adults, and the meanings they construct for a given piece of text may be different from the meanings constructed by their adult teachers or authors of instructional materials.

Knowledge About Reading and Writing

Any discussion of the factors that influence reading and writing would be incomplete without reference to terms such as *metacognition*. This term was introduced by developmental psychologists to refer to individuals' knowledge

FIGURE 2.3

Text Taken from Newspapers in Vermont and Australia

NIGHT AUCTION

Thursday, Oct. 9th 7:30 PM

Located on the so-called Harry Domina farm on Route #118 between East Berkshire and Montgomery, Vt. Watch for Auction Signs at Route Jct. #105 & #118 in East Berkshire, Vt.

50 Holstein Heifers 50

22 of the heifers are fresh within the last ten days and are milking between 50 to 60 lbs. of weighed milk, balance are all springing, 5 of these heifers are registered with papers that will be handed out the same night. Heifers have good size and condition and are going to be sold for cash regardless of price. Heifers have all been T.B., blood tested and inoculated from shipping fever and I.B.R. Heifers are open for inspection anytime on site where auction is to be held. Trucking available.

Auctioneer: **Ringman:**
Tel: **Berkshire, Vt.**
Sales held inside tent Tel:

Owners:
Berkshire, Vt. Tel.:

CRICKET MATCH
AUSTRALIA vs. ENGLAND

A hair-raising century by Australian opener Graeme Wood on Friday set England back on its heels in the third test at the Melbourne Cricket Ground. Unfortunately, living dangerously eventually cost the Australians the match. Wood was caught out of his crease on the first over after lunch. Within ten more overs, the Australians were dismissed. Four were dismissed by dangerous running between creases. Two were dismissed when the English bowlers lifted the bails from the batsmen's wickets. The three remaining batsmen were caught by English fieldsmen. One was caught as he tried for a six. When the innings were complete the Australians had fallen short of the runs scored by the English.

From "Developing Readers' Knowledge Through Analogy" by David A. Hayes and Robert J. Tierney, *Reading Research Quarterly*, Vol. 17, No. 2, 1982.

about and control over their own learning and thinking activities (Flavell and Wellman 1977; Brown 1978).

Metacognition in reading and writing refers to one's understanding of the reading and writing processes. This understanding is revealed in two ways. First, understanding involves the learner's knowledge of the nature of reading and writing; the purposes and goals of reading and writing; the various factors that influence reading and writing; and the what, how, when, and why of strategy usage in reading and writing. Second, learners' understanding is reflected in the control they have of their actions while reading and writing for different purposes. Active learners monitor their own state of learning, plan strategies, adjust efforts appropriately, and evaluate the success of their ongoing efforts (Brown, Armbruster, and Baker 1986; Raphael, Kirschner, and Englert 1988).

Research suggests that skilled learners know a great deal about reading and writing, and that this knowledge influences their ability to select and use appropriate strategies and skills in different reading and writing situations. It is becoming increasingly clear that learners need several types of knowledge in order to become proficient. First, they need to understand that a skill or strategy exists and is available to be used for reading/writing. For example, writers need to be aware that they can edit or revise their writing when it does not communicate their meaning as clearly. Many young and less-skilled writers seem unaware of this aspect of skilled writing. This type of knowledge is called *declarative knowledge* and requires only that the child know that a skill or strategy exists.

Knowing that a particular skill or tactic exists is not enough for successful performance. Learners also need to know how to perform the skill or strategy. To continue with our example, it is not sufficient to know that you can change your writing to clarify meaning; you must also understand how to go about editing and revising. This type of knowledge is called *procedural knowledge* because it refers to knowledge of the procedures necessary to execute and orchestrate the components of the reading process.

In the past, it was assumed that declarative and procedural knowledge would ensure application; that students who knew about the components and how to apply them would surely use this knowledge in the appropriate reading situations. Almost daily, however, teachers encounter students who appear to have mastered a skill or strategy sufficiently to employ it, but who fail to demonstrate any such competence during real reading situations. These children often fail to apply their existing skills and strategies because they lack a third type of knowledge, *conditional knowledge* (Paris, Lipson, and Wixson 1983). Simply stated, conditional knowledge is knowledge about when and why to employ a known strategy or skill. For example, skimming is obviously not a universally helpful approach to reading. Readers need to know when and why it is appropriate to use skimming. Conditional knowledge is essential for students to be able to apply the strategies and skills learned during reading instruction in other reading situations.

Skilled learners possess a wide range of knowledge related to reading and writing including knowledge of purposes and goals, knowledge of various text factors, knowledge of task requirements, and knowledge about the skills and strategies used in reading and writing. For example, they know that the purpose of reading and writing is "to make meaning" rather than "to say all of the words right" or "to write neatly." Skilled learners also realize that reading and writing will be easier if they know a great deal about the topic of the text they are reading or writing and if they are interested in it (Myers and Paris 1978). These examples may seem incredibly obvious, but there are many young and poor learners who do not have even these basic understandings about reading and writing.

Skilled learners also understand how various text factors can influence their reading and writing. Before we ever open a book or write the first words in a text, our knowledge of the type of text we are reading or writing influences the way we will read or write that text. We know about different types of texts such as encyclopedias, cookbooks, letters from friends, novels, newspapers, and so forth. We have expectations for how these texts are organized and for the types of information they contain, and this knowledge guides us in the selection of appropriate reading and writing strategies. For example, if you were reading or writing about a miracle cure for baldness from/for *Scientific American*, you would be likely to approach the task differently than if you were reading or writing about it from/for the *National Enquirer*.

Knowledge about the tasks that learners will be asked to complete in the course of reading and writing also affects strategy selection and usage. When we asked a group of fifth grade students to tell us why they thought their teachers wanted them to work in their workbooks, one child responded indignantly, "Do you know what she [the teacher] did? She gave us a test on the workbook. You're not supposed to remember that stuff!" His response reflected his awareness that in many classrooms students need not remember the material in their workbooks, but simply complete it and put it in the appropriate place.

Skilled learners also have knowledge about different skills and strategies for reading and writing and about how to use them. For example, they are aware of strategies for dealing with words and sentences they do not know (ask for help, use the dictionary, reread). They are also aware of the purposes for different strategies such as planning or prewriting (it helps you get out all your ideas, you can see how your ideas go together). It is not sufficient to know what the strategies are and how to use them; learners must also know when and why to use them.

Skilled learners not only have a great deal of knowledge about reading and writing, but they can also apply that knowledge to monitor and regulate their reading and writing. For example, they know when their answers to questions are not satisfactory (Garner and Reis 1981). There is also evidence that they can adjust their strategies in response to different reading and writing situations (reading and writing for fun, reading and writing for specific ideas or for general impressions, studying), and that they use specific strategies to meet the demands of specific reading and writing situations (for example, using different styles depending on their relationship to the intended audience of their writing). In summary, it appears that students' knowledge and control of the reading and writing processes play an important role in their reading and writing performance.

Attitudes and Motivation

Whether children perform or learn in a particular situation depends on whether they can do what must be done and whether they choose to do it (Adelman and Taylor 1977). Learning and performance require both skill and will (Paris, Lipson, and Wixson 1983). Factors such as interest, the amount of time and effort required, willingness to take risks, or perceived competence can influence children's decisions whether to use their skills or not.

The student's attitude toward reading and writing is a central factor affecting reading and writing performance. Good students generally have more positive attitudes toward reading and writing than do poor students. Attitudes, beliefs, and expectancies become more negative with failure. This results in less effort, which, in turn, maintains a cycle of failure (Dweck and Bempechat 1983). Positive attitudes and motivation can compensate for relatively weak skills, and negative attitudes can prevent a student from applying existing knowledge or from acquiring new information (Paris, Olson, and Stevenson 1983).

A related finding is that high interest in reading material results in greater desire to read and increased comprehension (Asher 1980). Clearly, students tend to have more knowledge about topics that interest them, so research on interest is somewhat confounded with prior knowledge, which is in itself a powerful factor in comprehension and composition. However, there is also evidence that interest enables students to read beyond their measured ability, and that low-achieving students are more affected by interest than high-achieving students (Shnayer 1969).

Research indicates that positive self-perceptions promote achievement-oriented behavior, whereas low self-perceptions lead to decreased motivation (Harter 1981). In addition, positive attitudes and self-perceptions are associated with a sense of control over reading and writing successes and failures. Perceived lack of control can grow out of repeated and prolonged failure experiences. This can have a debilitating effect, sometimes called *learned helplessness*, which in turn causes a general expectation that all events that happen to the person are uncontrollable. The end result can be passive behavior.

This cyclic pattern was demonstrated in a study by Butkowsky and Willows (1980). The poor learners in the study had significantly lower initial expectations for success than did average and good learners, and when confronted with failure, they persisted at the task for shorter periods of time. However, it also appears that children's beliefs about why they succeed or fail in reading and writing vary across reading and writing situations (Hiebert, Winograd, and Danner 1984). Therefore, it is likely that learners' willingness to exert effort also will vary from situation to situation.

Correlates of Reading and Writing Performance

There are a number of factors internal to the learner related to skilled reading and writing. These factors are frequently referred to as *correlates* of reading and writing ability/disability, because strengths and weaknesses in any of these areas are often correlated with reading and/or writing performance. When one or more of these correlates is strongly present in a student or a student population, these students may be considered *at risk* for school failure (Vacca and Padak 1990). It is important to understand, however, that a high correlation between some organic factor and performance in reading and writing does not ensure that the organic factor is the *cause* of the high or low performance. The research thus far has yielded only equivocal findings regarding the causal relationships between most correlates and reading and writing success.

Despite the lack of evidence supporting specific causal relationships, it is still important to be aware of these factors. In individual cases, they may either account for reading and writing difficulties or simply compound the problem. In other cases, they will be ruled out as playing any meaningful role in reading and writing disability. In the following sections, we describe briefly correlates of reading and writing performance in four major areas: social and emotional development; physical development; language development; and cognitive development.

Social and Emotional Development

An area related to attitudes and motivation is students' social and emotional development. Students who have trouble adjusting to various social situations with peers and/or adults may experience academic difficulties. Students with emotional problems may also have difficulty concentrating in school, which often has a negative effect on their learning.

It has been estimated that emotional problems are a contributing cause of reading and writing problems for about 25 percent of reading and writing disability cases (Kappelman, Kaplan, and Ganter 1969). However, it is frequently difficult to determine to what extent emotional and social maladjustment are causes or results of reading and writing problems. "Every poor learner is at risk for psychological disturbance, almost always as a result of, rarely as the cause of, and frequently as a further contribution to, the poor reading [and writing]" (Eisenberg 1975, 219).

Although Harris and Sipay (1985) note that studies have failed to demonstrate stable relationships between poor learners as a group and emotional or social difficulties, individual students may certainly exhibit reading and writing difficulties due largely to social or emotional problems. There are students for whom learning is made more difficult by family upheaval, by neglect, and by interpersonal problems in school. In addition, of course, physiologically based emotional problems (for example, from drug-related birth trauma) can lead to students who are easily discouraged or unable to relate to others. Regardless of whether emotional and social problems are the cause or the result of reading and writing problems, if they are interfering with learning and performance, they must be considered in developing an instructional program.

Language Development

The acquisition of language competence is a major factor influencing subsequent reading and writing achievement. As children learn language, they develop abilities in understanding and producing speech. This development involves learning how their language is structured, how humans use language to communicate, and the specific words and rules of their own language.

All languages have certain characteristics, described earlier in this chapter, which children must learn or acquire (see also Chapter 7). Humans use language for a variety of purposes, and understanding the functions embedded in language is critical to comprehending and composing messages. The communicative functions include regulating other people's behavior, expressing feelings, pretending and creating, conveying or obtaining information, and establishing and maintaining contact with others.

This highlights the importance of recognizing that language and culture are strongly interrelated (Ovando 1988), which means that the aspects of context (culture, setting, etc.) influence learner factors as well as performance. The influence of context, in other words, can affect the learner directly or interact with learner factors (and other context factors) to influence performance. As Ruddell (1993) has noted:

> Regardless of whether students are learning English as a second language or a third (or fourth) language, much of what they bring to school from their primary langauge is a part of the beliefs, attitudes, behaviors, and values of their primary culture as well. To teach bi- and multilingual students effectively, we need knowledge and understanding of their language and culture, and the relationships between the two. (325)

Children acquire language competence at varying rates and to varying degrees. With few exceptions, children will have mastered the language and communication patterns of their own families prior to entry into first grade. Not all language and communication patterns are equally good matches with the demands of school settings, however. Children with delayed, underdeveloped, or merely "different" language skills are likely to have difficulty with conventional reading and writing. Indeed, one factor that is likely to place students at risk of school failure is limited English proficiency.

Although it seems obvious to point out that children will not easily learn to read a language they cannot speak, not all schools are equipped to provide the foundations in oral language that may be required for many students. Nor are many schools prepared to offer a rich multilingual experience that capitalizes on the knowledge and expertise of the larger community (Moll and Gonzalez 1994). Children's knowledge of the structure of language forms the foundation for learning to read. If the child's language differs significantly from the language he or she is encountering in books, the resulting mismatch will make initial learning difficult.

As young children are engaged in experiences with language, thought, and print, they gain an increasing awareness about what is required to accomplish literacy tasks. Instruction in reading and writing, like most cognitive tasks, requires some degree of reflective ability, yet not all children have acquired appropriate abilities in this area. Some abilities, though potentially useful, are late in developing in all children. For example, children must understand that sentences are made up of separate words and that words contain separable sounds. This ability to separate words into distinct sounds is called *phonemic segmentation*. Research suggests that most kindergarten and many first grade children cannot segment speech by phoneme (Liberman and Shankweiler 1979). Because the assessment-instruction process needs to take these factors into account, we will return to the issue of language development in Chapter 7.

Physical Development

Within the area of physical development, there are several factors that may influence reading and writing performance; hearing, vision, general health, and maturation are all important.

Hearing.   There are several types of hearing loss. Some make it difficult for students to hear all sounds; others result in loss of hearing for particular sounds.

Both types of hearing loss can occur in the same person, and hearing loss can occur in one or both ears. Since written language processes are based on oral language processes, children who have difficulty hearing are at a disadvantage in learning to read and write. An appropriate referral should be made if there is any evidence of impaired hearing, and if at all possible, the loss should be corrected before any further specialized instruction occurs. Hearing loss resulting from more temporary physical conditions (for example, ear infections) can also interfere with learning and should prompt careful teachers to consider adapting their methods of instruction. For example, intensive oral phonics instruction is unlikely to benefit students with permanent or recurring hearing impairment.

Vision.   There are several types of visual impairments we need to be concerned about. People who are farsighted have difficulty in seeing objects up close, as when reading or writing. Nearsightedness, on the other hand, results in difficulties seeing distant objects, such as the chalkboard. Astigmatism results in distorted visual images, which could lead to problems such as keeping one's place while reading and writing. Other types of vision problems occur when the eye muscles do not work together in a smooth coordinated fashion. These types of problems can result in fatigue and discomfort that interfere with reading and writing.

Research regarding the impact of these visual problems on reading and writing achievement appears to be equivocal. Harris and Sipay (1985) conclude that there simply is not sufficient evidence to make any real judgment about the relation between problems of visual acuity, poor eye muscle coordination, and reading and writing ability. They also point out that these problems are not likely to be detected by the eye tests commonly used in schools, since the Snellen Chart is designed to detect only problems of nearsightedness. Although adequate visual and auditory acuity are clearly required to learn to read and write, these are often not assessed during reading and writing diagnostic workups.

General health and maturation.   Learning and cognitive development depend on acceptable overall development. Poor general health is related to failure in any or all areas of learning. Students who are in poor health—who suffer from poor nutrition or chronic illness, for example—may experience frequent absences from school, or fatigue and decreased attention while in school. Insufficient sleep may also contribute to fatigue and lack of concentration. It is important to recognize that these factors can play a role in learners' reading and writing. It may sometimes be appropriate to request a complete physical for a student who seems to be having difficulty with reading and writing to make sure that diet, sleep patterns, or physical problems are not implicated. A thorough assessment must include consideration of these components of overall development that may impede learning.

Cognitive Development

Reading and writing are specific examples of cognitive activity. Learning how to read and write require learning only a handful of skills and strategies that are unique to reading and writing. Many of the things that are required of readers and writers are required of people engaged in other learning and problem-solving activities as well. For example, students need to be able to listen, attend, and exert effort during learning. Normal reading and writing, like all cognitive abilities, are developmental processes. This means that beginners know less than experts, but it also means that the quality of their knowledge and skills is different. Therefore, "in relating cognitive factors to reading [and writing], both specific prior learning and more general developmental factors influence reading [and writing] performance at any given time" (Ringler and Weber 1984, 26).

As children grow and mature, they acquire an increasingly sophisticated repertoire of cognitive abilities. Developmental stages or shifts in perspective are often used to capture this changing and increasing knowledge base (Bruner 1964, Piaget 1960, Vygotsky 1978). Both Piaget and Bruner describe growth during the preschool and school years as a time when children are moving toward the ability to transcend the present and think flexibly about the world. Teachers need to understand how their students think about their world so that they can provide experiences that are appropriate to children's cognitive functioning and that move them to expand and restructure their knowledge.

Cognitive factors also include development in the areas of perception, attention, and memory, as well as encompassing traditional notions of intelligence and verbal ability. Although it is beyond the scope of this text to consider each of these aspects in detail, each will be discussed briefly below to provide an awareness of the scope of the cognitive-developmental factors that may influence reading and writing achievement.

Intelligence. Intelligence generally refers to overall mental ability. Included in the construct of intelligence are such indicators of ability as speed of learning, ability to solve problems, and ability to engage in high-level thinking tasks. Although most people believe intelligence is a broad-based attribute, most textbooks that deal with cognitive development discuss this topic almost exclusively in terms of the results of intelligence tests. In sum, intelligence is viewed as the ability to do well on the tasks presented on IQ tests.

Given the importance of judgments about intelligence in school settings, there are several points that need to be made here. First, intelligence is a construct. That is, the components of intelligence are not readily observable. Indeed, there is substantial disagreement about what the components are. Most psychological authorities note that intelligence is actually grounded in culture, and that different societies value different sets of skills and define intelligence accordingly (Okagaki and Sternberg 1991).

Given this situation, caution needs to be exercised in attributing reading and writing problems to limited overall cognitive ability. In our multicultural society, it is possible for different types of behavior and knowledge to mean different things to different individuals. For example, some cultural groups take aggressive display of information as totally inappropriate behavior—the mark of someone either not very smart or not very polite. Other groups teach children to provide creative, but not necessarily factual, answers to situational questions. Conclusions generated about intelligence in the absence of appropriate cultural context can be misleading.

In addition, newer theories of intelligence emphasize multiple intelligences rather than a single unitary intelligence (Gardner 1983, Sternberg 1985). As Bransford, Goldman, and Nye (1991) point out:

> A shift in the emphasis from academic intelligence to multiple intelligences carries with it the implication that intelligence is not a wholistic trait that characterizes an individual. Thus, an individual might be relatively intelligent in school but relatively unintelligent in other contexts such as the auto repair shop and vice versa. (152)

This supports the notion of an interactive view of learning and ability; rejecting the older view that intelligence was a relatively stable characteristic and, as such, was not susceptible to change via instruction.

Increasingly, it appears that intelligence, again as measured by existing tests, can be influenced by certain experiences and instruction (Campione, Brown, and Ferrara 1982). More importantly, there is an increased interest, not in static measures of intelligence as traditionally assessed, but in measures of potential to learn. The evidence to date suggests that measures of potential can contribute important information to the process of assessment and instruction and we will return to these in Chapter 11.

Information-processing abilities.   Student learning is also associated with the ability to process information in either written or spoken form. *Attention, perception*, and *memory* are all factors that influence learning and performance.

The ability and willingness to pay attention to important stimuli is a major factor in school success (Gage and Berliner 1988). Human beings are surrounded by stimuli, that is, all aspects of the environment that are present to be learned, enjoyed, and noticed. Clearly, if students cannot or do not attend to the parts of the environment that contain essential information, they cannot learn or retain new information and skills. Attention, however, is very selective and is influenced by a number of other factors, including motivation, maturity, context, and instruction. For example, people focus more attention on unusual or unique stimuli (larger print, boldface, etc).

The ability to impose order on sensory information is called *perception*. It too is central to student learning and performance. Like attention, perception is considered to be selective (Bruner 1964). This selectivity of perception is influenced by past learning and knowledge. This more active view of how people take in and process information suggests that we organize perceptual information, rather than passively perceive available stimuli. Perception, like attention and memory, is also developmental. That is, important changes occur during childhood and adolescence. Older children have more experience and knowledge, and this allows them to impose order on a greater array of stimuli, thus enhancing perception.

Finally, the development of memory is an important aspect of cognitive information-processing ability. *Memory* is the process of storing and retrieving information. For many years, psychologists and educators assumed that all perceived events were registered or stored in memory, and that the inability to remember information was due to a failure in retrieving what one knew. However, recent research suggests that limited memory can result from a variety of factors. As we have seen, perceptions of events can differ depending on prior knowledge, affecting what is noticed and stored. The less comprehensible the information, the less likely it is to be stored and retrieved effectively.

As with all cognitive abilities, memory changes and develops over time. Older children are better at storing and retrieving information than younger children, and adults tend to be better at this than children. These developmental differences may be due in part to capacity (increased space for coping with information), but most psychologists now believe that memory improves because the ability to organize incoming information improves with age. Older children and adults clearly have better concept formation and a more elaborate network connecting concepts (schemata) that allows for better organization of new information. In addition, older children and adults tend to have better strategies for coping with information, and they are better at understanding what they need to do in order to remember information.

It is easy to see how individual differences in these areas of development can affect students' abilities to cope with school tasks. It is also becoming increasingly clear that these cognitive abilities are not static. Attention, perception, and memory operate in relation to *specific types of information*. It is misleading to talk of children's information-processing abilities without specifying exactly what it is they are trying to perceive and remember (Gage and Berliner 1988). We see once again how culture, expectations, and experience can influence performance and potentially confound the measurement of these abilities.

CHAPTER SUMMARY

This chapter focused on the elements of skilled reading and writing performance and the contextual and learner factors that influence performance. The first section of the chapter described skilled performance as the ability to use reading and writing effectively and creatively for personal, recreational, academic, and civic purposes. The elements of skilled performance were defined as comprehension, composition vocabulary development, word identification, rate and fluency, spelling, grammar, usage, and the mechanics of writing.

The second and third sections of the chapter identified and described the contextual and learner factors that influence performance. The contextual factors were grouped according to settings, instructional resources, curriculum, instructional methods, and assessment practices. The learner factors were categorized as prior content knowledge, knowledge about reading and writing, attitudes and motivation, and correlates of skilled performance. The correlates of performance were defined as those social, emotional, linguistic, cognitive, and physical factors that are related to, but do not necessarily cause, strengths and weaknesses in reading and writing performance.

Consideration of the conventional aspects of reading and writing performance must be constrained by concerns for the ways in which learner and contextual factors interact to influence performance. Unless this complex and dynamic view of reading and writing is employed during assessment, we run the risk of developing a distorted picture of reading and writing processes. This poses serious problems for assessment, but even more serious concerns about the quality of instruction.

CHAPTER 3

Reading and Writing Disability and the Assessment-Instruction Process

INTRODUCTION

Chapters 1 and 2 focused on understanding the reading and writing processes. In this chapter and in much of the remainder of the book, we focus on understanding the nature of reading and writing disability and applying this understanding to the assessment and instruction of reading and writing. A plan for the assessment-instruction process is presented, and we explain the reasons for using this plan and describe each of the following steps:

THE STEPS IN THE ASSESSMENT-INSTRUCTION PROCESS

Step 1 Getting Started with Assessment
Step 2 Evaluating the Context
Step 3 Evaluating the Learner: Focusing on Reading and Writing
Step 4 Evaluating the Match Between the Learner and the Context
Step 5 Reflection, Decision Making, and Planning
Step 6 Identifying a Better Match: Diagnostic Teaching
Step 7 Adapting Instruction: Continuous Monitoring and Modification
Step 8 Reporting

UNDERSTANDING AN INTERACTIVE VIEW OF READING AND WRITING DISABILITY

In this text we use contemporary views of reading and writing ability and the lessons of history to detail an interactive perspective on reading and writing disability. We are suggesting that the interactive view of reading and writing *ability* be adopted for reading and writing *disability* as well. This means that reading and writing disability, like ability, would no longer be viewed as an absolute property of the learner, but rather as a relative property of the interaction between specific learner and contextual factors (Lipson and Wixson 1986).

An interactive view of reading and writing disability addresses several of the concerns we have about any theory of disability. First, we believe that a theory of disability should respond to recent conceptual and empirical evidence; it should account for the reading and writing behaviors of poor students but should also suggest new areas of investigation. Second, we believe that theories of reading and writing disability should enhance instruction. We now turn our attention to these issues.

A Theoretically Sound View of Disability

Current theory and research in reading and writing provide evidence that the ability to comprehend and/or compose varies for both able and disabled learners, as a function of various interactions with different reading and writing situations. For example, there is evidence that young children of all ability levels are better able to recognize words that contain regular phonic patterns, and that they are also more successful when reading high-frequency as opposed to low-frequency words (Juel 1988). The results of such studies suggest that children's performance on measures of isolated word recognition can be expected to vary as a function of the particular words on a given test.

Small samples of oral reading errors are often used to characterize a student's word recognition ability in all reading contexts. However, studies of oral reading errors suggest that children's word recognition ability is highly variable and is influenced by many factors. These factors include instructional method, type of prose being read, the student's prior knowledge of the materials being read, and the difficulty of the text (Wixson 1979). This means that oral reading errors reflect particular strategies a learner employs in interaction with a particular reading activity. As such, they may or may not be representative of the strategies used by a particular learner in other reading situations.

Comprehension performance is also subject to variability in both able and less-able learners. Both groups are similarly affected by differences in prior knowledge, by text organization, and by type of comprehension task. For example, Williams and her colleagues have demonstrated in a number of studies that both able and less-able students in Grades 3 through 7 were better able to identify the main idea when they were asked to select the best title than when they were asked to write a summary sentence (Williams, Taylor, and deCani 1984).

Finally, there is evidence that less-skilled learners perform like skilled learners under certain circumstances. For example, in an examination of the story comprehension patterns of sixth-grade learners, McConaughy (1985) found no differences between good and poor learners in either the quality or the accuracy of their recall summaries. Specifically, McConaughy reports that poor learners' story organization is as good as that of good learners of the same age when the structure of the text is explicit and learners are required to summarize what they think is important, rather than to recall as much as possible.

A related finding in the area of writing is that the relative difficulty of the expository text structures in writing tasks varies depending on the type of task that students are performing and the manner in which the writing is analyzed. If written productivity is evaluated, then an explanation text structure may be easier for students to produce than a comparison/ constrast structure. If text organization is evaluated, then the comparison/contrast text structure might be easier for students to produce than the explanation text structure.

The foregoing suggests that the strategies students employ as they read and write should be expected to vary as a function of a number of factors. There is evidence that both the awareness and application of reading and writing strategies varies in relation to the difficulty of the text and task. Evaluating strategic behavior in the absence of some consideration of potential sources of variability is problematic. As Jones (1983) has noted, "learning strategies cannot be defined or understood without reference to the text to which they apply because the cognitive processes vary according to the text condition" (p. 6).

When reading and writing disability are viewed from an interactive perspective, it becomes clear how difficult, and probably fruitless, it is to search for a single causative factor within the learner. Yet this is the approach that continues to dominate assessment and instruction in reading and writing disability today. Despite the increased sophistication of perspectives on reading and writing ability, our views of reading and writing disability are still wedded to the historic "search for pathology" (Sarason and Doris 1979). An editorial in the *The Learning Disability Quarterly,* a journal that publishes much of today's research on reading and writing disability, summarized this view very well:

> Our entire field is DEFICIT DRIVEN; we spend millions of dollars and hours looking for deficits, defining them, perseverating on them, imagining that we are exorcizing them, and sometimes even inventing them to rationalize our activities. (Poplin 1984, 133)

Research has amply demonstrated that variability in performance is a normal part of the reading and writing process. However, assessment and instruction for most disabled learners still depend on the use of commercial, standardized test instruments that assume that reading and writing processes are static, and that reading and writing ability can be measured at some point in time, using one set of materials and tasks to predict performance on other materials in other settings. This is especially problematic given the tasks that comprise existing reading and writing tests. Many existing instruments are based on dated and incomplete notions about reading and writing. When a mismatch exists between the theories used to define reading and writing competence and those used to drive assessment and instruction, the assessment information is of little value (Valencia and Pearson 1987; Wixson, Peters, Weber, and Roeber 1987). We will discuss the problems and advantages of standardized testing in Chapter 10.

An Instructionally Significant View of Disability

As a result of research and practice based on earlier views of reading and writing disability, we know a great deal about how people process various isolated words, construct grammatical sentences, and comprehend short, contrived texts. Less is known about the relationship between these skills and performance while reading and writing real texts for real purposes. What is needed is a view of reading and writing disability that results in improved assessment and instruction practices.

An interactive view is well suited to the understanding of reading and writing (dis)ability because it predicts variability in performance within individuals across texts, tasks, and settings. This perspective moves discussions of reading and writing disability away from simply specifying deficits and toward the specification of the conditions under which a student can and will learn. In this view, a student's performance on various reading and writing measures is considered an indication of what he or she can and will do under a specific set of conditions, rather than a set of fixed abilities and disabilities (Wixson and Lipson 1986). The necessity for identifying the disability is eliminated and our attention is refocused on how each student performs under different conditions and which set of conditions is most likely to facilitate learning.

An interactive view of reading and writing disability provides a unifying theoretical orientation for teachers and specialized support personnel. The clearest implication of such a reorientation is that the performance of both able and less-able students is subject to variability. The factors that influence the reading and writing process are the same for both populations of students. At present, there is a tremendous need for coordination of assessment and instruction between classrooms and specialized programs. If different views of reading and writing underlie the programs in these two settings, problems inevitably arise for students, and the prospects for potential transfer and learning are limited. Both classroom teachers and specialists need to recognize that the student who is experiencing difficulty in reading and writing is only one component in the reading and writing process.

An interactive view of reading and writing also provides a basis for communication between teachers and support staff. Personnel involved in the education of students with reading and writing problems can begin to talk about the specific contributions of the learner, the text, and the context as determiners of reading and writing performance. All educators need to understand the importance of recognizing this so that we can begin to work together. Since learner performance is likely to be influenced by a wide array of factors, pull-out programs are unlikely to be effective unless there is coordination between the classroom and the clinic. Teachers must provide opportunities for classroom practice and application of the skills and techniques developed in the clinic. Similarly, clinicians can no longer ignore the content and context of classroom instruction, believing that remediation of some specific disability will transfer to other settings.

Finally, an interactive view makes clear the important contribution of context. Both classroom teachers and specialists must be sensitive to the influences of their distinct environments on learner performance. Thoughtful teachers have always realized that information collected in one situation is not entirely helpful in another. Unfortunately, we have sometimes rejected information from various sources as unreliable because it did not coincide with our own. Such apparently contradictory information can be valuable in planning optimal student instruction. For example, it should no longer surprise us when a student performs differently as an individual, in small group settings, and in large group settings. The documentation of these differences can provide the basis for genuinely collaborative professional relationships—-relationships that will strengthen the prospects of learning for all students.

UNDERSTANDING THE ASSESSMENT-INSTRUCTION PROCESS

The problem of teaching and learning is the match between the student and the circumstances he or she encounters in the learning environment (Hunt 1961). The notion of the proper match between student and circumstance is what we must grasp if we are to be effective evaluators and instructors. Assessment and instruction need to be focused on an evaluation of the existing match and the identification of the optimal match between a learner and the conditions of the reading and writing context.

The purpose of assessment, then, is to find patterns of interactions that allow us to make relatively good decisions about instruction. Because few standardized tests provide this kind of information, we suggest a number of assessment strategies that are needed to supplement existing measures. We are not suggesting that current testing instruments be abandoned altogether, but rather that assessment move forward from a different perspective. Nor are we suggesting that the individual student is not an important factor in the assessment process, but that we must look to the individual in interaction with specific texts, tasks, and methods. In the past, such specification has been incidental to the goal of identifying the learner's problem. This text is designed to help educators accomplish this in an intentional and thoughtful fashion.

The long-range goal of the entire assessment and instruction process is to produce strategic, motivated, reflective readers and writers, and to develop mature readers and writers who can and will apply their skills and strategies independently and in a flexible manner—not to identify causes or provide labels.

To achieve an interactive approach to assessment and instruction, we need to gather information about the demands of the context (for example, what is required to read and write using various methods or materials) and explore how the context may influence a student's performance and learning. We also need to gather information about what the learner knows and how he or she behaves during reading and writing. We must also examine the interaction between the areas within these two components of the assessment-instruction process.

We emphasize that the assessment-instruction process continues to be an art, rather than a science. The best way to become proficient at the assessment and instruction of reading and writing is to learn as much as possible about learners, the contexts in which reading and writing occur, and how they interact to influence reading and writing performance.

A plan for proceeding with the process of assessment and instruction is described in the next sections of this chapter. This is a decision-making approach to assessment and instruction. Throughout this text, we provide information about areas to be assessed and also describe in detail tools and strategies for gathering information. In addition, however, we need to make decisions at every stage of the process because the complex of factors that interact is never quite the same for any two students. Effective decision making is dependent on knowing when and why we would engage in a particular activity, or use a particular test or instructional technique.

Implementing the Assessment-Instruction Process

The components of effective assessment and instruction are similar whether they are conducted in the classroom or in a remedial/support setting, by a classroom teacher or a specialist. However, the amount of attention devoted to each component and the procedures used to evaluate them are likely to be different. The classroom teacher has the benefit of daily contact with the student or students in question, but limited time to spend with individual students. The specialist or clinician has the benefit of individual time with the student, but limited knowledge about the student's daily interactions with reading and writing in the classroom.

It is important for classroom teachers to develop a repertoire of assessment techniques that can be incorporated easily into their daily instruction. (These will be discussed in the chapters that follow.) Those students who demonstrate difficulty on these assessments would then be seen individually or in smaller groups for further evaluation. The assessment of the methods and materials may be fairly straightforward for classroom teachers because of their daily access and repeated experience with them. Classroom teachers have the added benefit of being able to incorporate trial teaching procedures into the real context of their daily instruction.

The language arts specialist or clinician usually only deals with students who have already been identified by some means as having a problem. Specialists have the advantage of working closely in small settings with an individual student. This may provide in-depth information unavailable to the classroom teacher. However, if specialists do not work in the classroom, evaluating the learner in interaction with the reading and writing context may be more difficult, because they do not have daily contact with the student(s) in question in the context in which the problem is occurring. They must rely on limited examinations of the materials, classroom observation, and interviews with the parents, the teacher, and the students for this evaluation. Furthermore, they must be aware of and sensitive to the teacher's style and the organization of the classroom to develop trial teaching procedures that would be appropriate for use in the student's classroom.

Specialists who are operating in pull-out programs need to be especially aware of the potential difficulties in this situation. Too often, the students who are most in need of consistent, coherent reading and writing instruction are the ones receiving the most fragmented instruction. What is most important, however, is that students may be practicing and acquiring skills and abilities in one setting that are neither valued nor applied in another. Communication between classroom and clinic is of the utmost importance.

Increasingly, the advantages of these different settings are being tapped by innovative staffing configurations. Many schools have implemented student support teams composed of classroom teachers, special educators, and content specialists. The members of these teams confer about individual students and pool their insights, knowledge, and resources. Many assessment and instruction strategies will be tried by the classroom teacher, others may be implemented in the classroom by a Chapter 1 or special education teacher, and still others may involve pulling the student out for individual assessment or instruction.

The remainder of this book is designed to provide information about the what, how, when, and why of the assessment-instruction process. The next section of this chapter provides a step-by-step plan for carrying out this process. The steps in this plan provide the framework for the subsequent sections of this book, and the procedures involved in each step are discussed in detail in at least one or more of the following chapters (see Figure 3.1). Within each chapter, the specific information needed to implement the assessment-instruction process is provided in as much detail as possible, including examples of what procedures to use and how to use them, and explanations of when and why they are appropriate for use.

Steps in the Assessment-Instruction Process

The steps in the assessment-instruction process are guided by three questions that we have adapted from those used by Diane Sawyer (personal communication 1980). They are:

1. What is the current status of the interaction between the learner and the instructional context?
2. What is the primary source of interference with learning or performance?
3. How can learning or performance be established or improved?

The foundation of the assessment-instruction process rests on an accurate assessment of the existing match between the learner and the context. Using this information, our next task is to generate hypotheses about the primary source of interference with learning or performance. It is critical that the hypotheses generated in this phase of the process focus on problems of major importance. All readers and writers have minor difficulties with certain aspects of literacy, but these problems are rarely a primary source of interference with learning or performance. To ensure that we are focusing on major problems, it is sometimes helpful to ask ourselves "If I corrected this problem, would the individual in question be likely to demonstrate improved reading and writing learning or performance?" The steps focus on identifying the means by which learning or performance may be established or improved.

The steps of the assessment-instruction process are summarized below. We follow a case study through all the steps to illustrate how the process was carried out with one student. Detailed information on how to proceed with each step is provided in subsequent chapters.

Step 1: Getting Started with Assessment

The assessment-instruction process described here is not a standard set of tests and prescriptions to be used with all students. Rather, it is a dynamic process tailored to the needs of individual students and continually evolving as each additional piece of information is uncovered. The first step in the process involves identifying the presenting problem, gathering background information, and planning the initial evaluations of the learner and the learning context. Individuals are referred for, or seek out, help in reading and/or writing for a wide range of reasons. If there were only one or two sources of difficulty, our task would be relatively easy. Since that is not the case, and unlimited time is rarely available to explore all possible avenues, the initial phase of assessment must provide a focus for subsequent steps in the process.

Background information provided by the individual, parents, school records, interviews, and visitations can yield valuable insights into possible sources of difficulty. Information about both the learner and the context should be gathered. Trying to complete an assessment for an individual is rather like reading a good mystery. No clues should be ignored, no information overlooked in the early stages of the story. We cannot be sure at the beginning just what will turn out to be important, even when the evidence seems to lead to an obvious conclusion. The task in this first phase is not to arrive at conclusions, but rather to generate hunches that may be tested. In short, you should try to avoid coming to any conclusions in the early stages, and view your early findings as hypotheses to be tested against reality later on.

Case study.   Seth was referred to the clinic of one of the authors by Mr. Williams, his Chapter 1 teacher, who had several concerns. First, the available psychological data on Seth were not entirely helpful in planning an instructional program, and Mr. Williams wanted additional information to improve Seth's

FIGURE 3.1
The
Assessment-
Instruction
Process

program. Seth had been referred for evaluation for special education services but was not presently receiving them because of parental resistance. Therefore, Mr. Williams wanted additional information so that he could make a recommendation about the appropriate placement for Seth. Finally, Seth was failing to make good progress despite receiving remedial reading help in school for the past two years. At the time he was referred, Seth was in the mid-third grade and had repeated first grade once. Seth lived in a state with no compulsory kindergarten and he did not attend school at all prior to entry into the first grade.

In gathering background data on Seth, we spoke to his mother and to his older sister, who was a teacher in his school district. Seth was the youngest of six children and lived on a farm in a rural county. He was small for his age and had limited use of his left hand and arm, which were underdeveloped and deformed. Both parents were busy with farm chores, and Seth was expected to help as well. Because of the family's responsibilities, little time was available for other activities. Family life seemed to revolve around their shared jobs. Seth had little contact with children outside the school setting and had limited experiences with life off the farm.

The school records included annual report cards and a recent report by the school psychologist. The records suggested that Seth had been struggling with reading since he began his school career. At the time of the evaluation, he was placed in regular third-grade material in all areas except reading instruction, which was provided by a Chapter 1 reading program outside the regular classroom. Seth's written language abilities were also weak, but there was very little writing activity in the classroom and he received no special support in writing.

The records also indicated that Seth was inattentive to assigned tasks and that he frequently failed to complete his work. On a norm-referenced achievement test administered four months before this evaluation, Seth scored in the first percentile in reading comprehension. The psychologist's report included an estimate of ability within the low-average to average range. In addition, the psychologist suggested that Seth's left-side "paralysis" might be impairing neurological functioning and argued strongly for a "right hemisphere approach" to instruction, involving whole word and language experience activities.

Case discussion.   In this first step we gathered and considered a variety of preexisting information. Briefly, we concluded that, with regard to reading and writing, Seth was not learning or performing as well as might be expected based on his age, ability, and educational background. In addition, we had gathered enough background information to form some initial impressions that were used to guide subsequent evaluations of the learner and the learning context. These can be summarized as follows:

 A. Seth's background and interests suggested he may have had limited experience with and knowledge about reading and writing. This was an area we needed to pursue through interviews with Seth and his parents.
 B. Seth's apparent lack of interest in many school-related activities and his failure to complete assignments suggested he may have had little motivation for school in general, and reading and writing in particular. This area needed to be pursued through observations and interviews with Seth, his teacher, and his parents.
 C. Seth's history of poor performance, his test scores, and his difficulty completing assigned tasks suggested that his basic reading skills were very

poor. This hypothesis needed to be tested, and assessment of sight word recognition, word analysis, and comprehension skills were all planned.

D. Seth's failure to complete assignments and his dependence on the teacher suggested that the work he was being given may have been too difficult for him. This was an area that needed to be examined through informal measures and an evaluation of the materials and methods being used.

Step 2: Evaluating the Instructional Context

Despite wide recognition that teachers and teaching methods contribute to academic success, academic assessments rarely include evaluations of these factors. If teachers and methods are rarely considered, the contribution of materials or setting factors are examined even less frequently, especially the non-school literacy abilities that may accompany students from diverse backgrounds. Failure to even consider such factors leaves the learner as the sole source of difficulty, and is something akin to blaming the victim (Coles 1978; Stuckey 1991).

A variety of procedures should be used to assess the learning context, including classroom observations, interviews, checklists, and visual inspection and analysis. Since most of these procedures are informal, care must be taken to examine this information systematically. Observation guidelines are helpful here, as are checklists. Great strides have also been made in the area of materials assessment so that a variety of procedures such as text analysis, comprehensibility checklists, and holistic scans have been added to traditional readability measures. Teachers, students, and parents can also provide invaluable information as they describe important aspects of the cultural and instructional setting for learning.

It is not always possible, or even desirable, to evaluate all possible contextual factors. However, it is imperative that the student's performance be examined from the perspective contexts in which he or she is expected to learn and perform. Not infrequently, students' reading or writing problems are exacerbated, if not actually caused, by contextual factors.

Case study.   This step focuses on assessing the instructional context in which Seth was expected to perform and also the larger social context within which he was learning. During the interview with Seth's parents, they indicated that he did read a farm journal occasionally and that he received *Humpty-Dumpty* magazine at home. They confirmed that reading aloud to Seth was not a practice in their home. Instead, Seth, like other members of the family, was oriented to outdoor activities and farm chores.

Information about the instructional context was gathered during a half-day classroom observation and interviews with Seth's teachers. Seth received instruction both in a regular classroom and outside the classroom in a Chapter 1 reading program. He was not part of a regular reading group within the classroom, although workbook tasks were assigned frequently. It appeared that he was rarely expected to read full-length texts in either setting. However, when longer selections were assigned, there was generally no prereading preparation or during-reading support.

Although the teacher read aloud as a daily part of the instructional program, Seth went to his Chapter 1 reading class during much of this period. Contrary to federal guidelines, Seth did not receive reading instruction in his regular classroom, but only in the Chapter 1 classroom. His reading instruction was focused largely on word analysis, and work was assigned from a program that emphasized visual and auditory perception of letter clusters in words. The method of instruction used by this particular program emphasized the analysis of words into their constituent parts as opposed to beginning with word parts and blending them together to form a word.

The classroom teacher indicated Seth was responsible for the same assigned work required of all other children in the class and that there was no differentiation of tasks among students. The language arts, spelling, and social studies books used in Seth's classroom were standard third-grade texts with readability estimates ranging from a 2.5 to a 5.0 grade level. Seth was expected to complete all classroom assignments before going to recess. The teacher reported that Seth really liked recess and did not like to miss it, although he frequently did because his work was incomplete.

On the day we observed, Seth still had twelve math problems left to complete when recess time came, despite the fact that he had finished his art project earlier than most of the other children and returned to his seatwork, and despite the fact that he worked industriously and without distraction for the entire period. He repeatedly asked the teacher for help—on every item, in fact. As we observed Seth, we were able to determine that he had little idea about how to approach the math problems assigned. Each time Seth approached the teacher for help, he was given information about how to do the specific problem he was working on, but he never received additional instruction targeted at his lack of understanding about how to do this *type* of problem. More troubling still was our observation that at least some of the assigned work was explained while Seth was involved in reading instruction outside of the classroom. In this particular case, he had little recourse but to continue approaching the teacher for help.

Discussion with Seth provided additional information about his instructional context. After our visit to his classroom, we asked him about his favorite part of the day and he noted that he really enjoyed the time when his teacher read to the class. Seth had previously indicated that he enjoyed the period in the day when his teacher was reading *James and the Giant Peach*. During that earlier exchange, we had been concerned because, despite his obvious interest, he was unable to accomplish a coherent retelling of the story. This time, Seth explained that he had to go to Chapter 1 reading class during read-aloud time and was able to hear only the initial portion of each day's reading!

Case discussion. Our evaluation of the learning context revealed the following: instructional materials written at a third-grade level and above, little evidence of materials that Seth would be interested in and/or motivated to read, classroom assignments that emphasized task completion, no individualization of classroom assignments, large numbers of classroom assignments, lack of direction and explanation for classroom assignments caused in part by a "pull-out" reading program, no reading instruction in the regular classroom, Chapter 1 reading instruction focused on word analysis, and little opportunity to read longer texts for meaning.

Step 3: Evaluating the Learner

Each individual's abilities, skills, beliefs, interests, and instructional history influence reading and writing achievement. In Chapter 2 we outlined the components of reading and writing knowledge and skill that must be considered in any assessment. As in the evaluation of the context, a variety of sources should be used in evaluating the learner because each source of information provides only a small part of the picture. These include: classroom observations; interviews with parents, teachers, and the student; formal assessments; and informal assessments.

In the chapters to follow, we describe in detail the types of procedures that may be employed in evaluating the learner. Generally speaking, these procedures fall into three categories. First, *observational and interview data* are rich sources of information but are often considered unreliable or subjective (see Chapter 4). We discuss ways of increasing the reliability of data collected in these ways and also describe the unique contributions to assessment that are made by such procedures. Second, more traditional types of information about the learner result from using various *informal assessment* instruments and techniques (Chapters 7, 8, and 9). Both familiar and less-familiar strategies are presented. The third and best-known source of information about learners is *formal assessment,* using standardized, norm-referenced tests (see Chapter 10). Although widely used, most formal tests have significant problems in terms of the value of the diagnostic information they yield. However, a consideration of individual assessment would not be complete without a serious discussion of the role of such instruments in the assessment-instruction process.

Case study.   An initial interview with Seth confirmed that his life revolved around family and friends. He reported few other interests but became animated in his discussions of the animals and his exploits on his "four-wheeler." Seth said that he didn't like television very much, that he didn't like "being cooped up," and that he would rather play outside. Although he said he enjoyed stories, he reported that neither he nor his family read at home.

In response to questions focused on his knowledge about reading, Seth could not give a reason why people read, and said he read because he wanted to be "smart." He appeared to believe that reading involved only accurate word recognition, naming only "sounding out" as a strategy for analyzing unknown words. Similarly, he used neatness as an indicator of "good writing" and seemed unaware of personal uses for writing. When asked what his teachers did to help him become a better reader and writer, he could think of nothing for writing but said that they helped him sound out the words in reading.

During the interview with Seth's parents, Mrs. C. reported that Seth's health history was normal except that he had a series of ear infections during his first year of first grade. Tubes were inserted to correct this problem and no further difficulty was reported. She also noted that Seth's left arm "paralysis" resulted from a forceps delivery during which nerves were damaged. Thus, it seemed unlikely to us that neurological impairment was implicated in his problems.

Seth's classroom teacher reported that Seth seemed much younger than the other children in the class and that he sometimes asked questions or made comments that were "babyish." She indicated that Seth asked for help frequently to get attention. Further, she felt that Seth acted "cute" when he could not do something or wanted help, which was often.

Seth's abilities and behaviors were observed in both the classroom and the clinic. In the clinical setting, Seth appeared highly motivated to work hard in those areas where he felt he was competent and/or where he was succeeding. He enjoyed several of the instructional activities that were used and was always anxious to try reading on his own if appropriate prereading support had been provided. Seth sought help when he perceived work to be too difficult for him, and in those situations he put forth little effort. When pressed, he would attempt difficult tasks, but if success was not immediate, he shrugged and said he could not do it.

As described previously, Seth was also observed in his classroom. At the beginning of the observation period, Seth's teacher was phasing children into a painting project. Seth was one of the first students done with his project. While the majority of the class continued to paint, Seth washed his hands and returned to work at his desk. After returning to his desk, Seth looked up from his work only occasionally. Despite the noise level and the proximity of two groups of children chatting, Seth seemed undistracted. However, he was very reliant on his teacher. He asked questions frequently, requiring her help on nearly every individual task on which the examiner observed him working.

Informal assessments of several types were also employed with Seth. Information was collected using informal tests of isolated word recognition, informal reading inventories, and tests of word analysis skill. Formal assessments, including norm-referenced tests of reading achievement and vocabulary knowledge, were administered to obtain estimates of Seth's performance as compared to other children his age. The pattern of results indicated that, overall, Seth's reading achievement was at least a year and a half below what we might reasonably expect given his age and school experience. His sight word recognition was inadequate, and his word analysis skills were limited to the ineffective use of phonic analysis. Although his vocabulary knowledge was appropriate for his age, both his listening and reading comprehension were generally poor. In addition, his oral reading errors reflected little attention to meaning or contextual cues. However, in situations where he had adequate background knowledge and sufficient interest, he was able to answer questions successfully, retell a story, and/or generate a main idea. Finally, early informal work samples suggested that he was almost entirely unable to produce a written product. Even with considerable support, his ideas were disjointed and his narratives were limited to three or four sentences.

Case discussion.   At this point in the assessment-instruction process, several specific areas of difficulty had been identified. Seth's responses to interview questions and performance on informal measures suggested that both his reading and writing knowledge and skill were limited. For example, although Seth believed that he usually understood what he read, he had difficulty retelling stories in a coherent fashion, could not write coherent texts, and could neither identify nor generate a main idea. Seth did not appear to apply what skills and knowledge he had in a consistent way, so the products of his efforts were even less acceptable than might be expected. Although he was not actively resistant to reading or writing, Seth did not appear to be motivated to read or write nor to improve his skills; he greatly preferred to do other things. He worked hard when he experienced success, but application during difficult tasks was limited.

Step 4: Evaluating the Match Between the Learner and the Context

The fourth step is to evaluate the match between the knowledge, performance, and motivation of the learner and the materials, methods, and settings within the learning context, using the information gathered in the previous steps. This is the culmination of the first phase of the assessment-instruction process. It provides the answer to the first question guiding the assessment-instruction process: What is the current status of the interaction between the learner and the learning context?

Since an interactive view of disability predicts variability, it becomes relatively easy to see why some students appear to thrive in the very environments that befuddle others. Our job in this stage of the assessment-instruction process is to pull together all that we know as the result of our professional efforts and experience, and to evaluate how well existing demands, expectations, and supports of the context match the student's abilities, interests, knowledge, and level of independence.

Case study.   As we reached this point in the assessment-instruction process with Seth, we began to see that the match between Seth's abilities, interests, knowledge, and level of independence and the demands, expectations, and supports of his present placement was problematic in several ways. First, it appeared that his daily classroom assignments were mismatched with his knowledge and skills. The quantity of work was more than he could reasonably complete in the allotted time. In addition, the level of work was too difficult. He could not complete any of this work without additional help. This situation was aggravating his already strong personal tendency toward dependency. Our assessment suggested that he was receiving no in-class support that might help to compensate for limited knowledge and skill.

Second, Seth's interests lay outside the academic setting. He was not internally motivated to complete classwork in order to reap the rewards of school success. The content of the school's instructional materials and tasks was largely devoid of references to lifestyles or interests similar to Seth's. His experiences were limited and little prereading development was done to increase what appeared to be inadequate prior knowledge.

The emphasis on word analysis in Seth's remedial program appeared to represent a closer match to his existing needs and abilities; however, little attention was being given to his problems with comprehension. Finally, he was regularly denied access to the aspects of school life that he did enjoy—recess, book read-aloud time, and so on.

Case discussion. At this stage in the process, there were still many unanswered questions regarding the match between Seth's specific problems and particular instructional approaches. Although our assessment of the learner had revealed a number of problem areas, these needed to be prioritized and the most effective instructional approaches identified. The issue of instruction was especially critical since it appeared that the existing match was not ideal.

Step 5: Reflection, Decision Making, and Planning

The fifth step is to generate hypotheses from the evaluation of the existing match regarding the second guiding question: What is the primary source of interference with learning or performance? Probably the most critical feature of skilled assessment is the ability to reflect on available data and realize what it means. Collecting information about learners is relatively easy, compared to thinking about it and making sense of it. The assessment-instruction process must include sufficient time to reflect on information gathered. Indeed, the inexperienced clinician may need to spend as much time reflecting on the information as has been spent gathering it. In later chapters, we provide guidelines and formats for summarizing and reflecting on available data.

The answers we have generated in response to the question, "What is the primary source of interference with learning or performance?" are then used to identify possible solutions to the hypothesized problems. Not all things are equally possible, given the realities of school life and the state of our current knowledge. Decision making is both a thoughtful consideration of instructional priorities (What does the student seem to need most?) and a consideration of the available resources and feasibility of change (How much control do we have over the mismatch?). During decision making, we must specify which components of the problem might be changed in some way, and how this might best be accomplished. These decisions form the basis of the plans for the next steps in the process.

There is a temptation at this stage to begin mapping out a detailed instructional program. However, it is often the case that we are not ready to say with certainty exactly what needs to be done. As we reflect on available information, new questions are often raised that need to be addressed through further evaluation. Therefore, the focus of this step is to identify possible solutions that can be tried out in some systematic way.

Case study.   As we reflected on Seth, we had several hunches about his strengths and weaknesses as a reader and the best use of our resources. First, Seth's word identification skills were inadequate. His knowledge of sight words was far from automatic, and he was unable to analyze whole words into their constituent parts. Seth's failure to recognize that the whole was made up of parts was not limited to word analysis. For example, Seth seemed unable to analyze stories at a global level, often failing to see connections between one event in a text and another. His retellings were typically fragmented, and he seemed unable to remedy the problems, even with discussion. Not surprisingly, during oral reading Seth was often content to leave nonsensical miscues uncorrected, suggesting that he was not attending to meaning.

Despite these serious difficulties, Seth's strengths were notable. He had no difficulties in the areas of hearing or discriminating letter sounds. He both knew and regularly applied sound-symbol information for initial and final consonants. Seth's overall reading behavior indicated that he was inattentive to meaning, but he did demonstrate ability in this area during isolated reading events. For example, while reading a selection about a boy's dog being hit by a car, Seth's miscues were consistently meaningful and his responses to subsequent questions indicated a strong ability to bring relevant prior knowledge to bear on the text.

Case discussion.   We identified the primary source of interference with Seth's learning or performance as inadequate word identification skills, coupled with limited background knowledge, interest, and motivation. Secondarily, we were concerned with his ability to read for meaning. Our best guess at this point was that Seth needed an approach that would help him see how the various parts fit into the larger whole of identifying words and understanding what was being read. Therefore, we decided to try a holistic, language-experience approach with Seth, in an effort to address both his problems with word identification and comprehension, and with background knowledge, interest, and motivation. We planned to try out several different methods for enhancing Seth's word identification skills within the context of this approach. The specifics of these diagnostic teaching procedures are described in greater detail in the next section.

Step 6: Identifying a Better Match: Diagnostic Teaching

The sixth step involves continued assessment, based on the hypotheses and possible solutions generated in the previous step. The primary method of assessment used in this step is called diagnostic teaching. The two major purposes of diagnostic teaching are to provide additional diagnostic information about the interaction between the learner and the instructional context, and to identify instructional procedures that are likely to be effective in improving learning and performance.

Diagnostic teaching is a combination of assessment and instruction that provides information about how students perform under classroom-like conditions and how they might perform if we altered some aspects of the instructional setting. Diagnostic teaching usually involves systematically manipulating one or more components of reading and/or writing processes. Teachers are often gratified to know that there is a name for what may look like "messing around" or "trying out this and that." All instruction can be viewed as diagnostic teaching, as long as it is thoughtfully planned using our best guesses about what may work for a given student, and as long as we are prepared to monitor our work continually to see how adjustments have affected learning and performance.

Case study. Although we had a great deal of information about Seth, we also had several questions and concerns that needed to be addressed in order to be able to identify a better match:

1. What approach to instruction should be employed with Seth?
2. By what means does Seth learn most rapidly and retain most consistently?
3. Should the relative focus of instruction be placed on expanding Seth's repertoire of word recognition skills, or could some generic instruction improve both word analysis and passage comprehension abilities?
4. Could reading and writing inform each other in Seth's instructional program?

Based on our earlier reflections, we planned a series of diagnostic teaching episodes for Seth. The first component of instruction we manipulated involved word recognition and retention. Using three different approaches to instruction and three groups of five words, we systematically taught Seth to recognize the words instantly. We timed the instructional sequence so we would know how long it took under each set of instructional circumstances for him to learn the five words in each set, and we also retested him on these words after one and one-half hours to see how many words he had retained from each sequence. Thus, we are able to evaluate both effectiveness and efficiency. Finally, we asked Seth to tell us which method he thought had been most effective for him.

At delayed retesting, Seth knew at sight (two-second flash) all fifteen new words. It appeared that all three instructional approaches were effective. However, using one approach he learned the five new words in one and a half minutes, whereas using a different approach, it took ten minutes for him to learn the words! In terms of efficiency, Seth was likely to benefit from a phonics program that blends parts into wholes as opposed to a phonics program that breaks the whole into component parts. It should be noted, however, that he learned the words with equal ease when they were presented as sight words. The approach that was least efficient for Seth was the "whole-to-part" phonics approach similar to his current instructional program. Interestingly, Seth's perception conformed to these conclusions. He felt he had learned the words most easily in the "part-to-whole" phonics approach.

These results were a little disconcerting since, as noted earlier, we suspected that Seth could benefit from a "holistic" approach to instruction. In order to clarify issues related to approach and content, we initiated a language experience activity designed to allow Seth to read and write about topics of interest to him. During the first diagnostic teaching segment, we were chagrined to find that while Seth was enthusiastic about discussing a personal encounter with a "coy-dog" (half dog, half coyote), the story he dictated was sparse and incoherent. Subsequent work with a conference partner did nothing to improve the quality of the product. Two additional trials, yielding similar results, led us to conclude that this was not the most effective method for improving Seth's word recognition or comprehension skills at the present time.

Case discussion.   Recall that the questions we wished to address in the diagnostic teaching step of the process included, "What should be the focus on instruction for Seth?" and "What approach to instruction should be employed?" After several manipulations such as those described above, we concluded that Seth's program would need to contain strong elements of work in both word recognition and comprehension, and these might need to be somewhat separate for the time being. Despite our earlier conclusions, it appeared that Seth needed to develop a strong understanding of the component parts before he would benefit from more holistic instruction. For him, the rather counterintuitive benefits of part-to-whole instruction were obvious. However, he also needed as much exposure as possible to whole texts and read-aloud sessions as a means of increasing his understanding of the purposes for reading and writing.

Step 7: Focus on Instruction: Continuous Monitoring and Modification

The results of diagnostic teaching are used to plan an instructional program that is likely to respond to the most important needs of the individual reader. There are times when instruction will proceed before assessment is completed. At other times, the individual responsible for assessment will not deliver instruction. Wherever possible, of course, the preferred arrangement is for both assessment and instruction to be conducted by the same person.

In either case, initial instructional outcomes are established. Although attitude goals, information goals, and process goals may all be included in an individual's program, it is also possible that one or two of these will receive special emphasis. The information gathered in earlier portions of the process is used to inform decisions about what content to include and what delivery system to use. It is understood that these initial decisions may be changed or altered as further information is gathered.

Every instructional encounter with a particular reader is an opportunity for assessing and improving instruction. It is possible, and desirable, to continually monitor the effectiveness of the recommended instructional program and to make fine-tuning adjustments in the program as needed. Continuous monitoring of instructional progress is absolutely essential, and adaptive teaching involving modifications in texts, tasks, and materials is desirable. The full potential of this process can only be realized when it becomes part of daily practice.

Case study.   Since there was increasing evidence to suggest that a more part-to-whole approach would be effective for Seth, he received daily work that focused on the individual constituent parts of words. For phonically regular words, he received instruction in individual sounds and symbols and was supported as he blended these to form words and word parts. This focus on constituent parts was also used for high frequency sight words. In this case, though, the tutor used a visual and kinesthetic approach, having Seth trace a "new" word four times with different colors. Then Seth was directed to "get a picture" of the word in his head and the card was removed. As a next step, Seth was asked to talk about the word, in general: how many "tall letters," its shape, and any other unique features (for example double letters). Then, Seth was encouraged to spell the word, checking against the card. Finally, the word was added to the practice pile and counted as "learned" when he could recognize it reliably in print.

The parts-to-whole approach was also used to support comprehension through an adapted process writing approach. During the first phase, Seth dictated a story. When he believed it to be complete, the tutor then rewrote the story so that it included an introduction, episode, and conclusion. This revised piece was discussed, with the emphasis placed on the components of a strong story. Finally, one component (the introduction, episode, or conclusion) was deleted and Seth was encouraged to write a replacement. This process was continued until Seth had rewritten the entire piece. This practice proved especially helpful to Seth and was later coupled with "story frames" (Fowler 1982) to encourage Seth to construct whole texts that contained important component pieces. In addition, contact between school and clinic was maintained to good effect.

Although Seth continued to receive remedial reading support outside the classroom during the regularly scheduled reading instruction time, he no longer missed key components of the rest of the day. The support personnel in Seth's school also agreed to incorporate several of the recommended instructional procedures. For example, Seth's program was changed to include daily experiences with whole texts. He was read to daily, and these read-aloud sessions formed the basis for work in comprehension and writing. Similarly, direct instruction in word recognition was planned so that rapid application in text was featured.

Case discussion.   It is especially important to recognize that only parts of Seth's instructional program could really be accomplished in the clinic setting. Because some aspects of his progress in reading and writing were governed by the classroom and school setting, it was important to include teachers and specialists very early on in Seth's remedial program. He clearly needed, and could benefit from, some individualized instruction. However, he also needed a total instructional program that was more responsive to his needs.

Step 8: Reporting

This step involves the summarization of information obtained in the previous steps in written reports and/or oral conferences. It requires a clear statement of the presenting problem(s); a description of the information collected in the evaluations of the learner, the learning context, and through diagnostic teaching; a synthesis of this information into a clear statement of the primary difficulty; and recommendations for future practice, including descriptions and examples of appropriate materials and methods.

Although procedures for writing and reporting vary, the reporting format should parallel as closely as possible the goals of the assessment-instruction process. For now, it is important only to arrive at a general appreciation of how important clear, concise communication can be for students.

Case study.   As a result of the clinic's report, Seth's parents concluded that he did indeed need the help of special education placement, and requested that he be evaluated for determination of eligibility. The school, in turn, was anxious to use the information obtained from Seth's assessment in the clinic. Conferences were conducted with the Chapter 1 teacher and with the special educator, and the school effectively implemented the suggestions detailed in the final report. The special educator was especially interested in the mapping activities that had been done, and incorporated these activities in Seth's program. She also worked with the classroom teacher to find ways to provide prereading support activities for Seth in social studies and science.

You may also recall that there was reason to believe that Seth's daily class work was not entirely appropriate. The final report recommended that Seth's program would need to be individualized to accommodate his specific needs and abilities. Therefore, Seth's fourth-grade classroom placement was made with an eye to teacher flexibility. In particular, the teacher's ability to provide consistent and appropriate support and willingness to adapt and individualize instruction were considered. He was placed with a teacher who had demonstrated these abilities in the past and who was also capable of ensuring that Seth took responsibility for his work.

Case discussion.   In later chapters we discuss these aspects of communicating the results of the assessment-instruction process in some depth. In the meantime, you can find Seth's final report in Appendix A. Continuous assessment is critical, of course. In Seth's case, this will need to be done by the special education team as they conduct their periodic reevaluation of Seth's eligibility for their services. In addition, this will be done to make adjustments to the recommended program. It is likely that Seth will need continued support for some time to come. Only continuous assessment and adjustment will ensure his progress.

CHAPTER SUMMARY

This chapter considered an interactive view of reading and writing disability and its application to assessment and instruction. The first section of the chapter presented an interactive view of reading and writing *disability* that is consistent with the interactive view of reading and writing *ability* presented previously in Chapter 1 and which provides the theory that drives this text. An interactive view of disability suggests that students' performance on various reading and writing tasks is an indication of what they can and will do under specified conditions, rather than a set of fixed abilities and disabilities. Our attention is focused on how each student performs under different conditions and which conditions are most likely to facilitate learning rather than identifying the disability. The notion of the proper match between student and circumstance is what we must grasp if we are to be effective evaluators and instructors.

The second section of this chapter focused on an understanding of the assessment-instruction process. The long-range goal of the assessment-instruction process was described as the development of strategic, motivated, reflective learners who are able to apply their skills and strategies independently and in a flexible manner. Learning to read and write was characterized as a lifelong pursuit in which the knowledge gained from each reading/writing experience affects subsequent experiences. Because there are differences between instructional settings (classroom, resource room, clinic, etc.), different applications of the assessment-instruction process for these settings were discussed. Classroom teachers have the benefit of daily contact with students but limited time to spend with individual students. In contrast, the specialist or clinician has the benefit of individual time with the student but limited access to the student's daily interactions with reading and writing in the classroom. As a result, the amount of attention devoted to each component and the procedures used to evaluate them are likely to vary.

In the final section of this chapter, we described *procedures* for implementing the assessment-instruction process. The steps in the assessment-instruction process are guided by three questions: What is the current status of the interaction between the learner and the context? What is the *primary* source of interference with learning or performance? How can learning or performance be established or improved? The steps in the assessment-instruction process are as follows:

Step 1 Getting Started with Assessment
Step 2 Evaluating the Context
Step 3 Evaluating the Learner: Focusing on Reading and Writing
Step 4 Evaluating the Match Between the Learner and the Context
Step 5 Reflection, Decision Making, and Planning
Step 6 Identifying a Better Match: Diagnostic Teaching
Step 7 Adapting Instruction: Continuous Monitoring and Modification
Step 8 Reporting

SECTION *II*

Evaluating the Instructional Context

In the first three chapters, we provided both a theoretical and a practical framework for thinking about assessment-instruction. The theoretical framework provides the rationale for much of the remainder of the text. Frequent reference is made throughout to the ideas and concepts presented in Section I.

This section is divided into three subsections. As its name suggests, Chapter 4 includes a discussion of tools and strategies for initiating assessment. Chapters 5 and 6 provide the basis for the execution of Step 2 of the assessment-instruction process: *Evaluating the Reading and Writing Context*. Chapters 5 and 6 describe more fully the contextual factors of setting, instructional resources, approaches, and tasks. We discuss the contributions of these factors to reading performance and describe ways in which these factors can be evaluated for individual students. The measures we suggest are designed to help summarize information about the setting, the specific instruction, the reading materials, and the tasks students face in their literacy contexts. Each of these areas is considered in light of the most current research, and also in terms of the desirable outcomes for reading and writing instruction.

The third part of the Instructional Context is *Evaluating the Learner.* Recent attention to other aspects of reading, writing, and learning has been helpful, but there is not nearly so large a body of knowledge. Similarly, the traditional emphasis on the learner has resulted in the generation of more tools and strategies for assessment than have efforts in other areas. Each of the four chapters in this part contains information that will increase teachers' knowledge and understanding and also describes tools and strategies for assessment. These include norm-referenced tests and traditional informal measures (that is, Informal Reading Inventories), as well as innovative, teacher-based tools and strategies.

The steps in the assessment-instruction framework, presented in Chapter 3, guide us through the process and through this text. On the title page before each section, a flowchart of these steps is presented again, this time with one section highlighted. The highlighted section identifies the major focus in this section.

STEP 1
Getting Started
with Assessment
(Ch. 4)

STEP 2
Evaluating the
Context
(Chs. 5 & 6)

STEP 3
Evaluating the
Learner
(Chs. 7–10)

STEP 4
Evaluating the
Match Between
Learner and
Context

STEP 5
Reflection,
Decision Making,
and Planning

Ch. 11

STEP 6
Identifying a Better
Match: Diagnostic
Teaching

STEP 7
Adapting Instruction:
Continuous Monitoring
and Modification
(Chs. 12–15)

STEP 8
Reporting
(Ch. 16)

CHAPTER 4

Getting Started with Assessment

INTRODUCTION

Assessments of student reading and writing ability must begin somewhere. In this chapter, we provide a road map for the initial step of the assessment-instruction process: Getting Started. The procedures for collecting, interviewing, and observing described in this chapter are essential to a good beginning, but these activities don't end after this phase of the assessment-instruction process—as in, "That's done, now let's move on to the next step." Talking and observing with an eye toward assessment should be continuous activities in every classroom and clinical setting. Because these are such powerful tools, they are useful in virtually every phase of the assessment-instruction process and are discussed in almost every chapter of this book.

This chapter begins with a brief discussion of the nature of assessment and some guidelines that are important for the entire assessment-instruction process. The idea of a *Diagnostic Portfolio* is also introduced. As we use the term, it is both a way to think about assessment and instruction and a way to manage information. Then we provide a rationale and describe procedures for collecting background information and conducting observations and interviews, including a discussion of the sources of information that are useful in the Getting Started phase.

In the Getting Started step of the assessment-instruction process, we are less concerned with gathering information about students' application of literacy skills than we are with obtaining a general picture of the factors that may be influencing the performance data we will gather later. In this chapter, *observation, interviews,* and *work samples* are discussed as approaches to the problem of gathering *background information* for the purpose of getting started. We hope to gain an initial understanding of the learner and the context within which he or she is learning. The techniques described in this Getting Started step of assessment-instruction may save many hours of work later on.

UNDERSTANDING ASSESSMENT

Contexts for Assessment Instruction

Most students learn to read and write in *developmental* programs at the elementary and middle school levels. These programs are based on materials and tasks that have been developed so that they increase in difficulty and complexity across age and grade levels and are designed for use with large numbers of students. The assumption underlying developmental reading and writing programs is that the same (or very similar) base materials, content, instructional plans, delivery systems, and sequence are appropriate for all "normally developing" students. Consequently, everyone proceeds through the program in the same order and in the same way, although pace may vary for some students.

In most classrooms, however, there is a wide range of student achievement in reading and writing. Many teachers accommodate individual differences in their classroom by varying their instruction somewhat, within the parameters of the developmental program. When students fail to maintain the pace or make anticipated progress, they are generally referred for help in special programs.

Specialized programs of all sorts (often called "remedial" or "corrective" programs) exist to serve students who have not learned to read or write as well or as quickly as their peers or whose progress is slower than expected. Until quite recently special programs almost invariably involved identifying students based on formal achievement/diagnostic tests and then removing them from their regular classroom for some period during the day/week so that they could work with a specialist. Most of the instruction for struggling students was delivered by someone other than the classroom teacher and in an area outside the regular classroom (often called the "pull-out" model).

Although these configurations are still quite common, there are many schools and classrooms that have moved toward a new generation of procedures and processes for working with students "at risk" for failure. These alternatives generally provide additional diagnostic flexibility and also focus more attention on the role of the classroom and the teacher. There is an increased awareness that assessment and evaluation should be located in the classroom and be conducted by the classroom teacher, wherever possible. The vast majority of diagnostic information needed to plan and evaluate instruction can be gathered in the course of normal literacy events, as long as the teacher is knowledgeable and skilled.

The instructional value of collaborative and contextualized assessment procedures is likely to be much greater than could be realized by conventional approaches. In many schools, all teachers participate in team staffings designed to promote collaborative responses to individual strengths and needs. In this section and throughout the book, we try to suggest strategies that are compatible with a more integrated approach to working with students' reading and writing problems. At the same time, we recognize that traditional clinical settings and pull-out programs are still common and we try to suggest ways to create the best assessment-instruction context possible.

Guidelines for Assessment

Assessment must reflect our best and most current understandings of reading and writing. Certainly it appears that many traditional assessment practices have not provided information about important aspects of literacy. The International Reading Association and the National Council of Teachers of English have jointly published a document which details the *Standards for the Assessment of Reading and Writing* (IRA/NCTE 1994). The eleven standards are summarized in Figure 4.1. These standards are both implicitly and explicitly visible in the recommended practices we describe throughout the text. In addition to these standards, we offer the following few guidelines for assessment focused on students who are struggling in the areas of reading or writing.

For these students it is also essential that we assess directly the factors that are known to influence reading and writing, rather than ignoring them or attempting to create situations where they do not matter. What is needed is a structured approach to determine how an individual handles actual reading materials or writing tasks under conditions that simulate real reading and writing situations both in and out of the classroom. The following guidelines provide the basis for assessment practices that achieve these goals.

FIGURE 4.1
Standards for the Assessment of Reading and Writing

Standards for the Assessment of Reading and Writing

- **Standard 1:** The interests of the student are paramount in assessment.
- **Standard 2:** The primary purpose of assessment is to improve teaching and learning.
- **Standard 3:** Assessment must reflect and allow for critical inquiry into curriculum and instruction.
- **Standard 4:** Assessments must recognize and reflect the intellectually and socially complex nature of reading and writing and the important roles of school, home, and society in literacy development.
- **Standard 5:** Assessment must be fair and equitable.
- **Standard 6:** The consequences of an assessment procedure are the first, and most important, consideration in establishing the validity of the assessment.
- **Standard 7:** The teacher is the most important agent of assessment.
- **Standard 8:** The assessment process should involve multiple perspectives and sources of data.
- **Standard 9:** Assessment must be based in the school community.
- **Standard 10:** All members of the educational community — students, parents, teachers, administrators, policy makers, and the public — must have a voice in the development, interpretation, and reporting of assessment.
- **Standard 11:** Parents must be involved as active, essential participants in the assessment process.

Source: *Standards for the Assessment of Reading and Writing.* Prepared by the IRA/NCTE Joint Task Force on Assessment, 1994. International Reading Association.

Assess Meaningful Activities

To evaluate students' reading and writing abilities, we must assess students as they read and write real texts for real purposes. There are times when it may be reasonable to evaluate some component skill in isolation (for example, sight word vocabulary). However, we should avoid generating conclusions about the contribution of any single skill to overall reading and writing ability until we have also observed the component in context.

In addition, we must consider how relevant the component abilities are for real, or *authentic*, reading and writing activities (Goodman, Smith, Meredith, and Goodman 1986). Authenticity describes both tasks and materials. There should be a purpose for reading or writing that transcends assessment or instruction. School tasks and texts in reading and writing should be similar to those used by people in non-school settings. If they are not, questions of authenticity are raised.

Assessment Should Be Contextualized

The most informative assessments are those that occur within the everyday instructional context rather than artificial testing contexts. There is evidence that people are aware of the differences among contexts and alter their performance accordingly (Spiro and Myers 1984). Anyone who has ever puzzled over the discrepancy between students' performance in the classroom and their test performance is aware of this problem.

In general, students tend to consider formal testing situations to be more important than everyday classroom tasks. However, this perception can have very different effects on different students. Some students perform better in the formal testing situations because of increased motivation to do well, while others perform less well because of the anxiety created by the pressure to do well. Therefore, we do not want to collect information that tells us only how students perform in formal testing situations. We want to be able to make some predictions about students' performance in everyday instructional contexts.

Assessment and Purpose Should Match

No single assessment tool or strategy can do everything. We must think carefully about what we want to know and why we are assessing. If we need comparative data on large numbers of students, then informal, classroom-based assessment probably is not practical. On the other hand, if we want information that will help us plan instruction for individuals or groups of students, then standardized, norm-referenced tests are not likely to be helpful.

Even after the general type of assessment (formal versus informal) has been determined, we need to consider our purpose. For example, if we are interested in making placement decisions, then we do not need procedures that yield a fine-grained analysis of strengths and weaknesses. Alternatively, if we are trying to make decisions about whether to teach or reteach a particular component, then we will need a tool or strategy that provides an evaluation of a specific area.

Assessment Should Be Systematic

Whether we use formal, standardized tests or informal, classroom-based proce-dures, our assessments must be reliable or trustworthy indices of student per-formance (see Chapter 10). That is, we need to know that students' performance on a particular assessment would remain constant or stable if the procedure were to be readministered. The results of an assessment would have little meaning if they fluctuated wildly from one administration to the next.

The reliability of formal test instruments typically is addressed through the standardization process and reported in the manual. The trustworthiness of informal assessments depends on the extent to which we are systematic and consistent in our use of these techniques (Valencia, and Calfee 1991). When making comparisons among individuals, we must attempt to evaluate all of our students under the same conditions, with the same level of support. For exam-ple, we should attempt to formalize at least some of the probing questions asked during story retellings. If the student is given additional assistance, then it is important to record the information provided to clarify the conditions under which the performance occurred. Otherwise, the information will not be instructionally useful.

Assessment Should Be Continuous

Multiple samples of students' performance are always preferable to a single sample. Not only does continuous evaluation improve the reliability of the pro-cedure, it also permits us to observe the *patterns* of behavior that are most infor-mative for assessment and instruction. In addition, it casts assessment and instruction in their proper roles—as interacting elements of teaching. Viewing every instructional interaction with a student as an assessment opportunity enhances our diagnostic powers.

We have found that continuous assessment helps us to view both our own teaching and the student's ability in a different light. A student's failure to per-form can be viewed as an opportunity to gather information, rather than a reflection of some static and inherent ability (in either the teacher or the child). Teacher evaluations must be taken seriously. Indeed, the majority of assess-ments in reading and writing can/should be done continuously and in conjunc-tion with the daily instructional program as an aid to planning, adapting, and refining instruction.

The Diagnostic Portfolio and Thumbnail Sketch

Thoughtful reflection and good records are essential when a variety of stan-dardized and informal procedures are used to plan instruction, evaluate progress, and communicate with parents and administrators. We suggest creat-ing and using a *Diagnostic Portfolio* as a way to support and promote the ongoing and multisource type of assessment advocated in this text. According to Valen-cia, McGinley, and Pearson (1990), the term *portfolio* has both a physical and philosophical sense:

As a concept, the "idea" of a portfolio forces us to expand the range of "things" we would consider as data to use in instructional decision-making. It is also an attitude suggesting that assessment is a dynamic rather than a static process reflected most accurately in multiple snapshots taken over time. All who have a stake in contributing to the portfolio (students, teachers, and parents) have a right to visit it whenever they wish—to reflect on and analyze its contents. But it is also a physical entity, a container in which we can store the artifacts of our literacy—the examples, documents, and observations that serve as evidence of growth and development—so that they are available for visitation and reflection.

Diagnostic Portfolios, like other types of portfolios, are *organized* and *intentional* collections. Also like other portfolios, they include materials that exemplify the depth and breadth of a student's expertise. They include a variety of different types of information collected over time as indicators of growth in reading and writing, which make it easier for teachers, clinicians, and students to plan the experiences that will encourage additional progress.

The contents of the portfolio will vary in relation to the particular program of assessment and instruction in effect. As Valencia (1990a) notes, the range of items to include in a portfolio is almost limitless, but may include written responses to reading, reading logs, selected daily work, pieces of writing at various stages of completion, classroom tests, observational checklists, unit projects, and audio or video tapes. An important addition to these suggestions, for those who follow the assessment-instruction process outlined in this book, is the inclusion of measures designed to evaluate various aspects of the instructional context. "The key is to ensure a variety of types of indicators of learning so that teachers, parents, students, and administrators can build a complete picture of the student's development" (Valencia 1990a, 339).

There will also be information in a Diagnostic Portfolio that is unlikely to appear in conventional portfolios. Most contemporary descriptions of portfolios suggest that portfolios should be embedded in classroom instruction and that students should play a pivotal role in selecting, maintaining, and reflecting upon the portfolio contents.

A Diagnostic Portfolio has somewhat different functions and forms and the degree of student involvement will be quite dependent on the age and maturity of the student. The Diagnostic Portfolio is designed to improve teacher decision making through more comprehensive and representative assessment; to get a richer and more authentic view of the student's literacy knowledge and use in order to rethink and/or reshape instruction. As a result, the teacher is likely to have a more central role in the Diagnostic Portfolio than is typical for classroom-based portfolios. Since the purpose of this portfolio is much more highly focused, it is likely to contain at least some conventional assessment information and there will be many more pieces of evidence that speak to the teacher and to the specialist (see Figure 4.2).

We recommend that the contents of the portfolio be organized into several layers of information: the actual evidence, or raw data, and one or more levels of summary or profile sheets to help synthesize the information. Inclusion of

FIGURE 4.2
The Diagnostic
Portfolio
(labels)

- written responses to reading
- reading logs
- writing samples
- selected daily work
- pieces of writing at various stages of completion
- classroom tests
- observational checklists
- unit projects
- audio or video tapes
- running records
- informal reading inventories
- student self-reflection
- formal test results
- summary of interview results
- summary of school history
  ETC.

the raw data enables us to examine students' actual work and progress notes, rather than relying simply on a number or grade.

Summary or profile sheets assist us in analyzing and synthesizing the information in ways that help us make decisions and communicate with parents and administrators. We have found it helpful to use a summary chart we call the *Thumbnail Sketch* to facilitate and monitor decision making as we work through the steps of the assessment-instruction process (see Figure 4.3). This chart, or any form of written summary for that matter, forces us to think carefully about the important factors operating in individual cases. It can also identify areas about which we need more information. In this chapter we describe some of the tools and strategies for initiating the completion of information in Step 1.

Sources of Information

All students, even very young children, come to us with a personal and educational history. Students' physical, cognitive, affective, and sociocultural histories have a profound influence on what and how they learn. In some cases, assessments of reading or writing ability can be speeded immeasurably by the careful and thoughtful gathering and analysis of background information regarding these areas.

In the Getting Started phase of the assessment-instruction process, it is important to gather as much background information as possible from the home, the school, and the learner because we cannot know what information might be significant. There are several reasons to collect background information. First, it is helpful at the onset of assessment to establish that the primary source of difficulty is *not* a correlate (see Chapter 2) since some correlates should receive attention before assessment is continued (for example, poor vision). Second, we want to avoid, where possible, duplicating assessment

FIGURE 4.3
The Thumbnail Sketch

Getting Started (Step 1)	About the Reading and Writing Context (Step 2)	About the Learner (Step 3)	Decision Making (Steps 4 and 5)	Diagnostic Teaching (Step 6)
Background Name: Age: Grade: Key Correlates:	*Resources* *Instruction*	*Knowledge About Reading and Writing* *Reading and Writing Performance*	*Evaluating the Match* (What is the existing match?)	*Planning and Implementing* (What is most likely to (re)establish learning?)
Information About the Learner Knowledge about Reading and Writing: Motivation:	*Settings*	*Motivation*	*Reflection and Generating Hypotheses* (What does the learner need?)	*Evaluating the Diagnostic Teaching Sessions*
Information About the Context School History: Instructional Approaches: Experiences, linguistic and cultural context:	*Tasks*	*Reflection and Independence*		

information and efforts. Some students have already received a great deal of attention and testing. Unless there is a good reason to do so, we would not want to duplicate efforts. Finally, we want to gather as much information as possible in order to make good decisions as we proceed with the assessment-instruction process.

It is important not to leap to conclusions about etiology at this early stage. For example, although the failing marriage of a student's parents may be contributing to reading or writing problems, a great many students whose families are experiencing stress read and write well and prosper academically. The purpose of gathering background information is not to attribute cause but to provide insights that allow us to make good decisions about instruction.

Background information can be examined from a number of points of view, reflecting the contributions to reading and writing of both learner and context. The school gathers and reports information on students from a point of view that is different from a parent's. Similarly, the student's view of his or her history is likely to be different from either of these other sources of background information. Each of these points of view can provide important insights during the Getting Started phase. Using several sources of information allows us to examine performance from several perspectives. As Anthony et al. (1991) point out, this increases our confidence in the information and deepens our understanding of the student's reading and writing.

Home/Parents

Parents are particularly good sources of information about students' background, because they have enduring contact with them. They have information about their child's overall experiential background and developmental history that includes knowledge about physical, cultural, linguistic, affective, and cognitive factors. Parents are likely to have a somewhat different perspective about students than school personnel. It is often more personal and more graphic, including critical cultural, motivational, and attitudinal information.

Home and community expectations for learning and achievement have a profound effect on students and these should be explored as fully as possible with parents. Coming to understand how parents use reading and writing; what they believe about the value and nature of literacy; whether English is a primary language in the home; and how they try to teach knowledge and skills can be helpful in both assessment and instruction.

Parents also have a more long-range view of their child's school experience. They will remember and describe, for example, how first grade was such "a waste" because the teacher got sick in the middle of the year and they couldn't find a substitute teacher. Or, they will know, even if the school records don't reveal it, that their daughter's problems in writing started in third grade, when the school started a new approach to writing. Although this information does not necessarily inform us about the specific difficulties that the student is experiencing right now, it can help our understanding of the overall context of the reading or writing problem.

In addition to the value of the information itself, it is important to enlist parental support as early as possible. Their involvement and understanding is often necessary in order to achieve lasting change in reading or writing performance. Some parents are unaware of the need to provide continuous and supported reading and writing practice in the home or believe that only school personnel should work with their child. Some parents are literate and supportive in their first language but not in English, while others are distrustful of schools. An initial interview can provide information about the amount and type of reading and writing activity that takes place in the home and about how literacy and schooling are viewed there.

School

Sometimes teachers are reluctant to seek background information because they are worried that such knowledge will color their perceptions and treatment of students. They are aware of studies about the effects of teacher expectations on student achievement, often called "Pygmalion effects" (Rosenthal and Jacobson 1968). This is a more serious concern when reading or writing disability is viewed as a problem located entirely within the learner (see Chapter 3) than it is when disability is viewed from an interactive and contextual perspective.

From an interactive perspective, patterns observed in the past are not invariable or static, nor are they the only patterns possible. Past history merely reflects the student's performance in a specific setting, using particular materials, instructional approaches, and so on. Consequently, teachers and clinicians must have access to background knowledge so that they can begin to determine what their students have experienced and how they responded to these experiences, information about both the learner *and* the learning context.

In addition, of course, there is some information that is very straightforward and important to know. For example, if "Jennifer" missed a great deal of school because of illness, we know that she has not had the opportunity to acquire particular knowledge and skill. This background is different from the history of "Jason," of the same age and "disability," who was present during all instructional periods. Although we cannot know immediately why Jason has failed to benefit from instruction, we know that he was exposed to it.

School records. All schools keep records on student progress and achievement, although the amount and type of information available from schools varies widely from one school district to another. Today, most schools maintain and retain little except the most standardized information. In some areas, support personnel (for example, Chapter 1 teachers, speech therapists) keep their own records and this information may not be included in the overall school records. Permanent records normally contain only the results of standardized achievement tests, copies of periodic grading results, and perhaps a list of the curricular materials used by the student (for example, a listing of basal criterion test results). Some schools have established minimum competencies, and student progress in these areas would be noted. Similarly, some schools give periodic group "intelligence" tests (see Chapter 9) and these results would be included as well.

When students have been tested for eligibility for a special education placement, however, the school records probably contain a great deal more information. There would probably be an evaluation by a school psychologist, including the results of one or several individual intelligence and aptitude tests. In addition, there would normally be some sort of report from the classroom teacher regarding academic progress and overall functioning. It is important to note the dates associated with these types of information as an aid to interpretation. When comprehensive in-school assessment has taken place, the school records can eliminate the need for gathering certain types of information, although it is often necessary to supplement this formal information before drawing specific diagnostic or instructional conclusions.

Teachers. If the classroom teacher is not the person leading the assessment, then he or she is an obvious source of information about the student who is experiencing difficulty. Classroom teachers can quickly and efficiently provide information about students' performance in reading and writing and about the types of instructional programs or opportunities that the student has experienced. Less obvious is that teachers can also provide insight into the types of tasks that are considered important in their classrooms. In addition, they can describe the criteria used to evaluate students in this context. Students are rarely required or expected to do the same things in all settings and teachers can help us to understand the richer details of the instructional context.

Similarly, it is important to gather information from all teachers who work with a student. Recently, a Chapter 1 teacher with whom we work discovered that one of her students worked with five different teachers in the course of each week (in five different places in the building!). Each of these teachers had somewhat different expectations and programs. It turned out that no one had really realized this until they began a close assessment using a Thumbnail Sketch to pull the information together.

Learner

Probably the most neglected source of information regarding a student's performance is the student. Poor readers or writers are often surprisingly insightful about their difficulties. For this reason, we have devoted a large segment of this chapter to student interviews and observation.

In later chapters we will describe how the learner provides very direct performance information. Here we want to suggest how student interviews, work samples, and observation can help us to gather information about their background knowledge, their reading and writing knowledge and skill, and their attitudes and motivations about reading and writing. These approaches can also help us "get started" by providing us with student self-evaluation information and with information about how the student perceives his or her instructional setting.

This is always important but is especially so when the learner's primary culture or language are divergent from the school's expectations and values. Ovando (1993) has argued that "Because teaching practices are not always linguistically enlightened, language can become a main source of inequality surrounding the lives of students who come to school marked with a stigmatized speech variety" (223). Students can help us to understand their cultural, linguistic, or ethnic background and to make some early inferences about how these might interact during reading and writing events.

Work Samples

Unlike the other sources just described, work samples may seem an unfamiliar source of assessment information. Part of a general approach to newer assessments, called *performance assessment*, work sampling also has close ties to portfolio assessment approaches just described. Teachers have always used students' own products and behaviors to make decisions about instruction, further assessment, and/or referral. However, until recently, these sources of information have not been viewed as centrally important for appropriate, effective, and efficient assessment. Consequently, both teachers and specialists have tended to downplay their utility and even ignore the information altogether.

Work samples that provide evidence about students' understanding and interpretation of texts is especially useful. In particular, work samples can and should be selected so that they reveal students' *growth*, not just their present level of functioning. Some students who are not reading or writing at age-appropriate levels have, nevertheless, made great strides. Where possible, the same or similar tasks or products should be selected from several points in a student's school history. This can reveal quite vividly dramatic changes in students' performance or troubling evidence of failure to develop. They can also provide insight into the experiences provided by the instructional context and the task expectations encountered there.

TOOLS AND STRATEGIES FOR GETTING STARTED

Interviews

Although interviews are widely used in our society for a variety of purposes, these tools are not used often in the area of literacy assessment. Interviews can be time-consuming to conduct, but professionals have begun to realize that information elicited from interviews can enhance the diagnostic value of the overall assessment. Even when teachers talk to students and others, the information gleaned is rarely reported. This may be due to the fact that many teachers and administrators are distrusting of interview information, even though most teachers and administrators were hired on the strength of an interview and the presumed competence it revealed.

In part, this distrust results from the fact that interview information is *self-reported*. In the past, both school personnel and researchers have been troubled by a number of issues surrounding self-reported information (Cavanaugh and Perlmutter 1982; Nisbett and Wilson 1977). First, there is a possibility that students or parents might report information that is an inaccurate reflection of their true ideas, beliefs, or inclinations. In particular, it has been argued that students are likely to report what they think the teacher/adult wants to hear.

A second concern revolves around the ability of individuals, especially children, to talk about their ideas or abilities. This is a particular concern when students are either very young or have speech/language differences or difficulties. Of course, similar concerns arise when English is not the primary language in the home. It is clear that we must consider these potentially confounding factors just as we would the factors that can influence performance on other types of assessment instruments, and seek multiple indicators to confirm or validate their findings. However, it is also important to remember that current research suggests that interviews and other types of self-report strategies can provide both reliable and valid information that is difficult, perhaps impossible, to glean otherwise (Ericsson and Simon 1980; Lipson, Irwin, and Poth 1986).

Interviewing, like other informal assessment tools, requires a knowledgeable and skilled professional eye. It is important for teachers and specialists to structure interviews and to try to gather information in systematic ways, recording data in a consistent manner. Structured procedures, including tape recording, can increase the reliability of interview information and ensure that teachers interpret thoughtfully the results of such assessments. There is also an argument for collecting information in *less* formal contexts, by attending to the nature and content of everyday talk with students. These multiple and repeated conversations can provide both new and confirming ideas about students' reading and writing performance (Lipson 1995).

Parents

During the Getting Started phase of the assessment-instruction process, it is imperative to gather information about family background, parental expectations, health history, and support for reading and writing in the home. We prefer to do this through personal interviews. We try to be informal, using an interview form to remind us of important areas of discussion. It is usually sufficient to start the interview by asking the parent, "Tell me about your child's school experience," or, "Tell me about your child's reading/writing problems." This is generally enough to launch parents into a long monologue, because few people ever get enough time to talk specifically about their children.

Cultural differences among parents can obviously influence interviews. Understanding something about how authority figures are viewed by the cultural group of the parents and acquiring knowledge about appropriate conversational rules is professionally responsible. It can also help you to interpret more accurately the information you get. Of course, when parents' primary language is not English, you will need an interpreter if you are not fluent in their language.

Even if there are no apparent cultural or linguistic differences, parents are often confused and intimidated by professionals and their jargon. In addition, many parents of poor readers and writers are frightened and dismayed by their child's apparent inability to acquire these critical abilities. For many, this is interpreted to mean that their daughter or son is not very bright. Sometimes they are concerned that they have done or not done something that has caused the problem. It is important to be positive and supportive while working with parents, without raising any unrealistic hopes about magic remedies.

Several authors have suggested helpful guidelines for parent interviewing (McCloughlin 1987; McGinnis and Smith 1982). These include the following:

1. Meet in a private and confidential setting.
2. Avoid jargon.
3. Listen attentively and avoid talking too much.
4. Keep note-taking to a minimum although it's a good idea to summarize major points with them at the end.
5. When in doubt, clarify what was said to avoid misunderstandings.
6. Follow cues provided by the parent and be aware of variation in cultural expectations and rules for interaction.
7. Avoid making judgmental remarks.
8. Be tactful.
9. Encourage less talkative people by asking open-ended questions.
10. Do not be afraid of silences. They often elicit important information.
11. Respond forthrightly to parents' anxiety; try to reassure without painting an overly optimistic picture.
12. Remain relaxed and avoid defensiveness and sarcasm, at all costs.
13. Assure parents that the information will be treated confidentially and then make sure that it is.

A family information form is presented in Figure 4.4 that can be used either as an interview guide or, in cases when a personal interview is not possible or practical, as a written form to be completed at home by the student's family. It is important to remember that completing a written form can be intimidating to some parents. In particular, be alert to the possibility that the parents may not be literate themselves. This may be the case when forms are repeatedly "lost" or "forgotten," suggesting that an extra effort may be needed to make personal contact. It is entirely possible, for example, to have a satisfactory phone interview to gather key background information.

Whichever approach is taken, it is essential to gather information about the factors in a student's educational experiences, health history, attitudes toward school and reading and writing, and family background that may be related to problems in reading and writing. Although most parents do not mind sharing family history, some will be concerned. It may be necessary or desirable to explain certain questions, particularly those that refer to family history of academic success and early developmental and health history. Simply telling parents that these can be factors in students' achievement is usually enough.

FIGURE 4.4
Family Information Form

General Information: _____
_____
Languages spoken: _____
Preferred language: _____
Primary language spoken at home: _____

Family Members:
Mother's name, occupation, and age: _____
Father's name, occupation, and age: _____
Marital status: _____
Siblings' names and ages: _____
Has a family member experienced any health or learning problems? ___ If so,
please describe _____
Is there anything in the home that may be a source of difficulty for your child (e.g.,
moving, separation, remarriage, illness, financial problems?). ___ If so, please describe
_____

Educational History: _____
_____
_____

Health History and Development: _____
_____
_____

Reading and Writing Development:
What are your child's attitudes toward reading? writing? school? _____
What do you feel are your child's special learning needs? _____
What does your child do very well? _____
Does your child have any special interests? ___ What are they? _____
How does your child spend leisure time? _____
When did you first notice that your child seemed to be having some trouble in
reading or writing? _____
How do you feel your child's special needs have been handled? _____
What do you expect for your child's future? _____

Comments:
Please write about any other attitudes, behaviors, or information that you feel are
important for us to know. _____
_____

Parents are often unaware of the potential influence of routine childhood experiences. For example, a history of ear infections can have an inhibiting effect on both language development and phonological awareness. Similarly, unreasonable parental expectations, competition with older, successful siblings, or early entrance into academic programs can cause students to avoid reading tasks. Parents rarely offer this information spontaneously and an interview should elicit it.

Some parents attribute their child's difficulties to poor teaching and schooling. School history can, of course, be a critical factor in students' reading and writing development. Unsatisfactory initial instruction, poor classroom management, or simply lack of readiness for the program offered in the school can result in learning difficulties. It is important not to fuel this discontent, since the student (and the parents) will probably continue to depend on the school/teacher in question. On the other hand, being an empathic listener and an advocate for students is a responsibility you bear. If schools or teachers appear to be a factor in the student's problem, it is important to be tactful in responding to parents' concern, frustration, and anger, while also working to remove barriers to successful performance.

Finally, parents are potential sources of information about students' development in specific areas of reading and writing. Asking parents to report on their own observations of key literacy outcomes can be enormously informative. In Figure 4.5 there is a sample of the information that parents can provide and a notation about the outcomes related to those items. Parents would not, of course, receive the annotated version, but would respond only to the prompts in the left-hand column. Again, information about student performance from several perspectives can help us gain confidence in the emerging picture we have of an individual learner.

School

As with parent information, we seek information from the school that is uniquely theirs to offer. School records and personnel can suggest how well a student has functioned in an academic setting, what instructional materials have been used, and how far he or she has progressed in acquiring age-appropriate reading and writing knowledge and skill. As we have already noted, school information can also help us avoid the duplication of previous assessment efforts. When available, recent test results and observational data may provide invaluable direction for preparing an assessment plan. In the best cases, information is obtained about what has worked instructionally and what has not.

Student information should be accessed and handled discretely. Schools are sometimes sensitive to the permanence of student records, which are always available to parents at their request. Students may view their own records at the age of majority (Family Educational Rights and Privacy Act/Buckley Amendment, PL 93–380, 1974). If you are a teacher in the building, you may access and discuss any student information as long as you are planning instruction or

FIGURE 4.5

Observation Guide for Parents (Primary) Signifying Important Learning Behaviors

MY CHILD AS A LEARNER			
Name _____ Date _____			
Grade _____			
Indicate your observation of your child's learning in the following areas. Please comment where appropiate.			
	Yes	No	Comments/Examples
1. My child likes to listen to me read to him/her.	☐	☐	
2. My child likes to read to me.	☐	☐	
3. My child tries to read in everyday situations (street signs, cereal boxes, store signs).	☐	☐	
4. It is clear from the way my child talks that a book has been understood.	☐	☐	
5. My child tries to figure out new words for him/herself when reading.	☐	☐	
6. My child sometimes guesses at words but they usually make sense.	☐	☐	
7. My child sometimes chooses to write.	☐	☐	
8. My child likes to talk about & share what was written.	☐	☐	
9. My child voluntarily tries out new words or forms of writing.	☐	☐	
Questions: _____ _____ _____			

ATTITUDE

INDEPENDENT APPLICATION

FOCUS ON COMPREHENSION

STRATEGY

RISK-TAKING

SELF-INITIATED ACTIVY

From: Anthony, R.J., Johnson, T.D., Mikelson, N.J., & Preece, A. (1991). *Evaluating Literacy: A Perspective for Change*, p. 51. Portsmouth, NH: Heineman. Reprinted with permission.

making decisions. Schools are not permitted to distribute this information to any outside professionals without explicit parental consent, and most schools and school employees do not discuss individual students without it either. If there is any question about whether a parent would be concerned about the assessment processes being used, it is a good idea to obtain written parental consent before reviewing student records.

There appears to be a tremendous lack of coordination between the core instructional setting in many schools and the remedial settings taking place in those same schools. Johnston, Allington, and Afflerbach (1985), for example, found that only one-third of the remedial reading teachers interviewed knew what reading instructional materials were used in the regular classroom. Similarly, only 10 percent of the classroom teachers knew what materials were used in the resource rooms! Consequently it is important to gather information from both settings when students are involved in pull-out programs.

Personal conversations or written summary forms from key school personnel can add immeasurably to our understanding of the student and his or her reading and writing history. Figure 4.6 presents a school information form that can be used either as a guide for interviewing teachers and support personnel, or as a written form to be completed independently by them. We need to know as much as possible about the student's specific knowledge and skill. We also need to know exactly what types of instruction have been offered, how this has been received, and the school's perception of this student.

Student

Student interviews are especially important because they signal to students the importance and value of self-evaluation. They can help to establish a collaborative working relationship and they send a message early in the assessment-instruction process that students are expected to take some responsibility for their own learning.

Current research reveals that measures of reading and writing knowledge are strongly related to reading comprehension or writing performance (Paris, Cross, and Lipson 1984; Paris and Jacobs 1984; Englert et al. 1991). Interviews, or less formal classroom conversations, offer considerable promise as a method of assessment because they provide us with rich information about students' knowledge, understanding, and beliefs.

Indrisano (1982) describes the framework used at Boston University for an initial interview which begins with the interviewer saying:

> Today we'll try to discover more about you and the ways you learn. We'll need two kinds of experts, one expert on learning and one expert on you. I've studied about learning and have taught many people, so I could be called an expert on learning. You've been making discoveries about yourself all your life while you've been living there inside you. If we work together we will have the information we need to help you. I'll begin by asking a few questions. (13)

Following this introduction, the examiner asks five general questions:

Figure 4.6
School Information Form

Student Background

Name: _____ Birthdate _____

Age: _____ Grade: _____ Teacher: _____

School district: _____ School: _____

School address: _____ Phone: _____

Principal: _____ Teacher: _____

Parent(s): _____ Phone: _____

Parent address: _____

School attendance: Regular _____ Irregular _____ Reason _____

Ever repeated/skipped a grade? _____ If yes, what grade? _____
   What was result? _____

Is nonpromotion or special class placement now being considered? _____

What, if any, special services is this student now receiving? _____
_____

Describe the student's performance in reading, spelling, writing, math, science, and
   social studies: _____
_____
_____

What concerns, if any, do you have about this student's behavior and/or
   performance in the classroom? _____
_____

Reading/Writing Instruction

Instructional personnel	Materials and methods	Progress
Name: _____	_____	_____
Position: _____	_____	_____
Frequency of instruction: _____		
Name: _____	_____	_____
Position: _____	_____	_____
Frequency of instruction: _____		
Name: _____	_____	_____
Position: _____	_____	_____
Frequency of instruction: _____		

Describe any special methods or materials used to help this student: _____
_____

What are this student's strengths? _____
   Weaknesses? _____

Test Results

Type of test	Name of test	Date	Results	Examiner
Intelligence				
Achievement				
Vision				
Hearing				
Other				

Other information relevant to this student's performance in school: _____
_____
_____

1. What do you do very well?
2. What is it that you do not do well?
3. How have you learned to do what you can do well?
4. What does not work so well?
5. If you were to give expert advice about you and the ways you learn best, what would you say? (If further prompting is needed, Indrisano suggests asking, "What would you like your teachers to know about you and the ways you like to learn?" or, "How could they help you more?")

This type of initial interview sets the tone for a mutually supportive working relationship.

Subsequent interviews and conversations can focus on students' knowledge of the goals of reading and writing, the processes and skills involved in skilled reading and writing, and students' appraisal of their own reading and writing abilities (see Lipson 1995). Each of these aspects is discussed below.

Functions, goals, and purposes of reading and writing. When asked to talk about their knowledge of reading and writing and reflect on their abilities, students share with us their view of what it means to be competent. Several researchers report responses from students who possess mistaken notions about the goals of skilled reading (Paris and Jacobs 1984; Wixson, Bosky, Yochum, and Alvermann 1984). Our experience suggests that many struggling writers have similarly mistaken ideas about writing. When student theories of reading or writing are inaccurate, or their image of their own competence is askew, learning is difficult. Their theories compete for attention and can make them resistant to learning more efficient and effective strategies (see Johnston 1985b for several powerful case studies of adults whose concepts of reading have interfered with acquisition of reading skill).

Consider the following responses to the question, "Do you have trouble with reading?":

Jonathon, age l0: "I have to tell you something. I'm in the fourth grade, but I'm only using a third grade reader. That's not very good."
Michael, age 13: "I must, my Mom's making me come here [the clinic]."
Jane, age 11: "Yes, when I read, the stuff just seems to go out of my head."
Sara, age 7: "Yes, I read too softly."

Embedded in these responses are theories about reading. In their daily interactions with teachers, parents, and print, students construct a vision of reading in general and their ability to perform in particular. In the quotations above, note that both Michael and Jonathon estimate their ability only in terms of external factors. Sara, on the other hand, estimates reading competence using a criterion appropriate only for public performance. Such definitions can interfere with the ability to learn the important elements of skilled reading, because students often fail to understand the reason for instructional activities. Only Jane has provided a response that suggests she may grasp the nature and demands of real reading and has recognized a serious limitation in her own ability. Not surprisingly, these students perform differently in and out of school. Although each was classified as "at risk" in reading and/or writing, their problems are quite different, and these first responses in an interview setting provided important information that was pursued in later sessions.

Asked to respond to the question "What makes a good writer?" students reveal their theories as well. The following samples from several third and fourth grade students are suggestive of the range of responses to questions like these.

> *Brandie, age 10:*   A good writer would put his experiences in the story. Try to make the story sound real, and put voice in it.
>
> *Chad, age 9:*   They write good; periods, capitals, full sentences. Put your apostrophes in and spell right.
>
> *Heidi, age 10:*   They write neatly. Spell almost every word right.
>
> *Greg, age 10:*   Someone who has good thoughts, good description in their stories.

These students clearly have differing ideas about the goals and functions of writing. Both Brandie and Greg understand something about the personal value of writing as well as the variation in genre. Chad and Heidi, on the other hand, think in terms of mechanics and usage. Not surprisingly, their views of reading and writing are often, though not always, aligned. Greg thinks that a good reader, "is someone who knows what the book says, who really gets into the book and has a lot of feeling in the book." Heidi, on the other hand, thinks that a good reader is, "someone that knows every word in the book."

It appears that many young students believe that the goal of reading is flawless word calling or that effective reading is equivalent to verbatim memory of text. As well, many students appear to equate writing with neat handwriting and/or accurate spelling. Such inappropriate assessments by students may lead to a corresponding application of inappropriate strategies (pay attention only to the graphic cues, read it over and over again, write using only words that can be spelled correctly, etc.). These beliefs may also provide insight into classroom practices that need to be explored more fully.

Self-appraisal and goal-setting.   As noted previously, it is often helpful to ask students to appraise their own reading and writing abilities and to establish goals for their instructional work. Open-ended interview questions can provide insight into students' ability to engage in self-evaluation but also into the criteria they apply for responding.

In our experience, students are frequently very accurate in their appraisals of their difficulties and often select appropriate goals as well. Self-appraisal is particularly important when working with older students and adults. These individuals are likely to have fairly sophisticated abilities to reflect on their actions and skills. We were reminded of this quite painfully as we recently observed a conversation between a seventh grade boy and his special educator. He (angrily) proclaimed in a planning meeting that "this year I want to learn to read!" She retorted that she wished he would feel better about himself as a reader, since he really could read. He countered that "reading like a first or second grader didn't count." She reiterated her belief that he should view himself as a reader.

When both parties are communicating carefully, these early interactions can set the stage for a level of reflection by both the teacher and the student and for joint effort that can focus the assessment-instruction process. However, many students have not attempted this type of reflection before and self-appraisal may help them to start seeing their reading and study problems more clearly. The types of scripted interview questions that are particularly effective are summarized in Figure 4.7. These are, of course, just questions to begin a conversation. A skilled interviewer will follow the leads offered by children as they reflect on learning experiences, as well as more specific reading knowledge, melding the critical components of skill and attitude (see Figure 4.7).

Knowledge about reading and writing skills and strategies. Although students' knowledge of skills and strategies does not ensure their application, information about awareness can be gathered through interviews. Wixson et al. (1984) developed an interview specifically designed to evaluate readers' awareness of the goals and purposes of reading activities, the demands imposed on them by specific reading activities, and the strategies they have available to carry out specific reading activities. We have adapted it here for use with writing as well as reading (see Figure 4.8).

This interview assesses students' knowledge of much more than the goals and purposes. Because the interview is designed to be used with actual classroom materials (that is, a basal reader, a content-area text, workbook pages, writing samples), it reveals students' perceptions of their own abilities and the strategies they might employ in specific contexts they encounter daily.

Such systematic probing can lead to fairly detailed and differentiated profiles of students' understanding of the situations in which reading skills and strategies should be employed. For example, responses to the question "If your teacher told you to remember the information in this story (chapter), what would be the best way to do this?" asked in the context of several types of materials such as a basal reader, a trade book, and a content-area text, can provide information about a reader's level of strategy development and sensitivity to the varying demands that the same task can impose in different reading contexts. Some students provide responses such as "try hard" or "think about it" in both contexts, which may indicate a generalized lack of awareness regarding task demands and strategy usage.

Other students' responses suggest that they have developed context-specific strategies for dealing with a particular task. Within the context of writing, responses such as "think about the plot," or "use voice" suggest an awareness of the properties of narrative text that make narrative writing effective. Similarly, responses in the context of a content-area text such as "take notes and study," "write out the questions," "have someone quiz you," and "break it up into small parts and memorize it," suggest an awareness that remembering in this context requires a conscious effort on the part of the reader.

FIGURE 4.7

Student Interview

Questions designed to elicit students' awareness of various aspects of the reading and writing processes might include:

Functions, goals and purposes of reading and writing
- What is reading (or writing)?
- What are some of the reasons people write (read)?
- Why do people read (or write)? (see Chapter 6 for additional suggestions).

Self-appraisal and goal-setting
- Describe yourself as a reader (writer).
- Tell me two things you can do now in writing (reading) that you didn't used to be able to do?
- What would you like to do better as a reader (writer)?
- What is there about writing (reading) that you still don't understand?
- What kind of help do you think you need with reading? In writing?
- How long do you think it will take for you to read as well as you want or need to read?
- Who is the best writer (reader) you know?
- What does that person do that makes her/him such a good writer (reader)?
- How could you improve your reading (writing)?

Knowledge about reading/writing skills and strategies
- Do you read in a different way when you're reading different kinds of things?
- Are some things easier to write about than others?
- How do you decide what to read (write)?
- What do you do when you have trouble during reading and writing?
- How do you get started in writing?

Attitudes and motivation
- Do you write (read)? What?
- What are some titles of books that you've enjoyed?
- What topics do you enjoy writing about?
- Have you ever had a teacher who made reading/writing fun and exciting? Tell me about her/him.
- Have you ever learned something just by writing (reading) about it?
- Have you had some experiences that have made you want to read (write) about something?
- Do your parents (or someone else) read to you? How often?
- Do you have a library card? Books? Magazines?

FIGURE 4.8

*Interview for
Assessing
Student
Perceptions of
Classroom
Reading and
Writing Tasks*

Reading and Writing Interview

Name: _____ _____ Date: _____

Classroom Teacher: _____ Reading Level: _____

Grade: _____

Directions: Introduce the procedure by explaining that you are interested in finding out what students think about various reading and writing activities. Tell the students that they will be asked questions about their reading and writing, that there are no right or wrong answers, and that you are only interested in knowing what they think. Tell students that if they do not know how to answer a question they should say so and you will go on to the next one.

General probes such as "Can you tell me more about that?" or "Anything else?" may be used. Keep in mind that the interview is an informal diagnostic measure and you should feel free to probe to elicit useful information.

1. What hobbies or interests do you have that you like to read or write about?
2. a. How often do you read in school?
   b. How often do you read at home?
3. a. How often do you write in school?
   b. How often do you write at home?
4. What school subjects do you like to read about?
5. What school subjects do you like to write about?

Introduce reading and social studies books

Directions: For this section use the student's classroom basal reader and a content area textbook (social studies, science, etc.). If no basal is used in the classroom, select a piece of literature that is representative of classroom reading materials. Place these texts in front of the student. Ask each question twice, once with reference to the basal reader and once with reference to the content area textbook. Randomly vary the order of presentation (basal/literature, content). As each question is asked, open the appropriate text in front of the student to help provide a point of reference for the question.

6. a. What is the most important reason for reading this kind of material?
   b. Why does your teacher want you to read this book?
7. a. Who's the best reader you know _____?
   b. What does he/she do that makes him/her such a good reader?
8. a. How good are you at reading this kind of material?
   b. How do you know?
9. a. Do you write about this kind of material?
   b. Why does your teacher want you to write about this?
10. What do you have to do to get a good grade in reading?
11. a. If the teacher told you to remember the information in this story/chapter, what would be the best way to do this?
    b. Have you ever tried ____*(e.g. summarizing)*_____?
12. a. If your teacher told you to find the answers to the questions in this book what would be the best way to do this? Why?
    b. Have you ever tried ____*(e.g. asking yourself questions)*_____?

FIGURE 4.8
(Continued)

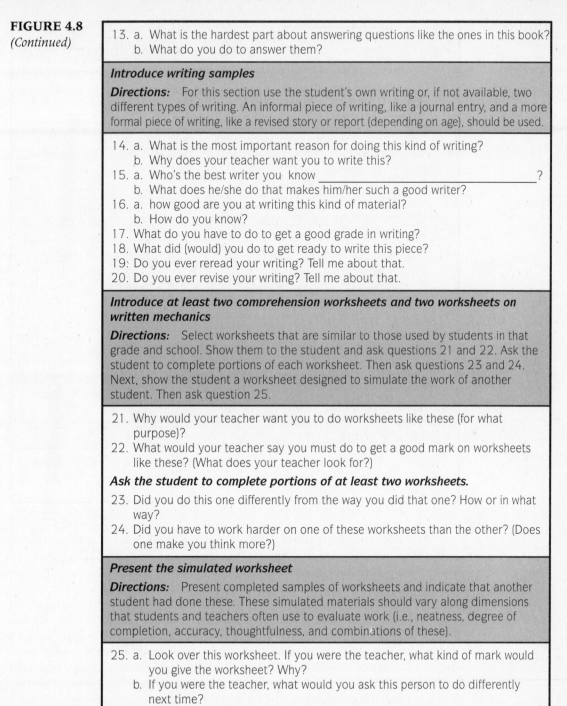

13. a. What is the hardest part about answering questions like the ones in this book?
    b. What do you do to answer them?

Introduce writing samples

Directions: For this section use the student's own writing or, if not available, two different types of writing. An informal piece of writing, like a journal entry, and a more formal piece of writing, like a revised story or report (depending on age), should be used.

14. a. What is the most important reason for doing this kind of writing?
    b. Why does your teacher want you to write this?
15. a. Who's the best writer you know _____?
    b. What does he/she do that makes him/her such a good writer?
16. a. how good are you at writing this kind of material?
    b. How do you know?
17. What do you have to do to get a good grade in writing?
18. What did (would) you do to get ready to write this piece?
19. Do you ever reread your writing? Tell me about that.
20. Do you ever revise your writing? Tell me about that.

Introduce at least two comprehension worksheets and two worksheets on written mechanics

Directions: Select worksheets that are similar to those used by students in that grade and school. Show them to the student and ask questions 21 and 22. Ask the student to complete portions of each worksheet. Then ask questions 23 and 24. Next, show the student a worksheet designed to simulate the work of another student. Then ask question 25.

21. Why would your teacher want you to do worksheets like these (for what purpose)?
22. What would your teacher say you must do to get a good mark on worksheets like these? (What does your teacher look for?)

Ask the student to complete portions of at least two worksheets.

23. Did you do this one differently from the way you did that one? How or in what way?
24. Did you have to work harder on one of these worksheets than the other? (Does one make you think more?)

Present the simulated worksheet

Directions: Present completed samples of worksheets and indicate that another student had done these. These simulated materials should vary along dimensions that students and teachers often use to evaluate work (i.e., neatness, degree of completion, accuracy, thoughtfulness, and combinations of these).

25. a. Look over this worksheet. If you were the teacher, what kind of mark would you give the worksheet? Why?
    b. If you were the teacher, what would you ask this person to do differently next time?

FIGURE 4.8
(Continued)

Summary Sheet

- What does the student perceive as the goal or purpose of classroom reading and writing activities (see questions)

  Basal reader or literature selections:
  Content textbook: _____
  Reading worksheets: _____
  Writing samples: _____

- What criteria does the student use to evaluate his/her reading and writing performance? (questions 7, 10, 11, 15, 17, 22, and 25)

  Basal reader or literature selections:
  Content textbook: _____
  Reading worksheets: _____
  Writing samples: _____

- What strategies does the student indicate he/she use when engaging in different comprehension activities? (questions 11, 12,13, 18, 19, 20, 23, and 24)

- Remembering information?
  Basal reader or literature selections:
  Content textbook: _____

- Answering questions?
  Basal reader or literature selections:
  Content textbook: _____
  Reading worksheets: _____

- Conveying information?
  Journals: _____
  Stories or reports: _____

Adapted from "An Interview for Assessing Students' Perceptions of Classroom Reading Tasks" by Karen K. Wixson, Anita B. Bosky, M. Nina Yochum, and Donna E. Alvermann. Reprinted with permission of Karen Wixson and the International Reading Association.

Attitudes and motivation. We can learn a great deal by asking students about their reading- and writing-related experiences, interests, habits, and attitudes. These initial interviews are most effective when we listen carefully, clarify when needed, and assume a nonjudgmental attitude.

Teachers have long recognized that students differ in their attitudes and motivation toward reading and writing. That poor readers or writers are less motivated than good readers or writers is hardly surprising. However, we may not realize the depth of these feelings. Juel (1988) reported on the results of a longitudinal study in which readers were periodically asked to choose preferred activities, with reading listed as one of the choices. One poor reader spontaneously offered the comment, "I'd rather clean scum off the bathtub than read!"

Interviews can also provide insights into learner motivations and attributions for success and failure. For example, Joey, age 9 and repeating the third grade, was recently referred to one of the authors' clinics. The results from interest inventories and unfinished sentence forms indicated that Joey did not read and would rather do almost anything else than read. As you read the following excerpt from an initial interview, think about what Joey is saying:

> *Interviewer:* "How do you think you do as a reader?"
>
> *Joey:* "I'd feel good about reading if I could learn how to read."
>
> *Interviewer:* "What do you think the problem is?"
>
> *Joey:* "I don't know. Something inside me stops me when I try to read. I can't spell either."
>
> *Interviewer:* "What do you enjoy reading?"
>
> *Joey:* "Nothing. I'm embarrassed 'cause I can't read."
>
> *Interviewer:* "What do you think might help you to become a better reader?"
>
> *Joey:* "I don't really know."

Joey is clearly not motivated to read at this point. It would be easy to attribute his reading problem to lack of motivation. During this portion of the interview, however, Joey revealed a much more complex picture of his underlying motivations and attitudes. He appears to be suggesting that his lack of motivation for reading grows from his awareness that he cannot do it. What is especially troubling is the fact that he appears to doubt that he will ever be able to read well.

Over time, feelings such as those expressed by Joey may very well develop into the generalized pattern of "learned helplessness" (Dweck 1975) described in Chapter 2. Importantly, the information gleaned through interviews can help teachers to understand the potentially conflicting goals of disabled readers and writers. As Johnston (1985b) so powerfully documents, these students may want to learn to read, or learn to read better, but other goals may inhibit their progress.

Many disabled readers and writers experience high anxiety about the task; many, like Joey, suspect that they cannot succeed in any event; and many may not want to admit to such "failure." Because discussions of motivation, attributions, and interest can be emotionally charged, we must proceed cautiously. Remember, it is important to have multiple indicators to interpret, confirm, and validate the information obtained through interviews.

As we are just getting started in the process, the value of these initial interviews lies in their ability to suggest hypotheses. These hypotheses can help to inform the evaluation process and may suggest directions that otherwise might never have been uncovered.

Observation

Although much information can be obtained through talk and testing, no other single tool can provide such in-depth information about the learner's actual use and application of knowledge and skill as observation. No other tool can demonstrate so clearly whether the reader or writer is both skilled *and* motivated. Nor, of course, can it provide such a quick view of the student's instructional setting; an overview of daily assignments, texts, and tasks, as well as the social environment for learning.

Observation, in the hands of an experienced evaluator, is one of the most powerful assessment tools a teacher/clinician can possess. Information about virtually every component of reading and writing can be collected using observation. We have provided in-depth discussions of how to observe specific components in other portions of the book. In this section, we limit our discussion to general observational guidelines and try to capture the power of this tool as a rich source of information about the learner and the general instructional context.

The quality and utility of observational information is subject to variation, since observational data may not be reliable. Reliability (Chapter 10) deals with the question of consistency. When we say that a measure is reliable, we mean that the results we attain tomorrow, using this tool, would be roughly the same as those we achieved today. Reliability " ... depends, for all practical purposes, on the adequacy of the behavior sample on which the score is based, which, in turn, depends on the stability of the behavior being measured. Our experience indicates that a score based on a single visit to a classroom seldom has adequate reliability ... Since reliability is primarily a function of the adequacy of the sample of behavior observed, reliabilities can be raised by increasing the number of visits" (Medley 1985, 101).

Because teachers have many opportunities to observe student behavior, their estimates of student strengths and weaknesses are often quite trustworthy. External specialists who may observe students only once or twice need to exercise caution in generalizing the results, for either student performance or classroom context.

Other factors, such as observer (teacher) objectivity, may also influence the quality and the reliability of observational information. Teachers must be aware that their observations are subject to personal bias. Like everyone else, teachers tend to see things from their own personal perspectives. Some teachers conclude that students are making satisfactory progress when they appear to be busy and attentive. Some teachers are prone to notice certain kinds of behavior and block out other kinds. Some only pay close attention to whatever disrupts classroom routine. Others are more concerned with symptoms of possible unhappiness (Almy and Genishi 1979, 7).

There are several ways to increase the reliability of observational data. First, teachers should determine exactly what will be noted before observing. Next, teachers plan how, when, and where to observe (Jaggar 1985). If these observation categories are important and well-defined, then observation accuracy will increase. Finally, teachers should use some type of format or observation guide that helps to systematize the observation.

The forms and ideas presented here are examples of the ways in which observations can be structured so that the information gathering is reasonably objective. Observing in a busy classroom requires fairly structured observations. This could involve making anecdotal records of what students say during different reading activities or during conversation, or making notations regarding the interactions in groups. "The important thing is that teachers think of observation as a form of problem solving; it is a selective search for knowledge to guide instruction" (Jaggar 1985, 6).

Perhaps the greatest strength of observation as an assessment tool is that students' performance and behavior can be evaluated in real settings as they are actually performing target tasks. Many teachers question the validity of standardized tests because they feel that students are being evaluated on tasks that are not meaningful or typical. Observation, of course, should normally avoid this problem. This is also a useful tool for those who are not the regular classroom teacher. Observations of a student functioning in the regular classroom can provide information that is not available in a one-to-one clinical setting.

Like all assessment instruments, the validity of observations is dependent on how carefully the behaviors to be assessed have been selected. Knowledge of the reading and writing processes is critical since the validity of observation is related to what is worth noticing. In reading and writing, this means looking for authentic literacy behaviors where students are engaged in a variety of activities under a variety of conditions—engaged in independent seatwork, sustained silent reading, writing for a specified audience, cooperative work projects, teacher-guided lessons, and so forth.

Observation can be used as a tool in almost any phase of the assessment-instruction process. For example, observation can be used to get to know individual students, evaluate groups, assess progress, appraise teaching techniques, and identify problems (Almy and Genishi 1979). In the following chapters, we provide specific and detailed ideas for evaluating the learning context (see Chapters 5, 6) and observation plays a central role in these discussions.

In the Getting Started phase, we use observation primarily to observe the student in context. No attempt is made to analyze or interpret detailed information about the setting or task, or about the student's specific reading or writing difficulties. Instead, we want to gather information that helps us to interpret the interviews and work samples we are collecting at the same time, to gain insight into the school climate and culture, and to understand the organization and structure of the classroom.

Teacher and Classroom

When students are struggling, it is critical to examine the context within which they function. Whether you are the student's classroom teacher responsible for the daily instructional setting, or a support teacher responsible for planning and implementing a specialized program, it is important to understand what the student is expected to do and how. If you are observing in someone else's classroom, you should make it clear to the classroom teacher that your observation is intended to help you understand the student's instructional program and that the goal is to benefit the student. If you are the classroom teacher for the student, "observation" of your own classroom is, of course, impossible. However, you can "take stock" using the questions and observation formats as guides for self-reflection.

If the student moves from one setting to another during the school day, your observations should include each one. Questions like the following can be used to organize your context assessment.

- What materials and tasks are used with this student?
- What types of classroom organization, expectations, and interactions are apparent?
- What types of instructional groups does the student participate in?
- Does the instructional approach in each setting seem congruent with the others?

In the early stages of the assessment-instruction process these types of questions can help us identify areas that may benefit from closer examination later. In Chapter 1 we introduced a number of context factors, or aspects of the classroom, that may influence learning. Observations or self-reflections that focus on these aspects can get us started in an efficient manner. A summary form may be helpful in conducting an initial classroom examination (see Figure 4.9).

The physical dimension is important because environmental factors like noise, distraction, or poor viewing positions can make it difficult for some students to learn (Polloway and Patton 1993). Other features of the physical environment, like seating arrangements, can contribute to behavior problems or may make certain types of teaching and learning difficult. Both the overall physical arrangement of a classroom and particular location of the individual student should be examined in the Getting Started phase observations.

The setting includes a variety of components, including a personal or social dimension of a classroom that has to do with the "psychological atmosphere of the classroom" (Palloway and Patton 1993). The social dimension of classrooms is strongly influenced by teacher factors such as philosophy of learning, ability to maintain order, and his or her approach to student-teacher relationships. Teacher attitudes and expectations are not the only things that contribute to this dimension, however. Others include student attitudes and self-concepts, the way faculty and staff overall deal and interact with students, and the involvement of parents.

Teaching and learning benefit from safe and orderly environments. When teachers and students spend too much time in transitions, in managing unruly behavior, or in explanations of routine tasks, there is less time available for teaching and learning. These management factors influence learning for all students, but for the student who is struggling it is important to notice whether there are unique management issues operating. For example, these students are more likely to leave the room for instructional purposes. Is this time being used effectively? How much time is taken in transitions?

The instructional dimension, of course, is paramount. We will return to this issue in Chapter 6. In the Getting Started step, observation and self-reflection will function at a fairly global level. Issues that may be examined at this time could focus on:

FIGURE 4.9
*Summary
Form for
Observing
Context*

Name: _____ Class: _____ Date: _____	
Observations: Classroom Dimensions	**Comments**
Physical Environment:	
Setting:	
Curriculum:	
Instructional Methods:	
Instructional Materials:	
Instructional Tasks:	

- What types of assessments are done in this setting?
- How has the teacher used assessment information in planning the student's program?
- How does the teacher respond to individual differences in the classroom? (Is there evidence of accommodations, modifications, etc?)

The context for instruction is of central importance, but different students interact with settings and materials differently. Observation of the student *in* the instructional setting provides the final, critical pieces of information as we get started.

Learner

Skilled teachers know that conclusions should not be drawn from one or even two instances of a particular behavior. Instead, when using observation, we are looking for *patterns of performance*. Patterns emerge when the same (or similar) behaviors are observed repeatedly over time. Alternatively, patterns can emerge that reveal the circumstances that influence reading and writing. You can see how the student performs *in interaction* with various texts and contexts (that is, subject area texts, children's magazines, library research, reading groups, and so on), watching for variability or stability. In this way, it is possible to determine what students can and will do under different conditions.

It should be easy to remember important events, but by the end of a busy day, we frequently have forgotten what we meant to remember. Finding a convenient and accurate way to record information is important. Many teachers find it useful to keep "Post-its" close at hand. Whenever you observe something of interest, jot down the time, date, and student information. Then, at your leisure, you can stick these "memos" in a notebook or portfolio tabbed for each student.

Many teachers use checklists such as the one in Figure 4.10 that provide a place to note students' overall interactions in the classroom. These should be created to facilitate observations of important classroom activities. The advantage here is that it focuses on multiple sources of information about students and can help us to establish patterns of behavior that can lead to fresh instructional approaches.

As we get started, it is unlikely that we will make detailed observations of students' application of reading and writing knowledge and skill. These are done as we get further into the assessment-instruction process. In the initial stages, a noticing teacher can find out a great deal about reading and writing interests by observing the students. Samples of the types of behavior we might want to look for to inform us about our students' knowledge of reading and writing are presented in Figure 4.10. More open-ended questions can be used to summarize our observations and are worth asking about all students:

- For what purposes does the student read/write—to accomplish classroom tasks, or for pleasure?
- How does the student respond to different types of comprehension questions? Writing tasks?

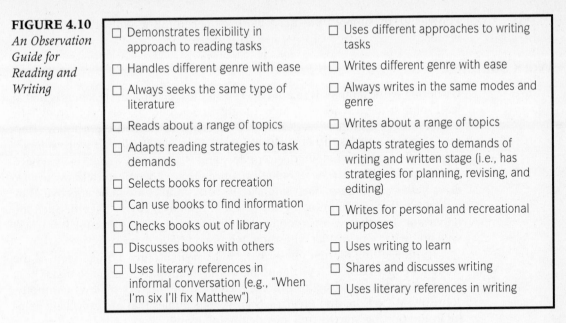

FIGURE 4.10
An Observation Guide for Reading and Writing

☐ Demonstrates flexibility in approach to reading tasks

☐ Handles different genre with ease

☐ Always seeks the same type of literature

☐ Reads about a range of topics

☐ Adapts reading strategies to task demands

☐ Selects books for recreation

☐ Can use books to find information

☐ Checks books out of library

☐ Discusses books with others

☐ Uses literary references in informal conversation (e.g., "When I'm six I'll fix Matthew")

☐ Uses different approaches to writing tasks

☐ Writes different genre with ease

☐ Always writes in the same modes and genre

☐ Writes about a range of topics

☐ Adapts strategies to demands of writing and written stage (i.e., has strategies for planning, revising, and editing)

☐ Writes for personal and recreational purposes

☐ Uses writing to learn

☐ Shares and discusses writing

☐ Uses literary references in writing

- How does the student adjust his/her rate, strategy usage, and writing approach to meet the demands of different purposes, texts, and tasks?

As we have already discussed, students' attitudes can have a significant and cumulative effect on their achievement. Often people do not like to read or write because they are not skilled at these tasks. However, it is also the case that skilled reading and writing require practice. Teachers and clinicians are obliged to help students find reading material and writing activities that respond to their individual interests and that help them to see the functional value of reading and writing.

One of the simplest and most effective ways of finding out students' interests is to watch their daily behavior and listen to their conversations (see Lipson 1995). The following are examples of the types of questions that can be used to guide these observations:

1. How do students approach reading and writing activities (active involvement or passive resistance)?
2. What types of reading and writing activities do students select during their spare time at school and at home?
3. Do students "stick with" reading and writing activities or give up easily?
4. Do students talk about reading? writing? What is the content and tone of these remarks?

Gathering information in response to these questions will not provide a solution to the problems. It can, however, indicate whether a student understands and appreciates the value of reading or writing and is willing or able to use this knowledge to support the hard work of becoming a skilled reader and/or writer.

Work Samples

Gathering work samples is relatively easy. In most classrooms teachers retain at least some student work and, increasingly, in portfolio classrooms there will be a wide-range of student work in work folders or in showcase portfolios (Tierney, Carter, and Desai 1991; Valencia and Calfee 1991). Not all work samples are equally useful in helping us to understand readers and writers, so we need some sense of *what to select*. In addition, once selected, we need to know *what to make of the work* that has been sampled. If work samples are to be effective, they must be collected intentionally to represent dimensions you have decided are important. In other words, you should know what types of samples you will seek and what you will do with them when you have them.

In the Getting Started phase, we will be trying to get a broad view of the student's experience with print and his or her abilities to respond to text. These may include story maps, illustrations, retellings, and literary reviews (Anthony, Johnson, Mickelson, and Preece 1991). Work samples that are especially helpful in the Getting Started step include the following:

- Samples of the types of reading and writing work that are generally required in the student's classroom
- Writing samples — unsupported writing about self-selected topics (this can come from the classroom portfolio if there is one, otherwise it should be collected)
- Lists of books that have recently been read by the student in and out of the classroom
- Examples of work completed for projects or other content areas

Work samples like these can, of course, help you make some initial judgments about the student's knowledge and skills in key areas. For example, Reading Logs (see Figure 4.11) can provide useful information about several aspects of students' literacy development, including the frequency and quantity of students' reading and the breadth of their experiences.

Similarly, writing samples from many contexts should be examined—journal entries, process writing folders, projects, letters, and notes. Not all of these reveal the same information about students' knowledge and skill in writing nor about their motivation to write.

FIGURE 4.11a

*Sample
Reading Log*

Name _____ Term _____

Date Completed	Title of Book	Author

Source: *Authentic assessment* by B. Hill and C. Ruptic. Copyright © 1994 Christopher Gordon. Used by permission.

FIGURE 4.11b *Sample Reading Log*

Name _____

Month/Year _____

| Title | Author | Start Date | | Value | Genre | # of Pages | Response |
		Finish	High—Low			
				1 2 3 4 5			
				1 2 3 4 5			
				1 2 3 4 5			
				1 2 3 4 5			
				1 2 3 4 5			
				1 2 3 4 5			
				1 2 3 4 5			
				1 2 3 4 5			
				1 2 3 4 5			
				1 2 3 4 5			
				1 2 3 4 5			
				1 2 3 4 5			
				1 2 3 4 5			
				1 2 3 4 5			
				1 2 3 4 5			
				1 2 3 4 5			

GETTING STARTED ON THE DIAGNOSTIC PORTFOLIO

Finding the time to conduct in-depth assessments on individual students is problematic. One solution to the problem of achieving both in-depth and ongoing evaluation is to create strong collaborative working arrangements among classroom teachers and specialists or resource personnel. Classroom teachers can benefit from the assistance of specialists in obtaining more detailed information about students and how they perform in a variety of settings. Resource personnel can benefit from the assistance of classroom teachers in obtaining continuous assessments of students' knowledge, skills, and attitudes in various classroom contexts. This type of collaboration also allows teachers and specialists to coordinate their instructional efforts and to evaluate the extent to which students are able to transfer their knowledge and skills from one setting to another.

Teacher reflection is a critical component of successful assessment. We have suggested that the Getting Started step requires the gathering together of existing information and the initial collection of some new interview and observational data. Specific artifacts, like work samples or written responses to interviews, should be used to begin the Diagnostic Portfolio.

The Cases of Marvin and Kyle

Information gleaned from oral interviews, observations, and work samples should be summarized on the Thumbnail Sketch. In Figure 4.12, you will find two samples of what this looks like in the Getting Started step. The information in this figure is a summary of the information about "Marvin" and about "Kyle" who will be used frequently throughout the book to illustrate ongoing assessment.

Marvin

Marvin's parents were concerned about his lack of progress in reading and writing. His classroom teacher was also concerned about "significant" reading difficulties. Marvin was referred to the University Reading Clinic.

Information gathered from his school records and his teachers revealed that he was eleven years old, in the beginning of fifth grade, and his reading level was at approximately the third-grade level. In addition, there was no indication that any physical, linguistic, or cognitive correlates were implicated in his reading problem. Interviews with Marvin indicated that he understood the purposes of reading and that he believed his problem was comprehension. Observations in the classroom and in the clinical setting suggested a pleasant, cooperative individual whose behavior did not change dramatically under different contextual conditions. No useful work samples existed because Marvin's school records did not include these and he had been in the current setting so short a time. The nature and extent of Marvin's specific reading and writing abilities remained unclear.

FIGURE 4.12a

Marvin's Thumbnail Sketch: Getting Started

Information about Marvin, gathered in the Getting Started step, is summarized here. Other information will be added later.	
Getting Started (Step 1)	**About the Reading and Writing Context (Step 2)**
Background Name: Marvin Age: 11 Grade: 5 Key Correlates: • Above average IQ • Normal vision, hearing, and overall health • Interests are science, sports, "taking things apart" **Information About the Learner** Knowledge about Reading and Writing: • Reports that people read to learn and for recreation: reports adjusting rate for text difficulty • Reports that own reading problem is comprehension • Names, "breaking words down" and "asking someone" as the only strategies for reading words that are unfamiliar Motivation: • Pleasant, cooperative demeanor during classroom and clinic sessions • Talks freely about affective responses to text and persists without prompting on difficult tasks **Information About the Context** School History: • School-administered achievement tests place him in the 35th percentile in reading • Multiple moves and family disruptions during K-1. Instructional Approaches: Experiences, Linguistic and Cultural Context: • English spoken in the home.	**Resources** **Instruction** **Settings** **Tasks**

**FIGURE
4.12b**

*Kyle's
Thumbnail
Sketch: Getting
Started*

Getting Started (Step 1)	About the Reading and Writing Context (Step 2)
Background Name: Kyle Age: 6 1/2 Grade: 2 Key Correlates: • Normal vision, hearing, and overall health/development • Difficult time "paying attention" *Information About the Learner* Knowledge about Reading and Writing: • Reports that own reading problem is knowing the words • Is able to reflect on his own reading and writing abilities Motivation: • Says he doesn't really like to read, would rather play and build • Cooperative and willing to work both in school and in extra sessions *Information About the Context* School History: • Successful preschool experience • Same multi-age K-2 classroom since kindergarten • Lack of progress in reading and writing noted at end of grade 1 Instructional Approaches: • Literature-based instruction in an inquiry-oriented classroom • Daily reading and writing Experiences, Linguistic, and Cultural Context: • English spoken in the home. • Both parents college graduates • Many books and book activities	*Resources* *Instruction* *Settings* *Tasks*

Interviews with Marvin's parents suggest that frequent moves and variation in school settings may be a factor. These need to be explored more fully in an investigation of the instructional context.

Kyle

Kyle's classroom teacher expressed concern about his slow progress. Kyle is in a multiage K–2 classroom. He has been with the same teacher, Ms. McIntyre, since kindergarten. She knows he has made progress but wants to review and evaluate his literacy development to make the most of his last year, as well as to ask questions about possible referral for special services.

School records include literacy portfolios in Kyle's school. A review of these indicates that Kyle knows a great deal about his own emerging abilities (see Figure 4.13). These portfolios also support the teacher's belief that Kyle has made progress. Writing samples from kindergarten and grade 1 clearly demonstrate his ability to apply his growing knowledge and skill (see Figures 4.14–4.15).

FIGURE 4.13

Kyle's Reflections on Writing Progress

name ___Kyle___   date __February 1994__
grade 1

Portfolio Reflection on Writing

When I write I used to...	Now I know how to...
I used to be sloppy,	do longer stories
	I put titles on my stories
and I didn't sound out the words	I sound out words better
I can't read my own words back,	I can read back my story better.
not make clear letters	now I know which way the letters go.
use one letter to spell a whole word	
use all upper case letters	use lower case letters
not leave spaces	

FIGURE 4.14
*Kyle's
Preferences
for Tasks,
Projects*

name Kyle _____   date MAR. 28 1994 _____

What have you enjoyed learning most this year? Why?

=Ltke werk-benct-bcus -
you can mac-anything.~

In addition, Ms. McIntyre has asked her students to reflect on their favored
activities and this feedback provides insight into Kyle's motivation for reading
and writing as well as his ownership of various activities. His own self-knowl-
edge is striking and powerful.

These clearly reveal that Kyle prefers action and choice to sitting and "paying attention." Not surprisingly, he readily notes in a casual conversation that
he really doesn't like to read.

An interview with Kyle's mother supports Kyle's view of himself. She notes
that he would prefer riding his bike to reading. She also says that although his
overall development was normal, he was a "fast mover." He was running at
nine months and his verbal development was very quick, "above normal"

FIGURE 4.15

Kyle's
Reflections
Re: Paying
Attention

name: APR. 5 — 1994   date: grade 1

Kyle *Thinking About Antarctica*

How do you feel about your study of Antarctica? Why?

I feel good bakus I
Lerd about glathers.

What was your favorite part about the study? why?

Makeing the glacter wosn't
I Lok to Paper mgha
     like

What was the hardest thing about studying Antarctica?
why?

paying otachin. I can'k halpit
     attention   help it.

according to her. Kyle's family is supportive of literacy. He has "always been surrounded by books; they've always been there" and he reads in bed every night. He has a younger sister who is reading well above grade level already.

As we move through the assessment-instruction process, further information about Marvin and Kyle can be added to their Thumbnail Sketches.

CHAPTER SUMMARY

The purpose of this chapter was to assist the reader by providing the knowledge and techniques necessary for getting started in the assessment-instruction process. We began with a set of guidelines that are important for the entire assessment-instruction process. These guidelines promote an approach to assessment that is contextualized; that examines how readers and writers perform in authentic classroom or other real-world settings. They are as follows:

- assess meaningful activities
- assessment should be unobtrusive
- assessment and purpose should match
- assessment should be systematic
- assessment should be continuous

In this chapter we also discussed the contexts for assessment and instruction and sources of information. We noted that students and teachers often work in more collaborative environments today and, although there still are some isolated remedial instructional settings, these are less common than in the past. Sources of information include the home, school (school records and teachers), and the learner. Finally, we advocate using a Diagnostic Portfolio to plan instruction, evaluate progress, and communicate with parents and administrators.

The second major section of this chapter describes the tools and strategies that are used in the Getting Started phase of assessment. Interviews and informational forms that can be used to gather information about both learner and context were described. Specific interviewing and observational techniques were described for the purpose of evaluating various aspects of students' knowledge about reading and writing and their attitudes and motivation toward reading and writing activities.

Finally, the chapter describes how to use a Thumbnail Sketch as a vehicle for summarizing information from the Diagnostic Portfolio. As we get started with assessment, Marvin and Kyle are used as examples.

STEP 1
Getting Started
with Assessment
(Ch. 4)

STEP 2
Evaluating the
Context
(Chs. 5 & 6)

STEP 3
Evaluating the
Learner
(Chs. 7–10)

STEP 4
Evaluating the
Match Between
Learner and
Context

STEP 5
Reflection,
Decision Making,
and Planning

Ch. 11

STEP 6
Identifying a Better
Match: Diagnostic
Teaching

STEP 7
Adapting Instruction:
Continuous Monitoring
and Modification
(Chs. 12–15)

STEP 8
Reporting
(Ch. 16)

CHAPTER *5*

Instructional Settings and Resources

INTRODUCTION

Traditional assessment looks only to the student as the source of reading and writing difficulties. Clearly, students' knowledge, skill, and motivation are crucial factors in reading and writing achievement. However, a growing body of research demonstrates that instructional context and methods can support learning or contribute to disability. Assessment that is intended to inform instruction requires careful descriptions of how different aspects of the instructional environment influence learning in general and how they match the needs of the particular student under consideration.

Gaskins (1988) notes that one of the strongest impediments to change in schools is the belief, even among very good teachers, that the need for change must reflect poor or incompetent teaching. An interactive view of reading and writing ability and disability suggests otherwise. School success and/or failure result from a complex interaction among many factors (Coles 1987). Some factors that seem to influence a particular student negatively do not affect a second student at all. Similarly, the program that has been successful in the past may not work for the student who is struggling now. The focus should be on assessing the context and method in terms of their likely impact on specific students' performance in reading and writing.

A recent analysis of fifty years of research suggests that "the different kinds of classroom instruction and climate had nearly as much impact on learning as the student aptitude categories" (Wang, Haertel, and Walberg 1994). Taken together, factors like classroom management, climate, instruction, and assessment and social interaction influenced learning as much as the learner characteristics. In this and the next chapter, we discuss how different aspects of the instructional environment influence reading and writing performance and describe methods of evaluating these factors (see Figure 5.1).

FIGURE 5.1
Components
of the
Instructional
Context

Instructional Settings	Instructional Resources	Instructional Approaches	Instructional Tasks
Teacher belief Literate environment Classroom interaction Classroom organization Grouping Writing instruction Congruence among settings	Text types, structure, and features Commercial programs	Curriculum Methods Assessment practices	Task type Task content, form, and implementation

This chapter begins with a discussion of literacy and the role of cultural context in defining the goals of literacy and continues on to describe the subtle interactions that can and do influence school achievement. Next, we turn our attention to understanding and assessing instructional settings, discussing five aspects of setting that merit attention: teacher beliefs; patterns of classroom interaction, classroom activity and organization; ability grouping; and congruence across instructional settings.

This chapter also focuses on the role of instructional resources in reading and writing performance. Specifically addressed are text type and structure and text features that influence comprehensibility. The complexity of factors related to instructional environments makes assessment very difficult. We have attempted, however, to provide ways to evaluate the aspects of instructional resources known to influence learning.

UNDERSTANDING LITERACY LEARNING ENVIRONMENTS

Before turning our attention to the instructional environment, we will briefly consider the relations among home/community and school settings. American children are often exposed to books in the home prior to formal schooling, and many children participate in social groups devoted to story time or reading and writing in settings such as daycare, preschools, clubs, and church groups. Becoming literate occurs in social situations that shape purposes, conditions, constraints, audiences, standards, and motivation to engage in reading and writing activities (Paris and Wixson 1987).

Relations Among Home/Community and School Settings

Every educator knows that literacy is not accomplished in schools alone. The children themselves contribute to learning and achievement, but so do parents, siblings, and the general community. Attributes that are important to consider regarding the larger literacy setting include: the nature of the linguistic community (language(s) spoken in the home/community), the literacy status of the home/community, the relationships between home/community and school, and the socioeconomic status of home/community. All of these factors in turn affect individual and community literacy goals.

Identifying attributes that contribute to school achievement should not be a process of laying blame. Rather, careful examination and description of the settings children encounter can promote both understanding and adaptation. Poor instruction is a less prevalent problem than instruction that is unresponsive to the needs of individual students. The ways in which various setting features interact can be both extremely subtle and profoundly important, affecting student learning and motivation. Teachers and clinicians must consider the results of recent research which offer insights into the ways that home experiences can produce a mismatch between student and teacher expectations. One of the most illuminating of these is a study by Heath (1983).

Heath studied the patterns of language use in three communities in the southeastern United States and concluded that patterns of language use and social interaction differed strikingly for children in homes from these communities. In "Maintown," a middle-class, school-oriented community, the focus of literacy-related activities was on labeling, explaining, and learning appropriate interactional patterns of displaying knowledge. Children learned how to use language in literacy events and were socialized into the interactional sequences that are central features of classroom lessons.

Families in "Roadville," a white, working-class community, also focused on labeling and explanations; however, they did not link these ways of taking meaning from books to other aspects of their environment. Consequently, children from these homes were well prepared for the literal tasks of early reading instruction, but not for reading assignments that call for reasoning and affective responses.

The third group of homes under investigation were located in "Trackton," a black, working-class community. The children in these homes were not taught labels or asked for explanations; rather, they were asked to provide reasons and express personal responses to events in their lives. As a consequence, these children were unprepared for the types of questions often used in beginning reading instruction and unfamiliar with the interaction patterns used in reading lessons.

These differences resulted in mismatches in the patterning of teacher-pupil interactions during reading and writing instruction (Heath 1981). For example, a predominant characteristic of teachers' questions was (and still is) to ask students to name the attributes of objects or events in isolated contexts. Trackton parents did not ask the children these kinds of questions, and Trackton children had different techniques for responding to questions. Teachers reported that it was difficult to get responses from Trackton students. Trackton parents reported that teachers did not listen or that "we don't talk to our children the way you do," and Trackton children reported that teachers asked "dumb" questions they already knew about.

Heath then shared with the teachers examples of how Trackton children interacted at home, and teachers incorporated questions similar to those the children were familiar with in their instruction. As a result, the children participated much more frequently, and in time the teachers were able to involve them in more traditional question-answering as well. This research illustrates the point that the children from these homes were initially disabled by virtue of the fact that they had not engaged in the type of interaction that is characteristic of classroom instruction, but that their disabilities were remediated by the social interaction they subsequently experienced with their teachers (Gavelek and Palincsar 1988).

Goals for Learning Literacy

Teachers and schools are often frustrated by the apparent lack of motivation and achievement among students. Recent research and reflection has lead to a more complex conclusion: all children are motivated to achieve, but they may direct their actions toward different goals, under different conditions, and for different reasons. It must be recognized that at least some children are motivated toward different goals than those emphasized by educators.

It is also important to realize the existence of different definitions of achievement and motivation. Students' achievement and motivation can only be understood in relation to the cultural contexts in which they live. Different cultures and different contexts dictate norms of behavior that vary. Individual behavior reflects, and is constrained by, these different norms. To the extent that subcultures define achievement goals differently, differences in observed motivation to achieve those goals would be expected.

Experts cannot agree on a single definition of literacy because the attributes and standards are relative to the context in which reading and writing are observed. An African boy chanting the Koran in a language he cannot understand, a teenager striving to read the driver's test manual, and a student in a classroom stumbling to pronounce words in a primer are all participating in literate activities. Literacy is a social and cultural phenomenon that encompasses much more than school-oriented values and practices. Furthermore, as cultures change so do definitions of literacy. New technological advances require new knowledge and skills, and societies expect both more and different abilities from literate individuals.

Because literacy definitions vary, many scholars describe literacy activities in terms of how print is used and how reading and writing fit into the total fabric of a cultural group (Scribner and Cole 1981). These uses and purposes partly determine the value that is placed on literacy by the community. They may also determine who has access to literacy within a particular culture. It is well known that literacy is given different levels of priority in various societies, and that many cultures restrict access to literacy to certain portions of the population (Downing and Leong 1982).

Although it is relatively rare today for cultures to restrict access to literacy by law or stricture, there are other, less direct ways to control access to literacy. Cultures define the social functions of literacy, methods of instruction, and standards of competence. For example, Western societies historically restricted females' access to scientific and mathematical literacy by denying women entry into certain types of employment and by establishing certain norms of behavior.

Similarly, the culture of the school informs students of acceptable forms of achievement behavior and motivation (Dreeben 1968). Schools do vary in the way they operate, and these differences may result in differing expectations for students to achieve. For example, a school may routinely provide excused absences from class and even classwork for certain students (athletes, student government representatives, job training participants). System features of the school, such as its size, neighborhood, formal structure, and informal climate, may also influence students' motivation and achievement by affecting their expectations for success, self-esteem, and time on task (Schmuck 1980).

Different cultural groups can have similar or dissimilar frames of reference for the functions and activities of literacy (Green and Bloome 1983). When students do not share with teachers the same expectations or rules for communication and participation in the classroom, they often devalue literacy or exempt themselves from instruction, thereby diminishing their opportunities to become literate. Although cultural setting is a vague and global term, it is important to recognize at the outset that the functions, values, and frames of reference in particular contexts influence who has access to literate activities and the opportunity to learn to read and write (see Fraatz 1987).

UNDERSTANDING THE ROLE OF INSTRUCTIONAL SETTINGS AND RESOURCES IN READING AND WRITING PERFORMANCE

In this section, we discuss how various aspects of instructional settings and resources interact with cultural and home environments to influence student learning and motivation.

Instructional Setting

Setting factors do not operate in isolation from other aspects of the instructional environment, rather they interact with each other and with other contextual factors. We have separated them somewhat for purposes of discussion and as a guide to the factors that must be considered in evaluating the instructional context. Wherever possible, however, we have tried to suggest the interrelationships between and among the elements.

Teacher Beliefs and the Literate Environment

Perhaps no single factor influences the instructional setting more than a teacher's knowledge and beliefs about teaching and learning. As we noted in Chapter 1, teachers are often unaware of the extent that their views about learning and literacy influence and shape classroom instruction and the learning experiences offered to students.

Beliefs will serve as a frame of reference for a teacher in selecting materials for instruction and for presenting and guiding the use of these instructional materials. These values will be communicated to the students, both verbally and nonverbally. Students will adhere to and improvise upon the contextual demands, or will find ways to change the nature of those demands through active, or passive, negotiation (DeFord 1986, 166). As a result, students' behavior and the degree to which they participate in academic tasks is often determined by what others expect of them.

Teacher expectations are shaped by their beliefs about learning and literacy in general. In turn, these beliefs influence the type of classroom environment that is established. Students attend to these subtle and not-so-subtle clues as they determine how to behave and what to learn. Evidence of how these beliefs and actions influence each other is provided by DeFord (1986), who studied three separate classroom literacy environments—traditional, literature-based, and mastery learning. The three teachers, who had all been identified as "exemplary," created dramatically different classroom settings as described below.

The context in the *traditional* classroom was formed by the teacher. Within this curriculum model, the teacher set up a series of general rules for classroom participation, some explicitly stated, others implied. Lessons were thoroughly planned, allowing for a limited number of child-initiated decisions, and usually structured so that they could be completed in one work period. Reading groups were generally organized according to the basal program, with seatwork consisting of workbook pages and phonics worksheets. If the seatwork was a writing activity, the topic was assigned by the teacher; very little writing was student-initiated. The overriding teacher concerns were for a productive, smooth-flowing, moderately quiet day, and to provide assignments that allowed students to work at levels that minimized confusion.

The children in the traditional classroom were responsible and cooperative. They participated actively in discussions led by the teacher and worked diligently to complete their assignments. Verbal interactions were most commonly teacher-child or teacher-group conversations, although quiet child-child conversations were allowed during seatwork time to discuss assigned work.

The teacher and children formed the context in the *literature-based* classroom together as they wrote, read, and explored the environment both in and out of their classroom. Teacher goals and student goals were negotiated to produce the curriculum and context. The rules, set by the teacher and children together, revolved around issues of productive work and social/child development. Reading and writing instruction were handled individually or in small-group situations, with the teacher assessing and teaching on a daily basis from information gathered during the work period. Instruction involved a variety of topics, materials, and methods, including numerous field trips that provided the content for reading and writing. Teacher planning for student projects usually extended from several days to several weeks, during which time progress was evaluated continuously until the projects were completed.

The teacher structured open-ended activities and helped students make decisions about personal outcomes. The children in the literature-based classroom were active, independent, and generally responsible for the social climate of the room. They helped each other and collaborated on projects. Child-child conversations and teacher-child conversations were most common, with fewer teacher-group interactions.

In the *mastery learning* classroom, "the literacy context was directed by the curriculum, the teacher serving as mediator and manager of the reading and writing program" (DeFord 1986, 174). Since the content of the curriculum was delivered within a highly structured management system, students worked independently at their seats a significant amount of the time. The teacher created an orderly and quiet work environment for the execution of these tasks. Reading groups met to receive teacher-directed instruction within the programmed materials. This instruction involved introducing, practicing, reviewing, and testing word lists and vocabulary. Assigned workbook and basal reader pages were executed independently, and tests were administered periodically.

Writing activities and oral exchanges occurred almost exclusively at the initiation of the teacher. Writing tasks were assigned each day, and discussions generally occurred only in teacher-led forums. Planning occurred only within the prescribed program materials, and work was assigned so that it could be completed in a half-day block of time.

This observational research (DeFord 1986) highlights the extent to which classroom organization, activities, and discourse may vary as a function of teacher beliefs about literacy and literacy education. The unique attributes of classroom settings influence the nature of students' literacy learning.

Classroom Interaction

Teachers rely on verbal interactions to make many educational decisions and judgments. According to Cazden (1986), "spoken language is the medium by which … students demonstrate to teachers much of what they have learned. Spoken language is also an important part of the identities of all participants" (432).

Variation in ways of speaking is a universal fact. When the variation is significant, it can lead to painful mismatches for individual students or groups, and these mismatches can affect achievement (Cazden 1986; Flanders 1975). Differences in how and when something is said may only require a temporary adjustment, or they can seriously impair effective teaching and accurate evaluation.

Teachers, like other groups of specialists, have unique ways of talking. Some of the more obvious features of teacher talk include asking known-answer questions and evaluating students' answers to questions. Teacher talk is often characterized by its preoccupation with control of behavior and of talk itself. Students must "learn how to participate in reading, what effective reading means, and the definitions of reading held by the teacher and school" (Green and Bloome 1983, 23) to be regarded as skilled in literacy activities in school.

Studies of cultural differences also suggest that students would be better served if teachers took differences in prior experiences in the home community into account more than they now do. Too often, "teachers now differentiate among their students in ways that may continue, even increase, the inequalities of information and skills that are present when students start school" (Cazden 1986, 445). Research evidence suggests that some children come to school with an oral style of discourse that is inconsistent with the teachers'. These children often do not gain access to the kind of instruction and practice required to develop a more literate discourse style, and as a result they perform less well in school-based literacy activities.

Linguistic and interactional patterns are important because teachers make judgments about students' abilities and behavior based on them. For example, Michaels (1981) studied first-grade, "sharing-time" experiences and found that when children's narrative styles were very different from the teacher's expectations, the event was generally unsuccessful. In addition, the teacher frequently made negative assessments of the students' ability and sanctioned the students' performance.

Because interaction styles are so subtle and interwoven with individual identity, they can be difficult to assess. However, there is evidence that when instruction is shaped to respond to these differences, achievement and interaction improve. Research with native Hawaiians provides an example of the importance of cultural compatibility of communication styles in reading lessons.

Boggs (1985) learned that native Hawaiian adults rarely ask children questions for information, as white, middle-class parents commonly do. They use direct questions primarily when reprimanding their children. When telling a story, Hawaiians cooperate in taking turns to construct the story with voices overlapping, an activity called "talk story." In addition, Hawaiians delegate household chores to an older child, who, in turn, is responsible for making certain that the work is done. Apprenticeship and observation, rather than explanation or discussion, are used to teach children new skills.

Consistent with this knowledge about the interaction patterns of native Hawaiians, Au (1980) observed that Hawaiian children were more successful in reading lessons using the participation structures of the talk story than with the conventional recitation pattern commonly used in reading lessons with children from the mainstream culture (Au and Mason 1981). Teachers using these two participation structures clearly provided different kinds of social events, and Hawaiian students demonstrated much higher levels of achievement-related behavior in the lessons incorporating the culturally compatible talk story pattern.

Classroom Organization

Over the past several years, research descriptions of classrooms have demonstrated what most classroom teachers know only too well: classrooms are busy places, and teachers are very active participants in classroom events. These features of classroom life are critical to understanding what is expected of students, and also whether teachers do think about individual students, instructional purposes, or content.

Because the environment is busy and demanding, organization is a major factor in classroom teaching. According to Doyle (1986), the activity is the basic unit of classroom organization. Activities are relatively short blocks of classroom time during which students are arranged in a particular way. Labels for activities reflect either their organizational focus (seatwork, discussion) or their focal content (reading, journal writing). More than thirty separate activities occur each day in the average elementary school class.

Teachers must also divide their attention among competing demands. For example, in a study of third-grade classrooms, approximately half of the teachers' acts involved instructional activities such as questions, feedback, and imparting knowledge (Gump 1969). The rest of the time the teachers were involved in organizing students for instruction and orienting them to tasks (23 percent), dealing with deviant behavior (14 percent), and handling individual problems and social arrangements (12 percent).

Consequently, management of activity can take precedence over instructional content. Indeed, there is evidence to suggest that subject matter is often reduced by teachers and students to a set of procedures to be followed in completing assignments in order to satisfy management demands (Doyle 1986). "Neither teachers nor students talk much about the meaning, purposes, or underlying operations of the content. The work is often done without understanding" (Doyle 1986, 417). This disturbing conclusion is consistent with the finding that while in class students often focus a significant part of their attention on information about how to do the work they are assigned as well as what behavior they are to display (King 1983). Clearly, the degree to which students have an opportunity to learn content or to practice significant literacy behaviors will depend, at least in part, on the types and quantity of classroom activity provided. In addition, teachers who can increase the amount of academically engaged time produce students who achieve at higher levels (Rosenshine 1979).

Examination of the types of activities can also provide an indication of how productive the classroom environment is likely to be. For example, student involvement is highest in teacher-led small groups (90 percent), slightly lower for whole-class recitations (80–85 percent), and lowest for seatwork (65 percent) (Kounin 1970; Rosenshine 1979). Open-ended, small-group activities result in higher levels of academic and intellectual engagement (Blumenfeld et al. 1983; Bossert 1979).

Differences among classrooms can and do account for differences in student performance and achievement. Although classroom organization and management may vary within and among schools, the predominant pattern continues to be the teacher-directed classroom, in which students are expected to work independently and to interact primarily with the teacher and the instructional materials. For some students, the traditional patterns of organization pose especially serious problems.

Increasingly, there are alternative classroom organizations in which teachers and students work more collaboratively, interact frequently about texts and tasks, and discuss reading and writing activities with peers in conferences and in literature groups. Some students may find this open-ended, process-oriented classroom structure difficult to manage.

Researchers contend that families and cultures vary considerably in the extent to which they prepare children for various settings (Fillion and Brause 1987). Children who are accustomed to assisting others in accomplishing tasks, collaborating on projects, and generally working together, are at ease in the cooperative classrooms in which these activities are rewarded, but uncomfortable in more traditional classrooms. Hispanic homes have been characterized as fitting into the cooperative format (Tikunoff and Ward 1983). Similarly, Philips (1982) found that Native American children were accustomed to independent activities and were unaccustomed to the noise and competition characteristic of many classrooms. Differences between cultural values and classroom values were so extreme as to alienate the children from their teachers and their classmates. These findings underscore the importance of examining the match between classroom organization and cultural or individual patterns of achievement.

Grouping

Grouping patterns in classrooms constitute a special type of organizational structure. Teachers need to exercise caution if they group students for instruction, because such arrangements have implications for student motivation and achievement. Key components of the grouping structure in the classroom include size and number of groups, basis for grouping, consistency of groups across content areas, stability of groups over time, labeling of groups, mobility of individuals among groups, number of groups functioning as groups at one time, and amount of time spent in individual, group, or whole-class structures (Marshall and Weinstein 1984).

Reviews of research on ability grouping for reading instruction suggest that instructional and social reading experiences differ for students in high- and low-ranked reading groups and that these differences influence student learning (for example, Allington 1983b; Hiebert 1983). The social properties of ability groups are derived, at least in part, from the fact that students are grouped with those defined to be similar and separated from those defined to be different. Group placement is based on socially valued criteria, so that group membership immediately identifies some individuals as better than others. Therefore, high- and low-ranked reading groups are likely to form unique instructional-social contexts that influence the learning outcomes of the individuals within those groups.

As a consequence, students make judgments about their own and others' competence. Reading assessment can be enriched by a clear understanding of the types of social distinctions that accompany grouping patterns in the classroom. For example, when researchers ask students about how they learn how smart they are, students commonly refer to group membership (Marshall and Weinstein 1984). We see this repeatedly when we interview students in our clinics.

Student feelings of efficacy and motivation are affected by grouping decisions, but research suggests that students in different groups also receive distinctly different instruction. Students in low-ranked groups spend considerably less time in actual reading tasks than students in high-ranked groups (McDermott 1977). High-ability groups read silently more often than they read orally, while low-ability groups read orally much more frequently than silently (Allington 1983b). In addition, teachers interrupt students following oral reading errors proportionally more often in low-ability than high-ability groups and are more likely to emphasize word identification with low groups and comprehension with high groups (Allington 1980).

The nature and extent of such differential treatment varies from teacher to teacher, and at least some of the variation can be seen as appropriate differential instruction (Brophy 1983b; Haskins et al. 1983). Too often, however, low groups receive less exciting instruction, less emphasis on meaning and conceptualization, and more rote drill and practice activities (Good and Marshall 1984).

The differential treatment, coupled with the simple fact of group membership, provides students with more messages about their potential for success in reading (R. Weinstein 1986). Average- and low-ability students who are in ability groups give lower self-evaluations than those who are not in ability groups (Rosenbaum 1980). Research suggests that most groups based on homogeneous ability levels are relatively stable over time with infrequent mobility of students from one group to another (Rosenbaum 1980) and that membership in reading groups of different ability levels contributes significantly to the prediction of reading achievement beyond initial individual differences (R. Weinstein 1976).

In sum, the evidence suggests that a low-group psychology develops wherever ability grouping is practiced, even in schools whose low-group students would be high-group students somewhere else (Good and Brophy 1987). Such students may be prime candidates to become underachievers because it may be easier for them to remain passive and to pretend indifference rather than risk failure by trying their best.

Before leaving this topic, it is important to note that some groups are formed for reasons other than ability, such as grouping for student interests or specific skill needs; promoting interaction among students of varying backgrounds; and promoting learning in all students (Marshall and Weinstein

1984). Research on cooperative learning groups has demonstrated a positive effect on achievement, race relations, and student self-esteem (Slavin 1983). In contrast to stable and homogeneous groups, students have greater opportunity to work with more of their peers and to observe their own and others' strengths in a variety of areas when a flexible grouping strategy is used. Where external rewards are distributed, more children have the opportunity to receive recognition than where stable hierarchical grouping strategies result in the high group consistently receiving more rewards and privileges.

In light of the foregoing, Good and Brophy (1987) offer the following guidelines for within-class grouping:

1. The number, size, and composition of groups should be determined by teacher goals.
2. Groups should not be formed for the sole purpose of altering the pace of instruction. Instead, they should promote differentiated instruction for individual students.
3. Assignments to groups should be flexible, not permanent, and the scheduling and instruction of these should be subject to change as well.
4. Students should be assigned to a group for a specific purpose and should be managed in such a way as to limit the impact on their other activities, both academic and social. For example, members of the same reading group should not be seated together, nor should membership in a reading (or other group) dictate the students' grouping for other subjects.
5. The organization and instruction of groups should result in extra instruction for low achievers.

In writing instruction, permanent ability grouping is rare. As a result, students who are poor readers may be relatively enthusiastic writers. If grammar, usage, and mechanics are not emphasized unduly, they escape the negative consequences resulting from grouping practices in reading.

Writing Instruction

Reading and writing development and instruction are intimately related. What children read will affect what and how they write. Eckhoff (1983), for example, found that the features of the basal texts read by children were reflected in their own writing. On the other hand, the writing instruction provided by teachers can be, and often is, distinct from the reading program, and this instructional program is likely to exert its own influence on students' writing performance.

> The social context in which students engage in writing has a powerful impact on the type of writing they produce (DeFord 1986). Key elements of successful writing programs include writing for a real purpose and a real audience in a supportive environment that provides frequent, if not daily, opportunities for sustained writing (Calkins 1983; Graves 1983). (Raphael, Englert, and Kirschner 1989, 265)

Writing instruction today, like reading instruction, has undergone considerable reconsideration. Historically, writing instruction was little more than assigning students to produce a written product and then evaluating it, with an emphasis on grammar, usage, and mechanics (Hoskisson and Tompkins 1987). The written work was generally done during a single class period and was unrelated to the reading program.

In the elementary grades, the focus was most often on producing narrative stories and writing time was often removed from spelling and grammar instruction. At higher levels, requests for products plus grammar instruction was the vehicle by which students were expected to improve their writing abilities.

While these practices still exist to one degree or another, there is a general recognition that students' writing improves by writing and by viewing and discussing good models of written work (Hillocks 1986). In addition, there is widespread interest in the process of writing. As Raphael, Englert, and Kirschner (1989) note, "Research on this subject describes writing as a nonlinear process. That is, it does not begin with simple tasks and work toward more complex tasks; instead it consists of a number of more holistic activities" (265).

The instructional program should provide daily writing opportunities to plan, draft, edit, revise, and/or publish written work. In addition, students need scaffolding during writing instruction in much the same way they do in reading. This support may take the form of conferences, modeling, and/or mini lessons. In recent years, teachers have sometimes focused on the process approach too rigidly and have sometimes abandoned the role of teacher too completely. In his new book, Graves (1994) remarks on this need for balance:

> … we've learned much more about the essentials of teaching writing and how to use our time more effectively. Readers of my earlier book will find *A Fresh Look at Writing* more assertive: although listening to children is still the heart of the book, I think we now know better when to step in, when to teach, and when to expect more of our students … We've learned that, right from the start, teachers need to teach more. (xvi)

Successful programs appear to share several common elements (Calkins 1983; Graves 1983, 1994; Raphael, Englert, and Kirschner 1989). First, the program provides for frequent, sustained time for writing that is both predictable and productive. Second, students write for real purposes and real audiences. Third, the environment is supportive and students are both challenged and encouraged. It is also organized so that students have access to materials and support. Finally, successful writing programs teach children the conventions of writing (Graves 1994).

What is very apparent is that writing performance, like reading, is influenced by the opportunities presented in the classroom and by the context for learning established at home and at school. Most significantly, children's understanding of what it means to write will be influenced by the types of writing that are promoted in the classroom and by the focus of the instruction.

Congruence Within and Across Instructional Settings
The school life of many poor readers and writers involves not one, but several, instructional contexts. Until recently, most poor readers and writers received

special instruction outside of the classroom (called pull-out programs), a configuration that is still quite common. However, many less-skilled readers and writers now receive their instruction via *inclusion* programs, receiving special instruction within the regular classroom. This instruction may still be planned and provided by a special teacher. In either arrangement, it is likely that students are experiencing two settings, two teachers, and, frequently, two sets of program materials.

Researchers such as Allington and Johnston have examined the relationships between supplemental reading and writing programs and regular classroom instruction (Johnston, Allington, and Afflerbach 1985; Allington and Johnston 1989). Their results revealed that an astonishing 80 percent of classroom teachers did not know what instructional materials were being used with the remedial students in their room. The data also indicated that only 50 percent of the specialists could specify the reading book used by classroom teachers. If classroom and supplemental teachers do not know this general information, it is, of course, extremely unlikely that they have coordinated any other aspects of the students' reading and writing instruction.

Examinations of the instruction students receive in the classroom and in the remedial setting suggest that there is little congruence. On a typical day, remedial students are receiving instruction on different skills, using different materials, and with a different focus in two different environments (Allington, Stuetzel, Shake, and Lamarche 1986). As Johnston and his colleagues (1985) point out, this means that the students who have the most difficulty integrating information and transferring learned skills to new situations are presently receiving the most fragmented, least unified instruction of all.

The coordination of efforts between the classroom and the special teachers is at the heart of most definitions of what Walp and Walmsley (1989) call "procedural congruence." These authors note that organized mechanical coordination does little to ensure that students will encounter a coherent and well-conceived instructional environment. Simple push-in programs will not assure congruent instruction either. "It is quite possible to have classroom and remedial teachers occupying the same space yet delivering unrelated programs" (Walp and Walmsley 1989, 365). It seems likely that congruence between instructional settings for remedial students will depend on teachers having serious discussions about the nature of reading and writing and the rationale for delivering "more of the same" or "different" instruction.

Instructional Resources

An increasing body of research suggests that the nature of the texts read and produced in instructional settings has a significant effect on their learning and performance. This realization has forced both educators and publishers to examine their assumptions about the sources of reading and writing difficulty and has encouraged special education practitioners to promote "curriculum-based evaluations" (see Howell and Morehead 1987). A reading and writing assessment for any individual is incomplete until we have identified the characteristics of the materials that are regularly used for instruction.

Text Type and Structure

Researchers have identified a number of text factors that influence readers' comprehension, fluency, memory, and enjoyment of selections. A major factor in determining students' reading performance is the type of text being read. Research in this area suggests that major differences exist between narrative (story) and expository (informational) texts. Narrative text is often characterized by specific elements of information such as problem, conflict, and resolution. Expository text, by contrast, is usually described in terms of organizational structures such as cause-effect, compare-contrast, or descriptive. Generally speaking, the evidence suggests that narratives of all sorts (even unfamiliar ones) are easier to understand than expository texts (Graesser and Riha 1984). Differences in text structure and organization, as well as purpose, probably contribute to the differences readers experience in reading narrative and expository texts. In the following section, we describe separately what is known about the structure of stories and informational texts and its influence on reading performance.

Narrative texts. A narrative tells a story about human events and actions. Researchers have concluded that narratives have an identifiable structure (see also Chapters 7 and 8). Although different types of narrative texts such as fables, mysteries, and adventures vary in specific ways, they also have some features in common. Common features of narrative include: characters; setting or time placement; complications and major goals of main characters; plots and resolutions of complications; emotional patterns; and points, morals, and themes (Graesser, Golding, and Long 1991).

The principal purpose for stories is often assumed to be entertainment, but "the range of purposes for telling a story is as varied as the motives that underlie human behavior. Thus, stories can be used to cause pain as well as pleasure (that is, to embarrass, to humiliate, to parody, to flatter, to console, to teach, to arouse guilt, etc.)" (Stein and Policastro 1984, 116). Readers and listeners use their knowledge of text purpose to anticipate text type and structure. For example, listeners expect different discourse features from a conversation or an amusing cocktail story than they do from a lecture.

Individuals build internal story structures and use them to aid comprehension during reading. Text organization helps readers predict, focus attention, and retain or recall content (McConaughy 1982). Both children and adults comprehend better when story content is organized so that it conforms to expectations (Mandler and Johnson 1977; Mandler 1978; Stein and Glenn 1979; Stein and Nezworski 1978). When stories have missing segments (for example, initiating events) or altered sequence, readers comprehend and remember less (Thorndyke 1977).

Because the internalized sense of story seems so central to comprehending narratives, it is important to understand something about its development.

Even very young children appear to have a rather well-developed sense of story. Recent evidence also suggests that poor readers, at least by sixth grade, have as well developed a sense of story as do good readers, and that they use it to enhance comprehension (McConaughy 1985). It should also be noted that these internal story structures appear to develop as children listen to and read well-formed stories. Thus it is extremely important that disabled readers are offered well-crafted stories containing strong story structures, so that they can develop this sense of story early and make the most efficient use of this knowledge.

Unfortunately, many of the reading selections used to teach children to read and to help remedial readers are poorly written. Beck, McKeown, and McCaslin (1981) concluded as they analyzed basal stories that these types of selections can pose serious impediments to comprehension since "the printed texts in the earliest school reading materials are not in themselves complete stories or even complete messages" (780).

The "story" in Figure 5.2 is typical of a certain class of selections encountered in schools. The most obvious problem with this text is that it simply does not conform to our expectations for either the content or organization of stories. In terms of content, for example, we expect that stories will revolve around some type of conflict—environmental conflict, interpersonal conflict, or internal conflict (Bruce 1984). The segment in Figure 5.2 contains no such elements, and it is difficult to imagine what would drive a reader through the text. The structure and organization of this selection do not conform to traditional story grammar descriptions. This reliance on artificial texts actually may make reading *more* difficult. Children find them uninteresting and difficult to comprehend, since they do not invite reader involvement (Bruce 1984). In addition, children need good writing models if they are to improve their own writing. Hillocks (1986), who conducted an extensive review of research on writing, concluded that "research indicates that emphasis on the presentation of good pieces of writing as models is significantly more useful than the study of grammar" (p. 249).

FIGURE 5.2
"The Shoemaker and the Elves"

Tap, Tap Story
Tap, tap, tap. See me work. I make good things.
See the red ones. See the blue ones. See the yellow ones.
No, no, no. I do not want red ones. I do not want blue ones.
I want green ones.
No, no, no. I do not want big ones. I want little ones.
No, no, no. I do not want little ones. I want big ones.
Oh, my. Oh, my. No one wants my things. I will go to bed.
I will work in the morning.
Tap, Tap Story from *Learning to Read in American Schools* by R. C. Anderson, J. Osborn, and R. J. Tierney. Copyright © 1984 by Lawrence Erlbaum Associates, Inc., Publishers. Reprinted by permission.

Informational texts.   Five common structures are used repeatedly in text-book writing, at least in the western hemisphere (Armbruster 1984):

1. *Simple-listing:* Information is presented in an unordered list.
2. *Comparison/contrast:* Ideas are described in terms of their similarities and differences.
3. *Temporal sequence:* Time order of ideas or events is used to organize the text.
4. *Cause/effect:* The presentation of ideas or events focuses on the causal relationships between and among them.
5. *Problem/solution:* Relationship between and among ideas or events are linked so that one represents a problem and the other(s) represents a solution to that problem.

Whereas even young children seem able to recognize and use story structure, it appears that even middle-grade students are either unaware of or unable to use informational or expository text structure to aid comprehension (Elliott 1980; Taylor and Samuels 1983). Several factors probably account for this.

First, there are many ways to organize information in expository texts, and the patterns aren't so clearly defined. The research in this area suggests that not all of these text patterns are equally easy for young readers. For example, under some conditions simple listing is more difficult than compare/contrast because it requires readers to impose an organization, often by inferring the relationships between and among listed items (Meyer and Freedle 1984). Although the ability to use text organization to increase learning and promote comprehension improves with age, reading ability differences are also noted by the middle grades. Good readers at the junior high level are better than poor readers at recognizing and using text structure in informational texts (McGee 1981, 1982).

A second reason why children may have less skill in reading expository text is that they typically have much less experience reading this type of material. Many schools do not use textbooks at the early levels for content area instruction, and basal reading programs have traditionally included more narrative than expository texts in their anthologies. In addition, differences between good and poor readers' ability to read exposition may be related to opportunity, since it appears that poor readers have even fewer opportunities to read informational text than good readers (Allington 1984).

Even when elementary students do have the opportunity to read, they are often offered poor examples of exposition. The quality of textual materials influences performance *for all readers* (see Shimmerlik 1978). Studies designed to compare readers' comprehension of organized versus disorganized texts have consistently demonstrated that comprehension and recall are strongly affected by the organization of ideas in text. Well-organized text that highlights the overall structure and supports the relationships between ideas contributes to comprehension and enhances recall. Poor readers appear to be affected by these factors more seriously than good readers (Meyer, Brandt, and Bluth 1980).

Well-structured text promotes the integration of knowledge so that more cognitive resources are available to process new, more complex information. In turn, these more-organized knowledge structures promote complex comprehension activities, such as generating inferences, summarizing, and evaluating (Anderson and Armbruster 1984a). Poorly written text is difficult even for proficient readers to comprehend and remember. Students, especially those with reading problems, need to read *good* informational texts.

Text Features That Influence Comprehensibility

The term *considerate texts* was coined by Armbruster and T. Anderson to describe texts that enable readers to gather appropriate information with minimal effort, as opposed to inconsiderate texts that require readers to put forth extra effort in order to compensate for the inadequacies of the text (Armbruster 1984; Anderson and Armbruster 1984a). Although the principles for analyzing considerate text were designed for subject area textbooks, we believe that they apply equally well to narrative materials. The features of text that contribute to its considerateness are discussed briefly in the sections that follow. They are coherence, unity, audience appropriateness, and adjunct instructional aids.

Coherence.   Coherence means "a sticking together" (Anderson and Armbruster 1984a, 204). The ideas and concepts in texts are tied together by an underlying cohesive structure. In coherent writing, the author has moved smoothly from one idea to the next, making it easier for readers to understand the big ideas. The author clarifies facts and helps the reader to understand the significance of these ideas or events.

According to Armbruster (1984), coherence is the text factor that exerts the strongest influence on comprehension and learning. When reading coherent (versus less coherent) text, readers take less time to read, they recall more, and the integration of ideas is improved (Goetz and Armbruster 1980). Readers are better able to build a model of the meaning of text when it has a strong cohesive structure, which functions like a "road map to understanding" (Binkley 1988, 104). For example, both reading time and recall are improved when authors repeatedly refer to key ideas (Goetz and Armbruster 1980).

There are many ways that authors tighten relationships and increase the flow of ideas (Grimes 1975; Halliday and Hasan 1976). Authors can make effective use of *reference* by using pronouns to link previous or forthcoming events, people, and things. Similarly, authors use *lexical repetition* and *synonyms* to tie ideas together—for example, by repeating key words several times or using other words with the same meaning (for example, *elephant* and *lumbering animal*). Coherent text also makes effective use of *intersentential connectives* such as *therefore* and *obviously* to tie ideas together.

Stories for young or less-able readers are frequently inconsiderate because of attempts to control difficulty by using roundabout language or by omitting information completely. This can result in highly contrived and incomplete selections such as the example provided in Figure 5.2. According to Green

(1984), this excerpt is from a version of *The Shoemaker and the Elves*. Key words such as *shoemaker, elves,* and *shoes* are never used (see Figure 5.2).

Both able and less-able readers appear to take a very long time to recognize fully and use most cohesive ties in text (Bridge and Winograd 1982). However, some aspects of cohesion seem to pose special problems for less-able readers. For example, simple conjunctions such as *and* appear more difficult for less-able readers than other types of connectives (Bridge and Winograd 1982). Since conjunction does little to illuminate the key relationships between and among ideas, readers need to make additional inferences, something that seems to be hard work for poor readers. Similarly, although the absence of explicitly stated connectives makes reading more difficult for all readers, the need to infer connectives poses more serious problems for less-able readers (Marshall and Glock 1978–79).

Unity. Although unity in text is closely related to coherence, they are not exactly the same thing.

> Unity refers to the degree to which the text addresses a single purpose. The author of a unified text has not strayed from the purpose by including irrelevant and distracting information (Anderson and Armbruster 1984a, 209).

The importance of unity can be seen quite clearly in the sample fifth-grade social studies text presented in Figure 5.3. Although this selection suffers from several problems, one of the greatest is its lack of unity. The reader is hard-pressed to know just what is important. Readers with little knowledge of the Civil War (most fifth grade students) will have a difficult time forming an integrated picture of the information in this section of text, since the selection moves from topic to topic so quickly. Similarly, poor readers will have trouble because there is little opportunity to use prior knowledge (either preexisting or garnered from text) as an aid to comprehension.

Text unity is likely to have an especially strong effect on both less-knowledgeable and less-able readers. In order for comprehension to occur, readers need to integrate text information with prior knowledge and also integrate the information from one part of the text with information from earlier parts. If this does not happen, readers' memory of the text will be limited because they will be forced to recall isolated facts rather than organized sets of information (Anderson and Armbruster 1984a).

Audience appropriateness. "Audience appropriateness refers to the extent to which the text matches the reader's knowledge base—knowledge both of the content and of discourse features such as syntactic and rhetorical structures" (Anderson and Armbruster 1984a, 212). Authors of books for young people, and the publishers who distribute them, have a responsibility to consider how appropriate both the content and structure of their materials are for those who are not yet expert in terms of either skill or knowledge.

Evaluating appropriateness can be extremely tricky for teachers who have had many more experiences in the world, and are themselves often content experts.

FIGURE 5.3
Social Studies Text

The North and the South at War

In 1861 Lincoln became the President of a divided United States. He took the oath of office on a high platform in front of the capitol in Washington, D.C. He was dressed in a black suit, a stiff white shirt, and a high silk hat. He carried a cane with a gold handle.

Lincoln stepped forward and placed his left hand on a Bible. Raising his right hand, he promised to "preserve, protect, and defend the Constitution of the United States." People wondered how he would do this. Seven states had already left the United States. Would Lincoln try to punish them? What would he say about slavery?

Lincoln did not answer all of these questions in his Inaugural Address. He said that no state had the right to leave the United States. He warned that he would protect the forts and buildings which belonged to the United States government.

War broke out only a few weeks after Lincoln became President. It became known as the Civil War.

The war began at Fort Sumter in South Carolina. Fort Sumter was on a small island in Charleston harbor. Find it on the map. It belonged to the United States government. Union soldiers from the North held the fort. South Carolina, now a part of the Confederacy, ordered Fort Sumter to surrender. When the commander of the fort refused, the food supply was cut off.

Lincoln had food shipped to Fort Sumter. This made Confederate leaders angry. Southern soldiers fired on the fort. Northern soldiers fired back. A fierce battle took place. At last the Northern soldiers had to give up. This was the first battle of the Civil War.

Thousands offered to serve in the Union Army. Thousands rushed to join the Confederate forces, too. Everyone hoped the war would be over soon. But it wasn't. It dragged on for four years.

During the second year of the war, both sides ran short of troops. They then drafted, or ordered, people into the armies. This was the first time in United States history that soldiers were drafted.

Both sides needed money, supplies, and troops. Money-raising events were held in the Union and in the Confederacy. Groups were formed to help the families of soldiers.

Women who had never worked outside their homes went to work in offices and factories. Some women ran the family farms and businesses for the first time. Others knitted and sewed uniforms and made bandages to use in the hospitals.

Doctors and nurses went to serve on the battlefield. Mary Walker was one of the doctors. At first, she was allowed to work only as a nurse. Later, though, she became an Army officer and worked as a doctor.

Clara Barton was called the "Angel of the Battlefield." She was born on a Massachusetts farm on Christmas Day, 1821. For a while, she taught school near her home. Later she moved to Washington, D. C. She was a clerk in one of the government offices.

When the Civil War began, Clara Barton carried medicines and food to injured soldiers. The officers ordered her away. They said the battlefield was no place for a woman. But she did not give up. In fact, she got other women to join her. After a time, she ran a large hospital for wounded soldiers.

Clara Barton served suffering people the rest of her long life. She helped to find missing Union soldiers. She took care of the victims of wars in other parts of the world. She helped people who had lost homes in fires, floods, and storms. She founded the American Red Cross.

Dorothea Dix was another nurse during the Civil War. She had spent years trying to make life better for people in prisons and poorhouses. During the Civil War, though, she took time out from her work to care for wounded soldiers. She was in charge of all the nurses for the Union Army.

From *Our Country of Tiegs-Adams: Our Land and Heritage.* © Copyright, 1979, by Ginn and Company. Used by permission of Silver, Burdett & Ginn Inc.

Teachers often fail to recognize inconsiderate text because they are familiar with its content. They need to keep in mind that their students lack most of the background knowledge needed to understand the vocabulary, concepts, difficult pronoun referents, and allusions (Wisconsin Department of Public Instruction 1989, 35).

Even when materials are generally appropriate for the intended audience, however, mismatches can occur. This is where the knowledgeable and thoughtful teacher will need to exercise judgment. When working with special student populations or when the overall school curriculum does not support the content, we must make sure that we are judging the contribution of these materials to reader performance. Under some circumstances, failure to comprehend has very little to do with reading skill.

Adjunct aids. Adjunct aids are the structural features of texts that are intended to supplement or complement the information in the written text. They include features such as illustrations, headings and subheadings, boldfaced type, charts and figures, introductions and summaries, and questions either within or at the end of a reading selection. These features are included specifically to focus and guide readers' understanding and are common in materials used for instructional purposes.

As with other features of the text, adjunct aids have an impact on students' comprehension and learning. For example, when topic sentences are clearly present, readers comprehend and recall text content better (Bridge, Belmore, Moskow, Cohen, and Matthews 1984). Furthermore, comprehension of main ideas is enhanced when they are stated explicitly at the beginning of paragraphs or text sections (Baumann 1986) or are highlighted in some way (Doctorow, Wittrock, and Marks 1978).

The mere presence of such features does not ensure enhanced comprehension. Students must be aware of these features and understand how they contribute to understanding. Many of the adjunct aids described above are unique to the materials used for instructional purposes, and students may need direct guidance and explanation from teachers in order to take full advantage of these text features.

Commercial Reading/Language Arts Programs

Commercially prepared reading/language arts programs are a type of material that can influence students' learning and performance. As recently as 1988–89, it was estimated that at least 90 percent of all classrooms in the United States use commercially prepared basal programs to teach reading (Goodman, Shannon, Freeman, and Murphy 1988), and that between 75 and 90 percent of the instructional time devoted to reading in American schools is occupied with the materials provided by basal reading programs (Osborn 1989).

Until recently, basal programs have reflected a skills approach to teaching reading/language arts. The professional literature has been critical of their use of contrived language, controlled vocabulary, and simplistic stories lacking in conflict, character development, and meaningful situations (K. Goodman et al. 1988). As a result of changing market demands over the past decade related to factors such as increased teacher involvement in decision making and policy initiatives to improve language arts education (Hoffman et al. 1994), basal publishers have moved to align their programs more directly with current theory and research.

Traditionally, basal programs include a multilevel series of materials for both the student and the teacher. At each level, student materials consist of an anthology of reading selections and a collection of independent exercises. The primary material for the teacher at each level is a teacher's guide that includes detailed teaching directions and suggestions. For many teachers, the basal series is their reading/language arts program. This makes it important to examine these materials to understand the nature of the instruction received by many of the students who are experiencing difficulty with reading and/or writing.

The student anthologies contain a variety of different types of reading selections appropriate for students at each grade/ability level. Although basal reading anthologies contain a variety of text types, narrative texts predominate. This is particularly true at the early reading levels where, for a long time, there was a prevalence of "pseudo-texts" that were created especially for these types of instructional materials. These selections contained highly controlled vocabulary and, often, distorted syntax intended to simplify initial reading experiences. They were not representative of any authentic text types that exist outside the instructional context, and they were often unnecessarily difficult because the language and story structure were artificial. This is not an accurate characterization of the selections in current basal series, since every major publisher has conducted at least one complete revision since 1990. However, it is not uncommon to find basal programs with outdated copyrights in many classrooms. It is even more common for old materials to be used in programs for students experiencing reading and writing difficulties. Below we summarize the most recent trends in basal reading materials and then provide some cautions for those who are still using older materials.

Recent developments.   Focusing primarily on beginning reading levels, a recent comparison revealed important differences between basals with a 1986/87 copyright and those with a 1993 copyright (Hoffman et al 1994). Notably, in contrast to the 1986/87 programs, the stories in the 1993 series were a higher quality and there were fewer adaptations of literature. The evidence also indicated that vocabulary control and repetition was either substantially reduced or abandoned altogether in the 1993 programs. Similarly, the total number of words in the 1993 programs was considerably less than in the 1986/87 programs; however, the 1993 programs included many more unique words than did the 1986/87 programs.

The tone of the teachers' guides was less prescriptive in the 1993 programs, moving in the direction of a "teacher-as-decision maker" model. Further evidence of this came from a change in the underlying instructional design of the teachers' guides. Especially at the earliest levels, 1993 programs had moved toward a shared reading model and away from the directed reading model of the 1986/87 programs (see below). Vocabulary was introduced more in the context of the story in the 1993 editions and fewer questions were provided in an effort to include more high-level questions. Assessment tools in the 1993 programs were broadened beyond the test-only model in the 1986/87 programs.

Even Wepner and Feeley (1993), whose analysis of basals was conducted using 1989 copyright materials, found that all had incorporated at least some of the contemporary language of instruction, such as *emergent literacy, modeling, literature-based,* and *cooperative grouping.* According to these researchers, perhaps the most dramatic change has come in the area of strategic reading. Although the programs do vary considerably, most are much stronger in the support they provide for students to become strategic readers, including such metacomprehension strategies as question generating, summarizing, paraphrasing, predicting and verifying, and thinking aloud (Wepner and Feeley 1993, 70–72).

In summary, teachers need to be aware that the evaluation of basal resources is critical since the date of publication may be far more important to determining appropriateness than the publisher or the fact that it is a basal. Hoffman et al. (1994) concluded that "innovations were being offered on a scale unparalleled in the history of basals. Notable was the fact that the differences between the old and the new versions were far greater than variations between publishers" (p. 65).

Concerns about traditional basals. We have already noted concerns about the quality of narrative literature in older basals. Poorly written and/or adapted texts predominated the anthologies through the 1980s. The situation with informational text is even more serious. First, traditional basal reading anthologies rarely included informational text and, when they did, the texts were often not representative of the full range of informational materials students encounter outside the context of reading instruction. For example, selections from subject area textbooks were (and still rarely are) included. According to Barr and Sadow (1989), the organization of reading selections can have a "profound effect" on teachers' use of fiction and nonfiction material, causing teachers to make more limited use of nonfiction material. Specifically, only when information and narrative texts were interspersed did teachers make effective use of the nonfiction materials.

Many students with reading and writing problems read only what is in their basal anthology. Consequently, the nature and organization of selections that students are exposed to in these materials can have a major impact on their reading and writing performance. If basal anthologies are the primary instructional material, teachers must ensure that the selections in the anthologies represent the full range of materials students of a given age/ability will read in all school and non-school settings. Students must have the opportunity to read many types of age-appropriate materials for a variety of purposes if they are to become competent readers and writers.

The anthologies are only one area requiring evaluation. Journals or workbooks that accompany each level of a basal series also require careful examination. Students in basal programs often spend the largest portion of their instructional time working in these materials, and the nature of seatwork activities can have a significant impact on students' understanding of the nature of reading and writing. The features of these and other types of instructional tasks and practice activities are discussed further in the next chapter.

Finally, the teacher's guides that accompany each level in a basal program influence classroom practice. The instructional activities teachers choose are generally those described in the teacher's guide (Barr and Sadow 1989; Durkin 1984; Shannon 1983). These guides provide a variety of information, including replicas of both the selections and the workbook pages that appear in the students' materials; organizational procedures to follow in implementing the program; specific directions for presenting prescribed skills; suggested questions to ask when discussing selections with students; enrichment activities for use as follow-up or culminating activities; and assessments that can be used to evaluate student progress.

Instructional design.   The instructional design, or framework, that has traditionally been used in basal reading programs is the *directed reading activity* (DRA). The DRA was first introduced by Betts in 1946 for the purposes of giving teachers a basic format for systematic group instruction, improving students' word recognition and comprehension skills, and guiding students through a reading selection. It has remained remarkably unchanged since that time. Wepner and Feeley (1993) found that all seven basal programs they reviewed used a DRA framework and, although Hoffman et al. (1994) report some movement away from this model at the earliest levels, it is still a common feature of contemporary basals.

In a DRA framework, instruction is organized around before, during, and after reading activities for each selection in the anthology.

Prereading activities in a DRA often include providing relevant background, creating interest, introducing meanings and/or pronunciations for new vocabulary, and establishing purposes for reading.

During-reading activities are intended to guide students' reading, and often include silent reading focused on answering purpose-setting questions, oral reading and responding to questions dealing with short sections of the text, and/or oral rereading to clarify or verify a point.

Postreading activities are of two types: activities focused on the reading selection, such as group discussion or end-of-selection questions; and activities focused on skill instruction and practice that may or may not be related to the reading selection.

Traditional basal lessons focus on content goals in teaching the reading selection, process or skills goals in separate skills lessons and activities, and largely ignore attitude goals. Furthermore, skills objectives have taken precedence over content and attitude objectives in traditional basal lessons; "that is, the stated purpose of each lesson is to learn a particular skill (which may or may not be relevant to understanding the reading selection). Students are often held accountable for their skill learning through practice exercises and end-of-unit or end-of-level tests. However, they are rarely held accountable for their comprehension of the reading selection, except through group questioning and discussion" (Wixson and Peters 1989, 22).

Effective reading lessons focus simultaneously on content, process, and attitude objectives. The goal is not simply to teach the content of given selections or to provide isolated skills instruction, but to promote strategic, motivated reading of a variety of materials for a variety of purposes and tasks (see Chapter 6). Conventional programs do little to advance these outcomes. For example, Morrow's (1987) analysis of six sets of basal readers, Grades K–3, suggests that little attention was focused on the goal of voluntary reading. She found that fewer than 5 percent of the overall instructional suggestions included activities designed to promote positive attitudes, to encourage book discussion, or to build knowledge of authors and illustrators. Though this has been remedied in many contemporary basals, these often appear as optional or supplemental activities. Only a few programs have highlighted these important outcomes.

The type of instruction typically associated with the DRA is characterized by teacher-centered activities designed to teach the reading selection, and isolated instructional procedures and independent student practice activities designed to teach skills. The traditional basal lesson plan directs the teacher to ask students to practice or perform a particular task or to ask questions with specific responses.

Among traditional programs there is a lack of scaffolded instruction involving the progression from teacher modeling and explanation to independent student practice and application (see Chapter 6). There is little support for engaging in instructional dialogue. Durkin's (1984) analysis of the teacher's guides of five major basal series supports these conclusions. Her analyses revealed that the guides provided few suggestions for comprehension instruction but many for review, application, and practice. In addition, she reported that the teacher's guide "mentions" the skills or strategy and then quickly moves to brief examples available in application formats. Although many students do eventually learn through these indirect practice methods, many do not, and some are actually misled by the questions and activities provided in basal lessons (Wixson and Peters 1989).

The traditional DRA promotes the role of the teacher as the presenter and the student as the receiver of information and encourages teacher-centered patterns of interaction. There is little opportunity for student-initiated involvement, and students have little opportunity to monitor and regulate their own reading. Although there is little direct evidence regarding the effects of different instructional frameworks, it seems safe to assume that a steady diet of teacher-centered exchange would provide different results than a more interactive pattern that placed increased responsibility on the reader (see Palincsar and Brown 1984).

Examining the content and method of instruction used to teach reading can help to determine whether there have been opportunities for a particular student to learn a given content. Not infrequently, students who have difficulty reading specific texts or with certain reading skills simply have not had the instructional or practice opportunities necessary to become competent. Such an evaluation can also provide information about what has *not* proved helpful in teaching individual children to read. When an analysis of the instruction and the instructional materials suggests ample opportunity to learn but the child has not benefited, further assessment and/or diagnostic teaching is needed (see Chapter 11).

Alternative frameworks and other commercial materials. Many teachers, particularly primary teachers, have turned from the classic DRA to a modified framework such as a Shared Reading approach. Modeled after a bedtime story reading time, the Shared Reading Experience (Holdaway 1979) encourages children to participate in reading and rereading activities in a supportive environment. Generally teachers use a big book so that a group of students can see the print as the teacher reads the book. After students have enjoyed the story, the teacher and students reread the book over several days — accomplishing a variety of tasks that may include comprehension and vocabulary work, concepts about print, phonics and decoding, or attention to narrative elements such as character or setting. Teachers provide scaffolded support through initial whole text reading, choral reading, and rereading. Over time, students acquire the confidence to read this and similar stories in small book form.

In addition to big books and the individual versions of big books, many teachers are using other materials in their classrooms. Some continue to use the basal as a primary resource, but have added other supplemental materials. Others have replaced the basal with children's literature (trade books) and/or one of the available series of "little books." These little book series have been created for use with beginning readers. The earliest levels have one word per page for a total of perhaps five words. Somewhat later levels have more words per page and make heavy use of repetition and/or predictable refrains. All books include multiple cues to aid word recognition — that is, strong picture-text correspondence and/or rhyming. Later levels contain fully developed short stories.

These materials have become popular with teachers who were concerned about the quality of basal materials. A particular strength is the comfortable size of these materials and the fact that each contains its own unique story — a contrast to the heavy anthology of the basal, even when it contains fine literature. These resources have problems, however. The heavy use of picture-text cueing can prevent some students from gaining independence with print, unless teachers are careful to move them along. At least one of these series of little books was published out of the U.S., with the result that specific vocabulary words are often extremely uncommon and unfamiliar to U.S. beginning readers. In addition, the stories, while clever, are generally not good literature. As Peterson (1991) has noted, " … none can offer the rich variety of story, language, and illustration of the many talented writers and illustrators in publishing today. On the other hand, the 'little book' series are valuable in that they provide simple, repetitive texts that quickly engage beginners in the process of reading" (120).

Other materials often used as substitutes for basals actually have many of the problems associated with older basal programs. In particular, most use readability formulas to control difficulty, resulting in awkward, sometimes difficult, narrative passages. These stories have generally been written specifically for a publisher and can be criticized for the same lack of quality as traditional basals. The single advantage is that they are contained within one book and thereby convey to students something about the authentic nature of reading. Finally, there are very few informational texts among these little book materials. The leveled "step" books have produced a growing body of informational text, some of it quite interesting to early readers.

To summarize, teachers need to examine the materials they use very carefully to determine what contributions to reading performance these texts may be making. If reading is made more difficult by obscure vocabulary or opaque stories, these books should be pulled from the collection, especially if children are struggling.

STRATEGIES AND TOOLS FOR ASSESSING INSTRUCTIONAL SETTINGS AND RESOURCES

In this chapter we are suggesting that it is important to observe the context for learning, not just the student in that context. This can be a tricky business. It can also be extremely important. Until recently assessments of the instructional context have been rare. Fortunately, there is now a sparse but growing number of strategies and tools for assessing instructional settings and materials.

Assessing Instructional Setting

In this section we describe some techniques for examining and describing instructional settings to determine how they may be contributing to a particular student's struggles or successes. The point is not to pass judgment, but to collect information that can be used to make sound decisions aimed at improving instruction for students who need our help.

The Literate Environment

Teachers' beliefs about reading and writing are often visible in their classrooms. To begin evaluating the literate environment, an overall observation can be helpful.

The summary sheet in Figure 5.4 draws from a variety of sources (Cooper 1993; Curry 1993; Louglin and Martin 1987). It is designed to focus your self-evaluation or observation of the various aspects of the classroom environment.

The types of learning that are valued by the teacher should be reflected in the classroom. Duffy and Roehler (1989) note that classrooms contain both a physical and an intellectual environment. The *intellectual environment* is established and affected by teacher expectations, student motivation, and literacy goals. Elements related to the development of an appropriate intellectual environment are discussed at length in the previous section on instructional method. Reflective assessment will ask questions which include:

- For what purposes do students read and write?
- Do students appear to read and write for authentic purposes?
- Do students discuss reading, challenge meaning, and confer about writing?

Although many authors suggest examining the *physical environment*, the focus is most often on assessing the general attractiveness and orderliness of the environment (for example, Glazer and Searfoss 1988). Observation and assessment can, however, focus more specifically on aspects of the environment that directly influence the acquisition of reading and writing skill. Reflective assessment questions about physical setting might include:

- Does the environment reflect the many types, functions, and uses of print?
- Are the students' own written works prominently featured in the classroom? (Are they displayed? Is there an "author's chair" and so on?)
- Is there a writing center where students can store writing folders, get materials, display and share work, and so on?
- Is there a reading corner where students have access to a wide array of print materials and opportunity to share books read?
- Are desks and chairs arranged so that students confer with each other?

The physical environment can communicate to students both what is valued and what is acceptable. Inaccessible reading and/or writing centers and uninviting activities and spaces affect students' understanding of the value and purposes for reading and writing. They also influence students' voluntary reading and writing. Similarly, rigid seating arrangements do little to advance the cooperative or verbal interaction patterns that are necessary for many students' literacy development. Consequently, these factors are related to the intellectual environment as well.

A sound knowledge base and a commitment to literacy are extremely important, but teachers must also know how to maintain a functional learning environment for fairly large groups of children. The teacher's ability to organize the classroom and manage the daily routine influences the amount of time available for teaching and learning. Some key focus questions for assessing the organizational factors in classrooms are:

FIGURE 5.4
Checklist for Evaluating the Literate Environment

IN MY CLASSROOM:	COMMENTS
1. There are many different kinds of books and other print materials	
2. There are many different types of writing materials and tools	
3. Students' work, messages, labels, and stories are displayed	
4. There are messages and or plans for the current day	
5. Print materials are displayed near objects, pictures, and other center displays	
6. Books or print displays about community, culture, or language are displayed	
7. Print has functional use—sign-ups, charts, etc.	
THE FOLLOWING AREAS ARE PRESENT IN MY ROOM:	**COMMENTS**
Library—well stocked, accessible, and comfortable	
Writing/publishing center—well stocked and accessible	
Listening/viewing area	
Group meeting place	
Conference area	
Place for sharing, performing, etc.	
I PROMOTE READING AND WRITING:	**COMMENTS**
Daily opportunities for sustained reading and sustained writing	
Students read for a variety of purposes	
Students write for real audiences and for a variety of authentic purposes	
Students have choices about what to read or write	
Students confer with me and with other students about reading	
I support (scaffold) students during reading and writing	
I teach the fundamentals of writing (conduct mini-lessons, teach conventions, provide spelling instruction)	

- Are there clearly understood classroom rules and routines?
- Are procedures for seeking help and getting supplies well established and nonintrusive?
- Do students share the responsibility for routine tasks?
- Are routine scheduling problems handled smoothly (for example, movement by some students to special services or activities)?
- Are transitions between activities handled smoothly and quickly?
- Does the teacher make effective use of the available instructional time?

These questions highlight various aspects of effective organization. Any continuing factors or conditions that make it difficult to deliver instruction smoothly should also be identified. Although we have adopted a teacher decision-making stance throughout this text, we are aware that there are a variety of constraints imposed on teachers that can influence the organization of their classrooms and their ability to make and execute good decisions (Mason, Roehler, and Duffy 1984). These should be identified and considered as the interactive case evaluation proceeds.

Classroom Interaction and Grouping

Teacher beliefs also dictate the type of *social-emotional environment* that is established in the classroom. According to Duffy and Roehler (1989), the social-emotional environment is strongly determined by social interactions, grouping practices, and a general sense of purposefulness. The amount and type of reading and writing that children do is influenced by the social-emotional context.

Although it is extremely important, the influence of classroom interaction is often very subtle. It is important to recognize how difficult it may be to describe the features of classroom interaction, much less assess its impact. Based on several short observations (See Figure 5.5), the following set of focus questions may be helpful in characterizing the general pattern of interaction in a classroom.

- What are the notable characteristics of the linguistic community of the students you are assessing?
- Who typically initiates language exchanges, decides on the form and content of written work, or directs discussions?
- How often do oral and written interactions serve the purpose of eliciting "set" or "known" responses, in contrast to open discussion or divergent responses?

The answers to these global questions can give a sense of the amount and type of verbal interaction that occurs in the classroom and the demands and opportunities likely to be present for individual students. In particular, this general observation can reveal unusual linguistic, cultural, or classroom characteristics.

Occasionally, a much closer examination is desirable or necessary to gather in-depth information about the interactions between the teacher and a particular child or group of children. In this case, careful and systematic classroom

FIGURE 5.5
Assessing Classroom Interaction and Grouping Practices

IN MY CLASSROOM:	COMMENTS
1. The amount of time spent in whole group *reading* instruction is:	**Purpose:** (direct instruction, practice, support, etc.) Type of activity:
2. The amount of time spent in whole group *writing* instruction is:	**Purpose:** (direct instruction, practice, support, etc.) Type of activity:
3. The amount of time spent in small group *reading* instruction is:	**Purpose:** (direct instruction, practice, support, etc.) Type of activity: **Nature of the group** (ability, interest, cooperative, skill work, etc.)
4. The amount of time spent in small group *writing* instuction is:	**Purpose:** (direct instruction, practice, support, etc.) Type of activity: **Nature of the group** (ability, interest, cooperative, skill work, etc.)
5. Amount of time spent working individually/ independently during reading/writing is:	**Purpose:** Type of activity:
6. Students read silently:	Length of time: Nature of materials:
7. Student-student interactions take place in reading:	Frequency: **Purpose:** Type of activity/interaction:
8. Student-student interactions take place in writing:	Frequency: **Purpose:** Type of activity:

observation will be necessary. A procedure described by Page and Pinnell (1979) is useful in both classrooms and clinics. This procedure involves tape recording a "conversation" with the student and then using a checklist to evaluate the types of exchanges that occur. The oral interactions are evaluated to see which conversational partner:

- asks and/or answers questions
- gives personal information about self
- gives information about something other than self
- refers to past events
- makes predictions
- draws conclusions
- makes evaluative statements
- gives orders
- makes requests

The authors report that teachers are often chagrined at the analyses that result, since the patterns are not always what they intended: "Teachers only asked questions and students only gave answers. As a result, the language of both was limited" (p. 62). When teachers use these initial results to shape subsequent interactions, there is often a dramatic increase in *verbal interaction* versus question-response patterns.

The type of grouping practice can influence verbal interaction patterns in the classroom. As we have seen, grouping practices seem to exert a strong influence on student achievement and motivation. Consequently, effective assessment must include a consideration of school and classroom grouping practices (see Figure 5.5). Teachers often use a variety of organizational patterns in their classrooms. It will be particularly important to identify the variety of patterns and their associated purposes.

Both observation and interviews may be necessary to get a clear picture of the complex ways in which students are organized. For example, it is important to determine what information teachers use to make their placement decisions. Although most teachers make careful and intentional grouping decisions using some systematic procedure, others generate groupings on the basis of "untested assumptions" (Good and Brophy 1987). An example of an untested assumption might be something like: "Her brother had trouble in reading and writing, so she will too." Placement decisions based on this type of reasoning are obviously problematic, especially because "teacher judgment" is often used to make other educational decisions as well.

The assessment of grouping practices should also examine the extent to which membership in a group for one purpose (a reading or writing group) defines *access* to other tasks, activities, and levels of achievement. This is a problem especially in middle and junior high schools where scheduling is complicated and the need to receive specialized instruction in reading and writing, for example, may dictate the classes and sections for all other subjects. To gather this information, it may be necessary to observe or inquire about the grouping arrangements and grouping characteristics for subjects other than language arts.

As we have already seen, one of the reasons this information about grouping is so important is that it influences the patterns of interaction that occur among peers and between teachers and students. The quantity and quality of these interactions may profoundly affect both achievement and motivation. In the next section we consider these issues directly.

Congruence Within and Across Settings

Among the most critical aspects of an assessment of the instructional context will be the degree of congruence from one setting to another. In essence, it will be necessary to observe and collect information about multiple settings. A first step involves collecting information about the relationship between classroom instruction and any supplemental or replacement instruction. Shake (1989) suggests using a simple form that could be completed with relative ease by both the classroom teacher and specialists to summarize instruction across settings by the day of the week. With two columns, one for the classroom teacher and one for the support classroom, each teacher writes a brief narrative for the day. A communication system such as this makes it easy to assess the degree of congruence between instructional settings for students receiving special services.

Once the instructional context for a particular student has been described, the information needs to be analyzed and evaluated. In particular, teachers need to examine the degree of similarity between instruction for average/above average students and that received by lower-achieving readers and writers. For example, teachers need to consider how much text students with differing skill levels are exposed to each day and/or week. In addition, it is important to consider similarities and differences in the approaches used to teach students with differing skill levels. If there are substantial and significant variations in the two programs of the sort described previously in this chapter, teachers and assessment personnel should examine the assumptions and rationale for these programs and procedures very carefully. Some students may require unusual programs, however, such decisions should be based on careful consideration, not unsupported assumptions.

Teacher Beliefs

From time to time we all need to carefully examine our beliefs and practices in light of new information and new innovations. Several questionnaires and interviews have been developed to help identify teachers' beliefs and theories about reading and writing. Most of these are quite long and time-consuming. Examinations of the literate environment often reveal what teachers believe about teaching, learning, and literacy. After examining the environment, it would be useful to ask yourself (or ask the student's teacher) questions such as these:

What does the teacher (or, do I) believe:
- is the purpose of reading and writing instruction?
- is necessary for students to know and do before they will become skilled readers and/or writers?

- are appropriate activities to promote reading and writing competence?
- are the most important priorities in literacy instruction?

Teachers are occasionally surprised to find that although they believe that something is important, they do not provide for it in their own program. For example, most teachers believe that prior knowledge influences reading and that building background is important, but many teachers actually do not include these features in their instruction. Recognizing mismatches between beliefs and practice helps teachers more clearly identify what steps to take to help a student who is struggling to become literate.

Assessing Instructional Resources

The idea that instructional resources might exert an independent influence on students' ability to read and write is not a new one. In this section, we review some older tools and techniques and present some newer alternatives for assessing different instructional resources. The purpose for evaluating instructional resources in the assessment-instruction process is actually twofold: (1) to predict the likely impact of instructional factors on performance—to assess the contributions of these factors to reading and writing ability; and (2) to gain insight regarding appropriate instructional materials—to match the failing reader and writer with materials that result in effective teaching and efficient learning.

Evaluating Text

Teachers have always been concerned about the materials their students read. They have generally recognized that "to teach reading effectively or to help students gain information from text requires a match between the difficulty of the reading material and the reading ability of the child" (Zakaluk and Samuels 1988, 122). Unfortunately, achieving this match is not as easy as it sounds.

We have already described the many factors that can influence how difficult a particular text is for a particular individual—the complexity of which was recognized at least 50 years ago:

> In its broadest sense, readability is the sum total—including interactions—of all those elements within a given piece of printed material that affect the success a group of readers have with it. (Dale and Chall 1948, 15)

The earliest discussions of "readability" assumed that factors such as the physical appearance and format of the print, the style of written expression, language usage, and the content of the text affected the difficulty of the text (Gray and Leary 1935). In the intervening years, researchers have demonstrated what teachers have long known: that interest, motivation, and prior knowledge also determine how readable a text will be.

Despite the early recognition that determining text difficulty was extremely complex, the tools used to measure readability have generally captured only limited aspects of text difficulty. Importantly, any serious analysis of the forms and functions of narrative and expository text did not occur until quite recently. Prompted by the desire to generate fast and efficient estimates of text difficulty, there has been a proliferation of "readability formulas." We are going to digress somewhat and present a fairly detailed discussion of them, because these formulas still dominate the area of text assessment. We will then turn our attention to a variety of contemporary alternatives.

Readability Formulas

Readability formulas are procedures that have been developed to assess difficulty objectively, generally by counting some text feature that can be easily identified. According to Klare (1988), the first readability formula was developed by Lively and Pressey in 1923. Since that time, over fifty readability formulas have been developed (Schuyler 1982). To understand the appropriate use and potential misuse of readability formulas, it is important to understand something about their development and notable features.

Developing a readability formula. General procedures used in development are quite similar for all readability formulas (see Conard 1984, for a complete discussion). Readability formulas are derived from detailed analyses of a small set of passages called criterion passages. The selection and validation of the original criterion passages is a critical first step, since the difficulty of all other passages will be determined by comparison with these criterion passages and tasks. If the texts and tasks are not similar to those used by teachers or read by students, then the predictive power of the formula will be weak. Most of the existing readability formulas were validated using extremely short criterion passages.

The criterion passages are then examined and text elements are specified as factors that are likely to contribute to passage difficulty. Once the possible text elements have been identified and quantified, analyses are conducted to determine which are the best predictors of passage difficulty. Finally, a mathematical formula is generated that provides the best description of the relationship between text elements and text difficulty.

Even the earliest readability researchers assumed that critical elements would include text features such as conceptual density and quality of writing. However, these abstract factors proved difficult to measure and were often either not selected for study or were dropped because they could not be counted reliably. The two elements that have proved to be the best predictors of text difficulty (at least using short criterion passages) are semantic difficulty and syntactic complexity of the sentences (Klare 1984). Semantic difficulty is most often estimated using vocabulary, as measured by either frequency/familiarity or length of words; syntactic complexity is most often measured by sentence length.

Because different formulas have been developed using different criterion passages and different tasks, caution is needed in using any of the existing formulas.

For example, the Spache Formula was developed so that it is only appropriate for primary grade passages, while the Dale-Chall is only applicable to materials above the fourth-grade level. In addition, only some formulas examine elements that have theoretical or empirical support from current views of the reading process, and no formula provides a totally satisfactory assessment.

Using readability formulas.   The greatest strength of readability formulas lies in their ease of use. But they must be used cautiously. One of the easiest and most frequently used formulas today is the Fry Readability Formula (Fry 1968). It assesses syntactic and semantic difficulty using only counts of syllables and sentence length (see Figure 5.6). Although this obviously provides a limited

FIGURE 5.6
Fry
Readability
Formula

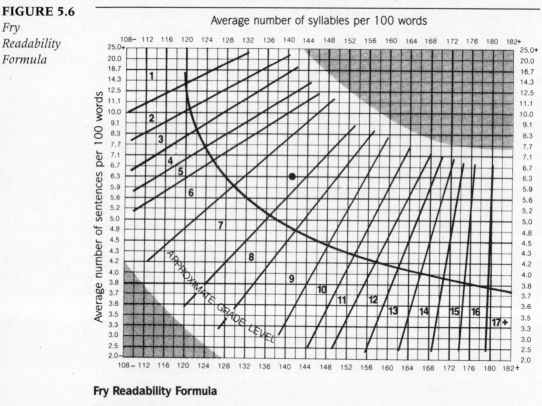

Fry Readability Formula

(Description):
1. Select three 100-word selections from the beginning, middle, and end of the text. Don't count proper nouns.
2. Count the number of sentences in each selection. Estimate to the nearest tenth of a sentence.
3. Average sentence count.
4. Count the number of syllables in each selection.
5. Average the syllable count.
6. Plot the two scores on the graph to get the grade level.

From "A Readability Formula That Saves Time" by Edward Fry (1968). *Journal of Reading, 11,* pp. 513–516, 578. International Reading Association. Reprinted by permission.

view of readability, at least the formula was developed using trade books and other real reading material.

The use of rich criterion passages makes readability formulas fairly reliable when used to rank real, noncontrived texts to be read by a general population (Klare 1984). If materials are grossly unsuitable for use in a targeted grade, readability formulas can reveal this fact in a time-saving manner so that decisions about text appropriateness may be made more rapidly. However, as the Commission on Reading (R. Anderson et al. 1985) notes, "readability formulas are useful only as a rough check on the difficulty and appropriateness of books" (81).

Studies suggest that interformula reliability is a cause for concern (McConnell 1982), especially in the upper ranges of the readability estimates (high school and college level texts). Differences of two or more grade levels in the estimates generated are not unusual when several formulas are applied to the same piece of text.

For placement purposes, the use of readability estimates alone clearly poses serious problems. When gross comparisons are needed, however, readability estimates can be helpful. If you are going to use these formulas, the tedium of analyzing text can be avoided by using one of the available microcomputer software programs (Schuyler 1982).

Criticisms and misuses of readability formulas.

Although formulas have proved quick and efficient, there are many concerns associated with them. Some of these have to do with the formulas themselves and others have to do with their use. As Cullinan and Fitzgerald (1984) noted, it is not what is measured by formulas that causes concern; rather, it is what is not measured. Among the many factors that have been shown to influence text difficulty but that are not accounted for by typical formulas are text structure, interest, motivation, and prior knowledge (Entin and Klare 1985; Fass and Schumacher 1978). In combination, these factors may critically influence the relative difficulty of a selection. A text that may be difficult for one reader may be relatively easy for another of the same reading skill.

One of the most serious concerns about readability formulas involves their misuse in rewriting existing materials, a practice promoted by early formula developers (Dale and Chall 1948; Flesch 1948). There has been an understandable temptation to revise text to make it easier and more accessible to readers. However, the indiscriminate use of readability indicators, such as sentence length, to rewrite text has often had the unexpected result of making text more, rather than less, difficult (Davison 1984; Davison and Kantor 1982; Pearson 1974–75). For example:

> *Version 1:* Because the law forbade blacks from sitting in the front of the bus, Rosa Parks was arrested and many black people decided to start a boycott.
> *Version 2:* The law forbade blacks from sitting in the front of the bus. Rosa Parks was arrested and many blacks decided to start a boycott.

Because version 2 requires readers to infer the relationship between two separate ideas, it is likely to be more difficult to comprehend. Most readers have more trouble understanding and remembering inferred material, but poor readers seem to find this especially difficult (Marshall and Glock 1978–79).

Text "simplifications" based on readability formulas can and do lead to incoherence and increased text difficulty. In addition, such materials place a heavy burden on readers' prior knowledge because the text provides fewer clues for constructing meaning. Indeed, it may actually be necessary to lengthen text through elaboration, paraphrase, and example in order to enhance readability when topics are complex or less familiar.

The benefits gained from using readability formulas need to be measured carefully against the potential dangers of their use. The joint IRA/NCTE Readability Statement (see Figure 5.7) provides guidance in the appropriate use of readability formulas. Importantly, these formulas should not be used to rewrite or write reading materials, and teachers should be cautious of texts that have done so. In addition, users need to be particularly alert to possible mismatches between the reader and the text; readers from nontraditional backgrounds may be influenced by factors not measured in the formula.

Finally, it is a good idea to remember that the purpose of these formulas is to *predict* the difficulty of materials. Formulas do not actually evaluate the relative difficulty that any individual reader experiences during reading of a particular text. As "tests" of reading materials (Chall 1984), they fall short of providing comprehensive answers to our questions about text quality and appropriateness. We need other ways to evaluate these issues, and we consider alternatives in the next section.

The Cloze Procedure as a Readability Measure

As we have noted, the problem with most approaches to text readability estimates is that they do not evaluate how specific text features might actually influence reading performance for a given reader. As Zakaluk and Samuels (1988) note:

> Readability is not an inherent property of text, but the result of an interaction between a set of particular text characteristics and the information processing characteristics of individual readers (Kintsch and Vipond 1979). Text factors alone cannot determine readability; readers' prior knowledge and understanding influence comprehensibility and recall. (128)

Efforts to develop interactive readability measures that take the reader into account are not new, but are still in need of refinement. The cloze procedure is one such development.

Since its development by Taylor in 1953, the cloze procedure has endured as a method for evaluating text to determine whether students can "understand" it. Although there is substantial disagreement in the reading community about the utility of the cloze procedure as a measure of comprehension, it does provide a quick estimate of the relative difficulty of a particular text for a given student.

FIGURE 5.7
The IRA/NCTE Readability Statement

Background Information Bulletin on the Use of Readability Formulae

Textbook adoption committees and other educators face important decisions when deciding whether instructional materials are of appropriate difficulty for the students who will use them. Many factors enter into determining the readability of materials, including the syntactic complexity of sentences, density of concepts, abstractness of ideas, text organization, coherence and sequence of ideas, page format, length of type line, length of paragraphs, intricacy of punctuation, and the use of illustrations and color. In addition, research has shown that student interest in the subject-matter plays a significant role in determining the readability of materials.

Matching students with textbooks at appropriate levels of difficulty, therefore, is a complex and difficult task. Various pressures have forced publishers to use readability formulae to assure purchasers that their textbooks are properly "at grade level." Unfortunately, these formulae measure only average sentence and word length to determine the difficulty of passages. Although long words and sentences sometimes create problems of comprehension, they do not always do so. For example, the sentence "To be or not to be" is short, but it includes difficult concepts. This sentence, "The boy has a big, red apple for lunch and some cookies for a snack," is long but simple. Readability formulae would allow the first sentence but not the second.

Serious problems occur when publishers use readability formulae. Authors of materials who are required to write to "fit the formula" often produce choppy sentences full of short words. The language doesn't sound natural to the student, who is a sophisticated speaker and whose own language may be full of complex sentences and multisyllabic words. A second problem is that complex ideas, which depend on complex sentences, cannot be adequately written in the prose style dictated by readability formulae; consequently, learning of the content may be impaired.

Third, there is a real danger that makers of instructional materials will avoid using interesting and important works of literature because those works, which often contain long words and long sentences, don't "fit the formula." Not only the student's interest but also the beginnings of the student's literacy education are lost by such omissions.

Educators and publishers should use alternative approaches for measuring text difficulty. Procedures should include:

1. Teacher evaluation of proposed texts, based on the teacher's knowledge of their students' prior information and experiences, and their reading ability and interests.
2. Teacher observations of students using proposed texts in instructional settings, in order to evaluate the effectiveness of the material.
3. Checklists for evaluating the readability of the proposed materials, involving attention to such variables as student interests, text graphics, the number and difficulty of ideas and concepts in the material, the length of lines in the text, and the many other factors which contribute to relative difficulty of text material.

If readability formulae are used at all, they MUST be used in conjunction with procedures that look at all the parts of a text which affect comprehension. Readability formulae are simply insufficient as a guide to matching students with books and other instructional material. It is not what readability formulae measure that concerns us; it is what they do NOT measure.

Informed educational consumers must demand that authors and publishers select and develop well-written, literate text materials for students, and all who are involved in preparing and selecting text materials for the schools should cease the practice of depending on readability formulae alone to determine what is readable.

The IRA/NCTE Readability Statement (Bernice Cullinan and Sheila Fitzgerald, 1984). *The Reading Teacher*. Reprinted by permission of the International Reading Association.

Cloze passages are created by deleting every *n*th (usually fifth) word from a piece of text, leaving both the first and the last sentences intact (see Figure 5.8). Students are then asked to read the selection, supplying the deleted words. The rationale for this approach is that students must understand the text in order to supply the deleted words. Concerns about the task itself are more serious when cloze is used to make judgments about reading ability than when it is used to estimate the "fit" between text and reader.

To avoid any difference in judgment between scorers, students' responses are counted correct only when they have provided the exact replacements for deleted words. Verbatim scoring is required in order to use the criteria established by earlier studies (see below). Importantly, verbatim scoring produces relatively the same results as the more time-consuming scoring of synonyms (McKenna 1980).

The cloze score is expressed as a percentage when the number of correct responses is divided by the total number of possible items. The following criteria, developed after substantial testing by Bormuth (1968), are generally accepted, although other criteria have been offered as well (see Pikulski and Tobin 1982):

> Above 57 percent Independent Reading Level
> 44–57 percent Instructional Reading Level
> Below 44 percent Frustrational Reading Level

It is evident that the cloze procedure provides information about text difficulty in terms of the *individual student.* "Formulas predict readability; cloze pro-

FIGURE 5.8
Sample Cloze Passage

New Guinea

New Guinea is a large island in the Pacific Ocean. New Guinea people live _____ tribes. Each tribe is _____ different but all of _____ decorate their bodies. It _____ important to the people _____ do this. In some _____ there are people called "_____ men." They cover themselves _____ river mud and put _____ masks made of mud. _____ other tribes there are "_____ men" who wear big _____ made of human hair.

_____ people in New Guinea _____ live as people did _____ thousand years ago. They _____ use sticks to plant _____ corn and other crops. _____ grow most of their _____ food and make the _____ they need.

Once a _____ tribes from all over _____ island come together for _____ big fair. This fair _____ called a sing-sing. People _____ their best animals and _____ crops to show to _____ . The judges decide which _____ the winners.

Then there _____ dancing and singing. The _____ and singers paint their _____ . They wear fur on _____ ears and headdresses with _____ feathers.

Source: Lipson, M. Y. (1981). Third Grade Readers' Use of Prior Knowledge in Inferential Comprehension. Unpublished doctoral dissertation, The University of Michigan.

cedure and other similar comprehension methods measure readability" (Klare 1984, 707). For clinicians this can be extremely useful. However, classroom teachers will need to make judgments about text appropriateness in different ways. In the next sections, we describe some tools for assessing the likely influence of text at a more general level.

Evaluating Text Type and Comprehensibility

It should be quite clear by now that readability estimates alone are unlikely to provide all the information teachers need regarding the difficulty and appropriateness of textual materials for their students. First, not all text types pose the same difficulties, nor are all equally easy to read, even if the readability formula suggests otherwise. Second, the factors not accounted for by readability formulas require attention. In this section we suggest some strategies for evaluating narratives, expository texts, and basal anthologies to determine whether they are "comprehensible" or "understandable" versus "readable."

Narrative text.   Two major issues must be addressed in evaluating narratives for comprehensibility. First, the text must be examined to determine if it is well structured, conforming to conventional expectations for story structure and language use. Next, the narratives should be evaluated to see if they are interesting and enjoyable. The large class of "narratives" encompasses a wide range of genres, including realistic fiction, folktales, fables, fairy tales, myths, mystery, and science fiction (Flood and Lapp 1987). However, all narratives have something in common and that must be captured in an evaluation of them; they are meant to be interesting and enjoyable.

When the characters and their relationships are well developed and their goals easily identifiable, children read with greater interest and understanding (Sundbye 1987). Because well-formed narratives are easier to read than more ambiguous ones, they should be evaluated for the common components of narrative texts (see also Chapter 8). The following set of questions adapted from Calfee (1987) might help highlight these important, but more difficult to analyze, aspects of text.

- How does the story begin (setting, time)? How powerful, weak, or dull is the "lead," or beginning of the story?
- Who are the main characters? Who is telling the story (point of view)? How much do we learn about the characters?
- What is/are the main problems or conflicts to be solved or resolved? Is the conflict interpersonal, with the environment, or internal to the character?
- How does the content of the story/plot teach a lesson or help readers learn about people, reasoning, problem solving, etc.?
- How does the story end (resolution)? Is the ending satisfying, interesting, and/or powerful?

In particular, the evaluation should identify the degree to which narratives have strong plots with well-defined characters whose motives and goals are clear. When these aspects of a narrative are obscure, poor readers have much more difficulty comprehending them.

Expository text.   As it has become clear how strongly text features can influence text difficulty, a number of guidelines for evaluating informational texts have been generated. One of the most comprehensive of these was offered by J. Irwin and Davis (1980) and is reproduced in Figure 5.9.

An especially helpful feature of this checklist is that several dimensions of text difficulty are distinguished and evaluated separately. For example, learnability and understandability are evaluated separately. Consequently, teachers can evaluate the strengths and weaknesses of texts based on the ways they wish to use them.

Expository text can be evaluated for understandability alone. However, when students are to be held accountable for learning and remembering information from textbooks, teachers need to evaluate texts somewhat differently. In the event that students have trouble learning information from text, an assessment of the textbook features may provide useful information about how to help them learn and remember more. Alternatively, an assessment may reveal the fact that the text obscures important or new information, making learning difficult.

A helpful procedure is described by Armbruster (1984) who suggests selecting a topic from the text and generating several questions that you would expect students to be able to answer after reading about such a topic. Then, read the text and make sure that it is possible to answer these questions using *only* the textual information. When the text does not provide the information or makes it difficult to understand, teachers must be prepared to compensate for the text's inadequacies or elect not to use the text at all.

Careful examination of the text is absolutely essential. Checklists like the one in Figure 5.9 can provide important guidance for evaluating texts with specific student populations in mind. A text that is appropriate for some students may not be for others. Some texts will be used as supplements, while others will be used by all students as the primary source of information about a discipline. The readability checklist permits a consideration of different responses given different purposes and different students.

Reading anthologies.   Collections of stories, informational selections, poetry, and drama often provide students with the core of the material they will use in reading instruction. These anthologies are generally embedded in sets of related instructional material which will be considered in the upcoming sections. For some students, these anthologies provide the only reading material they encounter, and the quality of their reading experience is determined by the content of the anthology. For these reasons, they require careful evaluation.

Osborn (1989) suggests examining the student reader for both the content and the appearance of the material. Others suggest examining the content for the types of thematic organization (Searfoss and Readence 1989). Still others suggest evaluating the quality of the message, or the "ethos"

FIGURE 5.9
Readability Checklist

This checklist is designed to help you evaluate the readability of your classroom texts. It can best be used if you rate your text while you are thinking of a specific class. Be sure to compare the textbook to a fictional idea rather than to another text. Your goal is to find out what aspects of the text are less than ideal. Finally, consider supplementary workbooks as part of the textbook and rate them together. Have fun!

Rate the questions below using the following rating system.

5 = Excellent
4 = Good
3 = Adequate
2 = Poor
1 = Unacceptable
NA = Not applicable

Further comments may be written in the space provided.

Textbook title:
Publisher:
Copyright date:

Understandability

A. _____ Are the assumptions about students' vocabulary knowledge appropriate?

B. _____ Are the assumptions about students' prior knowledge of this content area appropriate?

C. _____ Are the assumptions about students' general experiential backgrounds appropriate?

D. _____ Does the teacher's manual provide the teacher with ways to develop and review the students' conceptual and experiential background?

E. _____ Are new concepts explicitly linked to the students' prior knowledge or to their experiential backgrounds?

F. _____ Does the text introduce abstract concepts by accompanying them with many concrete examples?

G. _____ Does the text introduce new concepts one at a time with a sufficient number of examples for each one?

H. _____ Are definitions understandable and at a lower level of abstraction than the concept being defined?

I. _____ Is the level of sentence complexity appropriate for the students?

J. _____ Are the main ideas of paragraphs, chapters, and subsections clearly stated?

K. _____ Does the text avoid irrelevant details?

L. _____ Does the text explicitly state important complex relationships (e.g. causality, conditionality, etc.) rather than always expecting the reader to infer them from the context?

M. _____ Does the teacher's manual provide lists of accessible resources containing alternative readings for the very poor or very advanced readers?

N. _____ Is the readability level appropriate (according to a readability formula)?

Learnability
Organization

A. _____ Is an introduction provided for each chapter?

B. _____ Is there a clear and simple organizational pattern relating the chapters to each other?

C. _____ Does each chapter have a clear, explicit, and simple organizational structure?

D. _____ Does the text include resources such as an index, glossary, and table of contents?

E. _____ Do questions and activities draw attention to the organizational pattern of the material (e.g. chronological, cause and effect, spatial, topical, etc.)?

F. _____ Do consumable materials interrelate well with the textbook?

FIGURE 5.9
Continued

Reinforcement

A. _____ Does the text provide opportunities for students to practice using new concepts?

B. _____ Are there summaries at appropriate intervals in the text?

C. _____ Does the text provide adequate iconic aids such as maps, graphs, illustrations, etc. to reinforce concepts?

D. _____ Are there adequate suggestions for usable supplementary activities?

E. _____ Do these activities provide for a broad range of ability levels?

F. _____ Are there literal questions provided for the students' self-review?

G. _____ Do some of the questions encourage the students to draw inferences?

H. _____ Are there discussion questions which encourage creative thinking?

I. _____ Are questions clearly worded?

Motivation

A. _____ Does the teacher's manual provide introductory activities that will capture students' interests?

B. _____ Are chapter titles and sub-headings concrete, meaningful, or interesting?

C. _____ Is the writing style of the text appealing to the students?

D. _____ Are the activities motivating? Will they make the student want to pursue the topic further?

E. _____ Does the book clearly show how the knowledge being learned might be used by the learner in the future?

F. _____ Does the text provide positive and motivating models for both sexes as well as for various racial, ethnic, and socioeconomic groups?

Readability Analysis

Weaknesses

1. On which items was the book rated lowest?

2. Did these items tend to fall in certain categories?

3. Summarize the weaknesses of this text.

4. What can you do in class to compensate for the weaknesses of this text?

Assets

1. On which items was the book rated the highest?

2. Did these items fall in certain categories?

3. Summarize the assets of this text.

4. What can you do in class to take advantage of the assets of this text?

From "Assessing Readability: The Checklist Approach" by J. W. Irwin and C. A. Davis. *Journal of Reading*, November 1980, pp. 124–130. International Reading Association. Reprinted by permission.

content (Schmidt, Caul, Byers, and Buchman 1984). Of course, we also need to be sure that the content is a reasonable fit with the goals and expectations of the school and its programs. In evaluating student anthologies, the following should be considered:

Balance of Content

What proportion of the reading selections is narrative?
What proportion of the reading selections is exposition?

What other genre or type of reading is included?

If page count rather than number of selections were used to estimate proportion, would this balance change?

Does there appear to be a wide range of genre represented?

Are different narrative types represented?

Are different types of exposition represented?

Is it apparent that reading purpose might vary with the content?

Characteristics of the Selections

Are the selections representative of real reading materials or have they been written for inclusion in the anthology?

Are high-quality children's books and stories included? Have the materials been included in unabridged versions?

Are intact (versus excerpted) materials the rule? Are the selections representative of all racial and ethnic groups?

Are selections free of bias and "socially inappropriate allusions"? (Osborn 1989, 291)

Physical Qualities of the Materials

Are the reading materials attractively presented?

Is comprehension enhanced (rather than diverted) by the illustrations?

Is the print clear, appropriate, and uncluttered?

Anthologies are, of course, only as good as the books and excerpts included. So, within these guidelines, we need to consider the qualities and characteristics of the narrative and expository selections themselves (see above). If students read *only* from an anthology, the impact of exposure and practice must be carefully considered. For example, some children may have difficulty learning to read exposition, because they have limited experience with this type of text. Finally, these same questions can and should be posed for alternative reading materials (little books and other supplementary material).

Evaluating Basal Lesson Design

In most basal readers, the content, method, and tasks are dictated by the instructional framework used to teach each selection. As we have noted, this framework is divided roughly into prereading, reading, and postreading activities. It is especially important for teachers to evaluate the lesson frameworks and the content of commercially prepared lessons because these materials have been shown to have a powerful influence on classroom reading instruction.

Previously in this chapter we described the issues surrounding basal reading materials. Guidelines for evaluating basal lesson plans developed from a variety of critical reviews are provided in Figure 5.10. A program that does not meet most of these criteria is suspect, and its utility in promoting independent, motivated reading is doubtful.

PORTION OF THE LESSON	Yes	No	Some
Prereading			
Evidence of process, content, attitude goals?			
Does instruction inform students about the type of text they are asked to read, its properties, the purposes for which it might be read, and the strategies for reading it?			
Are students encouraged to tap their own experiences, interests, and background knowledge?			
Are there provisions for individual differences?			
Are there suggestions for different grouping or reading options?			
During Reading			
Are there different levels of support for students?			
Do activities and questions help students achieve content, process, and attitude goals?			
Do instructional activities encourage students to become actively engaged in reading and to take responsibility for their reading?			
Is strategic reading modeled throughout?			
Are there suggestions for assessment during reading?			
Are students encouraged to engage in self-evaluation?			
Is the focus on teaching students how to comprehend or merely on checking whether a student has comprehended?			
Postreading			
Does the text ask students for personal response to the literature?			
Do questions focus on major text concepts and elements?			
Do activities and questions focus on theme concepts?			
Are students asked to make intertextual connections (to think about this text in terms of previously read material)?			
Does skill instruction clearly relate to the literature?			
Are reading and writing connections made visible?			
Is there an integrated model of reading and language arts?			
Assessment			
Are there multiple types of assessment provided?			
Is assessment clearly linked to the instruction provided?			
Does assessment promote an appropriate view of reading and writing?			
Are students, as well as teachers, involved in assessment?			

The use of these procedures can be time-consuming. As Wixson and Peters (1989) point out, however, "over time, these procedures are likely to become more a 'mind set' than a series of discrete steps" (p. 60). In any event, the degree to which detailed evaluations suggest the need for extensive modification provides one estimate of the quality of the commercial plans.

THE DIAGNOSTIC PORTFOLIO

The Cases of Marvin and Kyle

Both Marvin and Kyle live in middle-class communities with intact families. They both speak English as their primary and only language. Their parents are hard working and each has a mother who has been deeply involved in his education from the beginning. Each presently attends a school that is highly regarded by the community.

During the context evaluation, entries in a Diagnostic Portfolio are likely to be primarily narrative, anecdotal notes. Both work and text samples might, of course, provide useful information. Kyle's teacher, for example, regularly copies a page from students' texts to place in their portfolios, with a date, to show what is being read.

Marvin

For the past three years, Marvin was in a parochial school. Parents and teachers alike generally value a highly structured approach to teaching and learning. Teachers believe that all students should be able to do "grade level" work. Skills are emphasized and teachers generally believe that these "basics" must be acquired before students can move on to more challenging reading and writing tasks. Both phonics and handwriting work are assigned often in the early grades. In that school (like the one Marvin has transferred to) teachers are using a dated basal reading program.

Teachers generally believe that all students should be doing "grade level" work. This, coupled with a large teacher-student ratio, means that all students are placed in the same materials for instruction. The general instructional framework has involved whole group instruction, with oral reading of stories from the basal, and workbook and seatwork follow up. Students sit in rows and move around the room very little.

In Marvin's new school, the classroom environment is much more relaxed. Students' desks are arranged in clusters of four and there is considerable movement around the room during the day. The teacher has organized instruction using ability groups and Marvin has been placed in the lowest group (with two other students) who are using the 3–2 basal. Although Marvin's old school had no library and made no provisions for silent reading time during the day, in his new placement there is a well-stocked library and the teacher has a fifteen-minute, sustained, silent reading time two to three times a week.

Students do very little writing in either school. What writing does occur is almost entirely closed task activity. In both settings there are some writing assignments, handwriting practice, and spelling tests.

Marvin has never received special services. The private school he attended did not make provisions for special needs and his new school is just now exploring the options for Marvin.

Kyle

Kyle is in a multiage K–2 classroom. He has been with the same teacher, Ms. McIntyre, since kindergarten. His mother volunteers in this room frequently. The literacy environment in this classroom is a rich one. As students enter each morning, they write their names in the sign-in book and also indicate with a ✓ whether they want milk, hot lunch, or both. They sign up for snack and make choices of activities each morning by moving their name tags to various activities being offered. There is a consistent message to students that they will read and they will write. There are books of every sort. The library corner is attractive and accessible; teachers discuss books with children all the time, and book dialogue journals start early. There are also small, teacher-made booklets for special purposes—tiny alphabet books for the youngest students and small handwriting booklets for everyone who needs to practice. There are big books, there are books in the science area and there are counting books by the basket of nuts, etc. There are different shapes of paper and many types of writing utensils.

Ms. McIntyre believes in a child-centered classroom and expects that students will learn to read and write by reading and writing. Her job is to ask the right question at the right time or provide the right prompt when things get stalled. She can most often be found in corners and on the floor, having quiet, but intense, conversations with children about their work. Children interact with her and with each other continuously. The most frequent type of interactions involve discussions of on-going work, activities, or personal responses. The children talk about their out-of-school experiences during share time and write about them in journals. The classroom is organized as a reading-writing workshop (see Chapter 6). There are no formal groupings of any sort, although Ms. McIntyre might call a group together to work on an area of interest or difficulty and children frequently organize themselves into groups to accomplish tasks—plan a puppet show, work on blocks, read together, etc.

In addition, there are multiple types of formats for writing. The children in Ms. McIntyre's room write a great deal: in journals, in process writing folders, about their themes, to record their exploratory findings, and to communicate with each other. For reading, the youngest children read each other's writing and they read from a set of early reading materials (predictable texts, picture-label books, etc.). Later, as they progress, they read from commercial "easy-to-read" controlled vocabulary books. There are also many children's literature trade books and these are read by children as soon as they are able. By second grade, most children are choosing easy "chapter books." These texts may be self-selected, "negotiated" between teacher and child, or assigned. In early second grade, Kyle was reading from the easiest of the controlled vocabulary books (*Little Bear*, by Minarik, for example).

CHAPTER SUMMARY

The content and discussion in this chapter are relatively unusual. Reading and writing assessment has traditionally looked to the student as the source of academic difficulties. However, a growing body of research demonstrates that many contextual factors contribute to literacy and can enhance learning or lead to difficulty. In this chapter, we acknowledge this fact and examine ways to include contextual information in a comprehensive assessment of individual reading and writing difficulties.

We briefly discuss the difficulty of defining literacy, noting that standards of competent performance are determined by culture. Following this brief discussion, we devote a large segment to key factors of the instructional setting that influence student performance. For example, differing teacher beliefs result in the creation of diverse learning environments that can result in problems for students whose own expectations and beliefs may be at odds with the teachers'. Similarly, the differential treatment teachers frequently offer to members of different ability groups can have a negative effect on student performance and perceptions. More subtle differences, such as those related to patterns of verbal interaction or the congruence between regular and remedial programs, are also described as contextual factors that influence learning.

This chapter also addresses the role of instructional resources in reading and writing performance. Specifically, we consider text type and structure and how the nature of text can influence reading and learning. We also examine the features of text that influence comprehensibility—the aspects of text that can make reading easier or more difficult, and learning productive or more tedious. Next, we examine the role of commercial reading/language arts programs as a particular example of reading texts.

The final section of this chapter describes strategies and tools for assessing instructional settings and resources. A variety of strategies and tools are described for assessing the instructional setting including guiding questions and checklists. Strategies and tools for assessing instructional resources ranged from highly structured readability formulas to more informal checklists. In addition, guidelines are provided for evaluating texts (narrative, expository, and anthologies).

CHAPTER 6

Instructional Approaches and Tasks

INTRODUCTION

We hope it is obvious by now that instructional approaches and tasks are intimately linked to the factors discussed under setting and resources in Chapter 5. This close relationship is acknowledged in the introduction of all contextual factors in Chapter 5 (see Figure 5.1, p. 124) and by the fact that we conclude this chapter with a discussion of all dimensions of the reading context as we reexamine Step 3 in the assessment-instruction process. Although the division may be somewhat arbitrary, we hope that it facilitates a closer examination of the contextual factors that can influence reading and writing performance.

In this chapter we continue the evaluation of the instructional context by focusing on the role of instructional approaches and tasks in reading and writing performance. We then describe ways to evaluate instructional practices including curriculum, methods, assessment practices, and tasks.

UNDERSTANDING THE ROLE OF INSTRUCTIONAL APPROACHES IN READING AND WRITING PERFORMANCE

In this portion of the chapter, we summarize research on effective approaches to instruction. There are two ways in which this research can help in the assessment-instruction process. First, descriptions of effective instruction provide a framework for specifying the important attributes of the instructional context. Second, it is important to understand what characterizes good instruction to evaluate its contribution to the reading and writing process for individual students.

The question of what constitutes effective instruction has been of consuming interest to educators and researchers for decades. However, during the past thirty years there has been a great increase in efforts to specify the attributes of successful schools, classrooms, and teachers. The important lessons from recent research are that students need to be actively engaged in order to learn, and that initial learning requires teacher modeling and explanation. There is also support for the general conclusion that students need multiple opportunities to learn (Cooley and Leinhardt 1980). These findings suggest that the effects of instructional method are intimately connected to the classroom management practices and teacher expectations described previously in Chapter 5. Unfortunately, the evidence also suggests that teachers are spending too much time managing and assessing children by assigning them activities and asking questions, and too little time teaching (for example, Durkin 1978–79). Existing methods often encourage teachers to view instruction as placement in a program rather than a series of decisions to be made about what content should be taught or what methods might work best.

In the following sections, we describe instructional approach in terms of curriculum (what to teach), instructional method (how to teach), and assessment practices. However, it is important to emphasize that research on effective instruction in reading and writing is far from definitive. Indeed, the research in this area is so diverse that it is possible to find evidence supporting contradictory practices. Effective teaching can occur within the context of many programs and many materials, but no one set of materials nor any single program is likely to address the needs of every student. Our instructional guidelines are derived from two sources of information: our conclusions about the best theoretical perspectives on the reading and writing process, and our understanding of the best available research evidence regarding effective reading and writing practices.

Considering What to Teach

Reading and writing instruction should be as consistent as possible with our understanding of the reading and writing processes. Both instructional activities and student outcomes should emanate from a definition of skilled reading and writing (see Chapter 1). If instruction is to be effective, especially for students who are struggling with reading and writing, then it must be linked to personal "sense-making" for the students. In addition, of course, students must acquire sufficient skill and control to use reading and writing to meet this sense-making goal. To accomplish these ambitious, but critical, goals, students need opportunities to learn about *all* aspects of reading and writing in situations that provide for as much authentic application and practice as possible.

Effective teachers establish curricular goals and objectives for specific lessons and students. Students who are made aware of goals and objectives prior to reading and writing are more successful than those who do not have this information. Despite this fact, many teachers are not clear about their goals, and many schools do not have well-considered program outcomes.

Evaluating the instructional context requires consideration of both *overall curricular goals* and *specific instructional objectives*. The fundamental questions to be asked regarding goals and objectives are: What is being taught? and Is the student likely to be a better reader and/or writer because she or he has achieved this goal or objective? The answers to these questions are explored for general curricular goals in the next section and for instructional objectives in the following section.

Curricular Goals

Reading and writing instruction in the United States has too often focused on easily measured subskills. Little attention has been directed toward the acquisition of important overall ability (Brown, Collins, and Duguid 1989). In a well designed language arts program, mastering the parts is not the end in itself, but a means to an end, and there is a balance between practice of the parts and practice of the whole (R. C. Anderson et al. 1985). Recent efforts to develop state and national content standards in English language arts represent attempts to translate current theory and research into student outcomes (Pearson 1993). These outcomes or standards are intended as guides for those who must develop classroom or district curriculum and instruction.

For the purposes of this text, we have distilled current standards and outcomes into the goal of developing *strategic, motivated, reflective readers and writers*. Strategic readers and writers are able to recruit their extensive knowledge of a wide range of skills for reading and writing. In addition, they can use this knowledge and skill flexibly, adapting their approach for different purposes, tasks, and materials. For example, strategic readers and writers recognize that recreational reading of light fiction does not require the same intentions or skills as assigned reading of a physics text. Not only do they recognize this, they act accordingly, making adjustments before, during, and after reading.

Motivated readers and writers are those who not only *can* read and write, but *choose* to do so for a variety of recreational and functional purposes. They generally understand the various purposes for reading and writing and are reasonably skilled at using reading and writing to meet their needs. Not all motivated readers and writers do enjoy and select the same types of reading and writing activities, but they do have one thing in common—they read and write voluntarily.

Reflective readers and writers are those who develop and use their own standards to evaluate their reading and writing and the meanings they construct. They set their own personal goals for developing reading and writing abilities and for learning from reading and writing. They are aware of both their efforts and their accomplishments.

In developing motivated, strategic, reflective readers and writers, much of the traditional content of reading and writing instruction will continue to be important, but students and teachers must not focus on the acquisition of knowledge and skill as an end in itself. Instead, the goal is for students to use their knowledge and skill as they read and write widely. The total reading and writing curriculum across ages and grades must attend to the interplay among these outcomes. A program that does not balance these primary aspects of reading and writing may produce students who can, but will not, read or write, or students who enjoy books but cannot read them independently. Both breadth and depth are desirable in the developmental reading and writing program, but the relative attention to different aspects of the curriculum may vary across the developmental continuum.

Just as the emphasis on different outcomes may vary across the developmental continuum, it will also vary for individuals who are experiencing reading and writing difficulty. Some students will need to acquire knowledge about reading and writing; others will need ample opportunity to apply and adapt their reading and writing skills; still others will need to develop an increased appreciation for the functional value of reading and writing practice. The issue here is a critical one: *both the content and the method of reading and writing instruction are factors in student achievement.*

Instructional Objectives

General curricular goals provide guidance and direction for the identification of more specific instructional objectives used for particular lessons and students at particular levels of development. It is important to understand that instructional objectives are not synonymous with activities (for example, journal writing, dictating stories). When objectives are equated with activity completion, both teachers and students are likely to misconstrue the purpose of instruction. In addition, successful instruction is likely to be measured in terms of the number or levels of activities completed, rather than the extent to which knowledge and/or competence have increased. This is an extremely important distinction that must be understood, both to evaluate and plan effective instructional programs.

The goal of developing strategic, motivated, reflective readers can be translated into three types of instructional objectives that relate to the outcomes required for students to become expert readers and writers (Duffy and Roehler 1989). Sound instruction must contain provisions for each of the following types of objectives:

1. *Attitude objectives:* Students need to develop the motivation and desire to read and write for a variety of personal purposes.
2. *Content objectives:* Students need to be able to comprehend and learn the content of texts and to create meaningful texts.
3. *Process objectives:* Students need to understand how the reading and writing process works and acquire skill in using this knowledge.

Until recently, the most neglected area in reading and writing instruction is that reflected by attitude objectives. Traditionally, many teachers have asserted that they want students to be motivated to read and write. Few instructional programs, however, have provided directly for the development of attitude objectives and fewer still have included assessments of attitude. Just as students vary in their knowledge and skill, they may differ in their attitudes and motivation toward reading and writing. Some students find reading and writing gratifying and, therefore, read and write widely outside of school. Others do very little reading and writing and may come to view skilled reading and writing as tedious activities required to complete a number of discrete tasks.

Attitude objectives are important, legitimate concerns for all teachers. The relations between positive attitudes and achievement suggest that students' expectations and values have a significant effect on both their effort and achievement (Covington and Omelich 1979; see Wigfield and Asher 1984 for a complete review). In order to become effective readers and writers, students must demonstrate both *skill and will* (Paris, Lipson, and Wixson 1983). If they are not willing to engage in independent reading and writing, students will not have sufficient opportunity to practice acquired skills, nor will they develop the facility to read and write flexibly for their own purposes.

If attitude outcomes have been neglected in the past, the same cannot be said about content outcomes. Many reading/literature lessons have traditionally focused almost exclusively on methods and techniques for helping students understand the content of specific texts. Teachers should not abandon their efforts to help students comprehend during reading. However, all reading does not entail studying and a detailed understanding of the content of text, and students should not be led to believe that it does. Nor should instruction aimed at an understanding of specific content be divorced from instruction in the processes and values associated with a particular type of reading.

Instruction designed only to help students understand specific stories or textbooks aids comprehension but does little to develop comprehension ability (Johnston 1985a; Paris, Wixson, and Palincsar 1986). Effective reading instruction must achieve the delicate balance between focusing on content and developing the ability to process different types of materials for different purposes. Students must acquire the skills and strategies required to comprehend and learn *on their own*, and teachers need to think carefully about how they address these important process objectives. Similarly, effective writing instruction must balance attention to the content of writing with the skills and processes essential for effective writing in a variety of situations.

What we want to avoid is instruction emphasizing content objectives at the expense of process objectives or vice versa. What is needed in both reading and writing instruction is a balance among attitude, content, and process objectives.

Considering How to Teach

Once important goals and objectives have been determined, attention can be directed to the best ways to help students meet these goals. This is the focus in the following sections, in which we move from *what* is being taught to the methods of instruction or *how* it is taught. This section is organized according to the practices associated with achieving the general curricular goals of developing motivated, strategic, reflective readers and writers.

Promoting Motivated Reading and Writing

Students should seek to gain the intended knowledge and skill benefits from instructional activities. They should also be motivated to set goals and use strategies that are appropriate for doing so. Students' motives, goals, and strategies developed in response to classroom activities will depend both on the nature of the activities themselves and on how the teacher presents these activities to the students.

Reading and writing achievement are powerfully influenced by motivation and attitudes (see Chapter 2). Good and Brophy (1987) concluded that most current research supports an expectancy x value theory of motivation. According to this theory, the effort that people will be willing to expend on an activity is a product of the degree to which they expect to be able to perform the task successfully if they apply themselves and the degree to which they value the rewards that successful performance will bring. This theory of motivation implies that teachers need both to help their students appreciate the value of school activities and to make certain that their students can achieve success in their school activities if they apply reasonable effort.

It is important that teachers use strategies designed to motivate their students to learn from academic activities. But Good and Brophy (1987) argue that certain preconditions must be in place in order for motivational strategies to be effective: (1) the teacher must create a classroom atmosphere that is supportive of students' learning efforts; (2) students must be given tasks of an appropriate difficulty level; (3) activities must be selected with worthwhile academic objectives in mind; and (4) the teacher must show moderation and variation in using motivational strategies. Once these preconditions are established, there are several different types of motivational strategies that teachers use to promote students' expectations for success and value of learning.

Motivational strategies. In order to meet challenging goals, students must possess confidence and be willing to take risks; they must *expect* to be successful. Good and Brophy (1987) describe strategies that teachers might use to promote students' expectations for success. Not surprisingly, the most basic strategy here involves assigning tasks on which students can succeed, if they apply reasonable effort, and instructing them thoroughly so that they know what to do and how to do it. Other strategies include helping students to: set appropriate goals; commit themselves to these goals; use appropriate standards for appraising their levels of success; recognize the linkages between effort and outcome through modeling, socialization, and feedback; and view effort as an investment rather than a risk.

Although most teachers are aware of these strategies, they take considerable thought and often additional effort to apply. Good and Brophy (1987) point out that the class as a whole may respond to one level of motivational support, but students who have become discouraged to the point that they give up at the first sign of difficulty or frustration need more intensive and individualized encouragement. Some students will require arranging instruction that virtually guarantees success. Such strategies are essential because students' expectations for success are often related to their judgments about why they succeed or fail, which affect their willingness to try difficult tasks. These judgments are called *attributions.*

Attributing success to ability and failure to lack of effort means the person generally will expect to succeed and will be willing to try more challenging tasks. In contrast, attributing success to a variable factor (like task ease) and failure to lack of ability means that the person will not expect to succeed. When the person fails, he or she will give up quickly since extra effort will not overcome the person's perceived lack of ability (Wigfield and Asher 1984, p. 425).

As a result, many less-able students may also benefit from "attribution retraining" (for example, Fowler and Peterson 1981). In this case, instruction is aimed at teaching students to: concentrate on the task at hand rather than worry about failure; cope by retracing their steps to find their mistakes or analyzing the problem to find an alternative approach; and attribute their failures to insufficient effort, lack of information, or reliance on ineffective strategies rather than lack of ability. It is important to understand that expectancy affects motivation. In addition, the degree of objective success that students achieve is less central than how they view their performance—that is, what they see as possible for them to achieve with reasonable effort, whether they define this achievement as successful or not, and whether they attribute their performance to controllable factors such as effective strategy usage or to uncontrollable factors such as ability.

Expectancy is not the only factor that influences student motivation. Remember that students must also value the activity. Good and Brophy (1987) suggest different strategies to address the *value* aspects of student motivation. These strategies emphasize motivation for *learning*, not merely performing. Much traditional instruction attempts to motivate students to learn in order to meet some performance standard (for example, to take a test).

> If students are motivated solely by grades or other extrinsic reward and punishment considerations, they are likely to adopt goals and associated strategies that concentrate on meeting minimum requirements that will entitle them to what they see as acceptable reward levels. They will do what they must in order to prepare for tests and then forget most of what they have learned (Good and Brophy 1987, 308).

Strategies focused on learning, on the other hand, should motivate students to study and learn because they find the information or skill interesting, meaningful, or worthwhile. Although the affective, emotional aspects of this approach to motivation are important, Good and Brophy (1987) argue that these will be insufficient for students in academic settings. Students should be focused on sense-making and importance, not just enjoyment. This, they argue, will result in effective and motivated student effort. Teachers, especially teachers of older students, should attend to these distinctions.

The three general features of classroom learning environments that support the development of student motivation to learn are: modeling of the thinking and actions associated with motivation to learn; communicating expectations and attributions implying motivation to learn in the student; and creating a supportive environment for learning by minimizing the role of factors that produce performance anxiety. In addition, there are a number of other strategies for inducing student motivation to learn that are more situation-specific. For readers and writers who are struggling in school settings, the issue of motivation and the importance of communicating the value of becoming literate cannot be overemphasized. Effective teaching requires the acquisition of a sophisticated repertoire of ways to focus students on learning.

Voluntary reading and writing.   The cost of failing to address motivational issues is high. Too often, repeated experiences with failure or school experiences that do not make the value of reading and writing evident result in students with poor attitudes and limited willingness to attempt reading and writing tasks. Students with strong negative feelings about reading and writing are not likely to read or write voluntarily. These attitudes, in turn, influence ability.

There is a strong association between voluntary reading and writing and general reading and writing achievement (Greaney 1980; Morrow 1983). For example, children who demonstrate voluntary interest in books are rated significantly higher by teachers on school performance than are children with low interest in books (Morrow 1986). They also score significantly higher on standardized tests and in work habits, social and emotional maturity, and language arts skills. Other evidence suggests that time spent in voluntary reading of books is the best predictor of reading achievement gains between second and fifth grade (Anderson, Wilson, and Fielding 1988). Finally, research suggests that independent reading is one of the major determinants of vocabulary growth, especially during and after third grade (Nagy and Anderson 1984).

It is clear that most reluctant learners will need experiences that go beyond the instruction provided in commercial programs if they are to become independent, voluntary readers and writers. Morrow (1983, 1986) has conducted a series of studies that examined instructional practice and its influence on students' motivation to read and its involvement in voluntary reading. Specifically, she has examined the influence of classroom environment, like library corners, and literary activities, like book talks, on students' selection of reading as a voluntary activity. The following practices appear to influence students' voluntary reading (Morrow, 1989):

1. *Print rich environment.* It appears that children need attractive and accessible library corners that provide a range of materials (books of all types, magazines, and so on).
2. *Active student involvement with reading.* Morrow suggests various teacher initiated activities and projects related to books. However, she also acknowledges the importance of ample practice time through recreational reading periods.
3. *Adult-child interactions focused on literature.* Teachers must invite children to interact with these materials by reading aloud and telling stories.

These practices are not new, but their importance has been reaffirmed. Teachers need to model their love of reading and writing, but they also need to consider the nature of their planned instructional activities. "If through a teacher's presentations, children learn to associate reading only with repetitive skill drills and testing, they will probably not be encouraged to reach for books on their own" (Morrow 1989, p 220). Reading and writing educators need to recognize how self-regard and motivation are influenced by instructional practices in order to avoid the negative consequences of repeated failure.

Promoting Strategic Reading and Writing

Good teaching must include instruction in how to read, remember, and think about text independently. This means both that students acquire reading and writing skill and that they are able to transfer this knowledge to a variety of reading and writing situations and tasks. The problem of how to maintain and transfer skilled and strategic behavior has become a major issue facing educators today. The traditional practice of teaching isolated component parts of reading and writing has proven less effective in improving reading and writing ability on transfer tests and on subsequent achievement tests than instruction that is embedded in more meaningful events.

Current research suggests that it is possible to teach students how to be strategic readers and writers. This research suggests a need for instruction based on the principle of gradually releasing responsibility for learning from the teacher to the student (Pearson and Gallagher 1983). In the initial stages of acquisition, the teacher has primary responsibility for students' learning. In the final stages of learning, the student has the primary responsibility for practicing and applying what has been learned. What comes between is a form of guided instruction that represents joint responsibility between the teacher and the student. These features are discussed at some length below.

During the acquisition phase of the instructional process, the teacher has the primary responsibility for learning. The attributes of teacher-based instruction that have demonstrably improved reading and writing performance include: clear teacher presentations (Roehler and Duffy 1984); good direct explanation (Paris, Cross, and Lipson 1984); modeling and guided practice (Palincsar and Brown 1984); high levels of active student involvement (Palincsar and Brown 1984); and providing for review and feedback (Adams, Carnine, and Gersten 1982). Using these techniques, researchers have demonstrated improvement in students' decoding abilities (for example, Cunningham 1990); vocabulary knowledge (for example, Pany and Jenkins 1978); and comprehension ability (for example, Paris, Cross, and Lipson 1984).

Although the relative contributions of these separate teaching practices have yet to be determined, it appears that clear, specific, teacher explanation is particularly important to students' improvement. Clear explanations provide students with knowledge about how to accomplish various reading and writing tasks. However, knowledge about *how* to perform a skill or strategy does not ensure that students will use it.

To increase the likelihood that students will use their skills, teachers must provide students with information about when and why to use the skills they are learning. Research suggests that this is a critical factor in students' ability to transfer the skills they have learned to other reading and writing contexts (Cunningham 1990; Paris, Lipson, and Wixson 1983). Although it may seem obvious to teachers, students frequently do not understand how skills acquisition is related to real-life reading and writing. Effective reading and writing instruction must also involve feedback on the utility of the action (Lipson and Wickizer 1989) and instruction in why, when, and where such activities should be applied (Paris, Cross, and Lipson 1984).

As the student becomes more skilled, the responsibility for continued learning becomes shared between teacher and student. A study by Gordon and Pearson (1983) can be used to illustrate how this gradual release of responsibility might actually be accomplished. In this study, learning to make inferences was conceived as involving four tasks: (a) posing a question, (b) answering it, (c) finding evidence, and (d) giving the reasoning for how to get from the evidence to the answer. Release was accomplished through four stages of instruction. In stage 1, the teacher modeled all four tasks; in stage 2, the teacher did (a) and (b) while the students did (c) and (d); in stage 3, the teacher took responsibility for (a) and (c) and the students did (b) and (d); and in stage 4, the students did all but (a).

Once students have acquired sufficient knowledge and skill to work independently, the primary responsibility for learning is transferred to the student. Effective instruction provides students with many opportunities to advance their learning by using their literacy skills in productive and authentic ways. The effects of practicing reading and writing in holistic settings have become increasingly evident in recent years. Beginners can enjoy intensified gains when provided with increased opportunities to read and write large numbers of texts (Pinnell 1985a); seven- and eight-year-olds enjoy significant increases in meaning vocabulary when they listen to good books (Elley 1989); individuals at many ages recognize more words after reading them in continuous text (Herman, Anderson, Pearson, and Nagy 1987; Nagy, Herman, and Anderson 1985); and both comprehension and vocabulary have been improved when students' recreational reading is increased (Anderson, Wilson, and Fielding 1988).

We will return to these issues in later chapters, but the point should be made, since the evidence is quite impressive: students need to read and write to become good readers and writers. Simple workbook completion activities do not provide enough substantial practice and may actually contribute to students' lack of motivation for reading and writing authentic texts outside of school. The following sections discuss three notable characteristics of the gradual release model of learning and instruction: scaffolding; social interaction or dialogue; and level of instruction.

Scaffolding.   The hallmark of instruction involving the gradual release of responsibility is *scaffolding*. Scaffolding has been described as instructional assistance that enables someone to solve a problem, carry out a task, or achieve a goal that he or she could not accomplish without support (Wood, Bruner, and Ross 1976). The metaphor of a scaffold calls attention to a support system that is both temporary and adjustable. Teachers should expect students to need their support in moving from one level of competence to the next so that, in time, they will be able to apply problem-solving strategies independently and wisely (Paris, Wixson, and Palincsar 1986).

Scaffolded instruction begins with selecting a learning task for the purpose of teaching a skill that is emerging in the learner's repertoire but is not yet fully developed. The task is evaluated to determine the difficulty it is likely to pose for the learner. This is done to facilitate decision making about how to make the task simpler and the learner more successful. Modeling, questioning, and explanation are used during instruction to make the task explicit and to represent appropriate approaches to the task (Palincsar 1986).

There is considerable emphasis on student participation in the learning activity for the purposes of providing opportunities to use the skills being instructed and evaluating student performance. This evaluation is conducted to determine the level of difficulty of the task, make appropriate adjustments in the level of instructional support, and provide the learner with information regarding his or her performance. Finally, the aim of scaffolded instruction is generalization to less-structured contexts. Such generalization is facilitated by the gradual withdrawal of the scaffold as the learner demonstrates increased competence (Palincsar 1986).

Dialogue.   Instruction in the gradual release model is also characterized by the ongoing interplay between teacher and learner in the joint completion of a task. These dialogues are the means by which support is provided and adjusted. When children engage in subsequent problem solving, they display the types of behaviors that are characteristic of dialogues they had when they were collaborating with a more expert individual. Palincsar (1986) suggests the following characteristics of dialogue:

1. The teacher supports students' contributions to the dialogue, eliciting and supporting responses at the idea level (versus asking for one-word, discrete responses).
2. The teacher uses student ideas and links those ideas to new information.
3. The dialogue has a focus and direction.
4. The teacher makes use of explicit instruction.
5. The teacher uses feedback constructively to help students improve their responses.

The relationship between teacher and learner in this supportive dialogue is to be contrasted with that observed when students are left to discover or invent strategies independently, or when students are passive observers who receive demonstration and are "talked at" regarding strategy use. When this type of dialogue occurs with initial instruction, it "enables learners to participate in strategic activity even though they may not fully understand the activity and would most certainly not be able to exercise the strategy independently" (Palincsar 1986, 75). The available evidence suggests that teachers often conduct monologues, not dialogues, and rarely use student ideas as the basis for discussion and teaching. Teachers are taught to "tell" and are rarely provided with instruction or guidance in conducting effective dialogues with students.

Level of instruction.   A gradual release model of learning and instruction draws heavily on Vygotsky's (1978) view of the relationship between instruction and cognitive development. According to Vygotsky, instruction is best when it proceeds ahead of development and arouses those functions that are in the process of maturing. In other words, instruction leads development. Cognitive skills that are emerging but not yet fully mature are considered to lie within the zone of proximal or potential development. This zone is defined as: the distance between the actual developmental level as determined by independent problem solving and the level of potential development as determined through problem solving under adult guidance or in collaboration with more capable peers. (Vygotsky 1978, 76). This means that instruction is likely to be most effective when teachers identify the zone or levels at which students can perform with some assistance and guide them to the point of independent learning.

A familiar example offered by Au and Kawakami (1986) may be helpful in describing what instruction within the zone of proximal development might look like. They observed skilled teachers conducting reading comprehension lessons and noted that these teachers consistently posed questions they knew their students were likely to have difficulty answering. This, the authors argue, demonstrates how the students were being challenged to perform at higher levels than they were able to achieve independently. They also observed that the teachers responded to incorrect answers by helping the students work out a better answer, rather than just giving them a correct response. Students were given the opportunity to carry out rather advanced comprehension skills, if only with considerable assistance.

The appropriate level of instruction may also be influenced by other factors, such as the difficulty of the materials in which students are placed. Many poor readers are placed in materials that are so difficult that they cannot identify even 80 percent of the words correctly (Juel 1988). Experts argue that an astonishing 50 percent (Guthrie 1980) to 60 percent (Ekwall and Shanker 1985) of all elementary grade students are working with inappropriate instructional materials for reading. This and other factors influencing the appropriateness of the level of instruction are discussed in greater detail in Chapter 5.

Promoting Reflective Reading and Writing
Without reflectivity, neither knowledge nor the skills for applying knowledge are likely to be used intelligently (see Onosko and Newmann 1994). Reflectivity encompasses a variety of traits including: a persistent desire to understand

the reasons for one's own and others' thoughts and actions; a tendency to take time to think problems through for oneself, rather than acting impulsively or automatically accepting the views of others; a flexibility to entertain alternative and original thoughts and actions; and a habit of examining one's own thinking processes and establishing personal goals. It is important that teachers design instruction explicitly to help students become reflective readers and writers.

Complex/authentic problems.   Although we discuss tasks in greater detail in an upcoming section, it is worth noting here the importance of employing authentic, complex problems and projects in promoting reflective readers and writers. Newmann and Wehlage (1993) use the word authentic to distinguish between instruction and achievement that are significant and meaningful rather than trivial and useless. They use three criteria to define authenticity more precisely: "(1) students construct meaning and knowledge; (2) students use disciplined inquiry to construct meaning; and (3) students aim their work toward production of discourse, products, and performances that have value or meaning beyond success in school" (p. 8).

Newmann and Wehlage (1993) caution that even activities that place students in the role of a more active, cooperative learner and that seem to respect student voices can be implemented in ways that do not produce authentic achievement. The challenge is not simply to adopt innovative teaching practices, but to work against two persistent problems that make conventional schooling inauthentic: the work students do often does not allow them to use their minds well; and the work frequently has no intrinsic meaning or value to students beyond achieving success in school.

As a result of their work with Project Zero, Walters, Seidel, and Gardner (1994) conclude that authentic, complex problems or projects embody many distinct dimensions that can only be sorted out through careful reflection. In contrast, simple problems or projects usually do not generate the same kind of reflection. Students generally refer to the accuracy and neatness of their work when asked about their performance on worksheets consisting of exercises for practicing a specific skill. In contrast, they mention a variety of dimensions such as their vision, planning decisions, compromises they had to make, and so forth when reflecting on their completion of authentic, complex tasks and projects. In short, we cannot expect students to become reflective readers and writers if we do not provide them with experiences worthy of reflection.

Self-assessment.   Central to reflectivity is the ability to monitor and evaluate one's own literate activity (Johnston 1992). A common feature of students having trouble with reading and writing is their failure to monitor and self-correct. They look to others to see if they are "doing it right." They do not feel able to evaluate their own performance.

Johnston (1992) describes a variety of practices that encourage self-evaluation. For example, it is important to recognize self-evaluation when it occurs. When a student becomes aware of a problem, we can say, "I like the way you noticed that yourself. That is a sign of a good writer/reader." The information conveyed is that self-evaluation is important to becoming a better reader/writer, not that they have performed as you wanted.

Other practices that promote self-evaluation include encouraging students to give it a try, anticipate, and check their predictions and attempts. It can also be encouraged by reflective responses that turn questions back to learners. For example, a question such as "How could we check whether that is correct?" might provide assistance since it opens up one or more strategies for self-checking. The student's response is also likely to give us information about the strategies the learner has available.

According to Tierney, Carter, and Desai (1991), students need opportunities to share their work with their peers. Reflecting on their work with other students becomes a vehicle for students to discover important ideas, explore new concepts, think in new ways, and refine their methods of communicating to different audiences. Ongoing charts can be created as a way to record student thoughts about reading and writing. Samples of student work can be used as examples of a certain feature that students think is important to emphasize. Charts developed from student input become the beginning of criteria for quality work that students recognize.

Once students have a variety of samples and have generated ideas about criteria for reading and writing, they are ready to start to apply their criteria to their own reading and writing. Student comments will not be as sophisticated as teachers' comments and may focus on features of reading and writing that are not that important when they are just beginning to develop the tools necessary to think critically about themselves as readers and writers. As they become increasingly responsible for judging the quality of their own work, they are learning to take control of their own reading and writing.

Self-evaluation and reflectiveness can also be overtly valued by making portfolios a central part of classroom evaluation. A portfolio can include entries selected by the students to represent their growth. Each entry can have attached to it statements as to why the work is important, what has been learned, and future goals. This gives the teacher information about what the student values and requires the student to be reflective.

Walters et al. (1994) observe that as students work on projects and collect artifacts for their portfolios, they can also be engaged in a continuing discussion of standards of quality. How does a student come to understand that one essay is more articulate than another? How do these judgments go beyond the issues of simple accuracy in spelling and grammar? Even very young students are quite capable of setting standards for themselves (see Higgins, Harris, and Kuehn 1994). Setting standards is an important ability in continuing to learn outside of school. We need to spend a greater portion of our time as teachers helping students set their own standards instead of always establishing those standards independently of the students and in advance of their experience.

For students to become reflective self-evaluators, they must feel themselves to be able knowers and evaluators. Students need to have confidence, self-respect, and to value their own knowledge to be self-critical and develop reflective commitment to their reading and writing. These conditions are most likely to occur when students feel that they have something to contribute. Students are made to feel this way when people actually listen to them and communicate that their ideas are not less valuable than those of the teacher or others.

The way we talk as teachers can make us appear to have all the knowledge and be all-powerful arbiters of quality, or it can suggest that the students are knowledgeable and able to judge their own reading and writing. Students' thoughts about reading and writing need to be accepted. When we begin to understand what our students think, we can offer appropriate guidance that promotes individual progress.

Considering Assessment Practices

This entire book deals with assessment in one way or another. This section focuses specifically on assessment practices as a feature of instructional contexts that influence reading and writing performance. Within this context, we need to be concerned with at least two dimensions of classroom assessment—those assessments required for external accountability purposes and those assessments selected and/or created by the teacher for evaluation and to inform instruction. We have grouped the types of assessments that can be used for these two purposes into two large categories—tests and alternative, authentic assessments.

Tests and Testing

Resnick and Resnick (1992) indicate that tests are the heritage of what they refer to as the "routinized" skill goals derived from the psychological theories of the first part of the twentieth century. Two key assumptions of standardized testing technology, referred to as decomposability and decontextualization, are compatible with this routinized curriculum. They are, however, incompatible with thinking goals for education and with what we know today about the way people learn.

Decomposability. According to the Resnicks (1992), built into the decomposability assumption is a metaphor that likens thought to a simple machine. One can build a machine by separately constructing each of the parts. When the parts are put together, if the design is good, the machine will run. This view suggests that in teaching mental competencies such as reading and writing, it will suffice to teach each of the components. It supports a notion of teaching and testing separate skills, reserving their composition into a complex performance for some indeterminate later time. This assumption has been seriously challenged by recent research which recognizes that complicated skills and competencies owe their complexity not just to the number of components they engage, but also to interactions among the components and strategies for calling upon them.

Complex competencies such as reading and writing cannot be defined just by listing all of their components. Efforts to assess reading and writing by identifying separate components of those abilities and testing them independently may interfere with effectively teaching such abilities. Assessing separate components encourages instructional activities in which isolated components are practiced. Since the components do not "add up to" reading and writing, students who practice only the components are unlikely to learn to do real reading and writing.

Decontextualization.   Closely linked to the decomposability assumption, decontextualization asserts that each component of a complex skill is fixed, and that it will take the same form no matter where it is used. This assumption suggests that if students know how to get a main idea, for example, they know how to do so under all conditions of text type, prior knowledge, and so forth. However, recent theory and research suggest that we can no longer teach a skill component in one setting and expect it to be applied automatically in another. We cannot validly assess a competence in a context very different from the context in which it is practiced or used.

There is widespread agreement among educators, researchers, and policy-makers that most standardized tests currently used in American schools do not tap many of the skills and abilities that students need to develop to be successful in later life and schooling (Darling-Hammond, Ancess, and Falk 1995). Consistent with the decomposability and decontextualization assumptions, the most frequent criticism of these tests is that they do not evaluate "higher-order skills" and students' abilities to perform "real world" tasks.

Although this discussion has focused primarily on standardized tests, it is worth noting that Chittenden (1991) defines tests as any situation in which the student is asked a question to which the questioner or examiner knows the answer. He also notes that although a lot of this type of interrogation goes on in our schools, whether under the guise of classroom discussion or standardized tests, it is not characteristic of normal everyday conversations and interactions. Tests, then, can be anything from standardized measures, to basal tests, to teacher-made examinations and questioning.

Alternative Assessments

In response to the concerns about standardized tests, many educators and researchers are developing alternative assessment practices that look directly at students' work as a means of evaluating student performance. These alternative assessments are referred to by a variety of labels, including authentic and performance assessments, and take a variety of forms including portfolios, observation, and performance tasks.

According to Wiggins (1989), alternative assessments have four common characteristics. First, they are designed to be truly representative of performance in the field. For example, students actually do writing—for real audiences—rather than taking spelling tests or answering questions about writing. The tasks are contextualized, complex, intellectual challenges involving the student's own research or use of knowledge. In addition, they allow student learning styles, aptitudes, and interests to serve as a source for developing competence and for the identification of strengths that may have been hidden previously.

Second, alternative assessments seek to evaluate "essentials" of performance against well articulated criteria. These are openly expressed to students and others in the learning community, rather than kept "secure" in the tradition of tests. Learning and performance are both supported when teachers and students know ahead of time what an assessment will evaluate. Performance-based criteria guide teaching, learning, and evaluation in ways that place teachers in the role of coach and students in the role of performers.

Third, alternative assessments help students develop the capacity to evaluate their own work against public standards. These assessments promote students' ability to revise, modify, and redirect their energies, taking initiative to assess their own progress. Finally, alternative assessments involve students in presenting their work publicly. This deepens their learning by requiring that they reflect on what they know and frame it in a way that others can also understand; it ensures that their apparent mastery of an idea, concept, or topic is genuine.

Impact on Teaching and Learning

Both tests and alternative assessments often have some accountability function whether to audiences external to the classroom or to the teacher and/or students themselves. It is the accountability functions of tests and assessments that result in the greatest impact on teaching and learning. Regardless of the form or frequency of assessment, to the extent that performances of students and classrooms are made visible and have consequences ranging from prestige and shame to merit increases and management constraints, the nature of assessments tends to shape teachers' practice and therefore student learning and performance. We agree with the Resnicks (1992) when they conclude:

> *You get what you assess*—teachers will teach to the assessment if the tests matter in their own or their students' lives; and
> *You do not get what you do not assess*—what is not integral to classroom assessment tends to disappear from classrooms in time.

Given these principles, the type and focus of assessment can make a big difference. For example, because most traditional standardized tests focus on isolated skills rather than on complex performances, they can and do drive instruction in the wrong direction. When tests are used as arbiters of many school decisions about placement, graduation, advancement, etc., they often exert great influence on what is taught, leading to a narrowed curriculum. Teachers are pressured to teach what is tested and to teach these things in the particular forms and formats used on the tests. This leads to an overemphasis on superficial content coverage and drill on discrete skills at the expense of in-depth projects and other complex tasks. It also leads to classwork in which students spend their time on test-like tasks, to shallow learning, and to misperceptions of students' abilities.

According to Darling-Hammond, Ancess, and Falk (1995), because most traditional tests provide only a limited measure of a narrow aspect of learning or development, they are poor predictors of how students will perform in other settings. This promotes a view of students as having deficits that need to be remediated rather than as having individual differences, approaches to learning, and strengths that can be supported and developed. Neither do traditional tests reflect or capture the diversity of students' backgrounds and experiences. They often contain assumptions and facts that are grounded in the context of the dominant culture, and fail to include relevant forms of knowledge from other cultures. This places students from nondominant cultures at a disadvantage in demonstrating what they know and can do (Garcia and Pearson 1991).

In contrast, alternative assessments can, although may not if improperly designed, impact teaching and learning in more positive ways. Because students are involved in developing, exhibiting, and evaluating their own work, alternative assessments help them develop a sense of responsibility and ownership of their work and encourage them to analyze and reflect on their progress regularly. Alternative assessments can encourage an intelligent, rich curriculum, rather than the narrowed one fostered by teaching and coaching for tests.

UNDERSTANDING THE ROLE OF INSTRUCTIONAL TASKS IN READING AND WRITING PERFORMANCE

The opportunity to learn is central to skilled reading and writing, and school tasks are central to this opportunity. Students learn what a task requires them to do and acquire the information and operations necessary for successful task completion. Tasks are defined by Doyle (1983) as a goal and the set of cognitive operations required to meet the goal. Academic tasks are defined by the answers students are required to produce and the routes they can take to obtain these answers. Tasks influence learners by directing their attention to particular aspects of content and promoting specific ways of processing information. Instructional tasks differ in both their content and their form, that is, in the procedures, social organization, and products they require. The elements of tasks vary from simple to complex and combine in various ways to shape how students think and how they work by determining how information is obtained, how it is processed, and how it is presented to the teacher for evaluation.

Task Content and Form

Task content refers to the cognitive complexity of the task and reflects the objectives students are expected to attain. Different learning objectives vary in difficulty for students, because they require different levels of cognitive processing and different prerequisite skills (Doyle 1983). Variations in the difficulty of task content affect student learning and behavior. For example, moderately difficult tasks produce greater motivation than do "easy" tasks (Clifford 1991). Moderately difficult tasks help learners calibrate their progress toward a goal by providing information about progress as well as concrete evidence of accomplishments (Schunk 1989). As a result, they enhance confidence and increase interest. Conversely, students may perceive minimally challenging situations or "safe" successes as evidence that others hold low expectations for them, which may reinforce a perception of their own low ability (Weiner 1992).

Students' reactions to content are also influenced by their beliefs about its inherent appeal, its difficulty, and their familiarity with the topic (Blumenfeld et al. 1987). For example, students are more likely to be discouraged when they confront difficulties with new material because they are more uncertain about their ability. Since performance in the classroom is public and subject to evaluation, few children are likely to be strongly interested in new material, where they may be confused, make errors, or have to exert a great deal of effort unless they are fairly certain they will succeed (Brophy 1983a).

Task forms also affect learning, irrespective of their content (Blumenfeld et al. 1987). As vehicles for the transmission of content, different forms vary in the extent to which learning objectives are evident to students. Forms differ in the obviousness of their purposes, the complexity of their procedures, the social organization in which they are carried out, and the products that result. For example, the purposes and procedures for completing worksheets are generally more straightforward than those surrounding a discussion.

Certain forms may exhibit more procedural complexity than others, but this can also vary within the same form. When tasks are procedurally complex, students may spend more time carrying out procedures than focusing on the content to be learned. In addition, forms differ in the prerequisite skills they require. The more prerequisite knowledge and skill required to accomplish the task, the more hesitant students may be to work at the task (Blumenfeld et al. 1987). Finally, task difficulty is determined by the nature of the product students must complete for evaluation and by the clarity of the evaluation criteria.

When the product can be evaluated according to numerous criteria, students—particularly younger ones—tend to focus on aspects that are more objective and easier to identify and define (like neatness or length) at the expense of concentrating on content or richness of ideas, clarity of explanations, or complexity of analysis (L. Anderson 1981; L. Anderson, Brubaker, Alleman-Brooks, and Duffy 1985). These tendencies are obviously strengthened when teachers' evaluative comments focus on neatness or effort. If teachers rely on assessment criteria ill-matched to the original cognitive purpose of the task, students will learn to process at the levels required by these criteria. These cumulative effects will be discussed in greater detail in the next section.

The Cumulative Effects of Task

Research suggests that students rely on prior experiences with lesson format and content as a guide to interpreting current tasks. They construct knowledge structures, learning strategies, and representations of the subject itself according to their experience. Even when conditions make such approaches inappropriate, students' approach to tasks is strongly influenced by their expectations concerning the form of the product and evaluative criteria to be used in assessment. If teachers do not provide information about product form or evaluation procedures, students will expect their performance to be assessed in the same way and at the same cognitive level as it was previously. So, for example, if students receive a steady diet of literal questions, they will tend to process the text at that level, and attempt to answer more thoughtful questions in the same manner as they have learned to respond to literal questions.

Generally speaking, students have to do two things as part of academic tasks: obtain information from reading/listening, and show teachers that they understand the information by producing a product. In some cases, the form in which information is obtained is different from the form of the product required for evaluation. In some of these cases, students will find it easier to obtain information than to display their knowledge/skill appropriately because the performance task is more complex. Blumenfeld et al. (1987) note that it is possible for students to possess the cognitive skills necessary to achieve the content goal, but to be unable to negotiate successfully the form in which they are required to display their knowledge. The actual problem may be failure to understand the form, rather than an inability to comprehend the content.

The more complex the task form, the more important it is for teachers to provide clear and specific explanation and feedback during the lesson to distinguish between the content- and form-related aspects of the learning task. Otherwise, students may spend considerable time on aspects of the task that are irrelevant to the learning objective. In such cases, actual time on task may remain high, although much of it may be devoted to aspects of the task that are irrelevant to the successful achievement of the objective.

The manner in which students approach and think about new information depends on their previous experience with the task forms. The more frequent the experience of similar task forms across subject matter, classrooms, and grades, the greater the consistency with which students approach and think about their work. If students are consistently exposed to tasks with simple forms, they will have little practice in the form-related skills of planning, organizing, selecting among several alternative strategies, and monitoring their progress toward a goal. The result is limited opportunities to learn those self-regulation skills essential for accomplishing a variety of tasks (Cormo and Mandinach 1983).

Similarly, this repeated exposure is likely to result in preferences for easy, clearly defined task forms that require minimal time or involvement on the part of the learner. This problem is further compounded when the complexity of either task content or form differs by ability group. To the extent that low achievers are assigned tasks with simple content *and* form, opportunities to develop higher level cognitive abilities become stratified and inequitable (Bowles and Gintis 1976).

Reading and Writing Tasks

Students are confronted with a wide variety of tasks during the course of reading and writing instruction. In many classrooms, they are expected to answer questions, complete workbook activities, read stories and books, produce book reports, write reports, keep a journal, engage in educational games, and complete projects. In some classrooms, they are expected to read for lengthy periods, a task that does not entail an obvious "product." In these classrooms, students are expected to respond in some way— by discussing the book in conferences, writing about the book, describing the book to others in a book talk, or creating an art project.

Tasks influence how students interpret and experience the reading and writing curriculum and may be particularly powerful for students just beginning formal literacy instruction. They are the "crucible" in which student motivation, cognition, instruction, and learning fuse (Turner 1995). The tasks within a particular classroom define for students what literacy is, why it is important, and what it can do. Tasks influence students' literacy learning in two ways: by predisposing them to link literacy with specific cognitive activities, and by focusing students on certain uses and purposes for literacy (Turner 1995).

A study by Turner (1995) in six basal and six whole language first-grade classrooms provides insight into the impact of literacy tasks on students' voluntary strategy use, persistence, and attentional control during task completion. Literacy tasks were classified as open (child-specified processes/goals, higher-order thinking required) or closed (other-designated processes/goals, recognition/memory skills required). The results indicated that there were both differences in the types of literacy tasks employed in basal and whole language classrooms and differences in the effects of open and closed literacy tasks on student behavior.

Although student tasks differed considerably between basal and whole language classrooms, few classrooms were completely consistent in selecting tasks that adhered to the type of instruction employed. The two most consistent structures in basal classrooms were individual seatwork and teacher-directed reading groups. The tasks in basal rooms were primarily, although not exclusively, of the practice type as exemplified in copying, workbook, and worksheet assignments. Within basal classrooms, 77 percent of all tasks observed were classified as closed.

Whole language classroom structure consisted primarily of small groups. Tasks were located at various centers in the classroom, such as the author's table, the library corner, and the listening center, and students were allowed some choice with regard to tasks and order of completion. Within these classrooms, 73 percent of all the tasks observed were classified as open.

Turner (1995) notes that her study focused on average readers from white, middle-class populations and that her results may not apply to others outside this group. Hiebert and Fisher (1991) report, however, that an increasing number of studies describe growth in students' learning as a result of changes in task structure such as increasing the diversity of the task "diet," student generation of oral and written language, use of students' prior knowledge, or authenticity of school tasks.

For example, one program shifted from word-by-word reading of English texts to discussion of story content, allowing students and teachers to switch to Spanish when needed to clarify the meaning of the text (Moll and Diaz 1987). By the third lesson, students were reading passages by themselves and answering comprehension questions at a comparable level to English monolingual readers at grade level. Similar results were reported in a case study of writing. Similarly, integrating a task-like teacher read-aloud on a regular basis can increase low-income students' involvement as readers and writers (Feitelson, Kita, and Goldstein 1986), and increased participation of ESL (English as Second Language) students in reading trade books has resulted in reading and listening comprehension at twice the previous rate (Elley and Mangubhai 1983).

Hiebert (1994) argues that open, or what she calls authentic, literacy tasks allow students without extensive literacy experiences to participate more fully in literacy events.

> Students who depend on schools to become literate are probably most in need of authentic literacy tasks. A regimen of skill and drill for these students fails to help them become readers and writers who engage in thoughtful, avid literacy as a life-long pursuit (Commins and Miramontes 1990; Moll and Diaz 1987; Moll et al. 1980). The opposite of the skill-and-drill syndrome, however, is not the answer either. As part of authentic tasks, students benefit from modeling and discussions about features of written language, including the graphophonic system. (405)

Hiebert and Fisher (1991) argue that task structures can be productively addressed in terms of the teaching and learning "diet" that students experience in schools. Although it may be tempting to view open tasks as always preferable and closed structures as less preferable, the real issue is determining which task structure(s) are most appropriate under different learning conditions. Because specific task structures tend to promote or enhance some educational outcomes more than others, choice of literacy goals must drive instructional design. The situation is further complicated because the fit between task and educational outcomes is not necessarily the same for students from different gender, racial, or sociocultural groups.

We agree with Hiebert's (1994) conclusion that many models of literacy tasks are needed, especially ones that attend to students of different ages and prior literacy experiences. The one-size-fits-all assumption that underlies many current authentic literacy practices, with the same activities recommended for all students, requires careful examination for the instruction of students who vary in developmental levels and literacy backgrounds. This one-size-fits-all assumption suggests that the same tasks will be effective for students who have had well over 1000 hours of literacy experiences before beginning kindergarten and those who enter first grade with the 100 hours or so of kindergarten literacy instruction. Hiebert (1994) indicates that this assumption is potentially damaging "because it encourages teachers to suspect that there is something wrong with children and their parents when immersion in literacy does not produce fast results" (407).

The following discussion highlights several different types of tasks that are commonly used in classrooms today: independent seatwork; reading comprehension questions; reading-writing workshop; and discussion.

Independent Seatwork

Widely published reports suggest that, on the average, elementary students spend fewer than ten minutes every school day reading connected text, and between 40 and 70 percent of their reading time doing seatwork (L. Anderson et al. 1985; L. Anderson 1984; Fisher et al. 1980). Since students spend so much time interacting with seatwork, close examination of both the content and use of these activities is essential. As Osborn (1984) has noted, well designed seatwork activities can facilitate the initial teaching of what is new and the maintenance of what has already been taught. On the other hand, poorly designed seatwork activities and practices force students to spend countless hours on boring and sometimes confusing activities that do not promote reading and writing competence.

Reviews of the content of traditional workbook and skill-sheet materials suggest that these materials are unlikely to benefit students in any significant way (R. Anderson et al. 1985). Criticisms of the content of traditional reading workbooks (Osborn 1984; Scheu, Tanner, and Au 1989) indicate that most of these materials involve very limited amounts of reading, focus on isolated drills of skills that are often only marginally useful in learning to read, involve little writing, and do not engage students in activities that would promote comprehension.

Basal programs are clearly intended to promote reading/language arts abilities and prepare students to read and write a wide range of authentic material (novels, reference books, content area textbooks, and so on). However, it is doubtful that this can occur with the steady diet of contrived texts that traditionally appear in workbooks. For example, some research suggests the transfer of knowledge and skill from one context to another is far from automatic. Hare, Rabinowitz, and Schieble (1989) found that many students who could identify the main ideas in basal-like skills texts were unable to construct main ideas in more complex, naturally occurring paragraphs.

Based on the evidence available, experts have offered a variety of suggestions about how to improve the seatwork tasks that are a large part of reading and writing instruction. With regard to the content of reading seatwork, Cunningham (1984; Cunningham et al. 1989) suggests that seatwork would be of more value if it focused on helping students to access background knowledge and set purposes for reading, follow the structure of the reading selection, become increasingly independent in the use of comprehension strategies, and understand why they are doing it and how it will help them become better readers.

Cunningham et al. (1989) also suggest that completed worksheets not be turned in and graded. Rather, students should bring them to the reading group where students should check their own worksheets. Answers should be given and the reasoning behind the answer should be explained. Students who have made mistakes should fix them before turning in the worksheet. Finally, they recommend that teachers let the students teach others by working together to complete their seatwork assignments. These suggestions can serve as the basis for further evaluation of reading seatwork activities.

In addition to the content of seatwork activities, we must be concerned with how seatwork materials are used. In an in-depth study of reading seatwork, L. Anderson et al. (1985) observed eight first-grade classrooms to determine what teachers and students do during the time devoted to seatwork, and how students attempt to understand and complete assigned work. Although there were some differences in seatwork assignments from one class to another, within each class the assignments were similar across time, with the same form of assignment often used two to five times a week. Also, in six of the eight classes observed, over half of the seatwork assignments were given to the whole class, despite the fact that students were assigned to different groups.

L. Anderson et al. (1985) also found that teacher instruction related to seatwork rarely included statements about what would be learned or how the assignment related to students' past learning. When teachers did attend to students doing seatwork, they most often monitored student behavior, rather than their understanding or task performance. Teachers generally emphasized keeping busy and finishing assigned work, not understanding what was being taught.

The seatwork assignments that low achievers received were particularly inappropriate. These students did poorly on their assignments and often derived answers by using strategies that enabled them to complete the assignments without understanding them. These findings are compounded by the evidence (see Chapter 5) that students assigned to lower reading groups spend even more time on worksheet exercises and less time actually reading than students in higher reading groups (Allington, Stuetzel, Shake, and Lamarche 1986). It is not surprising that these students are especially likely to believe that reading is "finishing the workbook pages."

L. Anderson et al. (1985) suggest that poor seatwork habits developed in first grade may contribute to a subsequent passive learning style. Low achievers, who often work on assignments they do not understand, may come to believe that school work does not have to make sense; therefore, it is not necessary to obtain additional information or assistance as an aid to understanding. In contrast, high achieving students rarely have difficulty with seatwork, so that any problems they have are more likely to motivate them to seek help.

Good and Brophy (1987) note that, because younger and lower-achieving students may spend between 300 to 400 hours a year doing reading/language arts seatwork, it is imperative that teachers find strategies and activities that enable them to use this time well. They suggest that "successful seatwork activities have the following characteristics: (1) allow students to work successfully and independently, (2) are interesting and reflect variety both in terms of the type of the assignment and how it is completed, (3) frequently allow students to read for comprehension and pleasure, (4) occasionally relate to students' personal lives" (Good and Brophy 1987, p 247).

Scheu, Tanner, and Au (1989) suggest a general model for the development of seatwork activities that calls for teachers to act as decision makers who consider both their students' needs as developing readers and writers and the qualities of selections to be read. According to this model, teachers should design and assign seatwork tasks based on the kinds of independent practice students need to understand specific selections and to become more proficient readers and writers in general. Activities need to be thoroughly integrated with the reading and writing lessons, because they give students the chance to work independently with the concepts and skills needed for a holistic understanding of a selection. The purposes of seatwork assignments should be explained and discussed. Finally, completed seatwork assignments should often serve as the basis for starting a discussion of the selection.

The increasing consensus among experts is reflected in the recommendations of the Commission on Reading: (1) children should spend less time completing workbooks and skills sheets; (2) children should spend more time in independent reading; and (3) children should spend more time writing (R. Anderson et al. 1985). According to Cunningham et al. (1989), "real" reading and writing activities should be a part of each student's daily seatwork. Unlike the time spent on traditional worksheet activities, time spent reading and writing has been shown to contribute to growth in reading ability. In addition, reading and writing are more interesting, enjoyable, and intrinsically motivating than worksheet activities.

Reading Comprehension Questions

Many different types of questions are used in a variety of ways each day in virtually every classroom. Questions are an integral part of teacher presentations, discussions, seatwork, examinations, homework assignments, and remedial instruction (Dillon 1988).

A variety of question taxonomies have been used to classify various types of questions. Traditional question taxonomies that classify questions separately from the text or information being questioned (Barrett 1976; Bloom 1956) are inadequate, given an interactive view of reading. Any interaction that occurs as a reader answers questions about a text will have a direct effect on comprehension and/or learning. Indeed, a large body of literature indicates that the type, content, and use of questions all influence student comprehension and learning.

A taxonomy of question-answer relations proposed by Pearson and Johnson (1978) provides one means for examining questions in a more interactive manner. Questions are classified in the context of, rather than apart from, the text or information being questioned. They identify three types of questions based on the probable source of the information the reader will use to answer the question (see Chapter 8). When the information needed is stated explicitly in the text, the question is textually explicit (TE). When the answer is implied rather than explicitly stated, the question is textually implicit (TI). Finally, there are some questions for which the appropriate answer is neither explicitly stated nor implied in the text, but relies heavily on the background information/prior knowledge the reader brings to the text. Pearson and Johnson call these types of questions scriptally implicit (SI), using script as a synonym for schema or knowledge structure.

Research by Wixson (1983a; 1983b; 1984) indicates that both the type and the content of questions promote different learning outcomes. Specifically, TE questions promoted verbatim reproduction of the text, TI questions resulted in the generation of text-based inferences, and SI questions led to the production of inferences based on prior knowledge. Furthermore, students learned and remembered best the information they were questioned about, regardless of whether it was important or trivial to the important ideas in the text. For example, 57 percent of the students who received the question for a passage on "Shrimp Farms" about where scientists started a new kind of farm included the information that shrimp farms were started in Japan in their recalls. In contrast, only 17 percent of the students who were asked different questions about this passage included this information in their recalls.

Indiscriminate use of questions can lead students away from, as well as toward, a desirable learning outcome. We must use questions in a manner consistent with the goals and purposes of our instruction. For example, in situations where less inferential processing is desirable—such as reading directions or conducting science experiments—explicit questions may be the most appropriate. When the integration of the ideas within a text is desirable, as is often the case in subject area reading, textually implicit questions may be most helpful.

We must also remember that if we ask questions that focus on unimportant information, students are likely to learn this information at the expense of other, more important content. Furthermore, repeated use of similar types of questions shapes the way students approach their reading assignments. Hansen (1981) found that students who received a steady diet of inferential questions were able to answer those kinds of questions more easily than students who had been asked only literal level questions.

Students' performance is also affected by the pattern of question-answering that teachers establish in the classroom. Effective questioning requires that students be allowed sufficient time to think about and to respond to questions, yet Rowe's (1974) study of teacher *"wait-time"* provided stunning evidence that students often had little opportunity to produce thoughtful responses. Her observations indicated that after asking questions, teachers waited less than one second for a response before calling on someone. In addition, after calling on a student, they waited only about a second for the student to give the answer before supplying it themselves, calling on someone else, rephrasing the question, or giving clues. Following these observations, Rowe (1974) investigated what would happen if teachers were trained to extend their wait-times to three to five seconds. These findings indicated that increased wait-times led to more active participation in lessons by a larger percentage of students, and an increase in the quality of the participation.

Subsequent research indicates that pacing and wait-time should be adjusted to the level of questions being asked and the objectives they are intended to address. A fast pace and short wait-time are appropriate for drill or review activities covering specific facts. A slow pace and longer wait times are appropriate when students are expected to think about the material and formulate original responses, rather than simply retrieve information from memory.

Currently, there is a shift away from answering teacher-posed questions with their implied "right" answers. Instead, teachers are often advised to solicit personal responses to reading (Rosenblatt 1978; Winograd and Johnston 1987). The long-term effects of this shift have yet to be determined. Although it appears that students can often respond to a piece of writing even though they cannot justify their responses (Galda 1982), a steady diet of tasks that permit only literal, "correct" responses can result in students who are unengaged in reading and writing as personally important activities (Moffett 1985; Parsons 1990). The tension between these two approaches permeates much of the educational field today.

Reading-Writing Workshop

The Reading-Writing Workshop represents a comprehensive approach to reading and writing instruction that has been formalized into an approach by Nancie Atwell (1987). The tasks associated with this approach are designed to engage students in meaningful literacy activities and to develop strategic approaches to reading and writing. Two main ideas behind the Reading-Writing Workshop are that students own their own reading and writing and the teacher's role is that of expert reader-writer and guide rather than evaluator. Students are responsible for selecting their own reading material and their own topics for writing. Teachers read and write for their own purposes along with the students and share their experiences with students. The four key elements of Reading-Writing Workshop as defined by Atwell (1987) are:

1. Time to read and write
2. Forums for response
3. Conferences with the teacher
4. Mini-lessons

Reading and writing workshops provide extended time for students to read and write. Guidelines are provided by Atwell (1987) for student behaviors that help all members of the class respect the reading and writing that are taking place and to keep reading and writing central to the activities in the classroom.

Guidelines for Reading Workshop time include that students: are responsible for having a book in their possession at the beginning of the session; must read a book for the entire period (no magazines or newspapers), preferably one that tells a story (no books of lists or facts where readers can't sustain attention, build speed and accuracy); cannot do homework or read material for another class; and may not talk to or disturb others. Guidelines for Writing Workshop time include that students: should write on one side of the paper only to make it easier to cut and paste; are not to erase, but save a record of their thinking by simply drawing a line through text they wish to change; and are to speak in quiet voices only, so others who are thinking will not be interrupted.

Along with time to read and write, Reading-Writing Workshop also provides forums for response to reading and writing. Responses can take both verbal and written forms. Verbal forms include literature response groups, peer conferencing, group sharing of writing, and conferencing with the teacher. Written forms include dialogue journals between teacher and student and note writing between students about their reading.

The primary basis for evaluation in the Reading-Writing Workshop is conferences between student and teacher that occur throughout the school year. Reading and writing conferences provide students with chances to review their progress toward old goals and to set new ones. Atwell (1987) describes four types of writing workshop conferences—status of the class, topic, draft writing, and evaluative.

The final element of Reading-Writing Workshop is mini-lessons to assist students with their reading and writing. Mini-lessons can include a variety of activities, from reading of poetry and literature, through short discussions of an author, to the presentation of reading strategies. The teacher makes choices about which mini-lessons to present based on students' dialogue journals and informal and formal conferencing. The key to mini-lessons is that they be relevant to students' actual reading or writing and that the topic can be addressed in a relatively short period of time.

Evidence of the impact of Reading-Writing Workshop comes from several sources. Atwell (1987) presents numerous examples of students who started reading in Reading Workshop because that was the expectation and ended up reading because they enjoyed it. Others have found that Reading Workshop has a positive effect on the attitude and involvement with reading of learning-disabled students (Oberlin and Shugerman 1989). McAuliffe (1993) reports that the peer feedback available in Writing Workshop helped second-grade students change their writing so that more of their classmates could engage with it.

Several issues have also been raised regarding Reading-Writing Workshop. Ash (1990) argues that although student ownership of reading is important, there is still an important role for whole-class or group readings of selected texts. Others point out that fiction/narrative texts are privileged at the expense of great nonfiction with which students need to become familiar.

Discussion
In a volume devoted to discussion as a means of promoting reading comprehension, Alvermann, Dillon, and O'Brien (1987) write that discussion is a curricular task selected by teachers for a variety of purposes. Some teachers may perceive discussion as a forum for raising important issues in relation to reading

assignments. Others may see discussion as an opportunity for identifying and clarifying students' misconceptions, and still others may view discussion as a way of checking on whether students read assigned material.

Alvermann et al. (1987) indicate that discussion is important both as a communication skill and as the foundation for developing higher level reading skills. As a means of defining discussion, they propose three criteria:

> Discussants should put forth multiple points of view and stand ready to change their minds about the matter under discussion; students should interact with one another as well as with the teacher; and the interaction should exceed the typical two or three word phrase units common to recitation lessons. (7)

Similarly, Goldenberg (1993) describes discussion as an interesting, engaging conversation that deals with an idea or a concept and has meaning and relevance for students. The focus remains discernible throughout and there is a high level of participation, without domination by any one person, especially the teacher. Teachers and students are responsive to what others say, so that each statement builds on, challenges, or extends a previous one.

According to Goldenberg (1993), teachers or discussion leaders question, prod, challenge, coax, or remain silent. They clarify and instruct when necessary, but without wasting time or words. They make certain that the discussion proceeds at an appropriate pace, knowing when to push to draw out an idea or to ease up to allow for more thought and reflection. In essence, they are skilled at "weaving individual participants' comments into a larger tapestry of meaning" (318).

Based on the experiences of practicing teachers, Goldenberg (1993) identifies the basic elements of discussion as instructional and conversational (see Figure 6.1). In one sense, discussions are instructional because they are designed to promote learning. Teaching through discussion requires a deliberate and self-controlled agenda. In another sense, discussion is conversational in that it appears to be natural, spontaneous, and free from the didactic practices associated with formal teaching. While maintaining specific curricular, cognitive, and conceptual goals, the teacher tries to establish a high degree of responsiveness and dynamic interaction with students.

Before leaving the topic of discussion, it is important to heed the experiences of a group of educators attempting to improve their discussion practices (Villaume et al. 1994). These educators observed a great deal of inconsistency in students' movement beyond the role of answer-giver in their early discussions. Some students assumed an active responsible role naturally, while others appeared uncomfortable and uncertain, and still others used the opportunity to be disruptive and silly. They determined that modeling was not sufficient, as only a few students had accepted their subtle invitation to engage in the behaviors modeled. They determined that instruction about discussion was needed and developed a series of strategies to teach their students about discussion.

The experience of these educators suggests that without significant effort on the part of the teacher, many discussions are not likely to achieve the lofty

FIGURE 6.1
Conversation Elements

Elements of the Instructional Conversation

Instructional Elements

1. *Thematic focus.*   The teacher selects a theme or idea to serve as a starting point for focusing the discussion and has a general plan for how the theme will unfold, including how to "chunk" the text to permit optimal exploration of the theme.

2. *Activation and use of background and relevant schemata.*   The teacher either "hooks into" or provides students with pertinent background knowledge and relevant schemata necessary for understanding a text. Background knowledge and schemata are then woven into the discussion that follows.

3. *Direct teaching.*   When necessary, the teacher provides direct teaching of a skill or concept.

4. *Promotion of more complex language and expression.*   The teacher elicits more extended student contributions by using a variety of elicitation techniques—invitations to expand (e.g., "tell me more about that"), questions (e.g., "what do you mean"), restatements (e.g., "in other words—"), and pauses.

5. *Elicitation of bases for statements or positions.*   The teacher promotes students' use of text, pictures, and reasoning to support an argument or position. Without overwhelming students, the teacher probes for the bases of students' statements—e.g., "How do you know?" "What makes you think that?" "Show us where it says _____."

Conversational Elements

6. *Fewer "known-answer" questions.*   Much of the discussion centers on questions and answers for which there might be more than one correct answer.

7. *Responsivity to student contributions.*   While having an initial plan and maintaining the focus and coherence of the discussion, the teacher is also responsive to students' statements and the opportunities they provide.

8. *Connected discourse.*   The discussion is characterized by multiple, interactive, connected turns; succeeding utterances build upon and extend previous ones.

9. *A challenging, but nonthreatening, atmosphere.*   The teacher creates a "zone of proximal development," where a challenging atmosphere is balanced by a positive affective climate. The teacher is more collaborator than evaluator and creates an atmosphere that challenges students and allows them to negotiate and construct the meaning of the text.

10. *General participation, including self-selected turns.*   The teacher encourages general participation among students. The teacher does not hold exclusive right to determine who talks, and students are encouraged to volunteer or otherwise influence the selection of speaking turns.

Source: Goldenberg, C. (1993). Instructional conversations: Promoting comprehension through discussion. *The Reading Teacher, 46,* 316–326.

goals articulated previously. Discussions that are not well developed are likely to have a variety of unanticipated consequences for students, especially those experiencing difficulty with reading and writing.

STRATEGIES AND TOOLS FOR ASSESSING INSTRUCTIONAL APPROACHES AND TASKS

Although the tools for assessing instructional approaches and tasks are somewhat limited, it is possible to gather information about the instruction received by specific students. Although some information may be collected by interviewing the teacher and/or the student and by examining materials and assignments (see also Chapter 5) reliable conclusions require some classroom observation. Because some teachers may be fearful about being observed (Stallings, Needels, and Sparks 1987), the purpose of the observation should be made quite clear. It is important to keep in mind that the purpose is not to pass judgment, but rather to try to determine what, if any, contextual factors might be altered to improve the match between what the student needs and what the classroom instruction provides.

Assessing Instructional Approaches

In the following sections, we describe several ways to assess the classroom curriculum, methods, and assessment practices that comprise the instructional approach.

The Curricular Focus of Instruction

Descriptions of the focus of instruction involve a number of interrelated issues. The curricular goals and lesson objectives generally provide the most relevant information about the instructional focus. However, because teachers frequently rely on commercially prepared materials to specify their instructional program, it will sometimes be necessary to infer an instructional focus from the content and materials being used (see Chapter 5) . In this section, we focus on ways to assess the *outcomes* and *balance* of the reading and writing program for particular students.

Recall that the overarching goal of reading and writing instruction should be the development of strategic, motivated, reflective readers and writers. To do this, teachers must provide instruction aimed at three large categories of outcomes: *attitude* outcomes, *content* outcomes, and *process* outcomes. One of the ways that assessment information about the instructional focus can be gathered is to ask teachers to complete "focus sheets" that suggest the degree to which their instruction is focused on one or another of these major outcomes. An example of a brief checklist that can be used to assess the instructional focus is provided in Figure 6.2. As always, instructional practice needs to be assessed *in relation* to important outcomes.

FIGURE 6.2

Instructional Focus Sheet

Checklist for Providing a Balanced Focus in Reading and Writing Instruction		
Are students being given opportunities to develop *positive attitudes* toward reading and writing? • Are you providing for daily SSR and independent writing? • In reading, are you encouraging students to immerse themselves in reading and responding? • Are students encouraged to share what they have read and/or written? • Do you provide guidance in selecting good books and support in reading them? • Are reading and writing activities authentic and relevant to students' needs and interests?	Are students directed toward important *content* in their reading and writing? • Are you providing support for students to identify the important information in text? • Are questions focused on important information in text? • Are students expected to integrate information from a variety of sources? • Do students read and write about important ideas and/or persistent issues reflected in literature?	Do students have ample opportunity to acquire important reading and writing *process skills*? • Do you provide direct instruction in reading and writing strategies and processes? • Do you model effective reading and writing strategies for students? • Do you help students to acquire important information about reading and writing? • Are students encouraged to recognize patterns in their reading and writing so that they can use the knowledge and skill they possess? • Are students provided with opportunities to reflect on their own progress?

Another indicator of the focus of instruction is the amount of time spent on various activities. One way to organize observational data is to summarize activities in terms of the amount of time allocated to them (Good and Brophy 1987). This type of observational system can provide useful information, especially if distinctions are made in terms of the amounts of actual reading and writing that are done. For example, one study of this type reported that students in the remedial classes observed spent only 10 to 20 percent of their time actually reading and writing connected text, even when a single paragraph is considered connected text (Allington, Stuetzel, Shake, and Lamarche 1986).

This type of assessment technique is especially useful because it can also suggest the degree to which the reading and writing program is *balanced*. In some classes, significant attention is devoted to isolated word-level work, but little attention is devoted to working with whole texts. In others, students are rewarded for completion of specific reading and writing products (reports or worksheets), but are not really expected to work independently during sustained reading and writing periods. In still others, students are expected to spend time with books, but praise and rewards are delivered for quantity of books read without attention to the significance or merit of these books. Each of these can create different student outcomes, different student attitudes, and/or different student knowledge. For this reason it is important to describe as fully as possible the range of time and activity spent on various outcomes to assess the balance of the program. This issue will be addressed further in an upcoming section on Evaluating Instructional Tasks.

Instructional Methods

Our discussion of tools and strategies for evaluating instructional methods is organized according to our goal of creating motivated, strategic, reflective readers and writers.

Methods and motivation.   As we have seen, instructional techniques and student motivation for learning are strongly related. Student interviews can be exceptionally useful in assessing the relationship between instruction and motivation. Some of the interviews we have already suggested may provide information about the quality and appropriateness of the instructional program (see Chapters 4 and 8), although these should clearly be designed or adapted to gather information about specific aspects of the setting or instruction that may be influencing the student.

For example, interviews can be structured to collect information about the motivational impact of units of instruction. Rogers and Stevenson (1988) asked students questions such as:

> What went well for you?
> What did you enjoy most?
> Should the study of __ be a part of everyone's education?

Interestingly, the last of these questions often provoked the most honest assessment of interest *and* learning. Perhaps asking a question that is more distant and less personal encourages richer thinking.

The interview information will, of course, be supplemented with data generated through observation. The instructional context should be examined for evidence of the motivational practices we described earlier (see Figure 6.3). Although these strategies *cannot* be quantified easily, this is not necessary. A strongly negative profile of instructional factors linked to motivation can provide important information about the achievement and progress of specific students.

Methods and strategic learning.   The issues that we have been discussing up to now have tended to be quite global, cutting across the curriculum and often touching on aspects of instruction that are important for all learning. In this section we describe some focus questions for assessing the salient features of the instructional approach to reading and writing method. Many of these issues were also addressed in Chapter 5 because the method of instruction is so

FIGURE 6.3
*Assessment of
Motivational
Strategies*

Motivational Analysis of Tasks and Activities

Use: Whenever particular classroom tasks or activities are observed
Purpose: To identify the motivational elements built into the task or activity

Check each of the motivational elements that was included in the observed task or activity.

A. Extrinsic motivation strategies
_____ 1. Offers rewards as incentives for good performance
_____ 2. Calls attention to the instrumental value of the knowledge or skills developed in the activity (applications to present or future life outside of school)
_____ 3. Structures individual or group competition for prizes or recognition

B. Intrinsic motivational features of the task or activity
_____ 1. Opportunities for active response (beyond just watching and listening)
_____ 2. Opportunities to answer divergent questions or work on higher level objectives
_____ 3. Immediate feedback to students' responses (built into the task itself, rather than provided by the teacher as in C.8 below)
_____ 4. Gamelike features (the task is a game or contains gamelike features that make it more like a recreational activity than a typical academic activity)
_____ 5. Task completion involves creating a finished product for display or use
_____ 6. The task involves fantasy or simulation elements that engage students' emotions or allow them to experience events vicariously
_____ 7. The task provides opportunities for students to interact with their peers

C. Teacher's attempts to stimulate students' motivation to learn
_____ 1. Projects intensity (communicating that the material is important and deserves close attention)
_____ 2. Induces task interest or appreciation
_____ 3. Induces curiosity or suspense
_____ 4. Makes abstract content more personal, concrete, or familiar
_____ 5. Induces dissonance or cognitive conflict
_____ 6. Induces students to generate their own motivation to learn
_____ 7. States learning objectives or provides advance organizers
_____ 8. Provides opportunities for students to respond and get feedback (asks questions during group lessons, circulates to monitor performance during seatwork)
_____ 9. Models task-related thinking and problem solving ("thinks out loud" when working through examples)
_____ 10. Includes instruction or modeling designed to increase students' metacognitive awareness of their learning efforts in response to the task (includes information about mental preparation for learning, about the organization or structure built into the content, about how students can impose their own organizational structures on the content to help them remember it, or about how to monitor one's own comprehension and respond to confusion or mistakes)

Notes:

From *Looking in Classrooms* 4th. ed by Thomas L. Good and Jere E. Brophy. Copyright © 1987 by Harper & Row, Publishers Inc. Reprinted by permission of HarperCollins Publishers.

closely linked—especially in elementary schools—to the instructional materials employed. Questions like the following should be used to evaluate classroom methods and approaches.

- Is the general approach to reading and writing basal-based? literature-based? based on subskills mastery learning curriculum? some combination of these?
- Does the teacher attempt to meet individual needs by grouping? altering content? changing the tasks? providing different levels of support? Does not appear to differentiate instruction in any way?
- Is language arts instruction defined (by the teacher) in terms of a specific published program? Does the teacher/school draw from a variety of sources and define the reading and writing curriculum in terms of clearly established outcomes?
- What is the relationship between the method used in this classroom and that used by other teachers in the building?

Asking yourself or the teacher these questions results in useful descriptions of the instructional method employed by the teacher. In some schools these components of instructional method may be dictated by the administration of the school. In others these are informally decreed between and among teachers so that deviation from these practices may result in ostracism from the mainstream of professional contact. However, in most schools, teachers have a great deal of discretion about how they deliver instruction, especially if they have demonstrated that they are reasonable, responsible professionals.

Two important aspects of instructional method are so individual that it will be difficult to evaluate the extent to which they are used without close observation in the classroom. These are the amount of scaffolding and the quantity and quality of dialogue. Although there are no good tools available to evaluate these critical features, there are some specific teaching behaviors we can look for as we observe in the classroom. For example,

Does the teacher encourage students' acquisition of new or difficult material?
Does the teacher support learning by modeling and/or providing guidance?
Does the teacher engage in dialogue with students (as opposed to lecturing)?
Does the teacher support students' contributions to dialogue?
Does dialogue have focus and direction?
Does the teacher use student ideas and link those ideas to new information?
Does the teacher use feedback constructively to help students improve their responses?

Few teachers have been well trained in these methods, but some have developed these skills to a high degree. The presence or absence of these methods will most likely influence the achievement or involvement of some less-skilled students.

   Methods and reflection.   The two aspects of instruction identified previously as essential for promoting reflective reading and writing are the use of authentic, complex problems and projects, and opportunities for self-assessment. It is not easy to determine the extent to which classroom practices promote reflection in individual students. Certainly, one can look to see if students are provided opportunities to reflect through activities such as complex assignments, open-ended discussion, individual conferencing, and portfolios involving self-assessments. It is clear, however, that the extent to which instructional practices facilitate reflection, and, for that matter, motivation and strategic behavior, is related to the classroom culture itself. It may be helpful then to consider the set of more broad-based standards developed by Newmann and Wehlage for evaluating instruction that engages "students in using their minds well" (p 8).

   The five standards developed by Newmann and Wehlage (1993) for evaluating the quality of instruction are as follows.

- higher-order thinking
- depth of knowledge
- connectedness to the world beyond the classroom
- substantive conversation
- social support for student achievement

Each standard is rated from 1 to 5 along a continuum from less to more and raters should consider the number of students to which the criterion applies and the proportion of class time during which it applies.

   Scores on the higher-order thinking scale range from a 1, which represents lower-order thinking only, to a 5, which means that higher-order thinking is central to the instruction. A score of 3 means that students primarily engage in routine lower-order thinking, but there is at least one significant question or activity in which some students engage in some higher-order thinking.

   Lower-order thinking activities are defined as those that ask students to receive or recite factual information or to employ rules through repetitive routines. Students are in the role of information-receivers and are asked to recall prespecified knowledge. In contrast, higher-order thinking activities require students to manipulate information and ideas in ways that transform their meaning and implications.

   The depth of understanding scale refers to the substantive character of the ideas in a lesson and to the level of understanding students demonstrate as they consider these ideas. Knowledge is thin or shallow when it does not deal with significant concepts and/or students have a trivial understanding of important concepts. Knowledge is deep or thick when it concerns important concepts and/or when students can make clear distinctions, develop arguments, solve problems, construct explanations, and otherwise work with relatively complex understandings.

On the depth of understanding scale, a score of 1 indicates "knowledge is shallow" and a score of 5 indicates "knowledge is deep." A score of 3 indicates that knowledge is treated unevenly during instruction; at least one significant idea may be presented in depth, but in general the focus is not sustained.

The third scale, connectedness to the world, measures the extent to which instruction has value and meaning beyond the school setting. A score of 1 is given instruction with little or no value beyond the school; students' work has no impact on others and serves only to certify their success in the instructional context. A score of 5 is given instruction that is connected to the world outside of school, and in which students address real-world problems and/or use personal experiences as a context for applying knowledge.

The fourth scale measures substantive conversation and scores range from 1, no substantive conversation, to 5, high-level substantive conversation. In classes with little or no conversation, interaction typically consists of teacher presentations that deviate little from a preplanned body of information and set of questions. The conversation is often choppy, rather than coherent, and there is often little or no discussion. High levels of substantive conversation are indicated by three features: considerable interaction about the ideas of a topic; sharing of ideas in exchanges that are not completely teacher-directed; and cohesive dialogue that builds on participants' ideas.

The fifth and final scale, social support for student achievement, involves high expectations, respect, and inclusion of all students in the learning process. Social support is low and earns a score of 1 when teacher or student behavior, comments, and actions tend to discourage effort or participation, or when the overall atmosphere of the class is negative. Token acknowledgments of student actions or responses do not necessarily constitute evidence of social support. Social support is high and earns a score of 5 when the teacher conveys the following: high expectations for all students; that it is necessary to take risks and try hard to master challenging work; that all members of the class can learn important knowledge and skills; and an understanding that a climate of mutual respect among all members of the class contributes to achievement by all.

The standards just described provide a framework through which to view assignments, instructional activities, and classroom conversations. Newmann and Wehlage (1993) caution that it is important to remember that these standards attempt only to represent the degree of authentic instruction observed within discrete class periods. Numerical ratings alone cannot portray how lessons relate to one another or how multiple lessons might accumulate into experiences more complex than the sum of individual lessons. The relative importance of the different standards also remains open for discussion.

Previous research indicates that teaching for thinking, problem solving, and understanding often has more positive effects on student performance than traditional teaching. The effects of high levels of adherence to this specific set of standards are not well established. Many educators believe that there are appropriate times for traditional instructional practices such as memorizing, repetition, and quiet study without conversation. Clearly the emphasis should be placed on moving instruction toward more authentic achievements for individual students, however that might best be accomplished.

Assessment Practices

According to Chittenden (1991), assessment is an attitude before it is a method. Through his work in elementary classrooms, he observed four quite different attitudes or stances teachers adopt with respect to monitoring and evaluating students' learning, which he refers to as keeping track, checking up, finding out, and summing up. He notes that although these views are largely complementary, they sometimes conflict.

A "keeping track" stance is characterized by attention to what activities students have been involved in such as what books a particular student has read, or which students have not yet completed certain activities. Teachers devise many ways to make records to meet their keeping-track needs. For example, they create informal checklists and inventories and gather material from students' journal entries. Over the year, a fairly substantial record of activities and accomplishments is often compiled in the name of keeping track.

A "checking-up" stance is often approached both formally and informally. Informal checking up involves observing and asking students questions. Formal checking up is focused on testing, defined as any situation in which the student is asked a question to which the questioner or examiner knows the answer.

The "finding out" stance is focused on inquiry or figuring out what is going on. The teacher is attending to what a particular student response meant or what a student understood from a particular story. Teachers may be asking questions, but clearly not with the intent of "checking up." Chittenden (1991) believes that the "finding out" stance is most critical to successful teaching and learning.

Finally, to complete the picture, is the "summing up" stance. This stance directly addresses the needs of accountability through reporting to parents, districts, and students. Attention is focused on organizing information in ways that are meaningful outside the classroom.

The types of assessments used and the manner in which they are used are likely to vary according to these stances. In contexts where all four stances are present, we would expect to see a full range of assessment instruments including both tests and alternative assessments. These various assessments may complement each other in the sense that they reflect a consistent view of literacy learning. Alternatively, they may be in conflict in that some reflect a more traditional, isolated skills approach to literacy learning and others reflect a more interactive, constructivist view of literacy learning. This situation can be confusing to students and lead to difficulties and/or mixed impressions related to reading and writing performance.

Still other contexts may evidence heavy reliance on one or two stances. This situation is likely to direct curriculum and instruction in specific ways that may or may not support student literacy learning. For example, too much emphasis on checking up and/or summing up may lead to instructional practices that do not promote independence, motivation, and the problem-solving skills necessary for successful reading and writing performance. Heavy dependence on these stances can also lead to misperceptions of students' abilities. Determining the extent to which these stances are present or absent within a particular instructional context and their potential impact on a student's reading and writing performance provides valuable information in the evaluation of the instructional context.

Evaluating Instructional Tasks

In this section, we review some techniques for assessing instructional tasks. The purpose for evaluating tasks in the assessment-instruction process is actually twofold: (1) to predict the likely impact of instructional tasks on reading and writing performance; and (2) to gain insight regarding appropriate instructional tasks in an effort to match less-skilled readers and writers with tasks that result in effective teaching and efficient learning.

Task Type

An interesting finding of the Turner (1995) study described previously was that the type of literacy task students received was a stronger predictor of behavior than whether they were in a whole language or basal classroom. Students used more strategies, persisted longer, and controlled their attention better during open as opposed to closed literacy tasks, regardless of the type of classroom in which these tasks occurred.

As you may recall from the previous discussion, closed tasks are those in which either the task or the teacher indicates the information to be used as well as the expected outcome. They offer limited opportunities for students to make decisions, and automatic application of practiced skills is often the goal. In contrast, open tasks are those in which students themselves can select relevant information and/or decide how to use the information to solve a problem. They invite more metacognition and decision making, which facilitates higher level cognitive processing. The factors in open tasks that appear to influence students' motivated, strategic, reflective behavior are opportunities for challenge, personal control, satisfying interests, and collaboration (Turner and Paris 1995).

The relationships between student performance and classroom task expectations is extremely important to ascertain. For example, some teachers actually evaluate students' reading competence not on their ability to read and write connected text but on their ability to complete workbooks or other worksheets. On the other hand, there are classrooms in which students are regularly

FIGURE 6.4
Summarizing Types of Instructional Tasks

Check the tasks that are present in the classroom. Use the space to the right of each task to estimate what portion of day/week is spent on that activity. Use the space under open or closed to comment on how the task is employed.

Tasks	Time Spent	Open or Closed
Reading Connected Text		
_____ teacher assigned	_____	
_____ student selected	_____	
Writing Connected Text		
_____ journal	_____	
_____ writing process projects	_____	
_____ interdisciplinary projects	_____	
Listening to Connected Text		
_____ teacher read	_____	
_____ other students	_____	
Conferencing		
_____ with teacher	_____	
_____ with other students	_____	
Discussion		
_____ whole class	_____	
_____ small group w/teacher	_____	
_____ small group w/out teacher	_____	
Workbooks/worksheets		
_____ commercial	_____	
_____ teacher-generated	_____	

engaged in fruitful reading and writing activity for extended periods of time. To understand the experience of a particular student requires a clear description of the kinds of tasks that are assigned and an examination of the proportion of time that is spent on different types of tasks. Completing a summary analysis such as the one provided in Figure 6.4 will quickly reveal what types of instructional tasks are used regularly.

Task Content, Form, and Implementation

Since students spend so much time interacting with instructional tasks, it is essential to examine in some detail their content and form, and how they are implemented. The questions provided in Figure 6.5 will help determine the content and form of instructional tasks as well as how they are implemented. Well-designed tasks can promote initial learning of what is new and maintenance of what has already been taught. On the other hand, poorly designed tasks require students to spend countless hours on tedious and sometimes confusing activities that do not promote reading and writing competence.

Turner and Paris (1995) identify five characteristics of literacy tasks that promote motivated, strategic, reflective reading and writing. Specifically, these tasks are designed to:

Provide authentic choices and purposes for literacy;
Allow students to make modifications so the difficulty and interest levels are challenging;
Show students how they can control their learning;
Encourage collaboration;
Emphasize strategies and metacognition for constructing meaning; and
Build responsibility, ownership, and self-regulation.

In designing these tasks, teachers recast activities to emphasize the enjoyment and the value of literacy. They demonstrate to students the many ways that a

FIGURE 6.5
Describing Task Content, Format, and Implementation

Generally describe the content and format of instructional tasks and how they are implemented. Use the following questions to guide your examination.

1. Do tasks reflect the most important aspects of what is being taught in language arts program?
2. Do tasks foster independence in the use of reading and writing strategies?
3. Do some tasks provide for a systematic and cumulative review of what has already been taught/learned?
4. Do tasks access background knowledge and set purposes for reading and writing?
5. Are skills taught in the context of real reading and writing tasks?
6. Is attention given to the integration of reading and writing skills?
7. Do tasks avoid fragmented, isolated skill drill?
8. Are tasks relevant to student needs?
9. Do tasks provide students with regular opportunities to share and collaborate?
10. Do tasks include both teacher-assigned and student-choice activities?
11. Is the teacher taking time to demonstrate, not just assign?
12. Do teachers make clear what students are to do, how to do it, why they are doing it, and how it will help them become better readers and writers?
13. Do teachers provide constructive support and feedback throughout the task completion process?
14. Do students know and understand how they will be evaluated?

task can be done. Concrete examples of successful, but different, approaches to tasks are provided. Students are taught to assess the difficulty of a task and how to adjust their goals and strategies accordingly.

They emphasize the positive aspects of help seeking and help giving. They teach students how to give clues rather than answers, and group evaluation is a regular part of literacy instruction. These teachers help students see that real learning comes from error, since errors provide information about problems. By emphasizing the value of effort and refining strategies, they equip students to attempt increasingly difficult tasks.

The Instructional Environment Scale (TIES)

The publication of *The Instructional Environment Scale* (TIES) by Ysseldyke and Christenson (1987) represents the first serious effort at systematically assessing the impact of instruction on student performance. TIES is based on this premise:

> Learning and behavior are not independent of their surroundings ... student per-
> formance in school is a function of an interaction between the student and the
> instructional environment. The relationship among student characteristics, acade-
> mic outcomes, and the nature (or quality) of the instructional environment is rec-
> iprocal. (l)

The focus is on evaluating individual students in their instructional environment. The authors describe two major purposes for using TIES: "(a) to systematically *describe* the extent to which a student's academic or behavior problems are a function of factors in the instructional environment, and (b) to identify starting points in *designing appropriate instructional interventions* for individual students" (3).

Three sources of information are tapped when using TIES to judge the quality of the instructional environment: a teacher interview, a classroom observation, and a student interview. At the heart of TIES is the *Instructional Rating Form*. Using research on teacher effectiveness as the basis for development, the authors created this scale of items for twelve component areas (see Figure 6.6). The scale used on the rating form ranges from "very much like the student's instruction" to "not at all like the student's instruction." Each of the twelve components is assessed using this scale. An extensive set of ''descriptors'' is provided to guide the judgments in each component.

The authors clearly state that this is not a norm-referenced test, but rather a qualitative scaling instrument. The technical adequacy of TIES appears to be acceptable for an instrument of this type. The authors rely heavily on inter-rater agreement in rating the instructional environment. Most reported that reliability coefficients are above .90 (with lower reliabilities reported for the two components of Cognitive Emphasis and Motivational Strategies). Although these suggest excellent reliability, it is very likely that untrained users of this test would generate much lower coefficients because of the large number of descriptors

FIGURE 6.6
TIES
Components

Instructional Rating Profile				
How characteristic of the student's instructional environment are indicators of effective instruction in each of the following areas:	(Circle one in each row)			
	Not at all	Not much	Somewhat	Very much
1. Instructional presentation	1	2	3	4
2. Classroom environment	1	2	3	4
3. Teacher expectations	1	2	3	4
4. Cognitive emphasis	1	2	3	4
5. Motivational strategies	1	2	3	4
6. Relevant practice	1	2	3	4
7. Academic engaged time	1	2	3	4
8. Informed feedback	1	2	3	4
9. Adaptive instruction	1	2	3	4
10. Progress evaluation	1	2	3	4
11. Instructional planning	1	2	3	4
12. Student understanding	1	2	3	4

From *The Instructional Environment Scale* by James E. Ysseldyke and Sandra L. Christenson. Copyright © 1987 by James E. Ysseldyke and Sandra L. Christenson. Reprinted by permission of PRO-ED.

and categories that must be considered. The extensive research base for the component categories supports the content validity of the instrument.

Despite some difficulties with TIES, it represents a welcome addition to the repertoire of tools available for assessment. First, it broadens the database upon which decisions about children will be made. Indeed, some states now expect that this instrument will be used to gather information when a special education eligibility determination is being made. A second benefit of TIES is less obvious. So exhaustive are the indicators included in the booklet that it may provide an educative function for some teachers and supervisors. As such, it may prove helpful as teachers and support personnel strive to improve the instructional environment for all students.

THE DIAGNOSTIC PORTFOLIO

The Cases of Marvin and Kyle

In Chapter 4 we introduced the Thumbnail Sketch as a way to summarize information that is gathered throughout the assessment-instruction process. The Thumbnail Sketches for Marvin and for Kyle have been updated based on our

Getting Started (Step 1)	About the Reading and Writing Context (Step 2)
Background	**Resources**
Name: Marvin	• Outdated basals and workbooks
Age: 11 Grade: 5	• Until recently, no recreational reading at all
Key Correlates:	**Instruction**
• Above average IQ	• Instruction focused on isolated phonics
• Normal vision, hearing, and overall health	• Reading assignments and practice without modeling
• Interests are science, sports, "taking things apart"	• No provision for development of motivation or strategies
Information About the Learner	• Whole group basal instruction; little prereading support
Knowledge about Reading and Writing:	• No cooperative work, book sharing and little discussion, especially promoting higher-order thinking
• Reports that people read to learn and for recreation: reports adjusting rate for text difficulty	• Limited reading outside the basal.
• Reports that own reading problem is comprehension	**Tasks**
• Names, "breaking words down" and "asking someone" as the only strategies for reading words that are unfamiliar	• In both old and new school, most tasks are closed
	• Workbooks; seatwork repetitive and isolated from instruction
Motivation:	• Questions used infrequently, most are text explicit, focused on detail
• Pleasant, cooperative demeanor during classroom and clinic sessions	• Almost no writing, except grammar worksheets and skills
• Talks freely about affective responses to text and persists without prompting on difficult tasks	**Settings**
	• English spoken in home. Few reading materials, limited interest in reading at home.
Information About the Context	• Placed in private parochial school from grades 2–4. Large student-teacher ratio, no support services. Policy of placing *all* students in grade appropriate materials.
School History:	
• School-administered achievement tests place in the 35th percentile in reading	
• Multiple moves and family disruptions during K-1	
Instructional Approaches:	
Experiences, Linguistic and Cultural Context:	
• English spoken in the home	

FIGURE 6.7b

Kyle's Thumbnail Sketch: Evaluating the Context

Getting Started (Step 1)	About the Reading and Writing Context (Step 2)
Background Name: Kyle Age: 6 1/2 Grade: 2 Key Correlates: • Normal vision, hearing and overall health/development • Difficult time "paying attention" **Information About the Learner** Knowledge about Reading and Writing: • Reports that own reading problem is knowing the words • Is able to reflect on his own reading and writing abilities Motivation: • Says he doesn't really like to read, would rather play and build • Cooperative and willing to work both in school and in extra sessions **Information About the Context** School History: • Successful preschool experience • Same multi-age K-2 classroom since kindergarten • Lack of progress in reading and writing noted at end of grade 1 Instructional Approaches: • Literature-based instruction in a inquiry-oriented classroom. • Daily reading and writing Experiences, Linguistic and Cultural Context: • English spoken in the home. • Both parents college graduates • Many books and book activities	**Resources** • Beginning readers: "little books" and own writing • Emerging readers: commercially controlled vocabulary and then trade books, children's literature • Journals, portfolios, theme booklets • Process writing folders • Many read alouds—literature **Instruction** • Child-centered curriculum • Individual conferences and whole group meetings • Inquiry-based theme work and choice time each day • Cooperative and collaborative groups • Problem-solving focus **Settings** • English only language spoken in home • Considerable home emphasis on reading and writing • Well-stocked library at school and home • School and community emphasize achievement **Tasks** • Almost all tasks are open • Reading time spent in reading continuous texts, conferencing with teacher, responding in many ways • Writing time spent writing original texts and revising for publication—in books, on walls, in class • Additional writing in journals, theme booklets, and correspondences • Students reflect on own work as select portfolio entries and evaluate own learning

evaluation of the context (see Figures 6.7a and b). This information provides the basis for our ongoing portfolio assessment.

Marvin

Marvin's school experience, while changing, has been dominated by closed tasks and dated literacy resources. In Marvin's old school, whole group oral reading followed by teacher directed questioning of content was the recurrent instructional frame. At no time during the day did Marvin make choices about what to read or write. The tasks that were assigned were almost entirely from commercially available instructional materials that focused on short answer responses to content questions.

In his new setting, Marvin's reading group meets with the teacher periodically to do round robin oral reading and to correct workbook pages. Also in this new school each child in the class has a reading folder that contains differentiated seatwork activities to be completed independently. Although Marvin is now expected to choose books for silent reading and to work on book projects from time to time, his daily tasks are still mostly closed in nature. The teacher does conduct discussions with the higher reading groups, but since Marvin's group struggles with decoding she focuses their independent seatwork on word-level assignments and these are corrected together.

The only assessment that takes place in either setting is externally provided. In both schools the children are evaluated every year on norm-referenced achievement tests and, in Marvin's new setting, the teacher uses the end-of-level tests that accompany her basal reading program to evaluate student learning.

Kyle

Kyle's classroom is one of many like it in his district. The school district has a well-articulated curriculum design. The outcomes clearly focus on students' literature-based reading and process writing.

Motivation to learn is shaped by the many activities and opportunities to explore personal issues. For example, Kyle wrote extensively throughout second grade about snakes—he conducted research, wrote a book, and made journal entries about snakes. There is a wide array of activities to engage different students. Some will spend their time building with blocks during "planning time" while others will work on a science experiment. However, *everyone* writes about what they have done when choice time is over.

Children expect to be successful because they see children of all ages around them being successful. Risk taking is supported through individual goal setting that Ms. McIntyre discusses with all students. In twice daily class meetings, Ms. McIntyre models how to solve problems, how to establish goals, and encourages children to do the same. Older students frequently model by explaining how they think or what they learned or plan to do.

FIGURE 6.8

*Kyle's
Dialogue
Journal*

OCT 16 1994

BARKLEY

I liked the tricks theat
Barkley did. I liked
the book.

MRS. BRILE'S MICE.

I Liked The Book. it wos grat
The littlist Mouse did what
he wanted to do.
She fed the finast cheese to
them. *10/27/94*
Dear Kyle

*I am enjoying reading about your
books, you are starting to tell more
about the characters and parts of
the story. You are becoming a fine
book reporter! You seem to be doing
a better job choosing books too! Do
you think so?* Yes *Love Ms M
Happy Halloween.*

In this classroom, there are very few whole group, or even small group lessons. Students do not receive direct instruction in skills except in response to their own reading and their own questions about print. Ms. McIntyre does discuss reading skills and strategies with individual children as they read and write. Conversations are explicit and the feedback to students about strategies (using picture cues, thinking about the middle and endings of words) is very focused and direct. Ms. McIntyre is adept at providing scaffolding for students—through the selection of predictable books, through shared and repeated readings, and in the instructional dialogue that she and others provide.

The use of scaffolding and dialogue is perhaps most visible in the dialogue journals used by Ms. McIntyre and her students. In Figure 6.8, Kyle and Ms. McIntyre have an exchange. Ms. McIntyre's response supports Kyle's ideas, provides him with correct spelling models, and challenges him to take on a new task.

There are no workbooks or worksheets in this classroom. The classroom is organized as a reading-writing workshop and most tasks in Ms. McIntyre's room are open ones. Students are expected to make good decisions during planning time and to write about the work they did during that time. They also read books, discuss them with their teachers, write responses to their reading in response logs, keep track of what they read in reading logs, write letters to their teachers in their dialogue journals, and write about personal experiences in their journals. In their writing folders they create drafts, keep notes, have conferences, rework some pieces, and publish writing regularly in public displays and in bound books.

There are no norm-referenced tests used in this school. Teachers have adopted a portfolio system and also worked to put in place an assessment system that reflects and challenges their own instructional and curricular designs (see Chapters 8 and 9).

The context for Kyle's literacy development is a rich, diverse instructional context. Like Marvin's, some, but not all possible arrangements are reflected in the description.

CHAPTER SUMMARY

This chapter continues the evaluation of the instructional context by focusing on the role of instructional approaches and tasks in reading and writing performance and techniques for assessing these factors. The first major section of this chapter focuses on instructional approach, which is defined here as the combination of curricular goals and objectives, instructional methods, and assessment practices that are evident within a particular instructional context.

We describe as our general curricular goals, developing motivated, strategic, reflective readers and writers. Motivated readers and writers are those who choose to read and write for a variety of recreational and informational purposes. Strategic readers and writers are able to recruit and use flexibly a wide range of knowledge and skill in reading and writing. Reflective readers and writers are those who develop and use their own standards to evaluate their own reading and writing. As a means of translating general curricular goals into instruction, three types of instructional objectives are described: attitude, content, and process.

Instructional methods are considered in terms of effective practices for creating motivated, strategic, reflective readers and writers. Instructional practices that promote motivation are those that help students to generate expectations for success and also help them to focus on learning versus task completion as a valued endeavor. Key among these practices are activities that promote voluntary reading and writing. Practices that promote reflective reading and writing involve the use of authentic, complex problems and projects as a stimulus for reflection and student self-assessments of their literate activities.

Creating strategic readers and writers involves instructional practices based on the principle of gradually releasing responsibility for learning from the teacher to the student. Three notable characteristics of the gradual release model of learning and instruction are: scaffolding that enables students to solve problems or achieve goals they could not accomplish without support; dialogue or the social interactions by which learning is accomplished; and the level of difficulty at which instruction is carried out.

Finally, classroom assessment practices are considered under the heading of instructional approaches. Tests and alternative assessments are described as two basic types of assessments used in classrooms, either for external accountability purposes or to inform instruction. The impact of assessment practices on teaching and learning is characterized by two principles: you get what you assess; and you do not get what you do not assess.

The second major section of this chapter focuses on reading and writing tasks as a means by which students define what literacy is, why it is important, and what it can do. Open literacy tasks are those in which the goals/processes are child-specified and higher-order thinking is required. Closed tasks are those in which the goals/processes are specified by someone other than the child, and recognition and memory are required. Different types of tasks promote different student behaviors and need to be evaluated accordingly. Independent seatwork, reading comprehension questions, reading-writing workshop, and discussion are examined as examples of different types of literacy tasks.

The third major section of this chapter describes techniques for gathering information about instructional approaches and tasks. These techniques include questionnaires and observational devices such as rating scales and checklists.

Most are informal and require some organization and reflection on the part of the person doing the evaluation. Finally, a relatively new standardized tool known as TIES (*The Instructional Environment Scale*) is described and evaluated, with the conclusion that it adds an important tool to the repertoire of evaluation strategies for assessing context.

STEP 1
Getting Started
with Assessment
(Ch. 4)

STEP 2
Evaluating the
Context
(Chs. 5 & 6)

STEP 3
Evaluating the
Learner
(Chs. 7–10)

STEP 4
Evaluating the
Match Between
Learner and
Context

STEP 5
Reflection,
Decision Making,
and Planning

Ch. 11

STEP 6
Identifying a Better
Match: Diagnostic
Teaching

STEP 7
Adapting Instruction:
Continuous Monitoring
and Modification
(Chs. 12–15)

STEP 8
Reporting
(Ch. 16)

CHAPTER 7

The Foundations of Literacy

INTRODUCTION

An understanding of the foundations of literacy is essential to the development of an appropriate program of assessment and instruction. A rich body of research produced over the last three decades has helped us to understand how the competence of young children emerges in the areas of reading and writing. These recent developments in the area of emergent literacy provide teachers and specialists with information that can be used to develop more effective assessment and instructional programs than have been possible with previous conceptualizations of readiness.

This chapter is divided into three major sections. The first section examines the historical context for thinking about beginning reading and writing, leading to the more contemporary perspective known as *emergent literacy*. The second section elaborates on two major areas of competence necessary for literacy learning derived from an emergent literacy perspective: language development and literacy experiences, which include developing print awareness, understanding the forms and functions of print, analyzing print, and controlling reading and writing processes. The last major section of this chapter describes strategies and tools for assessing the emergent abilities of young readers and writers.

UNDERSTANDING HISTORICAL VIEWS OF LEARNING TO READ AND WRITE

Over the last century, educators have differed in their views of how children learn to read and write. The ideas and beliefs associated with various perspectives are still present in the thinking of many teachers and administrators and in instructional programs provided to young children. Early educators argued that children

223

simply grow into *readiness*, much the way a tree or plant develops. Later, some teachers and theorists asserted that readiness is either caused or facilitated by the environment. Recent research has led to a reconceptualization of readiness as *emergent literacy*, or the gradual emergence of written literacy skills in the context of general cognitive and oral language development. Each of these views is described briefly, followed by a short discussion of instruction in today's schools.

Readiness

Developmental Views of Readiness

Historically, teachers were taught that readiness is an objectively measurable point that reflects the *moment* when an individual is sufficiently mature in cognitive, affective, and psychomotor areas to be *able* to learn to read. The concept of "readiness" is associated with reading, not writing. Until quite recently, students were expected to learn to read in kindergarten and first grade. Only after they had mastered most aspects of early reading was writing introduced.

The earliest views of readiness were clearly developmental ones. At the center of a developmental view of readiness are two related ideas: children's learning is biologically determined; and there is an orderly and predetermined development of abilities. These early views of reading readiness are attributed to Gesell, who during the 1920s described readiness as "neural ripening," arguing that "behaviors unfold automatically" (Teale and Sulzby 1986).

These developmental (often called "nativist") views of readiness received additional momentum in 1931, when Morphett and Washburne published a study concluding that children were unlikely to succeed in reading before they had attained a mental age of 6.6 years. Many educators believed that this finding validated the concept of readiness as an organically determined phenomenon. Mental age, perceptual-motor development, social maturity, and general physical development are all considered critical aspects of reading readiness.

The combination of neural ripening theories of development and the assertion of a set mental age for reading readiness created, perhaps unwittingly, an instructional mandate for inaction. The implications for educational practice seemed straightforward—instruction should be withheld until the child is "ready" (Teale and Sulzby 1986). Certainly, there is both intuitive and empirical evidence to indicate that children must arrive at some developmental milestones before they are able to cope with print. However, neither the available empirical evidence nor the anecdotal accounts of teachers and parents support an account of beginning reading development that is orderly and unchanging. In addition, it is not clear which, if any, of these traditional abilities are *prerequisite* to others.

Nativist views of reading readiness continue to exert strong influence today, evident in both assessment and instruction practices for preschool and kindergarten-age children. For example, in many parts of the United States, Gesell's developmental screening tests are still used to make decisions about students' readiness for entry into kindergarten and debates about the appropriate age for entry into kindergarten programs continue.

Educators who hold strong nativist views often argue that early print experiences or even the presence of print in the kindergarten environment is inappropriate. McGill-Franzen (1992) has countered that this version of learning is "a trap for poor children" because the kinds of experiences that might lead children toward literacy are considered inappropriate for kindergarten settings although they are generally offered to middle-class children in their homes. The available evidence certainly suggests that development, and therefore readiness for school tasks, is influenced by both experience and instruction.

An Experiential View of Readiness

During the 1950s and 1960s, educators began to move toward a notion of readiness as a product of experience. For example, Dechant (1970) wrote:

> There are both biological and environmental determinants of readiness for and achievement in reading. Among the more important factors are the child's intellectual, physical, social, and emotional development, his general proficiency in language, and his sensory equipment. Success in reading also depends on the child's proficiency in auditory and visual discrimination. It is assured by a wide background of personal experience, by a genuine interest in reading, and by an adequate instructional program. (Dechant 1970, 40)

Dechant, like others of this era (for example, Tinker and McCullough 1968), believed that instruction should be offered to develop readiness where there was none. This increased focus on teaching as a remedy for lack of readiness led to a wide array of training programs. With few exceptions, these programs were designed to train students in one or more subskill areas. Many of these subskills were similar to those tested on the earlier developmental readiness tests (perceptual motor ability, visual discrimination, and so on). Readiness training programs remain a common feature of many beginning reading programs.

It is important to understand that few of the early attempts at readiness training resulted in better reading achievement. One of the reasons that so few of these earlier readiness programs affected reading achievement is that many of the readiness skills described in older reading textbooks and embedded in most commercial readiness programs are not necessary for learning to read. For example, knowledge of shapes and colors may indicate overall cognitive development, but this knowledge is not required for students to begin to learn to read (see Durkin 1987; Shepard 1986). Similarly, many gross motor skills, once believed prerequisite for readiness, have proven unnecessary for learning to read. As a general rule, the only perceptual-motor training programs that have demonstrated any level of success in promoting reading achievement are those that move rapidly to involve children with letters and words, preferably in a meaningful context (see Klesius 1972; H. Robinson 1972).

Beginning Reading and Writing Instruction Today

In both assessment and instruction, content and procedures have been dictated by the views of reading readiness we have just described. Two points are especially important to understand: tests of reading readiness typically result in profiles of subskill abilities; and the appropriate response to lack of readiness has been a curriculum designed to train children in these subskills, and/or to delay instruction until these subskills have been mastered or "unfold."

Educators today often still talk about "readiness" as though they were describing a developmental phenomenon. However, when teachers say that a particular student is not ready to learn to read, they do not usually mean that the student is incapable of learning to read and write by some means that we might devise. Rather, they usually mean that the student is not ready to take advantage of the instruction that will be offered. This is problematic because kindergarten and first-grade programs typically offer only one type of beginning reading instruction. Thus, as Durkin (1978, 1987) notes, children have to adapt to the program rather than the other way around.

> The question of a child's readiness for reading has a two-fold focus: (a) his capacity in relation to (b) the instruction that will be available.... Ideally, of course, the educator's question would be: Given this child's particular abilities, what type of instruction can we offer that will make use of them and thus allow the child to experience success? (Durkin 1978, 162–163).

There *is* an increasing variation in the types of beginning reading programs used today and these generally reflect changes in knowledge and belief among teachers that have resulted from new bodies of theory and research. In the next section, we describe these issues in detail.

UNDERSTANDING EMERGENT LITERACY

Educators and researchers who have studied young children's literacy development have come to understand that children begin to acquire literate knowledge, skills, and behaviors at home during their earliest years. Teale and Sulzby (1986) note that "the first years of the child's life represent a period when legitimate reading and writing development are taking place. These behaviors and knowledge are not *pre-* anything, as the term *pre-reading* suggests" (p. xix). From an emergent perspective, readiness is reconceptualized as the *process of becoming literate* as opposed to a series of discrete, specifiable skills that must be developed before learning how to read.

An emergent perspective does not deny the developmental nature of literacy learning, but places it in a framework that identifies children's early years as a period of high activity rather than passive waiting for readiness to unfold. More contemporary developmental views, informed by the work of Piaget (1960) and Vygotsky (1978), see children as active constructors of knowledge. This view acknowledges the critical role of the learner, but also highlights the role of engaged adults:

> By talking with grownups and capable peers as they go about doing the kinds of things literate people do, children are able to construct meanings for tasks that

they could not understand on their own ... such instruction actually transforms the child's development so that tomorrow the child is able to independently do what he could do only with assistance today. (McGill-Franzen 1992, 58)

An emergent perspective also focuses our attention on all aspects of literacy, not just reading. Indeed, the relevant evidence suggests that many children will write before they read. At the very least the most recent research findings suggest that children are developing competence simultaneously in all aspects of literate behavior: reading, writing, listening, and speaking; and that children seem to acquire some of the readiness skills *in the process of learning to read and write* (Ehri 1979). Thus, reading and writing are seen as a continuum of socio- and psycholinguistic development that begins long before the onset of formal schooling and lasts a lifetime.

Current research suggests that there are many abilities that provide the underpinnings for literacy learning. It appears that these abilities emerge more or less simultaneously and that none is mastered before children enter school. Even at age seven, children continue to refine their understanding and control of literacy tasks (Lomax and McGee 1987). It is also clear that the acquisition of these early emerging abilities sets the stage for subsequent success or failure in school settings (Juel 1988).

In the sections that follow, we consider two important aspects of emergent literacy. First, we consider the nature of oral language development and how the acquisition of oral language competence prepares children for reading tasks and vice versa. Second, we discuss the types of literacy experiences necessary for effective emergence into conventional reading and writing. Four interrelated experiences are identified and discussed: developing print awareness; understanding the forms and functions of print; analyzing print; and controlling reading and writing processes.

Learning to Talk

Learning to talk is one of the first productive cognitive tasks confronting young humans.

> There is much for children to learn: not just the words, but their pronunciation and the ways of combining them to express the relationships between the objects, attributes, and actions to which they refer. They also have to learn how the more subtle distinctions of intention are expressed—indirect and direct requests; questions of various kinds, and expression of different attitudes, such as sympathy, anger, apology, and so on—through different selections and orderings of words and structures and the use of different patterns of intonation and facial and bodily gestures. (Wells 1986, 39)

The ways in which children accomplish this task can tell us a great deal about how humans learn to acquire cognitive competence in general.

Learning to read and write are highly correlated with oral language competence. This relationship probably exists for a number of reasons. First, reading and writing are language-based, cognitive tasks. Second, both written language and spoken language are communicative processes. That is, reading, writing and talking are used to exchange ideas, request information, demand and elicit help, share feelings, and so forth. Finally, both oral language communication and written communication are interactive, taking place in a context that influences the active search for meaning. By studying how children learn language, we can gain tremendous insight into the cognitive structures and strategies they will employ in learning to read and write.

The connections here are reinforced in an unexpected set of findings involving studies of learning to read and write among limited English proficiency (LEP) students. The research suggests that "LEP students who develop a strong sociocultural, linguistic, and cognitive base in their primary language (L1) tend to transfer those attitudes and skills to the other language and culture (L2)" (Ovando 1993, 225) and are more successful at learning to read and write in English (Hudelson 1987).

What Children Must Learn About Language
There are some features common to all languages that must be learned.

> When you know a language, you know unconsciously, intuitively, the set of possible sounds in that language, the set of possible meanings in that language, and a finite set of abstract principles for relating these meanings and sounds. (Lindfors 1980, 40)

Thus, one of the first tasks that confronts babies is to figure out that the auditory sounds of humans are meaningful. Although infants are typically surrounded by human talk, there is no reason to assume that they would automatically know that these sounds, in distinct combinations, had specific and special meanings.

The sounds of a language only provide the starting point, however. Children must learn how to express their intentions by using language. In order to accomplish this, they must figure out *how* to name the objects and ideas in their language. In addition, they must figure out the *grammar* of their language. This grammar is composed of the rules for mapping meaning onto words. The grammar typically dictates that various meaning relationships are described by particular word orders or syntactic structures (see Chapter 2).

Not all languages have the same rules for mapping meaning on strings of words. So, for example, in most romance languages (such as Spanish), adjectives follow the noun they are describing, whereas in English these modifiers are placed before the noun. Children must learn what word order is dictated by their particular grammar and the rules that tell them how to combine words.

There are other important skills and abilities required of the competent oral language user. For example, at very early ages children come to recognize a range of *language functions*. Halliday (1975) has studied and categorized the functions of language. In Figure 7.1, these functions are coupled with examples from a young boy from the ages of eighteen to twenty months.

Language is learned in order to express certain intentions and to perform certain functions. These intentions and purposes are executed in the context of

FIGURE 7.1
Functions of Language

Language Function	Example
Instrumental language the "I want" function; language used to satisfy needs	"I wanna the cookie too." Or, reaching for toy another child has "Mine!"
Regulatory language the "do as I tell you" function; language for controlling others	"I do it myself."
Interactional language the "me and you" function; language for interacting with others	"What you doing?" (Said over and over to elicit response from adult)
Personal language the "here I come" function; language for expressing feelings and personality	"I scared."
Imaginative language* the "let's pretend" function; language used to create own environment.	(Putting a construction worker's hardhat on his head): "Going to work. Bye-bye."
Heuristic language the "tell me why" function; language for exploring the environment	"Emma crying. What happened?"
Informative/representational language the "I've got something to tell you" function; language for communicating	"It's darking." (at the end of the day)

(*) As children get older, their use of language for imaginative play is very evident: "You pretend that you're sick and that's the hospital and I'll pretend I'm the mommy." (T's older sister, age 5).

Functions as described by Halliday (1975). *Learning How to Mean* (pp. 18–21). New York: Elsevier North Holland, Inc.

social interaction. It is our knowledge of language that allows us to translate the sounds speakers produce into a representation of the messages that they are trying to communicate. The end result of language learning is not simply mastering the language structures. Children master the forms of language in order to communicate. Mastery of vocabulary and word order results in nothing if the learner cannot use those forms for the purpose of producing and understanding thoughts, ideas, and feelings.

When individuals are competent in their primary or home language (L1), they know other things as well. According to Ovando (1993), there are five "culture-related" domains involved in learning a language. These include: (1) *discourse,* or knowledge of how to organize the language in longer chunks;

(2) *appropriateness*, involving knowledge of what types of language to use in different settings (for example, with friends versus in school); (3) *paralinguistics*, which captures the nonverbal aspects of communication such as gesture, distance from speaker, etc.; (4) *pragmatics*, or knowledge of the implicit norms governing communication in social settings, such as when to speak, how to pace talk, politeness rules, etc.; and (5) *cognitive-academic language proficiency*, which describes the language skills needed to learn specialized content. The complexity of this knowledge and the ways in which it interacts in different languages and cultures highlights how culture-specific language acquisition really is.

Of course, the social conventions of language are an important determinant of school achievement (see Chapter 5). They dictate how we should speak to different individuals in different contexts. "Languages grow and develop as tools of communication within a given environment. In this sense, there is no such thing as 'right' or 'wrong' language, only language that is appropriate or inappropriate in a given context" (Ovando 1993, 217). Mismatches between school conventions and the conventions that children have learned at home can lead to poor performance and wrong judgments about children's ability to learn in school.

How Language Is Learned

Most humans appear to move toward oral language competence through a series of more or less similar stages. The presence of these developmental stages across cultural and linguistic boundaries provides strong evidence that humans have some biological basis for language production. It is clear that children learn to speak their language using differing types of information and interactive styles (see Heath 1983). Thus, it seems that human babies have a biological predisposition toward learning language. However, it should also be noted that this predisposition is played out in environments where others interact through language and encourage children to participate (Wells 1986; Wong-Fillmore 1991). It is important to interpret so-called stage theories of development as general guidelines rather than rigid, unalterable stages.

Many parents would assert that they "taught their children to talk" and that children learn language largely through imitation and reinforcement/feedback. However, the available research evidence suggests otherwise. Children are not deliberately taught the language, and they don't learn to talk through imitation alone. Instead, it appears that children construct the grammar of their language through the internalization and generation of rules. What the child learns is not a set of utterances, but a set of rules for processing utterances. For example, young children frequently produce utterances such as these: "He *goed* to the store"; "It's *darking* outside"; or "I'm going to school today, *amn't* I?" These examples demonstrate how children produce speech that could not have been imitated, as no competent speaker of English produces them. The child creates order by generating hypotheses, testing them out, and then modifying them in the face of new evidence.

Children's mistakes reveal more about their knowledge than their lack of knowledge. As children generate rules for the language they are learning, their speech reflects this growing knowledge. For example, when children come to know that nouns can be converted to verb forms (as in "That room is a mess" and "You're messing up my things"), they may create errors that are consistent with this knowledge such as "We'll airplane to Florida" and "You're germing it all up." In these examples, we see that children search for regularities, create rules, simplify the task, and overgeneralize and extend the information they have to new situations. In short, they are engaged in the development of strategies.

Attention to meaning is a striking feature of early language development. From the beginning young children's utterances reflect semantic intent. Their productions reflect an awareness that the functional purpose of language is to create and communicate meaning. This is most evident at the two-word utterance stage, when children seem capable of producing only two-word constructions. During this stage, researchers have observed what is termed *telegraphic* speech, so called because children leave out the words that are left out in telegrams and retain only those most essential to convey meaning, for example "baby ride" and "Mommy cookie."

Although it is clear that children are not taught language, they do not learn it without help. Children need to have language available to them so that they can work out the regularities. In addition, they need responsive conversational partners who will help them to see how the language works and provide feedback on their efforts.

> Learning to talk should thus be thought of as the result of a partnership: a partnership in which parents and other members of the community provide the evidence and then encourage children to work it out for themselves. Andrew Lock sums it all up in a single phrase when he describes the process as "the guided reinvention of language. (Wells 1986, 51)

Oral Language and Its Relationship to Reading and Writing

It is probably not the case that learning to read and write are entirely dependent on oral language knowledge (Menyuk 1984). Preschool children have not acquired all the knowledge and skill they will need and use as they proceed through school. Children continue to acquire new vocabulary, more complex structures, and encounter new contexts for meaning as they grow and learn in school. In particular, children are exposed to new types of communicative encounters with different people, especially those out of their own linguistic community. And, finally, the language of books is not exactly the same as the oral language children have learned; although students from certain home environments use language that is more closely related to "book language" than other children.

However, it certainly is true that the development of oral language abilities lays the foundation for successful acquisition of reading and writing competence. Taking all the evidence together, oral language competence is important to reading and writing for these reasons:

1. In learning to talk, children develop (or demonstrate) a number of general cognitive strategies for learning.
2. In learning to talk (and listen), children acquire much that they will use to aid them in bringing meaning to print: vocabulary, understanding of syntax, the ways in which meaning is carried in language structures, and alternative structures for communicating similar and dissimilar ideas.
3. Children's oral language abilities permit them to use prediction and hypothesis testing to support their initial attempts at reading and writing.
4. Children's oral language structures will be reflected in the written forms and modes they produce in writing.
5. Children's degree of sophistication in vocabulary, syntax, phonological development, and usage will influence interaction with print during reading.

As we will see shortly, learning to read and write requires that an understanding of certain linguistic properties be brought to conscious awareness. Menyuk (1984) concluded that oral language development is important to learning to read because beginning readers who have not yet acquired certain features of oral language competence will not be able to bring them to conscious awareness for the task of reading. Similarly, writing appears to promote in children the ability to analyze language and speech in ways that had not been accomplished before.

Literacy Experiences

The foundations of literacy begin with language acquisition, but also include learning that print and speech are related, print encodes a message, pictures are guides to the message, some language units are more likely to occur than others, certain words in certain orders reflect particular messages, and memory may be used as a guide to understanding (Clay 1979).

These aspects of literacy are acquired in homes, parks, preschools, and stores—anywhere that children encounter and use print. Children are most likely to acquire useful and refined ideas about print as they observe and interact with literate adults. Researchers have consistently found that early and/or successful readers and writers share certain types of literacy experiences (Kastler, Roser, and Hoffman 1987, Ollila and Mayfield 1992):

1. Families provide a variety of writing materials.
2. Children observe others reading and writing.
3. Children are encouraged to experiment in writing.
4. Parents read aloud to their children.
5. Parents or others answer questions about reading and writing.
6. There are books in the home and/or children are taken to the library.

These experiences set the stage for learning to read and write, but also promote the acquisition of specific knowledge and skill. They are important for: developing print awareness; understanding the forms and functions of print; analyzing the task of reading; and gaining control of literacy behaviors/activities.

Learning about the Forms and Functions of Print

Children understand the functional value and significance of literacy when they experience it directly—through lap reading with their parents and as they send cards or help to write grocery lists.

Developing print awareness.   Children in our society are surrounded by print—on doors, cereal boxes, signs, etc. It appears that they acquire, at an early age, a fairly sophisticated understanding that these symbols convey meaning. Although some researchers question the utility of this generalized awareness (for example, Ehri 1987), it does appear that situational print awareness is part of a larger progression of acquired skill and knowledge. It is likely that most children understand something about the functions of print in environmental settings and use this information to arrive at key conclusions about the links between print and speech; however, it is also important to remember that some do not.

Just as children must come to understand the functional, meaningful nature of spoken language, they must come to appreciate that print is communicative, functional, and meaningful. Recent evidence suggests that most children in our society have a fairly well-developed "sense of print awareness in situational contexts" by the time they reach school age (Y. Goodman 1986; Heath 1983; Mason 1980). For example, Hiebert (1981) found that three-, four-, and five-year-old children were all sensitive to differences between print and drawing stimuli. In addition, when presented with words and letters in meaningful contexts, even very young children demonstrate competence in understanding concepts such as word and letter, provided they are not asked to use or understand specific terminology.

Children generally learn that print is meaningful prior to formal schooling as they observe print on pizza and cereal boxes, for example, and as they watch more competent others write notes or letters to friends and relatives. Many young children engage in "scribble writing" at a very early age and announce as three-year-old Theo did, "Oh, I think I'll write in cursive." What is especially revealing is that children's early scribbles vary from culture to culture—reflecting the characteristics of adult writing in that system. So, for example, while young U.S. children and young Egyptian and Israeli children all scribble, the physical appearance of the scribbles are very different although the purpose and intent are remarkably similar (Harste, Woodward, and Burke 1984).

Environmental print awareness is necessary for emergent literacy, but it clearly is not sufficient for success in conventional reading and writing. Children need to acquire much more specific ideas about how print is organized and why we read.

Understanding the language of books.   Despite many commonalities, oral and written language are not identical, and young children need to learn the language of books. *Read-aloud transactions* provide a pleasurable and supportive environment for this type of literacy learning. The Commission on Reading concluded in its 1985 report that "the single most important activity for building the knowledge required for eventual success in reading is reading aloud to children" (Anderson et al. 1985). One of the specific benefits of reading aloud to children in the preschool years is that children learn to "talk like a book" (Fox 1987). The following excerpt, for example, is hardly the stuff of daily conversations: " ... and he sailed off through night and day and in and out of weeks and almost over a year to where the wild things are ... " (Sendak 1963). During read-aloud transactions, children learn to deal with a different type of communicative style (book language) and with a communicator who is not present (the author). Children also become familiar with the look of print, the direction of it, the ways in which pages are turned to move through text, the fact that pictures and text are generally related, and so forth (Clay 1979).

This knowledge is as useful for writing as for reading. For example, one of the most important differences between spoken and written language is that written language is "decontextualized." This means that written language is produced so that it does not require the writer and the reader to share a physical context. In order to accomplish this, authors use a variety of cohesive devices to link information together in a meaningful whole. Children must learn to attend to the cues and referents that authors use so that they can sort out events and motives and to use them intentionally in their own writing so that others can understand the messages they compose.

Increasingly, researchers are studying not only the specific knowledge gleaned during reading aloud, but also the lessons learned from the exchanges themselves. These events often provide opportunities for adults to model appropriate thinking and feeling responses. This active interaction with text is necessary, of course, if children are to become competent readers and skillful writers. In addition, these read-aloud transactions teach children to question the meaning of text and encourage them to begin to think and use language in ways that will later be critical for school success (Altwerger, Diehl-Faxon, Dockstader-Anderson 1985; Wells 1982).

Understanding story structure.   Research suggests that young children need a well-developed sense of story to comprehend text fully. In addition, story sense appears helpful in generating predictions about upcoming text and also in remembering (or reconstructing) stories. Thus, children who have not yet formed a solid mental map of stories, or those whose experience has promoted a different frame, are likely to have more difficulty reading and remembering some information.

Read-aloud transactions help children begin to internalize different structures for different types of text. Well-read-to youngsters generate a mental map for stories during the many interactions they have with this type of text (Mandler and Johnson 1977; Stein and Glenn 1979). These mental maps, or "story schema," are generalized structures that people use to comprehend (McConaughy 1982). Several types of story structures have been proposed. The stories children encounter in school settings typically contain the following elements:

- Setting—generally the physical setting and characters
- Initiating event—"it all started when ..."
- Internal response—how the main character reacts to the initiating event
- Attempt—an action or series of actions by the character(s) to try to reach a goal or solve a problem
- Consequence—what happens as a result of the attempt
- Reaction—a final reaction or event that ties the rest of the story together (also called a resolution)

These elements actually describe the elements present in stories that come from the European folk and fable tradition (Stein and Glenn 1979). Other stories have different types of arrangements and are reflected in the stories children tell and in their comprehension of stories heard or read (Gee 1989; Minami and McCabe, in press). Many experiences with different types of texts encourage children to see that stories have certain predictable features and these can be relied upon to aid comprehension and memory.

The oral and written stories of less-skilled readers and writers are often less coherent and well-developed than those told or written by their skilled classmates (Montague, Maddux, and Dereshiwsky 1990). Research has consistently indicated that disabled readers produce poor narratives and have difficulty recalling narratives they have heard. In particular, they tend to delete causal and temporal connections from their stories (Dickinson and McCabe 1991).

Not surprisingly, children's ability to tell their own spontaneous narratives is also fueled by their language development and their experiences with stories. Students who have experienced stories that unfold in different ways, or have symbols and meanings different from European folktales, will have a different sense of story. They will have different mental maps available for comprehension. For example, the story structure of narratives told by African-American children (especially girls) tends to differ from that of white, middle-class children (Gee 1989). In addition, it is important to understand that children's primary language is a factor in assessment. Many L2 learners provide much more complete retellings if they are allowed to substitute their first language for key English vocabulary words they don't know or can't remember (Garcia 1991).

Similarly, our experience suggests that even when students demonstrate weak ability to tell classic narrative stories, they may have very strong ability to narrate other types. In Figure 7.2, for example, you will see Ian's attempt at telling a story, which is weak and ill-formed. You will also see that when asked to tell a personal narrative ("tell a story about something that happened to you") his knowledge and skill look far more impressive.

Ian is a young, first-grade child from an isolated rural community. His experiences with literature and formal school tasks were very slim. However, his large, extended family obviously provided considerable experience in telling and retelling personal narratives.

General literacy experiences such as read-aloud transactions provide children with the information they need to generate good hypotheses about

FIGURE 7.2
Ian's Story Telling and Personal Narrative

IAN, grade 2

I. Story Narrative: "Tell me a story"

Monster Meals. Monsters eat meals. Put some car doors, some old shoes, some nails. That's how monsters eat their meals. And I made that up.

II. Personal Narrative: "Sometimes people tell stories about a time when something exciting or sad happened; or about a good time with a friend. Did anything like that ever happen to you? Tell me a story about it."

When I was in kindergarten, my teacher told me to get off the ice. I didn't. I threw out a rock about this big and I went to go get it. I slipped and the rock landed on my thumb and I broke my thumb. And that hurt. (pause) They said my thumb was too small for a cast so they said, "gauze it up." So that's what my Mom and Dad put on it, gauze.

III. Retelling: "Now, tell *me* that story."

Dogger
There was this little boy that had a dog. He lost him. His parents and him were searching, but he didn't find him until they went to the fair and a little girl bought him. And he said, "Well," and his sister said, "Would you swap this teddy bear for my brother's dog back, please?" And she smiled. And then he said, "Did you like that teddy bear anyway?" She said, "No, I didn't like him because his eyes were too scary." And she said, "If I had another teddy in my bed there wouldn't be room for me." They used to walk him like a real dog, and his mother showed him how to wash him. And sometimes he'd pull him in a wagon.

---

conventional literacy. If children come to school without these experiences, the instructional program should build on the specific experiences children bring with them.

Analyzing Speech and Print

In order to become successful readers and writers children also must acquire the ability to analyze and to control their interactions with print (Bialystok and Ryan 1985). The special requirements of reading or writing print are not obvious to the novice. Young children typically demonstrate limited awareness of language itself. This *metalinguistic awareness,* or conscious knowledge of the linguistic elements of language, continues to develop throughout the school years. Yet, children must develop linguistic awareness in order to learn to read and write.

The concept of word. Because the strategy "pay attention to meaning" works so well for speech, young children seem not to be aware of the component pieces of language. For example, speech provides few cues to tell children about the word as a unit of analysis. Words that name objects are easily isolated, but in the flow of normal speech, individual words are not clearly marked. To be successful in reading and writing, though, children must acquire the ability to identify individual words in the context of other words.

The following example demonstrates how children who appear competent may have incorporated unanalyzed items into their language. A three-year-old sings "Baa-baa black sheep *have you any* wool …" (a favorite song which she has sung for months). Then she asks, "Mom, what's *pabuany*?" What has been understood by the informed listener (Mom) as "have you any" has actually been perceived and produced by the child as a single unit "pabuany." However, the child's question does indicate her growing demand for clarity in language.

As Downing (1978) points out, beginners must also learn what conventions are represented in print. For example, children must learn that words are bound configurations that are separated by white space in print and that the term *word* is used to refer to a specific aspect of language. The available evidence suggests that four- and five-year-old children have a difficult time selecting a word from among letters, numbers, phrases, and sentences (Ferriero and Teberosky 1979; 1982; Hare 1984). Reid (1966) interviewed five-year-old English children asking them whether a variety of stimuli were "words." Some identified whole sentences as words, some made only random guesses, and some said that words, phrases, and sentences were all words. Similarly, when U.S. kindergarten and first-grade children were given sentence strips and asked to "cut off" a word with a scissors, they sometimes cut off a word. Just as often, however, they cut off a portion of the word or cut off two words together (Meltzer and Herse 1969). Even when children are asked about reading and words with a book in front of them, many four- and five-year-olds demonstrate substantial confusion about what constitutes a word and what people look at when they read (Downing 1970).

Children do not acquire the concept of *word* in one flash of insight. As with all such knowledge and skill, the concept develops over time. A well-defined concept of word is probably not a prerequisite to reading and writing, although it clearly facilitates initial instruction. Many researchers have concluded that children learn about the concept of word *during* the process of learning to read and write (Ehri 1979; Hall 1976; Sulzby 1986a). That is, instruction in reading and writing is what leads children to develop the metalinguistic awareness of *word*.

Phonemic segmentation. The ability to separate words into constituent sounds, or phonemic segmentation, is one ability that increasingly appears to distinguish children who have difficulty learning to read and write from those who make good progress (Juel 1988; Stanovich 1986; Yopp 1988). For example, Juel's longitudinal study of a large group of "at risk" children suggests that children who are poor readers in first grade remain poor readers in fourth grade. One hallmark of those poor first-grade readers was very limited phonemic awareness. Indeed, Juel's findings suggest that although poor readers' phonemic awareness grew steadily in first grade, they left first grade with a little less phonemic awareness than the children who became average or good readers possessed upon entering first grade.

Clearly, children must be able to distinguish separate sound units in words before they will be able to identify letters in words that relate to these sounds. It is important to note that phonemic segmentation ability does not require that children know what letter stands for each sound they hear in a word. Phonemic segmentation is not the same as auditory discrimination, which refers to the ability to distinguish between two different sounds. Indeed, it appears that auditory discrimination tests are poor predictors of ability to segment speech (Yopp 1988).

Research suggests that young children may take quite a long time to acquire phonemic awareness. Liberman and Shankweiler (1979), for example, report the results of a study investigating the ability of four-, five-, or six-year-old children to segment speech into constituent phonemes and syllables. None of the children at age four was able to segment by phoneme, although half of these children could segment by syllable. Only 20 percent of the five-year-old children were able to segment by phoneme and, even at age six, only 70 percent were able to do so. Other authors have reported similar findings based on a variety of criteria (Calfee, Lindamood, and Lindamood 1973; Fox and Routh 1976; Hall 1976).

On the other hand, recent research suggests that there is a strong relationship between the rhyming abilities of children as young as three years old and their later success in reading (Bryant, MacLean, Bradley, and Crossland 1990). These researchers argue that this relationship is due to differences in children's ability to detect individual phonemes. Other researchers argue convincingly that children learn these individual phonemes when they receive instruction in school reading programs (Bowey and Frances 1991). They agree that phonological awareness is a critical factor in reading success, but that young children analyze only *onsets* and *rimes* (the initial consonants and a phonogram), not individual phonemes.

Most existing readiness programs do not include instruction designed to help children segment words into either phonemes or onsets and rimes. Since ability to segment speech into phonemic units appears to have strong predictive power, most researchers suggest that early instruction in this area is needed (Tunmer, Herriman, and Nesdale 1988). Indeed, recent research suggests that direct instruction in phonemic segmentation (A. Cunningham 1990) or onset and rimes (Goswami 1986) may be related to reading achievement at the beginning stages of reading development.

However, caution is needed in this area. Although the ability to segment sounds is clearly important, most researchers have also concluded that phonological sensitivity is necessary, but not sufficient, for reading achievement (Tunmer, Herriman, and Nesdale 1988). For most children, good instruction in reading and writing leads to greater linguistic awareness: "Being taught to read helps to develop awareness of phonological segments" (Menyuk 1984, 109). It is as though the child had never thought to analyze speech, but in learning to read and/or write had been forced to recognize units and subdivisions (Francis 1973). Thus, early successful experiences with print can develop students' abilities in this critical area (see Cunningham and Cunningham 1992; Pikulski 1994).

Speech-to-print match. As we have seen, children typically do not have the capacity to analyze speech into all its constituent parts until after instruction and/or practice in reading and writing have begun. Emergent readers and writers must begin to recognize that phonemes are represented in print with letters and letter combinations, and some direct information about this relationship is probably necessary before children can take control of their reading and writing.

In a longitudinal study of thirty children between the ages of three and six, Ferreiro (1980) examined the development of children's hypotheses and strategies for reading and writing. Her findings demonstrate that children's early "guesses" about the nature of these processes are quite different from those of older children. For example, children at first thought that similarities and differences between words were determined by the characteristics of the referent items, not by any similarities in sound. Thus, more letters were needed to write the name of a large item than were needed to write the name of a small one. Ferreiro (1980) provides the following marvelous example from a child in this stage:

> Maria (age four) was asked how many letters it would take to write her name. She said four (as many years as she was old). When asked how many letters it would take to write her mother's name, she responded six. But, for her father (a large man), she responded: "As many as a thousand."

There was considerable agreement among children as they moved through several stages. For example, at some point all the children she studied clearly evolved a "syllabic hypothesis." During this stage, the children believed that each letter represented one syllable. Clearly, when children arrive at the syllabic hypothesis, they have begun to see the formal relationships between speech and print. And, although the timing varied, all the children eventually realized that words are written with strings of graphemes.

In the same way that reading experiences promote phonemic awareness, writing appears to develop print level awareness and skill. As DeFord (1991) has noted:

> When young children write, the reading/writing process is conveniently slowed down; to form messages and print, children must work on a variety of levels. They have to think about what they want to say, what they hear and how they represent it, what they expect to see if they can't hear it and it doesn't look right, where they are in their message, and how they can make their message clear to other readers ... As young writers focus in on smaller or physical aspects of writing, they learn certain principles about print formation, letter sound relationships, spelling patterns, and the meaning of certain morphological forms. (86 and 88)

As children increase their understanding of the requirements of reading and writing, they begin to acquire more cognitive control over their own literacy skills.

The Development of Written Language

For many years, educators assumed that the ability to read preceded the ability to write. Reading was considered to be a decoding activity requiring reception of data, and writing an encoding activity requiring the production of data. Increasingly, research in the area of emergent literacy has brought these assumptions into question. Although the exact relationship between reading and writing has not been determined, it is clear that reading and writing behaviors emerge simultaneously and that the benefits are reciprocal.

> Given encouragement, children will begin to write before they begin to read ... Analyzing sounds in words requires an ability to make words hold still in the mind while the analysis is carried out, which in turn depends on having a stable concept of what a word is. (Gillet and Temple 1982, 163)

The Form and Function of Writing

It seems clear that young children acquire writing competence by writing—in much the same way that they become competent in speech by talking. This does not, of course, happen without a supportive and responsive environment. When children see others around them using writing for functional purposes, they will model their own behavior accordingly; writing lists and messages and signs during play and to signal wants and needs. Of course, these notes and signs will reflect the child's knowledge and skill in writing.

The following stages are evident in the writing development of most children (DeFord 1980, 162):

1. Scribbling
2. Differentiation between drawing and writing
3. Concepts of linearity, uniformity, linear complexity, symmetry, placement, left-to-right motion, and top-to-bottom directionality
4. Development of letters and letter-like shapes
5. Combination of letters, possibly with spaces, indicating understanding of units (letters, words, sentences), but may not show letter/sound correspondence
6. Writing known, isolated words—developing sound/letter correspondence
7. Writing simple sentences with use of inventive spellings
8. Combining two or more sentences to express complete thoughts
9. Control of punctuation—periods, capitalization, use of upper- and lower-case letters
10. Form of discourse—stories, information material, letters, and so on

Caution should be exercised in interpreting this information, because many of these characteristics will be evident simultaneously as children gain control over written forms.

Invented Spelling

The term *invented spelling* is a considered one. It is used to refer to a consistent phenomenon observed in young emergent readers/writers: the ability to invent spellings on their own. The underlying assumptions in the term are captured in the following quotation from Ferreiro (1978):

> In order to understand the writing system which society has forged for them, children must reinvent writing and thereby make it their own. (39)

It is increasingly clear that children's developing spelling abilities reflect their growing linguistic knowledge and control. As children acquire the conventions and the patterns of the language, these appear in their own writing.

The development of invented spelling in children should be supported because it seems clear that children are inclined to solve the puzzle of written language in much the same way they do oral language. For example, spelling errors across children are not random, as can be seen from the sample in Figure 7.3. This sample demonstrates how Kelly's "errors" reflect a rather considerable knowledge base; they are *not* mistakes. She can already isolate all initial and final consonants and represent them appropriately in print. Indeed, she can also represent most medial sounds.

In addition, studies of emergent readers and writers suggest that children appear to move through distinctive developmental stages—moving from very immature spellings to those that approximate standard spellings (for example, Beers and Henderson 1977; Chomsky 1981). Although there are some

FIGURE 7.3
Writing Sample (Age 6)

My brother and my sister are standing by my house

disputes about the content of each stage, the following distinctions are generally made.

Pre-phonemic spelling.   Children use alphabetic symbols to "write" words, but these are generally unrelated to the target word. There is no sound-symbol relationship present and these are likely to reflect earlier notions about how the writing system works (see Ferreiro above).

Early phonemic spelling.   Children exhibit a clear awareness that there is a relationship between phonemes and print. However, children represent very little of the phonemic information in print—sometimes the initial, sometimes the final, graphemes. The letters that are used represent specific phonemes from the word, but not all the phonemes are represented. Example: DR GML = Dear Grandma.

Phonetic (and letter name) spelling.   Children hear and produce sequences of sounds in words. At this stage, children may produce spellings that are quite readable (*wns* for *once* and *bik* for *bike)*. However, children at this stage are also often using a strategy that results in rather strange productions. As they try to represent more and more sounds in words, they begin to use a *letter-name strategy* (Beers and Henderson 1977). That is, they analyze the word they want to spell into its component sounds and then find a letter name to represent each sound. They then spell each sound by choosing the letter name that most closely resembles the sound they want to represent (Gillet and Temple 1982). Thus, children in this stage also produce such words as *lavatr* for *elevator* (Morris 1981). This approach causes problems in correct production of vowels and certain consonant combinations, in particular.

Transitional spelling.   Children's spellings bear a much closer resemblance to standard spellings. In this stage, children make use of visual as well as phonemic information (Gentry 1982). Children generally represent short vowels appropriately in this stage and also mark long vowels, even though these often represent overgeneralizations of learned rules. Thus, spellings such as the following are typical of this stage: *dres* for *dress* and *rane* for *rain*. As Morris (1981) notes, "These transitional spellings, which begin to appear in late first grade or early second grade, are to be welcomed by the teacher, for they signal advancement in the child's understanding of English spelling. No longer does the child believe that spelling is a fixed, simple code in which letters map to sounds in a left-to-right, one-to-one fashion" (664).

Children's inventive spellings can provide a great deal of information about their emergent literacy skills. It is important to understand that "when children reach the transitional stage, reading and spelling diverge from each other; that is, they may continue to make progress as readers at the same time that they continue to make many spelling errors.... Once the transitional stage is reached, it is not particularly productive to analyze spelling to learn about children's reading" (Gillet and Temple 1982, 187). It is, of course, productive to continue to attend to students' spelling as it reflects their knowledge and control of the writing process.

STRATEGIES AND TOOLS FOR ASSESSING EMERGENT LITERACY

Assessment of Emergent Literacy

Gathering dependable and useful information about the literacy abilities of young children can be a very tricky business. In the following section, we briefly discuss the theoretical problems involved in using most existing formal assessment instruments, saving a discussion of specific standardized tools for later in the text (see Chapter 10). In this chapter we describe a number of informal assessment strategies for observation, structured informal assessment, and diagnostic teaching. Before we turn our attention to these specific practices, it is important to consider the problems associated with the assessment of early literacy.

The match between readiness assessment and beginning reading and writing instruction has become increasingly poor as our knowledge and understanding of emergent literacy has continued to expand. Almost all of the readiness tests used today are variations of earlier tests that evolved from older, developmental views of reading readiness. Between 1930 and 1943, twelve readiness tests were published (Betts 1946), several of which are still used widely today in revised versions. As Teale, Hiebert, and Chittenden (1987) note, "Young children's reading and writing are being measured in ways that do not reflect an adequate conceptualization of early literacy development or sensitivity to the fact that children of 4 or 5 have special social and developmental characteristics" (773). Few readiness tests, for example, evaluate children's awareness of the purposes for reading; nor, for that matter, do they evaluate students' phonemic awareness. Similarly, none ask children to write or permit teachers to assess whether children know how to handle a book, understand the conventions of print, or understand the language that will be used in beginning reading instruction (Day and Day 1986).

In addition, most readiness tests include some tasks not directly related to the act of reading or writing (for example, identifying and/or matching geometric shapes). Finally, the demands of specific programs of beginning instruction have been ignored almost completely. "Because most (readiness tests) attempt to be nationally standardized tests, equally applicable to a variety of situations, none fully accounts for the questions of 'what methods' or 'what materials' will be used for instruction" (Nurss 1979, 43).

Now, however, the climate seems much more hospitable for examining children's literacy knowledge and abilities in more authentic ways. Teale, Hiebert, and Chittenden (1987) describe the attributes necessary for good emergent literacy assessment:

1. Assessment is a part of instruction.
2. Assessment methods and instruments are varied.
3. Assessment focuses on a broad range of skills and knowledge reflecting the various dimensions of literacy.

4. Assessment occurs continuously.
5. Literacy is assessed in a variety of contexts.
6. Measures are appropriate for children's developmental levels and cultural background.

These characteristics are entirely consistent with our approach to *all* assessment, but they are critical when evaluating the knowledge and skill of very young children. The Diagnostic Portfolio is an especially useful tool in the assessment of young, or very disabled, readers and writers.

Diagnostic Portfolio and Emergent Literacy

Gathering dependable and useful information about emergent literacy requires continuous observation of children in actual literacy settings. As assessment is planned, it is helpful to reflect on the following questions:

- What do I already know about this child?
- How do I know that?
- What do I still need to know to plan instruction?
- How can I find this out?

A summary form such as the one shown in Figure 7.4 should be used to organize information as it is gathered. This form can also be used to help determine what information is already available from sources such as those described in the Getting Started Phase (see Chapter 4).

Assessment strategies that can be conducted during everyday instructional exchanges are described in the following sections. These classroom-based strategies involve both careful observation of children engaged in normal instructional events and observations of children in situations that have been structured by the teacher to assess specific components of literacy (see Figure 7.5). Thus, for each technique described here, we indicate the types of information that can be gathered.

Informal assessments can provide rich data about children, but it is important to guard against hasty judgments and assumptions. Conclusions *must* be documented. The strategies and forms provided below can help with this task and the role of the Diagnostic Portfolio is key here. Young children's work samples and the observation checklists provide the evidence you need.

Observing Spontaneous Use of Knowledge and Skill

The procedures described in this section expand the focus of the observational techniques on knowledge and attitudes about reading, described in Chapter 4, to include observation of emergent literacy in the areas of oral language development and concepts about print.

Oral Language Checklists

Teachers need to assess oral language competence to ensure that children can accomplish the tasks required in school settings (see Chapter 2). School tasks

FIGURE 7.4

*Summary/
Planning
Form:
Emergent
Literacy
Assessment*

Student: _____ Age: _____ Date: _____

Examiner: _____

I. Oral language

II. Literacy knowledge/experience

    A. Print awareness (environmental)

    B. Book concepts (language, directionality, etc.)

    C. Concept of word (boundaries and linearity)

    D. Phonemic segmentation

    E. Speech-to-print match

III. Story retelling

    A. Story sense

    B. Dictated stories

    C. Language use

IV. Writing

    A. Forms and functions of writing

    B. Invented spelling

V. Observations and comments

demand language use that is quite different from the language used in homes and among peers. Thus, even if children have language development appropriate to their home environment, they may not have acquired language appropriate for functioning in a school setting.

Researchers and educators have come to realize that language is difficult to evaluate through short, controlled samples. Therefore, people who study language acquisition now frequently recommend evaluating language in naturalistic settings (see Lund and Duchan 1988). This means talking and listening to children engaged in everyday school activities. However, if children's primary language differs in important ways from school English, observations may be conducted in other settings as well to distinguish generalized linguistic problems from issues of context and culture.

What is needed is an inclination to notice and a willingness to make narrative notes. A framework is helpful to focus the "noticing." Previously in this chapter, we described Halliday's taxonomy of language functions. Halliday's categories are drawn from actual observations of children and can be used fairly easily as the basis for an evaluation checklist. This will provide information about students' functional use of language.

For more specific aspects of oral language, you might use Rubin's (1995) diagnostic checklist to focus attention (see Figure 7.6). As you observe the child,

FIGURE 7.5

Components of Emergent Literacy Assessment

Components of Emergent Literacy Assessment by Various Informal Techniques

Assessment Strategy	Oral Language Competence	Print Awareness	Concepts of Book Print	Story Sense	Phonemic Awareness	Speech-Print Match	Control of Reading–Writing
	Developmentally appropriate articulation and syntax / Adequate vocabulary / Elaborated use of language / Wide range of language functions	Recognizes environmental print / Recognizes various functions of print / Print carries a message	Parts of book / Directionality/orientation / Language of book print (word/letter) / Punctuation	Recognizes/recalls story elements / Produces well-structured stories / Retains structure during recall	Segmentation of words (oral) / Segmentation of syllables (oral) / Segmentation of phonemes (oral) / Rhyming	Matches spoken words to print / Some sight vocabulary / Sound-symbol correspondence (initial)	Attempts reading/writing / Knows letter names / Knows some sound-symbols / Uses some invented spelling
Informal Observation	X X X X	X X X	→				
Structured Interviews	X X X X	X X X	X X X X		X X		
Structured Observation		X X X	X X X X				
Retelling Guides	X X X X			X X X			
Dictated Stories	X X X X	X		X X		X X X	
Writing Samples	X X	X		X	X X X	X X X	X X X X
DLTA		X X	X X X	X X X			

note the time, setting, materials, and activity and indicate which functions of language are being used. In addition, specific examples of language used should be noted next to each function—the child's actual word usage and syntax can be quite revealing. This approach works well in most classrooms for young children, because there are often times when children are in several centers around the room. Teachers can target one or several children for observation on a particular day. Many teachers find sticky-backed notepads useful.

Checklists for Concepts about Print

Although there are several contrived ways to assess students' knowledge about the functions of literacy, evaluation in this area can be accomplished largely through observation. Many kindergarten and first-grade classrooms are print-rich environments. Print appears on labels, charts, schedules, and so on. In this type of environment, it is possible to observe how often and how well children employ print in their daily activities. As children use print to label, describe, and follow directions, teachers can document the growing competence of each child. For example, the teacher might watch children as they reread familiar books, charts, and papers. The following examples are suggestive of the types of events that are noteworthy:

> Example A: Four-and-a-half-year-old Nora picks up a newspaper and opens it appropriately, remarking: "Oh, here's some news."

> Example B: Five-year-old Joel works intently to make a label to describe his show-and-tell object so that people who see it on the science table "will know what it is."

These children clearly are acquiring a sense of the functional nature of print. Observations should focus on behaviors that demonstrate that children understand the various functions and conventions of literate behavior, not on accuracy (do they read/write correctly?).

As teachers watch for specific behaviors that will inform them about their students' emergent literacy, they should keep the following questions in mind:

- How well does the child distinguish print from pictures?
- How well does the child recognize the functions of print in the environment (signs, posted information, and so on)?
- How does the child reread familiar books (for example, does she "talk like a book," using the structure and vocabulary of book language)?
- What distinctions does the child make among pictures, scribbling, and print?
- In what ways does the child attempt to read familiar books, labels, charts, and so on?
- What distinctions can the child make among different forms of print (labels versus stories)?

Continuous observations of these types of behaviors yield a much richer picture of literacy knowledge than is permitted by formal measures alone.

Despite the usefulness of observation, relying on spontaneous use of knowledge and skill cannot ensure that we have gathered information about all that students can do. Thus, systematic task structuring can be helpful. Argiro (1987)

FIGURE 7.6
Oral Language and Speech Diagnostic Checklist

Student's Name:
Grade:
Teacher:
Diagnostic Checklist for Oral Communication and Speech Improvement

	YES	NO
Speech (general): The child's speech is		
1. distinct		
2. inaudible		
3. monotonous		
4. expressive		
Nonverbal Communication: The child		
1. uses facial expressions effectively		
2. uses hands effectively		
3. uses body movements effectively		
Vocabulary (general): The child's vocabulary is		
1. meager		
2. rich		
3. accurate		
4. incorrect		
Sentences:		
1. The child uses incomplete sentences.		
2. The child uses simplistic sentences.		
3. The child uses involved sentences.		
4. The child uses standard English.		
5. The child uses a variation of English.		
6. English is not the dominant language of the child.		
The child engages in conversation freely.		
The child respects other persons when he or she is speaking.		
The child enters into class discussions.		
The child can describe in his or her own words an event that has occurred.		
The child freely engages in these activities:		
1. creative drama		
2. role playing		
3. choral speaking		
4. finger play (primary grades)		
5. puppetry		
6. pantomime		
7. "show and tell" (primary grades)		
8. informal reports		
9. formal reports (intermediate grades)		
10. debates (intermediate grades)		
11. storytelling		

Source: Rubin D. (1995). *Teaching Elementary Language Arts: An Integrated Approach* (5th ed.) (pp. 116–117). Boston: Allyn & Bacon. Reprinted with permission.

developed a useful (and validated) battery of tasks to assess written language awareness (see Figure 7.7). This battery is based on the research of several authors and it pulls together many of the techniques we have described above. Much of this information can be gathered in daily encounters with students. However, some of this information requires simple structuring of either the task or the context so that a complete picture can be obtained of the child's abilities in these areas. This measure provides specific information about students' general print awareness and about their emerging abilities to analyze the task.

Writing Samples

Student writing samples can provide information about several aspects of emergent literacy. They provide teachers with information about children's knowledge of the sound-symbol system and about their understanding of the functions of writing.

If the child's classroom includes many opportunities for writing, spontaneous samples of children's work can be gathered easily. This is desirable because it permits an evaluation of not only what the child *can* do, but what he or she *does*. Genishi and Dyson (1984) suggest a number of questions that can be considered as various aspects of children's written work are observed (see Figure 7.8).

FIGURE 7.7
Checklist: Functions and Conventions of Literacy

I. Development of an Understanding That Print Conveys Meaning and Serves a Useful Function
Spontaneous use: Does child exhibit competence in using/reading:

Yes	No	
☐	☐	1. Labels
☐	☐	2. Cubbies
☐	☐	3. Signs
☐	☐	4. Name recognition
☐	☐	5. Book print

Structured observation: Present children with stimuli and evaluate ability to recognize by name or function.

1. Cartons or containers for common household foods
2. Advertisements/logos for local fast food chains (e.g., pizza or McDonald's)
3. Common directional signs (e.g., EXIT)
4. Newspaper, magazines, storybooks, adult novels

II. Development of an Awareness of Writing Conventions
Using the stimuli above:

Yes	No	
☐	☐	1. Can child show "where you read"?
☐	☐	2. Name any words or letters?
☐	☐	3. Show you how to read the print (directionality)?

FIGURE 7.8
Guidelines for
Observing
Kindergarten
Writing

When observing (watching, listening to, talking to children about) their writing, you might consider the following questions:

The Message
1. Does the child believe that he's written a message? If so,
2. Does the child know what the message is? That is, can he read it? If so,
3. Did the child freely formulate his own message? Or, did the child simply copy something? Or, was the message confined to a small set of words which the child could easily spell?
4. How long was the message?
    one word or a list of unrelated words
    a phrase
    a sentence
5. How does the child's written message relate to other graphics on the page?

The Encoding System
1. Can you read the child's message? If not,
2. Does there seem to be any system to how the child went from the formulated message to the print? For example, the child may have:
    put down a certain number of letters per object
    rearranged the letters in his name
    written a certain number of letters per syllable
3. If you can read the child's message, can you tell how the child encoded it?
    *For example, the child may have:
    recalled the visual pattern (e.g., *COOW*, child intended to write *moo*)
    based spelling on letter names (e.g., *PT*, which is read *Petie*)
    requested spellings from peer or adult
    based spelling on phonological analysis (e.g., *APL*, which is read *apple*)

The Written Product
1. How conventional are the child's written symbols? (Do they look like letters?)
2. Did the child follow the left-to-right directionality convention?
3. Is there any order to the way the letters or words are arranged on the page? Or, does it appear that the child simply put letters where there was empty space?

Message Decoding
1. Does the child appear to have written without any particular intended message? If so,
2. Did the child attempt to decode the written message?
3. If so, how did the child go from text to talk? The child may have:
    engaged in apparent fantasy behavior
    requested that an adult read the unknown message (e.g., "What does this say?")
    based the decoding on the perceived text segments (i.e., matched a number of oral syllables to the perceived number of segments in text)
    used a letter-name strategy (i.e., "read" a word containing the name of a written letter, as reading "Debbie" for *PARA NB*)
    based decoding on visual recall of a word similar in appearance

FIGURE 7.8
Continued

> **Writing Purpose**
> 1.   Why did the child write? Possible reasons include:
>   simply to write: no clearly identifiable purpose exists beyond this (e.g., "I'm
>   gonna' do it how my Mama does it.")
>   to create a message: the meaning of the message is unknown to the child
>   (e.g., "Read this for me.")
>   to produce or to practice conventional symbols (e.g., the *ABC*s, displayed
>   written language) without concern for a referent
>   to detail or accurately represent a drawn object (e.g., the *S* on Superman's
>   shirt)
>   to label objects or people
>   to make a particular type of written object (e.g., a book, a list, a letter)
>   without concern for a particular referent
>   to organize and record information (e.g., to write a list of friends)
>   to investigate the relationship between oral and written language without
>   concern for a particular referent (e.g., "If I do [add] this letter, what does
>   it say?")
>   to express directly feelings or experiences of oneself or others (i.e., direct
>   quotations, as in writing the talk of a drawn character), and
>   to communicate a particular message to a particular audience
>
> *It may be that the child *is* using one of these methods, but you simply cannot read it. After
> asking the child to read the paper, you may be able to detect patterns in the child's encoding
> system.
>
> From *Language Assessment in the Early Years* by Celia Genishi and Anne Haas Dyson.
> Reprinted with permission of Ablex Publishing Corporation.

Not all young children come from homes where reading and writing are modeled. More seriously, not all children enter school settings that support the relations between reading and writing. The writing of five- and six-year-old children:

> … is often not acceptable in schools, where conventional, adult-like writing may be the only writing of interest. As *Freddy* remarked, 'I used to write, but not anymore … I come to school now.' *Freddy* reported that he stopped writing when he started kindergarten…. (Genishi and Dyson 1984, 173)

Writing samples provided by *Teddy* at the end of kindergarten and the end of first grade provide dramatic evidence of the difficulties that can develop because of classroom practice. *Teddy's* work at the end of kindergarten is exemplified in Figure 7.9a. One year later, to the month, he was producing journal entries like those in 7.9b. During a portfolio review, another teacher was struck by the fact that there was virtually no evidence of *writing* in the most recent samples, so she asked Teddy to look at the two pieces and talk about them. He seemed impressed by his own production, as represented in the kindergarten sample, but did not offer an explanation. When the teacher remarked that he had done a lot of writing in kindergarten but there wasn't any in the first grade sample, Teddy sighed and commented, "You always have to be so *neat*—and spell the words right too." Clearly, his sample was less representative of what he knew how to do than what he chose to do, given the context.

Structured Interviews and Observations

In this section, we describe several techniques for conducting informal, but structured, interviews with very young children. We have used these techniques ourselves and found that they are manageable and also that they do discriminate among children who are more or less aware of the demands of beginning reading.

"Word" Reading

Ferreiro (Ferreiro and Teberosky 1979/1982) has devised a number of ingenious tasks that are quite easy to administer and that yield a number of insights into children's understanding of the conventions of print. The tasks are administered in a structured interview format that includes probing and discussing

FIGURE 7.9a
*Teddy's
Kindergarten
Journal*

This is picture of the Big Apple Circus.

children's responses to elicit more information about their print concepts. The interviews are designed specifically to explore children's ideas about what is readable and what can be written.

The word-reading task involves sorting word cards. The stimulus cards should include letter strings, real words, "possible" words, repeated strings, and numbers. Some sample items include:

two　　5　　zzzz　　me　　n　　iiio　　PIE　　jot

To administer this task, simply ask the child:

1. Which are something to read?
2. Which are not something to read?
3. Can you read the cards that are "good for reading?"
4. What do they say?

The examiner should also probe to determine what criteria the child is using to classify the cards.

In evaluating the child's responses, the following questions should be considered:

FIGURE 7.9b
*Teddy's
First Grade
Journal*

- What distinctions does the child make between words and numerals and words and letters?
- What distinctions does the child make based on the length of the display?
- How sensitive is the child to repeated elements?
- How do upper- and lowercase letters influence the child's decisions?

Patterns of response can indicate how aware the child is of the forms and conventions of written words.

Working with kindergarten children we found that some children argue that all the cards are "good for reading." As we noted above, an interview of this type allows us to explore responses. In defending this response, two explanations are common. Some children assert that although they could not read the cards, other "older" or "bigger" people could. Other children demonstrate that all the cards are "good for reading" by reading the letter names. Thus, the card "iiio" is read "i" "i" "i" "o," and the card *jot* is read "j-o-t." In neither case do these children appear to have satisfactory ideas about the forms and functions of reading and writing.

Reading with Pictures

Another task developed by Ferreiro combines pictures and word reading. Using cards or book pages that contain revealing pictures as well as print, the examiner/teacher engages in an open-ended dialogue with the child by asking the following questions:

1. Is there something to read on this card/page? (Have children point to it.)
2. What does it say? or What do you think it says?
3. (Using a portion of the child's response) Where does it say ?
4. Do you think it might say ?

A fairly typical exchange between Nicole and her teacher took place when Nicole's teacher showed her a card with a picture of a dog chasing a cat up a tree. Also printed on the card was the sentence: "*The dog runs.*"

Teacher:	Where is there something to read on this card?
Nicole:	Points to the words and runs her hands along the print.
Teacher:	What does it say?
Nicole:	I don't know.
Teacher:	What do you think it says?
Nicole:	The dog is chasing the cat.
Teacher:	Where does it say "The"?
Nicole:	Points to "The."
Teacher:	Where does it say "cat"?
Nicole:	Points to "dog."
Teacher:	Where does it say "dog"?
Nicole:	Points to "runs."
Teacher:	Where does it say "chasing"?
Nicole:	Laughs … There aren't any more of those … things.
Teacher:	That's right. What do we call those "things"?
Nicole:	Letters.… Or, numbers.

This conversation reveals a great deal about six-year-old Nicole's concepts of print. We find out, for example, that she knows that the print is what is read. She also has a well-established sense of directionality. However, she clearly lacks a sense of speech-print match. She also lacks clarity about the terminology associated with reading instruction.

It is helpful to consider the following questions in evaluating a child's performance on this task.

- How well does the child understand the speech-print match?
- How well does the child appear to understand word boundaries?
- How well does the child appear to understand directionality?

The purpose of these types of structured interviews is to delve into children's understanding and to gather instructionally useful information. Some of these same components are explored in the Concepts About Print test, discussed in the following section.

Structured Observations about Print Concepts

Some years ago, Clay (1985) created an informal test designed to assess young children's knowledge and use of print concepts. In its most recent form, the *Concepts About Print* (CAP) test is part of a diagnostic survey designed to detect reading difficulties among young children (Clay 1985). Two books, *Sand* and *Stones*, are used to assess children's knowledge of print conventions.

Using an interactive exchange, the examiner reads the book *(Sand* or *Stones)* asking twenty-four questions along the way. The child is told to help read the book by pointing to features in the book. These questions are designed to provide assessment opportunities related to the following concepts: how to hold a book for reading; print orientation; print, not pictures, carries the message; upper- and lowercase letters; punctuation marks; and directionality.

A recent review of the available research suggests that the CAP test is a valid measure of emergent literacy independent from intelligence (Day and Day 1986). For the classroom teacher, the CAP has the advantage of structuring observations. It can provide teachers with a place to start, and it also increases reliability, since the same tasks and materials are used for each child. In general, it can provide you with a quick assessment of children's experiences with books.

Of course, teachers can obtain similar information in more natural settings from regular picture books. Genishi and Dyson (1984) describe an adaptation that is quick and easy to use. Teachers select their own materials, including several different types of materials, for purposes of comparison. To implement this basic book-reading procedure, simply select a book and ask the child to do the following:

1. Show me the front of this book.
2. I'll read you this story. You help me. Show me where to start reading; where do I begin to read?
3. Show me where to start. Which way do I go? Where do I go after that?

4. Point to what I am reading. (Read slowly and fluently.)

5. Show me the first part of the story. Show me the last.

6. (On a page with print on both the left and right sides.) Where do I start reading?

Figure 7.10 provides a checklist of the concepts (distinctions between print and pictures, directionality, speech-to-print match) that can be used as a guide in evaluating the child's responses to these requests.

Structured Writing Assessments

Dictated Stories

Dictated stories are a rich source of information about oral language, print awareness, knowledge of the conventions of print, and story structure (Agnew 1982; Ringler and Weber 1984). Dictated writing samples are generally collected in one of two ways. In some classrooms, children produce journal entries

FIGURE 7.10

Print Concepts Checklist

				Yes	No	Sometimes
Name: _____			Date: _____			
Directions: Using a book the child has never seen before, test the following concepts.						
1.	Identifies front/back of book			☐	☐	☐
2.	Can indicate title			☐	☐	☐
3.	Identifies print as "what is read"			☐	☐	☐
4.	Can indicate picture			☐	☐	☐
5.	Knows where to start reading			☐	☐	☐
6.	Shows correct direction of print display			☐	☐	☐
7.	Indicates beginning of story on a page			☐	☐	☐
8.	Can show return sweep for a line of print			☐	☐	☐
9.	Indicates end of story			☐	☐	☐
10.	Identifies bottom of page			☐	☐	☐
11.	Identifies top of page			☐	☐	☐
12.	Can locate a word (by cupping, etc.)			☐	☐	☐
13.	Can locate two words that appear together			☐	☐	☐
14.	Can locate the space between words			☐	☐	☐
15.	Can locate a letter			☐	☐	☐
16.	Can locate two consecutive letters			☐	☐	☐
17.	Can indicate a period			☐	☐	☐
18.	Can indicate a comma, question mark			☐	☐	☐

several times a week. For very young children, this usually involves drawing a picture and "writing" any portion of the accompanying story that is possible. Then, the child dictates the message to the teacher, who writes it down exactly as produced. Alternatively, the teacher may set a topic for a child (or group of children) and then proceed as above. Some children provide only a label, while others generate text-length stories, sometimes continuing their story for several days (see Figure 7.11).

As children dictate and reread their stories, information about each component of emergent literacy can be gathered, using the type of form shown in Figure 7.12. After a dictation is completed, it is possible to gather information about other aspects of emergent literacy (Agnew 1982). Using the dictated story, simply ask the child:

- To find a word (by circling or framing it)
- To match a story word on a card to the story itself
- To find a letter and/or a sentence
- To find a word that begins the same as another
- To point "to the letters you can name"
- To point "to the words you can read"
- To "reread" the story

Collected over time, these dictated stories and journal entries can provide strong evidence regarding children's growth in many areas of emergent literacy.

Prompted Writing Activities

If spontaneous writing samples are not available, assessment information can be gathered by simply asking the child to write anything she or he knows how to write. It may be necessary to provide additional structure, because many young students balk at this. Two tasks that can be used to help generate writing samples are *All the Words I Know* and *Supported Writing*.

We have found that children often know how to write some words, even if they believe they are not yet writers. Thus, a paper headed *All the Words I Know* can sometimes produce results when the more generalized request to write has failed. Most children, for example, can write their own names, the names of some other people, and a few other high-potency words (Clay 1985). It also helps to probe further by asking the child to attempt to write specific words such as his or her mother's name, color names, the name of the month, the words on street signs or logos, and so forth. Such samples provide information about the child's word knowledge and attention to recurring environmental print.

Eliciting writing samples of connected text is important. The word-writing task just described cannot provide evidence of the child's awareness of text organization, directionality, or concept of word boundaries. These areas can only be assessed when children write several words or sentences. In addition,

FIGURE 7.11
*Lengthy
Dictated Story*

This is a house and it lives near a forest. There were two girls who lived together.

The girls names were Nava and Shoshana. One day they dis-Obeyed the rules and went out in the forest. They were'nt watch-ing and they Stepped in a hole.

Well, they were in the hole. A person was standing in the hole. up on earth. And the person had a rope.
    Nava and Shoshana called, "Help, send down the rope". But,

the person was a nasty person. And very nasty creatures came flying out. A hawk came flying out And a nasty bird came flying out.

FIGURE
7.12
*Dictated Story
Record Form*

Dictated Experience Story Summary Form

Name: _____ Date: _____

Directions: Present topic, object, or experience for student to discuss or experience directly. Ask them to tell you something about it.

Dictated Story:

Assessment:
Language Development

- Does the child speak in sentences. in single words, or word clusters?
- Does the child use descriptive names for objects and events or many ambiguous terms like "it," "that," "this thing"?
- Does the child provide adequate information to reconstruct the experience?
- Does the child use appropriate grammatical structure?
- How does the child use language appropriate to the task?
- How easily and fluently does the child dictate?

Literacy Development

- Does the child speak clearly and pace the dictation to allow the teacher to record?
- What does the child do as the story is transcribed?
- Does the dictation have clarity and organization (does it make sense)?
- Does the child provide a title that reflects the major ideas or themes of the dictation?
- How does the child (attempt) to read back his or her dictation?

At the conclusion of a dictated story activity, it is helpful to reflect on the following:

- What evidence is there that the child understands the concepts of word, sentence, paragraph, and story.
- What aspects of the speech-to-print relationship does the child understand?
- In what ways does the child use memory for text as an aid to reading?
- What sight vocabulary does the child appear to have mastered?
- How does the child use graphophonic information to read?

Comments:

the connected writing sample generally permits observation of the child's strategy for spelling unknown words.

Children will often be able to write some connected discourse if they are provided with a little support. *Supported writing* can be done in several ways. For example, the child can be asked to draw a picture, then write about it. Alternatively, it is possible to brainstorm with the child, generating several possible topics.

An analysis of children's writing strategies can provide much information about the status of emergent literacy. Students' development can be traced from scribbling through invented spelling to conventional orthography.

Using Stories to Assess Emergent Abilities

Since young children read or listen to many stories, it is relatively easy to embed this aspect of assessment into the regular instructional program.

Story Retelling Guides

Story retelling can provide a wide range of assessment information. Because this assessment strategy is discussed at length elsewhere (see Chapters 8 and 9), the discussion in this chapter is limited to two aspects of emergent literacy that can be assessed using retelling procedures: sense of story and oral language development.

The ability to recognize and use story structure clearly aids comprehension. As we assess children's retellings, we are looking for evidence that children have made use of the major components of stories to understand the text and to aid their recall. For young children, it is important to determine if they have noted characters, events, and resolutions. In addition, the children should make at least some sequential and causal connections between events and resolutions explicit and clear.

To conduct a story retelling, simply ask the child to retell a story that he or she has just heard or read. Ask the child specifically to retell the entire story just the way the author did. When the retelling has stopped, ask the child if there is anything else he or she can remember about the story. Record the child's retelling in writing and/or by audiotaping.

The form presented in Figure 7.13 can be used as a guide for evaluating the retelling with regard to the child's language and sense of story structure. In addition, it may be helpful to collect retelling data from children on both familiar and unfamiliar stories. Repeated exposure to the same material should also permit the child to capture the language of the text. If the quality and quantity of the retelling does not improve with repeated exposures, it is likely that the child needs more story reading opportunities or that oral language development (and experience) is not well-matched to the text. When used over time, retellings can help us evaluate and document a child's growth in a number of areas, including language fluency, complexity, vocabulary, usage, and knowledge about story structures. Children who

**FIGURE
7.13**
*Story Retelling
Form*

Child: _____	Date: ____	Story Title: _____

Language

	Yes	No	Sometimes
1. A variety of sentence patterns to express ideas	☐	☐	☐
2. Complete sentences	☐	☐	☐
3. Grammar, conventions	☐	☐	☐
4. Precise, descriptive words	☐	☐	☐
5. Overall fluency		Word count: _____	

Story Structure

	Yes	No	Sometimes
1. All basic structural elements present	☐	☐	☐
• setting	☐	☐	☐
• initiating event	☐	☐	☐
• the goal	☐	☐	☐
• one or more attempts or, all major events	☐	☐	☐
• the resolution	☐	☐	☐
2. Oral retelling is accurately sequenced	☐	☐	☐
3. Student can recall the "big idea"	☐	☐	☐
4. Student can sustain train of thought	☐	☐	☐

Comments

need greater support in comprehending stories may be evaluated on the Directed Listening Thinking Activity (DLTA).

Directed Listening Thinking Activity (DLTA)

Throughout this section, we have encouraged a type of assessment that can be embedded in daily classroom exchanges. Indeed, most of these assessments can and should be done as a part of regular classroom routines. The Directed Listening Thinking Activity (DLTA) was developed by Stauffer (1980) as an instructional strategy, but it is easy to use on a continuous basis for assessment because it fits naturally in the classroom routine.

The strategy simply involves the teacher reading a well-crafted story aloud to children. Before the story is read, the teacher asks children to make predictions about what the story will be about, what will happen in the story. Then, as the read-aloud proceeds, the teacher stops periodically to solicit predictions. The children are also directed to monitor their predictions to see if they were correct. Retellings can also be incorporated into the DLTA. Throughout the activity, the teacher asks the children questions such as:

1. What do you think this story will be about?
2. What clues did you use to help you?
3. Were your predictions right?
4. What do you think will happen next?

To assess an individual child's participation in a DLTA, you should ask yourself the following types of questions:

- Can the child predict from the title, cover, pictures?
- Are these predictions plausible?
- Are these predictions based on prior knowledge?
- Are these predictions based on an understanding of story structure?
- Is the child able to monitor predictions?
- Is the text used to revise predictions?

Teachers can evaluate change in students' knowledge and ability to perform various types of school tasks if they use and summarize DLTA data regularly.

THE DIAGNOSTIC PORTFOLIO AND EVIDENCE OF EMERGENT LITERACY: THE CASE OF KYLE

In Step 3 of the Assessment-Instruction Process we ask questions about "the learner's" knowledge of reading and writing; application of reading and writing skills; motivation; and independence and ownership. As we have noted, Diagnostic Portfolios have exceptional potential in the assessment and documentation of a child's emergence into conventional literacy. This emergence is, by definition, dynamic—we get an ever-changing view of children's emerging knowledge, skill, and affect. The portfolio, with its focus on continuous assessment, authentic tasks, and student involvement, is especially appropriate and well-suited for work with young children.

The Diagnostic Portfolio should contain a subset of work samples and evidence that had been collected in a classroom portfolio. Schools that use portfolios at all levels and/or settings that contain multi-age classrooms are ideal for collecting information over time; even information about the youngest learners. The samples we use in this section come from such a classroom—Kyle's multi-age teacher begins collecting information in kindergarten and continues to gather additional documentation and information for the three years that children are with her.

In the rich portfolios Ms. McIntyre and her class keep is evidence and information about each aspect of the learner's development. You may remember that some of this information was used to "get started" with Kyle (see Chapter 4). For example, we noted that Kyle's self-evaluations (prompted by Ms. McIntyre's periodic requests for reflection) suggested that Kyle was a very active child who enjoyed making things. In addition, he was aware that his writing was improving.

Samples of the extensive written work, including Kyle's own self-selected "best pieces," also go into a Diagnostic Portfolio (See Figure 7.14–15). Although many other children in this classroom are writing more and more skillfully, Kyle's progress from kindergarten to the end of grade one is obvious and clearly demonstrates his ability to apply his growing knowledge and skill.

In addition to these work samples, Ms. McIntyre summarizes his progress using a "Stages of Spelling Development" form developed by teachers in her district. Throughout kindergarten she noted his progress:

Pictures no words	9/21 and 10/5
Scribble or imitative writing	10/29
Random letters to represent words	9/21; *throughout fall*
Initial consonants to represent words	11/29 *"started making connection with teacher"*
Initial/final consonants for each word	3/8 *jp* for *jump* 3/25 *dk* for *duck*
Initial, final and medial consonants for each word	3/30 *sph dr* for *spider smt* for *cement*
Vowels used as place holders	
Approaching standard spelling	2/26 *my, dog, mom, me*

In combination, the evidence of the portfolio suggests steady progress in the area of developmental spelling.

Kyle continues to prefer action and choice to sitting and "paying attention." Not surprisingly, he readily notes in a casual conversation that he really doesn't like to read. On the other hand, his book logs reveal the rather large amount of reading that he does do under the strong encouragement of Ms. McIntyre.

To summarize, at the end of kindergarten, Kyle was at the early phonemic stage of spelling development and had not yet begun to read conventionally. He

FIGURE 7.14
Kyle's Writing:
Kindergarten

KYLE

(F) 1992-93

bY DHIS DAD

Me and my Mom and my sister and my friend
Brian are picking apples.

11/12

FIGURE 7.15
*Kyle's Writing:
Grade 1*

by Kyle   Jan. 15, 1994   ①

goiNgtoBoston
yesterday. I cam
hom frum Boston.
we leFt Saterday.
we drivj fer a lug tun
Finly we gotto Bostor
me and my sister plad inth
then we went in sid
we plad with my
cousin
csin. then we went to
bed then we woc up. then
we went to sleging then
we went hom.

Name Krle
Date FEB 17 1994
       FEB 16 1994

I selected this piece for my portfolio because
I sounded out my words and I
hardly had any mistakes, because it's my longest
story!

Krle
Signature

was able to reread familiar books and could recognize many high-potency words from his environment (labels, planning time choices, names, etc.). By the end of grade one, Kyle has begun to read and to write. His spontaneous writing suggests that he has arrived at the phonetic stage of spelling development. Observations by the teacher indicate that he has made steady, but slow, progress in reading. He can still read only a few familiar books, although his knowledge about sight words and phonics has increased. Although he is easily distracted, he has many opportunities to learn about interesting information and to do projects, which he likes to do. His oral language development is exceptionally strong and his retellings of both familiar and unfamiliar stories are detailed, accurate, and insightful. In the next chapters, we follow Kyle's progress as he moves toward conventional reading and writing; documenting and evaluating these changes using a wide array of tools and strategies.

CHAPTER SUMMARY

The first section of this chapter described two traditional views of reading readiness that underlie both readiness assessment and instruction in today's schools. The developmental view suggests that children simply grow into readiness, much the way a tree grows and develops. The experiential view emphasizes the role of the environment in developing readiness.

The second section of the chapter describes the more current conceptualization of reading and writing as emergent literacy. The gradual emergence of written literacy skills in the context of oral language development provides the perspective adopted for this chapter. Then we detailed two major areas of competence necessary for literacy learning derived from an emergent literacy perspective: oral language development and literacy experiences. Oral language development was described in terms of what children must learn about language, how language is learned, and the importance of language development in literacy learning. Essential literacy experiences were defined as developing print awareness; understanding the forms and functions of print, including the language of books and story structure; analyzing print, including the concept of a word, phonemic segmentation, and the speech-to-print match; and controlling reading and writing processes, including the form and functions of writing and invented spelling. We noted that most children acquire important literacy abilities long before they enter school.

The third section of this chapter described a variety of informal assessment procedures. These informal strategies can be used to gather information about a variety of different emergent literacy abilities. For example, dictated stories can be used to gather information about children's language development, sense of story, awareness of the speech-to-print match, and memory for print. Other strategies include guidelines for using structured observations and interviews, checklists, retellings, and writing samples.

Consistent with the guidelines for assessment provided in Chapter 4, the techniques described in this chapter allow for meaningful, unobtrusive, systematic, and continuous assessment of emergent literacy. Recognizing that readiness must be viewed within the context of the instructional program and tasks that children are going to encounter in school, many of the techniques described here are designed to be used with children during instruction and/or as they engage in tasks like those they will be expected to accomplish.

Finally, we provided examples of student work and observational records that contribute to a diagnostic portfolio. For young children, the collection over time can provide vivid and immediate diagnostic information.

CHAPTER 8

Informal Classroom-Based Assessment

INTRODUCTION

The information obtained through interviews and observations provides the background for further evaluation of the learner, using formal and informal assessment instruments. As a practical matter, students have always been referred for more specialized assessment on the basis of at least some informal classroom-based assessment. Until recently, however, few professionals viewed classroom assessment information as essential to the assessment and instruction of disabled readers and writers.

This chapter focuses on assessment strategies that are selected and/or created by teachers and clinicians interested in gathering information about each component of reading and writing. These classroom-based approaches differ from the norm-referenced standardized tests introduced in a later chapter because they tend to be more informal and because the content and tasks can be closely fitted to the type of knowledge and skill promoted by an individual teacher or school.

After a brief discussion of the role of the teacher in assessing students' reading and writing, we identify some critical issues in the development and use of informal assessment strategies. Finally, a wide range of strategies and tools are described for assessing component areas of literacy: word recognition, vocabulary, comprehension, studying, and writing. The assessment strategies described are almost exclusively *performance* measures. These are techniques for evaluating students' ability to *apply* their knowledge and skill. The variety of assessment strategies presented in this chapter are designed so that teachers can select from among a repertoire to examine some particular component area more closely. We describe assessment strategies and instruments that can be used for ongoing assessment of the student in interaction with reading and writing instruction. Many of these can (and should) be done as a routine part of the instructional program.

Retellings, for example, are an easy addition to the normal question-answer format that follows reading in most classrooms. Using a scoring form prepared ahead of time, teachers can collect information on each child over time (see also Chapter 9). In addition, teachers can easily collect samples of student oral reading during regularly planned reading activities (either individual or group) and examine these samples for patterns that may suggest instructional needs.

Finally, the information that is gathered about word identification, fluency, and comprehension, using the procedures described in this chapter, need to be collected on a continuous basis throughout the year for each student in a classroom. We describe an appropriate ongoing record or student portfolio that documents student progress and provides the basis for instructional decision making.

UNDERSTANDING INFORMAL CLASSROOM-BASED ASSESSMENT

The assessment-instruction process described in this text relies very heavily on the knowledge and skill of the teacher/examiner. Extensive description of formal tests, the traditional heart of reading and writing "diagnosis," is not the centerpiece of the process. Instead, we acknowledge the complexity of reading and writing processes and of learning to read and write. Like Simmons and Resnick (1993), we recognize that more *informal* assessment can often provide powerful and flexible evaluation strategies: "The most authentic and reliable estimate of students' capabilities comes from work they do over extended periods of time under the guidance of teachers" (11).

By virtue of their daily contact with students in a variety of reading situations, classroom teachers are in a position to incorporate the adaptations that form the basic assessment strategies described in this chapter directly into their regular reading instruction. Teachers can collect and interpret performance data, information about students' skills and strategies, as they read and respond to various school tasks.

One of the most serious problems with existing assessment practices is that they often lead teachers to believe that assessment and evaluation are someone else's job. When teachers rely too heavily on standardized test results, they may stop using their own good judgment (Valencia and Pearson 1987). The overreliance on formal tests may also cause teachers to discount or become inattentive to the high-quality information they themselves have. Teachers need the information they have before them because it provides evidence about students' ability to perform the actual tasks required in their instructional settings.

Teachers gather information from multiple samples on a daily basis as a function of the different types of texts, tasks, and methods that are employed as a part of their regular reading activities. The opportunities are great, but often go undetected. As Pinnell (1991) has argued, "teachers need assessment tools that help them become 'noticing teachers'" (81). This chapter describes many tools and strategies that will help teachers to "notice" the information available to them on an ongoing basis. It is more a matter of knowing what to attend to than a matter of having indefinite amounts of time to work one-on-one with students. Lipson (1995) has described ways in which conversations, even casual ones, with children can provide useful assessment information. "Noticing requires not only that teachers engage in careful observations of reading and writing as they occur in their own classrooms but also that they assign importance or significance to what they note" (Lipson 1995, 167).

The strategies suggested in this chapter should probably become a part of the repertoire of all teachers. Classroom teachers, in particular, are likely to start with these informal techniques first, because they are often less time-consuming than administering one of the more structured or formal assessments. Importantly, they also allow us to examine students' performance using familiar text forms and tasks. Of course, the quality and nature of these in-school tasks needs to be examined closely as well (See Chapters 5 and 6).

Another important advantage of classroom-based assessment is that evaluations can be responsive to the specific cultural and/or linguistic characteristics of individual students. This is critical, since standardized tests can distort information for some students as they tend "to reflect the language, culture, or learning style of middle- to upper-middle-class" students (Neill and Median 1989). In order to make good instructional decisions, teachers must come to trust that assessment is a continuous process that takes place within the instructional program. It should be designed to increase the "goodness" of the fit between each child and the materials and methods of instruction.

According to Johnston (1987), teachers can—indeed they must—become expert evaluators. We have already noted one of the most important attributes of an expert evaluator: the ability to listen. Another important characteristic of an expert evaluator is the ability to recognize patterns. Expert evaluators are not concerned about an isolated event or behavior, but are able to connect pieces of information to create an integrated vision of the student's knowledge and skill. Informal, classroom-based assessment can provide exceptionally powerful and helpful information. However, Valencia (1990b) reminds us that:

> The concept behind a "good" reading assessment, whether it is a standardized test or alternative classroom assessment, is the same. First it should be authentic; it should assess what we have defined and value as real reading. Second, it should be trustworthy; it should have clearly established procedures for gathering information and for evaluating the quality of that information. (60)

Classroom-based assessment requires reflection and planning. As Johnston (1987) points out, effective assessment requires procedural knowledge. Teachers must be able to create a context that elicits the types of reading/writing behaviors that they have decided to examine, and they must be skilled in managing all aspects of the assessment-instruction process.

As teachers turn to more informal assessment options, they should proceed cautiously. Informal tests offer no guarantee of excellence. Many common informal assessment tools need to be carefully considered. For example, skills mastery tests are a common feature in many classrooms, often used to place students in reading groups. Although much less common than they once were, many commercial reading programs provide for periodic end-of-level or end-of-unit testing to assess students' mastery of skills that have been taught.

The periodic administration of skills mastery tests can provide for continuous assessment of individual and/or class performance throughout the year. However, a major problem with these measures is that they frequently assess skills in isolation on a series of discrete subtests. For example, they often evaluate a skill such as main idea recognition under highly restricted conditions (for example, short, unfamiliar, informational passages with initial topic sentences) that do not reflect the complexity and variety of factors that are likely to influence students' ability to grasp a main idea under real reading conditions. In addition, mastery tests presume that the order of skill acquisition is invariable; that students must master a specific skill before proceeding to other skills and/or materials. Neither the assumption that reading skills are hierarchical nor the assumption that reading skills can be evaluated in discrete parts is warranted, given current knowledge about the reading process (Mason, Osborn, and Rosenshine 1977; Valencia and Pearson 1986).

To summarize, although informal tests can be a potent form of assessment, the techniques employed must be carefully examined for evidence that these capture what we know about skilled reading and writing. A serious problem in many existing tests, both formal and informal, is the lack of relationship between how reading and writing are measured and what we expect children to do during reading and writing. The truth is that we do *not* want children to know how to complete workbook-like pages or complete grammar exercises. Rather, we want children to be able to employ their skills during the reading and writing of real texts.

This means that we need to develop assessment procedures that assess more clearly the holistic terminal goals of reading and writing instruction and the factors that are known to influence reading and writing. As Wood (1988) notes, what is needed is a structured approach to determine how an individual handles the reading of actual textbook material under conditions that simulate the classroom situation. The guidelines for assessment offered in Chapter 4 should be reconsidered as guiding principles in teacher-designed assessment. These guidelines are important for *both* standardized and teacher-designed assessment. However, classroom-based assessment is too often discounted as haphazard, or unreliable. Consequently, teachers need to be especially careful to attend to important principles of assessment. Well-crafted informal assessment can assess meaningful reading and writing activities in a nonintrusive way, and teachers can ensure that it is systematic, continuous, and well-organized.

STRATEGIES AND TOOLS
FOR TEACHER-INITIATED ASSESSMENT

In the remainder of this chapter we describe specific techniques for evaluating the various components of reading and writing performance. These techniques—some old, some newer—can provide the initial repertoire for both classroom teachers and clinicians who want to expand their assessment practices. They are only suggestions, however. There are many other ways to evaluate performance informally. As teachers develop more refined skills for assessing students' knowledge and application of reading- and writing-related abilities, their confidence in making good assessment decisions will also develop.

Each of the strategies is designed to provide for ongoing student assessment during instruction. Throughout, we also provide forms that can be used to summarize and display this information. If a Diagnostic Portfolio is being used, these forms can facilitate analysis and interpretation. If this documentation is providing support or confirmation within a more traditional case evaluation, the summary forms are equally helpful in making sense of the documents.

Evaluating Word Recognition

Rapid and automatic word recognition, using a combination of strategies, is a hallmark of skilled reading. Not surprisingly, many poor readers have a limited repertoire of word recognition and word analysis strategies. Of course, the most effective way to assess children's word recognition and word analysis skills is to do so as children read aloud. It is possible to achieve a very detailed picture of students' word recognition and monitoring abilities by using the Reading Miscue Analysis (RMI) procedure (See Chapter 9). Because the RMI procedure is so time-consuming, few classroom teachers use it with any frequency. The Running Record, however, is tailored for classroom use.

Running Records During Oral Reading

The *Running Record* is a method of assessment that is ideally suited to continuous assessment. An adaptation of the RMI, "this task requires the teacher to observe and record the strategies the child uses 'on the run' while attempting to read a whole text" (Pinnell 1985a, 74). The technique was originally described by Clay (1979, 1985) and is based on the work of the Goodmans and their associates (K. Goodman 1969, 1973; K. Goodman and Y. Goodman 1977; Y. Goodman, Watson, and Burke 1987).

Although the Running Record may seem complex at first, it is especially useful for the classroom teacher because no special preparation is required ahead of time. A Running Record can be created as long as the text being read by a child is visible to the teacher. Therefore, it is possible to collect data any time you are listening to a child read aloud. It does take time and practice to do Running Records accurately. But it is well worth the investment because of the wealth of assessment information they provide, especially for younger and/or disabled readers. In Figure 8.1 you will find a sample Running Record of Kyle's reading in early grade two, along with a key to the various markings.

After the record has been taken, the teacher uses it to analyze oral reading performance. Although a full miscue analysis can be done (see Chapter 9), classroom teachers usually generate more global, less-specific inferences about what the child is doing to construct meaning from text and which strategies seem to be used most often to accomplish this (Pinnell 1987). A teacher's summary of the small sample you have examined in Figure 8.1 might read something like this:

> Kyle's most consistent miscues (oral reading "errors") are word substitutions. These substitutions are made using both language structure (syntax) and meaning (semantics) ("I tied it around a doorknob ..."). Kyle also monitors quite effectively for problems caused by weak graphophonic skills (he tries, for example, to self-correct mispronunciations of the words *winced, shuddered, admired*, etc.). He regularly uses rereading when meaning seems distorted. What Kyle does not do is to make full and effective use of the graphophonic information available, nor does he appear to have mastered all high-frequency sight words. Miscues in this area ("emperted," "winkered") are tolerated even when they result in loss of meaning. Kyle often rereads, but his self-correction attempts too often fail due to lack of sound-symbol information and decoding skill. Although he generally seems to "read for meaning," his comprehension is affected by word recognition.

Rhodes and Shanklin (1990) have devised a simplified assessment strategy for analyzing students' miscues in the classroom and it serves as a useful companion to the Running Record. The Classroom Reading Miscue Assessment (CRMA) (See Figure 8.2) is used as students read a whole text. Rather than analyze each oral reading miscue, teachers get an overall picture of the student's reading proficiency. First, the teacher determines the extent to which a reader is constructing meaning. To do this, each sentence in the text is considered separately. The teacher determines whether each sentence read by the child (after self-correction) is semantically acceptable or not. Then, a percentage of semantically acceptable sentences is computed by dividing the total number of semantically acceptable sentences by the total number of sentences read.

Rhodes and Shanklin suggest you may judge the student's overall performance using the following criteria: (1) proficient reading is 80 percent or higher; (2) adequate reading is 60 to 80 percent; and (3) poor reading is below 60 percent. It should be noted that these standards are much lower than those suggested by others (see Chapter 9). In addition, teachers record their observations about reading behaviors using a 5-point scale (see Figure 8.2).

As with any "test," Running Records provide a *sample* of behavior that may or may not be representative of the way a student interacts with different types of texts under different reading conditions. Students' miscue patterns vary depending on a number of factors (Wixson 1979). The best way to address the problem of variability in oral reading patterns is to obtain repeated samples of a particular reader's miscues under a variety of conditions. Detailed analyses of miscues is important in a complete assessment and we discuss this more fully in Chapter 9. However, Running Records provide classroom teachers with a practical assessment strategy and information

FIGURE 8.1

Sample Running Record for Norman Fools the Tooth Fairy

Norman was the only kid in his class who hadn't lost a baby tooth. One was sort of loose now. Instead of finishing his worksheet, Norman wiggled the tooth with his finger.

Later, while his teacher, Miss Harp, read them a story, Norman waggled the tooth with his tongue. How else was he going to get a tooth to put under his pillow for the tooth fairy?

His friends gave him lots of advice. "I tied a string around my loose tooth," said Toby. "Then I tied the other end to a doorknob, and my sister slammed the door." Norman winced.

"My dad pulled mine out," said Matt, "with his pliers."

Norman shuddered, but he admired the empty space between their teeth when they smiled. It showed that the tooth fairy had already paid them a visit.

"Try biting into an apple," said Sarah, "or eat lots of caramels."

Norman didn't have any caramels, but he did have a piece of licorice in his lunch bag.

Key for running record:

Accurate Reading ✓✓✓

Substitution $\frac{substitute}{text\ word}$

Appeal $\underline{A}$

Told $\overline{\overline{T}}$

Self-Correction Isc

Omission $\frac{\dot{}}{text\ word}$

Insertion $\underline{inserted\ word}$

Repetition ✓R

Return & Repetition ⌐✓✓✓ R

FIGURE 8.1
Continued

Page

1 ✓ ✓ ✓ ✓ ✓ ✓ ✓ ✓

✓ had/hadn't ↑ lots|SC/lost ✓ ✓ ✓ ✓ ✓ started/sort

✓ ✓ ✓   ✓ ✓ ✓ ✓

work study/worksheet ✓ ✓ his/the ✓ ✓

✓ ✓

2 ✓ ✓ ✓ ✓ ✓ Hop|Harper/Harp ✓

✓ ✓ ✓ ✓ ✓ ✓

✓ ✓ ✓ ✓ easy/else ✓ ✓ ✓ ✓

✓ ✓ ✓ ✓ ✓ ✓ ✓ ✓ from/for ✓

✓ ✓

3 ✓ ✓ ✓ ✓ ✓ ✓ ideas/advice ✓

✓ ✓ ✓ ✓ ✓ ✓ ✓

✓ ✓ ✓ ✓ it/the around/other ✓ ✓

✓ ✓ ✓ ✓ ✓ ✓ ✓

✓ Win-k-er | win-Kered|A/Winced |T

✓ ✓ ✓ ✓ ✓ ✓ ✓

✓ ✓ ✓

4 ✓ started|staggered/shuddered ✓ ✓ ad-ered|ordered|A/admired |T ✓

extra|ex-lemperted R/empty special|SC/space ✓ ✓ ✓ ✓ ✓

✓ ✓ ✓ ✓ ✓ ✓ ✓ ✓

✓ pretti|SC/paid ✓ ✓ ✓

✓ ✓ ✓ ✓ ✓ ✓ short|s-ā-r|shirley/Sara |T

✓ ✓ ✓ ✓ carmels/caramels

✓ ✓ ✓ ✓ ✓

✓ ✓ ✓ ✓ ✓ pin|pinch/piece ✓ liker/licorice ✓ ✓

✓ ✓

Accuracy

[E] errors = 17
[TW] total words = 169
TW-E / TW = 90%

about students' reading of multiple samples, since teachers can (and often do) collect information several times a week.

Word Sorts
The *word sort* (Gillet and Temple 1990) is a flexible assessment strategy that can be used to assess a variety of word level abilities. Gillet and Temple suggest using

**Classroom Reading Miscue Assessment
Developed by Coordinators/Consultants Applying Whole Language**

Reader's name _____ Date _____

Grade level assignment _____ Teacher _____

Selection read: _____

I. What percent of the sentences read make sense? Sentence by sentence tally   Total

_____ Number of semantically acceptable sentences

_____ Number of semantically unacceptable sentences

_____ % Comprehending score: $\dfrac{\text{Number of semantically acceptable sentences}}{\text{Total number of sentences read}}$ x 100

TOTAL _____

	Seldom	Sometimes	Often	Usually	Always
II. In what ways is reader constructing meaning?					
A. Recognizes when miscues have disrupted meaning	1	2	3	4	5
B. Logically substitutes	1	2	3	4	5
C. Self-corrects errors that disrupt meaning	1	2	3	4	5
D. Uses picture and/or other visual clues	1	2	3	4	5
In what ways is reader disrupting meaning?					
A. Substitutes words that don't make sense	1	2	3	4	5
B. Makes omissions that disrupt meaning	1	2	3	4	5
C. Relies too heavily on graphic clues	1	2	3	4	5

III. If narrative test is used:

	No	Partial			Yes
A. Character recall	1	2	3	4	5
B. Character development	1	2	3	4	5
C. Setting	1	2	3	4	5
D. Relationship of events	1	2	3	4	5
E. Plot	1	2	3	4	5
F. Theme	1	2	3	4	5
G. Overall retelling	1	2	3	4	5

If expository text is used:

	No	Partial			Yes
A. Major concepts	1	2	3	4	5
B. Generalizations	1	2	3	4	5
C. Specific information	1	2	3	4	5
D. Logical structuring	1	2	3	4	5
E. Overall retelling	1	2	3	4	5

Source: Rhodes, L. "Miscue Analysis in the Classroom." *The Reading Teacher* 44 (3): 252–254.
International Reading Association. Used by permission.

the word sort as a way to assess word recognition and/or word analysis, but we have also found it useful for evaluating vocabulary as well (see next section). This technique capitalizes on the fact that words are organized in human memory by patterns or relationships.

There are two types of word sorts: *open* and *closed*. In an open sort, no criteria for sorting the words are provided. Since students must impose their own organization on the words, it is possible to observe the types of relationships available to students. In a closed sort, the teacher establishes the criteria for sorting in advance. Using word cards prepared in advance (or selected by students from their own word bank), the teacher asks the student to:

- Put the words that go together in the same pile (open sort).
- Put all the words together that have the same beginning letter. Then, name the group (closed sort).
- Put all the words together that have something the same and label the characteristic.
- Put all the words together that have the same feature (for example, rhyme or spelling pattern).

As the student's performance is evaluated, it is helpful to consider the following questions:

- Does the child attend to meaning features or graphic features?
- Does the child recognize and use initial, medial, and final sounds?
- Does the child recognize and use structural cues (compounds, base words)?
- Can the child generate categories based on visual patterns (spelling patterns)?
- Does the child recognize multiple ways to represent sounds (the several ways to spell the short *e* sound)?

Some teachers we have worked with keep a class summary chart of the ways children choose to sort the words they provide. It provides important information on students' growing knowledge and flexibility in using aspects of phonics, categorization, and/or content information.

Evaluating Vocabulary

Knowledge of word meanings clearly influences reading performance. This fact has been unchallenged for decades, yet surprisingly few assessment techniques have been suggested for validating individual differences in this area. Most diagnosticians employ one of the available standardized tests to estimate relative vocabulary strength, and we have described several of these in Chapter 10. Most of these involve word-level assessments (finding definitions, picture associations, etc.).

A word is a label for a concept or idea. It has recently been suggested that vocabulary words are important, not because they are directly helpful in understanding text, but because the individual words reflect generalized knowledge about a topic. When a reader knows a word, he or she probably knows many other related words. The generalized knowledge (concepts) facilitates comprehension, not just the words (Anderson and Freebody 1981). For example, a knowledgeable sailor generated in a few seconds the following words when asked what she thought of when she heard the word *spinnaker:*

> spinnaker: jib; fore; aft; mainsail; port; bow; sheets; heel; winch; cleat; starboard; heading; gaff; sloop; schooner; 12-meter; galley; tack

It should be apparent that simply learning a definition for the word *spinnaker* would not be as helpful as the knowledge base that results in knowing *spinnaker,* but also knowing all those other words. Word meanings are related in such a way that they form concepts that are organized in a network of relationships. When asked to think about one word related to a concept, people generate many associated words. These concept relationships may be organized in a number of ways.

Class relations are hierarchical networks. Words are related to each other by superordinate and subordinate concepts. For example, *spinnaker* is part of a larger class, *sails.*

Examples are exactly what they appear to be. Every concept has associated examples and nonexamples. Thus, *spinnaker, jib,* and *mainsail* are all examples of sails, while sheeting is a nonexample of a sail.

Attribute relations provide us with organizational networks that focus on the characteristics of concepts. Thus, *mainsail, spinnaker,* and *jib* all have certain common features that connect them to the class of sails.

Although these organizations capture how sets of words may be related to concepts, there are other ways that words are related to each other. They may be organized according to aspects of language. For example, words are changed and interrelated by adding morphemes (affixes, inflectional endings). The richness and flexibility of students' vocabulary must consider these aspects of language as well as the conceptual density of the words and word networks. Vocabulary assessment must consider both aspects. In addition, the relationship between vocabulary and comprehension for each reader must be examined.

It is possible to get a general idea of the range and flexibility of students' vocabulary knowledge using word sorts (see above). As the student's performance is evaluated, it is helpful to consider the following questions:

- Does the child attend to meaning features or graphic features?
- Can the child generate relational categories?
- Does the child recognize multiple meanings for words?
- Does the child recognize and use affixes?
- Does the child recognize and use root words?
- Can the child generate superordinate categories?

Word sorts can easily be embedded in instruction and used repeatedly. This type of assessment strategy can be especially helpful if you are selecting content area texts, are examining students' ability to understand basal texts, or you want to compare your students' knowledge of some new theme or topic.

Multiple Measures of Prior (Vocabulary) Knowledge

Although general measures of vocabulary knowledge can be helpful, teachers also need to know how vocabulary is interacting with specific reading demands. Fortunately, vocabulary measures are relatively easy to incorporate into regular assessment-instruction efforts. Since prior knowledge can and does produce variation in reading performance, we suggest evaluating students' prior knowledge (vocabulary) throughout the assessment process.

Holmes and Roser (1987) identify and compare five techniques for evaluating prior knowledge that can be used during instruction and assessment: free recall, word association, structured questions, recognition, and unstructured discussion. The special value of the work of Holmes and Roser (1987) is that they have actually collected data to determine the utility and efficiency of these assessment strategies. The five strategies are easily adaptable to any assessment or instructional setting. Each approach requires only an observant teacher who understands his or her purpose in gathering such information.

Free recall: The teacher asks students: "Tell me everything you know about ____," and records the responses. Free recall provides the most information in the least time, but can pose problems for young and/or disabled readers who have retrieval problems and/or disorganized information.

Word association is much like the Prereading Plan (PReP) (see below). Teachers select several key words and ask children what comes to mind when they hear each one. These are quick to prepare and administer and generally yield more information than free recall.

Structured questions are posed to determine what students know *prior* to reading. This technique is both the most effective and efficient, yielding by far the most information. However, they are time-consuming to prepare.

Recognition requires that the teacher prepare several statements or key terms beforehand. Then, students select the words, phrases, or sentences they believe are related to the key terms or would be present in a particular selection. Recognition is second only to structured questions for efficiency and to free recall in effectiveness, and is helpful for children who have trouble retrieving information in production tasks.

Unstructured discussion is most like what is traditionally done in reading instruction, since students freely generate their own ideas about a topic, with no focusing from the teacher. However, this approach may not be worth the effort since it is the least effective and efficient procedure of the five.

Each of these techniques is designed to gather information that can be used to inform instruction and to provide quick, on-the-spot assessments of students' conceptual base regarding specific text information.

PReP

The Prereading Plan, or PReP, is a word association procedure designed to assess both the quality and quantity of students' prior knowledge. Developed by Langer

(1982, 1984), it has been well researched. PReP is a particularly effective strategy because it can be used for assessment purposes at the time of instruction.

To implement this procedure, preview the materials to be used and list two to four key concepts. The following questions are then used as the basis for a discussion:

What comes to mind when you hear/read ... ?
(Write the students' responses on the board.)
What made you think of ... ?
Given our discussion, can you add any new ideas about ... ?

Following the discussion, student responses are evaluated using the following classification scheme:

Much prior knowledge: precise definitions, analogies, relational links among concepts.
Some prior knowledge: examples and characteristics, but no connections or relations.
Little prior knowledge: sound-alikes or look-alikes, associated experiences, little or no meaning relations.

The technique can be used to generate diagnostic conclusions about how students' vocabulary (conceptual) knowledge is contributing to their reading difficulties, to make decisions about grouping and pacing, or to make decisions about appropriate instructional adaptations. If this information is needed for a group of students, Langer advocates creating a matrix. Students' names appear down one side and the three categories *(Much, Some, Little)* appear across the top.

To summarize, vocabulary assessment can, and probably should, be done in association with the demands of reading selections. Teachers will obviously need to make decisions about which of these vocabulary assessment strategies is most effective for their purposes. However, it is also important to note that different procedures may actually provide different types of information. Valencia et al. (1987) found that different measures seem to assess different aspects of vocabulary (prior) knowledge. Here again, it is important to recognize the value of multiple measures of prior knowledge. This is obviously most easily accomplished by a skilled teacher during actual instruction.

Evaluating Comprehension

The assessment of comprehension requires a dual focus. First, we are concerned with students' comprehension of a specific selection. Second, and more important, we need to assess students' growing comprehension *ability* (Johnston 1985a). In this section, the descriptions of tools and strategies for assessing comprehension are designed to evaluate whether students have understood what they have just read, and also to reveal whether they are developing the tools needed to understand other texts.

As we have already seen, a number of factors can influence reading performance. For example, students' ability to recall information and answer questions can be affected by the type and quality of the text (see Chapters 2 and 6). Therefore, it is important to assess students' comprehension of materials that are similar to those they are expected to read every day. These are likely to be much longer, more complex selections than any that appear on most commercially available tests. Because reading materials can exert such a strong influence on comprehension performance, we suggest becoming somewhat adept at analyzing the selections to be used for assessment purposes.

Comprehension Materials: Selecting and Analyzing Long Passages

An important first step in developing comprehension measures is constructing maps for the reading selections. The purpose of these maps is to identify important elements within each of the reading selections to ensure that test questions (or recall evaluations) are focused on important information. Stories and informational texts will, of course, differ. We expect students to recall the sequence of events from narrative texts, for example. On the other hand, recalls of informational text may not rely so heavily on sequence. Students' recalls should reflect an understanding of the relationships between and among key facts and ideas.

Story maps: Analyzing narrative text. Story maps reveal the underlying relationships between characters, events, and settings in a given story. They create a visual representation of the elements of setting, problem, goal, events, and resolution (Beck and McKeown 1981; Pearson 1982; Reutzel 1985). Story mapping generally begins with the identification of the problem, the attempt (or plan), and the resolution. The characters, events, and setting revolve around these elements. Sometimes, of course, these other elements are more important. For example, in many books by Ezra Jack Keats, the setting plays a central role (*Snowy Day, Evan's Corner*). Once completed, the maps are used to generate assessment questions (see below) and/or to generate alternative assessment tasks.

For *assessment* purposes, it is important to remember that the map should reveal the central ideas and should also capture the underlying relationships among events. To do this, teachers may need to use somewhat more elaborate maps. The more complex maps reveal how events are organized and how they are related to each other. In Figure 8.3, the map of a fourth-grade basal story reveals its problem-solution framework.

Although text mapping may seem time-consuming, we have found that teachers (even preservice teachers) can learn to do this with just a little practice. Careful analysis of texts is likely to increase both the reliability and validity of informal assessments. Structuring our assessment tasks around carefully analyzed reading material is likely to increase the degree they provide us with *trustworthy* (Valencia 1990a) information. In addition, most teachers report that they begin to view comprehension differently when they analyze selections carefully. They are much less likely to ask trivial, detail questions, and much more likely to pose thought-provoking, theme-related questions. Once the basic frameworks are learned, mapping takes relatively little time. Certainly, a battery of such selection maps could be developed by a small group of teachers working

FIGURE 8.3
Story Map for "The Sociable Seal"

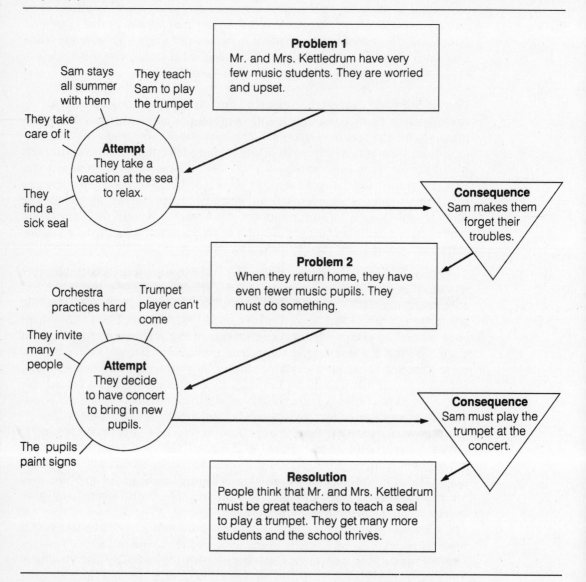

together, or teachers could work together to evaluate a set of "benchmark books" for use in classroom assessment (see Benchmark Books in Chapter 9 for more information).

Conceptual maps: Analyzing expository text. Few assessment instruments provide sufficient information about students' abilities to read nonfiction materials. Yet older students and adults read disproportionately more informational text than they do fictional material. There are simply no available commercial materials that provide good diagnostic information about this critical area of reading ability. For the purposes of evaluating comprehension in general, and studying in particular, it will be necessary to examine actual textbook passages closely (see Chapter 6).

A conceptual map is used to analyze informational selections, identifying relationships in the same way that story maps do for narrative selections. Conceptual maps visually display important elements such as central purpose, main and supporting ideas, and text organization. In Figure 8.4 you will see a conceptual map of a nonfiction selection from a second-grade basal reader.

Wixson and Peters (1989) provide a functional description of the steps involved in creating a conceptual map:

> Concept mapping begins with the identification of major concepts within the text, through reading and an examination of important text features such as headings and photographs. These concepts are then arranged hierarchically to form the first two levels of the concept map—central purpose(s) and major ideas. Then the map is expanded to include a third level of information—supporting ideas. Relations between concepts are highlighted by adding relational links specifying how the concepts are connected. The more clearly organized the text, the more coherent the concept map. If the relation between two concepts is not clear, a link cannot be established. (29–30)

It is important to identify any major organizational patterns and use these to guide your comprehension assessment.

The conceptual map in Figure 8.4 reveals a well-organized text. The ideas are linked together very clearly and each concept is connected by a linking concept which appears in parentheses (for example, first, types, steps). The map also shows that the relationships among the levels of information in this selection are clearly hierarchical. The first level (central purpose) involves describing the daily routine of the sea otter. Then the second level (major ideas) describes the sequence of sea otter activity during one day (hunting, eating, playing, and sleeping). Finally, the third level (supporting ideas) details the steps involved in these activities. This strong organizational pattern should be visible to, and used to support, students' comprehension of the text. It will also be used to evaluate the retellings generated by students after they have read the selection.

Retellings
Armed with a representation of the important elements of a particular text, it is possible to elicit recalls and assess lengthy selections with high levels of reliability.

FIGURE 8.4

Concept Map for "The Sea Otter"

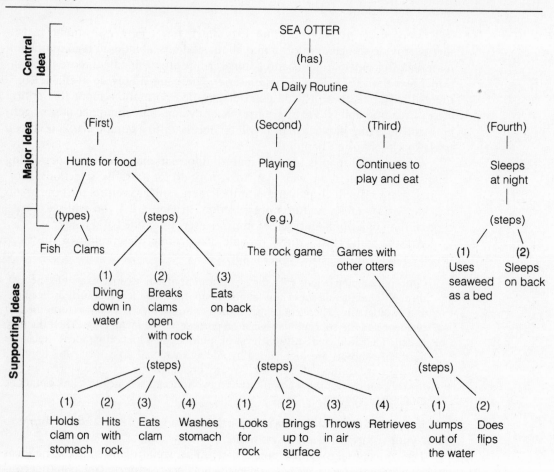

Readers' understanding of textual materials has traditionally been evaluated using question response scores. Indeed, the practice of answering questions is so pervasive that it is sometimes difficult for teachers to recognize that the ability to answer questions is not the same thing as understanding.

Retellings can add immeasurably to our understanding of readers' comprehension because they allow us to get a view of the quantity, quality, and organization of information constructed during reading. Readers' initial responses to the material should involve free recall of the text, without the interference of the teacher. Text recall is natural for children and does not necessarily bias them to process text in a particular way, as questions do. It provides the teacher with information about how the student is constructing meaning from the text without external influence. Because it is important to influence student response as little as possible, initial requests for retelling should be intentionally open-ended. The teacher can initiate the retelling of text with questions such as these:

- Tell *me* that story.
- Tell me what you have read, using your own words.
- What is the text about?
- Tell me as much information as you can about what you have just read. (Ringler and Weber 1984)

Students should be allowed ample time to recall and relate information, and it is important that the teacher not interrupt the student until the retelling is completed. This free recall can provide valuable insight into how the student processes text. Following the uninterrupted retelling, probing statements or questions can be used to elicit further information and to probe readers' understanding of the text. Probes constructed by the teacher should be based directly on the retelling. The following are examples of probes to be used immediately following the retelling:

- Tell me more about what you have read.
- Tell me more about what happened.
- Tell me more about the people whom you just read about.
- Tell me more about where this happened.

A caution is in order before definitive conclusions are made regarding students' ability to understand based on retellings. Some young or less-skilled readers have had little experience in retelling. In fact, they may be surprised that you are not asking them questions. For them, the novelty of the task may influence results, and you may want to attempt another retelling shortly after an initial attempt.

In addition to free and probed retelling, teachers and clinicians may also want to consider using structured questions. The teacher should avoid their use until *after* students have provided all possible information during free and probed retelling, since structured questions impose someone else's view of what is important on an evaluation of text understanding. Then, teachers can distinguish among information generated freely, information elicited with minimal cueing, and information generated through direct cueing.

Eliciting recalls. For fictional selections, it is often desirable to ask probe questions using elements of story grammar (Marshall 1983). Thus, questions such as the following are appropriate:

"Where did _____ happen?" (setting)
"What is _____'s problem?" (initiating event)
"What did _____ do about _____?" (attempt)
"How did _____ solve the problem?" (resolution)

Using these or similar probes, teachers can gather information about a child's ability to recall and infer important story information. Marshall suggests using a checklist to organize the assessment information (see Figure 8.5). It is possible to structure the retellings even more at this point by asking probe questions using elements of text structure appropriate to the type of reading selection. The following are examples of probe questions students might be asked for thematic stories and informational selections (Lipson and Wixson 1989):

Story Selections

What is the main problem the characters face? (problem)
What makes it difficult for the characters to solve their problem? (conflict)
How is the problem solved? (resolution)
What lesson(s) are there in the story? (theme)
What is the main thing that happens in the story? (theme)
What do you learn about the main characters? (characterization)
How is the setting of the story important? (setting)
Which event is a "turning point" in the story? (events)

Informational Selections

What is the central idea of this selection? (central purpose)
Using the headings to divide the text into sections, tell the main ideas in each smaller section. (major ideas)

FIGURE 8.5
Checklist of Retelling Behaviors

Student Names	Retelling Contains						
	Theme	Setting	Character	Goal/ Problem	Attempts	Resolution	Reactions

From "Using Story Grammar to Assess Reading Comprehension" by Nancy Marshall, *The Reading Teacher,* March 1983, p. 619. Reprinted with permission of Nancy Marshall and the International Reading Association.

What information does the text provide to tell more about (support) the important main ideas? (supporting details)

How does the author organize the information to tell you about the central and major ideas? (structure)

Analyzing recall information.   Gathering retelling data is the easy part of this assessment strategy, resulting in a wealth of rich information about students' ability to comprehend and about what students choose to share. The problem is less in the gathering than in the interpretation. How to make sense of, and evaluate, this wealth of information is an altogether different (and more difficult) job. It may be helpful to reflect on the following:

- What does the child recall about this selection?
- How does this recall compare with the map of the text (quantity and quality)?
- How does the student organize the recall?
- How does the recall rate as a whole?

Of course, some system for analyzing and interpreting recall data is needed in order to answer questions like these. Both quantitative and qualitative systems are available, some easier to use than others (Kalmbach 1986a; Morrow 1988).

The retelling guidelines suggested by Morrow (1989) involve a point system. The student's retelling is compared to an analysis of the original selection. To use this retelling procedure, point values are assigned to various aspects of the maps created earlier (setting, characters, problem statements, etc.). Then, the student's recall is evaluated according to how well it reflected these major components. Each retelling yields a score, with the total possible equalling ten points.

Figure 8.6 shows the transcript of Marvin's retelling of a full-length short story, *The Sociable Seal* (mapped in Figure 8.3). In Figure 8.7, you will find an analysis of this retelling using Morrow's (1989) system. Although Marvin did note the main characters, he did not refer to them by name (and, in fact, seems uncertain that "Sam" is the seal during probed questioning). In addition, his grasp of character development was very weak. More seriously, Marvin focused on events that were not central to the story. This significantly weakened his recognition of the plot and the theme. Note that when asked what the story was telling, Marvin concluded "That seals can play just as good as people, if not better," a theme that is not supported by the text analysis (see Figure 8.3).

The advantage to this type of system is that it is relatively easy to use and it reduces large amounts of data into manageable and reportable pieces. The disadvantage to any quantitative system is that it is possible to miss the qualitative aspects of the retellings.

Irwin and Mitchell (1983) have proposed a more holistic scoring system, borrowing from approaches used to assess writing, that is especially appropriate for evaluating students' recall of expository text. This system attends to the "richness of retellings," assessing not only such features as the inclusion of

FIGURE 8.6
Sample Retelling

Marvin's Retelling of "The Sociable Seal"

They were at their house. They went to the beach and saw a seal on the shore. When they first found it they took it, a boat, and went out to the sea. They left him and he came back and went to the shore as fast as he could. They couldn't believe it so they said they'd keep him 'til the end of the summer and they did. He wanted to stay. He took baths at night and they took baths at daytime in the morning. They had a music store and she needed people to play and one kid didn't show up so they went to get the seal to play the trumpet and he played it better than ever and they decided to keep him for as long as they wanted. They had a musical seal and he played good and everyone else did and they had sign-ups so you can play with him and all the people who wanted to sign up for practice with the seal and everybody signed up so they had enough people to play so they were happy and . . . um . . . that's the end.

Probe Questions and Marvin's Responses

1. Who found the seal?
   The people, Mr. and Mrs. Kettledrum.
2. What did they do for a living?
   They had a school music store.
3. What problem did the Kettledrum's have?
   They couldn't find a . . . A boy was sick and he couldn't play so they had to get somebody else so they picked the seal.
4. What was Sam like?
   Funny.
5. Where did the story take place?
   At the ocean and the music store.
6. What problem was the story trying to solve?
   That they couldn't keep the seal and they did because he didn't want to leave.
7. What do you think the story was telling you?
   That seals play just as good as people, if not better.
8. Why do you think they took Sam out to sea?
   So they could have him find his family, but he didn't want to. He swam back to shore and they saw him and decided to keep him.
9. Why did the Kettledrums go to the beach?
   Because they wanted to get away from all their problems.
10. What kind of problems were they having?
    They had problems with their orchestra and their school. Ummm. I dont' know.
11. Why do you think they had the musical?
    To get money.
12. Why were they happy at the end?
    Because the seal could play the instrument and they liked the seal so they kept him.

FIGURE 8.7
Evaluation of Marvin's Retelling

STORY RETELLING ANALYSIS

Student's Name: *Marvin*   Date: _____

Title of Story: *The Sociable Seal* _____

General Directions: Place a 1 next to each element if the child includes it in his or her presentation. Credit gist as well as obvious recall.

Characters and Setting

A. Begins story with an introduction   0

B. Names main character(s)   0

C. Describes character traits   0

D. Includes statement about time and/or place   1

Theme

Refers to main character's primary goal or problem to be resolved.   0

Plot Episodes

A. Recalls main events and episodes   1

B. Retells story in order and makes connections across text   1

Resolution

A. Names the problem solution/goal attainment   1

B. Ends story   1

Response to Literature

Includes a personal or critical response to the literature   0

Highest Score Possible (10)   **Child's Score:** 5

Comments:

Adapted from: Morrow, L. (1989). Using story retelling to develop comprehension. In K. D. Muth (Ed.), *Children's Comprehension of Text* (pp. 37–58). Newark, DE: International Reading Association. Used by permission.

major points and details, but also the degree to which students have gone beyond the text to generate cohesive generalizations and create a comprehensible whole.

The system employs a 5-point scale designed to assess the retelling as a whole. The criteria for assigning retellings to one of these levels are displayed in Figure 8.8. When Irwin and Mitchell's holistic scoring system is applied to Marvin's retelling, we would rate the richness of his retelling somewhere between 2 and 3. Marvin did include some major ideas and included appropriate supporting details. There is a cohesiveness and coherence to his recall. However, he did not include the major thesis (problem) of the selection in his retelling and, even with probing, failed to make appropriate connections between episodes, events, and problems.

To extend the diagnostic value of a qualitative assessment even further, specific aspects of the retelling can be summarized and evaluated (see Figure 8.9). The qualitative analysis in Figure 8.9 clearly demonstrates that Marvin had difficulty generating inferences from text, especially with regard to major ideas and themes. His abilities to summarize, generalize, and organize the text information were all weak. On the other hand, Marvin did recall detailed information from text and clearly responded affectively to what he read.

Both of the systems just described are typically employed to analyze *oral* retellings. With older students, written recalls may be employed. In either case, however, the task must be absolutely clear to students. As with all assessment procedures, task demands will most likely influence results. When written retellings are to be used, it is especially important that you differentiate a *retelling* from a *summary*. Although the evidence is slim, it does appear that written retellings are likely to generate more limited productions than oral ones. On the other hand, written retellings are frequently more coherent and organized. Ringler and Weber (1984) report good success using brief written recalls that focus attention on important story components. Using very holistic ranking procedures, we also have arrived at high degrees of reliability between teachers on such written protocols. When used over time, students' progress can be assessed and the effects of instruction can be demonstrated.

These techniques can be used to gather information about the child's ability to recall and infer important text information. In addition, affective responses to readings can be checked regularly with questions such as: Did you learn anything from reading this? Did you find this selection interesting? Did you enjoy reading this? Kalmbach (1986b) suggests that careful analysis of the retellings themselves can provide important information about students' responses to the text. "The way students structure a retelling will often tell you more about what they thought of the story than they can themselves" (p. 331). Although Kalmbach offers no specific suggestions, the following questions may focus evaluation:

- Is the child's personal interpretation evident from the retelling?
- Does the child make evaluative statements about the characters or events?

FIGURE 8.8
Guidelines for Evaluating the Richness of Retellings

Judging Richness of Retellings	
Level	**Criteria for establishing level**
5	Student generalizes beyond text; includes thesis (summarizing statement), all major points, and appropriate supporting details; includes relevant supplementations; shows high degree of coherence, completeness, comprehensibility.
4	Student includes thesis (summarizing statement), all major points, and appropriate supporting details; shows high degree of coherence, completeness, comprehensibility.
3	Student relates major ideas; includes appropriate supporting details and relevant supplementations; shows adequate coherence, completeness, comprehensibility.
2	Student relates a few major ideas and some supporting details; includes irrelevant supplementations; shows some degree of coherence; some completeness; the whole is somewhat comprehensible.
1	Student relates details only; irrelevant supplementations or none; low degree of coherence; incomplete; incomprehensible.

5 = highest level   1 = lowest level

Checklist for Judging Richness of Retellings				
5	**4**	**3**	**2**	**1**

	5	4	3	2	1
Generalizes beyond text	X				
Thesis (summarizing) statement	X	X			
Major points	X	X	X	?	?
Supporting ideas	X	X	X	X	?
Supplementations	Relevant	Relevant	Relevant	Irrelevant	Irrelevant
Coherence	High	Good	Adequate	Some	Poor
Completeness	High	Good	Adequate	Some	Poor
Comprehensibility	High	Good	Adequate	Some	Poor

The above matrix describes the evaluation of retellings in a holistic fashion on the basis of criteria similar to a procedure used to grade written compositions. This technique is an alternative to questioning for assessment of student comprehension of both narrative and expository text.

From "A Procedure for Assessing the Richness of Retellings" by Pi Irwin and Judy Nichols Mitchell, *Journal of Reading* February 1983, pp. 391–396. Reprinted with permission.

FIGURE 8.9
*Diagnostic
Summary of
Marvin's
Retelling*

Directions: Indicate with a checkmark the degree to which the reader's retelling indicates the reader's comprehension in terms of the following criteria:

	None	Low Degree	Moderate Degree
1. Retelling includes information directly stated in text.			
2. Retelling includes information inferred directly or indirectly from text.		✓	
3. Retelling includes what is important to remember from the text.		✓	
4. Retelling provides relevant content and concepts.			✓
5. Retelling indicates reader's attempt to connect background knowledge to text information.			✓
6. Retelling indicates reader's attempt to make summary statements or generalizations based on the text which can be applied to the real word.		✓	
7. Retelling indicates highly individualistic and creative impressions of or reactions to the text.			✓
8. Retelling indicates the reader's affective involvement with the text.			
9. Retelling demonstrates appropriate reader's language fluency (vocabulary, sentence structure, language conventions, etc.).			✓
10. Retelling indicates reader's ability to organize or compose the retelling.		✓	
11. Retelling demonstrates the reader's sense of audience or purpose.			✓
12. Retelling indicates the reader's control of the mechanics of speaking or writing.			✓

Interpretation: Items 1–4 indicates the reader's comprehension of textual information; items 5–8 indicate reader's response, and involvement with text; 9–12 indicate facility with language.

Source: Mitchell, J. N., & Irwin, P. A. The Reader Retelling Profile: Using Retellings to Make In Decisions. Submitted for Publication.

- Does the child attend to the language of the text, using it to support his or her interpretation?

Before making final judgments about students' ability to retell passages, be sure that the samples gathered represent the students' best efforts. The selections used for assessment should provide a good match for the students' interests, prior knowledge, and developmental ability. Of course, teachers can decide to gather information regarding performance on materials that are routinely assigned to the reader, regardless of appropriateness. The point to remember is that these procedures are sampling the reader's abilities, not measuring them in some definitive way. The goal is to learn more about the reader, and the selections teachers make should reflect their assessment purpose(s).

Questioning

Perhaps the most common form of informal reading assessment is questioning. Teachers use questions to evaluate all aspects of students' reading ability, although they are most often employed to assess comprehension. Although we believe that retellings enrich the picture, careful questioning can reveal much about students' understanding of a particular selection and about their ability to comprehend in general.

The comprehension that is revealed through questioning is, at least in part, a function of the questions that have been asked. Children's ability to answer questions is influenced by both the type and content of the questions they are asked (Pearson et al. 1979; Raphael, Winograd, and Pearson 1980). In addition, both the type and content of questions influence what children recall and the types of inferences they make (Wixson 1983a, 1984) (see Chapter 6). Because the demands of questions affect student performance, information gathered in this way requires careful consideration.

Since structured questions impose someone else's view of what is important, they should be asked *after* students have provided all possible information during free and probed retelling. In this way, distinctions can be made between the information generated freely, information elicited with minimal cueing, and information generated through direct cueing.

Many commercially available assessments (like those that accompany basal programs) use a classification scheme to label comprehension questions. These classification schemes are typically based on one of several well-known taxonomies (for example, Barrett 1976; Bloom 1956). However, there is little evidence that these taxonomies represent real differences in comprehension skills or in the level of difficulty of different questions. As an alternative to these question taxonomies, Pearson and Johnson (1978) suggested that question types should be determined by the source of the answer. They originally devised a three-level taxonomy that captured the relationship between a question and its answer source: text-explicit questions, text-implicit questions, and scriptally implicit questions.

This taxonomy has been extended and used widely as an instructional tool by Raphael (1982; 1986). Her latest refinement of these *question-answer-relationships* (QARs) includes the following categories:

1. *Right There QARs*. The answer is explicitly stated in the text, usually easy to find. The words used to make up the question and words used to answer the question are right there in the same sentence.

II. *Think and Search QARs*. The answer can be inferred from text information. The answer is in the story, but you need to put together different story parts to find it. Words for the question and words for the answer are not found in the same sentence.

III. *In My Head QARs*. These scriptally implicit questions (the question must be answered by referring to prior knowledge) have been divided into two types:

  A. *Author and You*. The answer is not in the story. You need to think about what you already know, what the author tells you in the text, and how it fits together.

  B. *On My Own*. The answer is not in the story. You can even answer the question without the story. You need to use your own experience.

Distinguishing between questions on the basis of the source of the answer is extremely important in assessment. If we are not sure what is required to answer the questions we ask, then it will be difficult to make instructional decisions about comprehension. For example, if we think the answer is right there, when in fact the answer requires connecting text information through inference, then we may incorrectly assume that students cannot locate detail information in text while the problem is actually related to inferential ability. Therefore, the first task in assessing students' comprehension with questions is to determine the task demands of the questions themselves (see Chapter 6).

Consideration should also be given to the effects of question placement. Most teachers regularly ask questions after the selection has been read. Questions in this position place a premium on student recognition of important information. However, if students come to expect that they will always be asked detail, text-explicit questions, they will attempt to remember small details at the expense of more global, inferential understanding. Another aspect of comprehension, however, is students' ability to locate and recognize information depending on their purpose. Thus, teachers may want to ask questions before reading. This permits evaluation of students' ability to read for differing purposes and/or to locate key information.

Finally, questions can be posed during reading. Questions asked during reading can help determine whether students are making connections and integrating relevant information. By refining the questioning strategies, important instructional information can be gathered.

Issues surrounding the quality and placement of questions in general are important, but so are concerns about the content and focus of questions. It is important to devise some means for mapping or outlining text. Maps or outlines like those we described earlier can serve as the basis for constructing comprehension questions. For example, the chart in Figure 8.10 was used in combination with story or conceptual maps when generating assessment questions for a new state test (Wixson, Peters, Weber, and Roeber 1987). Such a matrix can provide helpful structure to a novice teacher/evaluator. When the matrix is completed, an array of possible questions has been generated about important aspects of text. In addition, the various types of questions are well represented (the three types correspond directly to the three types of QARs described above).

Although these strategies may seem time-consuming, the instructional value of assessment information is enhanced. Students do not have to be characterized simply as "good comprehenders" and "poor comprehenders." Instead, teachers can describe quite precisely what and how they understand.

Evaluating Comprehension Processes

We have described a variety of ways to gather information about the products of comprehension. Analyzing students' recall and question responses can provide information about *how* students comprehend, but this information is indirect; it must be inferred. Recently, educators have tried a number

FIGURE 8.10
Narrative Question Grid

Story Components	Intersentence Level	Text Level	Beyond Text Level
Themes Main idea Level Abstract Level			
Plot Setting (Location and relation to theme)			
Characters (Traits and functions)			
Setting (Location and relation to theme)			
Characters (Traits and functions)			
Problem			
Conflict			
Resolution			
Major Events			

of newer assessment strategies designed to uncover the activity that goes on "inside the head."

Think-alouds. In a think-aloud procedure, readers are asked to stop at various points during their reading and "think aloud" about the processes and strategies they are using as they read. Wixson and Lipson (1986) suggest that think-alouds can produce insights into readers' approaches to text processing. They provide the following example of a student's verbal report:

Stacy:	(reads title) Space Ship Earth.
Tutor:	What were you thinking about when you read that title?
Stacy:	A space trip to earth. (reads first portion of text, haltingly and with many repetitions) Boy! I had a lot of trouble with that one.
Tutor:	What makes you think you had trouble with it?
Stacy:	I kept messing up.
Tutor:	What do you mean by "messing up"?
Stacy:	I kept reading sentences twice.
Tutor:	What do you think caused you to read sentences twice like that?
Stacy:	Not understanding it.
Tutor:	Okay, did any of the words give you trouble?
Stacy:	No. (139–140)

Stacy's verbal report reveals a view of reading that is governed by attempts to understand. "Although miscues were obvious during this segment, Stacy's 'fixup' strategy was driven by a desire not to sound good but to construct a sensible text representation" (Wixson and Lipson 1986, 140). Procedures for eliciting students' reports of mental activity generally include the following (Alvermann 1984; Lipson, Bigler, Poth, and Wickizer 1987; Wade 1990):

1. Teacher/evaluator selects a text (generally about 200 words, but longer selections have been used).
2. The text is segmented and marked so that students will stop at predetermined spots.
3. The teacher/evaluator reminds students to think aloud about the text and/or their thoughts as they read the text.

Sometimes students are asked to provide text-based think-alouds. Wade (1990), for example, has designed a think-aloud procedure that requires students to generate hypotheses about the text as they read. Students are told to "tell what is happening," and they are then asked to detail the portions of text that led to their hypotheses. Student reports are analyzed in terms of the information they yield about the reader's ability to make hypotheses and integrate and revise information during reading.

On the other hand, Lipson et al. (1987) focused on readers' use of mental processes. Consequently, they asked students "to tell what you were *doing* and *thinking* as you read that part." Using this approach, students' verbal reports are analyzed for evidence that they employed various strategies known to enhance comprehension (see Chapter 15). Paris (1991) describes a more prompted think-aloud which revolves around a specially created think-aloud passage, or TAP. In Figure 8.11, you see an example of a TAP and the guided questioning procedure, which allows teachers to observe students' strategy use during comprehension.

FIGURE 8.11

Example of Think-Aloud Passage

An Example of a Think-Aloud Passage

The Peabody Ducks

The Peabody Hotel in Memphis, Tennessee, is a very famous place. The Peabody is a beautiful hotel. It has large, nice rooms and fancy decorations. It is not famous for its looks, though. It is famous for its ducks!

Mallard ducks have been performing for guests of the Peabody for over 50 years. Every morning at 11:00 A.M., hotel workers roll out the red carpets in the lobby of the Peabody. Then they begin to play a marching tune.

The audience starts to smile and clap as the ducks waddle into the lobby. The ducks march down the carpet and into the fountain in the middle of the lobby.

The ducks swim in the fountain all day. At 5:00 P.M., they leave the fountain and follow their trainer, Edward Pembroke. They march to the elevator and ride back up to the roof of the Peabody. The hotel has built them a large cage on the roof. It is known as the Royal Duck Place. The place has fountains, pools, food, and even a fancy purple trat where the ducks sleep.

Edward Pembroke has trained ducks for the Peabody for almost 50 years. He teaches them to listen to his voice as he tells them what to do. He also teaches them to follow signals that he gives with a cane. Pembroke usually trains groups of five ducks at a time. Each duck only performs for three months. After three months, the trained ducks are sent back to farms. New ducks take their place. This way, the ducks don't get bored and neither does Pembroke!

As you can see, the Peabody Hotel is an unusual place! Maybe someday you'll get a chance to visit Memphis. Then you too can get a look at the famous Peabody ducks!

From Paris, S. G. (1991). Assessment and remediation of metacognitive aspects of children's reading comprehension. *Topics in Language Disorders, 12,* 32–50. He references: *Heath Reading Strategies Assessment* (1991). Lexington, MA: DC Heath © DC Heath and Company.

FIGURE 8.11
(Continued) Sample of Think-Aloud Passage

Name _____ M   F   Grade _____ Date _____

Teacher _____ School _____

Strategies for Constructing Meaning *The Peabody Ducks*—Grade 3

Identifying the Topic	Strategies	Observed	Notes
1a. Look at this page. What do you think the story will be about?	Scans text	_____	_____
	Looks at title	_____	_____
	Uses picture	_____	_____
	Refers to prior knowledge	_____	_____
	Establishes purpose	_____	_____
	Points out words	_____	_____
	Displays positive affect, expectations	_____	_____
	Other	_____	_____

1b. How did you know this?

If you don't know, how could you tell?

Predicting	Strategies	Observed	Notes
2a. What do you think will happen next?	Predicts based on prior knowledge	_____	_____
	Predicts based on text cues	_____	_____
	Rereads	_____	_____
Why do you think that?	Looks forward in text	_____	_____
	Use context cues	_____	_____
	Other	_____	_____

If you don't know, how could you find out?

Monitoring meaning	Strategies	Observed	Notes
3a. What do you think "trat" means in the sentence you just read?	Uses context cues	_____	_____
	Substitution looks or sounds similar	_____	_____
	Mentions other as resources	_____	_____
3b. How could you tell?	Mentions dictionary as resources	_____	_____
	Other	_____	_____

If you don't know, how could you find out?

Making inferences	Strategies	Observed	Notes
4a. Why do you think Edward Pembroke uses a cane?	Infers based on text cues	_____	_____
	Infers based on prior knowledge	_____	_____
	Scans forward	_____	_____
4b. How did you decide this?	Rereads	_____	_____
	Other	_____	_____

If you don't know, how can you figure it out?

FIGURE
8.11
(Continued)
Sample of
Think-Aloud
Passage

Summarizing	Strategies	Observed	Notes
5a. If you wanted to tell your friends about this story, what would you tell them?	Retells mostly main ideas	_____	_____
	Retells mostly details	_____	_____
	Organizes ideas in recall	_____	_____
5b. How did you decide what things to tell them?	Expresses opinions or reactions	_____	_____
	Connects to personal experiences	_____	_____
	Uses genre/structure to help recall	_____	_____
If you don't know, how do you think you could decide?	Displays appropriate affect	_____	_____
	Other	_____	_____

Reprinted with permission from *Heath Reading Strategies Assessment.* (1991). Lexington, MA: DC Heath: © 1991 DC Heath and Company.

It is important to understand that verbal reports reflect what readers are doing as they read a specific text with specific task directions. There is good evidence that students' reading behaviors may vary as texts and tasks change (Olshavsky 1978). Maria (1990) has pointed out that think-aloud assessment procedures are very intrusive and require considerable teacher time. In addition, single think-aloud excerpts will not capture the variability we noted above. Both concerns can be addressed if teachers turn to careful observations of strategy use during normal instruction.

Continuous comprehension assessment. The value of Think-alouds can be improved significantly by "specifying the factors related to text and varying them systematically (Wixson and Lipson 1986, 140). This generally requires regular, ongoing assessment of students as they read and interact with a variety of texts and tasks. Good assessment should capture the full range of students' comprehension ability; not just their best or worst efforts.

A versatile assessment procedure, designed by Wood (1988), is the Individual Comprehension Profile. As described by Wood, a profile, or matrix, is created using the results from information that has been gathered by the teacher/evaluator. The information is recorded as students read from their basal, under conditions that parallel the daily expectations in the classroom. Although Wood provides a sample profile, the matrix is meant to be teacher-made, allowing teachers to enter columns for whatever conditions appear most important for their program and student(s).

We have used a variation on this procedure to create an Individual Reading Record (see Figure 8.12). As students read, information relevant to their performance can be recorded. If students are thinking aloud (see above), for example, the information generated would probably be used to fill the "Process

FIGURE 8.12

Individual Reading Record

Name: _____   Teacher: _____

Grade: _____   School: _____

	Date	Text Description	Topic Familarity	Attitudes and Interest	Reading Task(s)	Process Knowledge/ Strategy Use	Reading Performance	Level of Support
Text 1								
Text 2								
Text 3								

Knowledge/Strategy Use" column. The data recorded, coupled with specific information about the texts and tasks (see Chapters 5 and 6), provide a very complete picture of a reader's knowledge, skills, and abilities, and how this varies across texts.

Studying

Studying is a specialized type of comprehension (Anderson and Armbruster 1984b). Studying involves intensive reading for specific purposes, typically to organize, retain, and retrieve information. Often the purposes for reading have been imposed by others. However, many of the skills required for studying in the school context are also required in work settings. Even students who have a good foundation in the skills and strategies of reading through the elementary years may find the special demands of study and work reading difficult. We recommend assessing the study skills and habits of all students who have reached the sixth grade or beyond, since weaknesses in this area often cause serious academic problems.

Although it is helpful and important to assess all components of reading ability in natural contexts, it is absolutely critical to do so when assessing study skills. If they are to provide any useful information, assessments of studying ability must be specific to the content to be learned and related to the materials to be studied (Rakes and Smith 1986).

Assessment of students' studying abilities should move forward cautiously. Clearly students may be aware of these skills and strategies but not use them during studying. In addition, many of these skills can be executed passively (for example, outlining by copying headings and subheadings). It should be apparent how important it is to determine what is really required to understand a particular text or accomplish a specific task.

In planning an assessment of study skills, Estes and Vaughan (1978) suggest the following steps:

1. Identify the study skills that students will need for success in their studying activities.
2. Construct a diagnostic checklist to record your assessments of students' studying abilities.
3. Prepare a student self-appraisal survey based on the study skills you consider important.
4. Construct informal activities to assess the study skills you have identified as critical.
5. Informally observe students' ability to use their study skills as they perform tasks during daily classroom activities (paraphrased, 114).

Developing a checklist of critical studying skills and strategies. The specification of skills and strategies as reading-studying abilities is somewhat problematic, since many of these might arguably be considered generic comprehension skills. Rogers (1984) has made a distinction between casual and study reading that is helpful: "Deliberate procedures for retaining or applying what is read are called study-reading skills. They permit people to complete tasks which they would not do as successfully if they read only casually" (346). Long lists of study skills generally include specialized abilities such as: alphabetizing, skimming, note-taking, outlining, scanning, and reading maps, graphs, tables, and diagrams. Such lists are not entirely helpful, however, because the use of these studying skills does not ensure good comprehension, nor do all good readers use all of these skills (Armbruster and Anderson 1981).

There are many checklists available to guide observations of students as they engage in studying activities. Rogers (1984) has collapsed the long lists of reading-study skills into three large categories: (1) special study-reading comprehension skills, (2) information location skills, and (3) study and retention strategies, and has designed a comprehensive checklist of discrete abilities (see Figure 8.13). As always, this checklist should be adapted to specific settings. As students are observed engaged in study activity, the teacher should consider the following questions:

- Does the student have an organized approach to the task?
- Does the student seem to know what to do and how to use the text to accomplish the task?
- Does the student exhibit enthusiasm and/or interest?
- Does the student appear to be using appropriate study skills and strategies?
- Does the student appear to read with a flexible rate?

Ideally, checklists like this one would become a part of the continuous and ongoing assessment (portfolio) for each student, an idea implied by Rogers: "It (the checklist) can be completed as opportunities arise for observing each student and it can be kept in the student's records" (347). As a matter of practicality, however, it may be necessary to create planned opportunities or informal tests to make these observations efficient.

**FIGURE
8.13**

*Study-Reading
Skills Checklist*

Degree of Skill	Absent	Low	High
I. Specific study-reading comprehension skills			
A. Ability to interpret graphic aids			
Can the student interpret these graphic aids?			
1. maps			
2. globes			
3. graphs			
4. charts			
5. tables			
6. cartoons			
7. pictures			
8. diagrams			
9. other organizing or iconic aids			
B. Ability to follow directions			
Can the student follow . . .			
1. simple directions?			
2. a more complex set of directions?			
II. Information location skills			
A. Ability to vary rate of reading			
Can the student do the following?			
1. scan			
2. skim			
3. read at slow rate for difficult materials			
4. read at average rate for reading level			
B. Ability to locate information by use of book parts			
Can the student use book parts to identify the following information?			
1. title			
2. author or editor			
3. publisher			
4. city of publication			
5. name of series			
6. edition			
7. copyright date			
8. date of publication			
Can the student quickly locate and understand the function of the following parts of a book?			
1. preface			
2. foreword			
3. introduction			
4. table of contents			
5. list of figures			
6. chapter headings			
7. subtitles			
8. footnotes			
9. bibliography			
10. glossary			
11. index			
12. appendix			

**FIGURE
8.13**
(continued)

Degree of Skill	Absent	Low	High
C. Ability to locate information in reference works			
Can the student do the following?			
1. locate information in a dictionary			
a. using the guide words			
b. using a thumb index			
c. locating root word			
d. locating derivations of root word			
e. using the pronunciation key			
f. selecting word meaning appropriate to passage under study			
g. noting word origin			
2. locate information in an encyclopedia			
a. using information on spine to locate volume			
b. using guide words to locate section			
c. using index volume			
3. use other reference works such as:			
a. telephone directory			
b. newspapers			
c. magazines			
d. atlases			
e. television listings			
f. schedules			
g. various periodical literature indices			
h. others ( )			
D. Ability to locate information in the library			
Can the student do the following?			
1. locate material by using the card catalog			
a. by subject			
b. by author			
c. by title			
2. find the materials organized in the library			
a. fiction section			
b. reference section			
c. periodical section			
d. vertical file			
e. others ( )			
III. Study and retention strategies			
A. Ability to study information and remember it			
Can the student do the following?			
1. highlight important information			
2. underline important information			
3. use oral repetition to increase retention			
4. ask and answer questions to increase retention			
5. employ a systematic study procedure (such as SQ3R)			
6. demonstrate effective study habits			
a. set a regular study time			
b. leave adequate time for test or project preparation			
c. recognize importance of self-motivation in learning			

**FIGURE
8.13**
(continued)

Degree of Skill	Absent	Low	High
B. Ability to organize information Can the student do the following? 1. take notes_____			
2. note source of information _____			
3. write a summary for a paragraph _____			
4. write a summary for a short selection _____			
5. write a summary integrating information from more than one source _____			
6. write a summary for a longer selection _____			
7. make graphic aids to summarize information _____			
8. write an outline of a paragraph _____			
9. write an outline of a short selection _____			
10. write an outline for longer selections _____			
11. write an outline integrating information from more than one source _____			
12. use an outline to write a report or make an oral report			

From "Assessing Study Skills" by Douglas B. Rogers, *Journal of Reading*, January 1984, pp. 353–354. Reprinted with permission of Douglas B. Rogers and the International Reading Association.

Open Book Reading Assessment. In the Open Book Reading Assessment (OBRA) (Bader 1980), as its name suggests, students have access to the text throughout. The OBRA is based on the following assumptions: "To determine the skills to be evaluated, one must give consideration to (a) the nature of the tasks to be performed with the material and the levels of comprehension required and (b) the enabling skills required to perform the tasks or comprehend the information." Bader suggests creating items about such things as technical vocabulary, use of context clues, using charts, and using book parts. In addition, she suggests testing students' ability to answer questions that require making inferences and interpreting text information.

To create an OBRA tailored for specific settings, examine the textbook carefully and consider the types of tasks generally expected of students (see Chapters 5 and 6). The OBRA is a very flexible assessment strategy since it can accommodate almost any type of text-task context. The example in Figure 8.14 was developed by a vocational education teacher who was concerned about his students' failure to do well on tests. He constructed the OBRA to accompany an assigned chapter entitled "Electronic Fuel Injection Systems." The chapter contained the following notable features:

- Chapter Preview
- List of Objectives
- Clearly labeled section headings (for example, 53.3, Fuel Flow System)
- Fourteen (14) complex figures with detailed labeling

**FIGURE
8.14**
*Sample
Open Book
Reading
Assessment*

Auto Mechanics

Name_____(KEY)_____

1. Circle the components of an airflow system (pages 536, 539)
   a. air flow meter
   b. main jet
   c. throttle chamber
   d. throttle valve
   e. injector
   f. choke plate
   g. air regulator
   h. electronic control unit
   i. back pressure relief valve
   j. throttle body
   k. fuel distributor
   l. turbocharger

2. Using the diagram on page 540, indicate the order that fuel flows through the following components, starting with the fuel tank

1	Fuel Tank
5	Fuel Distributor
3	Fuel Damper
6	Injector
4	Fuel Filter
2	Fuel Pump

3. Using the following chart, circle the cars that should have an idle speed of 800 RPM if equipped with automatic transmission.
   a. 84 AMC Alliance
   b. 82 Renault
   c. 83 Toyota 4 cyl
   d. 82 Ford Bronco
   e. 80 Toyota Cressida
   f. 83 Toyota 6 cyl
   g. 83 Renault Fuego
   h. 79 Toyota Supra

Idle Speed and Mixture Adjustments

Application		Idle Speed			Idle Mixture		Voltmeter Leads	
Year	Model	M/T	A/T	Adjustment Location	Voltage	Fluctuation	Positive	Negative
AMC								
83	Alliance	650	650	Thrott. Hsg. Screw	6.0–7.0	0.5	D2-2	D2-7
84	Alliance, Encore	700	700	Thrott. Hsg. Screw	6.0–7.0	0.5	D2-2	D2-7
Renault								
82–83	Fuego Turbo	750	...	Thrott. Hsg. Screw	6.5–7.5	0.5	8	2
82–83	All Others	800	650	Thrott. Hsg. Screw	6.5	0	8	2
Toyota								
79–80	Supra	800	800	Thrott. Hsg. Screw	•	0.5	VF	B+
80	Cressida	800	800	Thrott. Hsg. Screw	•	0.5	VF	B+
81–82	All AFC	800	800	Thrott. Hsg. Screw	3.0–9.0	•	VF	E!
1983	4-Cyl.	800	800	Thrott. Hsg. Screw	5.9–9.0	2.0	VF	E!
1983	6-Cyl.	650	650	Thrott. Hsg. Screw	0.1–0.2	0.1	10 or 20	B+

In my textbook, to find quickly:
4. _e_ Definition of technical word
5. _d_ A statement of the book's purpose and features
6. _b_ Name of the book's publisher
7. _c_ Outline of what is in the book
8. _a_ Location in the text of a key term

I would turn to:
a) Index
b) Title Page
c) Table of Contents
d) Preface
e) Glossary

On page:
9. 563
10. beginning
11. beginning
12. beginning
13. 566

Note: If a section does not have a page number, indicate if it is in the beginning, middle, or end of the book.

- A New Terms section, with new vocabulary in boldface and brief definitions
- Chapter Review
- Discussion Topics and Activities section

After the students have completed the OBRA, the following questions should be considered in evaluating students' performance:

- Do the students recognize the parts of the text?
- Are students able to make use of graphic materials?
- When the text is available, can students locate specific information?
- Can students use the text to figure out unfamiliar, specialized vocabulary?
- Does the problem appear to be ability to use the text or ability to retain information?

This information is summarized and used to plan and adapt instruction. Bader (1980) suggests using a chart to display the information for the class. The chart in Figure 8.15 displays a portion of the one generated by the vocational teacher who constructed and administered the OBRA described earlier. He learned, to his surprise, that most of his students were unable to make effective use of the diagrams and charts in their textbook. Similarly, few of them were adept at using the helpful features of the book to derive information. Whereas he had previously attributed the students' poor performance to lack of effort and/or motivation, he now realized that at least some students were unable to learn

FIGURE 8.15

Open Book Reading Assessment Summary Form

	Literal Details Content												Using Diagrams and Charts														Using Book Parts									
	1												2 (Diagrams)						3 (Charts)																	
	a	b	c	d	e	f	g	h	i	j	k	l	a	b	c	d	e	f	a	b	c	d	e	f	g	h	4	5	6	7	8	9	10	11	12	13
Lorie				✓			✓														✓	✓														
Jack				✓			✓																				✓		✓		✓					✓
Mark				✓			✓	✓																	✓											
Judy				✓			✓															✓	✓													
Shane				✓			✓	✓																	✓											
Mike				✓			✓	✓																					✓		✓	✓		✓		
Greg			✓						✓						✓		✓																			
Jack R.					✓	✓																									✓		✓	✓		✓
Keith				✓	✓	✓																									✓		✓			

the information using the text. Instruction in textbook use and/or additional support for reading and studying would be needed.

Again, teachers may be concerned about the time-consuming nature of these assessment strategies. Although short-cuts are possible, the information gathered will not be as useful. As Rogers (1984) has noted, "students' use of study-reading can best be assessed by observing them while they are engaging in studying-reading for some personal interest or need. Contrived situations such as often occur when students are asked to complete worksheet pages from published materials are not as effective for assessing and teaching study-reading" (352).

Writing

Traditionally, writing has been evaluated by examining written *products*, just as reading has traditionally been evaluated by examining the products of reading (for example, question responses). Product assessments have generally consisted of evaluating two aspects of written work: composition and mechanics (Cramer 1982). Increasingly, educators and linguists are concerned with students' grasp of the writing *process*. Clearly, it is possible to make inferences about students' growing knowledge and control of the process by examining written products. However, students' behavior as they engage in writing is also of concern. Most experts suggest that the writing process involves several stages: a planning stage, for clarifying purpose and audience; a composing stage, which involves writing, reading, and attention to mechanics; and a revision stage, during which rereading and editing occur.

Evaluating Written Products

Folders, or portfolios, of ongoing and completed work are a normal part of classrooms where a process writing approach is used. Samples of written work should be gathered and provide exceptionally good evidence regarding student growth. Daily work samples, journal entries, and work from writers' workshop all provide rich information about students' developing knowledge, skill, and motivation.

Graves (1983) recommends that evaluation start with what he calls *Folder Observation*. This entails evaluating the written work in preparation for other types of observation. "Trends in children's writing will be important observation points, along with the specifics that make up the trends" (Graves 1983, 287). In completing a Folder Observation, it may be helpful to reflect on the following:

- What types of writing is the student producing?
- What topics seem to fuel his/her writing?
- What new ideas are being generated?
- Is there evidence of topic or theme change/growth?
- What skills can and does this child employ?

These overall trends and patterns are very important, but teachers often need/want to evaluate students individual writing samples more closely. Written work can be evaluated holistically or analytically. Many norm-referenced tests of writing involve analytic evaluations of written products (see Chapter 10). Holistic scoring of written products is quite common both in classroom assessment and in large-scale assessment (even statewide assessment of writing) and can be especially useful for screening purposes. Holistic scoring involves assigning a piece of writing a score after examining it *as a whole* (Cockrum and Castillo 1991).

Holistic scoring.   Holistic scoring involves evaluating a composition as a whole piece of writing. Unlike analytic scores (see below), holistic scores "depend on comparisons with other pieces of writing rather than on comparisons against a predetermined scale" (Bratcher 1994, 52). These comparisons may be done in two ways; by comparing the piece to other pieces (called "anchors" or "benchmarks") or by comparing a piece to papers in a set of compositions.

In the first case, a teacher (or better yet a group of teachers) would collect a great deal of writing. For example, all fifth-grade teachers might collect research papers for the whole year from all their students. They would then read them and agree on an exemplary paper or two—considered "high." Similarly, one or two very poor exemplars would be selected—considered "low." Finally, several papers considered to be "middle" would be identified. These pieces of writing become the "anchor" papers. Whenever a teacher evaluates a student's research paper in future, it is compared, holistically, to these anchors and classified in terms of its similarity to one or another of these types of writing.

As described by Bratcher (1994), the other type of holistic scoring occurs when teachers read an entire set of papers through one time and place them in three piles: good, poor, and somewhere in between. Then, the papers are read a second time in order to validate the first impression. Papers can be moved from one stack to another and then they receive a holistic score of: +, √, or – .

Occasionally, holistic scoring proceeds using a scale to guide the evaluation. Millett (1986) provides the following example of a scale used in holistic scoring:

0-This score is given to papers that cannot be scored for one reason or another. Papers may be blank, unrelated to the assignment, or illegible.

1-This score is given to papers that do address the assignment, but do so inadequately. Papers may be too short, general, or only tangentially related to the assignment.

2-This score is given to papers that are incomplete, inconsistent, or too general. Organization and details may be problematic.

3-This score is given to papers that are generally well-organized and address the assignment. There may be lapses in organization or areas of confusion, but the author's message is understandable.

4-This score is given to papers that are complete, well-organized, and detailed. The style and vocabulary add clarity and interest.

Analytic scoring.   Sometimes, teachers or other evaluators want to analyze writing in terms of its component parts. "Analytic strategies of grading [sic] are based on an assumption that the quality of a piece of writing is the sum of the quality of each component of the writing" (Bratcher 1994, 44). Generally, scores or points are assigned to the various component areas and then totaled to obtain a score or grade. From a diagnostic viewpoint, it can be helpful to analyze students' writing so that instruction can be tailored to the particular aspects that are causing a student difficulty. Written products are typically evaluated in four major areas: context, content, structure, and mechanics (Bratcher 1994). In Figure 8.16, you see a type of analytic scoring sheet. This type of scoring device can help teachers to "notice" what is important in writing.

Analytic or holistic evaluations of written products can certainly provide rich information about students' writing abilities. However, it is extremely difficult (perhaps impossible) to evaluate students' control of the writing process by considering only final products. Evaluation of student control over the process of writing requires that students be observed, over time, in a classroom that values process writing and encourages author development.

Observation Checklists

An effective observation framework should include examination of written work, but it should also provide for examining the writer at work. Kemp (1987) has proposed an observational checklist of behaviors to watch for as children write. The results of these observations can be used to evaluate children's developmental progress and also to identify areas that might require instructional attention. The form, which appears in Figure 8.17, parallels the major stages of writing, focusing on the student during planning, composing ("drafting"), and revision phases. In addition, this checklist addresses the critical affective outcomes addressed by creating good written products and provides for evaluation of student attitudes.

Finally, teachers need ways to summarize the information they have about students' writing. Temple and Gillet (1989) suggest that in addition to the assessments of the writer in the writing process, students' written work should be evaluated in terms of the functions of the writing, writing style, writing fluency, and mechanics. The checklist devised by Temple and Gillet (1989) delineates the kinds of questions to ask during the evaluation of students' writing. These include:

Functions of Writing

- What types of writing have been produced? (stories, expressive writing, descriptive writing, etc.)
- What topics have been selected by the writer? Who is the audience for this child's writing? (teacher, classmates, etc.)
- How sophisticated is the writer's awareness of audience?

FIGURE 8.16
*Analytic
Scoring Sheet*

TOTAL POINTS POSSIBLE: 100   TOTAL POINTS EARNED: _____

Context (20 pts.)   Points Earned: _____
    purpose of the writing identified
    reader identified
    writer's stance identified

Content (20 pts.)   Points Earned: _____
    topic is narrowed
    ideas are complete
    main idea is clear
    details are tailored to the main idea

Structure (20 pts.)   Points Earned: _____
    sequence of ideas (beginning, middle, end)
    follows assigned structure (expository form)
    paragraphs contain topic sentences

Mechanics (20 pts.)   Points Earned: _____
    completion of thoughts as sentences
    use of transitions and conjunctions to connect ideas
    conventional word endings
    personal pronouns
    contractions
    singular possessives
    verb tenses
    subject-verb agreement
    conventional spelling
    punctuation
    capitalization
    sentence variety (simple, compound, and complex)
    use of homophones
    use of comparisons

Process (20 pts.)   Points Earned: _____
    prewriting turned in
    partner checklist for topic, audience, and purpose
    rough draft
    revising worksheet
    editing workshop
    final copy submitted for class book

Source: Bratcher, S. (1994). *Evaluating Children's Writing*. NY: St. Martin's Press, p. 45. Used by permission.

**FIGURE
8.17**
*Checklist of
The Writing
Process*

Name of Child: _____ Date of Assessment: _____

Name of Teacher: _____

Title of Sample: _____
(attached, if to be used in discussion with parent or teacher)

A. Orientation to Writing

1. Is able on most occasions to engage in discussion of a theme or topic.
2. Is positive on most occasions when given writing opportunities.
3. Responds well to 'conferencing' or seeks out others for trying out ideas or words.
4. Engages in writing without need of persuasion or direction.

B. Drafting

5. Manages, when motivation is high, to produce a draft.
6. Contributes drafts to a personal journal or writing folder.
7. 'Rehearses' with drawing, talking, verbal composing.
8. Takes risks in using words when their spelling or precise meaning are not known.
9. Aims to write.
10. Responds to conferencing whilst composing drafts.
11. Reflects on efforts so far.
12. Avoidance strategies are rare.
13. Appears on most occasions to have purpose, that is, to write for an audience and/or a publication or self.

C. Revising, Rewriting, Editing

14. Makes judgments about own writing.
15. Submits drafts for others' comments.
16. Can 'see the words as temporary' (and) 'the information as manipulable.'
17. Is prepared to work over drafts.
18. Is careful in final stages about mechanics, such as spelling.
19. Revisits 'risk' areas to work over them.
20. Understands that own writing can be manipulated for better effects and to match changing intentions.
21. Seeks information, facts, opinions to strengthen writing.

Comments

What signs are there of the child's self-direction, self-monitoring, and incentive to write?

What kinds of freedom does the child show in engaging in the first writing stages?

Is s/he an 'explorer' with words, styles, structures, ideas?

What successful changes have taken place between drafting and final writing?

What are some of your perceptions of the writer's recent development?

**FIGURE
8.17**
(Continued)

D. Production

22. Produces sustained writing effort from time to time.
23. Takes pride in a completed work.
24. Is sensitive towards the writing efforts of others.
25. Achieves a 'voice' in some writing.
26. Achieves completeness of some writing.
27. Final presentation is accurate in mechanics, such as spelling and handwriting.
28. Reads own and others' writing.

E. Additional Observations

Comments
What does the writer do with the final products?

Are the final products valued/re-read? With whom?

What were the most successful strategies used this time to sustain the writing?

From *Watching Children Read and Write* by Max Kemp. Copyright © 1987 Max Kemp. Reprinted by permission of Thomas Nelson Australia.

Qualities of Writing Style

- Does the writing reflect good choices in language use?
- Does the writer make good use of descriptive language?
- Does the writer maintain a focus throughout the work?
- Are papers well-organized, given the purpose of the work?
- Are the written products defined by effective openings and endings?

Mechanics of Writing

- How much control of standard English usage/grammar is reflected in the written works of this writer?
- Are complete idea units (sentences) used throughout?
- Are punctuation and capitalization used appropriately?

These examples demonstrate how teachers can focus on and gather evidence of the writer's reading interests, knowledge, and skill. It is possible to conduct much more extensive analyses of students' writing abilities.

Student Self-Evaluation

According to Valencia, McGinley, and Pearson (1990), one of the characteristics of newer perspectives on assessment is the realization that it should be *collaborative*. "The essence of collaborative criterion lies in collaboration with students. When we work *with* students in developing assessments, we communicate our support of their learning process" (Valencia, McGinley, and Pearson 1990). This means that students should share some responsibility for monitoring their own progress, but this also means that they must have access to information. They need to be clearly informed of the purposes for various work assignments, and important evaluative criteria will need to be shared with them as well. Collaboration necessarily involves at least some student self-evaluation. Indeed, the ability to evaluate one's own work should be viewed as an important goal in most literacy programs, since it is a necessary requirement of independence (Johnston 1987).

In writing, teachers use teacher-student and peer conferences to establish criteria for evaluating success and/or progress (see previous section). Then, students are invited to contribute by evaluating their own efforts (see Figure 8.18). These self-evaluations must be taken seriously and must become part of the total assessment process.

For our purposes, it is especially important to note the extent to which students' self-evaluations reflect their development and progress as writers. Comments such as the following reflect differences that are important to recognize: "I liked this story because it's long"; "I tried to make a good beginning to this story and I think I did"; "I was trying to make people understand how the boy in this story felt." We want to attend as well to changing self-evaluations. Students can

FIGURE 8.18
Self-Assessment Questionnaire

A Self-Assessment Questionnaire

Name _____ Date _____

Title _____

As you publish your writing, reflect on your writing processes and this piece of writing. Please respond briefly to at least three questions in each section.

Part 1:   Your writing processes
➤ What part of the writing process was most successful for you?
➤ What writing strategies did you use?
➤ What part of the writing process was least successful for you?
➤ What do you need help with?

Part 2:   This piece of writing
➤ What pleases you most about this piece of writing?
➤ Are you comfortable with this topic and genre?
➤ How did you organize your writing?
➤ Does your lead grab your readers' attention?
➤ Which type of mechanical errors cause you the most trouble?

Source: Tompkins, G. (1992). Assessment in the processes of students as writers. *Journal of Reading*, 36, pp. 244–246. (p. 246). International Reading Association. Reprinted by permission.

help us understand their purposes in this way, but they also show us whether they have begun to take risks in writing or have internalized new standards for their work.

THE DIAGNOSTIC PORTFOLIO: EVIDENCE FROM THE CLASSROOM

Marvin

Marvin's new teacher (remember he had only recently transferred schools, with very little information) used the end-of-level basal skills tests as her primary assessment. Marvin had been placed in a grade 3–2 basal (the lowest group). The one set of tests he had completed indicated that Marvin was weak in most areas of word analysis. His comprehension appeared stronger and he clearly enjoys reading. As we have seen, Marvin's comprehension of long text tends to miss the point. He attends well to details although he can be diverted by entertaining subplots.

Overall, however, there is not a great deal of assessment information available from the classroom. His teachers (old and new) relied quite heavily on formal tests and basal inventories. In the next chapters we see how structured inventories and diagnostic teaching provided a much fuller picture of Marvin's knowledge and skill.

Kyle

Kyle's teacher, on the other hand, engages in fairly continuous classroom assessment. Running records have been collected on Kyle since late kindergarten. These reveal a struggling reader who, nevertheless, has gained considerable knowledge. By fall of second grade, Kyle is gaining ground on his age peers. As we have seen, he is still struggling with word level skills; both graphophonic and sight. His comprehension is very good, except when his serious word recognition difficulties limit his ability to use his excellent language and prior knowledge.

Kyle's writing is similarly filled with good ideas, but it is difficult to read. His purpose is generally clear, the content is good, but the mechanics are weak. For example, in mid-grade two, Kyle's writing folder contained the following story:

> Once there was a eagle. He was different than the others. Some of the others teased him. He didn't have any friends. But he had one. He was a hawk. His name was Eric. One day they went fishing. They saw some poachers. They flew back and warned the others. They all were saved! They were always kind from then on.

This captivating and well-structured story was difficult to read because Kyle's writing is large and ill-formed and also because his spelling is still at the phonetic level. On the other hand, sentences were marked by periods and some capitals.

About the same time, Kyle reflected on his own writing. He noted that, "I used to.... *write one santins, only the bgining of werds, and no detal in pichers*" "But now I ... *put mor santosis, sownd it out, and more dtal in pichers.*" Kyle is clearly developing in all areas of literacy although his teacher and parents remain concerned.

CHAPTER SUMMARY

In this chapter, we described the role of the teacher in an effective program of assessment, arguing that high quality information about students requires knowledgeable teacher/evaluators. We described a number of informal assessment strategies for evaluating specific components of reading competence. We suggested ways to gather information as students engage in actual reading and writing activities. For example, we described methods for gathering information about students' vocabulary knowledge using strategies such as free recall and PReP. In the area of comprehension assessment, we suggested techniques for enhancing the information that can be gathered using traditional techniques like questioning and retelling. In addition, we have described a verbal report, or think-aloud, procedure for assessing students comprehension abilities. Strategies for gathering information about students' studying abilities were also discussed, stressing the need to assess this area in naturalistic contexts. Finally, several informal techniques for assessing writing were described, and a section of student self-assessment was provided as well.

In each case, the assumption has been made that the information will become a part of a systematic, continuous, and well-organized assessment designed by well-informed teacher/evaluators. Assessment is viewed as an ongoing process. Each encounter with a child must be seen as an opportunity for interactive assessment. In this manner, teaching and testing become integral events. By adopting this stance, we have taken a positive step toward providing instructional programs that are responsive to the needs of all children.

Educators must continue to press for assessment instruments and methodologies that provide instructionally useful and contextually valid information. The assessment efforts described in this chapter can and should provide much more specific information about how and what to teach, but they are suggestive only. Ingenious teachers will find many other ways to evaluate their students' performance for the purpose of making placement and curricular decisions.

Most of the assessment strategies we have suggested can be easily incorporated in daily instructional programs. Indeed, the strategies described may be difficult for a teacher in a pull-out program to implement without the cooperation of the classroom teacher. It does little good to evaluate component skills and abilities without observing them in action. Students can, and often do, perform differently on tests of isolated skill or on tasks in constrained and artificial environments, than they do in real classrooms accomplishing real assignments.

Certainly support personnel, who may have more time to analyze task demands or observe students in action, may want to engage in more systematic assessment for various audiences. We turn our attention to these strategies in the next chapters.

CHAPTER 9

Structured Inventories and Assessments

INTRODUCTION

Although the informal classroom-based assessments described in the previous chapter provide extensive diagnostic information, there are times when structured assessments are desirable or necessary. We pursue the evaluation of the learner in this chapter with a discussion of structured assessments—including informal reading inventories (IRIs), writing rubrics, informal word recognition tests, and school-based assessment "packages." In the hands of a skilled examiner, these structured assessments can yield exceptionally useful information about a student's knowledge and application of reading skills and strategies. Informal structured assessments generally capture the interactive nature of reading in ways that more formal tests cannot.

This chapter presents an overview of various structured procedures. The presentation of information about the IRI is extensive since it represents the most commonly used structured type of informal assessment. We discuss construction, administration, scoring, and interpretation of IRIs, as well as issues and problems with traditional IRIs. Also in this chapter are sections that describe innovations among some newer IRIs and how the addition of retelling, miscue analysis, and fluency ratings can expand the utility of older IRIs. Other assessment tools and strategies include tests of phonics and word recognition. Finally, tools and strategies for evaluating classroom writing are explained including the development and use of rubrics.

UNDERSTANDING STRUCTURED INVENTORIES AND ASSESSMENTS

When teachers want only to inform their own instruction, the tools and strategies described in the preceding chapter are what is likely to be most useful. However, sometimes we are concerned about individual children and want to take a closer look. At other times parents want specific information and, at still other times, we are required to share information about students at the school or district level. In these cases, the very informal "on the run" assessments that were so useful for planning and adapting daily instruction are not quite so appropriate.

The overriding issue concerns the interpretive accuracy of the information. There are many ways in which others may not interpret the results appropriately, including: (1) they may not understand how the information was collected; (2) they may be unfamiliar with the book or passage that was selected for Running Records; (3) they may use different scoring conventions to record student responses; or (4) they may use different criteria for judging performance.

Classroom-based reading and writing performance is likely to provide the most authentic picture of a student's knowledge and skill because the tasks and texts will be familiar, the procedures more or less "school-like," and the context informal. For all these reasons, informal assessment is a good idea. On the other hand, we want our information to be "trustworthy" (Valencia 1990a). When we communicate with other professionals, with parents, or with the larger community, the tasks and conditions used in collecting information must be clear and the criteria used to interpret the information commonly understood.

Teachers whose work is funded by external sources (Title 1 and Special Education) are generally required to collect and communicate information based on systematic assessment practices. Until recently, most were required to use norm-referenced tests to gather this information (see Chapter 10). Now, however, a defensible system of informal assessment is often acceptable, but the tools and strategies need to be carefully considered.

The structured assessments described in this chapter share several common characteristics. They contain the procedures and/or materials for creating consistent, systematic assessment tools that allow a student's performance to be compared across selections or to be compared to a commonly established standard or set of criteria. Thus, anyone using these tools will know that others are employing the same procedures, materials, or techniques for evaluating student performance.

Formal tests are designed to compare a student's score to that of other students (see Chapter 10). Standardized procedures are used to administer these tests to large numbers of students in order to establish the standards for comparison. Teachers or test examiners must administer formal tests in exactly the same way as they were administered in the standardization process in order for the scores to be valid. In contrast, IRIs and other structured assessments are designed to compare a student's scores against some criteria for acceptable performance (for example 99 percent word recognition and 90 precent comprehension) that have been established independently of how any particular group of students might perform on the same test.

A key feature of all these structured assessments is that the activities involved closely approximate the activities found in daily classroom reading instruction. For this reason, the results obtained are more likely to be generalizable to classroom performance than results obtained from formal tests using activities that are further removed from classroom practice. In addition, because they are informal measures, they can be used more flexibly than formal tests.

In short, these tools are designed to create assessment conditions that are as trustworthy as possible, while still retaining an informal assessment environment. We start with the informal reading inventory because it is probably the most widely known form of systematic informal reading assessment.

STRATEGIES AND TOOLS FOR STRUCTURED ASSESSMENT

Informal Reading Inventories

Overview

An informal reading inventory is an individually administered reading test composed of a series of graded word lists and graded passages that the student reads aloud to the examiner. The examiner notes oral reading errors as the student reads and asks comprehension questions when the student has finished reading each passage. Most informal reading inventories also include silent reading passages, and some provide passages that are read to the student to determine a listening comprehension level, along with comprehension questions for each. When the student has finished reading, errors are analyzed and percentage scores are calculated for word recognition performance on the graded word lists and the oral reading passages. In addition, the examiner tallies performance on the comprehension questions for the various reading passages.

Betts (1946) and Kilgallon (1942) are frequently credited with the development of the IRI, although similar techniques were suggested by others even earlier (for example, Gray 1920). As originally designed by Betts (1946), the IRI was to be constructed by the teacher, using reading materials in which the students might actually be placed and procedures for administration that were similar to those used in classroom reading instruction, such as silent reading followed by oral rereading. The intent was to evaluate students' reading performance under circumstances that were as similar to classroom reading conditions as possible.

Today there are many types of IRIs and a variety of administration procedures. Some teachers still construct their own IRIs, but many prefer to use IRIs that have been prepared by a publisher to accompany a particular basal reading series. Others use IRIs that have been prepared commercially, independent of any particular reading series (see annotated list of commercially prepared IRIs on p. 378).

The two primary purposes for administering an IRI are to place students in materials at the appropriate levels by establishing their *independent, instructional,* and *frustration* reading levels and to identify strengths and weaknesses in the areas of word recognition and comprehension by analyzing the amount and type of word recognition and comprehension errors.

Four different levels of reading can be identified by applying established criteria to a student's word recognition and comprehension performance.

1. *Independent level:* This is the level at which students read fluently and make very few word recognition or comprehension errors. The reader can handle material at this level easily without the assistance of the teacher. Free or recreational reading materials should be at this level, as well as reading assignments such as homework, tests, and seatwork that the student is expected to complete independently.

2. *Instructional level:* At this level, the reader makes some errors; however, word recognition errors are not excessive and comprehension is adequate. This is the level at which the student will benefit most from direct instruction. For each child, the materials used for direct instruction—such as basal readers, subject area textbooks, and skill activities—should be at this level.

3. *Frustration level:* This is the level at which reading is often slow and halting, and the reader makes an excessive number of errors. Materials at this level are too difficult for the reader, even with assistance. Students should not be placed in materials at this level because effective learning is unlikely to occur.

4. *Listening comprehension level:* This is the level at which the student can satisfactorily comprehend material that has been read aloud. This level provides a rough estimate of the student's receptive language comprehension and is often used as a measure of the student's potential reading level.

Many different procedures have developed since the IRI was first introduced. In order to avoid giving the mistaken impression that there is only one way to construct and/or use an IRI, we present a description of various traditional IRI procedures in the next section.

Components of an IRI

The basic components of an informal reading inventory are graded word lists, graded reading passages, comprehension questions, and a summary/analysis sheet. To help illustrate some of these components, examples of an examiner's copy of graded word lists, a graded passage, and a summary sheet are presented in Figure 9.1a–c.

FIGURE 9.1(a)
Sample IRI Components

Form B • Graded Word Lists • Performance Booklet

List B-B (Pre-Primer)	Timed	Untimed	List B (Primer)	Timed	Untimed
1. we	_____	_____	1. they	_____	_____
2. and	_____	_____	2. she	_____	_____
3. house	_____	_____	3. will	_____	_____
4. the	_____	_____	4. of	_____	_____
5. duck	_____	_____	5. blue	_____	_____
6. one	_____	_____	6. it	_____	_____
7. street	_____	_____	7. are	_____	_____
8. happy	_____	_____	8. his	_____	_____
9. lost	_____	_____	9. now	_____	_____
10. know	_____	_____	10. dress	_____	_____
11. do	_____	_____	11. if	_____	_____
12. at	_____	_____	12. from	_____	_____
13. very	_____	_____	13. morning	_____	_____
14. party	_____	_____	14. father	_____	_____
15. out	_____	_____	15. ask	_____	_____
16. find	_____	_____	16. back	_____	_____
17. goat	_____	_____	17. green	_____	_____
18. wish	_____	_____	18. time	_____	_____
19. first	_____	_____	19. who	_____	_____
20. sing	_____	_____	20. cookie	_____	_____
Number Correct _____	_____		Number Correct _____	_____	
Total Score	_____		Total Score	_____	

Scoring Guide for Graded Word Lists

Independent	Instructional	Frustration
20 19	18 17 16 15 14	13 or less

FIGURE 9.1(b)

Sample IRI Components, continued

BASIC READING INVENTORY PERFORMANCE BOOKLET

Jerry L. Johns
Northern Illinois University

Student _____ Grade _____ Sex ☐ M ☐ F Date of Test _____

School _____ Examiner _____ Date of Birth _____

SUMMARY OF STUDENT'S PERFORMANCE

Grade	Word Recognition		Comprehension		Listening	Estimate of Levels
	Isolation (Word Lists)	Context (Passages)	Oral Reading Form ___	Silent Reading Form ___	Form ___	
	Total Score / Level	Percent Correct / Level	Percent Correct / Level	Percent Correct / Level	Percent Correct	
PP						
P						
1						Independent _____
2						
3						Instructional _____
4						
5						Frustration _____
6						Listening _____
7						
8						

SCORING GUIDE FOR READING LEVELS

Percent Of Word Recognition in Context	100 99	98 97 96	95	94 93 92 91	90 or less
	Independent Level	Independent or Instructional	Instructional Level	Instructional or Frustration	Frustration Level
Percent of Comprehension	100 95 90	85 80	75	70 65 60 55	50 or less

INFORMAL MISCUE ANALYSIS SUMMARY

Type of Miscues	Frequency of Occurrence			General Impact of Miscues on Meaning		
	Seldom	Sometimes	Frequently	No Change	Little Change	Much Change
Substitutions						
Insertions						
Omissions						
Reversals						

Consistent Strengths (+) and Weaknesses (−)   Check (✓) Consistent Difficulties

Comprehension
- ☐ main idea
- ☐ fact
- ☐ inference
- ☐ evaluation
- ☐ vocabulary
- ☐ lower level
- ☐ higher level

Word Recognition
- ☐ use of context
- ☐ single consonants
- ☐ consonant clusters
- ☐ short vowels
- ☐ long vowels
- ☐ syllabication
- ☐ flexible word attack

Oral Reading
- ☐ fluency
- ☐ word by word
- ☐ ignores punctuation
- ☐ lacks expression
- ☐ loses place
- ☐ repeats from habit
- ☐ requests assistance

Observations

FIGURE 9.1(c)

Sample IRI Components, continued

B-B (Pre-Primer)

F   1. ___ What happened to Pete?   "I cannot find my ball," said Pete.
(he lost his ball)   "It is a big ball. My ball is red."

F   2. ___ What did the ball Jill found look like?   "Here is a ball," Jill said. "The ball
(blue and small)   is blue. It is small. It is not red."

E   3. ___ How do you think Pete lost his ball?
(any logical response)

I   4. ___ How did Pete know that the ball   "I see a ball," said Pete. It is red.
Jill found wasn't his?   It is big. It is my ball."
(any logical response; it was small
and blue; it wasn't red)

                                        Percent of Word Recognition ____

V   5. ___ What does "find" mean?
(to locate; to look for something   ____ WPM
and then see it)   )3000

Percent of Comprehension ____

Scoring Guide Pre-Primer

Percent of Word Recognition in Context

100 99	98 97 96	95	94 93 92 91	90 or less
Independent Level	Independent or Instructional	Instructional Level	Instructional or Frustration	Frustration Level
100 95 90	85 80	75	70 65 60 55	50 or less

Percent of Comprehension

Reprinted from "Basic Reading Inventory Performance Booklet" from *Basic Reading Inventory: Pre-Primer–Grade Eight, Third Edition,* by Jerry L. Johns. Copyright © 1985 by Kendall/Hunt Publishing Company. Used with permission.

Graded word lists. Most IRIs begin with lists of words that have been graded to correspond with the grade levels in basal reading series. Although not originally included in the IRI, graded word lists have become a standard part of today's IRIs. Graded word lists are used to determine accuracy of word recognition in isolation and to assist the examiner in determining the level at which the student should begin reading the graded passages.

Each graded word list typically contains between ten and twenty words and includes different types of words ranging from a large number of function words, such as *the* or *want* at the lower grade levels, to multisyllabic content words, that may or may not be easily decoded, at the upper grade levels. Series-linked IRIs generally, but not always, choose selections from the anthologies at each level. It is often unclear how the word lists have been generated for commercially prepared IRIs (Jongsma and Jongsma 1981). Some are created from previously published lists of graded words or word frequency lists such as *Dolch* (Dolch 1942) or *New Instant Word List* (Fry 1980). However the lists are created, there is generally an effort to represent high-frequency features in the language, sampling words that students who read a great deal would not find difficult to recognize.

Graded reading passages.   The graded word lists are followed by a series of graded reading passages. Most IRIs have two or three passages at each grade level, so comparisons can be made among oral, silent, and listening comprehension. Alternatively, the various forms for each level may be used as pre- and post-tests. The graded reading passages are used for evaluating comprehension and for examining oral reading accuracy in context.

Graded reading passages range in length from 25 to 350 words. Typically, the length of the passages increases gradually, from the lowest to the highest grade levels, along the following lines: preprimer and primer, 25–60 words; Grade 1, 75–100 words; Grades 2 and 3, 75–150 words; Grades 4, 5, and 6, 150–200 words; Grades 7 through 10, 200–350 words. The authors of commercially prepared IRIs often construct their own passages or select excerpts from children's materials found in the library. When teachers or publishers construct IRIs to accompany a particular series, the passages are selected excerpts from the readers in the series.

Passage difficulty is determined by the level of the material from which it is taken and/or through the use of readability formulas (see Chapter 5 for detailed explanation). A review of commercially prepared IRIs indicated that two of the eleven inventories reviewed included illustrations along with their passages (Jongsma and Jongsma 1981), though this has probably changed somewhat with the addition of new IRIs. It is also accepted practice to vary the size of the print type in a manner that is consistent with the grade level of the passage.

Comprehension questions.   The graded passages are accompanied by a series of open-ended comprehension questions. Most commercially prepared IRIs have between five and ten questions per passage. Most IRIs categorize the comprehension questions according to types such as main idea, detail, literal, inferential, vocabulary, sequence, and cause-effect. Guidelines for constructing IRIs recommend that different types of questions be used (for example, Johnson and Kress 1965; Silvaroli, Kear, and McKenna 1982).

Administering an IRI

IRIs are administered individually and require 30–90 minutes for administration. They can be administered in more than one session. IRIs typically are administered in a quiet place, with the examiner and the student sitting at different sides of a table. It is usually a good idea to audiotape the administration for later reference. As with all aspects of the IRI, there is no one right way to administer it. Decisions about how to administer the IRI must be based on the purpose for administration and the types of information desired.

Graded word lists. The word lists are introduced by saying something like, "I have some words I would like you to read for me today. Please read carefully, and if you come to a word you don't know, just try your best." The word lists are then presented, either as a whole or one word at a time, through a window cut in a manila folder or on individual index cards. Administration of the word lists begins with the list that is at least two years below the student's grade placement. If the student misses any words in the first list that is administered, the examiner drops to lower lists until the student achieves 100 percent accuracy. As the student reads, the examiner tallies all words read correctly and records exactly what the student says when a word is misread. The student is encouraged to read words that are unfamiliar, and the administration of the word lists continues until the student makes some specified number of errors (for example, five errors in a list, or three consecutive errors).

Some published IRIs only have a timed administration of the word lists, in which the student is given anywhere from two to ten seconds to respond. Some only have untimed presentations, where the student is given unlimited time to respond. Still others have some combination of the two; for example, a timed administration followed by an untimed administration of the words that were missed the first time. The combined administration provides the greatest amount of information.

Oral reading passages. Administration of the oral reading passages begins with the passage that is at the same level as the word list on which the student achieved some specified criterion (for example, 100 percent). If the student does poorly on the first passage, the examiner drops down one level at a time until performance is satisfactory. The examiner begins the administration by saying something like, "Now I have some passages I would like you to read out loud to me. Please read carefully, because I will ask you some questions when you are finished. If you come to a word you don't know, just try your best." Then the examiner reads the motivation statement, if there is one, and asks the student to begin reading. The examiner may also wish to begin timing the student's reading in order to calculate the oral reading rate.

As the student reads, the examiner uses a code to mark every deviation from the printed text on the teacher's response sheet. If the student stops reading at a difficult word, the examiner waits some specified amount of time (for example, five seconds) and then either pronounces the word or directs the student to skip it and continue. The administration of the oral reading passages is stopped when the student is visibly frustrated or is making excessive word recognition and comprehension errors. Since it is not always possible to score the test immediately, the decision to suspend testing is frequently based on the examiner's judgment.

The oral reading errors that are commonly coded include *omissions, insertions, substitutions, repetitions, hesitations, ignoring punctuation, prompts, reversals,* and *self-corrections.* The sample coding system presented in Figure 9.2 is just one of

FIGURE 9.2

Oral Reading Errors

Error	Sample Notation	Remarks
SUBSTITUTIONS— mispronunciations or word replacements	*cars* *dojes* I saw ~~cats~~ and ~~dogs~~.	*May suggest lack of word recognition skills, carelessness, or language differences/dialect usage. Students with consistent mispronunciations usually require help in any or all word analysis skills, but especially phonics and structural analysis.*
INSERTIONS—letters, syllables or words added to the text	I saw the cats and dogs.	*These errors may signal carelessness or an oral language ability that surpasses reading ability. Comprehension is assumed when insertions are contextually appropriate.*
OMISSIONS—words, letters, or syllables deleted from the text	I saw cat and dogs.	*Generally not serious errors if meaning is kept intact. Students may skip word parts of longer words indicating a need for instruction in word analysis. Some omissions, particularly those of word endings, may be due to language differences or difficulties.*
REVERSALS—reversed order of words	I saw dogs and cats.	*May be result of many factors. In beginning readers, due to inexperience with important perceptual distinctions. Reversals may accompany more serious problems in severely disabled readers.*
PROMPTS—words pronounced by the examiner	*p* I saw cats and dogs.	*Usually due to lack of sight vocabulary and/or word analysis skills. May also be due to lack of self-confidence in ability to identify strange words.*
PUNCTUATION— obvious omission of punctuation	I saw cats and dogs	*May simply indicate need to work on the meaning of various punctuation marks. In some cases may be symptomatic of more serious word recognition or comprehension problems.*
HESITATIONS— obvious pause	*H* I saw cats and dogs.	*A student with many hesitations usually lacks either sight vocabulary or word analysis skills, has formed a habit of word-by-word reading, or is experiencing difficulty of some kind.*
REPETITIONS—part of word, a word, or words repeated	I saw I saw cats and dogs.	*May indicate that student is trying to figure out word or phrase. Sometimes repetitions are due to nervousness. Some believe that repetitions are a sign of normal, effective processing. Others believe they indicate some type of reading difficulty.*
SELF-CORRECTIONS— spontaneous corrections by the reader	*cars* I saw cats and dogs.	*Generally considered to be the sign of effective processing and attention to meaning. Students who must self-correct too frequently may not have acquired automatic word recognition skills and may be overrelying on context as a decoding strategy.*

Adapted from Ekwall, E., & Shanker, J. L. (1983). *Diagnosis and remediation of the disabled reader* (2nd ed.), Boston: Allyn & Bacon.

many that can be used. Which particular system is used is not as important as becoming familiar enough with one system so that it can be used quickly and consistently. It is important to code all deviations from the text, so the student's performance can be reconstructed at a later time. Audiotaping the session helps with this, of course.

Silent reading and listening passages. In addition to oral reading passages, the examiner can administer silent and/or listening comprehension passages and may also want to time the silent reading to determine the student's silent reading rate. There are a number of variations in the order of administration for oral, silent, and listening passages. Several of these variations are listed below:

1. Oral reading only.
2. An oral reading passage followed by a silent reading, and possibly a listening comprehension passage, all at the same grade level before going on to higher levels.
3. Oral reading passages until frustration level is achieved, followed by silent reading passages starting at that level or one level below until frustration level is achieved, which is then followed by listening comprehension passages.
4. Silent reading followed by oral rereading of all or parts of the same passage.

A review of commercially prepared IRIs indicates that six of the eleven inventories examined either disregard silent reading or make it optional, probably to shorten administration time (Jongsma and Jongsma 1981).

Comprehension questions. After the student finishes reading, the passage is removed and the examiner says something like, "Now I am going to ask you some questions about the passage you just read." The examiner reads each question and provides ample time for the student to make a response. If the student does not respond, or appears to have misunderstood a question, the question may be asked again or rephrased. Additional information may be elicited by neutral questions, such as "Can you tell me more?" However, leading questions that provide information related to the answer should be avoided.

Scoring an IRI

Preliminary scoring occurs while the IRI is being taken, because scores are needed to make decisions about subsequent steps in administration. The final scoring is completed when the student has finished the IRI, and the scores are entered on a summary sheet. Most published IRIs provide a type of summary sheet for recording student performance on word lists, oral reading, and oral, silent, and listening comprehension at each grade level. These scores are used to determine a student's independent, instructional, and frustration reading levels, which are recorded on the summary sheet. Many summary sheets also provide for recording the numbers and types of oral reading and comprehension errors made by the student.

Graded word lists.   The examiner determines the percentage correct on each word list and enters the number and the placement level on the examiner's response sheets. Unfortunately, this is not quite as easy as it may at first appear. As soon as we attempt to score an IRI, we are confronted with the question, What is an error? or, conversely, What is an acceptable response? Once again, there is no one correct way; it depends on the situation.

The biggest decisions that have to be made in scoring the word lists are how to handle self-corrections and the time factor. In other words, does a student know a word if it takes ten seconds to identify it, or if it is misread and then self-corrected? Some commercially prepared IRIs provide no guidelines for time limits or how to score self-corrections. Those that do recommend time limits for acceptable responses suggest time limits ranging from ten to fifteen seconds. Some IRIs suggest that all deviations, self-corrected or not, count as errors, while others do not count self-corrections as errors. Clearly, when there are only ten to twenty words in a list, decisions about what constitutes an error are not trivial. Each error translates into a 5 to 10 percent difference in the scores, which can have a significant impact on decisions about placement levels and the entry level into the reading passages.

Oral reading passages.   The examiner counts the oral reading errors and determines the percentage of word recognition accuracy. The percentage of word recognition accuracy can either be determined from a scoring guide or calculated by hand using the following procedure:

1. Subtract the number of errors from the total number of words in the passage to obtain the total number of words correct.
2. Divide the total number of words correct by the total number of words in the passage.
3. Multiply the result by 100 to convert to a percentage.

The percentage of word recognition accuracy and the placement level, if provided by a scoring guide, are entered on the summary sheet. In addition, the number of errors of each type is calculated and recorded on the summary sheet.

The question of what constitutes an error becomes even more complex in scoring the oral reading passages. Guidelines for scoring oral reading range from counting every deviation from the text as an error, to the other extreme, counting only those deviations that alter the meaning of the text. Most scoring guidelines lie somewhere between these two extremes.

A review of the scoring guidelines of eleven commercially prepared IRIs indicates that the majority consider omissions, insertions, substitutions, reversals, prompts, and repetitions to be scorable errors. Self-corrections, hesitations, and punctuation are to be noted but not counted as errors (Jongsma and Jongsma 1981).

Comprehension questions.   The examiner determines if the answers to each comprehension question are correct, incorrect, or partially correct, based on the suggested answers and on an awareness of acceptable alternatives. The percentage comprehension score is calculated using a scoring guide, or by dividing the number of questions that were answered correctly by the total number of questions and then multiplying by 100. The percentage comprehension score and the placement level, when provided by a scoring guide, are then recorded on the summary sheet. In addition, the number of each type of questions missed is calculated and entered on the summary sheet. Because there are often as few as five comprehension questions per passage, scoring decisions have a major impact on the final results of the IRI.

Rate.   The examiner determines the number of words read per minute for silent and/or oral reading using the following procedure:

1. Convert the amount of time it took to read the passage to seconds.
2. Divide the number of seconds by the number of words in the passage.
3. Multiply the resulting number by sixty to reconvert it into words per minute.

When the rate in words per minute has been calculated, it is entered on the examiner's response sheets and the summary sheet, when appropriate.

Interpreting an IRI

The information on the summary sheet regarding the percentage of word recognition accuracy and comprehension at each level is evaluated to determine the student's independent, instructional, and frustration reading levels. In addition, the information on the summary sheet regarding different types of oral reading and comprehension errors is used to determine specific strengths and weaknesses.

Placement/"achievement" levels.   As we have noted, IRIs have been used traditionally to place students in commercial materials (basals) that have corresponding grade level notations. Increasingly, these so-called "placement levels" are being used by teachers who use a literature-based approach. These teachers do not necessarily place students in reading materials according to these results, but they do use the levels as indications of student *achievement.* This is especially true in schools that are no longer using norm-referenced achievement tests and that have also abandoned basal reading programs. Lacking easily available numeric indicators of students' reading levels, they are using IRIs to communicate with parents and with each other.

Some IRIs provide placement-level criteria for the graded word lists, while others do not. There is no general agreement among those that do provide placement levels as to what the criteria should be. A review conducted by the authors of a limited sample of commercially prepared IRIs provided the following range of placement criteria for lists of 10–20 words: independent level, 90–100 percent (0–2 errors); instructional level, 80–90 percent (2–4 errors); and frustration level, 80 percent and below (2–4 + errors).

Determining the criteria for a student's general independent, instructional, and frustration levels on the reading passages is a complex issue. The original criteria, established by Betts (1946) and still the most widely accepted today, are presented in Figure 9.3.

Reviews of commercially prepared IRIs indicate that the majority continue to use Betts's criteria. There are several problems associated with the use of these criteria. First, the procedures for administering IRIs have changed somewhat from those under which Betts's criteria were first developed. Most guidelines for administering either published or teacher-constructed IRIs call for oral reading at sight, rather than Betts's procedure of silent reading followed by oral rereading. Second, the criteria leave a scoring gap between the frustration and instructional levels that can make interpretation fairly difficult (for example, what happens to the student who scores 65 percent in comprehension?). Third, they were developed on the basis of a study with fourth-grade students, and subsequent research suggests the need for criteria that account for the differential effects of age, grade, and/or the difficulty of the materials (Cooper 1952; Powell and Dunkeld 1971).

As a result of the problems with Betts's criteria, some believe that different placement criteria should be used. Powell (1980) has suggested the criteria presented in Figure 9.4 to account for both the grade level of the materials and two methods of administration—oral reading at sight and silent reading followed by oral rereading. Clearly there is a considerable disparity between the Betts and Powell criteria, and the majority of commercially prepared IRIs have converged in the following range, which may be used as a guide for establishing reasonable placement criteria (Figure 9.5).

The traditional interpretation of oral reading errors is based on a preponderance of errors of a particular type (see Figure 9.2), which are often noted separately on the summary form. The interpretation of a student's comprehension skills is based on an analysis of errors on different types of comprehension questions. Students with a preponderance of errors on a particular type of comprehension question are believed to have difficulty with certain types of comprehension. Depending on the types of comprehension questions included on the IRI, these problems might include understanding literal ideas or factual information, drawing inferences, identifying main idea, etc.

Students' rate of reading is reported in terms of the number of words read per minute during oral and/or silent reading. A slow reading rate may indicate a reading problem, but an acceptable rate does not guarantee that the material is being comprehended at a satisfactory level. Desired silent reading rates are

FIGURE 9.3
*Betts'
Placement
Criteria*

	Word Recognition		Comprehension
Independent	99% +	and	90% +
Instructional	95% +	and	75% +
Frustration	90% or less	or	50% or less
Listening Comprehension			75% +

FIGURE 9.4
Powell's Placement Criteria

Reading Levels	Reading at Sight		Oral Rereading	
	Word		Word	
by Grade	*Recognition*	*Comprehension*	*Recognition*	*Comprehension*
Independent				
1–2	94% +	80% +	94% +	80% +
3–5	96% +	85% +	96% +	85% +
6+	97% +	90% +	97% +	90% +
Instructional				
1–2	88–94%	55–80%	92–94%	70–80%
3–5	92–96%	60–86%	95–96%	75–85%
6+	94–97%	65–90%	97–97%	80–90%
Frustration				
1–2	86% or less	55% or less	91% or less	70% or less
3–5	92% or less	60% or less	91% or less	75% or less
6+	94% or less	65% or less	96% or less	80% or less

FIGURE 9.5
Criteria Used By Published IRIs

	Word Recognition	Comprehension
Independent	96–99%	75–90%
Instructional	92–95%	60–75%
Frustration	90–92% or less	60–75% or less

similar to oral reading rates at first- and second-grade instructional levels, but begin to increase sharply at the third-grade instructional level when word identification becomes more automatic. It is also important to remember that reading rates will vary according to the conditions of the reading situation, and that norms or standards are good only for the conditions under which they were obtained. Guidelines provided by Powell (n.d.) for evaluating the oral and silent reading rates obtained on IRIs for students at different instructional levels are presented in Figure 9.6. When using these guidelines, it is important to remember that students' instructional levels may be different than their grade levels.

Issues and Problems: Evaluating and Selecting IRIs

Whether teachers are constructing their own or using available commercial versions, serious attention must be given to the issues and problems surrounding the use of IRIs. The information gleaned from them can be useful, but since the decisions made about children can be quite serious, it is important to understand fully how to evaluate or construct IRIs for ethical use.

FIGURE 9.6
*Reading Rate
in Words per
Minute*

Instructional Reading Level	Oral Reading Rate at Sight	Silent Reading
Grade 1	45–65	45–65
Grade 2	70–100	70–100
Grade 3	105–125	120–140
Grade 4	125–145	130–180
Grade 5	135–155	165–205
Grade 6	140–160	190–220

Construction.   The major area of concern regarding the construction of IRIs focuses on the representativeness of the reading selections. When a passage is selected from a basal reader for use in an IRI, it is assumed to represent the materials the student will find in that reader. This may have been an accurate assumption when IRIs were first suggested and the vocabulary and content of basal readers were more highly controlled than they are today. However, in today's basal readers, passages taken from a single level can vary from first to twelfth grade readability (Bradley and Ames 1977). A student's reading performance within an anthology may vary considerably depending on the passage selected for use in the IRI. In fact, Bradley and Ames (1976) used several passages from the same reader and found that approximately 40 percent of the students tested had scores that ranged from the independent to the frustration level. In addition, many teachers today do not use basals at all, choosing instead from a wide range of literature. Representing this literature can pose serious challenges.

A second problem related to the reading selections involves the comparability of alternate passages at each grade level. Although there is a clear advantage to having several alternate passages at each grade level, it is difficult to be certain that these passages are comparable. Some authors suggest creating different passages by using different portions of the same selection. However, there is also variability in readability within selections, although perhaps not as great as within a book. When passages from the same selection are used, there is also the problem of accumulated prior knowledge affecting performance from one passage to the next.

Most IRIs do not account for the fact that there are *many* text factors that are likely to influence a student's performance. For example, it has been found that the effects of interest are sufficiently strong to cause comprehension scores to vary between the frustration and instructional levels (Estes and Vaughan 1973). Another finding is that the type and length of the passage influences the number and types of oral reading errors (see Wixson 1979). Other factors, discussed in Chapters 5 and 6, include text organization and topic familiarity.

A third major area of concern in the construction of IRIs focuses on the nature of the comprehension questions. Peterson, Greenlaw, and Tierney (1978) constructed three sets of questions for a single IRI according to a popular set of guidelines that called for one vocabulary, two literal, and two inferential questions. When these three sets of questions were used in testing, approximately 65 percent of students examined were assigned two different instructional levels, and 10 percent were assigned three instructional levels. This suggests that different questions for the same passages can produce different results. Finally, we must also be concerned with the degree to which comprehension questions are *passage dependent*. Questions that are passage dependent have answers that depend on information provided in the passage, rather than on the reader's prior knowledge about the topic. To illustrate this problem, read and answer the following questions taken from Johns (1988):

1. Skyscrapers are different from other buildings because they are: a. bigger; b. higher; c. cleaner; d. prettier.
2. A person who "operates with a frying pan" uses the pan for: a. cutting fish; b. cooking fish; c. hitting fish; d. cleaning fish.

How did you do? Johns found that 134 of 160 fourth- and fifth-grade students answered the first item correctly, and 131 answered the second one right *without* reading the passages. These questions were part of a study in which students scored significantly better than chance when they answered the reading comprehension questions from a test *before* they read the passages.

Studies of IRI-type tests suggest that results may be influenced by questions that are passage independent. For example, an analysis of the comprehension questions on four IRI-type tests indicated that 23 to 31 percent of the questions were passage independent (Allington, Chodos, Domaracki, and Truex 1977). In addition, the analysis demonstrated that there was a large degree of variability in the number of passage independent items from one passage to the next within each test. In other words, the results of these studies suggest that in some cases the variability in scores observed between passages may be attributable to differences in the comprehension questions, not to real differences in ability.

Administration. The major issue in the administration of an IRI is the effect that different procedures might have on students' scores. For example, Brecht (1977) reports a study in which children were administered IRIs both with oral reading at sight and with silent reading followed by oral rereading. Only 20 percent of the students obtained the same instructional level under both types of administration. When the rereading format was used, 70 percent scored at least one grade level higher, and 10 percent scored at least one grade level lower.

Another factor in administration that may influence students' scores is the directions provided to both students and teachers. According to Jongsma and Jongsma (1981), some inventories clearly emphasize the importance of reading accurately and not making mistakes. Although this may seem trivial, they point to evidence that directions can influence the number and type of oral reading errors, the degree of comprehension, and the rate of reading. One inventory actually directs the students to decrease their speed for subject area material and to reread sections or words on which they made "careless mistakes." Two inventories direct the teacher to start all students, regardless of age or reading ability, at the lowest levels on both the word lists and passages. This practice could result in boredom and fatigue for both the student and the teacher.

A final issue to be considered in the administration of an IRI is the effect of different procedures for administering oral, silent, and listening passages. If passages are only administered orally, is it safe to assume that performance can be generalized to silent reading? Research has yet to provide a definitive answer to this question. However, an interactive view of reading suggests that there will be differences in performance under different reading conditions. This means that performance may vary when students are asked to read a passage orally, as opposed to silent reading followed by oral rereading. Therefore, caution is urged in generalizing from one reading situation to another. It may also be necessary to administer an IRI under various conditions that are representative of those the student encounters frequently in the classroom to obtain a complete understanding of a student's reading abilities (see Chapter 11).

Scoring. A major area of concern regarding the scoring of an IRI is that decisions about what gets counted as an error are going to make a difference in the scores used for determining placement levels. Betts (1946) was not entirely clear about what constituted an error; however, an examination of the summary sheets he used suggests that all deviations from the text were counted as errors. Much of the controversy about scoring oral reading errors centers around so-called good errors; that is, errors that do not disrupt the meaning of the text and appear to arise from the reader's meaningful processing of the text, rather than some faulty skill or strategy.

Repetition errors have received the most attention. Some argue that repetitions should not be counted as errors, because they represent the reader's attempt to preserve the meaning of the text (K. Goodman, 1973). Others argue that repetitions should be counted as errors, because failure to do so will result in readers becoming physiologically frustrated before they reach the percentage of errors normally recognized as the student's frustration level. Ekwall and Shanker (1983) sum up the situation as follows: "Although it may not seem 'fair' to a student to count repetitions because the student ends up with more errors, it is in reality less fair not to count these errors. If the student appears to be a better reader than is actually the case, the student will be given reading material that is too difficult" (374).

For our part, it is difficult to make a single rule that accommodates all situations satisfactorily. In general, we do not consider repetitions, especially those that are accompanied by self-corrections, to be scorable errors. However, there are instances when repetitions are so disruptive that they are clearly interfering with effective reading. In these cases, repetitions should be taken into account in scoring.

A second area of concern focuses on the practice of aggregating different types of oral reading errors across passages and looking for patterns. Research has shown that the type of errors that readers make is directly related to the difficulty of the material. In fact, Kibby (1979) found that including frustration-level errors in an analysis can give a distorted view of the reader's skills and strategies. Our position on this is that oral reading errors should not be aggregated across passages. If some aggregation is necessary, then errors should only be aggregated for passages on which the student's performance was relatively comparable.

A related problem is that many commercially prepared IRIs analyze oral reading errors in isolation (Jongsma and Jongsma 1981). The focus of this type of analysis is on letter-sound differences, without any attention to context, the effects of previous errors, and/or the reader's background knowledge. We believe that oral reading errors should be analyzed both in terms of letter-sound differences and in relation to the contexts in which they occurred (see Miscue Analysis below).

Finally, traditional IRI scoring procedures do not provide any mechanism for evaluating the interaction between oral reading and comprehension errors. Oral reading accuracy affects various types of comprehension differently. Nicholsen, Pearson, and Dykstra (1979) report the results of research that revealed the following:

1. Accurate word recognition is important for comprehension of specific information, but relatively unimportant for global interpretation.
2. Errors that make sense in a sentence (for example, *giant* for *gorilla)* are more likely to disrupt comprehension of specific information than errors that clearly do not make sense (for example, *wall* for *gorilla),* because students are more likely to maintain a faulty interpretation that makes sense than one that is unreasonable.
3. Comprehension questions that require students to relate the ideas in two sentences are affected more by the word recognition error rate than questions that require responses based primarily on prior knowledge.

Thus, it is important that oral reading and comprehension errors be examined in tandem to determine the interaction between word recognition and comprehension abilities for a particular reader.

Placement and achievement.   The biggest problem confronting those who use IRIs for placement and related purposes is that there is no evidence that reading levels established through IRI testing actually correspond to classroom performance. The validity of IRI placement levels hinges entirely on readability estimates of the IRI passages. The results of an IRI must be interpreted cautiously when placing a student in appropriate instructional materials, given the variability among commercially prepared IRIs (Jongsma and Jongsma 1981). Of course, even more caution should be exercised if the uses extend to communicating outside the classroom. Most IRIs, administered traditionally, simply are not constructed well enough to be used as indicators of overall student achievement in reading. In addition, the issues described below raise serious concerns about the use of IRIs (alone) to communicate about achievement.

Even if IRI levels are indeed indicative of classroom performance, the next problem is to decide on the criteria for placement (achievement). The decision about which placement criteria to use seems not so much a question of which are best, but rather which are most appropriate, given the administration procedures, criteria for scoring, and purposes for administering the IRI. Decisions about the appropriateness of placement criteria should not be made independent of decisions about administration and scoring.

For example, a decision to administer an IRI using oral reading at sight, to count all deviations from the text as errors, and to use the Betts criteria for placement would be the strictest test and is the most commonly used set of procedures in commercially prepared IRIs. A decision to administer an IRI with silent reading preceding oral reading, to count only those errors that alter meaning, and to use the Powell criteria would provide very different results, and a much less strict test of reading proficiency. Although the majority of published IRIs use the Betts criteria, there is still enough variability to make this an important concern. Variability in placement criteria *can* result in different placement levels. This is one reason why we are much less enthusiastic about using IRIs for placement, as opposed to the evaluative purposes discussed in the next section of the chapter.

A second area of concern is how well traditional error analysis reveals students' strengths and weaknesses in word recognition and comprehension. The major problem with these types of analyses is that they treat each error type as a separate entity, as though they occurred independently of each other. Research has demonstrated again and again that this is not the case; rather, error types are all interrelated and cannot be separated in this manner.

There are similar problems with using question types as a means of finding a student's relative strengths among an array of subskills (McKenna 1983; Schell and Hanna 1981), since we lack objective standards for classifying questions by subskill. In addition, IRIs have such a small number of questions per subskill that it is difficult to reliably classify a reader's comphension problems using these question types. Perhaps the most damaging of all is evidence which suggests that all questions are measuring the same skill (Drahozal and Hanna 1978). Therefore, traditional analyses of oral reading and/or comprehension errors should not be relied on to produce a complete picture of a student's strengths and weaknesses in these areas.

Guidelines for traditional usage of IRIs.   The significant concerns that have been raised about the construction, administration, scoring, and interpretation of IRIs indicate that caution needs to be exercised in developing or selecting IRIs for use in placing students in appropriate grade-level materials. The following guidelines, based on the information in this chapter and the recommendations of Jongsma and Jongsma (1981), McKenna (1983), and Pikulski and Shanahan (1982), are provided to assist those who choose and/or need to use IRIs for placement purposes. However, "keep in mind that when using an IRI, as with any test, you're just sampling behavior. On another set of passages, given on another day, you might get different results" (Jongsma and Jongsma 1981, 704).

1. Look for selections that correspond to regularly used instructional materials with regard to content, difficulty, style, and length. Be alert to differences in the interest level of passages for different groups of students.
2. Stay alert to readability problems. Don't assume that texts are representative of classroom materials, or that texts on alternate forms are comparable.
3. Ensure the passage dependency of questions by "field testing" them. Do not assume that questions on published instruments are passage dependent, and do not hesitate to replace some of them with your own.
4. In writing questions, limit the number of types. In using commercial tests, be wary of summary sheets that break down student responses into a large number of comprehension subskills.
5. Determine procedures for administering and scoring and placement criteria within the context of the purpose(s) for using the IRI.
6. Consider carefully how the oral, silent, and listening passages will be presented.
7. Be sure that instructions for administering, scoring, and interpreting are clear and complete. Consider carefully what student directions communicate to the students.
8. Carefully consider what constitutes an error on the word lists and oral reading passages.
9. Consider which factors should be weighed most heavily in establishing placement levels, that is, word recognition, comprehension, or rate.
10. Do not aggregate oral reading and comprehension errors across passages. Differentiate errors that occur at students' independent, instructional, and frustration levels.

In summary, we do not believe that the primary strength of IRIs and IRI-like measures lies in their use as placement procedures, and certainly not for use as every-pupil achievement measures. Furthermore, we object most strenuously to the use of a single (usually commercially prepared) IRI as the sole criterion for placement/achievement. Having said this, we also believe that the informal procedures embedded in IRIs, coupled with the addition of more contemporary strategies like miscue analysis and retelling, can provide valuable information. The following section addresses the use of IRIs and IRI-like procedures for the evaluative and diagnostic purposes for which they are best suited.

Contemporary IRIs: A Look at What's New

The close critical examination of IRIs that has occurred over the past two decades has resulted in changes. Several older IRIs have completed major revisions and several new IRIs have appeared. In some cases, authors have addressed criticisms related to passage selection, scoring ambiguities, quality of comprehension items, and/or difficulties related to content. In other cases, authors have worked from an interactive, constructive perspective and have attempted to create inventories that reflect a contemporary model of reading.

Qualitative Reading Inventory

The recently revised *Qualitative Reading Inventory-II* or QRI-II (Leslie and Caldwell 1995) is a contemporary IRI that responds to many of the concerns described above. The QRI-II is an IRI "designed to provide diagnostic information about (1) conditions under which subjects can identify words and comprehend text successfully, and (2) conditions that appear to result in unsuccessful word identification, decoding and/or comprehension" (Leslie and Caldwell 1995, 1).

The QRI-II has undergone extensive pilot testing to develop the procedures used to answer the following diagnostic questions:

- Can the student identify words automatically? more words in context than in isolation?
- When reading orally, does the student correct oral reading errors that do not make sense? use meaning clues? use graphic or letter clues?
- Can a student successfully comprehend narrative but not informational material? familiar but not unfamiliar text?
- What is the quality of the student's comprehension?
- Does the student organize recall in stories according to elements of story structure?
- Does the student organize recall in informational texts according to main idea and supporting details?
- Can the student answer questions that require inferences as well as those whose answers are explicitly stated in the text?
- Does prior knowledge influence the student's performance?
- Does the student have a low knowledge base overall?

Innovations. Although a complete description of the QRI-II is not possible here, there are important differences between the QRI-II and other IRIs that should be highlighted. First, the QRI-II provides both narrative and expository texts at each level. A significant improvement in the most recent QRI involves the use of pictures at the preprimer through second-grade levels. One narrative and one exposition at each level contain supportive pictures so that the examiner can explore the impact of pictures on print-reading, but also so that teachers can assess students using more authentic materials. At each level from grade three through junior high, there are three narrative and three expository passages. Both narrative and expository selections are intact texts, not excerpts, and are highly representative of the structure and topics of selections found in basal readers and subject area texts.

Next, the passages were developed/selected to provide intentional variation in familiarity, with some topics likely to be familiar to most students at that grade level and others likely to be unfamiliar. The QRI-II provides two ways to assess a student's familiarity with passage content. Each reading selection includes a conceptual questions task and a prediction activity that may be used to determine a student's familiarity with the topic of the selection. These tasks allow the examiner to identify each passage as either familiar or unfamiliar to each individual student. The use of passages that vary in familiarity enables the examiner to arrive at a more complete description of a student's reading ability.

In addition to evaluating prior knowledge, the QRI-II assesses comprehension using both questions and retellings. Each selection has an accompanying text map for recording and evaluating the student's unaided recall. The comprehension questions are of two kinds: explicit and implicit. Answers to explicit questions are directly stated in the text, and answers to implicit questions require the reader to make inferences from textual clues.

Another innovative feature of the QRI-II is that the word lists contain words taken from the reading selections. As a result, the examiner can assess students' use of context by comparing their word recognition during passage reading to their performance on the word lists. Finally, like some other contemporary IRIs, the QRI-II includes materials that support alternative analyses of oral reading errors (see Miscue Analysis below).

Scoring and Interpreting.   Although the QRI-II does provide quantitative scores, they will vary for many students as a function of the type of text read, the familiarity of the passage content, and the manner in which comprehension is assessed. The interpretation of the scores must therefore be qualified by the above factors. This is what sets the QRI-II apart from other IRIs and the reason it has been called *qualitative*. As the authors of the QRI-II suggest:

> While it was once common, it is now simplistic to talk about a single independent, instructional, or frustration level for an individual. The act of reading is highly complex and contextual. (Leslie and Caldwell 1995, 17)

The authors go on to explain that students who possess extensive background knowledge about a topic can read and comprehend at a higher level than in unfamiliar material. In addition to prior knowledge, the structure of the text can affect a student's reading performance, as can the mode of reading and the nature of the comprehension task. The variety of passages on the QRI-II allows the examiner to evaluate the effects of topic familiarity, text structure, and reading mode on the independent, instructional, and frustration levels of the student. "It is not inconceivable that a single reader may have different levels for familiar and unfamiliar text, for narrative and expository material, and for oral and silent reading modes" (Leslie and Caldwell 1995, 17).

The authors further note that the major strength of the QRI-II is that it provides a profile of an individual reader's strengths and weaknesses across different types of text and in relation to the familiarity of the reading selections. These comparisons are facilitated by the inclusion of two summary sheets—the Subject Profile Sheet and the Comparison Sheet. Kyle's performance on the QRI (between grades two and three) is summarized in Figure 9.7. The Subject Profile Sheet is designed to provide the examiner with maximum flexibility in the amount of information to be recorded for a given student. The Comparison Sheet is designed to facilitate comparison of a subject's reading ability across different contexts. Kyle's results, summarized in Figure 9.7, suggest generally very strong oral reading accuracy and comprehension on all materials through grade three.

FIGURE 9.7a
Qualitative Reading Inventory-II

Student Profile Sheet

Name _Kyle_   Birthdate _3/27/87_   Grade _2→3_

Sex _M_   Date of Test _____   Examiner _____

Word Identification

Grade	1								
Level/% Automatic									
Level/% Total									

Oral Reading

	Bear/ Rabbit	Trip to Zoo	Wool: Sheep to You	Johnny Appleseed	Amelia Earhart				
Passage Name									
Readability Level	1	3	3	4	4				
Passage Type	N	N	Exp	N	Exp				
Level/% Total Accuracy	94%	97%	95%	93%	95%				
Level/% Total Acceptability	100%	99%	98%	99%	92%	(skipped line)			
Familiar/Unfamiliar	F	F	F	F	UF				
# Explicit Correct	4/4	4/4	2/4	4/4	2/4				
# Implicit Correct	2/2	4/4	4/4	4/4	3/4				
Level/% Comprehension	IND	IND	INST	IND	INST				
Rate									
Total Passage Level									

Silent Reading

	The Friend	Where Do People Live	Cahokia						
Passage Name									
Readability Level	3	3	4						
Passage Type	N	Exp	Exp						
Familiar/Unfamiliar	F	UF	UF						
# Correct Explicit	3/4	4/4	4/4						
# Correct Implicit	3/4	4/4	4/4						
Level/% Comprehension	INST	IND	IND						
Rate									

**FIGURE
9.7b**
*Comparisons:
Describing
Specific
Reading
Behaviors*

Student *Kyle*

WORD IDENTIFICATION

How Accurate Is the Student in Identifying Words?
Words lists total score: Level —
Passage reading
    Word identification: Level —

How Automatic Is the Student in Identifying Words?
Word lists timed score: Level —
Oral passage reading: WPM
Silent passage reading: WPM

What Strategies for Word Identification in Context Are Used by the Student?
Percent: Graphically similar miscues:
    Initial position — *yes*
    Final position — *yes*
Percent: Acceptable miscues — *74%* ⎫ = 98%
Percent: Self-corrected miscues — *24%* ⎭

Is There a Difference Between a Student's Ability to Identify Words in Isolation and Words in Context?
Words lists total score: Level — NA
Passage reading
    Word identification: Level — NA

COMPREHENSION

Which Types of Text Can the Student Handle Most Successfully?
Narrative text: Level — *No Difference*
Expository text: Level
Text with pictures: Level — NA
Text without pictures: Level — NA

Which Modes of Reading Represent a Strength for the Student?
Oral reading: Level — 3-IND   4-INST
Silent reading: Level — ⎧ *Slight Advantage*
    ⎩ 3-IND   4-IND

How Does the Student Perform in Familiar and Unfamiliar Text?
Familiar text: Level — Oral-gr. 4 IND (INST)
Unfamiliar text: Level — Silent-gr. 4 IND

What Is the Extent of the Student's Reading Problem?
Highest instructional level — 4
Chronological grade placement — 3

Familiarity does not appear to influence his comprehension. Kyle does show particularly strong comprehension abilities on exposition. His comprehension is really only influenced by oral reading accuracy (a tendency to skip lines in print).

In summary, the QRI-II provides a set of procedures that is both conceptually and psychometrically sound and that represents a major step forward in the development of interactive assessment devices.

Other Special Features

Another new IRI designed to address earlier criticism is the *Stiegltiz Reading Inventory* (SIRI)(1992). It contains all of the major components described above and suggests scoring using traditional error categories (see Figure 9.2), but refers to these errors as "miscues." There are several aspects of the inventory that highlight the wide range of contemporary IRIs. First, the SIRI offers both narrative (Forms B and D) and expository (Forms A and C) selections. Second, the author suggests using *free recall* as one means of evaluating comprehension. The SIRI also suggests evaluating both *familiarity* and *interest*. The prior knowledge scale and the level of interest scale (ranging from 1–5) are self-reported measures that are administered *after* reading. The usefulness of these tools is tempered somewhat by the fact that there are few suggestions for interpreting the information that is generated, nor is there evidence of the extent to which these self-reports are reliable.

The SIRI also offers tools for *evaluating emergent literacy* using a dictated story method and includes checklists for evaluating the abilities of early readers. Similarly, the revised *Bader Reading and Language Inventory* (BRLI)(1994) also contains a "Pre-Literacy Assessment" which includes concepts about print assessment, an interview, and tests for blending and segmenting sounds in words. On the other end of the continuum, the revised *Classroom Reading Inventory* (CRI) (Silvaroli 1994) provides separate forms for elementary, junior high/middle school, and for high school/adults. At the elementary level, the CRI also offers the unusual contrast of passages in a "traditional subskills format," accompanied by questions and a separate form of passages in a "literature format," with retellings.

The newer and revised IRIs also tend to offer more options for examining word level difficulties. For example, on the SIRI the graded word lists can be evaluated in *context* or in isolation, and in the revised *Ekwall-Shanker IRI* (1993) there are provisions for evaluating both phonics and structural analysis skills in context. The BRLI also contains a test of spelling which includes solid interpretive information.

Specialized Inventories: Using Informal Study Skills Assessments

There are many commercially available informal tools that assess study skills and habits. For example, the *Shipman Assessment of Work-Study Skills* (SAWS)(Warncke and Shipman 1984) contains a number of subtests for evaluating alphabetizing, dictionary usage, ability to use reference sources, use of graphic materials, and organizing skills. The *Content Inventories: English, Social Studies, Science* (McWilliams and Rakes 1979) contains a similar battery of informal tests. These commercial materials permit teachers to gather a wide variety of information about groups of children quickly. Therefore, they are quite useful if screening data are needed. However, these tests are not generally linked to the books or curriculum used in the classroom. Thus, the amount of information generated about students' ability to actually perform in that setting is somewhat limited.

To collect information about students' application of knowledge and skill, teachers will need to construct their own inventories. A *Group Reading Inventory* (GRI) is designed for use in the classroom and is helpful for gathering information about how well students can read their textbooks (Rakes and Smith 1986). A GRI typically has two components: a book-handling component and a comprehension section. Both parts of the GRI are constructed using the actual textbook employed in the classroom. Resource room teachers, of course, will need to construct an inventory that samples several types of texts.

Part I of the GRI is constructed by generating ten to twelve questions about the various parts of the text (see Figure 9.8 for sample items). Part II of the GRI is akin to an IRI. A relatively short selection (about 500 words) is drawn from a chapter in the text. Ten or fifteen questions are generated to test comprehension. Whereas students are directed to complete Part I of the GRI while using their textbook, the questions in Part II are to be answered without referring to the book. The information gleaned from this type of assessment can be used to complete an observation checklist like the one proposed in Chapter 8.

In summary, many of the commercial IRIs have recognized the variable nature of reading performance and have made some attempts to offer tools for collecting multiple samples under some varied conditions. The extent to which these are useful depends heavily on the orientation of the instructional program and the beliefs of the teacher. In the next sections we describe various techniques designed to create a structured assessment for: (1) analyzing oral reading miscues; (2) analyzing fluency; (3) analyzing comprehension; and (4) analyzing written language.

When used in conjunction with each other, the procedures described here form an assessment system that provides a great deal of information about the reader in a fairly parsimonious fashion. Miscue analysis of a student's oral reading is used to evaluate word recognition strategies in relation to text comprehension. The Fluency Scale is then applied to the same oral reading samples to evaluate the student's oral reading fluency. Retellings are then used to evaluate various aspects of a student's oral, silent, and/or listening comprehension. Many of the new or revised IRIs have included some means of gathering retelling information and many have replaced the more traditional error analysis with a focus on miscue analysis (or added it to the traditional summary).

Retellings of IRI Selections

We discussed retellings at some length in Chapter 8. The overarching guidelines for evaluating retellings of full-length selections are no different from

FIGURE 9.8
Excerpt from a
Group Reading
Inventory

USING BOOK PARTS

Introduction: These questions are designed to help you understand the organization of your text and to enable you to use it more effectively. You may use your text in answering the questions.

1. Where would you look to locate a short story in the text if you could not recall the title or the author?
   a. Glossary
   b. Table of Contents
   c. Literary Terms and Techniques
   d. Index of Authors and Titles

2. If you came across the word "demagoguery" in your reading in the text, where would you look *first* for a definition?
   a. Table of Contents
   b. Literary Terms and Techniques
   c. Glossary
   d. The Composition and Language Program

Excerpted from "Assessing Reading Skills in the Content Areas" by Thomas A. Rakes and Lana Smith in *Reading in the Content Areas: Improving Classroom Instruction, Second Edition*, edited by Dishner et al. Copyright © 1986 by Kendall /Hunt Publishing Company. Used with permission.

those already described, so we will not reiterate them here. However, it is important to remember to start with open-ended requests to recall as much as possible.

Selecting and Analyzing Short Passages

Although the addition of retellings can enhance the diagnostic value of an IRI tremendously, some cautions are in order. As we have already suggested, a number of factors can influence the comprehensibility—and recall—of textual material. Both the quantity and quality of student recalls can be affected by the type and quality of the text. For example, when students recall stories, we would expect to see appropriate recall of sequence and story line. In contrast, recalls of informational text may not rely so heavily on sequence but should reflect an understanding of the relationships among key facts and ideas. The coherence of a text can also affect recall. Many IRI passages read more like fragments of text than intact stories or informational selections. This can hamper student recall because it may be difficult for students to organize and retrieve the content presented. Finally, remember that reader interest in or familiarity with passage content can affect understanding, memory, and recall. Familiarity appears to influence the content of recall, and both interest and familiarity seem to have an effect on the amount of inferential comprehension achieved during reading.

Before making final judgments about a student's ability to retell passages, it is important to be sure that samples of the student's best efforts have been gathered. To do this, the selections that are used should provide a good match for the student's interests, prior knowledge, and development ability. It is, of course, desirable to gather information regarding performance on materials that are routinely assigned to the reader in class (see Benchmark Books below).

The point is that we are simply sampling the reader's abilities, not measuring them in some definitive way. The selections we make should reflect our assessment purposes.

Scoring and Interpreting Short Passages

A number of systems for scoring and interpreting passage recall have been proposed in the past several years. One of the most useful and straightforward systems was designed by Clark (1982, 1993—revised, personal correspondence) specifically for use with IRIs. The steps in this "Free Call" procedure are as follows:

1. Break the passages to be used for retelling into pausal units by placing a slash wherever a good reader would normally pause during oral reading. The boundaries for these units typically fall at punctuation marks and at connectives such as *and, but,* and *because.*
2. Make a numbered list of the separate pausal units in the order in which they occur.
3. Rate the level of importance for each pausal unit by assigning a "1" to the most important units, a "2" to the next most important units, and a "3" to the least important units. To simplify this process, read through the units and assign a "1" to the major units, read through the units again and assign a "3" to the least important information, and then assign a "2" to all remaining units.
4. Record the order in which the pausal units are recalled by numbering them in the order in which they are retold. Give the student credit for responses that capture the gist of the unit.

Three types of information result from this technique: the amount recalled, the sequence of recall, and the level of recalled information. The assessment of sequence is purely subjective. A judgment should be made about whether the order of the retelling was reasonable. The amount recalled is determined by dividing the number of units recalled by the total number of units in the passage. The score is then converted to a percentage by multiplying by 100. There are no available guidelines to evaluate the amount recalled. Clark reports that generally acceptable levels will be below the 75 to 90 percent criterion level of the IRI, and numerous research studies have reported average recall levels ranging between 33 percent and 50 percent depending on the level of the students and the nature of the materials.

Finally, to get an indication of the level of information that was recalled, compute the percentage of ideas recalled for each level of importance. These are perhaps the most significant scores to result from the Free Call procedure. To compute these scores, add all the recalled units at a given importance value and divide by the total number of units *rated at that level*. The resulting average scores show if the most significant information (as judged by the examiner) has been remembered. For example, if there were a total of twenty idea units rated as level 1 importance and the reader recalled ten of these, the percentage of recall would be 50 percent for level 1. The same method is used to determine percentages for levels 2 and 3. Of this earlier revision, Clark notes that an ideal recall would be, in effect, a summary of the most important information.

> As a summary, it should contain virtually all of the important level 1 idea units and none of the level 3 units. The percentages for level 1 should therefore approach 100, while the percentages for level three should approach zero. I have also found that the recalls which I subjectively feel are best contain approximately 50% of the material from level 2. The nature and length of the text, the background of the reader, and the purpose for the reading all affect this distribution (Clark 1993, personal communication).

Clark cautions that it is important to remember that there is a normal developmental tendency; older, better readers recall more information at higher levels of importance and in better sequence, so comparisons among individuals of different ages and abilities is inappropriate.

A sample of Marvin's recall has been scored using this system and is provided in Figure 9.9. As can be seen, Marvin has recalled a reasonable amount of the text in good sequence. However, he has recalled only 33 percent of the possible level 1 material, 67 percent of the level 2 information, and 22 percent of level 3 content. In addition, the mean importance level of units recalled is good. It is also important to note that he has failed to recall any of the last portion of the text. This failure to report crucial information from throughout the text and, in particular, about the resolution of the problem presented in the early part of the passage is serious. It suggests that Marvin may not be sensitive to the overall text structure of the passage or that he has trouble separating important from unimportant information. It certainly warrants further investigation with additional samples, using this and other procedures.

Miscue Analysis

Miscue analysis describes procedures that attempt to identify how readers process print by analyzing their oral reading errors. Interest in the ideas underlying miscue analysis dates back to Huey (1908/1968) but is most often associated with Kenneth and Yetta Goodman (K. Goodman 1969; K. Goodman and Y. Goodman 1977) and their colleagues. The fundamental assumption underlying miscue analysis is that reading is a "psycholinguistic guessing game," in which readers use their knowledge of language to sample, predict, and confirm the meaning of a text. Therefore, oral reading provides a means for examining readers' use of the language systems that cue meaning—graphophonic, syntactic, and semantic.

Miscue analysis procedures provide a structure for analyzing students' oral reading behaviors, with special attention to times when oral reading deviates from the text. Oral reading "errors" have been renamed miscues because it is believed that they are not random errors, but rather are mis-"cued" by the graphophonic, syntactic, and semantic systems the reader uses to process written material. It is assumed that both expected and unexpected oral reading

FIGURE 9.9
Sample Retelling Evaluation

Importance Number	Pausal Unit	Recall Sequence
3	1. Joe sat down	2
3	2. on the sidewalk	
2	3. in front of the trading post	3
3	4. with his buckskin jacket thrown over his shoulder.	
1	5. He felt worried	1
1	6. because it was difficult to know what to do.	
1	7. "Grandfather told me	4
1	8. to sell these blue beads.	5
2	9. He said they would bring	
2	10. me good fortune and good health.	
2	11. Grandfather is a wise	12
2	12. and understanding man.	13
1	13. He is proud	
1	14. to be an American Indian.	
2	15. He remembers	6
2	16. when his grandfather	7
2	17. gave him these same beads.	8
2	18. He has often told me	9
2	19. many interesting stories	10
2	20. of how his grandfather	
3	21. rode horses and hunted buffalo	11
3	22. on the plains.	
3	23. Joe held the string of beads	
3	24. high into the air toward the sunlight.	
3	25. "These are	
2	26. perfectly beautiful beads,"	
3	27. he said out loud.	
1	28. "I can't sell them	
1	29. because I am too proud of my great past.	
1	30. Yes, I will keep the beads."	

Total number of units = 30

Number of units recalled = 13

Percentage recalled = 43%

Sequence Evaluation = Good

Percentage of important units recalled = 3/9 (33%)

Percentage of moderate units recalled = 8/12 (66%)

Percentage of unimportant units recalled = 2/9 (11%)

responses are produced by the same process. Therefore, miscues are viewed as a "window on the reading process" (K. Goodman 1973). The concept of miscues has become so popular that the term is commonly used when referring to oral reading errors, even when they are analyzed in a traditional manner.

Reading Miscue Inventory (RMI)

The miscue analysis procedures developed by the Goodmans and their colleagues were simplified for research purposes and published as the *Reading Miscue Inventory* (Y. Goodman and Burke 1972). A further revision and a set of alternative procedures for administration, depending on the purposes for which the inventory is to be used, were published more recently (Y. Goodman, Watson, and Burke 1987). The RMI is designed specifically to identify and evaluate the strategies used by a particular reader to process written material. The following is a summary of the basic procedure:

1. A reading passage providing a continuity of meaning is selected for the reader. The selection must be somewhat difficult and long enough to elicit a minimum of twenty-five miscues.
2. The selection is retyped, and each line is numbered to correspond with the appropriate page and line from the original text to be used as a code sheet for recording miscues.
3. The reader is asked to read aloud and informed that the reading will be unaided. The code sheet is marked as the selection is read. The reading is tape-recorded for future reference.
4. The substitution miscues are coded.
5. Miscue patterns are studied, interpreted, and translated into instruction.

The reader is encouraged to guess after a thirty-second hesitation. If hesitations are continuous, the reader is told to continue reading even if it means skipping a word or phrase. The RMI procedures also include a retelling of the selection, which is scored subjectively by the examiner. More will be said about retellings in the next section.

Although all types of miscues are marked, only substitution (including mispronunciation) miscues are coded, according to RMI procedures. Each substitution miscue is coded on the basis of the answers to a specific set of nine questions.

1. *Graphic similarity.* How much does the miscue look like what was expected?
2. *Sound similarity.* How much does the miscue sound like what was expected?
3. *Correction.* Is the miscue corrected?
4. *Grammatical acceptability.* Does the miscue occur in a structure that is grammatically acceptable? Does intonation signal author's syntactic intent?
5. *Semantic acceptability.* Does the miscue occur in a structure that is semantically acceptable? Does intonation signal author's semantic intent?
6. *Meaning change.* Does the miscue result in a change of meaning? Is a dialect variation involved in the miscue? (Optional) *Grammatical function.* Is the

> grammatical function of the miscue the same as the grammatical function of the word in the text? (Y. Goodman, Watson, and Burke 1987)

There is also some variation in how these questions are used within each of the alternative procedures presented in the revised RMI.

The major advantage of miscue analysis over traditional analyses of oral reading errors is that it recognizes that some errors are better than others. Miscue analysis emphasizes the quality of errors as a reflection of the quality of strategies students are using to process text. Quality exists along a continuum, from not-so-good to good.

Differences in the quality of miscues can be illustrated best by the following examples taken from Hood (1978). Suppose a reader encounters an unknown word during reading. Reader A may try to sound it out and pronounce either a real word that does not fit the context, or a nonsense word; or Reader A may just wait for the teacher to pronounce the word. Reader A's responses are poor ones because there is little attempt to focus on meaning. Reader B might pay more attention to the context and guess a word that makes sense, though it may or may not look much like the text word. This error is better than Reader A's because it shows more focus on meaning, but it still may represent a poor response. For example, suppose the error fits the preceding context but does not make sense when the rest of the sentence is read. In this instance, the error is not acceptable, and the reader should self-correct.

Reader C might take a quick look at the subsequent as well as preceding context before guessing an unknown word. If it fits the whole sentence context, Reader C's substitution is considered better than the errors made by Readers A and B. But what if the meaning of Reader C's sentence is different from what the author had in mind? Reader D uses context cues to predict several meanings that may be contained in the next bit of print, and uses print cues to decide which meaning may be the right one. When reading aloud, Reader D may substitute words that mean the same as the text, such as reading "frightened" for "afraid." In addition, Reader D may omit unessential words, for example, by reading "told what he heard" instead of "told what he had heard." Words may be inserted, such as reading "the little old lady" for "the old lady." The writer's exact words may be read correctly but in different order, such as reading "put the tent up" for "put up the tent." Unlike other errors which do not sound sensible, these specific examples are all good errors because they represent the same meaning as the words in the text. More importantly, they reflect the use of effective strategies to process the text.

There are no normative data to guide the interpretation of readers' miscue patterns. However, miscue analysis research does suggest the existence of several trends. A summary of these trends provided by Wixson (1979) includes the following:

1. Most readers, regardless of age or proficiency, produce a greater number of contextually acceptable miscues than graphophonically similar miscues.

2. As readers become more proficient, the proportion of graphophonically similar miscues stabilizes and the proportion of contextually acceptable miscues increases.
3. Less proficient readers make fewer attempts to correct their miscues than more proficient readers.
4. Less proficient readers tend to correct acceptable and unacceptable miscues at almost an equal rate; whereas more proficient readers tend to correct unacceptable miscues at a higher rate than acceptable miscues.

Problems with the RMI

Miscues should be interpreted with caution, however, because there is evidence that patterns vary as a result of the complex interaction among factors such as the instructional method; the reader's background, skills, and purpose for reading; and the specific nature of the written material. As with any test, miscue analysis provides a sample of behavior that may or may not be representative of the way a student interacts with different types of texts under different reading conditions. Miscue patterns are best regarded as a reflection of the particular strategies employed by a particular reader to satisfy his or her purpose for reading a particular passage.

The best way to address the problem of variability in miscue patterns is to obtain repeated samples of a particular reader's miscues under a variety of predetermined conditions (see Running Records, Chapter 8). The nature and content of the reading selections should be varied with regard to each individual reader's skills and background in an attempt to present the reader with a range of reading tasks and materials. An analysis of the miscues generated by a particular reader under a variety of conditions may reveal any pervasive problems the reader may have, as well as the particular conditions that present the reader with the greatest difficulty.

In addition to the problem of variability, the two biggest problems with the RMI are that it is designed to be used with materials that are at least one grade level above the student's reading placement level, and the administration and scoring are too complex and time-consuming to make them practical for either classroom or clinical use. Procedures we advocate to simplify miscue analysis are provided in the next section.

Modified Miscue Analysis Procedures

The first step is to select text materials at what is believed to be the student's instructional level of difficulty, so that information is being collected about the way the student is likely to perform during real classroom reading situations. Next, the substitution miscues are analyzed within the context of the following four questions:

1. Does the miscue change the meaning of the sentence?
2. Is the miscue contextually acceptable within the context of the whole passage?
3. Was the miscue self-corrected?
4. Is the miscue graphophonically similar to the intended word?

FIGURE 9.10
*Modified
Miscue
Analysis
(Marvin)*

Text	Marvin	Meaning Change	Contextually Acceptable	Self-Corrected	Graphophonic Similarity
1 me	him	no	yes	yes	no
2 these	this	no	no	no	yes
3 beads	bands	yes	yes	no	yes
4 would	were	no	no	no	no
5 me	my	no	no	no	yes
6 fortune	future	no	yes	no	yes
7 gave	came	yes	no	yes	some
8 beads	beds	yes	yes	no	yes
9 has	was	no	no	no	yes
10 rode	told	yes	no	yes	some

In reflecting on the answers to these questions, we can begin to discover patterns of performance. In particular, we can begin to determine whether the student is attending to the meaningfulness of text (Are most of the miscues acceptable? Does the student self-correct most of those miscues that are not acceptable?).

The chart in Figure 9.10 illustrates Marvin's miscues on several sentences from a level-three selection on the Burns and Roe *Informal Reading Inventory* (1985). One or two miscues of a particular type may not be significant. It is the *patterns* of performance that we are looking to reveal.

One of the most important findings of miscue research focuses on the self-correction patterns of skilled and less-skilled readers. Skilled readers tend to self-correct miscues that are contextually unacceptable and to leave uncorrected errors that are contextually acceptable. Less-skilled readers are just as likely to correct acceptable as unacceptable miscues.

If we examine Marvin's self-correction behavior, we see that there are six contextually unacceptable errors that we would expect a skilled reader to correct (2, 4, 5, 7, 9, and 10). Marvin corrected two of these (7 and 10) and left four uncorrected (2, 4, 5, and 9). There were also four contextually acceptable errors (1, 3, 6, and 8) that we would expect a skilled reader to leave uncorrected. Marvin corrected one of these (l) and left the other three uncorrected (3, 6, and 8). Although not entirely random, Marvin's pattern of self-correction for this text is more like that of a less-skilled than a skilled reader.

Additional information can be obtained by examining the graphophonic similarity of the errors to the text word. Eight of Marvin's ten miscues have at least some graphophonic similarity to the word in the text (2, 3, and 5–10). Even the two errors that are not graphophonically similar (1 and 4) are common sight word confusions. This pattern, coupled with the fact that only four of his ten errors were contextually acceptable, suggests that Marvin is relying heavily on the graphophonic cues in this text.

Finally, it is important to consider the effect of the errors on the meaning of the passage. In most cases, when an error is contextually acceptable, it will not change the meaning of the text, and vice versa, if an error is contextually unacceptable, it will change the meaning of the text. However, occasionally

FIGURE 9.11

Miscue Analysis Worksheet (Kyle)

Subject **_Level 3_** Level of Miscues: (Independent/Instructional) Frustrational

	Miscue	Text	Graphically Similar	Semantically Acceptable	Syntactically Acceptable	Self-Corrected
Wool	knit	knitted	yes	yes	no	—
	clothes	clothing	yes	yes	yes	—
	then	when	yes	no	no	—
	the	it	no	no	no	yes
	looks	locks	yes	no	no	yes
	dries	dry	yes	yes	no	—
	com-bed	combed	yes	no	no	attemped, unsuccessful
	form-at	formed	yes	no	no	—
	wove	woven	yes	yes	no	—
	clothes	clothing	yes	yes	yes	—
	hands	hand	yes	yes	yes	—
Zoo	the	their	yes	yes	yes	—
	class	classes	yes	yes	no	yes
	Mar	Maria	yes	yes	yes	—
	Angelina	Angela	yes	yes	yes	—
	want	wanted	yes	yes	no	yes
	the	one	no	yes	no	—
	Lipoz	Lopez	yes	yes	yes	—
	there	where	partial	yes	yes	—
	to	of	no	no	no	yes
	Luzpa	Lopez	yes	yes	yes	—
	He	and	no	yes	yes	—
Column Total Total Miscues Column Total/Total Miscues = %			_____ _____	_____ _____	_____ _____	_____ _____

unacceptable errors do not change the meaning of the text, and acceptable errors do. There are several examples of this among Marvin's errors. Errors 2, 4, 5, and 9 are contextually unacceptable, yet they do not change the meaning of the text. In Marvin's case, these errors are all examples of common sight word substitutions, adding to the evidence that Marvin still has not mastered the orthographic structure of high-frequency words.

Marvin also has two errors (3 and 8) that are contextually acceptable, but *do* change the meaning of the text. The first time he encounters the word *beads* he calls it *bands,* and the second time he calls it *beds.* This is a good error in that it suggests that Marvin is using both contextual and graphophonic cues and he does not correct it, because it makes sense in the passage. However, it is clear that this error is also likely to have a profound effect on his comprehension of this passage. Therefore, the meaning change column can provide further insight into readers' miscue patterns.

The QRI-II, administered to Kyle between grades two and three (see Figure 9.6) provides support for summarizing and interpreting oral reading miscues. The summary form is presented in Figure 9.11 with Kyle's results from two instructional level passages.

Unlike Marvin, Kyle's profile is more similar to a good reader than to a poor one. Sixteen of twenty-two miscues were semantically acceptable. Kyle attempted to self-correct four of the six remaining miscues. Only twice did Kyle leave uncorrected a miscue that was both syntactically and semantically unacceptable; substituting *then* for *when* and mispronouncing the word *formed.* In other words, Kyle is attending quite carefully to the semantic and syntactic cues in text. He also is making use of the graphophonic cues (only five of twenty-two miscues was not graphically similar). Kyle's miscues fall into two large categories: he frequently makes substitutions of high-frequency sight words (*the* for *it; there* for *where, to* for *of*); and he has problems with morphemes, frequently dropping or adding endings (*knit* for *knitted, dries* for *dry, class* for *classes*).

Before going on, it is important to remember that, for both Kyle and Marvin, this is a very small sample of miscues taken from one or two texts. In order to make generalizations or predictions about Marvin's reading, in particular, we must examine a large number of miscues taken from a variety of texts under a variety of conditions. This issue will be considered further in Chapter 11 as we examine multiple samples of Marvin's reading.

Oral Reading Fluency Scale

Fluency can be defined as the extent to which readers organize the words in sentences in a manner that preserves the syntax of the author and signals the relations among word meanings. It is a separate, though clearly related, aspect of oral reading. It is important to consider fluency, in addition to accuracy (and rate), because all readers make errors as they read (Goodman and Goodman 1994).

An assessment procedure used by the National Assessment of Educational Progress (NAEP), and similar to one developed by Aulls (1982), evaluates fluency by providing an estimate of whether or not a student consistently reads sentences predominantly word-by-word; in two-word groups with occasional word-by-word reading; in phrase groups with some two- or three-word groups; or in phrase groups.

Selecting Materials

Research with good and poor readers in Grades 1 through 6, using a procedure similar to the one described here, suggests that word grouping strategies change as a function of the difficulty of the material, reading ability, and years of exposure to reading and reading instruction (see Aulls 1982). Most good readers in Grades 5 and 6 read consistently in phrase groups when reading instructional level and even frustration level material. However, good readers in Grades 1 through 4 typically read material at the independent level with better word grouping strategies than they do material at the instructional or frustration level. What appears to be unique about poor readers at any grade level is that they group words in material at the independent and at the instructional level in the same fashion.

We recommend using material at the student's instructional level since most instruction is carried out at the instructional level, and since poor readers perform similarly at all levels, instructional level materials seem acceptable. The materials should be no less than 250 words in length. The longer the text, the better the estimate. Texts of 500 to 1,000 words are equally appropriate and have the advantage of offering a highly confident estimate of the student's ability to consistently organize words into groups when reading texts of similar readability and text organization or type.

Scoring

It is difficult to do a holistic scoring of fluency as you listen to students read. We recommend taping the oral reading sample that will be used for scoring. The Oral Reading Fluency Scale used by NAEP (Pinnell et al. 1995) is described in Figure 9.12. As the teacher listens to the oral reading sample, there are several "key elements" to consider. The first is *phrasing*. Phrasing patterns result from pitch sequences and pauses during oral reading. For the examiner, pauses provide the primary signal of the division of words into groups. Pitch provides a secondary signal of the meaning assigned to each group. Teachers who are assigning levels to fluency should also attend to how closely the reader *follows the author's syntax and/or sentence structure*. Stress placements and intonation can provide clues to guide the scoring. In addition, readers often insert pauses to signal meaning implied by the author. Finally, the fluency rating should consider the reader's *expressiveness* during reading. However, the degree of expressiveness expected will vary according to age/grade of the reader. Only in the later elementary grades would we expect students to exhibit consistently good expressiveness during oral reading.

If a student rereads a phrase or sentence, the word grouping used in the first reading is scored. This provides the best estimate of how the student typically and spontaneously performs. Students can and do self-correct word groupings, but the intent is to characterize their spontaneous patterns for organizing text information fluently, not their self-corrections of disfluent reading.

FIGURE 9.12
*NAEP Fluency
Scale Levels*

NAEP's Integrated Reading Performance Record Oral Reading Fluency Scale
Level 4 - Reads primarily in larger, meaningful phrase groups. Although some regressions, repetitions, and deviations from text may be present, these do not appear to detract from the overall structure of the story. Preservation of the author's syntax is consistent. Some or most of the story is read with expressive interpretation.
Level 3 - Reads primarily in three- or four-word phrase groups. Some smaller groupings may be present. However, the majority of phrasing seems appropriate and preserves the syntax of the author. Little or no interpretation is present.
Level 2 - Reads primarily in two-word phrases with some three- or four-word groupings. Some word-by-word reading may be present. Word groupings may seem awkward and unrelated to larger context of sentence or passage.
Level 1 - Reads primarily word-by-word. Occasional two-word or three-word phrases may occur — but these are infrequent and/or they do not preserve meaningful syntax.
Source: Pinnel et al. (Jan., 1995). *Listening to children read aloud.* OERI US Dept. of Ed. National's Report Card. Report # 23-FR-04. Washington, D. C. Used by permission.

In order to determine the fluency rating, you may wish to mark the phrase boundaries as students read. The sample markings below characterize different students' ability to organize words into groups:

1. Word-by-word: *The/brown/pony/galloped/toward/the fence. /It/was ....*
2. Beyond word-by-word reading, but not consistently in phrases: *The brown pony/galloped/toward/the fence. /It was/...*
3. Consistently in phrases: *The brown pony/galloped toward the fence./ It was/ ...*

In the first example, all words except two were read word by word. The words *the fence* were organized into a two-word group. Since the majority of words were read word by word, the student must be considered to be a word-by-word reader. In example two, only two of seven words in the sentence were read word by word, and other words were grouped in two-word groups. In the third example, the entire text was read in phrase groups. Even if *galloped* had been read as part of the first word group *(The brown pony galloped/toward the fence)*, it would still be an acceptable phrase group. The exact phrase grouping is not as important as the preservation of sensible word groupings.

To obtain an overall estimate of a student's word grouping during reading, the examiner considers the fluency across sentences, and assigns a holistic score that captures reading of this student. A sample of Marvin's fluency rating using this scoring procedure is provided in Figure 9.13. Marvin does read some small portions of the passage fluently (sentences 6 and 12, for example). Overall, however, two-word phrasings were Marvin's most consistent pattern of group-

FIGURE 9.13
Sample Fluency Rating: Marvin

Introductory Statement

"Joe wanted more than anything in the world to buy the electric train set in the trading post window. But should he do this? Please read the following story."

---

1. Joe sat down/ on the sidewalk in front of/ the/ trading post with his/ buckskin jacket/ thrown over his shoulder.
2. He/ felt worried/because/ it was difficult/ to know/ what to do.
3. "Grandfather told me/ never to/ sell/ these blue/ beads.
4. He/ said they would/ bring me/ good fortune and/ good health.
5. Grandfather is/ a wise/ and understanding man.
6. He is proud/ to be an American Indian.
7. He remembers/ when his grandfather/ gave/ him these/ same beads.
8. He/ has often told/ me/ many interesting stories/ of/ how his grandfather rode/ horses/ and hunted buffalo/ on the plains."
9. Joe/ held the/ string of/ beads/ high into the air/ toward the/ sunlight.
10. "These/ are perfectly beautiful/ beads,"/ he said/ out loud.
11. "I can't sell them/ because/ I too am proud/ of/ my great past.
12. Yes,/ I will keep the beads."

Source *Analytic Reading Inventory* Woods & Moe, 1985, Grade 3 Selection.

---

ing words. He is beyond word-by-word reading the majority of the time, is able to read some sentences in complete phrases, but is not consistent in doing so. In addition, his phrasing is not fluent and he has not maintained the author's syntax or sentence structure. Finally, Marvin reads in a monotone, with little expression to signal his understanding. We would place Marvin at a fluency level of 2.

Interpreting the Score

Aulls (1982) suggests that students at different levels of fluency are characteristically different from one another. For example, he notes that all readers whose scores are not completely fluent (Level 4) represent students who are acquiring word grouping strategies. A major distinction probably exists between Levels 2 and 3. At Levels 3 and 4 students seem to be able to give much more attention to the development of the more advanced strategies for processing sentence meaning (Aulls 1982).

Students at Level 1 need to become more fluent before moving on. They may need to be provided with easier materials until they have learned to group words better. Those students at Level 2 will be much more likely to be ready to refine the less complex sentence processing strategies involved in confirming word identification cues or integrating them. Once the student has attained a score at Level 3, the teacher should begin stressing the development of more sophisticated sentence processing strategies.

It appears that Marvin is just on the verge of becoming a fluent reader. His ratings here are encouraging, given the large numbers of miscues present in his readings. This score sheds light on his performance because it suggests greater fluency (and potential comprehension) than a simple miscue analysis would suggest. However, Marvin is in fifth grade, and the passage described is a third level selection from an IRI. His plight highlights the caution noted by Aulls (1982):

> When a poor reader is an older, intermediate grade pupil who cannot read material beyond third-grade difficulty at the independent level, it is very likely that all or part of the reading problem is inability to read words in phrase groups and/or inadequately developed strategies, or the lack of use of them, for processing sentence meaning. A teacher who cannot or does not assess the sentence processing strategies of poor readers may incorrectly conclude that teaching word identification cues will be sufficient to enable a poor reader to become a fluent reader. (622–623)

Tests of Word Recognition, Phonics, and Spelling

Word-level difficulties are very common among poor readers and writers. Indeed, most students who are identified as having reading or writing difficulties will have some weaknesses in the area of decoding, word identification, and/or spelling. Classroom teachers generally observe and assess students' performance informally and then bring their concerns to a staffing meeting or make a formal request for further evaluation. There are a number of structured, but still informal, evaluation tools that can be used to assess word-level skills and strategies. In general, information is needed regarding three areas of word-level performance: *sight word recognition, word analysis,* and *spelling.* The limitations of most structured word recognition tests is that they do not involve reading words in connected text. The results from these tests must, of course, be considered against information about students' word recognition performance during reading (see Running Records and Miscue Analysis). Similarly, although spelling tests can and do provide important information, students' spelling should be examined during writing.

Word Lists

As we have already noted, it is generally wise to evaluate component skills in use, rather than in isolation. Clearly, using a word list to test word recognition skills is a very constrained procedure. However, one attribute of skilled reading is *automaticity* in word recognition. Good readers are able to recognize large numbers of words rapidly. Allington and McGill-Franzen (1980) found that the scores generated by isolated word recognition tests were markedly different from those generated by in-context word recognition tests. The scores were especially divergent for less-able readers. It appears that context does facilitate word recognition, but it is used more heavily by poor readers than able ones. Thus, students' ability to recognize high-frequency sight words should be evaluated both in isolation and in context.

There are many lists of high-frequency sight words. One of the most widely used is the *Dolch Basic Sight Word Test* (Dolch 1942). This test consists of 220 high-frequency sight words, grouped into lists deemed appropriate from preprimer to third grade. The list has generated controversy and many prefer to use one of the more recently created lists (for example, Fry 1980; Johnson 1971). The *New Instant Word List* (Fry 1980) appears in Figure 9.14. Fry's analysis suggests that one-half of all written material is comprised of the first 100 of these instant words. The complete list of 300 instant words makes up 65 percent of all written material, and studies by a variety of researchers have confirmed the utility of various high-frequency core words (Durr 1973). Assessment of sight word skill is essential, since students will find fluent reading difficult if they do not master these words. Students can be expected, as a general rule, to have instant recognition of the entire list by the end of grade 3. Sight word lists are generally administered on flash cards. The cards are used to control the rate of presentation, so that students' instant recognition can be evaluated. Most specialists suggest presenting cards or words at a rate of one second per word. After the initial presentation is completed (or stopped due to frustration), the words that were missed can be presented again to assess students' word *analysis* abilities.

Most people suggest a criterion level of 90 percent or better for each list; however, Botel (1982) suggests a mastery level of 70 percent, arguing that since reading words in isolation is more difficult than reading words in context, the scoring procedure should be adjusted accordingly. In evaluating the student's responses to the word list task, the following questions should be considered:

- Does there appear to be any consistent pattern to the errors?
- Is the pattern of these errors comparable at each level, or does it change with increasing difficulty?
- Does the student substitute initial consonants? final consonants?
- Does the student attend to the medial portions of words?
- Does the student reverse letters or words?
- What is the student's overall level of mastery of high frequency sight words in isolation?

Although some authors recommend equating the results from a sight word list with reading level ability, we caution against this practice. All that can reasonably be accomplished by administering a word list is an appraisal of the reader's instant recognition of words, without benefit of context. This can provide a quick, efficient clue as to the student's in-text reading, and perhaps an idea of what may be impeding progress. Of course, it does not yield direct information about the student's word recognition during reading. Remember, children often misread different words in context and in isolation (Allington and McGill-Franzen 1980).

An important next step, then, is to compare students' word recognition during reading to word recognition in isolation. Different patterns of response can be suggestive. For example, some children perform much better during reading than on isolated lists. This suggests good use of context and is fre-

FIGURE 9.14
The Fry Instant Word List

The Instant Words: First Hundred

First 25 Group 1a	Second 25 Group 1b	Third 25 Group 1c	Fourth 25 Group 1d
the	or	will	number
of	one	up	no
and	had	other	way
a	by	about	could
to	word	out	people
in	but	many	my
is	not	then	than
you	what	them	first
that	all	these	water
it	were	so	been
he	we	some	call
was	when	her	who
for	your	would	oil
on	can	make	now
are	said	like	find
as	there	him	long
with	use	into	down
his	an	time	day
they	each	has	did
I	which	look	get
at	she	two	come
be	do	more	made
this	how	write	may
have	their	go	part
from	if	see	over

Common suffixes: s, ing, ed

The Instant Words: Second Hundred

First 25 Group 2a	Second 25 Group 2b	Third 25 Group 2c	Fourth 25 Group 2d
new	great	put	kind
sound	where	end	hand
take	help	does	picture
only	through	another	again
little	much	well	change
work	before	large	off
know	line	must	play
place	right	big	spell
year	too	even	air
live	mean	such	away
me	old	because	animal
back	any	turn	house
give	same	here	point
most	tell	why	page
very	boy	ask	letter
after	follow	went	mother
thing	came	men	answer
our	want	read	found
just	show	need	study
name	also	land	still
good	around	different	learn
sentence	form	home	should
man	three	us	America
think	small	move	world
say	set	try	high

Common suffixes: s, ing, ed, er, ly, est

The Instant Words: Third Hundred

First 25 Group 3a	Second 25 Group 3b	Third 25 Group 3c	Fourth 25 Group 3d
every	left	until	idea
near	don't	children	enough
add	few	side	eat
food	while	feet	face
between	along	car	watch
own	might	mile	far
below	close	night	Indian
country	something	walk	real
plant	seem	white	almost
last	next	sea	let
school	hard	began	above
father	open	grow	girl
keep	example	took	sometimes
tree	begin	river	mountain
never	life	four	cut
start	always	carry	young
city	those	state	talk
earth	both	once	soon
eye	paper	book	list
light	together	hear	song
thought	got	stop	leave
head	group	without	family
under	often	second	body
story	run	late	music
saw	important	miss	color

Common suffixes: s, ing, ed, er, ly, est

The instant word list, pp. 286–87 from "The New Instant Word List" by Edward Fry, *The Reading Teacher*, December 1980. Reprinted with permission of Edward Fry and the International Reading Association.

quently accompanied by better comprehension than word recognition. When there is a large discrepancy, it can be expected that students are actually over-relying on context. The student may not have achieved automaticity in word recognition and reading may proceed very slowly.

Other children demonstrate exactly the opposite pattern. That is, they perform better on isolated word lists than they do in context. There may be several reasons for this, but often these students have too little experience with real reading. This limited reading experience often occurs in classrooms where students learn words in isolation (by completing workbook tasks, using flash cards, or playing games). Thus, these students have competence in recognizing words (or analyzing them, see below) but have not learned to transfer this skill to reading continuous text.

Of course, students' sight recognition of other words can be assessed as well. For example, word lists can be prepared from the instructional materials used in classroom or clinic. Lists created from basal readers or required trade books can be helpful in evaluating readiness to read specific materials and/or in assessing progress. If students are participating in a literature-based reading program, it may be advisable to examine high-frequency words derived from the literature commonly used in such programs. To this end, Eeds (1985) has analyzed 400 books appropriate for grades K–3 and identified the high-frequency words in those books (see Figure 9.15). The 227 words listed account for 73 percent of all words in her sample of books. Specialists or other teachers who are assessing students who are learning to read in a literature-based classroom program should find this list more helpful in evaluating sight word knowledge. The booklist from which this list was generated appears in Chapter 13.

Informal Tests of Phonics and Structural Analysis

Although we favor analyzing knowledge and application of phonics during reading of actual text, most diagnostic batteries include some form of isolated assessment of phonics skill. Teachers sometimes find it helpful to use these commercial materials as they build their own knowledge base and increase their ability to reliably identify important phonic elements that may be influencing students' reading. Once information has been gathered about the student's knowledge and skill in phonics, it will be important to generate record-keeping forms that summarize the patterns of strength and weakness that were observed (see Figure 9.16). These may also be used to aid analysis of writing samples, which can provide powerful information about phonics skill (see below).

Both informal and formal tests of phonic and structural analysis typically contain lists of nonsense words that embody one or more of the sound-symbol patterns. A sample test might look something like the following:

1. fload
2. zam
3. drowt
4. dispount
5. strabble
6. mait
7. glavorful
8. kneef
9. jarf
10. bluther

FIGURE 9.15

Bookwords
High
Frequency
Sight Words

Final Core 227 Word List Based on 400 Storybooks for Beginning Readers

the	1334	good	90	think	47	next	28
and	985	this	90	new	46	only	28
a	831	don't	89	know	46	am	27
I	757	little	89	help	46	began	27
to	746	if	87	grand	46	head	27
said	688	just	87	boy	46	keep	27
you	638	baby	86	take	45	teacher	27
he	488	way	85	eat	44	sure	27
it	345	there	83	body	43	says	27
in	311	every	83	school	43	ride	27
was	294	went	82	house	42	pet	27
she	250	father	80	morning	42	hurry	26
for	235	had	79	yes	41	hand	26
that	232	see	79	after	41	hard	26
is	230	dog	78	never	41	push	26
his	226	home	77	or	40	our	26
but	224	down	76	self	40	their	26
they	218	got	73	try	40	watch	26
my	214	would	73	has	38	because	25
of	204	time	71	always	38	door	25
on	192	love	70	over	38	us	25
me	187	walk	70	again	37	should	25
all	179	came	69	side	37	room	25
be	176	were	68	thank	37	pull	25
go	171	ask	67	why	37	great	24
can	162	back	67	who	36	gave	24
with	158	now	66	saw	36	does	24
one	157	friend	65	mom	35	car	24
her	156	cry	64	kid	35	ball	24
what	152	oh	64	give	35	sat	24
we	151	Mr.	63	around	34	stay	24
him	144	bed	63	by	34	each	23
no	143	an	62	Mrs.	34	ever	23
so	141	very	62	off	33	until	23
out	140	where	60	sister	33	shout	23
up	137	play	59	find	32	mama	22
are	133	let	59	fun	32	use	22
will	127	long	58	more	32	turn	22
look	126	here	58	while	32	thought	22
some	123	how	57	tell	32	papa	22
day	123	make	57	sleep	32	lot	21
at	122	big	56	made	31	blue	21
have	121	from	55	first	31	bath	21
your	121	put	55	say	31	mean	21
mother	119	read	55	took	31	sit	21
come	118	them	55	dad	30	together	21
not	115	as	54	found	30	best	20
like	112	Miss	53	lady	30	brother	20
then	108	any	52	soon	30	feel	20
get	103	right	52	ran	30	floor	20
when	101	nice	50	dear	29	wait	20
thing	100	other	50	man	29	tomorrow	20
do	99	well	48	better	29	surprise	20
too	91	old	48	through	29	shop	20
want	91	night	48	stop	29	run	20
did	91	may	48	still	29	own	20
could	90	about	47	fast	28		

From "Bookwords: Using A Beginning Word List of High Frequency Words from Children's Literature K–3" by M. Eeds, *The Reading Teacher*, January 1985, p. 420. International Reading Association. Reprinted by permission.

FIGURE 9.16
Summary Chart of Phonic and Structural Analysis

Directions: As the child reads note how frequently she or he:			
	Always	Sometimes	Never
Recognizes major sounds of consonants	☐	☐	☐
Uses onsets and rimes (analogies)	☐	☐	☐
Uses major CVC vowel patterns	☐	☐	☐
Recognizes consonant influenced pattern	☐	☐	☐
Uses major CVVC clusters	☐	☐	☐
Uses other patterns (clusters/phonograms)	☐	☐	☐
Uses structural analysis	☐	☐	☐
Uses morphemic analysis	☐	☐	☐
Uses a combination of context/decoding	☐	☐	☐

The *El Paso Phonics Survey* (Ekwall 1979), the *Sipay Word Analysis Tests* (SWAT) (Sipay 1974), and the *Gates-McKillop-Horowitz Diagnostic Tests* (Gates, McKillop, and Horowitz 1981) are among the commercially available informal tests of this type. The advantage of nonsense words is that it is possible to evaluate students' knowledge and application of word analysis strategies as they are used with totally unfamiliar "words." The disadvantage of this practice is that reading nonsense words is a more difficult task than reading real words in context (Harris and Sipay 1990). Baumann (1988) devised a phonics survey that compensates for this difficulty to some extent. The *Baumann Informal Phonics Test* requires children to read both real and nonsense words involving the same phonic element. For example, *walk, chalk, falk,* and *jalk* all appear on this test. In this way, students' recognition of phonic elements in familiar words can be compared to their performance on nonsense words. However, these words still appear in isolation, and it will be necessary to contrast performance on this type of test with performance during reading. This is especially important since some children consistently attempt to make real words from nonsense words. Their attempts to make meaning override the visual display. Consequently, they may appear to have limited sound-symbol knowledge when, in fact, they regularly employ word analysis strategies during reading, in combination with their meaning-seeking strategies.

Spelling Inventories

Virtually all experts in the area of English language arts agree that teachers should evaluate students' level of spelling and target instruction appropriately. In order to do that, of course, we need tools to help us. More importantly, we need to be clear about what content to teach. We discuss spelling instruction later in the text (See Chapter 13). For assessment purposes there are basically three sources of words to use in evaluation. Earlier educators advocated teaching students, through rote memorization, the most frequent words in the language (Dolch 1942).

While it is important for students to learn to spell these words, they don't really provide useful information about students' overall spelling development. Consequently, some authors suggest using any one of the available graded spelling lists from a commercial program to determine grade level performance. Structured spelling tests are then created by selecting a sample of, perhaps twenty-five, words from each level. The word lists are administered to determine at what level of difficulty students should be receiving instruction.

A different approach was suggested by Henderson (1992). He created a listing of words that reflected the recurrent spelling patterns of the English language. Building on this work, both Henderson, and later Templeton (1995), argue that spelling knowledge proceeds through several developmental stages, and effective assessment should be focused on determining which of these stages represents a student's present level of knowledge. We discussed the earliest of these stages in Chapter 7 (roughly equivalent to the pre-phonemic, early phonemic, and phonetic spelling stages). In that chapter, however, we simply called the next phase "conventional spelling." However, many students have difficulty in the next stages, what Templeton calls "syllable juncture" and "derivational constancy" (see Chapter 13 for additional discussion). In the syllable juncture stage, children make errors at the juncture of syllables (for example *hury* for *hurry* or *capcur* for *capture*). Students in the "derivational juncture" stage make spelling errors based on their lack of understanding of base words and affixes (*compisition* for *composition*, for example).

Templeton (1995) describes a structured inventory for evaluating students' stage-level knowledge of spelling. The Qualitative Inventory of Spelling Knowledge (see Figure 9.17) is designed for individual administration. Students are asked to spell words as best they can. If a student spells the first ten words on a list correctly, testing moves to the next level. Teachers are advised to stop testing when a student misspells more than 60 percent of the words on a list. Templeton suggests interpreting results about levels using the following guidelines:

- Independent Level: Over 90 percent of the words are spelled correctly
- Instructional Level: Between 40 percent and 90 percent of the words are spelled correctly
- Frustrational Level: Fewer than 40 percent of the words are spelled correctly. (322)

Evaluating Writing Samples

In today's classrooms, children write more than they ever have, and teachers have more information available to them about how to evaluate students' writing. The available options range from the very informal (see Chapter 8) to the very formal (see Chapter 10). Many norm-referenced tests of writing involve

FIGURE 9.17
Qualitative Inventory of Spelling Knowledge

Level 1	Level II	Level III	Level IV	Level V	Level VI
bump	batted	find	square	enclosed	absence
not	such	paint	hockey	piece	civilize
with	once	crawl	helmet	novel	accomplish
trap	chop	dollar	allow	lecture	prohibition
chin	milk	knife	skipping	pillar	pledge
bell	funny	mouth	ugly	confession	sensibility
shade	start	fought	hurry	aware	official
pig	glasses	comb	bounce	loneliest	inspire
drum	hugging	useful	lodge	service	permission
hid	named	circle	fossil	loyal	irrelevant
father	pool	early	traced	expansion	conclusion
track	stick	letter	lumber	production	invisible
pink	when	weigh	middle	deposited	democratic
drip	easy	real	striped	revenge	responsible
brave	make	tight	bacon	awaiting	accidental
job	went	sock	capture	unskilled	composition
sister	shell	voice	damage	installment	relying
slide	pinned	campfire	nickel	horrible	changeable
box	class	keeper	barber	relate	amusement
white	boat	throat	curve	earl	conference
	story	waving	statement	uniform	advertise
	plain	carried	collar	rifle	opposition
	smoke	scratch	parading	correction	community
	size	tripping	sailor	discovering	advantage
	sleep	nurse	wrinkle	retirement	cooperation
			dinner	salute	spacious
			medal	treasure	carriage
			tanner	homemade	presumption
			dimmed	conviction	appearance
			careful	creature	description

Source: Templeton, S. (1995) Spelling: The foundation of word knowledge for the less proficient reader. In L. Putnam (ed.), *How to become a better reading teacher* (317–329). Englewood Cliffs, NJ: Merrill. Reprinted with permission.

analytic evaluations of written products (see Chapter 10). Holistic scoring of written products is quite common both in classroom assessment and in large-scale assessment (even statewide assessment of writing). Using a holistic scoring system, you arrive at a rating that represents a global judgment about the overall quality of the written product. Using an analytic approach, specific aspects of the writing press are judged: syntax, vocabulary, and so on.

These judgments are guided by criteria, which are established before scoring begins. The tool that is used is called a *rubric*. According to Marzano and his colleagues, "a scoring rubric consists of a fixed scale and a list of characteristics describing performance for each of the points on the scale"

FIGURE 9.18
Sample Scoring Rubric for Writing

Writing to Inform	
4	These responses are well-developed and have provided more than enough information to inform the reader about the topic. The information is extended and expanded through specific details. A. These responses contain numerous specific details that more than adequately explain the topic. B. The organizational plan is established and consistently maintained. C. The writer addresses the intended audience. D. The writer fluently uses language choices to enhance the text in a manner consistent with the purpose.
3	These responses are adequately developed and have provided enough information to inform the reader about the topic. The information is presented clearly, and irrelevant information does not interfere with clarity. A. These responses contain some specific details that adequately explain the topic, although some details may not contribute to the development of the explanation. B. An organizational plan is established and generally maintained. C. The writer addresses the intended audience. D. The writer uses language choices to enhance the text in a manner consistent with the purpose.
2	These responses contain little development and have a minimal amount of information. The information included does not clearly explain the topic, and irrelevant information interferes with clarity. A. These responses have details, but the details may be inaccurate or may not adequately explain the topic. B. An organizational plan is established and minimally maintained. C. The writer addresses the intended audience. D. The writer seldom uses language choices to enhance the text in a manner consistent with the purpose.
1	These responses provide sufficient evidence that the writer saw the prompt and attempted to respond to it. The responses lack development and have little information. The information included may be vague or inaccurate. A. These responses lack sufficient details to explain the topic. B. An organizational plan, if established, is not maintained. C. The writer may not address the intended audience. D. The writer does not use language choices to enhance the text in a manner consistent with the purpose.
NSR	A. Blank B. Off topic/off task C. Unscorable

Source: *Prince George's County Scoring Guide for Reading/Writing/Language Usage.* (p.54). Prepared by P. Norris, P. Millen, R. Womack, and S. Kowzun. Used with permission.

FIGURE 9.19
Standards for Evaluating Narrative and Expository Writing

Standards for Evaluating Composing Skills for Narrative Writing

	Low	Middle	High
Story structure	No identifiable beginning, middle, or end. Story problem unclear. Action and characters not developed or related. Essential details missing or confusing. Story problem not solved, or resolution unrelated to events.	Beginning, middle, and end present, but not always identifiable. Story problem presented, but not completely developed. Some conversational or descriptive details included. End may not show logical resolution of problem.	Identifiable beginning, middle, and end. Characters introduced and problem presented. Characters and problem well-developed with appropriate conversational or descriptive detail. Story ends with believable resolution of problem.
Story setting	Setting of the story not identifiable. Details inappropriate and confusing.	Time and place of story are hinted at. But uncertain. Further references to setting may be inconsistent with original time or place.	Time and place of story clearly set. Specific details related to setting given in appropriate context. Setting consistent throughout.
Story characters	Characters not believable. Details related to character development are inconsistent, inappropriate, or missing. Difficult to distinguish one character from another. Action of characters unrelated to problem.	Characters somewhat believable. Some descriptive or conversational details given. Details may not develop character personality. Action of characters not always related to problem. Major and minor characters not clearly discernable.	Characters believable. Descriptive or conversational detail develops character personality. Action of characters relates to problem. Major characters more fully developed than minor ones.
Story conversation	Conversation among characters haphazard, incomplete, or muddled. Much of the conversation inappropriate to circumstances and to personality of story characters. Conversation seems unrelated to story being told.	Conversation sometimes appropriate to circumstances and to characters. Conversation may reveal character personality or relationships among characters. Conversation sometimes not clearly related to story.	Conversation appropriate to story circumstances and to personality of each character. Conversation used to reveal character and develop interrelationships among characters. Conversation clearly relates to story.
Story idea	Story idea is trite or otherwise uninteresting. Story lacks plot or plot is vague. Story ends abruptly or reaches no definite conclusion.	Story idea is interesting. Idea may lack freshness or imaginativeness. Story has a plot. Plot may not be well-developed or entirely consistent. Story ending may not be satisfying or interesting.	Story idea is fresh or imaginative. Story plot is well-developed, is consistent, and comes to a satisfying, surprising, or otherwise highly effective ending.

FIGURE 9.19
(Continued)

	Standards for Evaluating Composing Skills for Expository Writing		
	Low	**Middle**	**High**
Quality of ideas	Most ideas vague, incoherent, inaccurate, underdeveloped, or incomplete. Details often unrelated to topic. Nothing imaginative or thoughtful about the ideas.	Unevenness in completeness and development of ideas. Most ideas related to the topic; a few unrelated. Sound, but unimaginative ideas.	Ideas relevant to the topic, fully developed, rich in thought and imagination, and clearly presented.
Quality of organization	Introduction, development, and conclusion unclear. Emphasis of major and minor points indistinguishable. Sentences and paragraphs seldom related by transitions. Overall lack of coherence and forward movement.	Introduction, development, or conclusion not easily identified. Emphasis on major or minor points sometimes not well-balanced. Transitions between sentences and paragraphs used, but without consistency. Forward movement variable.	Introduction, development, and conclusion well-structured, complete, and easily identified. Emphasis of major and minor points well-balanced. Sentences and paragraphs clearly related by transitions. Logical forward movement.
Selection of words	Word selection inexact, immature, and limited. Figurative language seldom used.	Word selection usually suitable and accurate. Over-used words and clichés somewhat common. Figurative language may lack freshness, when used.	Facility and flair in word selection. Writer experiments with words in unusual and pleasing ways. Figurative language used, often in interesting and imaginative ways.
Structure of sentences	Not variety in sentence structure; often only simple sentences are used. Transitions limited to such words as **then**; conjunctions to **and**. Awkward and puzzling sentences common. Run-on sentences and fragments often appear.	Some variety in sentence length and structure. Transitions used when necessary. Few sentence constructions awkward and puzzling. Run-on sentences and sentence fragments appear, but do not predominate.	Sentence length and structure varied. Sentences consistently well-formed. Smooth flow from sentence to sentence. Run-on sentences and sentence fragments rarely appear.
Structure of paragraph	Topic sentences seldom used. Irrelevancies common. Order of details haphazard. Little or no command of the four common paragraph types.	Topic sentences usually stated. Irrelevancies uncommon. Order of details usually suitable. Limited ability to use the four common types of paragraphs.	Topic sentences stated and supported with relevant details. Appropriate variety used in ordering details (chronological, logical, spatial, climactic). Four types of paragraphs used when appropriate (narrative, explanatory, descriptive, persuasive).

FIGURE 9.19
(*Continued*)

Standards for Evaluating Mechanical Skills for Narrative or Expository Writing			
	Low	Middle	High
Grammar and usage	Frequent errors in the use of nouns, pronouns, modifiers, and verbs.	Grammatical conventions of inflections, functions, modifiers, nouns, pronouns, and verbs usually observed. Grammatical errors sometimes occur.	Grammatical conventions of inflections, functions, modifiers, nouns, pronouns, and verbs observed. Grammatical errors infrequent.
Punctuation	End punctuation often used incorrectly. Internal punctuation seldom used. Uncommon punctuation is almost never used correctly.	Sentences usually end with appropriate punctuation. Internal punctuation used, with occasional errors. Uncommon punctuation sometimes used, but often inaccurately.	Sentences consistently end with appropriate punctuation. Internal punctuation and other less common punctuation usually correctly used.
Capitalization	First word of sentence often not capitalized. Pronoun/often a small letter. Proper nouns seldom capitalized. Other capitalization rules usually ignored.	First word of sentences nearly always capitalized. I always capitalized. Well-known proper nouns usually capitalized. Other capitalization rules used, but not consistently.	First word of a sentence and the pronoun/always capitalized. Well-known proper nouns nearly always capitalized. Good command of other capitalization rules regarding titles, languages, religions, and so on.
Spelling	Frequent spelling errors. Shows a frustration spelling level (less than 70%). Unable to improve spelling accuracy in edited work without help. Misspellings often difficult to recognize as English words.	Majority of words spelled correctly. Shows an instructional spelling level (70 to 80%). Approaches 90% accuracy in edited work. Misspellings approximate correct spellings.	Nearly all words spelled correctly. Shows an independent spelling level (90%). Approaches 100% accuracy in edited work. Misspellings close to correct spellings.
Handwriting/ neatness	Handwriting difficult or impossible to read. Letters and words crowded. Formation of letters inconsistent. Writing often illegible.	Handwriting usually readable, but some words and letters difficult to recognize. Some crowding of letters and words.	Handwriting clear, neat, and consistent. Forms all letters legibly with consistent spacing between letters and words.

From *Language: Structure and Use. Teacher's Edition* 8 by Ronald L. Cramer et al. Copyright © 1981 Scott, Foresman and Company.

(Marzano, Pickering, and McTighe 1993, 29). Similarly, Garcia and Verville (1994) describe a rubric as a "hierarchy of acceptable responses. It identifies the qualities one would expect to see in a response at several points along a scale" (238).

Using these rubrics, general evaluations are made about the written work, typically using a three- or four-level scale (1–4, High, Middle, Low). An example of a rubric that is applied holistically to a specific type of writing is presented in Figure 9.18. Generally, these types of rubrics are task-specific. That is, the performance assessment, or genre of writing, is clearly specified and the attributes of excellent performance in that mode are identified. Other attributes are identified for other tasks. Of course, some guidelines may be used both holistically or analytically to judge writing samples (see Figure 9.19). As you can see,

FIGURE 9.20
Student Self-Evaluation Rubric

REASONING STRATEGY 8; ANALYZING PERSPECTIVES

a. I find and describe a topic on which people disagree and explain the areas of disagreement

4 I find and accurately describe a topic on which people disagree. I explain the obvious and specific areas of disagreement, but I also find and explain less obvious causes of disagreement.

3 I find and accurately describe a topic on which people disagree and explain the areas of disagreement.

2 I find a topic on which people disagree, but I make errors in explaining the specific areas of disagreement.

1 I find a topic on which people disagree, but I do not find or describe any specific areas of disagreement.

b. I state an opinion on the topic and explain the reasons for that opinion.

4 I clearly state an opinion on the topic and explain the reasons for that opinion. I also describe the thinking that might lead to the opinion, and I explain the strengths, weaknesses, and errors in that thinking.

3 I clearly state an opinion on the topic and explain some of the important reasons for that opinion. I do not explain the thinking that might lead to the opinion.

2 I clearly state an opinion on the topic, but I do not clearly explain the reasons for that opinion.

1 I do not state a clear opinion.

Source: Marzano, R. J., Pickering, D., & McTighe, J. (1993). *Assessing student outcomes: Performance assessment using the dimensions of learning model.* Alexandria, VA: ASCD. (p. 114). Copyright ©1993 Association of Supervision and Curriculum Development. Used with permission.

a composition is judged separately for narrative and exposition, whereas mechanical skills are judged together.

Rubrics can also be designed by or for students so that they may engage in more effective self-evaluation. An example of a rubric to be used by students in reflecting on one aspect central to effective writing is shown in Figure 9.20. As Marzano, Pickering, and McTighe (1993) point out," . . . rubrics provide important information to teachers, parents, and others interested in what students know and can do. Rubrics also *promote* learning by offering clear performance targets to students for agreed-upon standards" (29). Everyone is a winner in this situation. Assessment is proceeding with authentic tasks and the assessment criteria provide useful instructional targets and a focus for learning. In addition, these rubrics provide the systematic structure that allows teachers across classrooms to discuss and evaluate students' work with a common vision and a uniform set of standards.

A Classroom System: Benchmark Book Events

Despite the relatively informal nature of these tasks and despite the vastly improved nature of the texts and procedures among IRIs, many educators are still concerned that they represent a contrived set of materials and tasks that don't fully reflect the kinds of reading their students are doing. As a result, some schools and school districts have begun to create their own "assessment events," systematic assessment procedures to be carried out with real books using classroom-based techniques (Au 1994; Bembridge 1994; Valencia and Place 1994).

What distinguishes these assessments from the strategies described in Chapter 8 is the extent to which procedures and policies are prescribed and the whole process made more systematic. These events are intended to be used to inform instruction in the classroom but also to report results to audiences *outside* of the classroom. Teachers want to make sure they and their colleagues are evaluating students in a comparable way, using agreed upon materials and assessment tools. In this section the system devised by one such school is described. Teachers there have been working for two years to improve the consistency and trustworthiness of the information they pass along to colleagues and parents.

The teachers in the school determined early on in the process to use portfolios in their classroom. In Kyle's classroom, the collections began in kindergarten, but by first grade all the teachers in the building had agreed to a set of "core items" that they would all document in the portfolios. After much discussion, the teachers in this primary building determined that each teacher/child would collect writing samples three times a year, collect continuous information about independent reading using a book log, evaluate students' word recognition using the Bookwords list (see Figure 9.15), and document students' oral reading using Running Records (see Chapter 8) three times a year. Many other work samples were placed in the portfolios optionally.

The portfolio items reflect the ongoing progress of students in their class-rooms, and teachers also use an observational system by Meisels (1994), which provides developmental standards that are reflective of work at the national level. After one year, though, teachers felt strongly that they would like to have a means of evaluating students' growth in reading *in relation to* a set of increasingly difficult reading materials. These texts would provide benchmarks for estimating the appropriateness of students' progress as compared with students that age and might also serve as a means of identifying students who were in difficulty.

They began the process of identifying a set of benchmark books that could be used for examining accuracy (Running Records) and could also provide important information about students' comprehension abilities. The word "benchmark" was used to indicate designated points in reading development that are characterized by specific criteria and books and that are associated with increasing degrees of proficiency. A student's ability to read a particular benchmark book would provide information about his or her progress in reading and about developmental reading ability in terms of a series of stages.

Two primary concerns drove the identification of these materials. First, teachers wanted the books to reflect the authentic literacy abilities that children were acquiring in their classrooms. No teacher in this building uses basal readers; although many use the leveled materials for beginning readers described in Chapter 5. The basic materials for instruction in this building are trade books of children's literature. Therefore, they wanted an assessment that relied on book reading.

A second concern was that the books represent an accurate estimate of increasing difficulty. The benchmarks needed to be trustworthy. Teachers spent a year establishing criteria and selecting books that exemplified those criteria (see Figure 9.21). They also created assessment items to accompany the books. The books were "protected" from circulation and instructional use; saved for assessment purposes. Then, they began to validate these materials against student performance on previously used tools, the *Spache Diagnostic Reading Scales*. These teachers have elected not to assign grade levels to the books, but instead to describe five benchmark book levels that correspond to the expected progression of students through the three grades (K–2) in their building. The majority of students will "exit at E." Gratifyingly, after the first pilot year, the teachers determined that the majority of students did, in fact, read at or above the Level E benchmark.

The benchmark Books provide a structured assessment system that yields useful information about students. As we have seen, Kyle's progress was monitored during grade 2 by his teacher who made regular notations of his progress using running records (see Chapter 8). In addition, however, she evaluated him three times using benchmark books. In November, Kyle's word recognition accuracy on a Level C book was 99 percent, so

FIGURE 9.21
Benchmark Books: Criteria and Samples

Level	Descriptors	Example
A	Picture book with 1–3 words/page. Repetition of words and patterns. Picture clues drive recognition of unknown or unique content words.	*Baby Chimp* (R. Williams, The Wright Group, 1990)
B	Picture book with 4–25 words/page. High frequency Bookwords #1–60. Repetition of words, phrases, and events. Picture clues for unique words. Some phonically regular, decodable words. More difficult books may appear IF there's a familiar storyline (i.e. Little Red Hen).	*Good Morning Bears* (J. Hollands, Houghton Mifflin Read Alone, Lev. A, 1991)
C	Text-to-picture ratio changes (more text). Print is still enlarged. Average number of words/page variable but may go as high as 20–40. High frequency Bookwords #1–120. Less repetition and an increase in decodable words. Story structure with dialogue.	*Beef Stew* (Brenner, Random House, Step 1, STEP into Reading book, 1990).
D	Fully developed narrative stories and exposition. Smaller print size. All Bookwords (#1–227) may be used. Longer sentences (8–10 words/sentence). Books are longer and more dense, with 48–60 pages per book and 45–80 words/page. Pictures support comprehension vs. word ID.	*Molly and the Slow Teeth* (J. Cole, Houghton Mifflin, 1993).
E	Smaller print size. 90–120 words/page. Longer sentences in a longer book: 10–13 words/sentence and 20–40 pages/book. More complicated concepts and narratives. Developed dialogue, events, and characters.	*Christina Katarina and the Time She Quit the Family* (P. Gauch, Putnam, 1987).
F	This level builds on the others. Most distinctive feature: much longer and denser text, with more challenging vocabulary. Require that students have the "stamina" to stick with these longer, more complicated materials.	*The Knight at Dawn.* (M. Osborn, First Stepping Stone Book, 1993).

FIGURE 9.22

Kyle's Results on Benchmark Book, Level E

Kyle May 11, 1995

Christina Katarina, by P. Gauch

    This delightful story tells the tale of a strong-willed girl, Christina, who, having gotten fed-up with her family (younger brother bothering her, mom and dad yelling at her) decides to "quit the family." She changes her name to Agnes, and with the tacit approval of her mother, occupies half of the house. At first Agnes enjoys her new-found freedom, but she quickly finds that being on her own means that there is no one to help with chores and small disasters. She also finds that she misses her family. In the end, mom "convinces" her that the rest of the family really cannot get along without her and Christina returns to the family.

Oral Reading Accuracy: 96% accuracy

Comprehension:

1. Would you like to read more stories about Christina? Is she anything like you? (personal response)
   Kyle: *No. I wouldn't want to quit the family. I wouldn't put things all over the place.*

2. Why did Christina quit her family? (text explicit)
   Kyle: *Because she didn't like how her mother nagged too much. Her brother followed her too much. She liked her dad, but he got angry at her too much.*

3. How could Christina quit the family and still stay in the house? (text implicit)
   Kyle: *She quit the family, not the house. Her mother wanted her to stay. They put places for her to be in the house and places for her not to be.*

4. Who is Agnes? (text implicit)
   Kyle: *Her, but she changed her name in the old part of the house.*

5. Name three things that Agnes did in the story. (text explicit)
   Kyle: *She marked her areas out. She started to get missing with her family. She ate underneath the table.*

6. Did she enjoy herself when she quit the family? (text explicit).
   Kyle: *In the beginning, yes. They didn't tell her what to do, she could do what she wanted.*

7. Was there any time in the story when being on her own was not a good idea? When? (text implicit)
   Kyle: *No, I guess not.*

8. What happens at the end of the story? (text implicit)
   Kyle: *She joined back the family because she missed getting helped tucked in.*

9. During the week that Christina quit the family, what did Christina learn? (theme)
   Kyle: *That you can't just do it all by yourself because you need other people.*

Total Comprehension: 8/9 (89%)

Ms. McIntyre had him read from a Level D book, which yielded an accuracy score of 95 percent. Coupled with his good comprehension for the portion read, she judged this to be his instructional level. At the end of the year, Kyle was evaluated on one of the challenging Level E books. Figure 9.22 contains a summary of Kyle's oral reading and comprehension at that level. His total accuracy, 96 percent, makes this a comfortable instructional level for Kyle. He corrected two of six miscues and two others were mispronunciations of proper nouns. In addition, his comprehension, as measured on the comprehension questions, was very strong, revealing his excellent verbal skills and response to literature.

The Benchmark System demonstrates how the basic strategies and frameworks of IRIs, miscue analysis, and retellings can be applied to everyday materials to create a structured-assessment system for use at the school/district level.

THE DIAGNOSTIC PORTFOLIO: EVIDENCE FROM STRUCTURED INVENTORIES

Marvin

Marvin's performance on the informal reading inventory (Burns and Roe 1985) suggested that his word recognition abilities were weak. Although he was a fifth grade student, the test yielded an instructional level at grade 2 and a frustrational level at grade 3 (see Chapter 11 for further details). The miscue analysis suggests some ability to self-correct and an inclination to attend to meaning. It also reveals an over-reliance on graphophonic cues, coupled with poor abilities in this area. Finally, Marvin's orthographic knowledge is very weak, resulting in limited sight word recognition.

The results also suggested that his comprehension is somewhat stronger than his word recognition, although that also was below grade level. He had a difficult time comprehending implicit main ideas and inferences, in general, which posed particular problems. His ability to recall was less developed than his ability to answer questions. The analysis of his retelling indicated that he remembered less-important information than would be expected of a good reader, supporting the findings of retelling discussed in Chapter 8. His writing was meager and he was reluctant to participate. Marvin is clearly struggling in many areas of literacy.

Kyle

The new assessment system in Kyle's school generated good information. Benchmark book results during fall and early winter suggested that Kyle was still struggling. However, his comprehension was often very good and his word recognition abilities were growing. He had not yet acquired the more complex consonant-vowel patterns of the language.

FIGURE 9.23a
Edited Writing:
Grade 2, Kyle

Dear Animals of the Earth

Kyle

May 10, 1995

Dear Animals of the Earth,
     I give you your mountains. I give you
your habitats. I am your mother. I am the earth.
I am just as small as you are in this big universe of
planets and galaxies. The people are your brothers
and sisters even though they pollute my skies and
oceans. I am working on a letter to the humans to
tell them that you are their brothers and sisters and
the beauty they are destroying and soon, I will be so
sick. I will die and there will be no more earth.

Love,
Mother Earth

FIGURE 9.23b
Self-initiated Writing: Grade 2, Kyle

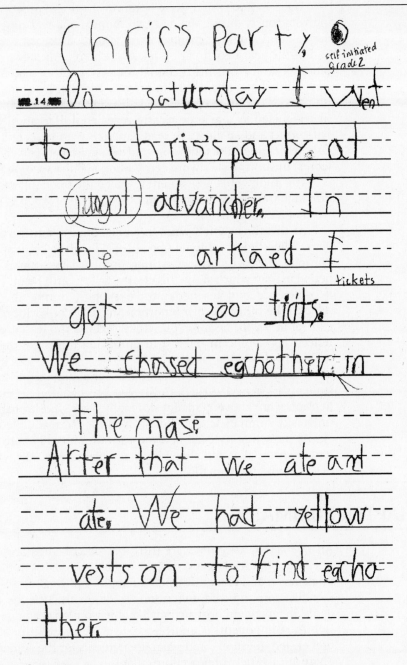

Chris's Party
On Saturday, I went to Chris's party at Jungle Adventure. In the arcade I got 200 tickets. We chased one another in the maze. After that we ate and ate. We had yellow vests on to find each other.

Then, in late winter, Kyle began to show real progress. He had been reading voraciously during the past two months and was now tackling much more difficult and lengthy "chapter books" (*Ralph R. Mouse,* by Beverly Cleary). The end-of-the year Benchmark Book Assessment indicated that Kyle's word recognition accuracy was instructional for easy grade 3 material, that his ability to stay with a longer book had improved, and that his comprehension was flourishing with the more complicated ideas in these new books. The miscue analysis conducted at that time clearly revealed a dramatically increased ability to self-correct and an ability to read materials without benefit of picture cues. The only remaining difficulties in word recognition involved longer, multisyllabic words. In short, Kyle's word recognition abilities were reaching independence.

The Bookwords Assessment revealed the same increasing abilities to recognize high frequency words at sight. At the end of grade 2, Kyle missed only one word of 227 Bookwords.

At this time, Kyle's writing, while conceptually very interesting, had not yet reached the transitional stage of spelling development. In Kyle's Diagnostic Portfolio are two pieces of writing produced by Kyle in the same two-week period in May which show this clearly. Kyle's earth poem (9.23a) is the result of a conference and teacher-editorial support during the writing stage. Kyle selected the other piece, a report on snakes to be included in his portfolio (see excerpt in 9.23b) because, he writes, "its has the leased words wrong." It also reflects his significant interest in nonfiction topics and his willingness to stick with difficult writing tasks.

At the end of the year, Kyle's teacher administered an IRI, required for all students (Spache 1981). Both his word recognition accuracy and his comprehension were above grade level. Finally, Kyle's performance at the end of the university summer school clinic was evaluated using the QRI-II. These results clearly show that Kyle has become a strong, and still improving, reader who can handle material at and above his grade placements. His written language abilities are more problematic.

CHAPTER SUMMARY

An *Informal Reading Inventory* (IRI) was described as an individually administered informal reading test designed to place students in materials at the appropriate levels and to identify their strengths and weaknesses in the areas of word identification and comprehension. Traditionally, IRIs are used to identify students' independent, instructional, and frustration reading levels.

The components of an IRI include graded word lists, graded passages, comprehension questions, and separate materials for the student and the examiner. There are a variety of procedures that can be used for administering and scoring an IRI, and different procedures produce different test results. Similarly, the criteria used for interpreting students' placement levels can have a significant effect on the results of the IRI.

The first half of the chapter concludes with some guidelines for the traditional use of IRIs for placement purposes. These include looking for selections that correspond to regularly used instructional materials; evaluating the passage dependency of the comprehension questions; and determining administration and scoring procedures, and placement criteria, together and within the context of the purpose for using the IRI.

The second half of the chapter describes additional tools and strategies, some of which may be used to adapt IRI administration. The techniques described in this section include:

1. Procedures for evaluating a reader's comprehension using retellings.
2. Procedures for analyzing readers' oral reading miscues to determine the language cue systems (i.e., graphophonic, syntactic, and semantic) they are using as they process a particular text.
3. A fluency scale designed to identify the extent to which a reader organizes the words in sentences in a manner that preserves the author's syntax and signals the relations among word meanings.
4. Informal, but structured, tools for evaluating sight word and phonics knowledge.
5. Procedures for using rubrics to evaluate student writing.
6. Strategies for using IRI-like procedures to create study inventories and for creating benchmark books to evaluate students' studying and also their word identification and comprehension skills.

IRIs and IRI-like procedures are potentially high-utility techniques for both classroom teachers and clinical personnel. For placement purposes, it is important that anyone using IRIs understands the issues associated with the representativeness of the reading selections to the materials in which a student is being placed. Although some might argue that IRIs should not be used for placement purposes, in reality there is no one measure that can serve this purpose adequately. The key to successful placement, both in the classroom and in the clinic, is the use of multiple indicators of performance on materials comparable to those in which the student is to be placed.

For the purpose of evaluating reader strengths and weaknesses, the issues of IRI usage differ somewhat between the classroom and the clinic. Classroom teachers obviously do not have the time to administer a traditional IRI individually to each student in their class. Even if they did, it is not clear that this would be entirely appropriate or necessary. However, using classroom materials and IRI-like techniques (as in benchmark books) can create the sort of structured assessment that can be useful to others.

In contrast to classroom teachers, specialists and clinical personnel often do not have the amount of regular contact with individual students necessary to successfully implement the classroom-based strategies described in Chapter 8. However, the interactive nature of the QRI-II makes it an excellent alternative for clinicians and resource personnel. The QRI-II also fits well with the purposes for which resource personnel are likely to find IRI-like procedures most useful. Whereas classroom teachers are likely to find procedures for ongoing assessment and instructional decision making most useful, clinical personnel and specialists are most likely to find these procedures useful for making programmatic curricular and instructional decisions for a given student.

Resource personnel must be particularly sensitive to the potential abuses of IRIs, given the limited amount of time that they are likely to come in contact with individual students. In particular, it may be difficult to predict a student's performance in the classroom from a small sample derived from administering just one IRI. However, in the hands of a skilled specialist, IRIs can provide a great deal of valuable information about the reader within a relatively short time period.

ANNOTATED BIBLIOGRAPHY OF IRIS

Burns, P. C., and B. D. Roe 1989. *Informal reading inventory* (3rd ed.). Boston: Houghton Mifflin. Grades 1–12. Two graded word lists and four sets of graded passages per grade level (preprimer-grade 12). Eight questions at preprimer to grade 2 levels, and ten at the other grade levels.

Ekwall, E. E., and J. L. Shanker 1993. *Ekwall/Shanker reading inventory* (3rd ed.). Boston: Allyn & Bacon. Grades 1–9. Each of four forms consists of eleven graded word lists (preprimer-grade 9). Five comprehension questions at the preprimer level and 10 at the other grade levels. Also contains tests of letter knowledge, basic sight words, the San Diego Quick Assessment (graded word list) and the El Paso Phonics Survey, as well as tests of phonics and structural analysis in context.

Johns, J. J. 1988. *Basic reading inventory* (4th ed.). Dubuque, IA: Kendall/Hunt. Grades 1–8. Each of three forms consists of ten graded twenty-word lists (preprimer-grade 8). Four comprehension questions at preprimer level; ten at other grade levels.

Silvaroli, N. J. 1994. *Classroom reading inventory* (7th ed.). Madison, WI: Wm. C. Brown & Benchmark. Grade 1-adult. There is a "Subskills" format (Form A, levels PP–8) and a "Literature" (Form B, levels 1–5) format for elementary level passages. There are also separate forms (Subskills format, levels 1–8) for use with junior high and with high school students-adults. Five comprehension questions on all forms but the Literature format, which uses a retelling to evaluate comprehension. No guidelines are provided for using the retelling rubric.

Spache, G. D. 1981. *Diagnostic reading scales.* Monterey, CA: CTB/McGraw-Hill. Criterion and norm-referenced battery for Grades 1–7. Three word lists (forty to fifty words each), two sets of eleven graded passages (preprimer-grade 7) with seven to eight comprehension questions each. Twelve supplementary decoding tests yielding grade equivalent scores.

Woods, M. L., and A. J. Moe 1989. *Analytical reading inventory* (4th ed.). Columbus, OH: Merrill. Grades 1–9. Each of three forms consists of seventeen graded twenty-word lists (primer-grade 6) and ten graded passages (primer-grade 9). Six comprehension questions at primer and grade 1; eight at the other grade levels. Two expository subtests consist of graded social studies and science passages (Grades 1–9).

CHAPTER 10

Formal Assessment

INTRODUCTION

Formal assessment devices typically are published tests that provide standardized methods of administration, scoring, and interpretation, and are often at the heart of the procedures used in traditional diagnoses of reading and writing problems. That these types of measures have not been considered until more than halfway through this text is intentional. The reason is simply that most formal tests do not reflect current definitions of reading and writing. Despite this fact, most professional educators are required to evaluate, use, and interpret both formal and informal assessment instruments. This chapter is intended to provide teachers and specialists with information about the properties of formal instruments that are important for intelligently evaluating the usefulness of available tests, in light of their purposes for assessment.

The first half of this chapter describes the aspects of standardized testing that are essential for evaluating formal tests including issues of type and purpose, important statistical concepts, validity, reliability, the characteristics of norming populations, test fairness, and the interpretation of test scores. The second half of this chapter provides detailed examples of formal reading and writing tests of different types, including survey, diagnostic, emergent literacy, and other areas related to reading and writing performance.

UNDERSTANDING FORMAL ASSESSMENT

In many districts, classroom teachers annually administer achievement batteries that survey several subject areas as a measure of student progress. When these tests are administered at the beginning of the year, they are often used to assist in placing students into groups or materials, and to screen for referral to special programs. When they are administered at the end of the school year, they may be used for decisions about promotion and retention and about placing students in summer programs or fall classes. Many districts also involve kindergarten and first-grade teachers in the administration of tests of readiness and emergent literacy for screening and program placement.

Teachers are also likely to encounter formal diagnostic and psychological tests when dealing with students who are participating in special programs, such as Title/Chapter 1, or receiving special education services. Classroom teachers are unlikely to actually administer these tests, but they are likely to receive reports describing the results of the administration of these types of tests by the reading specialist, special education personnel, or school psychologist. Because the classroom teacher often spends considerably more time with these students than the specialists, they shoulder a major portion of the responsibility for understanding the nature of these students' special needs and addressing them through their classroom activities. This is why it is extremely important that classroom teachers are knowledgeable about the tests being administered to their students, so they can follow up the results with informal measures in the classroom that will lead to appropriate classroom practice.

Specialists are more likely to have direct contact with diagnostic tests and those focusing on other language arts and related areas than are classroom teachers. Resource personnel are most likely to use these tests to demonstrate program effectiveness with individual students, to identify specific strengths and weaknesses as an aid to program planning, and as an aid in the identification of students with special needs. Even when the limitations of formal tests in these areas are recognized, there is still a need for their administration, because of legislative mandates and the need to have common measures that cut across schools, districts, and states. This makes it that much more important that the individuals administering and interpreting these tests have a clear understanding of what they can and cannot tell us.

Concerns

Important information can be obtained from formal tests of reading, writing, and related areas. Many of the most serious problems with formal testing involve test abuse, that is, people using test information inappropriately. It is absolutely essential that both teachers and resource personnel be critical consumers of formal tests to ensure that they are used properly.

It is our belief that instructional decisions should never be made solely on the basis of formal assessment instruments. It is absolutely essential that formal tests be followed up with informal measures that are more reflective of classroom demands before decisions are made about placement or about instructional programs.

The public appetite for numerical answers to literacy questions has been fed by the educational community. Classroom teachers and clinic personnel are often caught in the middle, forced to teach content they do not believe is useful so that students can perform well on standardized tests. We need to help the public understand both the uses and limitations of test information. In particular, educators need to be especially alert to the types of information *not* available from traditional standardized tests, especially information about students' abilities to read and write the different types of complex texts that are important in today's society.

Much of what we know to be important in reading and writing processes is not reflected in formal assessment devices. We know that reading and writing are holistic, constructive processes that vary as a function of the interaction among learner, text, and contextual factors (see Chapter 1). However, most existing formal instruments treat reading and writing as aggregates of isolated skills. As noted in *Becoming a Nation of Readers* (Anderson et al. 1985):

> If schools are to be held accountable for performance for reading test scores, the tests must be broad-gauged measures that reflect the ultimate goals of instruction as closely as possible. Otherwise, the energies of teachers and students may be misdirected. They may concentrate on peripheral skills that are easily tested and readily learned. Holding a reading teacher accountable for scores on a test of, say, dividing words into syllables is like holding a basketball coach accountable for the percentage of shots players make during the pre-game warm up. (100)

Most existing formal reading and writing assessments also imply that reading and writing are static processes—that students can be evaluated under one set of conditions and that this performance will be representative of their performance under all conditions. For example, formal tests evaluate students on passages that are much shorter than those students are expected to read in their classroom texts, and on tasks that do not represent authentic writing activities. It is then assumed that the results will generalize to reading and writing both within and outside the classroom. These tests do not take into account differences in genre or the purposes for the reading and writing activities. Neither do they consider how students' reading and writing performance is affected by their background knowledge or their attitudes and motivation toward reading and writing. Teachers need to be aware of these limitations and take them into account in interpreting the results of these tests.

The widespread use of formal reading and writing tests makes it important to understand a number of different aspects of standardized testing in order to become a critical consumer of these types of assessment devices. The information provided in this section of the chapter provides the basis for guidelines for test evaluation that are discussed in the second section of the chapter.

General Test Characteristics

Test selection and evaluation begin with an understanding of the purpose for which a test is being given. Information relative to a particular test must always be examined in relation to the purpose(s) for which it is being used.

Identifying the title, author, publisher, and date of publication reveal information about a test's quality and the appropriateness of its purpose and content for different students or testing situations. For example, a test with the word *survey* in the title suggests that the test will provide general information about a student's achievement, rather than specific information about strengths and weaknesses. Similarly, the reputation of the test author and/or publisher in reading, writing, or testing may suggest something about both the content and quality of the test. A recent date of publication or revision increases the likelihood that the test reflects the most recent theory and research, and that any norms used for scoring are current.

Other general characteristics of a formal test that are important for determining its appropriateness for specific students or testing situations include the level of difficulty and type of administration. Some tests are intended for a wide range of age, grade, and ability levels, while others are intended only for restricted levels. Still others have different forms for different levels. Therefore, it is important to determine that a test is appropriate for the age, grade, and ability of the student with whom it will be used.

The appropriateness of the test administration for specific students and purposes depends on factors such as whether the test is group or individually administered, and whether it is timed or untimed. Group tests are efficient to administer, but tend to provide more general information than individual tests and do not allow for the variety of response formats (for example, oral reading, extended writing activities) that are allowed by individual tests. Individual tests require significantly more time to administer than group tests, but tend to provide more specific information about the student. Timed or speed tests determine what a student can do under specified time constraints, whereas untimed or power tests evaluate a student's performance without any time constraints.

The two basic types of test interpretations we discuss in this chapter are norm-referenced and criterion-referenced. Criterion-referenced interpretations are designed primarily to provide information that relates easily and meaningfully to specific objectives and specific standards of performance that are often determined independently of the measurement process. The emphasis is on describing the level of performance of individuals and groups on the behavior a test is measuring.

Norm-referenced interpretations examine a given student's performance in relation to the performance of a representative group. The emphasis in norm-referenced testing is on the individual's relative standing, rather than on absolute mastery of content (Salvia and Ysseldyke 1988). Although the term *standardized* is often used synonymously with tests emphasizing norm-referenced interpretations, tests that emphasize criterion-referenced interpretations can be, and often are, standardized. *Standardized* means only that all students complete the same tasks under uniform directions (Swanson and Watson 1982).

The difficulty of test items and the manner in which items are selected also differ between tests, emphasizing norm- as opposed to criterion-referenced interpretations. Test items that produce a wide range of scores and discriminate well between high-scoring and low-scoring individuals are desirable for norm-referenced interpretations that determine an individual's relative position in comparison to a group of his or her peers. Therefore, the best norm-referenced items are those which 40 to 60 percent of the students answer correctly, because they produce the greatest variance in test scores. In well-constructed tests using norm-referenced interpretations, half of the population will score above the average, and half will always fall below the average.

According to Swanson and Watson (1982), there is a shift in emphasis between criterion- and norm-referenced interpretations from items that best measure performance in a domain of knowledge to items that provide the greatest diversity in scores. They further note Popham's (1978) conclusion that the procedures used to construct tests emphasizing norm-referenced interpretations are likely to result in the exclusion of items that measure the major instructional emphases of the schools.

Important Statistical Concepts

Tests use statistics to describe and summarize data. As a result, there are several statistical concepts that must be understood to evaluate the utility of formal tests for specific purposes. In this section we briefly summarize several major statistical concepts: normal distribution, measures of variation and centrality known as the standard deviation and the mean, and a measure of relatedness known as correlation.

Normal Distribution
One way of summarizing test data is to describe the distribution of test scores. The two characteristics of a distribution that are most important for the interpretation of educational tests are the mean and the standard deviation. The mean is the arithmetic average of the scores, and provides a central value or representative score to characterize the performance of the entire group. The standard deviation is a unit of measurement based on the degree to which the scores deviate from the mean. A large, standard deviation indicates greater spread around the mean than a smaller one. Test scores can be referred to in terms of the number of standard deviations they are above (+) or below (–) the mean, depending on whether the score is greater than or less than the mean.

A normal distribution of the behaviors or psychological characteristics we are interested in observing means that scores are distributed symmetrically around the mean. The normal curve is symmetrical and bell-shaped and has many useful mathematical properties. One of the most useful for test interpretation is that when it is divided into standard deviation units, each unit under the curve contains a fixed percentage of cases (see Figure 10.1). This means that in any normal distribution:

1. approximately 68 percent of the population will be between +1 and –1 standard deviations from the mean;
2. approximately 95 percent of the population will fall between +2 and –2 standard deviations from the mean; and
3. approximately 99.7 percent of the population will fall between +3 and –3 standard deviations from the mean.

FIGURE 10.1
*Normal
Distribution
and Sample
Test Scores*

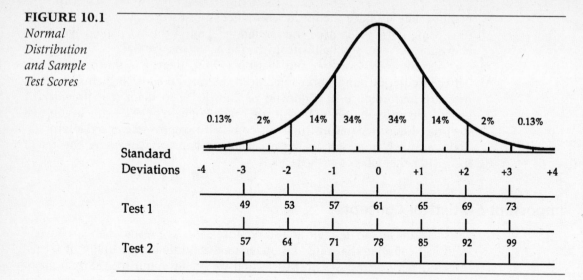

Raw scores from two different tests have been placed beneath the row marking the standard deviations in Figure 10.1 to illustrate how knowing the standard deviation and the mean contribute to the understanding of relative position within a group. Test 1 has a mean of 61 and a standard deviation of 4. Test 2 has a mean of 78 and a standard deviation of 7. Therefore, a score of 65 is equivalent to +1 standard deviation on Test 1 and a score of 85 is equivalent to +1 standard deviation on Test 2. Knowing the mean and standard deviation permits us to convert raw scores to a common scale that has equal units and that can be interpreted readily in terms of the normal curve.

Salvia and Ysseldyke (1988) use the example of intelligence tests to present another illustration of why it is important to understand the mean and standard deviation in interpreting test scores. The Stanford-Binet Intelligence Scale, a well-known intelligence test, has a mean of 100 and a standard deviation of 16. Assuming the scores on this test are normally distributed, approximately 68 percent of the school population would be expected to fall within +1 or −1 standard deviation of the mean, which translates into IQ scores between 84 and 116. Another well-known intelligence test, the Slosson Intelligence Test, has a mean of 100 and a standard deviation of approximately 24. If scores on the Slosson are normally distributed, approximately 68 percent of the school population would be expected to have IQ scores between 76 and 124.

The fact that the meaning of a score depends, in part, on the mean and the standard deviation of the distribution is often overlooked, according to Salvia and Ysseldyke (1988). Specifically, they cite the example of states that use an absolute score in the school code for the placement and retention of mentally retarded children in special educational programs; for example, a score of 75

(+5 or –5) for determining eligibility for placement. On the Stanford-Binet, a score of 80 is more than one standard deviation below the mean; on the Slosson, a score of 80 is within 1 standard deviation of the mean. If a single absolute score is specified, different levels of eligibility for special education classes could be unintentionally built into the school code.

Correlation

Another statistical concept that is important in the interpretation of test data is correlation. While the mean and standard deviation describe a single distribution of scores, correlations describe the degree of association between two or more sets of scores. This measure is important in describing the relationship of test scores to other variables of interest and is critical to the evaluation of reliability and validity.

The strength of the correlation is expressed using a *correlation coefficient.* The values of correlation coefficients range from +1.00 to .00 to –1.00. A positive correlation (+) indicates that high scores on one variable are associated with high scores on the other variable. A negative correlation (–) indicates that high scores on one variable are associated with low scores on the other variable. A correlation coefficient of .00 between two variables means that there is no relationship between the variables; the variables are independent, changes in one variable are not related to changes in the other variable. A correlation coefficient of either +1.00 or –1.00 indicates a perfect relationship between two variables (Salvia and Ysseldyke 1988).

Measures of correlation provide useful information about the various components of tests and can also be used as an index of test validity and reliability (see below). However, educators must use correlational information sensibly, which means, in part, understanding that correlation is not the same as causation. Correlation is a necessary but insufficient condition for determining causality. The mere presence of a correlation between two variables does not imply that one causes the other. An extreme example of this principle is the likelihood that there is a positive correlation between the contents of a family's garbage can and their children's early reading success. It is well known that early success in reading is correlated with socioeconomic status, which will likely also result in differences in the contents of one's garbage can. This does not, however, mean that a certain type of trash causes success or failure in reading.

Salvia and Ysseldyke (1988) point out that "for any correlation between two variables (A and B), three causal interpretations are possible: A causes B; B causes A; or a third variable, C, causes both A and B" (80). Correlational data do not tell us which of these three possible interpretations are true; therefore, we must never draw causal conclusions from such data. So, for example, the simple fact that there is a positive correlation between reading achievement and factors such as balance-beam walking or alphabet knowledge does not, by itself, mean that these factors cause skilled reading.

Validity

Validity is the most important concern in evaluating formal tests according to the 1985 *Standards for Educational and Psychological Testing* (1985 Standards), which was jointly prepared by the American Educational Research Association (AERA), the American Psychological Association (APA), and the National Council on Measurement in Education (NCME). The 1985 *Standards* represent the most current consensus among measurement experts on the topic of validity; however, it should be noted that these standards were under revision at the time of this writing. According to the 1985 *Standards*, the concept of validity is defined as "the appropriateness, meaningfulness, and usefulness of specific inferences made from test scores" (AERA, APA, and NCME 1985, 9).

Given the 1985 *Standards'* definition of validity, it is inappropriate to talk about the validity of a test, rather, validity refers to a particular inference, interpretation, or action based on a test score. Validity is related to the claims made by users of the test information. The valid use of tests is the responsibility of both the test author and the test user. A major factor in the valid use of tests is the extent to which there is a match between the test's and the test user's conceptualization of the domain being measured. We agree with Salvia and Ysseldyke (1988):

> Validity is the only technical characteristic of a test in which we are interested. All other technical considerations, such as reliability, are subsumed under the issue of validity and are separated to simplify the issue of validity ... Adequate norms, reliability, and lack of bias are all necessary conditions for validity. None—separately or in total—is sufficient to guarantee validity. (142)

Tests may be used and interpreted in a variety of ways, and evidence must be collected to support each interpretation and use. For example, standardized achievement tests are used both to provide accountability information to the public about schools and districts and to place students in particular classes and programs. Each of these purposes implies a different interpretation and use of test scores, which must be validated by accumulating appropriate evidence.

The 1985 *Standards* indicate that tests should include evidence of validity that specifies what inferences can be made reasonably. In addition, this document argues that test consumers should be warned against making specific kinds of inferences if the evidence that these inferences are warranted is not available. Again, it is the range and accuracy of possible inferences to other real-world phenomena (other tests, classroom performance, future success, etc.) that constitute evidence for the validity of a particular interpretation or use of a test score.

Content-, Criterion-, and Construct-Related Evidence of Validity
The following sections describe the three categories of evidence the 1985 *Standards* indicate should be considered in the process of test validation: content-, criterion-, and construct-related evidence of validity. These three categories of evidence are often treated separately, giving the false impression that they are

alternatives or options. Rather, they are intended as aspects of a unified view of validity which integrates evidence across categories.

Content-related evidence of validity.   Content-related evidence of validity "demonstrates the degree to which the sample of items, tasks, or questions on a test are representative of some defined universe or domain of content" (AERA, APA, and NCME 1985, 10). For example, the universe or domain of content may be an academic curriculum, a description of the behaviors required to perform a job, and a description of the psychological or educational characteristic being evaluated. The evidence usually involves professional judgments of the fit between the test items and the description of the domain.

Content validation involves a careful examination of the content of a test in relation to the universe or domain of content being assessed. This is often done by the test developer and described in the test manual. Walsh and Betz (1990) indicate that the most common type of evidence presented in support of content validity is the judgment of those who construct the test, or of other experts familiar with the domain of interest. Given that this type of evidence is usually somewhat subjective, they assert that it should be accompanied by a detailed definition of the domain being measured and a clear specification of the methods used to select items.

The test user can also gather content-related evidence of validity. Salvia and Ysseldyke (1988) identify three considerations that should be addressed in gathering content-related evidence of validity. The first deals with the appropriateness of the types of items included on the test. To examine this factor we must ask, "Is this an appropriate test question?" and "Does this test item really measure the domain?" So, for example, one should question the validity of the items on reading and writing tests that require the use of skills that are not used outside the testing situation in real reading and writing contexts, or the use of skills that are not age-appropriate.

The second consideration is the completeness of the item sample. For example, one would reasonably expect a test of writing achievement to include a far broader sample than a multiple-choice test of grammar and spelling. The third area concerns the representativeness of the task demands imposed by the format of the items. For example, reading skills can be evaluated in a variety of ways, including multiple-choice items, open-ended questions, retellings, oral reading samples, and so forth, and multiple formats may be required to adequately test the domain.

As models of literacy have changed, the match between the definitions of reading and writing and the content and methodology of standardized tests has become weaker (Wixson, Peters, Weber, and Roeber 1987). Indeed, the degree of mismatch between theory, instruction, and assessment has become quite alarming. Valencia and Pearson (1987) provide a summary of some of the ways in which information about the reading process is poorly aligned with testing (see Figure 10.2).

There is a clear threat to validity when test content is a poor reflection of the reading and writing processes as we understand them. Literacy professionals

FIGURE 10.2

Issues in Reading Assessment

A Set of Contrasts Between New Views of Reading and Current Practices in Assessing Reading

New views of the reading process tell us that . . .	Yet when we assess reading comprehension, we . . .
Prior knowledge is an important determinant of reading comprehension.	Mask any relationship between prior knowledge and reading comprehension by using lots of short passages on lots of topics.
A complete story or text has sturctural and topical integrity.	Use short texts that seldom approximate the structural and topical integrity of an authentic text.
Inference is an essential part of the process of comprehending units as small as sentences.	Rely on literal comprehension test items.
The diversity in prior knowledge across individuals as well as the varied causal relations in human experiences invite many possible inferences to fit a text or question.	Use multiple choice items with only one correct answer, even when many of the responses might, under certain conditions, be plausible.
The ability to vary reading strategies to fit the text and the situation is one hallmark of an expert reader.	Seldom assess how and when students vary the strategies they use during normal reading, studying, or when the going gets tough.
The ability to synthesize information from various parts of the text and different texts is a hallmark of an expert reader.	Rarely go beyond finding the main idea of a paragraph or passage.
The ability to ask good questions of text, as well as to answer them, is a hallmark of an expert reader.	Seldom ask students to create or select questions about a selection they may have just read.
All aspects of a reader's experience, including habits that arise from school and home, influence reading comprehension.	Rarely view information on reading habits and attitudes as being as important as information about performance.
Reading involves the orchestration of many skills that complement one another in a variety of ways.	Use tests that fragment reading into isolated skills and report performance on each.
Skilled readers are fluent; their word identification is sufficiently automatic to allow most cognitive resources to be used for comprehension.	Rarely consider fluency as an index of skilled reading.
Learning from text involves the restructuring, application, and flexible use of knowledge in new situations.	Often ask readers to respond to the text's declarative knowledge rather than to apply it to near and far transfer tasks.

From "Reading Assessment: Time for a Change" by S. Valencia and P. D. Pearson. *The Reading Teacher,* April 1987, p. 731. Reprinted with permission of S. Valencia and the International Reading Association.

must understand these issues and carefully evaluate the content-related evidence of validity provided by test developers. Too many of the existing standardized tests of reading, writing, and language arts distort the process by testing nothing more than subskills, or by requiring students to answer only multiple-choice questions. Instructional interventions aimed at improving the reading and writing abilities of poor readers must be evaluated using tests that do not trivialize the process.

Criterion-related evidence of validity. Criterion-related evidence of validity "demonstrates that test scores are systematically related to one or more outcome criteria" (AERA, APA, and NCME 1985, 11). The criterion refers to the behavior or performance of primary interest for which test scores are intended to be used as a predictor. Consider the example of college admissions tests, which are used to predict success in college as measured by first-year grade-point average. Success in college is the behavior of interest, and the strength of the relationship between scores on admissions tests and success in college is important evidence of the validity of the test.

There are two types of criterion-related evidence of validity—concurrent and predictive. Concurrent evidence refers to the relation between a person's score and an immediate criterion. Salvia and Ysseldyke (1988) suggest, for example, that if we were developing a test of achievement, the basic question would be: "How do we know that our new test really measures achievement?" To establish concurrent evidence of validity for this new achievement test, we would first have to find a valid criterion measure of achievement. Since there are no perfect measures of achievement, we can use other achievement tests that are presumed to be valid and/or teacher judgments of achievement. If our new test presents concurrent evidence of validity and elicits test scores corresponding closely to teacher judgments and scores from other achievement tests presumed to be valid, we can conclude that our new test is a valid measure of achievement.

The second type of criterion-related evidence is predictive. Predictive evidence refers to the relation between a person's score and performance on some measure at a later time. It is used when there is interest in how present status on the test predicts future status on the criterion measure. If we were developing a test to determine reading placement, for example, we would ask, "Does knowledge of a student's score on our reading placement test allow an accurate estimation of the student's ability to perform successfully in certain materials?" Successful placement in reading materials can be evaluated by another assessment (presumed valid) or by teacher judgments. If our placement test has adequate content-related evidence of validity and corresponds closely with either subsequent teacher judgments of appropriateness of placement or validly assessed ability to read certain materials, we can conclude that reading placement is a valid use of our test.

The nature of the criterion is extremely important in gathering both concurrent and predictive evidence of validity. In effect, the value of the test is being established by comparing it to another measure. To do this, the other measure must be appropriately effective or representative of the behavior under investigation. Therefore, the criterion measure clearly must be valid itself (Salvia and Ysseldyke 1988). The 1985 *Standards* urge test developers to provide thorough, accurate descriptions of the criterion measures and a rationale for using them. Finally, test developers and publishers are expected to provide complete, accurate statistical information regarding the degree of relationship between the target test and the criterion measure(s).

Construct-related evidence of validity. Construct-related evidence of validity is more complicated to describe, because it can encompass a variety of types of evidence (P. Moss 1994). The 1985 *Standards* indicate that construct-related evidence of validity "focuses on the test scores as a measure of the psychological characteristic of interest" (AERA, APA, and NCME 1985, 9). Examples of constructs provided in the 1985 *Standards* include reasoning ability, reading comprehension, and endurance. The process of construct validation is characterized as follows:

> The construct of interest for a particular test should be embedded in a conceptual framework, no matter how imperfect that framework may be. The conceptual framework specifies the meaning of the construct, distinguishes it from other constructs, and indicates how measures of the construct should relate to other variables. The process of compiling construct-related evidence for test validity starts with test development and continues until the pattern of empirical relationships between test scores and other variables clearly indicate the meaning of the test score (AERA, APA, and NCME 1985, 9–10).

The 1985 *Standards* then cite examples of the many different kinds of evidence that can support construct validation. These include relationships among responses to test items, the relationship of test scores to other measures of the same and different constructs and to other nontest variables, questioning test takers about the strategies they used in responding, questioning judges of constructed responses about their reasons for their ratings, and collecting content- and criterion-related evidence. In each case, the evidence is evaluated in terms of its consistency with the proposed interpretation.

Most theorists now argue that all validity research should be conducted within a construct validity framework (P. Moss 1994). This means that validity research requires an explicit conceptual framework, testable hypotheses deduced from it, and multiple lines of relevant evidence to test the hypotheses.

> Construct validity begins with descriptions of the purpose for which the assessment is being developed and one or more constructs appropriate to the purpose. The construct is the proposed interpretation or meaning for the test score (for example, reading comprehension) and the purpose is the use to which it will be put, such as certification for high school graduation. The construct description should locate the construct in a conceptual framework, no matter how informal, that defines the construct and distinguishes it from other constructs. The description of the purpose should specify the desired outcomes of test use, the population of persons for whom the test is intended, and the situations in which the test will be used. Hypotheses to be tested in subsequent studies concern the fit between the

descriptions of construct and purpose and the evidence collected. Construct validation rarely results in a summative decision about whether or not a given interpretation is justified. More typically, the outcomes of a given study or line of research
result in the modification of the test, the construct, the conceptual framework surrounding the construct, or all three. Thus, construct validity is as much an aspect
of test development as it is of test evaluation. (P. Moss 1994, 1104)

In evaluating construct-related evidence of validity, both convergent and
discriminant evidence should be considered (P. Moss 1994). Convergent evidence indicates that test scores are related to other measures of the same construct and to other variables that they should relate to as predicted by the
conceptual framework. Discriminant evidence indicates that test scores are not
unduly related to measures of other, distinct constructs. For example, within
some conceptual frameworks, scores on a multiple-choice test of reading comprehension may be expected to be more "convergent" with other measures of
reading comprehension, perhaps using other passages; conversely, test scores
may be expected to relate less closely to measures of the specific subject matter
knowledge reflected in the passages on the text.

Construct validation is most efficiently guided by the testing of rival
hypotheses which suggest alternative explanations or meanings for the test
score (P. Moss 1994). Prominent rival hypotheses or threats to construct validity
include construct underrepresentation and irrelevant test variance (Messick,
1989). Construct underrepresentation refers to a test that is too narrow in that
it fails to capture important aspects of the construct. Irrelevant test variance
refers to a test that is too broad in that it requires capabilities irrelevant or extraneous to the proposed construct. Continuing with the above example, a potential rival hypothesis to the claim that a test measures reading comprehension is
that it reflects "test irrelevant variance" because it depends unduly on specific
subject matter knowledge.

The utility and value of tests rely on evidence of their validity. No matter
what else is true, if the behavior or performance is not characteristic of the student in other related settings/tasks, then the scores are misleading.

Reliability

Reliability is another major consideration in evaluating a test. Reliability refers to
the consistency or stability of test scores and involves the extent to which some
attribute has been measured in a systematic and therefore repeatable way. When
we administer a test, we need to be confident that those taking the test would
earn similar scores if tested again with the same instrument. Test results would
have little meaning if they fluctuated wildly from one occasion to the next. We
would not administer a test if we knew that the student's score might be 15 or 20
points higher or lower if retested. For a test to be useful, it must be reliable.

The 1985 *Standards* indicate that "reliability refers to the degree to which test
scores are free from errors of measurement" (AERA, APA, and NCME 1985, 19).
Differences between scores from one administration to another or from one form
to another may be attributable to errors of measurement. These differences are

not attributable to errors of measurement if factors such as maturation or instructional intervention have made these differences meaningful or if inconsistency of response is a characteristic of the construct being measured. Measurement errors reduce the reliability and, as a result, the generalizability, of a test score.

The importance of a particular source of error depends on the specific use of the test. According to the 1985 *Standards*:

> Fundamental to the proper evaluation of a test are the identification of major sources of measurement error, the size of the errors resulting from these sources, the indication of the degree of reliability to be expected between pairs of scores under particular circumstances, and the generalizability of results across items, forms, raters, administrations, and other measurement facets (AERA, APA, and NCME 1985, 19).

The reliability of a test is usually expressed as a correlation coefficient (reliability coefficient) which provides an estimate of how much error there is in the test. Different reliability coefficients can be based on various types of evidence, and each type of evidence suggests a different meaning. It is essential that the method used to estimate reliability takes into account the sources of error of greatest concern for a particular use and interpretation, for example, random response variability, changes in the individuals taking the tests, differences in the content of the forms, and differences in administration, and so forth. Not all sources of error are expected to be relevant for any one test.

Estimates of the reliability of a test should consider not only the relevant sources of error, but also the types of decisions anticipated to be based on the test scores and on their expected levels of aggregation, that is, individual versus groups. Test developers and publishers have primary responsibility for obtaining and reporting evidence concerning reliability and errors of measurement related to the intended uses. Although the test users usually do not conduct separate reliability studies, they do have a responsibility to determine that the available information is relevant to their intended uses and interpretations.

Reliability Measures

There are several methods of estimating a reliability coefficient, depending on the intended uses and interpretations of the test. The two we describe here are test-retest and alternate form reliability. Test publishers should report reliability estimates and the methods used to obtain them. Test users should look for reliability information in test manuals in order to evaluate the adequacy of the test for a particular purpose.

Test-retest.   Test-retest reliability measures the stability of tests scores over time. It assesses the degree to which test scores are similar after a time delay versus the degree to which they change or fluctuate with repeated testing (Walsh and Betz 1990). If test scores are relatively stable across repeated testings, there is some basis for believing that the test is measuring something in a consistent manner. The procedures for establishing test-retest reliability usually involve two administrations of the same test to the same individuals, with a time interval of at least one week between the administrations. The test-retest reliability coefficient is the correlation between the sets of scores obtained at the two administrations of the test.

Alternate form.   Alternate form reliability assesses the degree to which two different forms of the same test yield similar or consistent results. If scores on one form of a test are similar to scores on an alternate form of the same test, we have increased confidence that the test forms are measuring some common domain in a relatively consistent manner (Walsh and Betz 1990). The procedures for establishing alternate form reliability involve developing two equivalent forms of the same test, and then administering both forms to a single sample of students. The reliability coefficient is the correlation between the scores obtained on the two forms of the test.

It is important to keep in mind that equivalent or parallel forms of a test are never perfectly correlated or reliable. Errors of measurement occur because the two tests differ somewhat in item sampling. This can be an important factor in interpreting pre- and post-test scores using alternate forms of the same test. Slight increases or decreases in scores are more likely to reflect measurement error than real gains or losses in the area being tested.

Standard Error of Measurement

One of the primary reasons for obtaining a reliability coefficient is to be able to estimate the amount of error associated with an individual's obtained score (Salvia and Ysseldyke 1988). The standard error of measurement (SEM) permits the test user to do this. The SEM provides information about the certainty or confidence with which a test score can be interpreted. When the SEM is relatively large, the uncertainty is great. When the SEM is relatively small, the uncertainty is minimized.

The SEM can be used to suggest the distance between individuals' true scores, with all the sources of error removed, and their actual scores. An individual's true score actually may be either above or below the obtained score. Using the SEM, we can define a range, or confidence interval, within which we can be relatively certain the individual's true score lies. Several options are available, depending on how "confident" we wish to be.

Since the SEM is based on a normal distribution of scores, we can say that 68 percent of the time the individual's true score will fall within + or –1 SEM of his or her obtained score. Therefore, if an individual's obtained score is 60 and the SEM is 4, the person's true score is somewhere between 60 + or –4, or between 56 and 64. This means that an individual's score fluctuates within 4 points on either side of the true score 68 times out of 100. This also means that the obtained score is likely either to underestimate or overestimate the student's true score about 30 percent of the time. If we want a higher degree of confidence, we can expand the size of the interval. A 95 percent confidence band is represented by + or –2 SEM and provides the interval within which an individual's true score will lie 95 out of 100 times.

It is important to realize what the SEM means for the interpretation of test results. When we say that someone's raw score corresponds to a grade equivalent of 4.5 (see section on scores), it sounds very precise. But consider the SEM and the confidence intervals. If the SEM is .3, we are only 68 percent certain that the true score falls between 4.2 and 4.8 and 95 percent certain that it falls somewhere between 4.0 and 5.1—a range of over one year. A larger SEM would mean even larger intervals. Swanson and Watson (1982) offer a related example of a child who has scored 75 on an IQ test with an SEM of 5. A 68 percent confidence level represents an interval of 70 to 80 and a 95 percent confidence level represents an interval from 65 to 85. Even though the student's score was at a level typically labeled as mentally retarded, it is possible that the true score was in fact in the low-normal range.

Desired Standards

As Salvia and Ysseldyke (1988) indicate, no test can be valid unless it is reliable, and no score is interpretable unless it is reliable. Therefore, it is important for test authors and publishers to present sufficient information about test reliability for the test user to interpret test results accurately. Reliability information for each type of score should be reported for each age and grade.

In terms of the level of error that is acceptable, Salvia and Ysseldyke (1988) recommend three standards or cutoff points for reliability coefficients. If test scores are to be reported for groups rather than individuals and are to be used for general administrative purposes, a reliability coefficient above .60 is acceptable. If test scores are to be used to make decisions about individual students, the standard should be much higher. For important educational decisions, such as placing a student in a Chapter/Title 1 class, a reliability coefficient of .90 should be considered minimum. For more general purposes such as initial screening, a reliability of .80 is acceptable.

Test Interpretations

The raw score, or the number of points received on a test, is usually the basic score in tests emphasizing either norm- or criterion-referenced interpretations. These raw scores alone tell us very little, since we neither know how other individuals performed nor how many total points might be reasonable or possible on the test. As Gronlund (1985) notes, "we can provide meaning to a raw score either by converting it into a description of the specific tasks that the pupil can perform (criterion-referenced interpretation) or by converting it into some type of derived score that indicates the pupil's relative position in a clearly defined reference group (norm-referenced interpretation) (347). Each of these modes of interpreting test performance can be useful under some circumstances and occasionally both are reasonable.

Criterion-Referenced Interpretations

Criterion-referenced test interpretation permits us to describe an individual's test performance on some preestablished standard, or criterion. In this way, it is not necessary or even desirable to refer to the performance of others. Students' performance might be described in terms of the speed with which a task is performed, the precision with which a task is performed, or the percentage of items correct on some clearly defined set of learning tasks.

Although percentage correct scores are often used as the standard for judging whether a student has mastered each of the instructional objectives measured by a criterion-referenced test, there are many ways to report these scores. Swanson and Watson (1982) present five measures, or *metrics*, commonly accepted as appropriate for criterion-referenced interpretation, several of which are basically raw scores:

1. A rate metric simply refers to the time it takes to complete the specified task.
2. A sign metric indicates the mastery or nonmastery of the task.
3. An accuracy metric gives the proportion of times the examinee is successful.
4. A proportion metric specifies the portion or percent of the population of items in a domain on which the student performs.
5. A scaling metric describes the point along a continuum at which the student's performance occurs (55–56).

Gronlund (1985) points out that criterion-referenced interpretation of test results is most meaningful when the test has been designed to measure a specific set of clearly stated learning tasks. In addition, there is sufficient coverage to make it possible to describe test performance in terms of a student's mastery or nonmastery of each task. The value of criterion test results is enhanced when the domain being measured is delimited and clearly specified and the test items are selected on the basis of their relevance to the domain being measured. There should be a sufficient number of test items to make dependable judgments concerning the types of tasks a student can and cannot perform.

Performance on the items on tests emphasizing criterion-referenced interpretations can range in difficulty from 0 to 100 percent accuracy, depending on the nature of the specific learning tasks to be measured. If the learning tasks are easy, the test items should be easy. Little attempt is made to modify item difficulty, or to eliminate easy items from the test to obtain a range of test scores. On a test emphasizing criterion-referenced interpretations, we would expect all or nearly all students to obtain high scores when the instruction has been effective (Gronlund 1985).

Although standardized tests typically have been designed for norm-referenced interpretations, it is possible to apply criterion-referenced interpretations to the test results. This simply involves analyzing each student's test responses item by item and summarizing the results with descriptive statements. Some test publishers aid this type of interpretation by providing a list of objectives measured by the test, with each item keyed to the appropriate objective, and by arranging the items into homogeneous groups for easy analysis.

However, as Gronlund (1981) notes, "just because it is possible to make criterion-referenced interpretations of standardized survey tests does not mean that it is sensible to do so. Since these tests were designed for norm-referenced interpretation, they have built-in characteristics that are likely to make criterion-referenced interpretations inadequate" (369). Norm-referenced survey tests typically do not provide a satisfactory basis for describing the specific learning tasks that students can and cannot perform. However, if such criterion-referenced interpretations are attempted, the following factors should be taken into account:

1. Norm-referenced tests often contain a conglomerate of learning tasks with relatively few items representing each specific type of task. This makes it difficult to obtain dependable descriptions of the tasks a student can and cannot perform.
2. The easier items are often omitted from the test during construction to obtain maximum discrimination among individuals taking the test. This can severely limit the description of what low achievers can do.
3. Many norm-referenced tests use only recognition-type items that may or may not be a relevant measure of the objectives. This may distort any criterion-referenced interpretation of the results (Gronlund 1985, 1981).

Norm-Referenced Interpretation

Norm-referenced interpretations indicate how an individual's performance compares to that of others who have taken the same test. According to Gronlund (1985), the simplest type of comparison is to rank-order the raw scores from highest to lowest and to note where an individual's score falls. Noting whether a particular score is second from the top, about in the middle, or one of the lowest scores in relation to a particular reference group provides a meaningful report to both teachers and students. If a student's score is second from the top in a group of 10 or more, it is a relatively high score whether it represents 95 or 60 percent of the items correct. The fact that a test is relatively easy or difficult for the students does not alter the interpretation of test scores in terms of relative performance.

Although the simple ranking of raw scores may be useful for reporting the results of a classroom test, it is of limited value beyond the immediate situation. To obtain a more general framework for norm-referenced interpretation, raw scores are typically converted into some type of derived score based on norms. The concept of comparing one person's test score to those of other people is the basis for test norms, that is, the test scores of a representative sample of people. Test norms usually are obtained using a standardization sample representative of the people by whom the test is designed to be taken. Based on the responses of this standardization, or normative sample, raw scores obtained from any subsequent examinee can be converted into a measure of relative standing in comparison to the normative group.

There are two important points related to the fact that test scores are based on the performance of individuals in the normative sample. First, even the slightest variation of the administration procedures for norm-referenced tests from those used with the standardization sample will render the norms, and therefore the test scores, invalid.

The second point is that norms are only applicable to individuals of the same age and/or grade as the students in the normative sample, which can be a major problem when testing students with serious academic difficulties. If a test at the appropriate age/grade level is administered, the norms are of questionable value because the student is at the extreme end of the distribution (not to mention the student's frustration at taking a test that is far too difficult). However, if a test designed for younger or lower-grade students is administered, the norms are inappropriate because older students were not included in the normative sample. To get around this problem, some tests provide norms for out-of-level testing that make it possible to obtain valid scores for students on tests that approximate their skill level more closely than their age/grade level.

According to Salvia and Ysseldyke (1988), norms are important because the normative sample is used to obtain the various statistics on which the final selection of test items is based, and an individual's performance is evaluated in terms of the performance of the individuals in the normative sample.

> Even if a test is reliable and otherwise valid, test scores may be misleading if the norms are inadequate. The adequacy of a test's norms depends on three factors: the representativeness of the norm sample, the number of cases in the norm sample, and the relevance of the norms in terms of the purpose of testing. (Salvia and Ysseldyke 1988, 114)

An evaluation of representativeness requires particular attention to demographic variables because of their theoretical and/or empirical relationship to what the test is intended to measure. According to Salvia and Ysseldyke (1988), representativeness hinges on two questions: Does the norm sample contain individuals with the same characteristics as the population that the norms are intended to represent? and, Are the various kinds of people present in the sample in the same proportion as they are in the population represented by the norms? Among the factors that must be considered in answering these two questions are the age, grade, sex, acculturation of parents (socioeconomic status and education), geographic factors, race, and intelligence of the individuals in the norm sample in relation to the characteristics of the population for whom the test is designed.

Another often overlooked consideration in assuring representativeness is the date the norms were collected (Salvia and Ysseldyke 1988). Ours is an age of rapidly expanding knowledge and rapidly expanding communication of knowledge. Children of today know more than the children of the 1930s or the 1940s, and probably less than the children of tomorrow. "For a norm sample to be representative it must be current" (Salvia and Ysseldyke 1988, 102). Finally, tests used to identify children with particular problems should include children with such problems in their standardization sample.

According to Salvia and Ysseldyke (1988), the number of subjects in a norm sample is important for several reasons. First, the sample should be large enough to guarantee stability. If the size of the sample is small, the norms will be undependable because another group might produce significantly different results. The larger the sample, the more stable the norms. Second, the sample should be large enough so that infrequent elements in the population can be represented. Third, the sample should be large enough to produce a full range of scores. As a rule of thumb, the norm sample should contain a minimum of 100 subjects per age or grade, although in practice the sample should have more than 100 cases.

The third factor related to the adequacy of norms is the extent to which individuals in the norm sample can provide relevant comparisons in terms of the purpose for which the test was administered (Salvia and Ysseldyke 1988). For some purposes national norms are the most appropriate, whereas in other circumstances norms developed on a particular portion of the population may be more meaningful.

A final note concerns the ethical issues associated with reporting and using tests with inadequate norms. If the test publisher or author recognizes that the test norms are inadequate, the test user should be explicitly cautioned (AERA, APA, and NCME 1985). "The inadequacies do not, however, disappear on the including of a cautionary note; the test is still inadequate" (Salvia and Ysseldyke 1988, 107). Inadequate norms can lead to serious misinterpretation of test results.

Test Scores

The following are descriptions of the most common types of derived scores: percentile ranks, standard scores, and grade and age equivalents.

Percentile Ranks

A percentile score or rank indicates a student's relative position in a group in terms of the percentage of students scoring below a given raw score. For example, if we consult a table of norms and find that a student's raw score of 31 equals a percentile rank of 70, we know that 70 percent of the students in the reference group obtained a raw score lower than 31, and that this student's performance surpasses that of 70 percent of the reference group.

Percentiles should not be confused with the familiar percentage scores. The latter are raw scores, expressed in terms of the percentage of correct items. Percentiles are derived scores, expressed in terms of percentage of persons scoring below a given raw score. A raw score of 90 percent could have either a low or high percentile rank depending on the performance of the other individuals in the group. We must always refer to the norm group used for comparison when interpreting a percentile rank.

A student does not have a percentile rank of 75. It is a percentile rank of 75 in some particular group. For example, a raw score on an achievement test may be equivalent to a percentile rank of 88 in a general group of high school seniors, 66 in a group of college-bound seniors, and 27 in a group of freshmen in a highly selective college. Relative standing varies with the reference group used for comparison. Therefore, a test must have separate norms for each group to which students are to be compared.

The major limitation of percentile ranks is that they are not equal units on all parts of the scale. A percentile difference of 10 near the middle of the scale (for example, 45th to 55th percentile) represents a much smaller difference in test performance than the same percentile difference at either end of the scale (for example, 5th to 15th or 85th to 95th percentiles). This is because the largest number of scores fall in the middle of the scale and relatively few scores fall at the extreme upper or lower ends of the scale. The difference between the 45th and the 55th percentiles represents fewer raw score points than the difference between the 5th and 15th or 85th and 95th percentiles (see Figure 10.3). Percentiles show each individual's relative position in the normative sample but not the amount of difference between scores.

Standard Scores

Standard scores express individuals' scores in terms of standard deviation units from the mean. There are a number of different types of standard scores used in testing; however, only the most common ones are discussed here. These are deviation IQs, stanines, and normal curve equivalents.

Deviation IQ. One widely used standard score is the deviation IQ where the mean is set at 100 and the standard deviation at 15 or 16, depending on the

FIGURE 10.3
Score
Comparison

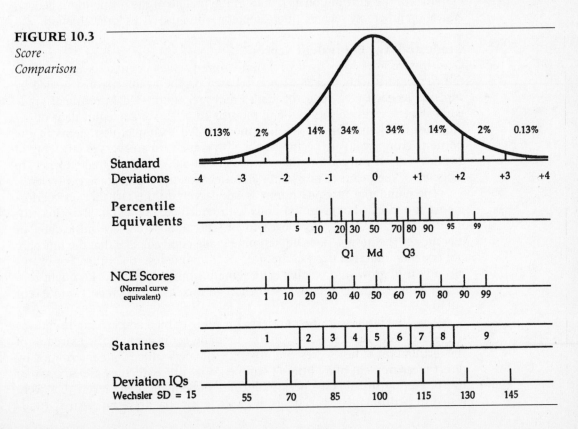

particular intelligence test. Thus, a score of 100 has been taken to indicate the average IQ, an individual with an IQ score of 84 or 85 falls one standard deviation below the mean, and an individual with an IQ score of 115 or 116 falls one standard deviation above the mean.

Stanines.   Stanines are standard-score bands that divide a distribution into nine parts with a mean of 5 and a standard deviation of approximately 2. The fifth stanine is located precisely in the center of the distribution and includes all scores within one-fourth of a standard deviation on either side of the mean. The remaining stanines are evenly distributed above and below stanine 5. Each stanine, with the exception of 1 and 9, which cover the tails of the distribution, includes a band of raw scores the width of one-half of a standard deviation unit.

Normal curve equivalents (NCEs).   NCEs are like percentile ranks with equal units. The NCE scale has been set with a mean of 50 and a standard deviation at 21.06. NCEs of 1, 50, and 99 correspond to percentiles of the same values. However, unlike percentiles, NCEs are equal units of measure whether they are at the low, middle or high range of the distribution. A gain of five NCEs represents the same amount of improvement in performance for students at the extremes of the distribution as it does in the middle of the distribution. Federal education programs such as Title/Chapter 1 often use NCEs for evaluation.

Grade and Age Equivalent Scores

Grade norms are widely used with standardized achievement tests, especially at the elementary school level. They are based on the average scores earned by students in each of a series of grades and are interpreted in terms of grade equivalents expressed in years and months (that is, a grade equivalent of 4.7 indicates the fourth grade, seventh month). For example, if students in the norming groups who are beginning the fifth grade earn an average raw score of 24, this score is assigned a grade equivalent of 5.0. Tables of grade norms are made up of such pairs of raw scores and their corresponding grade equivalents.

The popularity of grade norms is due largely to the fact that test performance is expressed in common units with which we are all familiar. Unfortunately, this familiarity often leads to interpretations that are misleading or inaccurate. The most serious limitation of grade equivalents is that the units are not equal on different parts of the scale or from one test to another. For example, a year of growth in reading achievement from grade 3.0 to 4.0 might represent a much greater improvement than an increase from grade 1.0 to 2.0 or 7.0 to 8.0.

A related problem is the uncertain meaning of high and low grade equivalent scores. Raw scores, corresponding to grade equivalents at the extremes of the distribution of test scores, are usually estimated rather than determined by direct measurement of a norming sample. More precisely, they are *extrapolated* by "projecting the average performance of students at grade levels that were tested to performance of students at grade levels that were not tested" (Baumann 1988, 37). In interpreting grade equivalents at the extremes, therefore, it is well to remember that they do not represent the actual performance of students at these levels. Indeed, because of the widespread misinterpretation of grade equivalents, the International Reading Association passed a resolution in April, 1981, that their use be discontinued in reading assessment and several major diagnostic tests have excluded these scores in their most recent revisions.

A common misinterpretation is that grade norms are equivalent to performance standards. It is especially important to remember that grade equivalents indicate the *average* score obtained by the students in the standardization sample at a particular grade level. This means that half the students in the norming group at this grade level scored above and half the students scored below this norm. Therefore, we should not interpret a particular grade norm as something all of our students should achieve. It is important to remember that the norm represents the typical performance of average students in average schools and should not be considered a standard of excellence to be achieved by others (Gronlund 1985).

A related misconception is that students who earn a certain grade equivalent score in a subject are ready to do work at that level. For example, we might conclude that a fourth-grade student should be doing sixth-grade work if she earns a grade equivalent of 6.0. However, students at different grade levels who earn the same grade equivalent score are apt to be ready for quite different types of instruction. It certainly could not be assumed that she has the prerequisites for sixth-grade reading. This would be especially true at the outer reaches of scores where no individuals from the grade group were included in the norming sample.

Age norms operate on the same principles as grade norms. Therefore, they have essentially the same characteristics and limitations as grade equivalents. Specifically, they are based on the average scores earned by students in the norming group at different ages and are interpreted in terms of age equivalents. Thus, if students who are 10 years and 2 months of age earn an average raw score of 25, their score is assigned an age equivalent of 10–2. Conversely, a student with a reading age of 11–6 has earned a score on the reading test equal to that of the average $11\frac{1}{2}$-year-old in the norming sample (assuming that age group was represented).

The major differences between age and grade equivalent scores are that test performance is expressed in terms of age levels instead of grade levels, and the expression of months in age equivalents runs from 0 to 11 months to reflect the calendar year as opposed to a range of 0 to 9 months that reflects the school year in grade equivalents. As with grade equivalents, age equivalents present test performance in units that are apparently easy to understand, but can be misleading. Literal interpretations of either should be avoided.

Comparison of Scores

Assuming a normal distribution and comparable norm group, we can compare different types of scores to the normal curve as presented in Figure 10.3. This figure illustrates the interrelated nature of various types of scores for reporting relative position in a normally distributed group. For example, a raw score that is 1 standard deviation above the mean can be expressed as a percentile rank of 84, a deviation IQ of 115, or a stanine of 7. Various scoring systems provide different ways of presenting the same information and, again, if we assume a normal distribution and comparable norm groups, we can convert back and forth from one scale to another.

The selection of which particular type of score to use depends on the purpose of testing and the sophistication of the consumer. In the opinion of many, grade and age equivalents should never be used because they are so easily misinterpreted (Salvia and Ysseldyke 1988). Standard scores are convenient because they allow test authors to give equal weight to various test components, can be converted easily to percentile ranks if the distribution is normal, and are useful in developing individual profiles. Percentile ranks require the fewest assumptions for accurate interpretation and present test results in terms that are easily understood (Salvia and Ysseldyke 1988).

Test Fairness

Gronlund (1985) describes well the increasing attention in recent years to the issue of test fairness to racial and cultural minorities. Concern with the fairness of tests parallels the general public concern with providing equal rights and opportunities to all citizens. Critics have charged that tests are biased and discriminatory and provide barriers to educational and occupational opportunities for minorities. The charge of test bias, or lack of fairness, can be examined from two perspectives: the possible presence of bias in the test content and the possible unfair use of test results.

Much of the concern with bias in test content focuses on the fact that minority group members frequently earn lower test scores than their more-advantaged peers. At the most fundamental level is the fact that tests are, almost by definition, culture-bound. It is impossible to construct a test that is independent of a cultural content, and to assume that tests can be made culture-free is as erroneous as the assumption that behavior and attitudes can be made culture-free (Walsh and Betz 1990).

According to Gronlund (1985), standardized tests of the past typically emphasized content and values that were more familiar to white, middle-class students than to racial or cultural minorities and students of lower socioeconomic status. For example, Garcia (1991) examined the English reading test performance of Hispanic children as compared with the performance of Anglo children enrolled in the same fifth- and sixth-grade classrooms. The results of this investigation suggest that the Hispanic students' reading test scores seriously underestimate their reading comprehension potential. Their test performance was adversely affected by their limited prior knowledge of certain test topics, their poor performance on certain types of comprehension questions, their lack of familiarity with vocabulary terms used in the test questions and answer choices, and their tendency to interpret the test literally when determining their answers.

Special efforts are now being made to correct preexisting problems. Major test publishers employ staff members representing various racial and cultural minorities, and new tests being developed are routinely reviewed for content that might be biased or offensive to minorities. Statistical analyses are also being used to detect and remove biased test items. Gardner (1978) cautions, however, that low test scores do not necessarily indicate test bias. It is important to distinguish between the performance the test is intended to measure and factors that may distort the scores in a biased manner.

Gronlund (1985) indicates that the most controversial problems concerning the fair use of tests with minority groups are encountered when tests are used as a basis for educational and vocational selection or placement. Much of the difficulty lies in the definition of fair test use. One view is that a test is fair, or unbiased, if it predicts as accurately for minority groups as it does for the majority group. This traditional view, which favors a common standard for selection, has been challenged as unfair to minority groups because they often earn lower test scores; thus, a smaller proportion of individuals tends to be selected. Alternative definitions of test fairness favor some type of adjustment for minorities such as separate cutoff scores or bonus points.

Walsh and Betz (1990) remind us of the importance of understanding that the quality of a test and the uses of test scores are two separate issues. The existence of bias in tests is a psychometric issue involving the concern about how tests are constructed and evaluated, while questions concerning how and when tests should be used are social issues. A test can be valid and relatively free of bias, yet still produce scores that have negative effects for minorities. In short, answers to validity and test bias questions do not provide answers to social policy issues.

Taylor, Harris, and Pearson (1988) note a fairness issue related specifically to reading assessments that is often overlooked. Because most poor readers are also poor test takers, formal tests may not fully reveal the competence and knowledge of these students, since they may be penalized by the way in which they are asked to display their knowledge. Similarly, the total test score for a poor reader may have little to do with what he or she actually knows or can do. As Taylor et al. (1988) point out, the majority of the items on norm-referenced tests are geared to the level being tested. Although a few easy and a few hard items are included, not enough of either are included to provide a reliable spread among students at the extreme ends of the distribution. As a result, the tests are likely to fail to measure what low-achieving students do know.

Some teachers feel that it is best to give students who have reading and writing problems a standardized test that matches their achievement level rather than their age/grade level. However, there are also certain problems inherent in this procedure. First, there may not be a content or format match with the student. Second, great care must be taken in interpreting the results. The scores have been determined on age/grade peers and are not appropriate for use unless the publisher has also developed out-of-level norms. Even when out-of-level norms are available, teachers should study the population on which these norms were developed to determine whether there is a match with their students.

Guidelines for Evaluating Standardized Tests

In the sections to follow, we consider a variety of formal assessment tools. The quality and usefulness of these tools should be considered in terms of the information we have just presented. Informed educators need to be critical consumers of assessment information. To do so, they must consider a variety of test characteristics within the context of its use and interpretation. Specifically, they must consider evidence of the validity and reliability of the assessment tools for the purposes for which they are used. In addition, they must consider the methods for reporting and interpreting test scores. Finally, concerned educators need to evaluate tests for potential sources of bias, and exercise care in administering and interpreting results with special populations. The outline in Figure 10.4 can be used to guide the evaluation of formal assessment tools.

FORMAL ASSESSMENT TOOLS

Educators do not need to be experts on the technical or psychometric properties of formal tests, but they can and should be careful consumers of test information. They should be able to evaluate critically the information provided by the tests themselves and know where to find critical reviews if necessary. In this portion of the chapter, we describe several types of formal assessment tools in the area of language arts and provide detailed descriptions and evaluations of exemplars of each test type. The tests described in this section are grouped according to the primary purposes for which they were intended to be used: survey, diagnostic, tests of general cognitive and verbal abilities, and readiness/emergent literacy assessment.

Each type of test is described briefly before we begin the description of specific tests. No effort has been made to evaluate all published tests. Instead, the most commonly used tests are used as prototypes, and the guidelines for test evaluation (see Figure 10.4) are used to focus the discussion. At the end of this chapter, there is a special test resources section that lists sources of information on tests and test reviews.

Survey Tests

Survey tests emphasize norm-referenced interpretations of global achievement in a variety of academic areas including the language arts. Generally speaking, the purpose of survey tests is to compare the performance of students or groups of students. They are most commonly used to screen large numbers of students

**FIGURE
10.4**
*Guidelines
for Text
Evaluation*

General Information

Name: _____ Publication date: _____
Authors: _____ Focus area(s): _____
Target ages: _____ Type of administration: _____
Scores: _____
Interpretation of results: (Criterion-referenced, norm-referenced, or both?)

Type and Purpose

Type: Note if a survey or diagnostic test and subtest areas
Purpose: What purposes are stated by the author(s)?

Validity

Content-related, criterion-related, and construct-related evidence of validity:
    Definition of domain assessed; Are items representative of defined domain?;
    concurrent and/or predictive evidence; evidence of support for testable
    hypotheses derived from defined domain

Reliability

Measurement: Are reliability coefficients, test-retest, and alternate form data
    acceptable for intended use?
Standard error of measurement: Is this acceptable?
Other factors: Sufficient numbers of items to test specific components, to determine
    a year's growth, etc.?

Norms and Scores

Norming: Consider whether the norms and norming procedures are acceptable and
    the norming sample comparable to your students
Scores: Note the types of scores generated and interpretations provided

Special Considerations

Test fairness: Consider both content and use in terms of examinee's background.
Provisions for students with special problems: Consider administration flexibility,
    content, and interpretation (e.g., provision for out-of-level testing)

General Evaluation

Special features/problems of this test: Consider length, novel formats, etc.
Appropriateness for purposes and students: Consider ease of administration, time
    to score/interpret, difficulty, etc.
What do others say about this test? If possible, consult specialized colleagues,
    written reviews, etc.

Recommendations

Would you use this test?
For what? With whom?
What cautions should be exercised?

for approximate levels of achievement in specific academic areas and to identify those who may have serious problems.

Survey tests are also often used to make general judgments about program success. For example, many Title/Chapter 1 programs use a global test of achievement in reading or mathematics for program evaluation purposes. Under these circumstances, educators should be especially concerned that the evidence of validity supports the use of a test for this purpose. Average scores on these tests should parallel acceptable performance on the tasks assigned or expected in that age bracket.

Survey tests are easy to administer and score, and are useful screening devices. Although survey tests are generally designed for group administration, this is not always the case. Because of their general nature, survey tests often lack content depth; they evaluate language arts in a most cursory fashion, using limited samples of behaviors. Also, because survey tests are intended for large general populations, they tend to estimate more accurately the ability of average students than those who are either very skilled or unskilled. The general scores do little to indicate specifically what a student knows or has trouble with. A low score indicates only that a difficulty exists, but does not reveal the nature or degree of difficulty.

A Group Survey Test: *Gates-MacGinitie Reading Tests*

One of the most commonly used group survey tests of reading is the *Gates-MacGinitie Reading Tests* (MacGinitie and MacGinitie 1989). A major revision of this test was underway at the time of this writing, but not available for review. This review deals with the third edition which, like its predecessors, has two subtests at Grades 1 through 12: Vocabulary and Comprehension. Vocabulary is measured on this test in terms of students' ability to identify synonyms in a multiple choice format. Comprehension is defined as the ability to answer multiple choice questions after reading brief paragraphs in a timed forum.

There are two parallel forms for Grades 1, 2, 3, 4, 5/6, 7/9, and 10/12. The administration of this test is timed, with the vocabulary tests taking twenty minutes and the comprehension tests taking thirty-five minutes. Raw scores are converted into percentile ranks, stanines, grade equivalents, NCEs, and extended scale scores.

As with previous versions, there is also a level *R* test designed for use in first grade. This is primarily a test of initial and final consonants and other sound-symbol information. There is also a PRE-level test for use in kindergarten. This untimed test includes items related to Literacy Concepts, Reading Relationship Concepts (for example, word meanings), Oral Language Concepts (including phonemic segmentation), and Letter and Letter-Sound Correspondences.

Consistent with its purpose as a survey test, the authors indicate that the Gates-MacGinitie Reading Tests are useful for teachers and schools to know the general level of reading achievement of individual students throughout their entire school careers.

> This objective information obtained from tests, complemented by teachers' evaluations and other sources of information, is an important basis for selecting students for further individual diagnosis and special instruction, planning instructional emphases, locating students who are ready to work with more advanced materials, making decisions about grouping, evaluating the effectiveness of instructional programs, counseling students, and for reporting to parents and the community. (Directions for Administration 1989, 29)

The authors describe specific efforts to provide evidence of the content validity of the Gates-MacGinitie, including careful selection of vocabulary and balancing passage content across several disciplines. However, they do not directly provide either construct- or criterion-related evidence of validity. Instead, the authors are careful to state that users should evaluate the test for validity in terms of their specific school and students.

Evidence of the reliability of the Gates-MacGinitie is acceptable for its stated purposes. Measures of internal consistency were determined for each level and generated reliability coefficients from .88 to .94. Alternate form reliabilities are also acceptable for the total score, but less so for subtests. Similarly, the norming procedures for this test are good, but becoming dated (the 1970 census was used for the stratified sampling). Approximately 5,000 students per grade were assessed and the norming sample includes a representative proportion of black and Hispanic students. The test also provides norms for out-of-level testing. In addition, the authors have made extensive efforts to remove bias from the test items and from the scoring.

Individually Administered Survey Tests

Reading and writing achievement are commonly surveyed in batteries of general academic achievement. Both the *Peabody Individual Achievement Test-Revised*, or PIAT-R, (Markwardt 1989) and the *Wide Range Achievement Test 3*, or WRAT3, (1993) have been used extensively, because they are easy to administer and provide a general measure of achievement in several academic areas. Tests such as these are often used to determine if there is a discrepancy between ability (usually IQ) and achievement sufficient to establish eligibility for placement in special education programs.

The PIAT-R is a general achievement battery containing six subtests in the following areas: general information, reading recognition, reading comprehension, math, spelling, and written expression. Scores are available as percentile ranks, stanines, grade and age equivalents, standard scores, and normal curve equivalents (NCEs) for all the subtests except written expression and for total reading and total test, which also excludes written expression. Grade-based stanine and developmental scaled scores are available for the written expression subtest.

The PIAT-R is designed for use with students from kindergarten through Grade 12 and is considered a screening tool, although the author also suggests that it can be used for individual evaluation and program planning. It is an untimed test that is estimated to take one hour to administer.

The content- and criterion-related evidence of validity for the PIAT-R are somewhat suspect. For example, on the reading comprehension subtest, students read isolated sentences, then turn the page and match the sentence from memory to one of four picture choices. No contextualized story comprehension is involved, nor are students expected to answer questions or summarize information. As an illustration, students read, "The puppy is in the pan," and select from one of the four pictures as displayed in Figure 10.5.

In addition, the spelling subtest is a series of multiple-choice items that progresses from tasks such as identifying a specific letter, to words that begin with a specified sound, to identifying the correctly spelled word. The written expression subtest involves writing a story from a picture prompt without any opportunity for prewriting or editing. Furthermore, the only criterion-related validity that is offered is a correlation with the *Peabody Picture Vocabulary Test-Revised* (Dunn and Dunn 1981), a test of verbal ability that seems an inappropriate benchmark for comparison. Other construct-related evidence of validity comes from data on developmental changes and factor analyses on test intercorrelations.

The evidence of reliability of the PIAT-R is substantially improved from the PIAT. Both the test-retest and the internal consistency coefficients are generally well within the acceptable boundaries for such an instrument. Test-retest reliability composite scores range from the low to the upper .90s. Most subtest correlations fall in the mid .80s to high .90s, with low values at Grade 6 in reading

FIGURE 10.5
PIAT-R Item

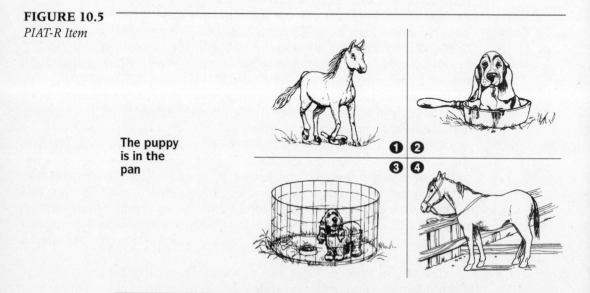

The puppy
is in the
pan

"The puppy is in the pan." *Peabody Individual Achievement Test—Revised PIAT–R Manual* by Frederick G. Markwardt, Jr. Copyright © 1989 American Guidance Service, Inc. Reprinted by permission.

comprehension (.78). Separate reliability data are reported for written expression, which suggest lower reliability for this subtest. For grades 2 through 12, the coefficients range from .69 to .91. Interrater correlations for each grade range from .30 to .81, and alternate-form coefficients range from .44 to .61 for the five grade levels investigated.

Although there are generally at least seven items per year's growth on the test, reading comprehension is a notable exception. This is especially problematic at the upper grades where the limited item pool restricts its utility. With a SEM of 3.8 for reading comprehension and 2.6 for reading recognition, there is reason to exercise caution. Finally, although the norming procedure is adequate, this test is often used to determine eligibility for special education programs, yet there were no special education students included in the norms.

In summary, the PIAT-R is a generally reliable screening instrument that can provide some information to teachers who know very little about the student they are testing. Because of serious concerns about the validity of the reading comprehension subtest, however, teachers might find more useful survey data upon which to rely.

The PIAT-R is most often compared to another individual achievement battery, the *Wide Range Achievement Test 3,* or WRAT3, (1993). The 1993 edition of the WRAT is intended for use with individuals aged 5–75, and is designed to measure the basic academic skills of word recognition (written decoding), spelling from dictation (written encoding), and arithmetic computation. It has two alternate forms and takes from fifteen to thirty minutes to administer. The two alternate forms may be administered together as a single combined form.

The WRAT3 was given to a norm sample of approximately 5,000 individuals selected to represent the appropriate mix of gender, ethnicity, regional residence and socioeconomic level for each age group as indicated by the 1990 Census data. The median reliability coefficients range from .85 to .95 over all the WRAT3 tests. Alternate form correlations across the age groups range from .87 to .99 for Reading, and from .86 to .99 for Spelling. Corrected test-retest coefficients range from .91 to .98. The SEM for most age levels is 5 for Reading and Spelling for the separate forms, and 3 and 4 respectively for the combined form.

Although content- and construct-related evidence of validity is provided, many continue to criticize the WRAT Reading test for its emphasis on letter and word recognition in isolation from any supporting context. The manual indicates that the WRAT was intentionally designed to eliminate the effects of comprehension. In so doing, it suggests the WRAT can be used to determine whether a student's problem is due to an inability to learn the codes necessary to acquire the skill or to an inability to derive meaning from the codes, and to prevent teaching errors that arise from the failure to differentiate these problems. We agree with Salvia and Ysseldyke (1988) when they said "A teacher who adjusted a student's reading curriculum on the basis of scores obtained on the Reading subtest of the WRAT-R would be on shaky ground indeed" (343).

Diagnostic Tests

Diagnostic tests are designed to provide a profile of a student's relative strengths and weaknesses. According to Gronlund (1985), diagnostic tests differ from survey tests in three major ways: they have a large number of subtest scores and a larger number of items; the items are devised to measure specific skills; and difficulty tends to be lower in order to provide adequate discrimination among students with problems. For example, rather than providing one or two general scores that represent a student's overall performance in reading, diagnostic tests break the domain of reading into various components such as knowledge of phonics, structural analysis, literal comprehension, inferential comprehension, and reading rate, and provide scores for each of these areas. The rationale underlying diagnostic tests is that instruction can be planned to help a student improve in areas where performance is low.

To have confidence in a diagnostic test, test users must satisfy their concerns for construct-related evidence of validity. It is entirely possible that a subtest is measuring nothing of consequence or that it measures something that does not lend itself to instruction. Ultimately, the utility of diagnostic tests relies entirely on the relationship between the subtests and the prevailing conceptions of what is important to learn in a particular area or discipline—both the users' views and those of the school curriculum.

Diagnostic tests can be individually or group administered, and provide either norm- or criterion-referenced interpretations or both. For example, the 1995 *Stanford Diagnostic Reading Test* (Karlsen and Gardner 1995) is designed for group administration, while the *Woodcock Reading Mastery Tests-Revised* (Woodcock 1987) is an individually administered diagnostic reading test. Others include IRI-type oral reading tests such as the *Gray Oral Reading Test–3* (Wiederholt and Bryant 1992). Finally, some diagnostic tests are embedded in criterion-referenced skills management systems. *The BRIGANCE Diagnostic Inventories* (Brigance 1976) provide an example of this type of testing.

A Group-Administered Diagnostic Test:
The Stanford Diagnostic Reading Test

The fourth edition of the *Stanford Diagnostic Reading Test*, or SDRT4, (Karlsen and Gardner 1995) is the latest version of a widely used group diagnostic test. There are six test levels from first grade through junior college: Red, Grades 1.5 and 2.5; Orange, Grades 2.5 and 3.5; Green, Grades 3.5 and 4.5; Purple, Grades 4.5 to 6.5; Brown, Grades 6.5 to 8.9; and Blue, Grades 9 to 12.9. It is a multiple-choice test, with a single form at each of the first three levels and two alternate forms at each of the upper three levels.

The manual indicates that the SDRT4 views reading as a developmental process that encompasses four major components: decoding, vocabulary, comprehension, and scanning. The subtests of the SDRT4 reflect this view. For example, auditory vocabulary is assessed only at the lowest two levels, and phonetic analysis at the lowest three levels. Reading vocabulary is measured at all levels but the lowest, and scanning is measured only at the top three levels. Reading comprehension is measured at all levels, but with some variations such as the use of cloze in addition to comprehension questions at the lowest two levels.

The stated purpose of the SDRT4 is to diagnose students' strengths and weaknesses in the major components of the reading process. The SDRT4 results can be used to help teachers challenge students who are doing well and provide assistance for others who lack some of the essential reading skills. Although the manual suggests that this test is appropriate for evaluating program effectiveness, measuring student gains, and reporting to the community, we believe that most people prefer a more global test of reading behavior for these purposes.

The SDRT4 is a timed test, requiring from one and a half to two hours, depending on the level. Raw scores, for both subtests and total tests, are easily converted to percentile ranks and stanine scores. Schools may also choose scoring options that include scaled scores, grade equivalents, and normal curve equivalents. In addition, criterion-referenced interpretation is offered.

Critics of the previous edition of the SDRT found the data on validity unconvincing (for example, Salvia and Ysseldyke 1988). Unfortunately, the manual for test interpretation was not available in time for us to include information here about norming procedures and evidence of validity and reliability for the SDRT4. This information will need to be obtained directly from the publisher or from other more current reviews of the SDRT4.

Individually Administered Diagnostic Reading Tests
The individually administered diagnostic reading tests described here are the *Woodcock Reading Mastery Test-Revised,* or WRMT-R, (Woodcock 1987), the *Gray Oral Reading Test, Third Edition,* or GORT–3, (Wiederholt and Bryant 1992), and the *Test of Reading Comprehension, Third Edition,* or TORC–3, (Brown, Hammill, and Wiederholt 1995).

The Woodcock Reading Mastery Test-Revised. The WRMT-R (Woodcock 1987) is a battery of individually administered tests designed to diagnose students' readiness for reading and their mastery of various components of the reading process. The six distinct subtests are grouped and reported as a readiness cluster, a basic skills cluster, and a comprehension cluster. There are two parallel forms of the WRMT-R. Form G contains all three clusters while Form H is used to measure basic skills and comprehension only (see Figure 10.6).

The WRMT-R is untimed, requires between forty-five and ninety minutes to administer, and emphasizes norm-referenced interpretations. It is designed for use with students from kindergarten through college. This test provides several options for scoring and interpretation. Included among these are percentile ranks for total reading score and relative performance indices (RPIs) for subtests. RPIs indicate the individual student's percentage of mastery for tasks that the norming group performed with ease (90 percent mastery). With somewhat

FIGURE 10.6

Table of the WRMT-R Subtests and the Clusters

Test or Subtest

Readiness Cluster (Form G only)
  Test 1: Visual-Auditory Learning
  Test 2: Letter Identification

Supplementary Letter Checklist
  Capital Letters
  Lowercase Letters

Basic Skills Cluster
  Test 3: Word Identification
  Test 4: Word Attack

Reading Comprehension Cluster
  Test 5: Word Comprehension

  Subtests
    Antonyms-Synonyms (combined)
    Analogies

  Vocabularies
    General Reading
    Science-Mathematics
    Social Studies
    Humanities

  Test 6: Passage Comprehension

more effort, it is also possible to generate grade and age equivalents, a variety of standard scores, and confidence bands for the RPIs.

The test manual provides little documentation of validity, and it will be left to users to decide if reading has been appropriately tested by the subtests. The Readiness Cluster contains two subtests: Visual-Auditory Learning and Letter Identification, and Word Identification. The Visual-Auditory Learning subtest, taken from the *Woodcock-Johnson Psychoeducational Battery* (Woodcock and Johnson 1978), requires students to learn rebus-like graphics for familiar words and use them to read sentences. On the Letter Identification subtest, students are asked to name twenty-seven capital letters and thirty-six lowercase letters written in several different type faces and is the only criterion-referenced portion of the WRMT-R.

The Basic Skills Cluster also contains two subtests: Word Identification and Word Attack. The Word Identification subtest requires students to read real words in isolation. On the Word Attack subtest, students encounter forty-five nonsense words used to measure phonic and structural analysis skills. This subtest is among the most controversial since many critics feel that reading nonsense words in isolation does not parallel normal reading. Clearly, the reader can neither check the approximation against known vocabulary words nor use the syntactic and semantic clues available in connected text. The WRMT-R authors defend its use, however, arguing that this does approximate real-life decoding.

The Comprehension Cluster is comprised of Word Comprehension and Passage Comprehension. The Word Comprehension test has been expanded in this latest edition, and students are now required to display word knowledge by generating antonyms, synonyms, and analogies on three separate sections of the test. The Passage Comprehension subtest consists of sixty-eight sentences or short paragraphs containing a missing word (a modified cloze activity). Students are required to read each segment and supply the missing word.

Norming procedures for the WRMT-R are reasonable, although the sample size for adults (ages 20 to 80) is quite small. Most users who want to use this test in K–12 school settings will find adequate representation for their purposes. The manual reports somewhat dated information asserting acceptable evidence of concurrent validity with unspecified editions of the *Iowa Test of Basic Skills, PIAT* reading subtest, and the *WRAT* reading subtest (see WRMT-R manual 1987, 100). Internal consistency reliability coefficients are reported for all subtests and range from .34 on letter recognition to .98 on word identification. The reliabilities for all clusters are above .80 and most are above .90. No test-retest reliability data are provided.

The results of the WRMT-R will be most helpful to teachers with a skills approach to teaching reading. In addition, general areas of difficulty can be highlighted using the clusters making it useful in identifying students for special and remedial services. We believe, however, that this test should be used cautiously, recognizing that it provides little new information to those who have extensive diagnostic information from other sources.

The Gray Oral Reading Test, Third Edition.   First published in 1915 as the *Gray Oral Reading Standardized Paragraphs,* this test has been revised and published most recently as the *Gray Oral Reading Test, Third Edition,* or GORT–3 (Wiederholt and Bryant 1992). The GORT–3, like its predecessor GORT-R (Wiederholt and Bryant 1986), has two alternate equivalent forms, each containing thirteen passages of increasing difficulty. Five comprehension questions follow each passage, and each passage is timed. The authors suggest four purposes for using the GORT–3 that involve identifying students with oral reading problems, evaluating the strengths and weaknesses of individual students, documenting progress in remedial programs, and measuring reading ability in research investigations.

Targeted for ages 7 to 18, the test is similar to an informal reading inventory in format and construction. However, norm-referenced interpretations of scores are available for reading rate, accuracy, a combination of rate and accuracy called the passage score, and comprehension. Standard scores and percentile ranks are both reported. In addition, an oral reading quotient is generated which is a combination of the oral passage reading score and the comprehension score. Finally, guidelines and scoring aids are provided to conduct a miscue analysis of oral reading behaviors.

The two types of content-related evidence of validity provided for the GORT–3—a detailed rationale for the structure and content of the passages and comprehension questions and the procedures used to select items—appear reasonable. Criterion-related evidence of validity is provided in the form of correlation coefficients (median = .57) from a series of smaller studies with a variety of other assessment instruments. Construct-related evidence of validity is provided through a procedure that first identifies constructs presumed to account for test performance, then generates hypotheses based on these constructs, and, finally, tests these hypotheses either logically or empirically. An aspect of this test that concerns some is oral reading without any preparation or opportunity to read silently.

Norming procedures for the GORT–3 appear nationally representative, although the number of individuals sampled at each age level is minimal. The evidence of reliability appears acceptable for the purposes for which it is intended. A limited sampling of students was used to conduct internal consistency estimates of reliability and all but one of the resulting subtest coefficients are greater than .80. Alternate-form reliability coefficients for a larger sample range from .80 to .82 with the exception of the comprehension score which is .62. The SEM at each age level is reported as 1 for subtest scores and 3 for the oral reading quotient.

The GORT–3 is relatively easy to administer and can provide guidance to a novice diagnostician, since the record form is quite comprehensive and helps to organize information (see Figure 10.7). Although most of the information provided can also be obtained by using an IRI (see Chapter 9), the availability of normative data is desirable when reporting of standardized scores is necessary.

The Test of Reading Comprehension, Third Edition.   The TORC–3 (Brown, Hammill, and Wiederholt 1995) is a silent reading test designed for use with students ages 7 to 17. The test should be administered individually, although group

FIGURE 10.7
Sample of Completed Page of Profile/Examiner Record Booklet

Summary of GORT-3 Test Results

Section I. Identifying Information

	Year	Month	Day
Date tested	91	7	13
Date of birth	84	6	5
Chronological age	7	1	8

School _Austin Elementary_   Grade _2_

Examiner's name _Dr. Pearson_

Examiner's title _Diagnostician_

Section II. Record of GORT-3 Scores

PRETEST: __✓__   POSTTEST: _____

Story	Rate	Accuracy	Passage Score	Comp. Score
1	3	2	5	3
2	2	2	4	3
3	0	1	1	0
4				
5				
6				
7				
8				
9				
10				
11				
12				
13				
Raw Score	5	5	10	6
Grade Equiv.	2.5	<1.9	1.9	<1.9
%ile	63	37	50	16
Std. Score	11	9	10	7

Sum of Std. Scores _17_

%ile _27_

Oral Reading Quotient (ORQ) _91_

Section III. Record of Other Test Scores

	Test Name	Test Date	GORT-3 Equiv.
1.	DLA-P:2	6/91	98
2.	FRI SRQ	6/91	104
3.	TORC Para. Reading	6/91	90
4.			
5.			

Section IV. Profile of Scores

From *Gray Oral Reading Test—3* by Wiederholt and Bryant, 1992. Reprinted by permission of PRO-ED.

FIGURE 10.7

(Continued) Examiner's Worksheet.

Section V. Worksheet for Recording GORT-3 Miscues

NO.	LINE	TEXT WORD	MISCUE	Meaning Similarity	Function Similarity	Graphic/ Phonemic Similarity	Multiple Sources	Self-Correction
				Categorized Miscues				
1	1	perched	sitting	1	1	0	1	0
2	1	a	the	1	1	0	1	0
3	1	for	at the	0	1	0	0	0
4	2	flown	flied	1	1	1	1	0
5	2	that	the/	1	1	1	1	1
6	2	moment	minute	1	1	1	1	0
7	3	flew	flied	1	1	1	1	0
8	5	unable	able	0	1	1	1	0
9	5	felt	fell	0	0	1	0	0
10	6	struck	hit	1	1	0	1	0
11	6	gathered	gained	0	1	1	1	0
12	7	dropping	dripping	0	1	1	1	0
13	8	last	least	0	1	1	1	0
14	8	fill	full	1	1	1	1	0
15								
16								
17								
18								
19								
20								
21								
22								
23								
24								
25								
			Number	8	13	10	12	1
			Percentage	57	93	71	86	7

Section VI. Summary of Other Reading Behaviors

OTHER MISCUES

Type		Number
Omissions	⌒	4
Additions	∧	2
Dialect	∨	0
Reversals	∼	0

OTHER OBSERVATIONS

Type	Check	Type	Check
Posture		Disregard of punctuation	
Word-by-word reading	✓	Head movement	
Poor phrasing		Finger pointing	
Lack of expression		Loss of place	
Pitch (too high) or low	✓	Nervousness	✓
Voice too soft or strained		Poor attitude	
Poor enunciation		Other _____	

administration is possible. The four subtests of the TORC–3 are: General Vocabulary, Syntactic Similarity, Paragraph Reading, and Sentence Sequencing. Optional subject area vocabulary subtests are available as well. Scores from required subtests are combined to determine a basic Comprehension Core, expressed as a Reading Comprehension Quotient, or RCQ. Raw scores can also be converted to standard scores, percentile ranks, and grade equivalents.

In addition to information about general reading comprehension ability, diagnostic information of a sort can be generated by comparing results from the various subtests. Other than Paragraph Reading, the subtests represent fairly unusual assessment formats and techniques. General Vocabulary, for example, requires students to read and consider three words that are related in some way by meaning. Then, the students read four other words, selecting two of the four that are most closely related to the original three. The Syntactic Similarity test requires students to select two sentences that have the same meaning expressed with different syntactic structure, and the Sentence Sequencing test requires students to reorder randomly presented sentences into meaningful paragraphs.

Two types of content-related evidence of validity are provided for the TORC–3—a rationale for the content and format of the subtests and the procedures used to select items. Criterion-related evidence of validity is provided in the form of correlation coefficients from six studies comparing the TORC–3 with other measures of reading comprehension. Median correlations for the subtests across measures range from .45 to .60. Construct-related evidence of validity is provided through a procedure that first identifies constructs presumed to account for test performance, then generates hypotheses based on these constructs, and, finally, tests these hypotheses either logically or empirically. Despite this evidence, some still are concerned that this test does not adequately represent the types of abilities necessary to read and understand connected text (see Hood 1985).

All new normative data were collected in 1993–94 for the TORC–3. The sample appears to be representative based on the 1990 Census data, and included students with disabilities who were enrolled in general classes. The reported reliability coefficients of the RCQ are above .90 for all age groups and range from .85 to .97 on the subtests. The test-retest reliability coefficients reported for a small sample of high school students are .85 for the RCQ and range from .79 to .88 on the subtests. The SEMs are 1 for the subtests and 3 for the RCQ at every age level.

The TORC–3 provides reasonable evidence of the overall reading comprehension ability of individual students using the RCQ score. Diagnostic information derived from subtest analysis, however, is likely to be both less reliable and less valid. The information generated from the TORC will be most useful in meeting federal or state guidelines for screening purposes.

Individually Administered Diagnostic Writing Tests

The examples of individually administered diagnostic writing tests described in this section are the *Test of Written Language 2*, or TOWL–2, (Hammill and Larsen 1988) and the *Test of Written Spelling, Third Edition*, or TWS–3, (Larsen and Hammill 1994). A third edition of the TOWL (Hammill and Larsen

1996) was scheduled for release in 1996 but unavailable at the time of this writing.

Test of Written Language, Second Edition.   The TOWL–2 (Hammill and Larsen 1988) is a test of both receptive and expressive language designed for use with students ages 7 to 17. Students are asked to read, listen, and write in response to several stimuli. Both contrived and spontaneous writing formats are employed. With the exception of the fifteen minutes allocated to story writing, the TOWL–2 has no set time limits. The test takes approximately two to two and a half hours to administer, and inexperienced examiners should allow considerable additional time for scoring.

The TOWL–2 has two alternate forms and includes ten subtests that can be reported as raw scores, percentiles, subtest and composite standard scores, and written language quotients. Five of the subtest scores are generated by analyzing a spontaneous writing sample, a story that is written in response to a picture stimulus: Thematic Maturity, Contextual Vocabulary, Syntactic Maturity, Contextual Spelling, and Contextual Style. Extensive checklists are provided for this purpose.

The other five subtests involve more contrived writing tasks. For example, subtest 4, Logical Sentences, requires students to rewrite sentences that have something wrong with them so "that it makes perfect sense" (21). Spelling and Style are both evaluated using the same dictation task, and the Vocabulary subtest requires students to write thirty stimulus words in sentences.

The content-related evidence of validity of the TOWL–2 is derived from the theoretical orientation of the test and from examination of the types of tasks generally required of students in school settings. Item development and selection seem adequate. Adequate criterion-related evidence of validity is provided from two studies comparing students' performance on the TOWL–2 to their language arts composite score on the SRA Achievement Series and to scores on student essays. Test-retest coefficients range from .59 to .99, with most in the high .80s. Interscorer reliabilities are reported ranging from .93 to .99.

The norming procedures for the TOWL–2 are carefully described and appear acceptable. The stratified standardization sample included over 2,000 students, distributed in a representative fashion across geographic areas and other demographic factors. The authors provide reasonable evidence regarding the reliability of the TOWL–2. The overall reliability of the test, using interscorer reliability, content sampling, and time sampling, ranged from .87 to .96.

In general, the TOWL–2 is a reasonable standardized measure of writing. Teachers and students who are accustomed to a writing process approach, however, will find this a somewhat limited view of writing competence since students are given the opportunity only to write one story with no prewriting or editing allowed. Although the TOWL–2 does not really generate any information that could not be collected by a knowledgeable teacher during classroom instruction and observation, the standardized information can be used to document and substantiate students' weaknesses in written language.

The Test of Written Spelling, Third Edition. The TWS–3 (Larsen and Hammill 1994) is a standardized measure for students ages 6 years and 6 months to 18 years and 5 months. It contains two subtests: Predictable Words, a measure of skill in spelling words that conform to phonic rules and generalizations, and Unpredictable Words, a measure of skill in spelling irregular words. The authors indicate that the TWS–3 may be used to identify students who might need interventions designed to improve spelling, to determine areas of relative strength and weakness in spelling, and to document overall progress in spelling, but that they are insufficient as the basis for instructional planning.

The TWS–3 uses a dictated word format, and results are reported as standard scores, percentile ranks, spelling ages, and grade equivalents. Content-related evidence of validity for the TWS–3 is derived from the content of the subtests and from the results of item analysis procedures used during item selection. Item development and selection seem adequate. Based on evidence of the equivalence of the 1976 and the 1994 TWS, criterion-related evidence of validity is provided from studies of performance on the 1976 TWS correlated with the spelling subtests of six other tests. Subtest correlations range from .59 to .97, and total score correlations range from .71 to .97.

Construct-related evidence of validity is provided through a procedure that first identifies constructs presumed to account for test performance, then generates hypotheses based on these constructs, and, finally, tests these hypotheses either logically or empirically. Given the constructs and hypotheses presented, the TWS–3 presents reasonable construct-related evidence of validity for use as indicated in the manual.

The subtests and total score of the TWS–3 were normed on a large sample of students in grades 1 through 12. Appropriate demographic characteristics of the sample were keyed to the 1990 Census data. The reported reliability coefficients for the total score are at or above .94 at all age levels, and, with one exception, above .90 for the subtests at all ages. The test-retest reliability coefficients reported from two studies are, with two exceptions, above .90 for the total score at all age levels and range from .71 to .98 for the subtests. The SEM for most age levels is 3 on the subtests (with some at 4 and one at 6 at the lower age levels), and ranges from 2 to 3 on the total score.

The TWS–3 is easy to administer and interpret (see Figure 10.8). Also, the availability of normative data is helpful when evaluating students general performance in this area.

An Individually Administered Diagnostic Test of Oral Language:
Test of Oral Language Development, Second Edition, Primary.
The TOLD–2 Primary (Newcomer and Hammill 1988) is an individually administered test designed for use with children ages 4.0 to 8.11. Norm-referenced interpretations are provided for scores on seven subtests evaluating a student's skills in specific language areas. The phonological aspects of language are evaluated in the Word Articulation and Word Discrimination subtests. The semantic

FIGURE 10.8
Sample Page 1 of Completed Summary/Response Form

TWS-3

Test of Written Spelling
Third Edition

SUMMARY/RESPONSE FORM

Section I. Identifying Information

Name Jim Bowie   Female ___ Male ✓
School Alamo Elementary
Examiner D. Crockett
Referred by Ms. Dickenson, teacher
Reason for Referral failing spelling

	Year	Month
Date of Testing	93	10
Date of Birth	83	5
Test Age	10	5

Section II. Record of GORT-3 Scores

TWS-3 Scores	Raw Scores	Std. Scores	%iles	Spelling Ages	Grade Equivalents
Predictable Words	11	82	12	7-3	1.5
Unpredictable Words	16	87	19	9-0	3.2
Total Words	27	83	13	7-10	2.3

Section III. Other Test Scores

	Name	Date	Std. Score	TWS-3 Equiv.
1.	TONI-2	93-5	12	112
2.	WRAT (Spelling)	93-5	76	76
3.	CTBS (Reading)	92-11	4	92
4.				

Section V. Test Conditions

A. Place Tested Crockett's office

		Interfering			Not Interfering	
B.	Noise Level	1	2	3	④	5
C.	Interruptions	1	2	3	4	⑤
D.	Distractions	1	2	3	④	5
E.	Light	1	2	3	④	5
F.	Temperature	1	2	3	④	5

G. Notes and other considerations _____

Section IV. Profile Scores

From Test of Written Spelling–3 by Larsen and Hammill, 1994. Reprinted by permission of PRO-ED.

aspects of language are tested in the Picture Vocabulary and the Oral Vocabulary subtests, and the syntactic aspects of language are represented in the Grammatic Understanding, Sentence Imitation, and Grammatic Completion subtests.

The TOLD–2 Primary is intended for use in identifying children whose language development is atypical, providing information about the strengths and weaknesses of individual children, and documenting progress in specialized programs. Administration time ranges from thirty minutes to an hour. Raw scores can be converted to percentile ranks and standard scores for both subtests and composites.

Fairly extensive criterion-related evidence of validity for the TOLD–2 Primary is offered in the manual. The authors compared the subtests of the TOLD–2 to nine criterion tests, with the correlation coefficients for all students ranging from .69 to .84. The coefficients for subtest scores for various age groups were smaller, however. Content-related evidence of validity is presented in the form of expert judgment. Although the tasks are similar to those used on many formal tests of language, Westby (1988) asks "Do the test tasks represent anything that the child actually does with language in the real world?" She concludes that the test has serious flaws in this area and suggests using it for screening only, supplementing it with language samples gathered in more natural language contexts.

The authors provide a good discussion of reliability and provide coefficients that consistently exceed .80. Using a measure of internal consistency, the composites range from .91 to .95, with subtests somewhat lower. These results suggest that the test has adequate reliability at both the subtest and composite level for screening purposes. For diagnostic conclusions at the subtest level, only some ages and subskills attain a .90 coefficient. Test-retest reliability information is limited to a small sample and reference to previous editions.

The norming procedures appear acceptable, with representative stratified sampling of acceptable numbers of students. However, the norms are based on speakers of mainstream English only and there is some evidence that dialect or bilingual speakers may perform poorly on this test (Westby 1988). The TOLD–2 is most likely to be useful in providing normative screening data to language arts professionals, especially when they are considering a referral to a language specialist. However, test users should be especially careful about possible dialect usage and should also be alert to evidence of acceptable language use in normal daily discourse.

A Criterion-Referenced Diagnostic Test:
The BRIGANCE Diagnostic Inventories

As we have already noted, tests emphasizing criterion-referenced interpretations (CRTs) are designed to assess students' abilities and describe their strengths and weaknesses without making comparisons to other students. CRTs have proliferated since their initial appearance in the 1960s. The success and utility of a CRT depends on the degree to which the tasks and behaviors sampled on the test are closely related to a reasonable view of skilled performance and are like the tasks and behaviors teachers intend to address.

The *BRIGANCE Diagnostic Inventories* (Brigance 1976) provide an example of this type of testing. There are five different BRIGANCE inventories aimed at evaluating a wide range of ages and skills, from preschool early development through the basic skills of the elementary years to a test of essential skills designed for use with secondary students. There is also a test designed to screen students for kindergarten and first grade. The inventories focus on a variety of skill areas including oral reading, reading comprehension, word analysis, vocabulary, listening, spelling, writing, and areas in mathematics and life skills. Each of the inventories contains a listing of 100 or more skills to be tested. The tests produce grade level scores for each of the skills, and teachers are encouraged to plan their instructional programs based on the specific items missed.

Unfortunately, the tests provide no information regarding the validity of these skills for developing competent readers and writers. The assumption is made that if children master each of the subskills in the hierarchy, they will be successful. This absence of validity information is especially troubling given that the BRIGANCE inventories have enjoyed wide use, in part because the results are so easily translated into instructional objectives of the sort used by many special educators to write IEPs. Indeed, any item that is not mastered on this test is likely to be listed as a desirable outcome on an IEP.

The BRIGANCE also provides no information about either the reliability or developmental appropriateness of the test(s). As a result, it is not reasonable to use the BRIGANCE as a placement tool, a purpose suggested by the author (Smith and Mitchell 1985, 216). The most defensible use of the BRIGANCE is to reveal fairly quickly to the uninformed or busy teacher some of the areas that may require further testing or evaluation. However, Brigance himself notes that the test should be used together with other information, such as classroom observational data and work samples.

Tests of General Cognitive and Verbal Abilities

Educators often require information about student performance in areas other than language arts. This may include information related to the learner factors contributing to reading and writing performance (see Chapter 2), such as general cognitive ability or emotional/physical development. Assessments in these areas may be necessary in order to eliminate or identify these factors as central in understanding performance.

The role of general cognitive development in influencing reading and writing achievement is well documented. As measured by standardized tests, the relationship between verbal ability and literacy learning is very strong. It is important for educators to examine the issues surrounding intelligence testing and to use this information cautiously, since test scores are obviously influenced by what is measured and by students' opportunity to learn what is expected (see Chapters 2 and 6). However, limited verbal ability *can* contribute to problems in reading and writing, and in the case of students who have significant limitations in verbal ability, special placements and provisions should be considered.

In addition to the usual cautions about test use and misuse, one major caveat regarding intelligence test information is in order. Many schools continue the practice of routinely collecting IQ data using group tests of intelligence. Sometimes the tests are piggybacked on the group achievement tests used by the district or school, and at other times schools use the available independent group intelligence tests. There are a wide range of problems associated with the use of these tests (see Salvia and Ysseldyke 1988). Most are not adequately normed and have limited evidence of validity as measures of intelligence. In addition, the reliability coefficients for individual test scores are often low. For these reasons, group intelligence data are not permissible as data when making major placement and eligibility decisions (for example, special education determinations). Given the limited utility of this information and the volatile nature of the data, it is hard to understand why schools persist in this practice.

Although we cannot possibly review all of these types of instruments in this text, some are administered or encountered so frequently by educators working in the language arts areas that they need to be addressed here. Specifically, we describe three tests that are commonly used to make decisions about students' cognitive abilities: the *Bender Visual Motor Gestalt Test* (Koppitz 1963, 1975), the *Peabody Picture Vocabulary Test* (Dunn and Dunn 1981), and the *Slosson Intelligence Test* (Slosson 1983). Each has serious limitations that are also described to help school personnel evaluate these and other similar tools used to make judgments about students.

Bender Visual Motor Gestalt Test (BVMGT)

Although this test is not, strictly speaking, a test of general cognitive ability, it is used to draw conclusions about minimal brain dysfunction and emotional disturbance. According to Salvia and Ysseldyke (1988), "the test has become one of the most frequently administered psychometric devices" (280).

The BVMGT requires only that students copy nine geometric designs, which are then scored according to a system described by Koppitz (1963, 1975). Shape distortion, perseveration, integration, and rotation errors are scored, generating a raw score that can be converted to age equivalents and percentile ranks. It is administered individually and norms are available for use with children ages 5 to 11.

Inter-rater reliability scores suggest that it is possible to score the BVMGT reliably. Test-retest reliability coefficients, however, are much lower. The mean reliability coefficient for studies reported in the 1975 manual was .71 (Salvia and Ysseldyke 1988). This does not meet the criteria of stability we would demand of a test used to make the types of serious judgments described above.

However, the most serious problem with the BVMGT is the lack of evidence establishing its validity. Neither the original test as described by Bender (1938) nor the descriptions and guidelines offered by Koppitz adequately support copying of geometric figures as a measure of visual perceptual functions. In addition, there is inadequate evidence offered as to the validity of Koppitz's (1963) suggestions that the test can be used as a measure of intelligence, brain dysfunction, and emotional disturbance.

Despite admonitions to use this test cautiously, the suggestion that perceptual-motor skills such as copying can predict success in reading, writing or other academic areas is difficult to justify. Indeed, the available evidence now suggests that there is no causal relationship between perceptual motor abilities and reading/writing success (see Chapter 2). Certainly, the suggestion that tests of copying could provide adequate evidence of general cognitive ability is even less reasonable.

Peabody Picture Vocabulary Test-Revised

The PPVT-R (Dunn and Dunn 1981) is an individually administered test of receptive vocabulary that provides norm-referenced interpretations of scores. It is designed for use with people from the ages of 2–1/2 through 40 years and contains two parallel forms. Each form consists of an easel-booklet of stimuli plates. Each plate page contains four pictures, one of which illustrates the meaning of the stimulus word that is read by the examiner. Students need only point or gesture to the correct picture. Administration time is approximately twenty minutes.

Raw scores can be converted to standard scores (mean of 100, SD of 15), percentile ranks, stanines, and age equivalent scores. In addition, the scores are displayed so that confidence bands appear around each of the derived scores. The norming procedures for the PPVT-R are good, both in terms of representativeness and stratified sampling methods. The norms for the group 2–1/2 to 18 are more reliable than those for adults, since there are 200 individuals per age group in this range, but many fewer to cover the ranges above age 19.

The authors offer no criterion-related evidence of validity, nor is there much information regarding content validity. In general, the authors simply assert the general utility of vocabulary measures in measuring cognitive ability. Although procedures for item development appear to be adequate, Jongsma (1982) notes that there is no evidence offered for the curricular relevance of these words. The manual reports reliability coefficients for internal consistency, test-retest, and alternate forms. These range from .61 to .91 and are generally acceptable for screening purposes. As the authors advise using this test for those purposes only, the reliabilities seem reasonable.

The PPVT-R is a reasonably reliable test that is quick and easy to administer and score. Although the test offers little evidence of validity, the authors suggest that it serves as a measure of achievement when viewed as a test of receptive vocabulary. It can also be considered to be a quick global measure of one aspect of verbal ability. Previous versions of this test resulted in so-called intelligence quotients and the test was frequently, but wrongly, viewed as an IQ test. In this latest version, the authors are careful to characterize the test as a receptive vocabulary test only and to caution against using it as a comprehensive test of intelligence. Like the TOLD–2, however, it can help educators decide whether they wish to recommend further testing.

Slosson Intelligence Test

The SIT (Slosson 1983) is a short, easy-to-administer, individual screening tool. It yields an estimate of intelligence as measured by a subset of items taken from the *Stanford-Binet Intelligence Test* (1972). The test requires only about fifteen minutes to administer, and scoring is also quite simple.

Although the test manual implies that it is appropriate for individuals as diverse as infants and adults with significant handicaps, the 1981 norms used to interpret the data from this test were developed on a sample of people from 27 months to 17 years, 2 months. This standardization group, although apparently representing diverse demographics, consisted of a narrow sample drawn solely from the New England states. In addition, the numbers of individuals per age group was inadequate at ages 2–6 and 13–18, rendering age equivalent (mental age) scores suspect. Scores can also be converted to deviation IQs (mean of 100, SD of 16), percentile ranks, NCEs, and stanines.

Items at the earliest levels (age range two weeks to two years) are derived from the *Gesell Developmental Tests of School Readiness* (Ilg and Ames 1965) (described in a subsequent section of this chapter). The remainder of the test is comprised of a subtest of items from the Stanford-Binet test. All items are administered orally, and examinees are not expected to read or write, except for several items requiring that they draw a circle, square, etc. Not surprisingly, the SIT scores are highly correlated with scores derived from the Stanford-Binet, which serves as the basis for its validity. Most troubling, however, is the author's assertion that the SIT is reliable, although the data presented are actually generated from the Stanford-Binet test-retest coefficients.

The SIT may be used as a global screening measure, since its correlation to the Stanford-Binet Intelligence Test is understandably strong. However, the absence of evidence of reliability renders this relationship suspect for any individual child. At the upper age ranges of the test, the number of items per age equivalent is quite thin (there is only one item for age 27, for example). Extreme caution in using and reporting the information from the SIT is suggested.

Readiness/Emergent Literacy Assessment

Traditional tests of reading readiness are intended to determine whether students are ready to learn to read (see Chapter 7). As a result, they are judged useful if they predict students' subsequent success in reading or appropriately place students in beginning instructional programs. Indeed, many school systems continue to use readiness tests for both screening and placement purposes, often as the basis for recommending special classes or delayed entry into school.

Most existing readiness tests share several significant problems. First, test results of very young children are often unreliable, and existing readiness tests are no exception. Second, few provide sufficient evidence of predictive validity to warrant making judgments about students' future performance. As Shepard and Smith (1986) note:

> The lack of high correlations with later school success is caused by the instability of the very traits we are seeking to measure. Four- and five-year-olds experience developmental bursts and inconsistencies that defy normative charts. In addition, the

cognitive domains that can be sampled at younger ages are only moderately related to the cognitive skills demanded later by reading and other academic tasks. (p 83)

A third problem relates to the degree to which readiness tests reflect recent advances in our knowledge of literacy development. Many commercially available readiness tests were first developed fifty years ago and generally do not provide information regarding the foundations of literacy that may be used to differentiate among students in instructionally meaningful ways.

More recently, tests developed in response to an emergent literacy view of reading and writing development have begun to appear. In fact, some tests we classified as traditional readiness tests in the first edition of this text have been revised in a manner more consistent with current views of emergent literacy. For example, in 1991 we described the Metropolitan Readiness Test or MRT (Nurss and McGauvran 1976/1986) as a prototype of a subskills readiness test. Although not all of the information on the revision was available at this writing, the information we did have presents the MRT6 (Nurss and McGauvran 1995) as part of a larger Metropolitan Early Childhood Assessment Program (M-KIDS). Level 1 of MRT6 is now individually administered, and the list of sub-tests for Level 2 appears far more representative of areas key to emergent literacy than in the previous edition.

Although the newer tests of emergent literacy are not without flaws, they offer different types of information than traditional readiness tests. Tests such as the *Test of Early Reading Ability–2* (Reid, Hresko, and Hammill 1989) attempt a global assessment of emergent literacy, while tests like the *Test of Awareness of Language Segments* (Sawyer 1987) examine some single component assumed to be critical to literacy development.

Gathering dependable and useful information about the literacy abilities of young children can be a very tricky business. We have addressed many of the salient issues in previous portions of this text (see Chapter 5). Before we examine some of the widely used standardized tools, it is helpful to consider the recommendations made by Nurss (1979) over a decade ago for the improvement of commercial, standardized tests in this area:

1. Readiness tests should include information about Language Concepts (understanding of the reading task, words, sounds, and letters).
2. Prereading assessment in the future should be based on reading-like tasks using actual letters, sounds, and words.
3. Readiness tests should assess instructional skills that can be related to specific methods and materials.
4. Prereading measures should focus upon content validity related to instruction rather than upon predictive validity.
5. The focus of prereading assessment should shift from readiness to beginning reading skills … The skill scores should be related to beginning reading so that they can be used to suggest which beginning instructional steps should be tried for each child (versus which kids aren't ready) (Nurss 1979, 55–56).

The following sections provide some prototypic examples of developmental tests of readiness, followed by examples of several more recent tests of emergent literacy.

Developmental Readiness Tests

Many school systems continue to use developmental tests, most often to make judgments about whether children are ready to enter school programs (Durkin 1987). They are also commonly used to make decisions about placement into special programs (that is, transitional kindergarten/first grades) or to limit entrance into kindergarten (who should stay home for a year). These tests often evaluate readiness using global data regarding physical and cognitive development. The *Gesell Developmental Tests of School Readiness* (Ilg and Ames 1965) is such a test. Alternatively, developmental readiness is often evaluated using measures of conceptual achievement. The *Boehm Tests of Basic Concepts-Revised* (Boehm 1986) and the *Test of Basic Experiences–2* (M. Moss 1979) are examples of this type.

Gesell Developmental Tests of School Readiness. The *Gesell* (Ilg and Ames 1965), as it is often called, consists of a small battery of interview and manipulative tasks to be used with children ages 5 to 9. Students are required to build with blocks, complete a picture of a man, copy forms and letters, name animals, and so forth. A subset of these tasks comprise the *Gesell School Readiness and Kindergarten Screening Test* (1978), which is to be used for children entering kindergarten.

Normative responses and age trends are provided in a separate document, *Scoring Notes: The Developmental Examination* (Ilg 1982). However, there is inadequate information about both the norming procedures and the validity of these tools. There is reasonable evidence of face validity for some tasks, but others are very questionable. For example, during the interview portions of the test, children are asked to respond to a number of inquiries, such as to tell how old they are, to show their right and left hands, to identify body parts, and to name their interests. During other portions of the test, children are asked to copy figures from memory and to manipulate number concepts. These tasks might very well elicit some reasonable information about language and cognitive development important to school performance. However, in other portions of the screening, the examiner is asked to consider such factors as the time and development of tooth eruption activity.

Still widely used, the Gesell tests have recently been singled out as questionable instruments for making decisions regarding children's readiness for reading (Shepard 1986; Shepard and Smith 1986). Shepard and her colleagues note that these tests do not meet guidelines put forward in the 1985 *Standards* (AERA, APA, and NCME 1985) for establishing validity, reliability, or norming procedures. In particular, they note that although the reliability is so questionable that distinctions between 4-year-old and 5-year-old performance are not possible, this is precisely the difference that is used to decide who should start kindergarten and who should not. Accordingly, teachers and administrators should exercise exceptional caution when making important decisions based on these tests.

Tests of basic concepts. Estimates of verbal and conceptual readiness are less controversial than estimates of physical and emotional development, but no less difficult to evaluate in young children. One advantage to tests of basic concepts is that they are often simple to give and score. For example, the *Boehm Test of Basic Concepts-Revised,* or BTBC-R, (Boehm 1986), is a group-administered test that takes only fifteen to twenty minutes to administer and provides normative data.

The BTBC-R is designed to measure students' knowledge of concepts thought to be important for school achievement. According to the author, it can be used to identify children who are at risk for learning problems and children who have not mastered basic concepts so that remedial instruction can be planned. The test evaluates students' understanding of fifty concepts representing various relationships (for example, *next to, inside,* or *several)* by having them mark pictures that reflect concepts read by the teacher. The author provides documentation that these concepts are generally important to school settings.

Alternate test forms are available for pre- and post-testing. Pass-fail scores are generated for each item and percentile ranks are available for total scores. The normative sample does not appear to include any children in special programs, and the data regarding socioeconomic status are questionable. Similarly, reliability coefficients are weak for test-retest estimates. Salvia and Ysseldyke (1988) conclude that "the device has inadequate reliability and norms for purposes other than screening" (442).

The *Test of Basic Experiences–2 or TOBE–2,* (M. Moss 1979) also relies on students' concept achievement to judge readiness for school learning. Most of the test assesses vocabulary knowledge; however, there are also items related to letter recognition and letter-sound associations. There are additional sections on vocabulary knowledge for mathematics, social studies, and science. Like the BTBC, the TOBE–2 is group-administered and takes approximately forty-five minutes to give (there is also a twenty-minute practice test). There are two forms of the TOBE–2: one for kindergarten and one for first grade. The norming procedures seem entirely acceptable, and the reliability of this test is acceptable.

Unfortunately, there is little information regarding validity. Indeed, the author relies on its similarity to other accepted tests to demonstrate face validity. Without a well-conceived description of the readiness framework used to construct the test, there is reason to question the rationale and the predictive validity of this instrument.

Tests of Emergent Literacy

Although many schools administer one or another of the types of readiness tests just described, there are other options. Instruments such as those described in the following sections have been developed recently to evaluate individual skill and knowledge of the foundations of literacy. Other tests in this category not discussed here include the *Test of Early Written Language, Second Edition* (Hresko, Herron, and Peak 1996), or TEWL–2, *Test of Phonological Awareness*, or TOPA (Torgesen and Bryant 1994), and the *Linguistic Awareness in Reading Readiness Test*, or LARR, (Downing, Ayers, and Schaefer 1983).

Test of Early Reading Ability-2. The TERA–2 (Reid, Hresko, and Hammill 1989) is designed to identify students who are below the average in reading development and to monitor progress in intervention programs. It is individually administered and takes fifteen to thirty minutes to complete. The TERA–2 test items relate to three component areas of early reading behavior: Constructing Meaning, Alphabet Knowledge, and Conventions of Print.

The original TERA, published in 1981, was "a significant departure from current readiness tests in that it provides a norm reference for the direct measurement of reading behaviors of preschool children" (S. Wixson 1985, 544). The revised edition (TERA–2) has maintained the strong features of the previous edition test while remedying some of the problems. For example, the stimulus materials are now bound in a spiral book, and some items include advance preparation in order to avoid cultural or geographic bias. The authors note the serious problems associated with age-equivalent scores, and these are not provided in this second edition. In addition, standard scores, percentile ranks, stanine scores, and instructional target zones are available (see Figure 10.9)—the set of items that lies between the child's chronological age (the solid line) and his or her mental age (the dotted line).

Normative data from a large sample are provided in the manual and generally seem adequate. Although the manual suggests that the TERA–2 is designed for use with children from 3.0 to 9 years 11 months of age, the standardization group is best for ages 5, 6, and 7. The reliability of this test is supported using internal consistency coefficients, which exceed .90 for both forms. The reliability coefficients for ages 8 and 9 are weaker.

The item selection and test construction of the TERA–2 appear reasonable, but its validity really rests on its theoretical orientation. The TERA–2 is notable for its attempt to assess areas of emergent literacy that have been identified by recent research. The Constructing Meaning portion of the test contains items designed to assess environmental print awareness, knowledge of relationships among vocabulary words, print awareness in connected discourse, and the ability to anticipate written language (a cloze test). Examiners must prepare cards with logos of local stores, common grocery items, and so forth prior to testing. On the Alphabet Knowledge portion, students are required to name letters, recite the alphabet, and read orally. Conventions of Print measures students' knowledge of left-right orientation, punctuation, spatial presentation of the story on a page and general book-handling ability.

Students respond to retelling a story, choosing correct answers, comparing answers, filling in a missing word, or finding a mistake in printed material. The test manual suggests basal levels of various ages of children. Unfortunately, the

**FIGURE
10.9**

*Summary
Form from
TERA-2*

Section V. Instructional Target Zone

Age	TERA-2 Constructs			Age
	Meaning	**Alphabet**	**Convention**	
10–0	46		44, 45	10–0
9–9				9–9
9–6	43			9–6
9–3				9–3
9–0			42	9–0
8–9				8–9
8–6			41	8–6
8–3	40			8–3
8–0	38	39		8–0
7–9		37		7–9
7–6	34, 35		36	7–6
7–3	32, 33			7–3
7–0	30, 31			7–0
6–9		28, 29		6–9
6–6	- - - - 26 - - - -	- - - - 27 - - - -		6–6
6–3		23, 24, 25		6–3
6–0		22	20, 21	6–0
5–9	19	18		5–9
5–6			16, 17	5–6
5–3		15		5–3
5–0	12	13	14	5–0
4–9			11	4–9
4–6			10	4–6
4–3			8, 9	4–3
4–0				4–0
3–9		6, 7		3–9
3–6				3–6
3–3	3, 4	5		3–3
3–0	2		1	3–0

Section VI. Interpretations & Recommendations John's score on the TERA-2 indicates that his early reading ability is above average. His DTLA-P aptitude score is also above average. Comparing the results of these two tests indicate that John is achieving at a level that is to be expected. Thus, his instruction should continue at its current pace, with emphasis on the content covered by items on his Instructional Target Zone (see above).

score sheet does not permit notation regarding specific components of each item passed or failed. This limits the amount of diagnostic information that is targeted, and even a sophisticated examiner has no place to organize the data.

The TERA–2 has acceptable levels of reliability for testing concepts related to emergent reading. Of the available readiness tests reviewed in this chapter, the TERA–2 is the best match with current models of readiness. Several traditional aspects of readiness (for example, letter knowledge) are assessed, as well as several aspects of metalinguistic awareness. The test is reliable, and young children seem to enjoy it and find the format nonthreatening.

Test of Awareness of Language Segments. The TALS (Sawyer 1987) is based on a body of research that suggests phonological segmentation ability is necessary for successful early reading achievement. It is designed for use with children ages $4\frac{1}{2}$ to 7 to "assess a child's ability to segment the stream of spoken language into words, syllables, and phonemes (sounds)" (Sawyer 1987, 1).

There are three subtests in the TALS, each focusing on a different element of speech analysis. Part A tests children's ability to segment sentences into constituent words, Part B asks children to segment words into syllables, and Part C requires children to segment one-syllable words into phonemes. Part A is administered to all students, while Parts B and C are offered depending on age and performance on the other parts.

The results of the TALS are interpreted in terms of "readiness for basal instruction," and three cutoff points are provided. Students are classified as "Ready for Instruction in Basal Reading Series," "Approaching Readiness for Basal Reader Instruction," and "Not Ready for Basal Reader Instruction." In addition, however, there is an exceptionally good chapter in the manual that describes how to plan instruction based on TALS results. Not only is the kindergarten-Grade 1 teacher informed of procedures for adapting instruction, research data are provided to demonstrate the advantages of these adaptations. In general, these adaptations involve teaching phonemic segmentation and blending with a language experience or reading-writing program.

The content-related evidence of validity for the tests is good. Predictive validity data are provided that suggest the test adds considerable information about students' future success in reading. Although the reliability is acceptable (Part B is low), the norming population is somewhat limited and caution should be exercised when interpreting scores since all subjects (about 250) were from a single geographic area.

CHAPTER SUMMARY

The chapter began by emphasizing that much of what we know to be important in reading and writing processes is not reflected in formal assessment devices. However, the widespread use of formal tests in reading and writing makes it important to understand a number of different aspects of standardized testing.

The general information necessary to become a critical consumer of formal assessment devices was the focus of the first half of the chapter. The topics discussed were general test characteristics, important statistical concepts, validity, reliability, test interpretations, test scores, and test fairness.

The discussion of general test characteristics included information such as the importance of determining the appropriateness of the level of difficulty and type of administration for the students with whom the test will be used and the purposes for which it is intended. Important statistical concepts for understanding normal distribution and correlation such as *mean* and *standard deviation* were also discussed.

Validity was described as the most important concern in evaluating formal tests as specified by the 1985 *Standards for Educational and Psychological Testing* (AERA, APA, and NCME 1985). Validity is related to the claims made by users of the test information and the valid use of tests is the responsibility of both the test developer and the test user. The three categories of evidence that should be considered in the process of test validation were described as content-, criterion-, and construct-related evidence of validity after the 1985 *Standards*.

Content-related evidence of validity refers to the extent to which the test's content is representative of the universe of content being sampled by the test, and requires that we have a precise definition of the domain the test items are intended to reflect. *Criterion-related evidence of validity* demonstrates that test scores are systematically related to one or more outcome criteria. The two types of criterion-related evidence of validity are concurrent and predictive. *Concurrent evidence* refers to the relation between a person's score and an immediate criterion. *Predictive evidence* refers to the relation between a person's score and performance on some measure at a later time.

Construct-related evidence of validity focuses on test scores as a measure of the psychological characteristic of interest. Most theorists now argue that all validity research should be conducted within a construct validity framework that requires an explicit conceptual framework, testable hypotheses deduced from it, and multiple lines of relevant evidence to test the hypotheses.

Reliability was also described as a major criterion of test acceptability. Reliability refers to the consistency or stability of a test and involves the extent to which some attribute has been measured in a systematic and therefore repeatable way. The two types of reliability discussed here were *test-retest* and *alternate-form*. The *standard error of measurement* (SEM) was also described as helpful to the test consumer in determining the confidence with which a test score can be interpreted.

Norm-referenced test interpretations were described in terms of the adequacy of the test norms. The size and representativeness of the norm sample are important because an examinee's performance is evaluated in comparison to the performance of the individuals in the normative sample. Based on the responses of the normative sample, raw scores obtained from any subsequent examinee can be converted into a variety of *derived scores* designed to measure relative standing. For example, *grade* and *age equivalents* are derived from the average scores earned by students in the normative sample at a particular grade or age level. Other types of derived scores discussed include *percentile ranks* and *standard scores*.

Criterion-referenced test interpretations were described as evaluating an individual's test performance on some preestablished standard, or criterion. The issue of *test fairness* to racial and cultural minorities was discussed in terms of the possible presence of bias in the test content and the possible unfair use of test results. The first half of the chapter concluded with summary guidelines for evaluating formal assessment instruments.

The second half of the chapter described several types of formal assessment tools and provided detailed descriptions and evaluations of exemplars of each type of test. *Survey* tests were described as norm-referenced tests of global reading achievement used to screen large numbers of students for approximate reading levels and to identify those who may have serious reading and/or writing problems.

Diagnostic tests were described as designed to provide a profile of an individual's relative strengths and weaknesses. Tests of general cognitive and verbal abilities were also described. Finally, traditional tests of reading readiness were discussed, as were more recent tests of factors associated with emergent literacy.

In conclusion, this chapter suggested that formal tests should be used with a great deal of caution; and that they should be used primarily as general estimates of various aspects of reading and writing, to be followed up by more in-depth, instructionally valid, informal measures such as those described elsewhere in this text.

ASSESSMENT SOURCES AND RESOURCES

Professionals in the fields of reading, writing, special education, and psychology often find it helpful to refer to test reviews and critical analyses completed by experts in these fields. Perhaps the most commonly used reference is a series of books called the *Mental Measurements Yearbooks*. Started and edited for almost fifty years by Oscar Buros, these references are often called simply "Buros," although they are presently edited by Mitchell. These volumes are unique because they provide independent, critical analyses of the tests by knowledgeable professionals. In addition to the *Mental Measurements Yearbooks,* Buros published a descriptive volume of reading test reviews that is now somewhat dated (Buros 1975). These and other critical reviews or descriptions can be helpful to those who need to evaluate tests.

Tests Cited

Bender, L. 1938. *A visual motor Gestalt test and its clinical use* (Research Monograph No. 3). New York: American Orthopsychiatric Association.

Boehm, A. E. 1986. *Boehm Test of Basic Concepts-Revised.* San Antonio, TX: The Psychological Corporation.

Brigance, A. H. 1976. *BRIGANCE Diagnostic Inventories.* North Billerica, MA: Curriculum Associates.

Brown, V. L., D. D. Hammill, and J. L. Wiederholt, 1995. *Test of Reading Comprehension,* 3rd edition. Austin, TX: PRO-ED.

Downing, J., D. Ayers, and B. Schaefer, 1983. *Linguistic Awareness in Reading Readiness (LARR) Test.* Slough, England: The NFER-Nelson Publishing Company.

Dunn, L. M., and L. M. Dunn, 1981. *Peabody Picture Vocabulary Test-Revised.* Circle Pines, MN: American Guidance Service.

Gesell School Readiness and Kindergarten Screening Test 1978. Gesell Institute of Child Development. Rosemont, NJ: Programs for Education.

Hammill, D. D., and S. C. Larsen, 1996. *Test of Written Language–3.* Austin, TX: PRO-ED.

Hammill, D. D., and S. C. Larsen, 1988. *Test of Written Language–2.* Austin, TX: PRO-ED.

Hieronymus, A. N., H. D. Hoover, and E. F. Lindquist 1986. *Iowa Test of Basic Skills.* Chicago, IL: Riverside Publishing.

Hresko, W. P., S. R. Herron, and P. K. Peak, 1996. *Test of Early Written Language, Second Edition.* Austin, TX: Pro-Ed.

Ilg, F. L., and L. B. Ames 1965. *Gesell Developmental Tests of School Readiness.* Lumberville, PA: Programs for Education.

Karlsen, B., and E. Gardner, 1995. *Stanford Diagnostic Reading Test,* 4th Ed. San Antonio, TX: Harcourt Brace.

Koppitz, E. M. 1963. *The Bender Gestalt Test for Young Children.* New York: Grune and Stratton.

Koppitz, E. M. 1975. *The Bender Gestalt Test for Young Children: Volume II: Research and Application, 1963–1973.* New York: Grune & Stratton.

Larsen, S. C., and D. D. Hammill, 1994. *Test of Written Spelling, Third Edition.* Austin, TX: Pro-Ed.

MacGinitie, W. H., and R. K. MacGinitie, 1989. *Gates-MacGinitie Reading Test,* 3rd Ed. Chicago: Riverside Publishing.

MacGinitie, W. H., J. Kamons, R. L. Kowalski, R. MacGinitie and T. McKay, 1978. *Gates MacGinitie Reading Test–Readiness Skills.* New York: Columbia University, Teachers College Press.

Markwardt, F. C. 1989. *Peabody Individual Achievement Battery—Revised.* Circle Pines, MN: American Guidance Service.

Moss, M. 1979. *Test of Basic Experiences–2 (TOBE–2).* Monterey, CA: CTB/McGraw-Hill.

Newcomer, P., and D. D. Hammill, 1988. *Test of Oral Language Development–2 Primary.* Austin, TX: Pro-Ed.

Nurss, J. R., and M. E. McGauvran 1995. *Metropolitan Readiness Test, Sixth Edition.* San Antonio, TX: The Psychological Corporation.

Nurss, J. R., and M. E. McGauvran. 1976/1986. *Metropolitan Readiness Test (MRT).* San Antonio, TX: The Psychological Corporation.

Reid, D. K., W. P. Hresko and D. D. Hammill. 1989. *The Test of Early Reading Ability–2 (TERA–2).* Austin, TX: PRO-ED.

Sawyer, D. J. 1987. *Test of Awareness of Language Segments (TALS).* Rockville, MD: Aspen Publications.

Slosson, R. L. 1983. *Slosson Intelligence Test* (2nd Edition). East Aurora, NY: Slosson Educational Publications.

Torgesen, J. K., and B. R. Bryant. 1994. *Test of Phonological Awareness.* Austin, TX: Pro-Ed.

Thorndike, R. L. 1972. *Stanford-Binet Intelligence Scale,* (Third Revision, Form L-M). Boston: Houghton Mifflin.

Wide Range Achievement Test 3 1993. Wilmington, DE: Wide Range Inc.

Wiederholt, J. L., and B. R. Bryant. 1992. *Gray Oral Reading Test–3.* Austin, TX: PRO-ED.

Woodcock, R. W. 1987. *Woodcock Reading Mastery Tests-Revised.* Circle Pines, MN: American Guidance Service.

Woodcock, R. W., and M. B. Johnson. 1977. *Woodcock-Johnson Psychoeducational Battery 1977.* Allen, TX: DLM Teaching Resources.

Interactions

THIS SECTION IS CENTRAL to understanding the relationship between assessment and instruction. As noted previously, the interactive nature of the assessment-instruction process requires careful observation of the ways in which the various factors may be influencing reading, writing, and learning in individual students. The single chapter in this section stands alone because it focuses exclusively on the relationship between assessment and instruction—on that moment in the assessment process when informed decision making is required of the teacher, and when the expertise and knowledge of that teacher will determine how the instructional planning to follow will proceed. Since reading and writing ability are not viewed as static, teachers must be prepared to describe the variability observed within the individual student under different conditions, and to engage in continued explorations of this variability through diagnostic teaching.

The steps of the assessment-instruction process addressed in this section are shaded in the figure on the following page. They are: Step 4—Evaluating the Match Between Learning and the Context; Step 5—Reflection, Decision Making, and Planning; and Step 6—Identifying a Better Match: Diagnostic Teaching.

CHAPTER *11*

Interactive Decision Making

INTRODUCTION

Assessment is not simply the gathering of information. The success of the assessment-instruction process depends on the teacher's ability to make informed, effective decisions. Although we can provide guidance in decision making, we cannot prescribe it. Ultimately, the quality of decision making relies on the professional knowledge, experience, and judgment of the decision maker. Therefore, it is incumbent upon teachers and specialists to learn as much as possible about all aspects of development, learning, and teaching in order to make informed decisions.

Informed decision making also requires a clear sense of the desired outcomes of the assessment-instruction process. We agree with Johnston (1987) when he writes, "the most fundamental goal of all educational evaluation is optimal instruction for all children and evaluation practices are only legitimate to the extent that they serve this goal" (744). Similarly, Duffy and Roehler (1989) note that the first characteristic of teachers who are instructional decision makers is that they "think in terms of what students should learn, not in terms of assignments for students to complete" (16). We would also like to emphasize the value of experience in implementing the assessment-instruction process for becoming an expert evaluator and decision maker. One of the most important characteristics of expert evaluators is their ability to recognize patterns. They not only know what patterns to look for, but also the conditions under which the patterns are most likely to occur.

This chapter addresses the understanding and implementation of three steps in the assessment-instruction process: Step 4—evaluating the existing match between the learner and the context; Step 5—reflection and generating hypotheses about what the learner needs, making decisions, and implementing a plan; and Step 6—determining how to (re)establish learning through diagnostic teaching. The first half of the chapter addresses the understanding of the procedures involved in these three steps. The second half of the chapter illustrates the implementation of these three steps through the use of three case studies.

UNDERSTANDING STEP 4: EVALUATING THE MATCH BETWEEN LEARNER AND CONTEXT

Using the information gathered in Steps 1–3, we are now ready to evaluate the match between the knowledge, skills, and motivation of the learner and the settings, methods, and materials/tasks within the instructional context. This step provides the answer to the question: What is the current status of the interaction between the learner and the instructional context? Our job in this stage of the assessment-instruction process is to pull together all that we know as the result of our professional efforts and experience and to evaluate how well existing demands, expectations, and supports of the context match the learner's abilities, interests, knowledge, and level of independence.

The match between the learner and the instructional context includes information about areas in which the fit is both good and poor. The information in this section comes both from an evaluation of interactions between these two sets of factors and from an evaluation of the interactions observed within the assessment itself; that is, how the student performed differently under different conditions during assessment.

By the time we get to this step in the process, many of the successful and unsuccessful interactions will be obvious. If we are still uncertain about how the learner and the context interact in ways that either facilitate or inhibit learning and performance, we can examine the information in each of the categories of learner factors (background; knowledge about reading or writing; skills application; and attitudes and motivation) and ask ourselves how it fits with what we know about the contextual factors (settings; methods; and materials and tasks) and vice versa.

For example, the information about skills application might suggest that the reader relies too heavily on graphophonic cues for word analysis and not enough on contextual analysis, while the information about methods indicates that instruction is focused on contextual analysis using a modified cloze procedure. This is a good match, because this instruction is likely to meet the reader's need to develop a better balance between the use of graphophonic and contextual cues in word identification. Conversely, the information about materials may suggest that writing instruction relies almost exclusively on drill sheets with brief sentences and that the writer performs better when producing stories to be shared with an audience. This is not a good match, because the writer needs different materials to facilitate learning. Other examples of poor matches that might be observed include:

- A third-grade student with a history of ear infections who has failed to acquire any functional sight vocabulary or word analysis strategies who is placed in a 2–2 reader and is receiving remedial instruction in isolated phonic skills.
- An eighth-grade student who does not read independently in or out of school and whose sight vocabulary and word analysis skills are below grade level on tests of isolated skills, but closer to grade level when reading coherent, full-length selections, who is receiving isolated word analysis skill-drill and is not permitted to advance beyond these isolated practices because of his weak performance on criterion tests of those skills.
- A highly verbal first-grade student who does not have the concept of a word, nor can he voice-point, whose instruction does not include writing with invented spelling, nor any explicit explanation about the conventions of print, and the purposes of learning to read or write.

Although it will often be quite clear how effectively the instruction and the students' needs are matched, there are times when conclusions remain ambiguous. In these cases, we need to carry our questions and concerns into the next step (see below). In other cases, we will have concluded that aspects of the match are clearly inappropriate, and in these cases our questions and concerns will involve generating hypotheses about ways to remedy the mismatch. In either case, it is time to step back and really think about what we know or suspect and what can be done about it.

UNDERSTANDING STEP 5: REFLECTION, DECISION MAKING, AND PLANNING

After the match between the learner and the context has been evaluated, we need to reflect on this information and generate hypotheses about the second question guiding the assessment-instruction process: What does the learner need? At this point in the process, not everything will be guesswork. We already know some things about what the learner needs as a result of our previous analyses. Other things will still be unclear, however, and we need to begin to make some decisions about the relative importance of the various problems/needs we have identified.

Remember that we can always find a problem if we are looking for one, but that every problem is not of equal importance to the progress of the student. In evaluating the importance of the problem(s) we have identified, we should ask ourselves, "If I changed (the source of interference), is this student likely to become a better reader or writer?" If the answer is "no," or we suspect that this intervention is unlikely to go very far in solving the problem, the problem we have identified is probably not a primary source of difficulty.

Another guide to determining what the learner needs is to reexamine the information gathered about the learner and the instructional context to determine if any of the materials, methods, or settings were more effective than others. It is important to remember that we cannot decide what the learner needs without knowing the context in which the problem exists. Otherwise, we look only to the learner for the source of the problem, when in fact it is more often the interaction between learner and context.

For example, a writer with sufficient skill and major anxiety or attitude problems may display skill deficiencies, but does not need more skill instruction. What is needed instead is instruction that takes the pressure off and/or motivates the practice and application of skills. Additional examples of different types of learner needs include instruction that capitalizes on strengths while attending to weaknesses, changes perceptions of the purposes and goals of reading and writing, or explains the how, when, and why of strategy usage rather than simply providing practice.

Generating hypotheses about students' needs is always a matter of informed decision making. It requires the use of all our knowledge and experience. Examples of specific student-needs hypotheses we have generated are listed below.

- A third-grade student with adequate word recognition skill who believes that the purpose of reading is saying all the words right needs instruction that promotes understanding of the goals of reading and practice with outside reading.
- A highly verbal first-grade student who does not understand print concepts needs exposure to written language in a variety of contexts.
- A fifth-grade student with adequate reading skills who is uninterested and unmotivated to complete assigned reading activities and to read in or out of school needs instruction that interests and motivates him.
- A fourth-grade student who functions normally at a second-grade level but is placed in a fourth-grade reader needs opportunities to read easy materials.
- A second-grade student who functions best in holistic, contextualized instruction who is placed in beginning material because she lacks mastery of parts, needs to be placed in more challenging materials and taught more whole-to-part than vice versa.

It is also important to recognize that many of these needs would never be identified if students were not examined within the instructional contexts in which their problems exist. Once hypotheses about learner needs have been generated and prioritized, we can begin planning the diagnostic teaching activities that will be used to evaluate the hypotheses.

UNDERSTANDING STEP 6: DIAGNOSTIC TEACHING

Following Steps 4 and 5, in which we reflected on the existing match and generated some preliminary hypotheses about what the learner needs, we need to address the third question guiding the assessment-instruction process: What is most likely to (re)establish learning? At this point in the process we are concerned with identifying a better or optimal match between the learner and the instructional context. To accomplish this goal, we rely primarily on the technique of diagnostic teaching. The following sections describe the purposes and procedures of diagnostic teaching.

Definition and Purposes

The idea that we might use sample lessons as a diagnostic procedure is not a new one. According to Harris and Sipay (1985), the procedure was developed first by Harris and Roswell in 1953. Current interest in interactive views of learning has resulted in significant advances in the development and implementation of these techniques. These types of procedures are referred to variously as "trial teaching" (Harris and Sipay 1985), "dynamic assessment" (Cioffi and Carney 1983; Feuerstein, Rand, and Hoffman 1979), "intervention assessment" (Paratore and Indrisano 1987), "clinical diagnosis" (Chall and Curtis 1987), and "diagnostic teaching" (Harris 1977; Wixson and Lipson 1986). Although there are differences among these related procedures, they do share a critical feature: they are interactive assessments that provide for systematic modification of the instructional situation in order to observe what a student does under specified conditions.

We prefer the term *diagnostic teaching* because it reflects the dual purposes for which we use this procedure. First, the procedure is *diagnostic* because it allows the collection of additional information in order to clarify and test the hypotheses generated during the initial steps of the assessment-instruction process. Second, the procedure is *instructional* because it provides opportunities to try out methods that may be successful alternatives for working with a student. This last is a critical feature of diagnostic teaching, because it allows us to explore a student's performance under circumstances more like those encountered in the classroom on a regular basis.

Throughout this book we have introduced numerous cautions, caveats, and concerns about traditional assessment practices. Diagnostic teaching procedures are flourishing, in part, as a response to these difficulties. The failure to test students under a range of conditions that represent authentic reading and writing events can result in both inaccurate diagnoses and erroneous conclusions about the focus for intervention.

Problems with the static, product-oriented results of traditional assessments have also raised serious questions about *equity* issues in assessment, particularly with the use of standardized tests of achievement and intelligence. For example, Campione and Brown (1987) note that although the scores individuals attain on static tests represent only estimates of competence, all too often the unwarranted inference is made that they are measures of ability level that are relatively permanent and resistant to change. In many cases, particularly for children from culturally diverse backgrounds, these scores may provide a dramatic underestimate of the potential level of performance under different circumstances. There is a growing body of evidence to support the conclusion that diagnostic teaching/dynamic assessment procedures provide better measures of learning potential by evaluating how a student can and will perform under different conditions (Spector 1992; Day and Cordon 1993).

The assessment procedures described in the preceding chapters are predicated on the assumption that we need to collect information about a range of learner and contextual factors. Until now, we have not really suggested gathering information specifically to confirm predictions about the nature of the problem and how to address it. However, diagnostic teaching is hypothesis-driven. It assumes that teachers are intentionally setting out to examine more closely something that has come to their attention.

Most instruction can be viewed as diagnostic teaching, particularly if it is carefully planned using our best predictions about what may work for a given student, and if we are prepared to monitor our work continually to see how adjustments have affected learning and performance. Diagnostic teaching permits the teacher to manipulate in a planned way any of the factors that are suspected to be contributing to or inhibiting reading and writing achievement. In addition, diagnostic teaching allows us to explore the "conditions that call forth learning" (Hunt 1961).

Skilled teachers consistently engage in "diagnostic teaching." However, because this technique is so fluid and nonstandardized, most teachers undervalue the assessment information that is generated and fail to document it. At the same time, they recognize the significant value of the instructional information it yields. Without diagnostic teaching, we have few alternatives but to believe that all students with similar presenting problems will benefit from the same instructional program. Diagnostic teaching provides an opportunity for truly integrating instruction and assessment.

Diagnostic Teaching Procedures

The procedures used for "diagnostic teaching" vary considerably from situation to situation. Because each situation is unique, it is impossible to provide step-by-step procedures for conducting diagnostic teaching sessions. However, we can describe the process of diagnostic teaching including its characteristics and tasks. The process we describe below involves three related tasks: planning, executing, and evaluating the diagnostic teaching effort.

Planning

When we reach the diagnostic teaching stage of the assessment-instruction process, we are ready to focus our efforts, rather than to continue gathering more general information. We have noted elsewhere in this text that assessment should be continuous and that diagnostic information is available any time we work with a student. However, we are using "diagnostic teaching" here to describe specific, intentional activity, rather than a general mind-set for observing instructional interactions.

It is important to keep in mind that we are attempting to verify hunches about both the source of the problem and the instructional manipulations that are most likely to call forth learning. Because of this dual focus, diagnostic teaching requires modification and manipulation of learners and instructional contexts. In order to identify the student's potential for learning under different instructional conditions or the factors and conditions that facilitate or inhibit learning, we need to view diagnostic teaching as "an interaction between an examiner-as-intervener and a learner-as-active-participant, which seeks to estimate the degree of modifiability of the learner and the means by which positive changes in cognitive functioning can be induced and maintained" (Lidz 1987, 4).

During planning, we need to determine how we will focus the diagnostic teaching to address the hypotheses generated in Step 5. As we have stated many times, the problems learners experience often lie in the interaction between knowledge, skills, and motivation and the settings, methods, and materials of the instructional context. Although the problem usually lies in the interaction between learner and contextual factors, when it comes to diagnostic teaching, it is easier to think about the contextual factors that can/should be altered than about manipulating learner factors. This is why Step 5 focuses on "what the *learner* needs"; it helps place the emphasis in diagnostic teaching (Step 6) on the *settings, methods,* and *materials* that are amenable to modification and manipulation (Campione and Brown 1987; Paratore and Indrisano 1987; Walker 1988).

Changing the setting.   Using the elements of the context described in Chapters 8 and 9, the first area we might consider manipulating is the instructional setting. For example, we might consider attempting to alter the student's goals for literacy learning, acquired from the instructional context. We might also consider altering the organization of instructional activities and groups (for example, from lecture to discussion; from a teacher-led group to a cooperative work-group or individual instruction). Finally, we might consider altering the interaction patterns or "participation structures" used during instruction (for example, from asking "known-answer" questions to more student-centered open discussion or peer writing conferences).

Changing the methods.   The methods of instruction comprise a second element of the instructional context we might consider manipulating. Within this area, we might consider altering what is being taught (focus) and/or how it is being taught (approach). For example, we might consider changing the focus of writing lessons from a heavy emphasis on individual skill instruction to the practice and application of skills in the service of writing for real audiences.

We may also wish to consider altering the methods of instruction being used to create motivated and/or strategic learning. For example, we may wish to change from extrinsic motivational techniques to those that are designed to enhance a student's desire to understand rather than simply comply with directions. We may also consider moving from methods that rely heavily on independent student practice to those that provide increased teacher support during the initial stages of learning. Some authors have suggested systematically varying the level of teacher support in the administration of traditional assessment procedures as a means of obtaining better instructional information. For example, Cioffi and Carney (1983) suggest a variety of modifications for administering an IRI, including eliminating time constraints, providing appropriate prereading instruction, observing miscues under prepared and unprepared conditions, and introducing instructional aids as needed.

Changing the materials and tasks.   The third area of the instructional context we might consider manipulating in diagnostic teaching consists of materials and tasks. The characteristics of the texts a student is reading can have a profound effect on learning and performance, and are therefore serious candidates for manipulation. Those that are easily modified include text type (for example, various types of stories and/or informational materials), length, readability, familiarity, organization (temporal sequence, cause-effect), coherence/unity, and structural characteristics (headings/subheadings, illustrations, charts, italics, etc.). Similarly, the type of writing that students are asked to produce may influence their performance. Again, familiarity with the mode and experience with the process can be powerful predictors of success.

It is also important to consider how the task demands that are being placed on the learner might be manipulated. Specifically, we might consider altering the content (that is, cognitive complexity) and/or the form (purpose and procedural complexity) of the tasks in which a student is asked to engage. This might include alterations such as changing from recognition tasks to open-ended or discussion tasks, or from low- to high-level tasks, or altering factors such as the quantity, mode of presentation and response (oral, written), and/or the clarity of task directions.

Generally, we should anticipate using multiple setting, method, materials and task options as we engage in diagnostic teaching. We are really attempting to set up the diagnostic teaching to represent or test certain interactions. However, not all interactions will be tested. It is important to recall that diagnostic teaching is hypothesis-driven. Only those factors and influences that appear to be likely candidates for improving learning and performance need be attempted.

Executing

It is clear that there are many ways to proceed with diagnostic teaching sessions. However, it is important to keep in mind that designing the diagnostic teaching to provide information about how a student performs under several different or contrasting conditions can help us clarify our hypotheses about what the student needs. The many options provided above suggest at least two ways that this might be accomplished. The first is to conduct diagnostic teaching sessions that try out several distinct alternatives to solving a particular problem. For future reference, we are calling this the *alternative methods* approach.

In contrast to the alternative methods approach, we can conduct diagnostic teaching sessions in which a particular procedure is modified by providing different levels of support to the learner. This approach uses the instructional technique of scaffolding described in Chapter 6 as an assessment device and will be referred to subsequently as the *scaffolding* approach. Whichever approach is selected, the procedures need to be viable instructional techniques that are appropriate for the setting in which they will be used on a regular basis.

Alternative methods approach. The alternative methods approach involves a comparison of two or more different instructional procedures for teaching the same content or skill. An example of the alternative methods approach can be seen by rereading the case of Seth in Chapter 3, in which we described how we explored possible teaching interventions. Recall that Seth was experiencing serious word recognition problems, and in addition, he seemed to have difficulty learning either new words or the skills needed to learn new words. Therefore, our diagnostic teaching efforts involved trying out three distinct instructional approaches: phonics instruction that taught him to break the whole into component parts, phonics instruction that taught him to blend parts into wholes, and sight word instruction.

As noted in Chapter 3, Seth recalled the words he was taught using each approach equally well. However, he learned the new words in the part-to-whole phonics approach and the sight word approach in a fraction of the time it took him to learn the words using the whole-to-part phonics approach. These results, combined with Seth's perception that he had learned most easily in the part-to-whole method, led to the recommendation that he be taught to recognize words using a part-to-whole phonics approach.

Although the alternative methods approach has been used for many years (Mills 1956), current innovations in pedagogy have led to broader applications. For example, this approach was used in one of the author's clinics with a bright, articulate, first-grade student who needed to use context more as an aid to word recognition in her reading. The alternative approaches tried during diagnostic teaching included repeated readings, reading text presented in a modified cloze format, and reading text altered to include self-monitoring "checkpoints" throughout.

Scaffolding approach.   This approach involves the teacher or examiner presenting the student with a reading or writing activity, observing the response, and then introducing modifications of the task. These modifications are really hypotheses about "the minimal instructional adjustments necessary for the child to succeed in materials at or near his or her grade placement" (Cioffi and Carney 1983, 768).

The predominant form of these modifications is introduction of "layered" prompts, or increasingly explicit hints (Day and Cordon 1993). The prompts continue until the student can perform the desired task and it becomes clear how much support is needed. Consider the case of a reader who is not able to answer questions about a grade level passage, even though word recognition is acceptable. We could plan an intervention that provided for activating background knowledge, preteaching vocabulary, focusing purpose setting, and guided reading questions. This type of instruction represents a heavy dependence on the teacher, however. As an alternative, we could teach a lesson providing only the one component of this instructional plan that we believe is crucial to improving the match so that the reader can perform effectively. For a very young or inexperienced child, this may involve just the preteaching of vocabulary. For another child who has limited stamina for long texts, it might be providing only the guided reading questions.

The point is that we would start with one type of minimal support and increase it only as we see that the child requires it. We would prioritize, or layer, the prompts or supports so that we can clearly identify the intervention of least assistance. It is sometimes even possible to generate a highly specified set of "ordered hints" (Brown and Campione 1986; Campione and Brown 1987). These hints go from least support to most support and can be documented for assessment passages as we begin to use diagnostic teaching. Imagine, for example, that a student cannot edit her own writing for spelling and mechanical errors. We can add a sequence of ordered hints such as the ones listed below and record the point at which the student *can* answer the question(s).

1. What could you do to make your story easier to read?
2. Do you know if there are problems with the writing?
3. Can you figure them out?
4. Is the information you need available?
5. Where could you find help?

If the student still cannot respond appropriately,

- Ask the student to reread her story to find any problems.
- If the student's response is inadequate, ask her to reread a specific piece of the text to identify a problem (that is, misspelling, word left out, punctuation missing).
- Narrow the search to a sentence or two if necessary.
- Finally, provide direct feedback if that is required.

The next steps would involve actually engaging in instruction designed to help students locate spelling errors, recognize run-on sentences, or clarify meaning (whatever is required by the text and task). In this manner, it will be possible to specify how much support is likely to be necessary for this student to perform under the various conditions that have been explored.

These approaches are not mutually exclusive. In fact they can be, and often are, apparent in combination within a diagnostic teaching session. An example of this comes from a diagnostic teaching session for a fourth-grade student with poor vocabulary knowledge in one of the author's clinics. The diagnostic teaching session employed vocabulary development activities both within and outside the context of reading connected text. In addition, the procedures that accompanied the text reading included the use of layered prompts to determine the level of support necessary to enable the student to identify, learn, and apply unknown words in the context of her reading.

Thus far, we have emphasized the intentional, well-planned nature of diagnostic teaching. Before leaving this section, however, it is important to understand that diagnostic teaching is also *opportunistic* and *flexible*. This means that a knowledgeable teacher who is able to set aside his or her own preconceived ideas about what will happen, and who can listen, is likely to gather a wealth of information from which to confirm hypotheses and plan instruction (Lipson 1996). The following exchange occurred during a diagnostic teaching session in which the tutor was using a think-aloud procedure (see Chapter 8) to explore more carefully her hunch that "Andrew" did not have many comprehension strategies available for use during reading.

Teacher: Tell me what you were doing and thinking as you read that part.
Andrew: Not much.
Teacher: Did that part make sense to *you?*
Andrew: Not really.
Teacher: Well, do you think it would be helpful to go back and reread that part to see if you can understand it?
Andrew: I don't know. You tell me. You're the teacher!

This rather extraordinary, and unexpected, exchange demonstrates how much students can tell us about their reading and writing if we will listen. It is true that Andrew uses few comprehension strategies during reading, but this exchange demonstrated the more serious fact that he is willing to be compliant but not responsible for his behaviors during reading.. It appears that he approaches reading and reading instruction passively rather than as an active participant (see Johnston and Winograd 1985).

Good diagnostic teaching requires flexibility in order to take advantage of opportunities as they arise. Over time, we develop a repertoire of both assessment and instruction procedures which can be used to respond to unexpected results or remarks. They will only be useful, however, to the extent that we recognize what is happening when it occurs and are prepared to revise our plans on the spot. This is opportunistic assessment-instruction. In the case we just described, the teacher decided to follow-up this exchange by asking Andrew what he thought it meant to be a good reader. She confirmed her new hypothesis; he believed good reading was flawless word calling and he relied heavily on the teacher to set purposes and to monitor both word recognition and comprehension. Consequently, he paid no attention whatsoever to meaning and could not set purposes for reading. In subsequent sessions, she pursued a line of diagnostic teaching aimed at discovering how he might learn to be a more active participant in generating meaning from text.

Evaluating

The examples provided above suggest that diagnostic teaching is not usually a one-time event. Diagnostic teaching is cyclical and continuous. Generally, the results of diagnostic teaching will be used either to establish a new focus for diagnostic teaching or to plan an instructional program or sequence.

> Optimal methods of instruction and levels of difficulty suggested by trial teaching thus provide the initial approaches that teachers use in remediation. However, as students progress and their needs in reading change, additional tryouts of methods and materials occur. (Chall and Curtis 1987, 786)

The thrust of the evaluation of the diagnostic teaching is to determine the impact of the manipulations on the student's learning, performance, attitude, motivation, and/or knowledge. When alternative methods have been used, this involves noting similarities and differences in a student's performance, motivation, and/or knowledge during and after the administration of the different interventions.

In the case of Seth, described above, this might mean several different types of evaluation. First, we would probably want to posttest his learning of new words under the different instructional methods to compare the relative effectiveness of the different interventions. Second, we would want to observe the extent to which he participated actively in each of the interventions. Other things being equal, the extent to which he was willing to engage in the instructional activities—that is, the extent to which the techniques "made sense" to him—is perhaps the most important criterion for future success. No matter how good the instructional technique, it is unlikely to be successful if the learner resists, rather than participates actively.

When the scaffolding approach has been used, the evaluation would focus on a comparison of the student's learning, performance, knowledge and/or motivation at various levels of support from unaided to the greatest amount of support provided. The purpose of this comparison is to find an optimal level of support; that is, the level at which the student is challenged enough to learn, but not so much that he or she gives up in frustration, or so little that he or she does not have to become actively involved. Regardless of the nature of the diagnostic teaching, comparisons can and should be made with information about a student's performance, skill, and motivation obtained through the observations, interviews, and formal and informal measures used in Steps 1–3.

We should also not overlook the invaluable information that can be gained by interviewing the student during and/or after the intervention. We have found the following types of questions to be extremely useful indicators of student learning and knowledge.

1. What do you think we are trying to learn and why? Why am I asking you to do _____?
2. Tell me how you figured out _____?
3. What would you have done differently if you were (I asked you to) _____?
4. Which procedure/activity did you like best and why? Which did you think helped you the most and why?
5. What did you learn, how do you do it, and when would you use it/how would it help you to read better (to write better)?

These simple but powerful questions can reveal a great deal about students' understanding of how to use a new skill or strategy, as well as *their* attitudes and motivation for engaging in particular activities. These questions also serve an instructional purpose in that they convey to the student the need to consider when and why a skill would be used during other reading and writing events (Paris, Lipson, and Wixson 1983).

The need to accomplish both the implementation and evaluation of diagnostic teaching as efficiently as possible is obvious. The tremendous advantage to diagnostic teaching, as we have already noted, is that it melds assessment and instruction so that we need not take a great deal of time away from teaching. At the same time, it can save months that might be wasted implementing an instructional program that has little or no impact on the learner.

IMPLEMENTING STEPS 4, 5, AND 6 OF THE ASSESSMENT-INSTRUCTION PROCESS

Thumbnail Sketch

We introduced the Thumbnail Sketch in Chapter 4. It is a useful way to summarize information from the various steps of the assessment-instruction process. The first column of the Thumbnail Sketch summarizes the information gathered about the learner as part of Step 1 (Chapter 4, Getting Started). The second column summarizes the information gathered about the context in Step 2 (Chapters 5 and 6). In the third column, we summarize information gathered about the learner (Chapters 7–9).

Whenever possible, the information summarized in this part of the chart should describe the actual statements, behavior, or performance of the student rather than making interpretations about these events. When generalizations or interpretations are necessary, it is helpful to indicate the sources of the information upon which they are based. It should also be noted that it is not necessary to include every piece of evidence that has been gathered. It may already be clear that certain pieces of information are irrelevant and should be disregarded. However, if there is uncertainty as to the importance of the information, it is probably best to include it. The Thumbnail Sketch for Marvin, summarizing information from Steps 1–3, is displayed in Figure 11.1.

The procedures necessary for completing the third and fourth columns of these charts are described in this chapter. The fourth column summarizes the decisions made about the nature of the existing match (Step 4), and hypotheses about what the learner needs (Step 5). The fifth, and last, column summarizes information about the nature and results of the diagnostic teaching used with the student (Step 6).

The types of information provided in the last two columns of the chart are, of necessity, more interpretive than descriptive. However, whenever possible, it is still desirable to note the evidence leading to a particular conclusion. The remainder of this chapter is devoted to illustrating the implementation of Steps 4, 5, and 6 and the Thumbnail Sketch through the description of three case studies.

FIGURE 11.1

Thumbnail Sketch: Marvin, Steps 1–3

Getting Started (Step 1)	About the Reading and Writing Context (Step 2)	About the Learner (Step 3)
Background Name Marvin Age: 11 Grade: 5 Key Correlates: • Above average IQ • Normal vision, hearing and overall health • Interests are science, sports, "taking things apart" **Information About the Learner** Knowledge about Reading and Writing: • Reports that people read to learn and for recreation: reports adjusting rate for text difficulty. • Reports that own reading problem is comprehension • Names "breaking words down" and "asking someone" as the only strategies for reading words that are unfamiliar Motivation: • Pleasant, cooperative demeanor during classroom and clinic sessions • Talks freely about affective responses to text and persists without prompting on difficult tasks **Information About the Context** School History: • School-administered achievement tests place him in the 35th percentile in reading • Multiple moves and family disruptions during K-1 • English spoken in home. Instructional Approaches: Experiences, Linguistic and Cultural Context:	**Resources** • Outdated basals and workbooks • Until recently, no recreational reading at all **Instruction** • Instruction focused on isolated phonics • Reading assignments and practice without modeling • No provision for development of motivation or strategies • Whole group basal instruction; little prereading support • No cooperative work, book sharing and little discussion, especially promoting higher-order thinking • Limited reading outside the basal **Tasks** • In both old and new school, most tasks are closed. Workbooks; seatwork repetitive and isolated from instruction. Questions used infrequently, most are text explicit, focused on detail. Almost no writing, except grammar worksheets and skills **Methods** • Practice without modeling • Focus on lower-order thinking • No cooperative or collaborative groups • Little connection to outside **Settings** • English spoken in home. Few reading materials, limited interest in reading at home • Placed in private parochial school from grades 2–4 • Large sutdent-teacher ratio, no support services. Policy of placing *all* students in grade appropriate materials	**Knowledge about Reading and Writing** • Reports that people read for recreation; reports rate adjustment for text difficulty • Reports misperception of own problem (believes it is comprehension) • Names "breaking words down" and "asking" as the only strategies for reading unfamiliar words • Good phonics knowledge but poor structural analysis and sight vocabulary **Performance in Reading and Writing** • Achievement test results (end of grade 4): PR-33; Stanine-4 • Word recognition lower than comprehension • Comprehension poor for complex, ambiguous, or symbolic texts • Has difficulty inferring main ideas, problem-solution, and linking events to self-generated theme **Motivation** • Pleasant, cooperative demeanor during instructional sessions • Talks freely about affective responses to text and persists without prompting on difficult tasks • When reading in the "instruction comfort range," laughs and comments on text **Strategic Abilities** • Uses prior knowledge to aid comprehension **Self-reflection** • Unclear

The Case Study of Marvin

Figure 11.1 presents a summary of the information gathered on the learner and contextual factors involved in Marvin's case, most of which has been discussed extensively throughout the text. Normally, we would proceed to evaluate the match between Marvin and his instructional context and to attempt promising interventions. In Marvin's case, however, the information seemed inadequate. There was very little information available from the classroom context. In addition, we suspected that his weak performance on the one IRI might itself have been the result of a poor match. Thus, our next step was to continue assessing, this time with the explicit intent to explore the circumstances under which he might perform well and less well.

Adding Information

Two additional IRIs were added to the one already used. Taken together, the three IRIs used in Marvin's case are the Burns and Roe (1985) *Informal Reading Inventory,* the *Analytic Reading Inventory,* or ARI (Woods and Moe 1985), and the *Classroom Reading Inventory,* or CRI (Silvaroli 1982). These three IRIs were selected because they vary considerably in several important ways that offer possible insights into Marvin's performance (see Figure 11.2).

ARI. Through grade 4, the ARI passages are narrative excerpts. From Level 5 on, they are expository selections of a much more technical nature. All passages are preceded by introductory statements that compensate for incomplete texts and provide useful purpose-setting information. The selections gradually increase in length, from approximately 50 words per passage to 250 words at Level 7. Eight questions of variable quality follow each selection. Most are reasonable and require a range of text processing, but some passages are weighted fairly heavily toward recall of details.

CRI. The Silvaroli CRI has been revised in its latest edition (1994). Marvin read selections from the 1982 edition. All passages except the primer selections are very short exposition (the longest is only 118 words in length). Each is prefaced by a motivational statement and accompanied by a picture. The selections are straightforward presentations of factual information, followed by five questions of varying quality. Most questions require recall of stated details, but many questions can be answered without reference to the text. For example, two of the five questions in the Level 3, Form C selection of this IRI are: "What does the word 'sip' mean?" and "Where do baby birds grow up?"

Burns and Roe IRI. All selections are narrative excerpts, and many continue from one form to the next, with the story introduced, for example, in Form A and continued in Form B. Many have a rather weak story line and ambiguous story events. One Level 4 passage, for example, describes how a little girl comes to understand death by watching a snowflake melt. The introductory sentences are central to student performance because, in some cases, the selection can only be understood with reference to the introductory

FIGURE 11.2a, b, c

Marvin's Results (Multiple Administration of IRIs)

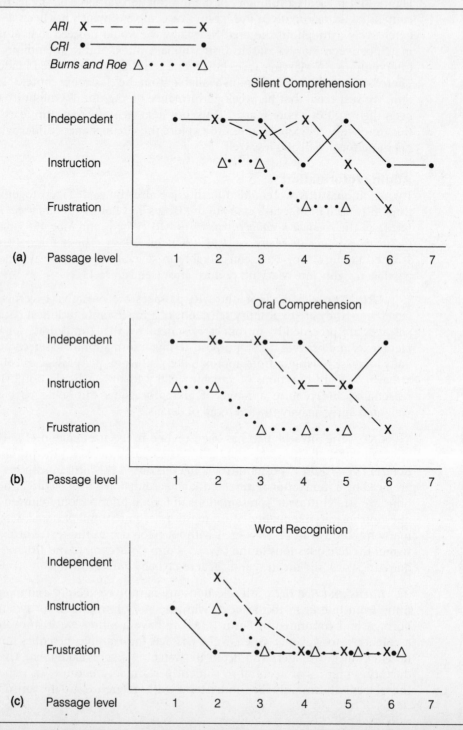

(a) Passage level

(b) Passage level

(c) Passage level

remarks. In a few cases, questions are posed about information presented only in the introductory remarks. The selections at the lowest levels are relatively long (65–100 words), but they increase in length only slightly over the reading levels (for example, Level 7 has 171 words).

Patterns and variations. Figures 11.2a, b, and c compare Marvin's performance on the three IRIs in the areas of silent reading comprehension, oral reading comprehension, and word recognition. Both the similar patterns and the considerable variability provide important information about Marvin's reading. Regardless of text, for example, his word recognition scores are consistently poor, and he reaches frustration level on word recognition at Level 3 on all three IRIs (see Figure 11.2c). On the other hand, his comprehension scores are consistently higher than his word recognition scores, and on two IRIs, he does not reach frustration level in comprehension until Grade 6 or 7. The disparity between his word recognition and his comprehension performance is substantial. However, he also demonstrates differential ability across texts and tasks. Note both his peak (silent reading at Level 5 on the CRI) and his valley (frustration comprehension at Level 3 on the oral reading, Burns and Roe).

In order to make interpretive sense of these results, we need to consider what we know about the text and task attributes of these IRIs. Although Marvin's comprehension abilities are quite good, it is obvious that the Burns and Roe IRI was more difficult for him than any others. Marvin's weakest performances occurred while reading several of these rather ambiguous passages. All three were fragments from longer texts, and none have very strong story grammar structures (see McConaughy 1985).

Although neither the type of text (narrative versus exposition) nor the type and number of questions significantly affected Marvin's performance, his performance *was* affected by factors such as coherence and conformity to expected story structure. In particular, Marvin's comprehension performance appears to have been affected by the degree to which he could generate a meaningful framework for interpreting a text (using introductory statements, prior knowledge, pictures, text structure, etc.).

An analysis of Marvin's miscues across these texts is also helpful. Marvin's miscues were overwhelmingly similar in graphic appearance to the text. He clearly attends to the print, but appears to have somewhat limited word recognition abilities. However, Marvin's performance in word recognition was also affected by different texts. Recall that his performance overall was not strong. But, when self-correction rate and the percent of contexually acceptable miscues are computed, his performance on these three IRIs looks quite different. On the CRI, Marvin's combined rate of self-corrected miscues and contextually acceptable miscues is 70 percent. On the ARI, this rate is 55 percent. On the Burns and Roe IRI, this rate is only 29 percent. Thus, the miscue analysis parallels previous conclusions. Marvin's overall performance seems tightly linked to his ability to comprehend reading materials.

This new information from several IRIs indicated that his word recognition skills were weaker than his comprehension skills and that he did not always seem to use the phonic knowledge he possessed during reading. Although generally strong, his comprehension was variable under different reading conditions, with areas of strength that had not been apparent earlier.

With this information in hand, we were ready to proceed with making some decisions regarding the appropriateness of the existing match, the nature of Marvin's needs, and how to change the match in ways that would lead to improvement in Marvin's learning and performance. The first step in this process was evaluating the existing match between Marvin's strengths and weaknesses as a learner and the characteristics of the settings, methods, and materials in which he was placed.

Evaluating the Existing Match and Generating Hypotheses (Steps 4 and 5)

A summary of our evaluation of the existing match (Step 4) and of the hypotheses we generated about what Marvin needed (Step 5) is provided in the fourth column of the Thumbnail Sketch presented in Figure 11.3. Recall that we said one way to evaluate the existing match between a learner and the characteristics of the context in which he must operate is to examine the information in each of the categories in the learner column and ask ourselves how it fits with what we know about the context and vice versa. Using this technique, we found more weaknesses than strengths in the existing match.

FIGURE 11.3

Thumbnail Sketch: Marvin, Steps 4 and 5

Decision Making (Steps 4 and 5)	Diagnostic Teaching (Step 6)
Evaluating the Match (Step 4) What is the match? a. Reading level placement below potential performance; below grade placement. b. Better reading in text is poor match to isolated phonics approach. c. Has trouble reading long/complex selections but receives no instruction in this area. d. Is expected to read long texts in science and social studies without preparation. ***Reflection and Generating Hypotheses (Step 5)*** What does the reader need? a. Increased practice in reading connected text b. Better prereading preparation for reading complex or lengthy selections c. Additional skill and practice in WR to improve fluency	***Planning and Implementing*** What is most likely to (re)establish learning? ***Evaluating the Diagnostic Sessions***

First, we noted that his approximate reading level (3–2) was considerably below his grade placement level (5). Second, his knowledge about and ability to use phonics skills during reading, combined with his lack of familiarity and ability with other word attack strategies did not match well with his current instructional emphasis on isolated phonics. Third, his problems comprehending complex texts and dealing with "high-level" comprehension tasks were not well matched to an instructional method that contained no teacher modeling and explanation of comprehension. Finally, the lack of cooperative work assignments and authentic reading and writing tasks in his instructional environment did not capitalize on his knowledge about the purposes of reading, or his positive attitude toward reading. In short, there were a number of areas in which the match between learner and reading context might be improved in an effort to promote Marvin's learning and performance in reading.

Step 5 provided the opportunity to reflect on the existing match and generate hypotheses about what Marvin needed if he was to become a better reader and writer. This meant setting some priorities among the various needs that had been identified. As a result of this reflection, the following priorities were established for Marvin. First, he needed to acquire much more fluency in applying the word recognition and word analysis skills he already possessed. Marvin also needed additional knowledge and skill in word analysis; particularly in the area of structural and morphemic analysis.

Second, Marvin needed to learn more about how complex stories and expositions are organized and needed many instructional opportunities to read such materials with guidance and support. These two problems converged in the need for Marvin to acquire skill in reading the type of lengthy reading assignments often expected of middle-grade students. With our priorities established, we were now ready to move on to more focused assessment using diagnostic teaching.

Diagnostic Teaching (Step 6)

Once we had generated and prioritized our hypotheses, we were then ready to plan, implement, and evaluate the diagnostic teaching to be used to confirm or deny our hypotheses and identify a match that would promote Marvin's learning and performance (see Figure 11.4).

Planning.   Marvin's strength was comprehension. However, his performance in comprehension was not universally strong. Marvin's consistently poor performance was limited to selections with unstated main ideas or problems, ambiguous themes, or complex text structures (the Burns and Roe IRI) and longer texts (see Chapter 8). These types of selections seem to embody what caused Marvin difficulty. We suspected that he could perform better if he were provided with more information prior to reading since he seemed to make such good use of all available information in constructing meaning. Indeed, he even appeared to make use of information available *after* reading (better performance on questioning tasks than retelling ones).

**FIGURE
11.4**
*Thumbnail
Sketch:
Marvin,
Step 6*

Decision Making (Steps 4 and 5)	Diagnostic Teaching (Step 6)
Evaluating the Match (Step 4) What is the match? a. Reading level placement below potential performance; below grade placement. b. Better reading in text is poor match to isolated phonics approach. c. Has trouble reading long/complex selections but receives no instruction in this area. d. Is expected to read long texts in science and social studies without preparation.	**Planning and Implementing** What is most likely to (re)establish learning? a. Use difficult texts with appropriate prereading preparation. b. Practice in reading connected text to build fluency. c. Additional skill in word recognition. Question: Direct instruction *or* • Try layered prompts w/IRI • Try Talking Dictionary
Reflection and Generating Hypotheses (Step 5) What does the reader need? a. Increased practice in reading connected text b. Better prereading preparation for reading complex or lengthy selections c. Additional skill and practice in WR to improve fluency	**Evaluating the Diagnostic Sessions** Increased work in reading should improve fluency Performs better with preparation Can read grade-appropriate text with support

Thus, one focus for diagnostic teaching involved looking at the interaction between text, prereading support, and Marvin's ability to comprehend. Because Marvin also clearly needed additional decoding skills and a great deal of attention directed toward increasing his automaticity, a second focus for diagnostic teaching involved testing out an approach to this problem. As we reflected on Marvin's needs and on what we could manipulate to "call forth learning," the following seemed to invite consideration:

What Can/Should Be Changed to Improve the Match?

1. Amount of prereading support
2. Type of prereading instruction/support
3. Length of text
4. Knowledge about structural analysis
5. Ability to infer main ideas
6. Reading fluency (automaticity in word recognition)

Not all of our conclusions about ways to improve Marvin's performance needed to be pursued through diagnostic teaching. Although diagnostic teaching is an invaluable addition to our assessment-instruction repertoire, it is not required in all situations. For example, there was no real reason to use diagnostic teaching to confirm that Marvin lacked knowledge about how to analyze multisyllabic words. We had very good evidence about this from previous assessment efforts.

FIGURE 11.5
Sample IRI Selection

> **About the story:** Read this story to find out about a boy named Pete and a problem that he has.
>
> "I see in the papers that the world is coming to an end," said Mr. Peters, reading the newspaper at the breakfast table. He chuckled.
>
> Pete swallowed his bit of toast. "When?" he said.
>
> His mother looked at his father and frowned, warningly.
>
> "Not this afternoon," she said hastily to Pete.
>
> Mr. Peters shrugged. "It doesn't say this afternoon," he agreed.
>
> Peter munched his crisp cereal thoughtfully. If it wasn't this afternoon it wouldn't do him much good, he thought. For the test would be this afternoon—the test the substitute teacher had prepared for them.
>
> Thinking about the test, Pete plopped into his seat at school with an unnecessary plunk. Miss Dingley frowned at him.
>
> Burns, Paul C., and Betty D. Roe, *Informal Reading Inventory*, Second Edition. Copyright © 1985 by Houghton Mifflin Company. Used with permission.

Executing: Comprehension focus. Because the Burns and Roe IRI selections caused Marvin difficulty, our first diagnostic teaching efforts were focused on these selections. Of course, we could have selected passages that were similar in text structure and theme. However, our major concern during this diagnostic session was to confirm our hypothesis that Marvin's comprehension was influenced by ambiguity or complexity of theme and main idea and that it could be improved by instructional support.

Marvin had reached frustrational level on a selection without a title that dealt with a young boy's concern about a test (see Figure 11.5). Marvin missed the subtle main idea and construed the selection to be about imminent war. Having construed the selection that way, Marvin missed several related questions, resulting in a frustration level comprehension performance. Since it appeared that Marvin might be able to understand material (even at this level of difficulty) if he had some organizational support, he was asked to reread the selection, this time imagining that the story was entitled, "Peter Worries About a Test." Given that much support, Marvin answered all the questions posed correctly and was able to provide a coherent and accurate summary of the selection. The exercise was repeated with two other selections, and each time Marvin was totally successful in his comprehension efforts.

Given a general idea of the topic, Marvin had no difficulty linking ideas, locating information, or supporting inferential conclusions. Our evaluation of this diagnostic teaching effort led us to conclude that Marvin could benefit from rather minimal supports in comprehending text. Next, of course, we would need to teach him to generate and use structural supports independently. This required recycling to establish a new focus, one designed to try out instructionally powerful interventions for accomplishing this. In the meantime, we wanted to attempt a trial teaching lesson directed at his rather significant word recognition/automaticity problems.

Executing: Word recognition focus.   In this diagnostic teaching session, we tried a variation on a repeated reading strategy, Talking Dictionary (see Chapter 12). This technique was used for two reasons: first, we believed that Marvin's poor word recognition efforts during reading might result from limited reading practice; and second, we hoped to arrive at an approach that would permit him to use his good comprehension abilities to read grade appropriate text. The supported oral reading activity we tried permits students to ask how a word is pronounced during a first reading and evaluates the extent to which they remember these words and build fluency during a second reading of the same material. Using grade level material (Grade 5), Marvin read seventy-six words correctly in a two-minute period during the first read-through (asked for eight words, misread five). During the second two-minute read of the same material, Marvin read 115 words correctly, miscalling only three words and correctly reading all eight words that he had requested during the first read.

Evaluating. As we evaluated our diagnostic teaching efforts for Marvin, we examined the impact of our manipulations on his performance. In the first instance, it was apparent that our instructional manipulation during the pre-reading phase had produced better performance than we had observed in the unaided condition. Similarly, our hypothesis that Marvin could benefit from greater exposure to print in a supported context seemed worth continuing. The word recognition/fluency manipulation was repeated in a second session during which Marvin read sixty-four words correctly in the first two-minute read and 127 words correctly in the second two-minute period. Given the effectiveness of this approach, we then integrated it into his instructional program.

The diagnostic teaching sessions generated several instructional options. In the second case, the diagnostic teaching resulted in a decision to include a specific instructional method into his ongoing program. We incorporated the repeated reading activity into every session to encourage Marvin to use his word recognition knowledge more automatically and to build fluency. In the first case, our diagnostic teaching resulted in a recycling to establish a new focus. We determined that Marvin could work, with support, in grade level material, and used it whenever possible.

Because he obviously needed more understanding of complex stories, we also initiated a new series of diagnostic teaching lessons designed to help Marvin recognize and impose story structure on lengthy narratives. Story maps (see Chapters 8 and 14) were used to guide him through text. They both supported him during reading and forced him to reconstruct meaning (generating connections) during a postreading retelling. After each of these sessions, Marvin's response to the three evaluative questions was recorded. After the first of these sessions, Marvin responded:

What did you learn?	I learned about story maps.
How do you use it?	You think about the people in the story and what they do and put it down on the chart.

> When would you use it?   During reading, you look for this informa-
> tion. Then you don't panic.

Clearly, continuous assessment will be necessary. The results of just two small diagnostic interventions, however, yielded exceptionally good information about what types of instruction would benefit Marvin.

The Case Study of Kyle

Kyle is unusual in the sense that we have been able to follow his progress over a relatively long period of time because of the strong assessment system in place in his school and classroom. Ms. McIntyre had made decisions at many intervals along the way; decisions about how and what to teach. The end of second grade was an important time to stop and take stock since he was moving on to a different school for grade 3 and also because he would be attending a university literacy clinic during the summer. The Thumbnail Sketch in Figure 11.6 summarizes the information that had been gathered about Kyle's reading and writing development. Using this summary of the information gathered in Steps 1–3, we turned our attention to the decision making steps in the assessment-instruction process.

Evaluating the Existing Match and
Generating Hypotheses (Steps 4 and 5)

A summary of the existing match (Step 4) and of the hypotheses we generated about Kyle's strengths and needs (Step 5) is provided in the excerpt of Kyle's Thumbnail Sketch (see Figure 11.7). First, we celebrated the fact that Kyle's reading performance had not only improved considerably, both his word recognition and his comprehension were age and grade appropriate. Indeed, his reading comprehension was quite exceptional. The match between his rapidly changing (growing) abilities and the classroom had been an exceptionally good one. When Kyle's emerging abilities converged with the motivation to read a whole series of books, he had a teacher who was alert to the moment and waiting to make the most of it, and a classroom structure that supported his exceptional growth during the last half of grade two. In addition, Kyle's classroom had provided him with opportunities to be highly active and personally engaged in various literacy (and other) activities.

The only area of significant need remained his weak skills in the conventions of writing and spelling. Kyle needed to acquire a better sense of the conventional spelling and to manage, edit and revise his own writing for better readability. In the normal course of Kyle's developmental reading program, he would also need instruction in some additional areas. For example, given the difficulty of the material he was now capable of reading, he needed better word analysis skills for longer and multisyllabic words. In addition, he needed instructional support for monitoring his reading of these more complex materials.

FIGURE 11.6
Kyle's Thumbnail—Steps 1–3

Getting Started (Step 1)	About the Reading and Writing Context (Step 2)	About the Learner (Step 3)
Background Name Kyle Age: 6 1/2 Grade: 2 Key Correlates: • Normal vision, hearing and overall health/development • Difficult time "paying attention" **Information About the Learner** Knowledge about Reading and Writing: • Reports that own reading problem is knowing the words • Is able to reflect on his own reading and writing abilities Motivation: • Says he doesn't really like to read, would rather play and build • Cooperative and willing to work both in school and in extra sessions **Information About the Context** School History: • Successful preschool experience • Same multi-age K-2 classroom since kindergarten • Lack of progress in reading and writing noted at end of grade 1 Instructional Approaches: • Literature-based instruction in an inquiry-oriented classroom • Daily reading and writing Experiences, Linguistic and Cultural Context: • English spoken in the home. • Both parents college graduates	**Resources** • Beginning readers: "little books" and own writing • Emerging readers: commercially controlled vocabulary and then trade books, children's literature • Journals, portfolios, theme booklets • Process writing folders • Many read alouds—literature **Instruction** • Child-centered curriculum • Individual conferences and whole group meetings • Inquiry-based theme work and choice time each day • Cooperative and collaborative groups • Problem-solving focus **Settings** • English only language spoken in home • Considerable home emphasis on reading and writing • Well-stocked library at school and home • School and community emphasize achievement **Tasks** • Almost all tasks are open • Reading time spent in reading continuous texts, conferencing with teacher, responding in many ways. • Writing time spent writing original texts and revising for publication—in books, on walls, in class. • Additional writing in journals, theme booklets and correspondences. • Student reflect on own work as select portfolio entries and evaluate own learning.	**Knowledge about Reading and Writing** • Reports that people read for enjoyment and to find out things • Can articulate ways to improve written work **Performance in Reading and Writing** • By end of grade 2, instructional reading level at grade 3–4 (Spache results, QRI-2, Benchmark Books) • Ability to answer questions and recall passages better than word recognition, but gap closing • Excellent comprehension of complex stories and materials • In writing, good control of topic, purpose, and voice • Spelling at phonemic level (approaching transitional) • Slow and illegible handwriting **Motivation** • Highly motivated to improve reading, less interested in actually reading • Easily distracted, but cooperative and funny • By beginning of grade 3, able to manage difficult tasks with perseverance • Enjoys writing about personal events and activities and also about science topics **Strategic Abilities** • Highly developed strategies in reading: uses picture cues, context, and graphophonic information; uses prior knowledge, monitoring, and rereading • In writing, strategies for managing lengthier texts and for revision are not developed **Self-reflection** • Exhibits exceptional self-evaluation and goal-setting behaviors. • Provides specific information about task difficulty and can identify areas of growth

FIGURE 11.7

Kyle's Thumbnail Sketch: Steps 4 and 5

Decision Making (Steps 4 and 5)	Diagnostic Teaching (Step 6)
Evaluating the Match (Step 4) What is the match? a. His reading level is grade appropriate. b. Reading materials change as Kyle's skills/abilities develop. c. He is showing more interest in reading now that he can handle more difficult and lengthy "chapter" books. d. In these longer books, though, he sometimes fails to monitor word recognition failures and has some word/sentence tracking problems. e. Has difficulty paying attention during more academic tasks, but his preference for action is addressed in his present classroom. f. Both his spelling and written language abilities are still weak. **Reflecting and Generating Hypotheses (Step 5)** What does the learner need? a. Continued support for self-selected, high-interest reading. b. A literacy program that focuses on authentic reading and writing. c. Some flexibility about activities. d. A more structured spelling program. e. Instruction in editing and revising his own written work.	**Planning and Implementing** What is most likely to (re)establish learning? **Evaluating the Diagnostic Sessions**

Diagnostic Teaching (Step 6)

We noted earlier that diagnostic teaching is not required in all situations. We really did not need to use diagnostic teaching to confirm Kyle's areas of on-going need, nor the type of instruction to which he would be responsive. For the most part, his remaining difficulties could and would be addressed in the course of a good responsive literacy program. Both his teachers and his parents were aware that his placement for third grade could be critical. Kyle continued to require a flexible classroom context that encouraged self-control and focused on authentic reading and writing tasks. Self-selection and activity remained central to maintaining Kyle's motivation and momentum. Acting as advocates, Ms. McIntyre and Kyle's parents helped to place Kyle in a classroom where he would, in all likelihood, continue to flourish.

Over the summer, Kyle participated in a summer literacy clinic sponsored by the local university. The work there focused on adjusting rate for text difficulty and on encouraging a self-control strategy for spelling and writing. With very little tutor support, Kyle was able to "talk through" some strategies for editing his written work. He generated the following description: "You write and check the spelling. You reread and see if it makes sense. Make sure it says what you want it to say." In spelling, his work focused on spelling patterns and an analogy strategy (see Chapter 13). Ms. McIntyre had provided all her students with self-addressed stamped postcards so that they might write to her over the summer. At the end of August, Ms. McIntyre received a postcard from Kyle that said, "I am a reader!"

A Case Study of Tom

Tom's parents enrolled him in a university-based clinic at the beginning of second grade. A summary of the information gathered on the learner and contextual factors involved in Tom's case is presented in the Thumbnail Sketch chart in Figure 11.8. Tom was seven years old and had just started reading in the first preprimer. Of the possible physical, linguistic, or cognitive correlates, the only likely factor in his reading problem was his language background as a dialect speaker.

Tom's interviews and performance suggested that he had prerequisite knowledge for learning to read and some awareness of his own reading difficulties. His performance on the TERA confirmed his readiness for reading and, more importantly, indicated that he performed better on story-based tasks such as retelling than on isolated letter and word tasks. Evidence from the word lists and the IRI confirmed good comprehension of what he could decode, accompanied by poor word recognition skills. Finally, his performance in the initial assessment revealed positive attitudes and motivation when dealing with tasks related to story reading contrasted with negative attitudes and motivation for isolated letter/word tasks.

There were several notable features of the reading context in Tom's case. First, his home setting was characterized by storybook reading experience with his mother, and his school placement was a small second-grade class reserved for remedial students. Second, the exclusive focus of his literacy instruction was on readiness activities such as sight word recognition and sound-symbol correspondence. In addition, the method of instruction was practice of isolated skills with no modeling or explanation and little opportunity to apply skills in any type of authentic reading or writing activities, including reading in the basal or writing in a journal.

Given this summary of the information gathered in Steps 1–3, we were then ready to proceed to Step 4 and an evaluation of the existing match between Tom's strengths and weaknesses and key features of the reading context.

Evaluating the Existing Match and
Generating Hypotheses (Steps 4 and 5)

A summary of our evaluation of the existing match (Step 4) and of the hypotheses we generated about what Tom needed (Step 5) is provided in the

FIGURE 11.8
Tom's Thumbnail Sketch, Steps 1–3

Getting Started (Step 1)	About the Reading and Writing Context (Step 2)	About the Learner (Step 3)	Decision Making (Steps 4 and 5)	Diagnostic Teaching (Step 6)
Background: Name: Tom Age: 7 Grade: 2 Key Correlates: • Dialect speaker • Normal vision, hearing, development **Information About the Learner** Knowledge about Reading and Writing: Motivation: Reading/writing Performance: **Information About the Context** School History: • Placed in special remedial class Instructional Approaches: • Grade 1, Basal-skills based Experiences, linguistic and cultural context: • Black dialect spoken in home and	**Resources:** Reading placement level PPI • Basal worksheets and skill sheets • Some oral reading from reader **Instruction** • Focused on isolated word rec. skills • Practice without modeling or explanation • Little time spent with reader or other books **Settings** • Mom reads to him at home • Placed in special class with 18 low-achieving second graders	**Knowledge About Reading** • Understands purpose of reading (interview) • Demonstrates knowledge of story structure (retelling) • Knows he has trouble with accurate oral reading **Reading-Writing Performance** • Missed 42 of 1st 100 words on Fry list • IRI:PP level word recognition 1st + level composition • TERA: Reading age = 6.8; performed better in retelling than isolated letter/word tasks **Motivation** • Withdrawn when asked to do traditional letter/word tasks • Animated when discussing books his mother reads to him and when retelling stories	***Evaluating the Match*** (What is the existing match?) ***Reflection and Generating Hypotheses*** (What does the learner need?)	***Planning and Implementing*** What is most likely to (re)establish learning? **Evaluating the Diagnostic Teaching Sessions**

FIGURE 11.9
Tom's Thumbnail Sketch, Steps 1–5

Getting Started (Step 1)	About the Reading and Writing Context (Step 2)	About the Learner (Step 3)	Decision Making (Steps 4 and 5)	Diagnostic Teaching (Step 6)
Background: Name: Tom Age: 7 Grade: 2 Key Correlates: • Dialect speaker • Normal vision, hearing, development ***Information About the Learner*** Knowledge about Reading and Writing: Motivation: Reading/writing Performance: ***Information About the Context*** School History: • Placed in special remedial class Instructional Approaches: • Grade 1, Basal-skills based Experiences, linguistic and cultural context: • Black dialect spoken in home and	*Resources:* Reading placement level PPI • Basal worksheets and skill sheets: • Some oral reading from reader *Instruction* • Focused on isolated word rec. skills: • Practice without modeling or explanation: • Little time spent with reader or other books. *Settings* • Mom reads to him at home • Placed in special class with 18 low-achieving second graders	*Knowledge About Reading* • Understands purpose of reading (interview). • Demonstrates knowledge of story structure (retelling). • Knows he has trouble with accurate oral reading. *Reading-Writing Performance* • Missed 42 of 1st 100 words on Fry list; • IRI:PP level word recognition 1st + level composition • TERA: Reading age = 6.8; performed better in retelling than isolated letter/word tasks *Motivation* • Withdrawn when asked to do traditional letter/word tasks: • Animated when discussing books his mother reads to him and when retelling stories.	*Evaluating the Match (Step 4)* (What is the existing match?) Existing Match There is a poor fit between: • Good knowledge about reading and instruction focused on isolated readiness skills. • Good comprehension and decontextualized word resource instruction. • Motivation to read and lack of opportunity to read • Active learning style and passive instruction. *Reflection and Generating Hypotheses (Step5)* What does the learner need? • Better word resource skills. • "Contextualized" instruction. • Active involvement in his own learning.	*Planning and Implementing* What is most likely to (re)establish learning? **Evaluating the Diagnostic Teaching Sessions**

third column of the Thumbnail Sketch presented in Figure 11.9. As in Marvin's case, the match between Tom's knowledge, skills, and attitudes and the settings, methods, and materials that confront him within the reading context was not a good one. Generally, the organization, methods, and materials of his instruction maximized his weaknesses in the knowledge and application of decontextualized skills, and minimized his ability to use his understanding of reading to comprehend and attack unfamiliar words. A number of specific interactions between learner and context supported this conclusion.

First, Tom's excellent knowledge about reading did not fit well with an instructional context that focused almost exclusively on isolated prereading skills; he did not understand what his instruction had to do with what he knew about reading. Second, his instruction did not capitalize on his strength in comprehension as a means of aiding his word recognition. Third, his instruction did not take advantage of his increased motivation when dealing with meaningful, connected text rather than isolated skill drill. Similarly, there were virtually no opportunities to link reading and writing, nor any authentic writing activities. Finally, the remedial setting in which he had been placed minimized the types of interactions that were likely to be most successful with Tom.

Our evaluation of the existing match provided us with the information needed to generate hypotheses about what Tom needed to progress as a beginning reader and writer. Our assessment was that Tom needed two things. First, he needed instruction that capitalized on his strong knowledge about reading while attending to his weaknesses in word recognition. In other words he needed "contextualized" word recognition instruction that would enable him to learn new word attack skills and apply those he had already acquired and learned. In the long term, he will also need to use writing to strengthen his print knowledge. The second thing that Tom needed was to become more actively involved in his own learning and instruction.

Diagnostic Teaching (Step 6)

At this point in the process, we were ready to engage in diagnostic teaching as a means of confirming our hypotheses and identifying possible instructional interventions. A summary of Tom's diagnostic teaching and its results is presented in the Thumbnail Sketch in Figure 11.10.

Planning. In the planning phase of diagnostic teaching, we needed to determine the specific nature of the interventions that would address the needs identified in Step 5. To do this, as we have noted previously, it is easiest to think in terms of the features of the settings, methods, and materials that can and should be modified and manipulated. In Tom's case, there were several aspects of the classroom setting (for example, grouping and interaction patterns) that needed to be modified to improve his involvement in his own learning and instruction. However, since we were not in a position to modify this setting, these factors were not good candidates for manipulation in diagnostic teaching. Despite this fact, there were still a variety of options that could be implemented in the tutorial program.

FIGURE 11.10

Tom's Thumbnail Sketch, Step 6

Getting Started (Step 1)	About the Reading and Writing Context (Step 2)	About the Learner (Step 3)	Decision Making (Steps 4 and 5)	Diagnostic Teaching (Step 6)
Background: Name: Tom Age: 7 Grade: 2 Key Correlates: • Dialect speaker • Normal vision, hearing, development *Information About the Learner* Knowledge about Reading and Writing: Motivation: Reading/writing Performance: *Information About the Context* School History: • Placed in special remedial class Instructional Approaches: • Grade 1, Basal-skills based Experiences, linguistic and cultural context: • Black dialect spoken in home	*Resources:* Reading placement level PPI • Basal worksheets and skill sheets • Some oral reading from reader *Instruction* • Focused on isolated word rec. skills • Practice without modeling or explanation • Little time spent with reader or other books *Settings* • Mom reads to him at home • Placed in special class with 18 low-achieving second graders	*Knowledge About Reading* • Understands purpose of reading (interview) • Demonstrates knowledge of story structure (retelling) • Knows he has trouble with accurate oral reading *Reading-Writing Performance* • Missed 42 of 1st 100 words on Fry list • IRI:PP level word recognition 1st + level composition • TERA: Reading age = 6.8; performed better in retelling than isolated letter/word tasks *Motivation* • Withdrawn when asked to do traditional letter/word tasks • Animated when discussing books his mother reads to him and when retelling stories	*Evaluating the Match (Step 4)* (What is the existing match?) Existing Match There is a poor fit between: • Good knowledge about reading and instruction focused on isolated readiness skills. • Good comprehension and decontextualized word resource instruction. • Motivation to read and lack of opportunity to read • Active learning style and passive instruction. *Reflection and Generating Hypotheses (Step 5)* What does the learner need? • Better word resource skills • "Contextualized" instruction • Active involvement in his own learning	*Planning and Implementing* What is most likely to (re)establish learning? Compare two "contextualized" approaches to word recognition instruction: • Teaching sight words taken from his dictated stories. • Teaching him to use graphic and contextual cues together to identify missing words in modified cloze passages. **Evaluating the Diagnostic Sessions** Dictated stories better than cloze because: • 100% of words learned vs 75%. • He reported preferring the "cutting" activity to all others. • More attentive, animated behavior

The characteristics of the methods, materials, and tasks of Tom's instructional context offered several alternatives for diagnostic teaching. Specifically, the instructional method could be modified to include methods and tasks that provided Tom with more support and elicited his active involvement in his own learning. In addition, his reading materials could be altered to provide him with more and better examples of interesting, connected text for use in learning and applying a variety of word recognition skills.

After considering the various alternatives, we decided to try out two alternative approaches for providing contextualized word recognition instruction. These approaches could roughly be characterized as a dictated stories approach and a cloze approach.

Executing.   The dictated stories approach was a modification of the traditional language experience approach. This procedure was designed to promote Tom's active involvement in learning sight words in the context of reading his own stories. The steps used were as follows:

1. Tom dictated and the examiner transcribed a short "story" on a topic of interest (for example, the upcoming holidays).
2. Tom read the story orally in its entirety.
3. The story was cut into sentence strips, the sentence strips were scrambled, and Tom was asked to put them in the correct order and reread the story.
4. The sentence strips were cut into word cards which were then scrambled, and Tom was asked to reorder the words into sentences and read aloud each sentence.
5. Tom targeted words to be entered into his word card file for future study and review.

The dictated story procedure required Tom to become actively involved in multiple readings of new words in the context of reading material he had generated for himself. In contrast, the cloze approach employed traditional early reading selections that had been altered to elicit Tom's active engagement in the application and integration of graphophonic and contextual word analysis strategies. Specifically, Tom was asked to read and supply the missing words for text in which all but the first letter of the targeted decodable words had been omitted. The targeted words were then added to his word bank for future study and review.

Both the dictated story and the cloze procedure were administered in a manner that included explaining to Tom the reason for each of the activities. In addition, he was asked frequently to reflect on what he was doing and why. This was done to help Tom understand the connections between reading instruction and independent reading activities.

Evaluating.   Several methods were used to evaluate the relative effectiveness of these two approaches. First, Tom was post-tested on his retention of the targeted words at the end of the session and after an intervening activity in which he listened to the examiner read. The results of this method of evaluation indicated that Tom recalled 100 percent of the words learned in the dictated story intervention and 75 percent of the words learned in the cloze approach.

The second method of evaluation involved asking Tom to describe the purposes of the two procedures and his feelings about completing the different activities. Tom described the purposes for both activities as learning to read words, but indicated that he liked cutting up the sentences the best.

The last, and possibly the most important, method of evaluation focused on the observation of Tom's interest and involvement in the various activities. Tom's behavior during the dictated story activities was animated and attentive. He was so interested in these activities that we had a hard time disengaging him when we needed to move on. In contrast, he was quite passive as he engaged in the cloze activities. Perhaps this procedure was too reminiscent of the activities he found so uninteresting in school. Whatever the reason, he showed a clear preference for the dictated story approach.

As a result of this diagnostic teaching experience, we devised a tutoring program based on the dictated story approach to which we added think-aloud and cloze activities that used his own stories. Tom never lost interest in this approach to learning, and proved to have a phenomenal memory for new words. We were able to introduce as many as ten new words in each session, and our frequent reviews indicated he rarely needed reteaching. At the end of twenty tutoring sessions, Tom's word recognition level on a repeated administration of the IRI had improved from a preprimer to a first-reader level on the word lists, and from a primer to a second-grade level for passage reading. The diagnostic teaching cycle was continuing, however, with interventions that would teach Tom to expand his repertoire of word recognition strategies from memorization and contextual analysis to the use of graphophonic information he will need as he begins to encounter more complex texts.

For both Marvin and Tom, the benefits of diagnostic teaching were both immediate and long-term. Each was quickly engaged in an instructional program that held promise of addressing their needs. In addition, the tutors were able to shape these sessions to obtain good information for planning and extending the reading programs of each. It does not always happen that our first diagnostic teaching sessions yield so rich a reward. One thing is abundantly clear, however. The quality of these sessions was directly related to two factors: the quality of the assessment information that was gathered before diagnostic teaching, and the thoughtfulness of the planning that went into the diagnostic teaching segment.

DIAGNOSTIC PORTFOLIOS: MAKING DIAGNOSTIC TEACHING WORK

Diagnostic teaching requires a solid knowledge base, a willingness to explore variation in student performance, and a repertoire of activities and materials for creating instructional adaptations. In the chapters to follow, we provide many suggestions for planning, adapting, and delivering good reading instruction. Many of these ideas can be incorporated into diagnostic teaching. Decision making and diagnostic teaching require that classroom teachers and clinicians make their hunches (hypotheses) explicit, set priorities, and use them to plan and execute instructional adaptations. Maintaining a Diagnostic Portfolio, and reviewing the contents periodically, can set the stage for this reflective teaching. When students' work and performance is reviewed over time and across multiple tasks and texts, it is often easier to inform instruction—to think about what might work or what should be attempted.

Good teaching requires that teachers establish and maintain their focus to accomplish assessment or instructional purposes. However, good teaching is also opportunistic and flexible. Interactive decision making during instruction is a hallmark of effective instruction (Duffy and Roehler 1986). This requires careful listening and refocusing.

In order to capitalize on the diagnostic teaching procedures we have described in this chapter, classroom teachers and clinicians will need to acknowledge the strengths and limitations of their own settings. Few classroom teachers will find the time to engage in continuous full-blown diagnostic sessions such as the ones we have described, and clinicians may even find it difficult to make this a part of their regular routine. Therefore, we suggest two specific practices that may prove helpful, depending on the setting.

Target Selections for Diagnostic Teaching

Classroom teachers who are using a basal reading system can designate specific selections in each level for use as diagnostic teaching selections. In this way, conditions can be set up that reflect the focus of classroom instruction. For example, predetermined selections can be used to:

1. conduct an individual assessment that examines students' progress outside their usual group setting;
2. set up conditions that are analogous to classroom instruction and compare those to students' unaided reading of the selection;
3. manipulate aspects of the lesson that are critical for student(s) in a particular classroom; and
4. select texts that make different demands as a means of exploring student flexibility.

If selections are targeted periodically, it is possible to do more elaborate assessment from time to time, rather than attempting it on a daily or even weekly basis.

Classroom teachers who are using a trade book/literature-based program can accomplish the same thing by establishing "assessment books." The benchmark books described in Chapter 9 are an example of this approach. We know of another school system that so values this approach that they have established a database for over 150 books so that teachers (and students) at Grades 1 through 3 can select from a wide array of regular library books to accomplish these assessments. Teachers who may be concerned about compromising the entertainment value of these books must remember that students need practice reading for a variety of different purposes. Furthermore, if the student's personal affective response to reading is an important goal of classroom instruction, then it should be included as part of the assessment.

A Collection of Diagnostic Teaching Selections

For both classroom teachers and clinicians, the time and attention demands are so great that diagnostic teaching is more likely to be employed if the materials and tasks are readily available. Paratore and Indrisano (1987) have developed a set of materials they use for diagnostic teaching that include graded (or progressively more difficult) passages and a set of tasks and prompts to accompany these passages. These materials permit them to explore a range of student responses "on the spot." To be effective, a collection of diagnostic teaching selections must be organized and grouped for easy use and clearly labeled so that adjustments can be made during the assessment session. In addition, we recommend using a set of clearly tabbed task cards to facilitate administration. The following types of materials should be considered for inclusion in a diagnostic teaching collection:

- Selections ranked by difficulty or a list of books to be used for assessment purposes.
- A listing of the types of tasks that can/should be used and the order in which these will be presented.
- A series of statements for each selection/book that could be expected in an adequate retelling of the text, and a place to note these.
- A summary sheet that includes key words to be used for assessment of vocabulary and/or word recognition.
- A place to make notes about student comments.

These ideas are, of course, only suggestions. Once started, a well-organized collection can and will grow. Furthermore, teachers who are committed to a portfolio approach to assessment find this type of organization absolutely essential to the effective implementation of ongoing assessment activities.

CHAPTER SUMMARY

This chapter focused on the point in assessment when informed decision making is required to determine how instructional planning will proceed. Specifically, this chapter dealt with understanding and implementing the steps in the assessment-instruction process that involve evaluating the match between learner and context (Step 4), reflection and generating hypotheses (Step 5), and diagnostic teaching (Step 6).

Evaluating the match between the learner and the instructional context (Step 4) involves using the information gathered in Steps 1–3 to determine the fit or match between the knowledge, skills and strategies, motivation and reflectivity of the learner and the settings, instruction, resources, and tasks within the instructional context. After the match between the learner and the instructional context has been evaluated, we need to reflect on this information and generate hypotheses (Step 5) about what the learner needs. This step is designed to help us make decisions about the relative importance of the various problems/needs we have identified.

Following Steps 4 and 5 in which we reflected on the existing match and generated some preliminary hypotheses about what the learner needs, we need to identify a better or optimal match between the learner and the context in order to (re)establish learning. To accomplish this goal, we rely primarily on the technique of *diagnostic teaching*. This procedure is both diagnostic, because it allows for the collection of additional information in order to clarify and test hypotheses, and instructional, because it provides opportunities to try out methods that may be successful alternatives for working with a student.

The process of diagnostic teaching involves three related tasks: planning, executing, and evaluating. During planning, we need to determine how we will focus the diagnostic teaching to verify our hunches about both the source of the problem and the instructional interventions that are most likely to call forth learning. Executing involves administering diagnostic teaching sessions using either the alternative methods or scaffolding approach to gain information about how a student performs under several different or contrasting conditions. Successful execution also requires the flexibility necessary to be able to take advantage of opportunities as they arise.

The primary thrust of the evaluation of the diagnostic teaching is to determine the impact of the manipulations on the student's learning, performance, attitude, motivation, and/or knowledge. Diagnostic teaching activities can be facilitated in both the classroom and the clinic through procedures such as using targeted selections in basal reading programs or preselecting a collection of diagnostic teaching materials.

SECTION *IV*

Instruction

THE PRECEDING CHAPTERS have focused on assessment and diagnostic teaching as a means of gathering information and gaining insight into individual learners. Decisions about how and what to teach are based on the resulting knowledge and understanding. Good decision making also requires an awareness of available instructional strategies and tools. Fortunately, there has been an upsurge of interest in recent years in advancing and promoting "best practices" in reading and writing instruction. Thoughtful teachers now have a wide array of effective instructional interventions from which to select their own preferred methods.

This section is divided into two subsections. Chapter 12, Getting Started with Instructions, provides guidelines for creating effective literacy environments and planning good initial instruction. In the second section, Adaptations, we deal directly with Step 7 of the Assessment-Instruction Process. In these chapters we describe instructional interventions that address specific components of literacy. Chapter 13 is devoted to adapting instruction to focus on word recognition and spelling, Chapter 14 to adapting instruction to focus on vocabulary, and Chapter 15 to comprehension, writing, and studying. Consistent with the focus throughout this text, these specific instructional techniques have been selected for discussion because they are a close match to the theoretical perspective of this text or because they have demonstrated their utility.

CHAPTER 12

Getting Started in Instruction

INTRODUCTION

Effective reading and writing instruction relies heavily on the decision-making powers of individual teachers. To make good decisions, teachers must orchestrate knowledge and skill in endlessly changing ways. In previous chapters we provided information about how to begin making good decisions using high-quality assessment information. In this chapter, we point out the types of instructional decisions that must be made and describe some effective instructional strategies for getting started.

Like assessment, instruction must begin somewhere. Of course, the multiple types of information that have been gathered, summarized, and examined quite closely in earlier steps of the assessment-instruction process (see Chapter 11) can now be used to plan an instructional program. However, it is often necessary to launch an instructional program before the assessment picture is completely clear. As we have already noted, the assessment-instruction process is continuous and requires adaptive teaching. Consequently, the issues addressed in this chapter are on the *beginnings* of instruction. This chapter lays the foundation for several chapters that follow, where more specific ideas about instructional intervention are offered.

In the next three sections of this chapter, we address three key aspects of instruction. First we discuss long-term curriculum planning, describing the types of decisions that must be made to establish a program focused on important curricular goals. Next, we describe some specific instructional activities that have such high general applicability that it makes sense to use them with nearly all students. Using these techniques, it is possible to get started with a student or students even when there is still some doubt about the details of the instructional program. In the final section of this chapter, we address the issue of lesson planning for individual students, providing guidance in specifying objectives and selecting activities. The more detailed planning described in that section leads from the "getting started," "high-utility" strategies described in this chapter to the narrower instructional focus of the remaining chapters of the book (see Chapters 13, 14, and 15).

MAKING DECISIONS: LONG-TERM PLANNING

Studies of school effectiveness suggest that instruction has the most impact when goals are clear and student progress is frequently monitored (Edmonds 1980; Rupley 1976). It is clear that teachers and the programs they implement are central to student learning (see Chapters 5 and 6). The basis for effective instruction is, of course, careful planning and preparation. Teachers make both long-term and short-term plans. In this section of the chapter, we describe some of the long-term, overarching decisions and plans that must be made by teachers: deciding on goals and objectives, selecting an organizational pattern, and selecting materials.

Goals and Objectives

There is always a variety of ways to help students learn information and acquire competence. Effective teachers control a wide range of instructional tools that they can use flexibly. However, specific instructional activities that might be used to teach students are of far less importance than knowing what is to be accomplished. Objectives are devised by teachers as they consider what they know about reading and writing processes, skilled performance, and the student. We turn to the first of these now, and to the second near the end of the chapter.

Even without exceptionally focused information about individual students, it is possible to make some judgments about appropriate practice based on an understanding of reading and writing processes. The curricular goals described in Chapter 6 also provide important guidance in initial planning. As we stated there, the goal of reading and writing instruction should be to create and encourage strategic, motivated, and reflective readers and writers. In refining these goals, we noted the need for specific lesson objectives to address *attitude*, *process*, and *content* objectives.

The first step toward accomplishing these ambitious long-term curricular goals is to create a context for success—an environment in which learning important outcomes is possible. We will return to the issue of lesson planning in the final section of this chapter.

Establishing a Literate Environment

The instructional context can and does influence learning and performance (see Chapters 5 and 6). Attempts to separate a particular learner's problems from setting, resources, approaches, and tasks are fruitless, since this separation ignores the interactive nature of reading and writing. Similarly, instruction is most effective when the texts and tasks mimic real reading and writing and the teaching occurs in integrated contexts. For example, there is evidence to suggest that students' reading achievement is enhanced by reading connected text with the support and guidance of a teacher, whereas there is little relationship between reading achievement and students' engagement in games or workbook activities (Leinhardt, Zigmond, and Cooley 1981; Zigmond, Vallecorsa, and Leinhardt 1980). Similarly, there is no evidence to support teaching formal rules of grammar as a means of improving speaking or writing (Hillocks and Smith, 1991). Rather, researchers such as Stotsky (1983) suggest that the abstract knowledge that proficient writers have about text comes from wide reading and writing experiences.

The first step in effective instruction, especially for less-skilled readers or writers, is the creation of a literate environment. Below we provide guidelines for establishing a literate environment using descriptors related to the three aspects of classroom contexts (Duffy and Roehler 1989) described in Chapter 5: the print environment (the physical environment), meaningful enterprise (the intellectual environment), and social exchange and interaction (the social-emotional environment).

The Print Environment

The first step in establishing a literate environment is establishing accessible, inviting, and well-trafficked reading and writing centers. The reading center, or library corner, should invite students to read. The rug(s), cushions, or soft chair(s) establish this as an area of comfortable interaction with print. Characters from books may be prominently displayed in the form of stuffed animals, drawings, illustrations, or book covers, depending on the age of the group.

The available print matter should offer students a wide range of reading options. Stocking a classroom library requires some knowledge and commitment on the part of teachers. Many teachers are well-informed about books, but there is evidence that others have not developed knowledge and expertise in this area. Mangieri and Corboy (1981) reported that 71 percent of the 571 elementary school teachers they surveyed could not name a single children's book published in the five preceding years. Only 9 percent of the total could name three or more such books.

The print materials should include all manner of real texts and reading materials used by literate individuals both in and out of school. The classroom reading collection might contain several books by the same author, books and stories created by students in the class, information about authors, and reference materials such as maps, atlases, and schedules. Materials that reflect a variety of cultural perspectives, especially those of the students in the class, are also important. These materials can help students feel accepted and promote understanding and respect for the language and the historical and personal heritage of different cultures.

Some materials will be intended for recreational, self-selected reading, while others will be used more selectively by students as they complete projects or acquire information. The materials in reading/writing centers or libraries should be consulted whenever possible. When a map is needed, students should be aware that they can consult the atlas in the reading center. When they need a good book for silent reading time, they should expect to find one there as well, along with written critiques of books by children who have already read them. In addition, this area would ideally contain newspapers, magazines, and other everyday print materials.

A literate environment also contains a well-stocked and accessible writing/publishing center. Students' writing folders may be kept in this area, but it should also contain writing materials, dictionaries, and, for older students, a thesaurus. Writing conference guidelines should be posted here. Many teachers and students like to have a word wall in this area. The word wall is simply a large, blank paper on which the students or teacher can write words that are frequently needed but difficult to spell, words that someone has found interesting and wants to share, or theme-related words that will be useful only for a particular period. If possible, this area should also contain at least one computer with word processing software and materials for illustrating and "publishing" books (paper, book bindings, markers, and so on). Samples of writing can also be posted, for inspiration or sharing.

Meaningful Enterprise

A key feature of any setting that promotes literacy is the provision for *meaningful enterprise*. In describing the attributes of a literate environment, Raphael and Englert (1989) note that students need to read and write for "real purposes and audiences," and they need many experiences that invite sharing and extending self-generated work. This is especially true for students of diverse backgrounds who don't understand the significance of schooling or becoming a good reader and writer for future life opportunities. If classroom activities are uninteresting or structured in ways irrelevant to students' lives, they are likely to "tune out" or become uncooperative (Au 1993; D'Amato 1987).

The point is that students must have opportunities to use their literacy skills for their own purposes, as well as others'. Classrooms where students read and write only for the teacher, using teacher-generated topics and guidelines, are less likely to produce people who read or write for their own purposes as lifelong learners. Using activities and materials that promote a meaningful approach to literacy, students are more likely to see the purpose behind them as genuine. As a result, they are more likely to transfer the knowledge and skill to new settings.

Much of the instructional and practice material designed for remedial work has been excessively contrived. The temptation is great to get started in instruction by using one of the packaged remedial programs involving extensive isolated skills work. However, remedial students are generally those who have the least appreciation for reading and writing as meaningful activities. Therefore, the first approach should focus squarely on the communicative nature of reading and writing, and students should be encouraged to use their skills in authentic ways. Students may find it rewarding to:

- read/write to younger students
- share humorous or moving portions of stories with others
- read/write to find out specific information or answer a question
- read/write in order to report to others
- read/write to compile information
- read to learn how to do something or to follow directions
- read to find out how others feel or react
- read/write for emotional support and guidance
- write to tell a personal story
- read/write for enjoyment

Whenever possible, the materials and tasks students use to learn to read and write should permit them to advance in their appreciation of the purposes for which they are acquiring these skills. Mastering a skill so that you can use it at the next level in a program is not a good enough reason for learning. Both students and teachers should understand how the new skill or knowledge can be used in real world reading and writing activities.

Social Exchange and Interaction

Another critical feature of literate school environments is the degree of *social exchange and interaction.* To become literate—to acquire the language and thinking skills needed to read and write effectively—students need many opportunities to discuss, collaborate, assist, and present information and ideas. Although we will be focusing our attention on techniques that are especially useful for working with individual students, the general environment in the school/classroom is critically important. We assume that all of the specific techniques to be discussed in this and future chapters are backed by an environment that involves large amounts of speaking, listening, reading, and writing.

According to Au (1993), research indicates that it is important to encourage nonnative speakers of English to use their native language to help them learn to read and write in English. For example, Moll and Diaz (1985) found that fourth grade students whose native language was Spanish could deal with grade-level texts and produce answers to comprehension questions comparable to their English-speaking peers when they were allowed to respond in Spanish. Building on students' native language abilities enhances their confidence and self-esteem by showing respect for their home languages and cultures.

In many classrooms there needs to be much more dialogue as opposed to lecture and formal presentation than is generally present in classroom settings (see Chapter 6, and Reciprocal Teaching in this chapter). Students need more opportunities to speak to each other, again as opposed to the formal oral presentations that are most common in schools. The smaller, less formal environments that are often characteristic of remedial instructional settings provide the perfect opportunity to promote a very dialogic, interactive mode of instruction. Unfortunately, many teachers of less-skilled students feel that they must deliver a specific skills-based program of instruction, and they often miss opportunities to promote literacy acquisition in a socially meaningful context.

Teachers who are interested in establishing a social context for learning can prompt literary responses, versus answers to questions, and can encourage students to challenge and comment on their reading and writing. Cooperative and collaborative arrangements can support this intention. Acting on decisions to alter the classroom context or the way that instruction is delivered requires careful consideration. In the next section we pursue these issues in some detail.

Other Long-Term Planning Considerations

Effective teachers make many decisions that require thoughtful reflection. Recent research and innovation in teaching suggest that even experienced teachers may want to examine such basic instructional decisions as how to group students and organize instruction. Similarly, new and exciting materials are available, and teachers may need to replace or supplement older texts with new books and materials.

Selecting Organizational Patterns

There are many ways to organize students for instruction. The range of acceptable practice is quite extensive, including classrooms with individualized arrangements, learning centers and open space, and team teaching with cross-class groupings, multiaged groupings, and whole class instruction in self-contained settings. In remedial settings, one-to-one tutoring is occasionally employed. However, the most common way to meet individual differences as discussed in Chapter 5 is to organize students into ability groups (Shake 1989) or to form homogenous ability groups in remedial settings. This type of arrangement has prevailed since the 1920s (Otto, Wolf, and Eldridge 1984) and there is extensive, but conflicting, evidence of its effectiveness. Although the research suggests that students *do* benefit from placement in groups (Rosenshine and Stevens 1984), there is less evidence that these groups need to be formed on the basis of ability. Indeed, an increasingly strong body of research suggests that students of all abilities benefit from organizational patterns that involve *cooperative groups* (Dansereau 1985; Johnson and Johnson 1986; Slavin 1983; Slavin, Stevens, and Madden 1988).

A widely recognized approach to cooperative grouping for reading and writing is Cooperative Integrated Reading and Composition (CIRC). Based on the cooperative learning principles developed by Slavin (1983; Stevens, Madden, Slavin, and Farnish 1987), CIRC couples traditional basal reading instruction with nontraditional grouping patterns. The result has been fairly dramatic reading achievement gains for students of all abilities. As an alternative to traditional patterns, it is worth a close look, either to be used in concert with other planned arrangements or as a substitute.

Students in the CIRC program belong to two groups: their own reading group (a traditional basal program) and a mixed ability team that is composed of members from two reading groups. Students work cooperatively to help each other master the material that has been assigned to them. The reading assignments are one component of the CIRC work; various writing activities associated with a process approach to composition are another. Students work together in a variety of supportive ways: reading to one another, summarizing stories, responding to stories, and practicing a variety of reading-related tasks. Group certificates are awarded to teams based on the average performance of all team members on all reading and writing activities.

In addition to cooperative grouping arrangements, special and support teachers are confronted with a wide array of choices about how to deliver reading and writing instruction. In some contexts it is undoubtedly better to provide in-class instruction (inclusion), especially if students join a mixed ability cooperative group after leaving their reading support group. In other cases, students will receive more focused and effective instruction in "pull-out" programs involving small groups of like-ability students. However, specialists need to be sure that their grouping arrangements are not promoting negative attitudes and/or dependency behaviors in poor readers or writers.

There is also evidence that elementary students of diverse backgrounds may benefit from the opportunity to learn in peer work groups (D'Amato 1988; Jordan 1985). Like other instructional approaches, however, the effectiveness of peer work groups may be strongly affected by cultural differences. Teachers need to "understand that peer work groups may need to be organized differently, and that peer teaching-learning interactions may take different forms, depending on the students' cultural background" (Au 1993, 87). It is important to build on cultural patterns of interaction to further literacy learning.

Executing any alternative grouping patterns requires careful consideration and planning. Long-term planning is required to alter the delivery of instruction in any significant way. However, given the rapidly changing knowledge-base regarding grouping practices, teachers should remain open to the development and evolution of different approaches as the evidence of successful interventions or arrangements grows.

Selecting Materials

Selecting materials is always something of a challenge for teachers of less-skilled readers and writers. The challenge becomes even greater when we demand that the texts and tasks students encounter be high-quality, authentic ones. In reading, students need whole texts that offer authentic reading models. Stories should offer strong narrative structures that entertain and speak to students' personal experience or interests. Expository texts should be accurate and considerate, providing students with opportunities to learn and remember important information.

Careful examination of the materials to be used for direct instruction is absolutely essential. We strongly recommend that available materials be evaluated using the guidelines suggested in Chapter 5. In addition, it will be helpful to refer to a variety of resources to build a collection and a repertoire. We have included a listing of award-winning fiction books (see Appendix B) as well as some sources of multicultural literature (see Appendix C). Materials especially designed for less-able readers and writers should be examined carefully to make sure that the text resulting from application of readability formulas or vocabulary control is not terribly stilted. The literary quality of these books is very uneven, but poor readers can often find a satisfying story between the covers.

In Appendix D, we have provided a listing of predictable and pattern books that will be useful for teachers of young or very disabled learners. Teachers who work with disabled readers or writers need a variety of these texts so that students can either acquire or practice their reading and writing skills in a supported print context. Some of these books are highly predictable at the level of word or syntax level (for example, *Brown Bear, Brown Bear,* by B. Martin), while others can be predicted only by attending to sound and symbol (for example, *Marvin K. Mooney,* by Dr. Seuss). Other books are predictable because there is an overall pattern and students can anticipate upcoming words and events using highly familiar or meaningful context (for example, *Little Red Hen).*

Not all students are excited by reading stories or poetry. Some would prefer nonfiction. Although it can be challenging to find good informational texts, the selection is expanding each year. Two exceptionally fine resources for selecting nonfiction and content-related books are: *Coming to Know: Writing to Learn in the Intermediate Grades* (Atwell 1990) and *Eyeopeners* (Kobrin 1988). Magazines and periodicals written by and for young people such as *Cobblestone, Cricket, Highlights, National Geographic World, Ranger Rick, Sesame Street, Sprint,* and *Stone Soup* should also be available in classroom settings. For more extensive descriptions and summaries, please refer to *Magazines for Children* (Stoll 1990).

Establishing an environment that promotes and encourages literacy is of the utmost importance. The materials and tasks provided for in the environment and the organizational patterns used will influence students' attitude and motivation for learning, and most likely what they learn about reading and writing as well. However, the instructional activities that take place in that environment also affect what students learn. In the following section, we provide descriptions of several instructional techniques that we have chosen to call *high-utility strategies.*

GETTING STARTED USING HIGH-UTILITY STRATEGIES

As a practical matter, teachers often want or need to begin some types of instruction even without a complete assessment picture. It is not possible for us to anticipate all the ways the information presented in this text might be used. Teachers can and do need to implement the steps and use the techniques of the assessment-instruction process in a variety of ways. The need to be flexible and to exercise professional judgment is an ever present mandate when working with students and schools.

The strategies we offer in this section are admittedly selective; we might have chosen others. However, we consider these to be high-utility because they: are theory-driven; have at least some empirical base to support their efficacy; have broad-based applicability; and address significant literacy outcomes.

The strategies we have selected generally share the following key features relative to current theory.

1. They provide for reading and/or writing in meaningful contexts for meaningful purposes.
2. They encourage social exchange or interaction focused on reading and writing activities.
3. They integrate skills and strategies in whole text reading and authentic writing activities.
4. They offer flexibility in terms of what can be done with the activities and the types of materials that can be employed.

Although many activities have been developed to promote reading and writing improvement, few provide evidence of their effectiveness. Most teachers are shocked to find that long-established practices often have no empirical base. For those strategies that we expect to use with all or most students (for example, high-utility strategies), we should demand demonstrated worth. In addition to empirical evidence supporting the efficacy of the strategies described here, we have used them in our own work with less-skilled readers and writers. These techniques are manageable for teachers who have not used them before and effective for students.

In the Getting Started phase of instruction, the flexibility of instructional activities is especially important, and the techniques described below offer almost unlimited adaptability. Together these activities encompass the full range of reading and writing abilities, offering a rich beginning context for any other instruction that might be required. The fact that each technique is designed to promote skilled, independent, and self-regulated reading and/or writing is also important. Instructional strategies must be planned to embody good practice, but also to address the important goals and objectives denoted in long-term planning.

In the following sections we describe six high-utility strategies selected according to the criteria described above: Sustained silent reading (SSR); dialogue journals; dictated stories; repeated readings; reciprocal teaching; and K-W-L.

Sustained Silent Reading

Sustained silent reading (SSR) practice promotes reading power and fluency, helps students develop positive attitudes toward reading, and is easy to implement in any school setting and at any grade level. Hunt (1970) provided the first descriptions of this practice, dubbing it Uninterrupted Sustained Silent Reading (USSR). In recent years, variations of the practice have been offered including: SQUIRT (Sustained Quiet Reading Time), DEAR (Drop Everything and Read), and SSR (Sustained Silent Reading). Across all adaptations, however, the heart of the technique remains the same: students read silently from self-selected materials for extended periods of time for their own purposes.

When students are permitted to read from materials that they choose, *and* when teachers model silent reading themselves, insisting that no student interfere with that experience, everyone benefits. The benefits of SSR are most clearly evident at the level of increased interest in, and motivation for, reading (Allington 1975; Cline and Kretke 1980; Sadowski 1980). It is also likely that SSR has a positive effect on students' abilities to read long, complex texts for their own purposes. As Hunt (1970) noted, SSR addresses the "essence of reading power; the ability to keep going with ideas in print" (150).

Despite the ease of implementation of SSR and the demonstrable positive benefits, some teachers abandon the practice after some initial attempt, and still others are reluctant to try it. Two reasons are most often offered. First, many teachers say that there is so little time in the day that they feel guilty if they are not "teaching." This is especially true for reading support teachers, such as special educators and Title/Chapter 1 teachers, and for high-school teachers, since they see students for so little time. This concern is obviously rooted in the idea that teaching only occurs during direct instruction. Although direct instruction *is* important, it is not the only way to teach. Indeed, some important literacy outcomes simply cannot be achieved via direct instruction. Such is the case with reading stamina and motivation.

With indirect instruction such as SSR, however, teachers must understand the importance of *modeling* (McCracken and McCracken 1978). Although it is tempting to use this period for other things (grading papers, conferencing, etc.), it is critical that students see teachers and other adults reading. This communicates that teachers think reading is important—so important that other things are put aside for the serious, albeit pleasurable, business of reading real books.

Launching SSR

Starting and monitoring SSR time is like implementing any other important aspect of the curriculum. There is no substitute for careful planning and good preparation. Teachers need to take time to create interest among students on the one hand (Gambrell 1978), and to clearly specify rules on the other (McCracken and McCracken 1971). Unfortunately, some students will never have been expected to read for sustained periods of time and will not know how to do it. Teachers must carefully prepare students and then be aware that some will need time to become proficient silent readers. The following steps should be considered before starting and during the initial stages:

1. *Talk to your students.* Clearly describe to them what will happen and what types of behavior you expect of them. The rules for SSR should include

provisions that everyone read a book that they have chosen, that everyone is quiet, and that there is no moving around during SSR.

2. *Help your students select books.* Do not assume that all of your students know how to choose a book that is good for them. Some younger or very unskilled students may need to have several books with them during silent reading period so that they do not need to move around to get a different book when they have chosen badly, or finish a short picture book.

3. *Start with success.* Initially, choose a short block of time (as little as five minutes for young or less-skilled readers) during a period of the day that is generally quiet and productive. One of the goals of SSR is that students begin to realize that they *can* stick with books, and that they can read and enjoy longer selections. The first periods should be so short that children should have no difficulty meeting the challenge (Mork 1972). Do not launch SSR during a period of transition. Using SSR to "quiet" students after recess or lunch period, for example, only works after both teachers and students are experienced at reading silently for sustained periods. The silent reading period should gradually be extended so that primary grade students are reading for fifteen to twenty minutes daily. Intermediate grade students should read for thirty to forty-five minutes. Aim for this length of time, even if this means that SSR cannot occur every day at the upper grades.

4. *Remember that you must read during this period also.* Select a book that you are presently reading or are genuinely interested in.

5. *Plan for it, include it in the schedule, and treat it seriously.* Recently, a first grade child told one of the authors that she did not do silent reading because her "work" was not done. Sustained silent reading is "work" and students will value its importance only if teachers do.

Adapting SSR

At first, some students will not use the period wisely-—a fact that should tell the teacher how much this period is needed. Teachers must be patient with students, while insisting that no individual disrupt the period. However, some students, including very young or very unskilled readers, may experience such difficulty that adaptations are needed. The most obvious adaptation is in the time provided. Some may be unable to sustain even the five minutes of initial time. Teachers should not hesitate to start with as little time as one minute! Some teachers find that it is helpful to set a goal together with the students and then use a kitchen timer in the beginning.

Guiding students in book selection can take care of many difficulties. Indeed, Hong (1981) has suggested that the key to success during SSR is the quality of the books. Other ways to adapt SSR that still retain the emphasis on book reading include the following:

1. Institute a "recreational reading time" (Morrow 1989) or "booktime" (Hong 1981) instead of SSR. This is a time when students are permitted

some interaction and movement. For example, buddy reading might be permitted, students might be allowed to select new books, or the teacher might be available to provide some reading help. Morrow also suggests that any book-related activity might be permitted during this period.

2. Introduce books to students so that they can choose a book based on some knowledge. All teachers have experienced the rush of enthusiasm for a book that has just been read aloud. Reading aloud is one of the best ways to introduce books to students. Other ideas for introducing books include doing book talks, preparing puppet shows using the characters and events from a book, and making book-tape combinations available for students.

We do not find that these adaptations are necessary in remedial settings, since there are generally fewer students. Occasionally we have had to remind students about how to read silently and how to attend to print during silent reading, and we have sometimes had to constrain students' choices so that they select appropriately. These adaptations are removed as soon as students have some experience successfully sustaining themselves with print. Students with any significant experience reading connected text do not generally need these supports.

Students who cannot sustain themselves in print may have had too much experience with isolated skills. There *are* students who have no experience reading ordinary books, and as a result have little idea that reading is a sense-making process. The benefits of SSR for these students include recognizing the purposes of reading, providing practice and transfer opportunities, and providing experiences with meaningful reading material.

Finally, SSR must be maintained in the curriculum, with its usefulness and purpose reviewed periodically. Although students should not be interrogated about the materials they read during SSR, they can be encouraged to keep a record of their reading. Teachers can then use this to shape the rest of the reading program. Hunt (1970) suggests that student self-evaluation is an important feature of SSR, allowing students and their teachers to monitor progress (see Figure 12.1). Other methods also provide this type of continuous assessment information. Graphing the number of words or pages read or keeping reading logs of all selections read can provide excellent documentation of the instructional program and rewarding feedback to students who need visible proof of their growing competence.

Dialogue Journals

Both attitude and process objectives can be addressed with well-crafted writing activities. Dialogue journals are especially well-suited to settings dealing with less-skilled students and have been used to help bilingual students develop their English skills (Flores and Hernandez 1988). As the name suggests, dialogue journals involve written exchanges between a teacher and his or her students, or less often, among students in a group (Atwell 1987; Fulwiler 1980). A dialogue journal contains a genuine conversation, written rather than spoken. The

**FIGURE
12.1**

*Questions for
Readers and
Writers*

How Well Did I Read and/or Write Today: A Self-Check

Today's Date _____ My Name _____

Titles of Books Read: _____ Authors: _____

Titles of My Writing(s): _____

This sheet contains sample questions to be used with students in evaluating
progress in individualized reading and writing programs. The questions are designed
for two purposes: (1) to have the student be more reflective about his/her own
reading and/or writing processes; and (2) to provide a check for the teacher on the
student's attitudes toward his/her own performance.

Any or all questions can be used to fit a particular program regardless of level of
student and teacher needs. Each teacher is free to select those items of greatest
worth.

Part One

1. Did you have a good reading/writing period today? Did you read/write well?
2. Did you read/write better today than yesterday?
3. Were you able to concentrate today on your silent reading? on your writing?
4. Did the ideas you were reading/writing about hold your attention?
5. Were you constantly moving ahead with the ideas you were reading/writing about?
6. Was it hard for you to keep your mind on what you were reading/writing today?
7. Were you bothered by others or by outside noises?
8. Could you keep the ideas in your reading/writing straight in your mind?
9. Were there words you did not know? How did you figure them out?
10. What did you do when you got to the good parts? Did you read/write faster? or slower?

Part Two

1. Why did you read this particular book/write this piece?
2. Was this a good choice?
3. Could you tell what was happening all the time you were reading/writing?
4. Was this book/piece of writing hard or was it easy for you to read/write?
5. What made it hard or easy?
6. Would you choose the same kind or a different kind of book/piece of writing next time?
7. Did you want to keep on reading/writing? Or did you have to force yourself to keep going?

Adapted from "A Self-Check" from "The Effect of Self-Selection, Interest, and Motivation upon
Independent, Instructional, and Frustrational Levels" by L. C. Hunt, *The Reading Teacher,*
November 1970, pp. 148–149.

interactive format of equal turns on the same topics is quite different from the traditional personal student journals, in which a teacher may sometimes make some kind of marginal comment on a student's entry, but often days or weeks after the student wrote it. The distinguishing characteristics of dialogue journals are their interactive, functional nature and the creation of mutually interesting topics (Staton 1987, 49).

Dialogue journals are frequently used to encourage students to reflect on specific content to be learned, books that have been read, or ideas that are triggered by recent reading/writing activities. Like SSR, dialogue journals are useful for most students because they are aimed at addressing broad reading/writing goals. In addition, they are easy to initiate, and with commitment, easy to sustain.

Atwell (1987) has provided extensive documentation regarding the benefits of journal activity with middle-school students, concluding:

> Through our dialogue journals my students learned, too, about the world of written texts—what good writers do, what good readers do, how readers talk, what books are for and how kids can get in on it. (170)

Atwell and her students have catalogued the topics addressed in hundreds of journal entries. These included sophisticated exchanges involving plot and action, authors and authors' craft, genre, applications to students' own writing, reading strategies and students' affective responses, judgments regarding book recommendations, and editorial topics and mechanical advice. Finally, there is a wealth of personal anecdote and mutual support that permeates the samples Atwell provides (see Figure 12.2).

Launching Dialogue Journals

The success of dialogue journals will probably rely on the teacher's commitment to read and respond honestly to students' entries. Because many students (and many teachers too) have had little experience with writing, it is important to think about how to get students started. Although a dialogue journal can be as simple as several sheets of notebook paper stapled together, we have found that something more substantial invites students to take the activity seriously. Fulwiler (1987b) suggests that students use a small looseleaf notebook for all journal entries so that any writing too personal to share can be extracted before it is turned in to the teacher.

Inexperienced students will need more than an attractive journal to overcome their reluctance to write, however. The following ideas should help the teacher launch the dialogue journal.

1. *Provide students with material or questions that invite response.* Reading a provocative book aloud or sharing something interesting or compelling about an author will be enough for some students. Others will need a specific question that prompts thoughtful response, like this one offered by Staton (1987, 49):

   Kelly: I like to read. Ev'ry time I woth a skery movy I have a drem.

FIGURE 12.2

Atwell Dialogue Journal Samples

At the start of the school year Libby's letters to me stayed on the outside of written texts. She gave daily blow-by-blow accounts of plot, of what characters were up to, as in this letter about June Foley's *Love by Any Other Name*.

9/11

Dear Ms. Atwell,

Billie is getting restricted because of Bubba and his friends mostly, and partly herself. First she got restricted for being late. And then she got restricted for sitting with Bubba's friends (and a day before they got a lecture on food fights) and a girl (a friend of hers) brought in a table cloth, wine glasses, china plate ware, napkins, champagne, for them and the table! And so they all got detention for a week! But why would they get a detention, because of the champagne? Probably.

Your friend,
Libby

P.S. Have a nice day!

Every time I wrote back to Libby I wrote back about the author, using the author's name and speculating about why he or she had decided to have characters behave as they did. My response to the letter above is typical:

9/11

Dear Libby,

Well, I do think champagne is a little bit much for a cafeteria lunch, but it's a good example for what Foley is trying to do here. Can you see how she's trying to show how far and foolishly Billie is willing to go to be in with the in crowd? (And can you guess what's going to happen to Billie by the novel's end, how Foley is going to have Billie end up? I can see it coming.)

Ms. A

I nudged right through the first two months of school, modeling author talk like crazy, and by the end of October Libby had begun to come inside.

10/24

Dear Ms. Atwell,

I have started reading *That Was Then This Is Now* by S. E. Hinton. It is a pretty good book! I didn't know that she had Ponyboy Curtis in the book as a character. That surprised me! I like the way she writes. It's like you are there in the book. You can picture what it is like and stuff.

Sincerely,
Libby

P.S. Have a nice day!

10/24

Dear Lib,

I know just what you mean. Hinton puts us inside the characters. She tells so much about what they're thinking and feeling that we see things through their eyes and feel with their hearts. In *The Outsiders*, with Ponyboy as her narrator, she really puts us there, in the book.

I loved it that Pony showed up in *That Was Then* . . . It was like an in-joke. You had to know *The Outsiders* to pick up on the reference: sort of like, be a member of the Hinton Club.

Ms. A

P.S. I'll be really anxious to know what you think of how Hinton decided to conclude this one. She shook me up but I think she was right.

Teacher: Scary movies give me bad dreams, too, Kelly. Maybe we shouldn't watch them. What good books have you read?

Kelly: The little red hen and Dick and Jane. I have problms some times well I hav this problm it is I am not very god on my writeing.

2. *Provide students with some model or idea of what is expected.* Gambrell (1985) suggests that students think about a format similar to letter writing and that they ask the teacher a question. Alternatively, teachers can start by asking the students a question that requires them to respond. Then, in the teacher response, appropriate dialogue exchange is modeled over several entries.

3. *Respond in ways that encourage individual students.* This encouragement will be based on knowledge of specific students and is likely to vary. According to Atwell (1987):

> My responses grow from what I've learned about a reader and how I hope to move the readers' thinking. In general my comments do three things, to *affirm*, *challenge*, or *extend* the reader's thinking. These comments take various forms: gossip, questions, recommendations, jokes, restatements, arguments, suggestions, anecdotes, instruction, and "nudges." (275)

Probably the most important key to maintaining the success of dialogue journals is the teacher's commitment to respond to students' entries. As a result, it is important to give some consideration to the management of journals. Many teachers, for example, find that they cannot read everyone's journal every night. Gambrell (1985) suggests starting dialogue journals with only a small group of students so that it is not necessary to juggle an entire class initially. After students have some experience with this activity, some teachers require that everyone write each day but they respond to only one-third each day. If a student really wants or needs a response on a particular day, however, the system should allow for this.

Maintaining and Extending Dialogue Journals

Once teachers have made the commitment to read and react to students' writing, dialogue journals can add immeasurably to the instructional program. They can "provide a 'window' into the students' cognitive activities during writing and reading … giving teachers opportunities to highlight students' idea generation, planning, predicting, and monitoring" (Raphael and Englert 1989, 238). Teachers' skills in this area are typically not well developed, so they should not expect to feel comfortable making responses initially. However, Atwell (1987) offers some "lessons" that are worth sharing (276):

1. *"One good, thoughtful question is more than enough."* Atwell's experience suggests that students' least interesting or insightful responses came when she asked didactic questions that sounded as though she were testing the students.

2. Respond *"as a curious human being."* Dialogue journals seem to work best when they are genuine dialogues between two people who are really expressing their own ideas and sharing their own experiences.

3. *"Make no corrections on students' letters."* Dialogue entries are not final writing samples. Atwell suggests responding to mechanics only when journals cannot be read.

4. *"The journals contribute to class grades."* The grades are based on a minimum quantity (one entry per week), thoughtfulness of the responses, "use of classroom independent reading time, and progress made toward a few, individual goals set at the beginning of each quarter."

Dialogue journals can be adapted for use across the curriculum (see Fulwiler 1987b). Classroom teachers should look for opportunities to use journal entries during non-language arts periods. It is becoming increasingly clear that when writing is used in content area disciplines, everyone benefits. "Journal writing in class stimulates student discussion, starts small group activity, clarifies hazy issues, reinforces learning experience, and stimulates imaginations" (Fulwiler 1982, 15). Resource teachers should consider asking students to write about topics that are being studied in their regular classrooms.

Dictated Stories

As an instructional technique, the dictated story has its roots in the Language Experience Approach (LEA) to reading (Stauffer 1969, 1980; Allen 1976). As a beginning reading method, LEA promotes student awareness of the relationship between oral and written language by having students produce a "language experience story." This story then becomes the reading material that is used for the delivery of instruction. Because this eliminates problems of a mismatch between the student's language and the reading materials, the technique has been widely used for very beginning learners, for bilingual students (Wilson and Cleland 1989), with middle-school remedial reading students (Sharp 1990), and with adults (Mulligan 1974; Newton 1977). Clearly, LEA addresses process outcomes while attending closely to both attitude and motivation.

LEA stories have traditionally been created by individuals or collaboratively by groups. For example, one of the authors was assigned to work with seventeen fifth- and sixth-grade boys whose reading level was below first grade. Collaborative LEA stories revealed the group's consuming interest in football, specifically the local professional team. Using this topic and the weekly game results, students wrote, revised, and worked with football stories all fall. Newspapers, sports magazines, and special edition sports periodicals were brought into the classroom and the students began to realize that they could read the specialized accounts of football activity. In the process, they learned to analyze the patterns of print; to recognize letter combinations, compound words, base words, and to master some high frequency sight vocabulary. The average reading gain for this group was over two grade levels in nine month's time. Most were still not exceptionally strong readers, but they had made good progress, had control over some essential skills, and more importantly, believed they could read and saw at least a few reasons for doing so.

As a practical matter, classroom teachers are likely to generate group stories when they have shared an experience (for example, a field trip) or are planning an activity (for example, a class party). Indeed, the first step in a Language Experience Story is the provision of an *experience* (e.g., the unexpected appearance of a skunk on the playground, a fire in a nearby building, and so on). Rich group stories can result from such experiences.

For the purposes of working with very unskilled readers or writers, individual stories may be preferred. Individual dictated stories need not be prefaced by some formal experience. In fact, sharing personal stories, memories, and moments is an important way for students, especially those of diverse backgrounds, to feel part of the classroom community (Mikkelsen, 1990).

Launching the Dictated Story

As the name suggests, these stories are created as a student dictates to a recorder (teacher, parent, older student). Always start by talking with students about what they would like to say. Some students will be ready to dictate, and a brief discussion will quickly reveal this. Other children will be floundering or have little idea about what they wish to say. The youngest or most unskilled students may want only to label. Like the other activities already suggested, dictated stories permit a range of responses and all students should be able to participate, although the responses may vary profoundly. Bridge (1989) offers the following guidelines for the dictation process:

1. Students should be able to read back the story, so it shouldn't be too long.
2. If possible, wait until the student's thought is complete, then record exactly what the student says.
3. Say each word as you write it, asking the student to watch.
4. As you record, provide some reading instruction appropriate for this student (e.g., note that there are spaces between words, that certain words begin the same way, that the story has an excellent beginning, and so on).
5. Read the story aloud for the student, encouraging students to join as they are able.
6. Have the student read the selection independently when he or she is able (this may require several readings).

Students will become more and more adept at producing dictated stories and, like the silent reading and the dialogue journals described above, this can form the core of a set of regular instructional activities. Simply producing a dictated story will be beneficial for the less-able student

The goal is to allow students to role play themselves as successful students, even in the early stages of becoming readers and writers. Through repeated readings of the words in the familiar context of the dictated stories, students will add the words to their sight vocabularies and develop oral reading fluency and confidence in themselves as readers (Bridge 1989, 195).

Adapting and Using Dictated Stories

Once the dictated story has been created, it can become the focus of all kinds of effective instruction. As noted above, it can be the reading material used to deliver reading instruction. The stories can be retyped or copied for instructional purposes. Students can then underline, highlight portions, or cut the stories apart. Dictated stories around the same or similar themes can provide opportunities to develop rich vocabulary and repeated exposure to some words.

Ideally, the use of dictated stories will be reduced and a more student controlled version of writing initiated as soon as students are able to take over the mechanics of writing (see Graves 1983; Temple, Nathan, Burris, and Temple 1988). Student-produced writing should not replace dictated stories until students are able to produce with some ease as much as they can dictate in a comparable period of time. Until then, students should create personal journals and drawings as well as dictated stories. This is true for both native and nonnative speakers of English, as research suggests that the writing development of ESL students parallels the writing development of students who speak English as a first language and that ESL students can begin writing in English before they have complete control over the systems of English (Hudelson 1986).

Dictated stories can provide the basis for remedial or basic instructional work of the following sort.

1. Create cloze passages using these stories to provide practice in using context and writing frequently-used or favorite words.
2. Select words to focus on—sight words that appear in repeated frames, words that have the same initial sound, base words used in interesting ways—whatever is appropriate for the student.
3. Look for themes that are worth pursuing with this student. Some may require the teacher to read aloud, but others may offer reading options for the student.
4. Look for opportunities to link the dictated story to something that has been read. One way to introduce new vocabulary and linguistic patterns is to encourage students to explore using book models.

If the stories are placed on a classroom computer, these types of multiple revisitings for various instructional purposes are obviously made much easier. Students may also be able to manage the transition from dictated stories to some independent writing if a program with voice synthesis is available.

Repeated Readings

Although very young children often hear the same story many times, once they enter school they are generally expected to read a story just once, with good fluency and comprehension, and then move on to another. The value of repeated experiences with books and stories has too often been missed by educators. The point of repeated reading is simply to persuade and induce children to read a particular text several times so that they can improve fluency through increased familiarity and additional practice. As such, it has proven to be an extremely useful tool for teachers working with less-skilled readers.

One of the most potent reasons for revisiting reading materials is to build fluency. We agree with Allington (1983b) who notes: "Limitations [of the research] aside, a preponderance of empirical and clinical evidence supports the relationship of fluent oral reading and good overall reading ability" (560). Although there are a variety of procedures for developing oral reading fluency (see Smith, 1979), the most widely tested technique involves *repeated readings* (Allington 1977; Chomsky 1978; Samuels 1979).

Like the other strategies already discussed, repeated reading offers both ease and flexibility in implementation. One of the most powerful characteristics of a repeated reading technique is the increased opportunity for practice reading continuous and connected text. Many teachers expect resistance from students when they are asked to reread material because, on the surface, this seems to be such a mechanistic and repetitive task. However, young children often choose to reread material themselves as they try to read real texts (Rasinksi 1986). They will return to the same piece until it is familiar and can be read with understanding. Less skilled readers generally do not get the opportunity to read much at all, much less reread material for control and fluency (Allington 1977). Repeated readings offer them this opportunity.

Finally, repeated readings permit students to experience reading something that is (or has become) relatively easy for them to read. Allington (1983b) has suggested that this experience of reading relatively easy material may be essential in the development of fluency. Whatever the reason, we have not only found limited resistance to a repeated reading strategy, we have generally found that this is a favored activity. Repeated readings focus specifically on one aspect of the reading *process,* but the strong success experiences that are evoked often produce positive attitude outcomes as well.

Launching Repeated Readings

The easiest way to initiate repeated reading is to mark off a segment of print in a text that the student is already reading and to ask the student to read and reread that section until he or she has reached some predetermined level of fluency. For example, Samuels (1979) suggested that students read repeatedly until they could read the section at a rate of 85 wpm. Others have suggested that speed is not a sufficient criterion. For example, Allington (1983b) suggests lightly marking segments of text in phrase units. Students' repeated readings are then judged in terms of improved phrasing. Still another possibility is simply to dictate how many rereadings of a text will be required (Ballard 1978). In any event, it is necessary to decide what students will be told about how the technique will be used and when they can move on to new material.

Some sensible guidelines for the beginning stages of repeated readings might include the following:

1. *Select materials that lend themselves to fluent oral reading.* Material that is too choppy or artificial, as commercial beginning materials can be, probably will not result in rewarding renderings of the text, nor in increased fluency.

2. Be sure to *talk to students about why they are doing this activity.* They should be helped to see that they are practicing a *part* of reading, much the way an athlete or musician might practice a small part in order to improve the overall performance. Emphasize that increased expression, knowledge of words, use of context, and so on will help them to comprehend text more easily. Students must see that the goal isn't exceptionally fine oral reading.

3. Since the student will be rereading the material several times, *don't hesitate to select material that will be somewhat challenging.* Clearly, it is also necessary to use good judgment about task difficulty as it affects individual students.

4. *Students should be encouraged to practice (reread) silently as much as possible.* The only real danger of repeated readings is that they may supplant other productive silent reading experiences.

Maintaining and Adapting Repeated Readings

Samuels (1979) suggests several ways to maintain interest in repeated reading. One of the easiest is to keep track of the experience by graphing or logging the results (see Figure 12.3). Students, especially discouraged students, find this simple practice extremely gratifying and are often anxious to share their progress with family and friends. Indeed, graphing or visually displaying progress is an excellent practice for young or less-skilled students, one that can be used with many activities and goals.

A caveat is in order, however. Feedback in the form of graphs and other displays should be individual and private. The purpose is to compare the student's performance with his or her earlier performance; any competitive comparison or public display is probably not helpful. Public competition is only rewarding for those who are highly successful. However, individual progress forms can help students to see their growth even when it has been slow. Other adaptations can be initiated as practical considerations and student needs dictate (Samuels 1979, 1988). For example, students can be encouraged to practice rereading by reading along with an audiotape. This is especially helpful for students who require a fluent model to guide them. Alternatively, students can work in peer groups to practice with a "buddy" (see Chapter 13).

As suggested, there are many ways to involve students in repeated reading. One of these, Talking Dictionary (Ballard 1978), has been especially successful for students who require high levels of support in repeated readings. Talking Dictionary involves reading, and then rereading a specific piece of text with the help of a "talking dictionary," or teacher. Talking Dictionary is implemented as follows (see Figure 12.4):

First Read:

1. The procedure is explained to the student.
2. The teacher selects, or helps the student to select, material that is too long to be read in one three-minute sitting.

FIGURE 12.3

*Repeated
Reading Chart*

If you repeatedly read the same passage, you will soon read it smoothly and easily. This sheet will help to record your progress in reading.

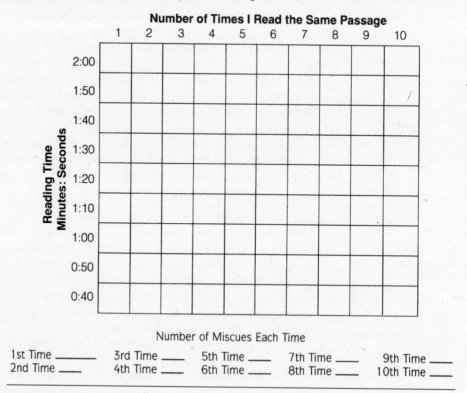

"Repeated Reading Chart," p. 5, in QUEST *Desert Magic* Unit 1, *Electric Butterfly and Other Stories* by Mark W. Aulls and Michael F. Graves. Copyright © 1985 by Scholastic Inc. All rights reserved. Reprinted by permission.

3. The student is asked to begin reading the selected portion of text aloud and continues reading for three minutes.

4. Whenever the reader encounters an unknown word, he or she asks for the pronunciation ("word please") and the teacher provides it *without* comment. The reading continues.

5. The teacher's job is to keep track of time (either two or three minutes is a reasonable amount), to provide unknown pronunciations, and to count the number of words read correctly.

Second Read:

1. The student returns to the starting point and repeats the process, again asking for any unknown words.

2. Once again, the teacher provides all requested words without comment, keeps track of time, and tallies correctly read words.

FIGURE 12.4
Talking Dictionary

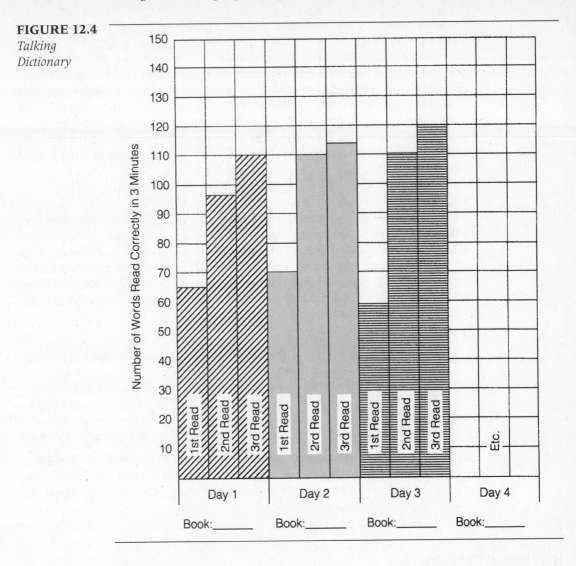

Third Read:

1. The process is repeated.
2. When the three minutes are completed, the results of the three reading attempts are graphed.

The procedure can be used quite easily by parents, who are often searching for an activity that will support their child's reading growth. One advantage of Talking Dictionary is that it permits only positive and helpful responses. In every way, the technique communicates to the student that the adult is there to provide support and will also celebrate the increased fluency that invariably results.

Students not only have an opportunity to practice reading connected text but also to do so in a supportive environment.

Generally speaking, teachers should expect that during the second and third renderings, students will recognize at least *some* of the words that were requested and read further into the text. If, after several attempts (graphed along the model presented in Figure 12.4) there is still *no* improvement, some adaptation should then occur. The most common adaptations involve the need to choose an easier (or more difficult) text, remind the student that it is desirable to request help when print does not make sense, or examine the role of anxiety in the student's oral reading fluency.

Although increased fluency is the most straightforward benefit to be enjoyed from repeated reading activities, it is not the only one. For example, there is evidence that young students' recognition of sight vocabulary improves when they are encouraged to reread texts (Bridge and Burton 1982; Bridge, Winograd, and Haley 1983; Chomsky 1978). There is also evidence from teacher read-aloud research that when students have repeated opportunities to hear the same stories again, their comprehension improves. Martinez and Roser (1985) report four changes that occur as students become increasingly familiar with a story:

1. Students produced more verbal responses.
2. The nature of these responses changed such that self-initiated comments and judgments became more frequent.
3. The focus on discussion changed so that students "tended to talk more about story language, events, settings, and titles as the stories became familiar" (785).
4. Students appeared to gain greater insights into some segments of stories.

Because of these other benefits, teachers should find the practice of "revisiting" texts potentially powerful even if they do not use one of the more structured repeated reading procedures. We will describe some other ways to repeatedly use text later in the chapter.

Reciprocal Teaching

Reciprocal Teaching, like several techniques that have been validated in recent years, is focused on process outcomes. The strategy was devised to promote the effective use of complex comprehension knowledge and skill and has proved effective in studies with remedial readers in middle school (Palincsar 1984; Palincsar and Brown 1984). It has also been used successfully to enhance the listening comprehension instruction of first grade students whose test score indicated that they were at-risk for reading problems (Palincsar 1986). The effectiveness of Reciprocal Teaching is evident by the improvement in the dialogue during instruction, the improvement in scores on measures of comprehension including standardized tests, the continuation of improvements for up to six months after training, and the improvement on classroom tasks that were similar to but distinct from the instructed activity.

Palincsar and Brown (1984) identified several major activities that are generally accepted as integral to comprehension ability. Skilled comprehenders understand a variety of explicit and implicit purposes for reading, activate prior knowledge, focus on important versus trivial content, and maintain this focus throughout the selection. In addition, they make critical judgments about the relationships between and among ideas in text, judge the content against prior knowledge, monitor reading for comprehension, and make inferences for the purposes of predicting, interpreting, and drawing conclusions about reading material. Reciprocal Teaching is intended to teach students to accomplish these activities as they read connected text.

Launching Reciprocal Teaching

This strategy requires that teachers have selected several expository passages and that they are prepared to work collaboratively with their students. The following steps describe the basic pattern of interaction in Reciprocal Teaching.

Step 1. The teacher meets with a small group (five to fifteen students) and models four comprehension-fostering strategies (predicting, self-questioning, clarifying, and summarizing). Then the teacher applies these strategies while reading a paragraph or segment from content area materials. After the procedure has been modeled by the adult teacher with several segments of text, the students take over the role of teacher.

Step 2. If the passage is new to the group, the adult teacher asks students to predict what the text will be about based on the title. If the passage is familiar, students are asked to recall and state the topic of the passage as well as the important points already covered.

Step 3. The adult teacher assigns a segment of the passage to be read (usually a paragraph) and either tells the students that she will be the teacher (especially for the initial days of instruction) or assigns one of the students as teacher for the first segment.

Step 4. When the group finishes reading the segment silently, the teacher for that segment proceeds to *ask a good question or two, clarify* the hard parts, *summarize* the paragraph or segment in a sentence, and then (starting the cycle all over again) to *predict* what the next paragraph or segment will discuss.

Step 5. Whoever is in the role of teacher for each segment must help answer the questions or suggest alternative questions, clarify the unclear parts of the text, revise the summary, and agree or disagree with the prediction.

Step 6. The adult teacher provides the guidance necessary for the student teachers to complete the preceding activities through a variety of techniques:

> *PROMPTING:* "What question did you think a teacher might ask?"
> *INSTRUCTION:* "Remember, a summary is a shortened version, it doesn't include a lot of detail."
> *MODIFYING the activity:* "If you're having a hard time thinking of a question, why don't you summarize first?"

REQUESTING the help of other students: "Who can help us out with this one?"

Step 7. The adult teacher provides praise and feedback specific to the student teachers' participation: "That was an excellent summary. You provided the most important information," or "You worded that question well, but it was about a minor detail. Can you ask us about some more important information?" After this feedback, the adult teacher models any activity that continues to need improvement: "A question I would have asked is . . ." or "I would summarize by saying . . ." The procedure continues in this manner with the teacher supporting and modeling as needed.

Maintaining and Adapting Reciprocal Teaching

The dialogic and interactive nature of Reciprocal Teaching demands a commitment on the part of teachers to engage in discussion and to respond to students' knowledge and skill. Over time, we would hope that students would not need teachers to help them craft good questions or clarify text. However, many students will need this support during difficult text reading, even after they have mastered the general approach. It is important to remember that Reciprocal Teaching is a *simulation* of the process of reading and comprehending. The specific strategies are not as important as the process itself. These should not be viewed as discrete activities to be trained and mastered. Instead, students (and teachers) should approach the task as a cognitive activity that is being launched interactively.

The original activity was designed for students who had adequate word identification skills but poor comprehension. It has been demonstrated to be effective with this group. However, Palincsar has subsequently adapted the technique to be used with very young or very unskilled students. In the adapted form, the text is read to students, and they are encouraged to think it through during a listening task. This approach has reaped benefits for these students as well.

K-W-L

Many students who require additional help in reading have particular difficulties reading and studying expository text. Reading for informational and/or study purposes may be unfamiliar for many less-skilled readers, and too often they approach reading passively, as a word-recognition task. Carr and Ogle (1987) provide a vivid description of the problem:

> When they (middle school and secondary readers), begin to read, they do not perceive that they should learn, rather than simply "look at text." They are unaware of basic techniques, such as identifying key ideas and summarizing. When we asked one sophomore what she did when she read, she responded, "I try to take in the words and hope the teacher won't call on me." (p. 626)

Ogle (1986, 1989) has developed a simple teaching strategy known as K-W-L that has high utility for many students across disciplines and is an appropriate choice for students who need support in accomplishing specific content outcomes. K-W-L is a three-step procedure to promote thinking and active reading. The letters stand for What I know (K), What I want to know (W), and What I have learned (L) (see Figure 12.5).

K-W-L can easily be used to adapt the traditional Directed Reading Activity (see Chapter 5) since the technique parallels the before, during, and after phases of the DRA. However, teachers who are accustomed to high levels of teacher control and direction will need to guard against too much interference. With too much teacher direction, students will quickly come to see that they are really just reading for the teacher's purpose, and there is little point in using the K-W-L strategy. Remember that the point of K-W-L is to help students become more actively involved in reading and to enhance their memory for information identified as personally important.

Launching K-W-L

In the first step (K), the teacher helps students to activate prior knowledge about a topic and organize it into useful categories. In the second step (W), the teacher helps students to ask themselves questions and set purposes for reading on the same topic. As students read, however, they are permitted to add questions to their list. In the final step (L), students record answers to questions they have asked and the group discusses the questions and answers. Of course, students may be jotting down answers to questions as they read.

It should be apparent that K-W-L requires no special training. It does require that a teacher be willing to help students identify what they know and permit them to pursue questions of their own determination. When introducing K-W-L, teachers should prepare a large sample worksheet so that all members of the group can see how the procedure is done. During subsequent experiences

FIGURE 12.5
K-W-L Strategy Sheet

K-W-L Strategy Sheet		
K-What we know	W-What we want to find out	L-What we learned and still need to learn
1. Brainstorming 2. Categories of information we expect to use A. _____ B. _____ C. _____ D. _____		

Adapted from "K-W-L: A Teaching Model That Develops Active Reading of Expository Text" by Donna M. Ogle (1986). *The Reading Teacher,* February 1986, p. 564.

with K-W-L, students can complete their own strategy sheets with diminishing amounts of teacher guidance.

Teachers can help to shape students' question-asking behavior through skillful modeling and discussion. For example, teachers are expected to model the categorization process during the K step. Similarly, in the final discussion, students should be encouraged to see that some questions were not answered in the piece just read, or alternatively, to see that they now have new questions as a result of reading:

> The teacher helps students keep the control of their own inquiry, extending the pursuit of knowledge beyond just the one article. The teacher is making clear that learning shouldn't be framed around just what an author chooses to include, but that it involves the identification of the learner's questions and the search for authors or articles dealing with those questions. (Ogle 1986, 569)

Because of these features of K-W-L, an excellent time to introduce the strategy is at the beginning of a new content area unit in which students are expected to pursue some topic for a report or presentation.

Maintaining and Adapting K-W-L

Maintaining K-W-L requires some investment in time. As Ogle (1986) notes, however, the increase in acquired knowledge makes the technique worthwhile. In addition, Ogle reports some evidence to suggest that repeated use of K-W-L encourages students to use the technique spontaneously during the reading of informational text. To increase the likelihood that students will transfer the strategy to other settings, the K-W-L technique has recently been adapted (Carr and Ogle 1987). The revised technique, K-W-L Plus, adds concept mapping and summarization components to the original strategy to enhance its power and utility, especially for secondary students.

Both concept mapping and summarizing are helpful techniques for studying and are natural outgrowths of K-W-L (see Chapter 15). For example, concept mapping requires students to categorize information—something that has already been done as part of the basic K-W-L activity. Carr and Ogle suggest that students use the text title as the central portion of a concept map and the category labels developed during K-W-L as the major concepts in the map (see Figure 12.6). In this way, students can visually display the information, helping them to understand and organize it for subsequent study.

The final step in K-W-L Plus involves using the concept map as an outline for a text summary. Carr and Ogle ask students to number the portions of the concept map in the order they wish to present information in their summary. Since the information is already quite concisely displayed, writing a summary is a relatively straightforward matter.

The important thing about K-W-L Plus is how clearly it demonstrates the value of linking *any* instructional strategy to important learning tasks. Furthermore, the adaptation combines several separate learning tools into one generally useful and powerful technique that can be used flexibly by teachers.

FIGURE 12.6

*K-W-L Plus
Worksheet on
Killer Whales*

K (Know)	**W** (Want to Know)	**L** (Learned)
They live in oceans. They are vicious. They eat each other. They are mammals.	Why do they attack people? How fast can they swim? What kind of fish do they eat? What is their description? How long do they live? How do they breathe?	D—They are the biggest member of the dolphin family. D—They weigh 10,000 pounds and get 30 feet long. F —They eat squids, seals, and other dolphins. A—They have good vision underwater. F —They are carnivorous (meat eaters). A—They are the second smartest animal on earth, D—They breathe through blow holes. A—They do not attack unless they are hungry. D—Warm blooded. A—They have echo-location (sonar). L —They are found in the oceans.

Final category designations developed for column L, information learned about killer whales: A, abilities; D, description; F, food; L, location.

Concept Map of Killer Whales

Abilities (2)
kill for food
detect pebble sized
    aspirin tablet in 30
    feet of water
find food in cloudy water
echo-location

Description (1)
warm blooded
dolphin family
second smartest animal
    next to man
born alive
10,000 lbs.
30 feet long
blow holes

Killer Whales

Location (4)
all oceans
sea worlds

Food (3)
small dolphins
carnivorous (meat eaters)
400 lbs. salmon daily

(1) through (4) indicate the order of categories the student chose later for writing a summary.

From "K-W-L Plus: A Strategy for Comprehension and Summarization" by E. Carr and D. Ogle (1987), *Journal of Reading*, 30, pp. 626–631. International Reading Association. Reprinted by permission.

Teachers can focus on the aspects of K-W-L Plus that will be most helpful to their students. For example, students who approach text passively, without engaging their own preexisting knowledge base, can be encouraged to spend considerable time on step K. Other students will require significant help in answering their questions and identifying additional ones.

MAKING DECISIONS: PLANNING FOR INDIVIDUAL STUDENTS

Setting the stage for literacy instruction and setting in motion some effective activities are important first steps. It is possible to make these initial decisions using the knowledge base established throughout this text. However, a repertoire of techniques, no matter how good, is not sufficient. Skilled teachers and specialists need to consider programs and planning simultaneously in a more systematic fashion. In this section we consider instructional planning in greater detail.

Lesson Planning

Students, especially less-skilled readers and writers, cannot afford to waste instructional time engaged in activities that they do not need or that will not help them to become more proficient. The goals and objectives that are designed for specific students must be clearly related to the assessment that has gone before. The most important thing to keep in mind is that there should be a clear relationship between the information that has been gathered through assessment and diagnostic teaching, the tentative conclusions about areas of need and action, and the instructional activities devised. Indeed, this is the heart of good planning—the matching of information about individual students with appropriate objectives that are, in turn, used to decide upon appropriate activities and materials.

Most teachers have been taught to use some type of generic lesson plan format. A typical lesson plan format has the following major components: (1) Topic or Focus; (2) Objectives; (3) Materials; (4) Activities/Procedures; and (5) Evaluation Plan. Clearly, writing the lesson plan following this or some other format is not what leads to success in teaching. Successful lesson planning rests on careful reflection. Using the information that has been gathered about the particular student(s) we are working with, we decide on some specific objectives. These objectives are in turn used to adapt and refine the instructional program, making changes in either the delivery or content of instruction as appropriate for individual students.

Objectives

The available evidence suggests that effective teachers establish goals and objectives for students (Rupley 1976). In addition, informing students of lesson objectives prior to reading and writing improves students' performance (Duell

1974; Maier 1980). Despite both empirical and practical evidence that students benefit from carefully considered objectives, there is some misunderstanding about the role and function of objectives. The objectives that are developed for a student should be clearly related to the diagnostic assessment that has gone before. It should also be evident how the objectives promote the larger important outcomes of skilled reading and writing.

Importantly, an objective should be focused on what *students will* learn or be able to do as the result of instruction. It *is not* a statement of instructional activities. For example:

OBJECTIVE: Jerry will increase his interest in, and his ability to sustain himself during, silent reading.

This objective provides guidance about what to focus attention on and how to accomplish the instructional jobs that are required. Because it is not a statement of the activities to be used, it is possible to imagine a variety of activities that might address Jerry's needs. Jerry's increased knowledge and skill, not the particular program or tasks, are what is important.

The use of objectives sometimes generates concern among educators. Indeed, some believe that objectives constrain teaching and limit teachers' ability to be creative or student-centered. It is true that more mechanistic models of teaching have sometimes reduced teaching and learning to easily measured, relatively trivial behaviors. However, good objectives make it more, not less, likely that students' needs will be noticed and that important outcomes will receive attention. The format of the objective is less important than the extent to which it focuses instructional attention. There are just two principles to keep in mind when writing objectives:

1. Objectives should define what the student will do and learn—not what you will do as teacher.
2. Objectives must be clearly related to some demonstrated need as determined by sound assessment.

The types of objectives that are generated for a particular student are heavily dependent on what we have learned about that student and our assessment of the match (see Chapter 11). The objectives established for some students may be largely attitude objectives. For others, the objectives generated will be more clearly process objectives, while a third group of students may need content information. Despite these variations, all students require some balance among the three types of objectives, and their programs should reflect this.

Activities

After the objectives have been determined, teachers can turn their attention to planning the specifics of the lesson they believe will best address these outcomes. This involves selecting specific materials and tasks, and/or designing activities that will promote learning in identified areas. Some teachers select activities simply because they enjoy using them or think that their students will like them. Similarly, many novice teachers base their judgments of lesson success on the smoothness of execution or the degree to which students exhibit enthusiasm. These are not trivial issues because they may influence student learning. However, the central criterion for making instructional decisions is the degree to which students make some progress toward becoming more skilled and/or motivated readers and writers.

We start with an array of instructional strategies that are useful to many students (see the previous section on high-utility strategies). Variations of these, as well as additional techniques, are then considered (see Chapters 13 and 14). Major considerations in planning and selecting activities include the following:

1. Is this activity closely linked to the student's needs? Does it address the objectives that have been established?
2. Do the tasks, in combination, form a comfortable flow of activity?
3. How close is the fit between this activity and what is expected of the student during normal reading, writing, and content area instruction?
4. What level of support is required for the student to participate and how does that fit with the total instructional setting?

It is particularly important to think about what level of support needs to be provided to ensure that students can learn what is being taught. Expect that efficient use of learned skill and knowledge will take considerable time, and that the level of teacher support should diminish as students become more adept. This often entails adapting activities or existing programs to meet the individual needs of students.

Although some activities have high utility and are very flexible, planning must also involve selecting specific approaches or techniques to use with the particular student(s). It is important to recall that we are not describing a developmental literacy program for all students. Although a balanced program is always desirable, the instruction for some individuals may reflect a more constrained focus. Some students, for example, simply have greater needs in the area of word analysis and word recognition than in comprehension or composition.

It is also important to realize that activities are not important in themselves. Teachers must guard against viewing their instruction as merely the management of activities (see Chapter 5). The instructional program should always be designed to provide the best possible fit for specific students. In the chapters that follow, we describe specific techniques that permit teachers to make adaptations in a basically effective program in order to focus more closely on one aspect or another of reading and/or writing.

Putting It All Together: Planning Lesson Frameworks

As we note in Chapters 5 and 15, there are a number of basic lesson frameworks that have been employed in reading and writing instruction. Most of these are organized around a before, during, and after reading pattern. In general, we favor starting with a consideration of these frameworks because they assume that teachers are working with actual reading material.

Select Materials

We have already discussed the issue of materials selection in considerable detail. In this section we wish to emphasize selecting materials for more specific purposes. Reading materials should always be evaluated along general lines and judgments made about the quality and merit of them. It is especially important to select materials that encourage and invite strong reader response whenever possible (see Chapter 15). However, teachers also need to consider texts in relation to their more focused goals and objectives.

Because of the rich variety of available literature, teachers need to think about print materials as they might be used in teaching. Different books, authors, and genres invite and permit varying instructional efforts. For example, young children often enjoy the *Curious George* books by H. A. Rey, a series of books that invites discussions of cause-effect. Effective comprehension work might be done with causal relations, since the stories generally revolve around a series of events that are related only by George's curiosity and the trouble that results. On the other hand, these books would not be a good choice for teaching students about story structure, since the traditional structure of stories is not obvious in them. When teachers think about reading instruction this way, lessons can become more text-driven than skills-driven. As Wixson and Peters (1989) point out:

> Consideration of the importance of the reading selection and its role in instruction refocuses our attention on teaching students how to read a particular type of text for particular purposes, rather than on the traditional instruction of isolated sub-skills. (24)

Effective comprehension requires careful consideration of the relationships among the text, the objectives, and the activities. Wixson and Peters (1989) recommend that teachers engage in a three-step process: analyze the text, establish goals, and plan or modify instruction.

Analyze the Text

Map the text so that the key concepts and relationships are revealed (see Chapters 5 and 8). For stories, it is important to examine the characteristics of text that may cause problems for students or which suggest powerful response opportunities for students. These might include recognizing various plot patterns (see Figure 12.7) or looking for challenging character, setting, or theme characteristics. The text should also be scrutinized for interesting or potentially troubling uses of words and illustrations. In analyzing expository text, teachers will need to consider different issues. Central purposes, major ideas, and supporting ideas must be identified so that teachers can see what content is present and how difficult it will be for students to read and learn from this material (Hayes and Peters 1989; Wixson and Peters 1989).

FIGURE 12.7

Structure of Reading Materials

Kind of Pattern	Description	Graphic to Clarify the Design
Step-by-step	Events flow logically one into the next. Ending can almost be anticipated. Example: James Herriot, *Bonny's Big Day* (New York: St. Martin's Press, 1987).	
Turn-about	Events flow logically one into the next, but ending takes an unexpected twist. Examples: Chris Van Allsburg, *The Garden of Abdul Gasazi* (Boston: Houghton Mifflin, 1979), and Jane Yolen, *Picnic with Piggins* (San Diego: Harcourt Brace Jovanovich, 1988).	
Circular	Events flow logically one into the next, but the action carries the main character back to where he/she began. Example: Maurice Sendak, *Where the Wild Things Are* (New York: Harper & Row, 1963, 1988).	
Just Imagine	Events repeat; each repetition varies slightly but action can be anticipated. Example: Joseph Low, *Mice Twice* (New York: Atheneum, 1981).	

Note: Encourage children to use their hands to demonstrate patterns in stories they read.

Hennings, D. G., *Communication in Action: Teaching the Language Arts*, Fourth Edition. Copyright © 1990 by Houghton Mifflin Company. Used with permission.

Establish Objectives

Select content, process, and attitude objectives appropriate for the text and student (see Chapters 6 and 11). In establishing goals, teachers should be clear about how the objectives contribute to the development of major reading and writing outcomes. They should also be sure that the text advances and invites instructional work on these objectives. Some samples of the relationship between comprehension instruction and selected materials are displayed in Figure 12.8.

Plan or Modify Instruction

For commercial materials, examine the suggested instructional activities carefully to see that they provide acceptable levels of direct instruction or that they focus on important aspects of the text. If trade books are used, appropriate levels of support need to be established and focused activities planned. The important thing is that these activities be closely related to the objectives established using text analysis and student assessment.

FIGURE 12.8

Texts and Possible Outcomes

Text	Notable Features	Content	Process	Attitude
Amos and Boris, by W. Steig	Language usage, descriptive metaphors, characters are vivid, settings strong, plot structure parallels story grammar.	Theme of mutual aid; characteristic work of author. Story events.	Recognizing story structure; author's use of language; cause-effect; inference (theme).	Love of language, appreciation of author's craft, enjoyment of characters.
Ira Sleeps Over by B. Waber	Strong problem-solution format, first person narrator, identifiable characters with clear sequence of events.	Theme of friendship; attend to events and character feelings (response to problem).	Use problem-solution story structure to aid comprehension; identify events (details) that contribute to theme.	Enjoy reading about someone like them; identify with character; seek to read other similar stories.
My Father's Dragon by R. S. Gannett	Fantasy. Series of vignettes that rely on cause and effect surrounding animals' outrageous problems. Setting is intriguing; thin character, fairly weak plot.	Dream-like quality of the adventure; story-teller's feel to the text recognizing the problems.	Prediction of events; fantasy is a genre. Cause-effect.	Enjoy genre and humor. Appreciate a story that can be told.

A literacy lesson framework developed by Tancock (1994) specifically for low-achieving readers and writers offers a guide to instruction that can be adapted to the needs of individuals or small groups. This framework includes the following five components:

1. Familiar reading (fluency)—approximately five minutes
2. Guided reading—approximately thirty minutes

Before-reading activity (generating prereading questions, introducing the book, or making predictions)

During-reading activity (teaching for strategy use, Directed Reading-Thinking Activity)

Postreading activity (answering prereading questions; evaluating predictions; or clarifying, extending, or refining thinking about the selection)

3. Writing (shared writing, cut-up sentences, writing process)—approximately fifteen minutes
4. Word sorting—approximately five minutes
5. Book sharing—approximately five minutes

In the familiar reading part of the lesson, the teacher selects several familiar, independent level texts for the student to choose from. The student reads and rereads, both orally and silently, books on many successive lessons, practicing the strategies learned in previous lessons. This portion of the lesson serves as a confidence builder and warm-up for the instruction to follow and provides opportunities for the teacher to model and teach fluency.

For the guided reading portion of the lesson, the teacher selects a book that will provide opportunities for the student to practice using strategies that he or she is beginning to develop. The before, during, and after reading activities are drawn from those commonly associated with the traditional directed reading activity (see Chapter 5) and from those detailed in upcoming chapters. These activities may include writing and should be related to the specific objectives for an individual or group of students.

The writing portion of the lesson may take the form of a shared writing procedure followed by a cut-up sentence activity, a more general writing process activity, or independent writing. Shared writing is adapted from the work of Clay (1985) and is used with emergent writers who are not yet fluent in developing content or in the mechanics of writing. The student generates a message by saying the words slowly, listening to the sounds, and encoding them with the appropriate letters. When the student needs help, the teacher writes a known word that contains the same spelling pattern and shows the students how to figure out the unknown from the known. New words are added to a writing vocabulary inventory. The student continually rereads the sentence as more words are added on, which allows for checking the message for errors in content.

After the message has been written, the teacher copies it onto a sentence strip while the student reads it. The teacher then cuts apart the words in the sentence and the student reassembles and reads it without looking at the original sentence. The teacher can also cut the sentence into segments that provide practice with certain letters or sounds.

More proficient writers can develop a piece of writing over several lessons, moving from planning to composing, revising, and publishing. These activities may be linked to books the student has read in guided reading or books she or he has heard in the book sharing portion of the lesson.

The word sorting portion of the lesson involves grouping words with common spelling patterns, or sounds, or those that share meaning. The words used for word sorting are gathered from a variety of sources including familiar and guided reading texts, and the student's own writing. Word sorting gives students practice in learning how to analyze and generalize common features of words, which is useful for both decoding in reading and encoding in writing

The final component of the lesson is the sharing of quality children's literature. The student listens to the teacher read aloud texts that they cannot read on their own. The teacher selects books on topics of interest and that are likely to stretch the student's imagination. As the instruction progresses, the teacher documents student progress in literacy portfolios that include the original assessment information, lesson artifacts, and progress reports by the teacher and the student.

It is important for teachers of less skilled readers and writers to remember that teachers—not materials—should be the instructional decision-makers for classroom reading and writing instruction (Wixson and Peters 1989). This perspective should guide all teaching, but it is absolutely essential for specialized personnel to remember, since their students are likely to be less flexible and less able to transfer or make connections from diffuse and poorly organized experiences.

An Example: Getting Started with Marvin

As we noted earlier, there are many ways that students might come to work with teachers and many contexts in which this occurs. In this section, we describe the Getting Started phase of working with Marvin. This instructional program was started in the university clinic setting of one of the authors. Unlike many of our students, Marvin came to this setting with a great deal of assessment information already complete.

Background and Setting
At the time of the original referral, Marvin was placed in a regular classroom, receiving no special support or services in reading or writing. His parents referred him for assessment because of their concerns about his academic problems. The assessment-instruction process was initiated by one of the authors who was working with the school. As a result, steps 1 through 6 of the assessment process were executed outside of the regular classroom setting by someone other than the teacher. Marvin's instructional program, the context for literacy, and to some extent, the materials he would use in that setting were already determined.

In the university clinic setting, the decision was made to pair Marvin with another student. It was felt that there were benefits to an arrangement that was *not* one-to-one tutoring. Specifically, we felt Marvin needed opportunities to discuss reading and writing in a socially supportive environment. He was himself a gregarious young man, and many of his interests revolved around people and social interaction. In addition, his reading difficulties and the subsequent instruction he received had tended to isolate him from his peers.

Selecting High-Utility Strategies
The information derived from the assessment and the diagnostic teaching sessions (see Chapter 11) suggested that there was merit in selecting at least two high-utility strategies to begin Marvin's program: SSR and Talking Dictionary.

Indeed, except for those students who require teacher read-aloud as the only way to interact with books, SSR is a standard part of all our students' programs.

Although there was fairly extensive and focused individual information available about Marvin, these two high-utility strategies have merit for a wide range of students in many programs, and Marvin's case was no exception. Marvin needed to increase his ability to handle longer segments of text; reading fluency was a significant problem as well. Although it seemed likely that Marvin could benefit from K-W-L (and we might have used this had we had less information initially), the decision to use this technique was deferred until later.

Selecting Materials

It is our experience that the appropriateness of text and task materials can have a significant effect on the success of the instruction. In Marvin's case, all of the materials were chosen with two major criteria in mind. Only full-length stories or books were to be used, since this constituted an area of need for Marvin, and these would involve fully developed complex stories with a strong goal structure. *Bones on Black Spruce Mountain* is a strongly evocative narrative involving two male characters and a strong adventure/suspense series of episodes. It was among several choices offered to Marvin during the first instructional setting, and one that sustained his interest over several weeks. In later sessions, it provided a rich source of multisyllabic words from which to teach and practice structural and morphemic analysis.

The selections in the *Quest* materials are all fully-developed short stories or expository narratives (two to six pages) of high interest. Marvin found these challenging, but he retained an interest in them. Only stories were selected initially, and we chose those with a sophisticated story structure. These short stories were used for direct instruction to develop both fluency and comprehension. In later sessions, these selections provided excellent material for use with both story mapping activities and a think-aloud strategy (see Chapter 15).

Planning for Marvin

The substantial amount of information available on Marvin could be used almost immediately to establish objectives, decide on materials, and begin to select activities. The objectives grew directly out of the diagnostic teaching sessions described in Chapter 11, and the specific activities are essentially adaptations of the high-utility activities we have already described. The specific objectives and activities established for Marvin's initial sessions were:

1. *Objective:* To develop reading fluency and motivate recreational reading.
   Activity: SSR for five minutes without interruption using *Bones on Black Spruce Mountain* (Budbill 1978).
2. *Objective:* To increase word recognition and reading fluency.
   Activity: Fifteen-minute taped read-along of connected text with fluency support using "Something Queer Is Going On" from *Electric Butterfly, Quest* (Aulls and Graves 1985).

3. *Objective:* To increase comprehension.

Activity: Identify characters and the goal structure (including problem-solution) of a complex story using taped read-along of "Something Queer Is Going On" from *Electric Butterfly, Quest* coupled with a story map.

Marvin's case illustrates what happens over time as planning and instruction proceed. The high-utility strategies used initially are sometimes retained (e.g., SSR), however, as students develop increased competence, some aspects of the initial plans are changed and adapted. The combination of initial instructional intervention and strong assessment information permits careful planning for an individual student like Marvin. The interweaving of assessment and instruction and a commitment to continuous assessment result in subtle, yet sometimes major, adjustments in the instructional program. Most often, the program becomes more and more focused as the teacher/tutor adapts to growing competence or finds that a more and more refined focus is appropriate. These more refined techniques for building an instructional repertoire are described more fully in the following chapters.

CHAPTER SUMMARY

In this chapter, we discussed some of the long-term, overarching decisions and plans that teachers must make. Guidelines for establishing a literate environment were provided along with information on selecting organizational patterns and materials.

In addition, teachers need to have a repertoire of instructional strategies that can be used in the initial stages of work with students. This section also included detailed descriptions of six, selected, *high-utility* instructional strategies: Sustained Silent Reading (SSR), dialogue journals, dictated stories, repeated readings, reciprocal teaching, and K-W-L. These specific instructional techniques were provided in this chapter, "to get started in instruction," because they are consistent with current views of reading and writing, have been proven effective, can be shaped to meet individual needs, and can be used to address some aspect of the attitude, process, and content objectives of a literacy program. In discussing each of these, we provided a description of the technique, guidelines for launching the technique in the classroom, and then discussed ways to adapt and/or maintain the technique for special purposes of groups.

In the final sections of the chapter, we provided information about how to plan for individual students using the specific, focused assessment information that has been gathered in earlier steps of the assessment-instruction process. In addition, we described a literacy lesson framework for low-achieving readers and writers that can be adapted to the needs of individuals or small groups. Finally, we returned to Marvin to provide an example of how the instructional program was initiated with him.

CHAPTER 13

Adapting Instruction to Focus on Word Recognition and Spelling

INTRODUCTION

Using the assessment information gathered in the previous steps and the guide-lines for sound instruction and planning as described in Chapter 12, a teacher might conclude that a student (or students) needs to concentrate more closely on acquiring or enhancing competence in word recognition, vocabulary, and/or spelling. Word recognition, spelling, and vocabulary are *word level aspects* of reading and writing. Of course, knowledge and skill in these areas often affect comprehension, composition, and studying.

The various components of reading and writing are intertwined in complex ways. However, it is often necessary to focus attention more closely on a partic-ular component of skilled reading or writing. In this chapter and the next chap-ter, we describe the instructional approaches and materials that may be used to adapt instruction so that it provides increased instruction and support in the areas of word identification and/or vocabulary strategies.

Problems at the word level, in either pronunciation or meaning associa-tion, generally pose major obstacles to wide reading and effective writing. These difficulties may influence students' rate, fluency, comprehension, or enjoyment of reading. They may also influence students' fluency, effectiveness, or willingness in writing. It is important to understand that in skilled reading and writing the boundaries between difficulties in word recognition, meaning, vocabulary, and spelling can be blurred. With regard to reading, Wilson and Hall (1990) note:

Meaning must be the focus of all reading and word analysis must be viewed in conjunction with helping readers derive meaning from printed language. Sometimes word analysis is erroneously interpreted as being merely the use of sound-letter correspondences for deciphering unknown words. However, sentence structure (syntactic information) and the stock of word meanings and concepts (semantic information) are key elements in deriving meaning from printed language and in figuring out unfamiliar written words. (iii)

The information about word recognition and spelling in this chapter is presented in three large chapter sections. First, we will discuss critical issues in word level instruction. These include a description of the components of word recognition and spelling ability, the debates surrounding the appropriate way to help children become competent, and the distinctions about students' word recognition and spelling based on a developmental continuum. Next, we will provide instructional guidelines that focus on word recognition and analysis and spelling. Finally, we will describe promising instructional techniques for focusing on these areas.

ISSUES IN WORD RECOGNITION, WORD ANALYSIS, AND SPELLING INSTRUCTION

A sizeable number of disabled students have difficulty with some aspect of word identification. Many of them also struggle with other aspects of written language, particularly spelling. Despite the prevalence of print skill difficulties among disabled readers, there is no unified vision of the type of instruction that should be delivered to these students. This is partly because of confusion about word identification and spelling directly and partly because of a failure to distinguish between various developmental stages and student abilities.

Components of Word Identification and Spelling

Rapid and efficient word recognition requires that readers know a number of words instantly at sight and also that they have acquired a repertoire of word identification techniques for analyzing words that are unfamiliar to them in print. In Chapter 2 we described the various components of word identification and spelling. Competent readers and writers possess knowledge and skill in using sight word recognition, meaning-based analysis, graphophonic analysis, and structural analysis. Effective students possess a repertoire of skills and strategies that are used in concert to pronounce words and retrieve their meanings, resulting in fluent reading and accurate spelling.

Although word pronunciation often involves meaning associations or "lexical access" (Gough 1984), it is clearly possible for readers to be able to pronounce or decode words without having any meaning associations for them. Skilled readers of English are capable of "reading" (pronouncing) large numbers of words without assigning meaning. Indeed, they can read "pseudo-words" with equal ease (Ryder and Graves 1980), demonstrating the degree to which good readers have internalized the sound-symbol system and structural aspects of our language. *Word identification, word analysis,* and *decoding* are all terms that have been used to describe a reader's ability to pronounce words. This ability requires "translating written words into spoken or subvocal words" (May 1990, 34).

The tools of word identification can be placed in three large categories, with supporting skills employed as necessary:

Sight Word Recognition
    High Frequency
    High Potency
Meaning-Based Word Analysis
    Contextual Analysis (Using Syntax and Semantics)
    Morphemic Analysis (Structural Analysis)
Graphophonic Analysis
    Phonics
    Structural Analysis—Syllabication

In a balanced reading program, provisions are made for ensuring development of each of these components of word identification. Some commercial programs attempt to teach only sound-symbol information and introduce phonics (and later structural analysis) by using nonsense words, without teaching students to make simultaneous use of other cueing systems. Other programs teach only contextual cueing (for example, cloze formats) without providing sufficient information about the graphophonic cueing system. Teachers and others concerned about literacy need to be clear about the relationships between and among the various word identification abilities. It is especially important to recognize that word identification and phonics are not exactly the same thing.

Phonic analysis, or the use of letter-sound correspondences, is one tool among several available to the skilled reader. Knowledge and skill in using the graphophonic cueing system is essential but not in itself sufficient for good reading. Anderson et al. (1985) conclude that "all that phonics can be expected to do is help children get approximate pronunciations of written words" (41). Similarly, Groff (1986) notes that phonics is not an exact science. Instead, application of phonics knowledge results in "rough estimates of the sounds that letters represent" (921). Because phonics results in inexact renderings, and because reading requires more than word calling, students must attend to several aspects of print at once, *syntax cues, semantic cues,* and *graphophonic cues,* using these to help make inferences about what the exact print word is.

Spelling requires attention to many of these same issues. For example, although many people believe that accurate spelling relies on "sounding out," the evidence is clear that, "beyond its most primitive stage, learning to spell has little to do with sounding a word out" (Henderson 1990, 88). Correct spellings rely on knowledge of sight words, morphemic and structural analysis, and an emerging awareness of spelling patterns. Experts agree, also, that knowledge of spelling patterns and vocabulary should be built on a foundation of experiences in reading and writing.

Clearly, knowledge of the ways in which the sound-symbol system works is critical to becoming a skilled reader and writer. Similarly, it is clear that students must be able to use their knowledge of the graphophonic cueing system, and the orthographic structure of the language, with ease and efficiency during reading. As Adams (1990) points out, the fact that students need to acquire this knowledge and skill is really not an area of dispute. *How* they should acquire this knowledge and skill and what knowledge is essential to becoming a skilled reader are areas of uncertainty.

Atomistic versus Integrated Instruction

Much traditional word identification and spelling instruction employs an atomistic approach to teaching. Reading is separated into constituent parts and instruction is delivered in small pieces. The temptation to do this is great because it is relatively easy to break word identification into associated subordinate tasks. Atomistic instruction also generally involves the introduction of these separate components in isolation and does not usually involve any presentation of words in text. Providing even sentence-length context has been relatively rare, and embedding instruction in longer patterned text is a very recent practice.

Whether students learn best when proceeding from parts to whole or from whole to parts is a debate that strikes at the heart of word identification instruction, and the answers often appear contradictory. For example, the overwhelming evidence from American researchers indicates that students learn basic sound-symbol correspondence more efficiently when they receive systematic and intensive instruction in synthetic (parts-to-whole) phonics (Johnson and Baumann 1984). In addition, the research suggests that students who receive direct instruction in segmenting sounds and in blending are generally more adept at word recognition than students who do not receive this training (see Adams 1990).

At the same time, it appears that such training does not result in enhanced comprehension (Resnick 1977). Newer models of reading suggest that sound-symbol information is not the only source of information available for word identification. It is clear, for example, that meaningful context aids word identification (Goodman 1965; Weber 1970; West and Stanovich 1978). As we have seen, pronouncing words during normal reading entails the use of a number of cueing systems in a coordinated fashion. However, good readers and skilled adults rely on context less heavily than do younger and poorer readers (Stanovich 1980, 1986), presumably because they have reached high levels of word recognition proficiency.

Into these apparently conflicting results we must also insert a discussion of fluency. Some reading professionals argue that reading fluency depends on automaticity in word recognition (LaBerge and Samuels 1974). In this view, students must learn to rapidly identify words using the sound-symbol information without depending on other cueing systems. Others argue that readers can only perform fluently when they attend more to constructing meaning from several sources and rely less on print (Clay 1979; Goodman 1976).

A more unified view is proposed by Barr, Blachowicz, and Wogman-Sadow (1995):

> The capability to read fluently depends on two conditions: (1) instantaneous recognition of an extensive set of printed words, and (2) considerable practice reading contextual selections. Some skillful young readers achieve fluency in their first year of reading. Many, however, require several years of reading experience before they acquire sufficient word knowledge and contextual practice to read unfamiliar material fluently. (65)

It seems apparent that rapid and automatic word identification is desirable. However, in the early stages of reading acquisition, it is helpful for students to encounter words in the supported context of meaningful print. This does not mean that these words cannot be removed for examination. Indeed, there are good reasons for doing so, and later in the chapter we will describe ways to focus on individual words in a less fragmented program.

Unless students are showing no growth in word recognition using a more integrated approach to reading instruction, we would argue for instruction that provides students with opportunities to see words in connected text first. Poor readers too often do not transfer the information they received during isolated skill instruction to more realistic reading materials and settings; many never receive sufficient practice in using the various component skills together. Consequently, they never achieve the high levels of automatic word identification that are the hallmark of skilled adult readers (West and Stanovich 1978).

> Children need to be *taught* to use the cue systems interactively. They need to be shown how these systems are interwoven, and then they need to be given a great deal of practice in anticipating words through using the semantic and syntactic systems and in confirming these anticipations through using the graphophonic system. They need to be *taught* strategies for changing their decisions when subsequent information proves them wrong. (Spiegel 1984, 5)

As with phonics instruction, one of the persistent issues surrounding sight word instruction is the debate regarding the appropriate presentation of new words. Although the evidence is not conclusive, there is reason to believe that students benefit from the presentation of new words in meaningful contexts (Ehri and Wilce 1980). In addition, it appears that poor readers recognize more high-frequency sight words during connected text reading than they do in isolation (Krieger 1981), and they should have opportunities to practice in these relatively more successful settings.

In an extensive review of the literature on sight word instruction, Ceprano (1981) concluded that some students benefit from isolating the words for examination. However, more recent studies suggest that this can and should be done within a program that employs meaningful, even predictable, contexts for the reading (Bridge, Winograd, and Haley 1983; Leu, DeGroff, and Simons 1986). In addition, the research in writing and invented spelling suggests that opportunities to write provide students with natural contexts for analyzing sound-symbol correspondence. Writing focuses students' attention on segmenting and isolating speech sounds. This ability seems to be a prerequisite to effective acquisition of other word identification strategies (Clay 1979) and practices that help children to isolate and blend sounds have repeatedly proven successful (Groff 1986).

In summary, the issues surrounding atomistic versus integrated approaches to word recognition and word analysis are complex ones. Isolated, fragmented instruction with limited opportunity to read and write real material seems doomed to failure, especially for children who are experiencing reading difficulty. On the other hand, teachers should not hesitate to provide students with information about sounds, symbols, and patterns and to pull individual words and sounds out of meaningful text experiences in order to help students notice key features (Adams 1990). Timely, systematic, and focused information about how to decode should be available to all students.

The parallels in spelling instruction are striking. Spelling instruction has traditionally remained separate from both reading and writing in the elementary curriculum and has involved presenting students with isolated lists of words. Although older lists were questionable, most contemporary lists contain words that have been selected for their age/grade appropriateness and that are united either by frequency or spelling pattern. This does not, of course, assure that students know these words or are motivated to learn to spell them.

In particular, students who are struggling are often asked to study lists that they cannot read and learn to spell words they are unlikely to use. As Henderson (1990) notes, "strange words, even nonsense words, may be memorized by anyone for a short period, but unless words are used in writing, they are likely soon to slip beyond recall" (92).

Identifying Areas of Instructional Need

Using the information gathered in previous stages of the assessment-instruction process, teachers can determine which aspects of word identification or spelling are posing the most serious difficulties for students. It is not uncommon, however, for students to demonstrate difficulties in more than one arena. For example, a student with extremely limited print skills may have weak phonics skills and limited graphophonic knowledge, but that same student may also have a weak repertoire of sight vocabulary. This should not be too surprising, since a student with few print skills tends not to try reading. Over time, students who don't read fail to acquire other abilities that result from repeated exposure to texts (Snider and Tarver 1987; Stanovich 1986).

It is particularly important to recognize when direct instruction in sound-symbol associations is unlikely to be beneficial. Cohn and D'Alessandro (1978) studied the word recognition errors of 100 students referred to their clinic and concluded that "only in a small percentage of cases is it true that poor word analysis performance in decoding a list of words is attributable to a lack of knowledge of the sound-symbol relationship involved" (343). In this study, students received some on-the-spot diagnostic teaching probes, such as "Please look at that word carefully and try it again." Given just this much prompting, students corrected roughly 50 percent of all initial miscues. If this prompt did not elicit a correct response, students were asked, for example, to examine the first letter(s) and produce the sound. This type of prompt resulted in the correction of another 29 percent of the miscues. Thus, at least 79 percent of all miscues resulted from something other than lack of sound-symbol knowledge.

Of the errors that remained uncorrected, there appeared to be three sources of difficulty: words with irregular phonic patterns (for example, *tongue, guard)*, lack of control over sound-symbol information which resulted in students sometimes pronouncing the phonic element correctly and other times not, and appearance on a word list versus in context. Like Allington and McGill-Franzen (1980), these authors found that less-skilled readers made errors on lists that they did not make in context. Cohn and D'Alessandro (1978) sensibly conclude that it is dangerous and foolish to reteach sound-symbol relationships, since it would be an attempt to "correct a situation that does not exist" (343). These students do need help, however, and might benefit from instruction that was designed to promote fluency, control, or flexibility.

Developmental Differences in Word Identification and Spelling

The issues surrounding instruction in word identification are often confounded by age and developmental stage. Teachers must recognize that differences exist among learners at different developmental stages. The very beginning stages of reading and writing involve somewhat different tasks and behaviors than later stages. For example, a developmental study by Shanahan (1984) suggests that the overall reading abilities of beginning readers are influenced most strongly by the word-level skills of word identification and spelling, whereas range of vocabulary affected older readers to a great extent.

One of the biggest problems facing teachers of struggling readers and writers is that much of what we know about word identification instruction and spelling is based on studies of young, normal learners. Students who are experiencing difficulty do not generally parallel the general population in their reading and writing achievement or progress. Therefore, describing word recognition or spelling techniques in terms of the normal stages of reading development can be problematic.

As a practical matter, students with word identification problems who appear in clinical or remedial settings generally fall into three categories: students with no or almost no print skills, students who have some print skills, and more advanced students whose print skills are not fully developed for reading multisyllabic words or specialized texts. In the following sections we will highlight the major word identification tasks of these groups.

Word Recognition and Spelling
for Students with No Conventional Print Skills

Literacy professionals often are called upon to work with students who have acquired no functional print skills. The special education eligibility guidelines in most states require a discrepancy between ability and achievement, a standard difficult to attain in very young children who are at the beginning stages of reading acquisition. Consequently, many youngsters who are struggling are served by developmental reading or compensatory education teachers in the earliest years of schooling. Increasingly, however, school districts are providing for specialized early intervention programs (see below) for these youngest students.

There are also some individuals who are not young but who have acquired virtually no functional print skills. Bilingual or LEP (Limited English Proficiency) students, in particular, require special consideration. Perhaps the most critical instructional issue for this group of students involves the careful consideration of emergent literacy and the degree to which the foundations of school literacy have been well-established.

Careful consideration of the literacy, linguistic, and cultural environments is essential for planning effective instructional programs. As a general rule, bilingual or LEP students need to acquire some pool of sight vocabulary. They will generally require systematic introduction of sound-symbol knowledge as well as careful support for a developing view of the functional value of reading and ample opportunities to read, write, speak, and listen.

In terms of word recognition, perhaps the major hurdle for bilingual or LEP students is the fact that, "even if the student can sound out a word more or less accurately, the word may not be recognized because it is not a part of the student's oral vocabulary" (Chamot and O'Malley 1994, 89). In addition, these authors note, bilingual or LEP students are likely to employ some of their own first language phonemes as they read, leading to confusions about pronunciation versus understanding of sound-symbol correspondence. Like other struggling young readers, bilingual and LEP students must learn to decode English print. Unlike other students, however, they do not have control over the language used to read.

There is little consensus about how to approach the dual needs of such students: the need to learn to speak English and the need to become literate in English are not precisely the same problem. In addition, the challenge may not be the same for all students. For example, different solutions may be needed depending on students' literacy in their native language.

Some programs, like ESL (English as Second Language), have assumed that students must acquire proficiency in Standard English prior to literacy instruction. However, May (1990) concluded there is no evidence that learning to speak Standard English fluently is required to learn to read. "It is likely that they need abundant *exposure* to Standard English before they are expected to read it well, but fluent *speech* in Standard English is probably not necessary" (479). There is relatively strong evidence to suggest that students possess an underlying language competence that can be used when learning a new language (Pflaum 1986). Proficient speakers of one language use their knowledge of how languages work to learn a second one. Similarly, the skills used to become literate in a native language are available when learning to read and write a second language. Of course, students who are illiterate in their native language do not have these resources to draw upon.

There are differences of opinion about how to proceed with the instruction of bilingual and LEP students. "There is not, however, any disagreement that children learning a second language should be learning in a language-rich environment" (Pflaum 1986, 100). Indeed, common sense would suggest that the educational programs of bilingual and LEP students should incorporate the attributes of effective instruction. May's (1990, 479) suggestions for instruction are consistent with the kinds of practices suggested for all students acquiring initial print skills. Teachers should:

1. Read aloud every day. Additional read-aloud experiences with peers and Big Books are also advised.
2. Provide ample practice for students to practice using English. Cooperative work groups and paired groupings work best.
3. Have students read predictable, patterned books and use these structures for writing as well.
4. Permit students to make limited verbal responses initially and provide guided support for increased proficiency.
5. Make use of drama and role playing.

Students whose language proficiency or literacy knowledge is not well developed will have a difficult time taking advantage of formal literacy instruction. These must be addressed as students work to acquire an awareness of language as an object of learning, as they learn to analyze spoken language into constituent sounds, and as they begin to assign symbols to sounds in their reading and writing activities. These important tasks must be accomplished or students will not prosper (Juel, Griffith, and Gough 1986; Williams 1980).

Spelling, like reading, is developmental in nature. These issues were discussed in detail in Chapters 7 and 9. Students in the earliest stages of spelling development may not attend to relationships between sound and print at all, but they quickly begin to represent some sounds in print. It is at this stage that students' knowledge of reading and spelling are most aligned. As students move toward greater skill in reading, the relationship between their word recognition and spelling knowledge and skill will weaken (Henderson 1990).

Word Recognition and Spelling Instruction for Students with Some Conventional Print Skills

Most students who receive specialized reading instructional support have some print skills. Indeed, it is generally the case that a referral is made only after some significant attempts have been made to teach the student to read and it has become apparent that the pace or efficiency of learning is problematic.

Although the majority of remedial students have some, but not all, of the requisite print skills required for skilled reading or writing, this is definitely not a homogenous group. It will typically be impossible to predict which print skills have been learned, which are underused, what cueing system is used most often, or whether students have generated any systematic approaches to dealing with print. Again, the careful review of assessment information is required. Although some teachers use the same commercial program for all students regardless of their specific knowledge and skill, this is clearly very undesirable.

The major differences between these students and those who have no print skills are that these students have demonstrated their ability to learn some aspects of the reading process and their skills can be used as the basis for additional learning. This information can often prove useful in planning the program. For example, students who have mastered the alphabetic principles of English orthography but who have limited sight vocabulary may require help in retaining the visual appearance of words. Many need to be informed that some words are not decodable using phonic knowledge, and may benefit from work in writing/spelling and seeing words in familiar settings. Since such students frequently underuse context, it may be necessary to teach them these skills as well.

Sometimes students do not exhibit a specific area of difficulty. Rather, they may have what appears to be a general weakness in all aspects of word identification (and, generally in these cases, spelling also). An examination of the students' miscues, for example, would suggest that there is no single major area of difficulty. Miscues appear in many component areas (high-frequency sight words and several different phonic patterns), and effectiveness in using meaning-based strategies for self-correction is erratic. Such a profile suggests that the student has not achieved control over the knowledge and skill that has been taught. Lack of experience with print, or haphazard instruction, is the likely source of difficulty.

For young, poor readers it makes a great deal of sense to intensify the reading experience, but to mimic developmental reading programs wherever possible. These students have time in their future school lives to become proficient, and, with support, to practice sufficiently to regain some of the ground that was lost in the early years. Indeed, effective congruent programming may have the greatest payoff for these students.

Limited or inadequate word identification abilities are not the exclusive domain of young students, however. Many older disabled readers have partial knowledge or mastery of word identification. This partial knowledge can be troublesome since these students generally know that they are supposed to use sound-symbol information to "sound out" unknown words. They often attempt to do so, relying on inadequate or underdeveloped information. We frequently encounter young people who have a jumble of half-known rules and homilies stored away but little ability to identify the regularities of print or to recognize the familiar words they have seen many times. These same students have typically failed to internalize the regular spelling patterns of the English language as well.

For somewhat older students, it is important to analyze performance and knowledge in terms of opportunities to learn. If the student has already received substantial experience with one type of instruction but failed to thrive, it may be especially important to consider alternatives. This might include intensive, nontraditional training in some aspect of word recognition (for example, the ABD program developed by Williams, 1980; described in the next section). It might also include supported reading of connected text (for example, the Heckelman Impress, discussed on page 539) and will, most certainly, need to include some specialized programs attending to the spelling patterns to learn new words.

Although it is clear that the most desirable situation involves early acquisition of decoding skill, the appropriate intervention is not always apparent for students who have not become skilled readers. Some of these students may not have received good initial instruction, while others may not have been positioned to take advantage of traditionally successful programs (for example, LEP children and students with poor phonemic segmentation abilities). What is clear is that many older students who have some print skills also have a history of school failure (Torgesen 1977; Stanovich 1986). This fact cannot be ignored in planning the instructional program for an individual student. In these cases, it is necessary to work with the existing complex of interactions.

"Jenny" is an example worth noting. Jenny was a nine-year-old second-grader when she came to our clinic. She had repeated both kindergarten and first grade and had been receiving specialized remedial help for several years. She had extremely limited mastery of phonics and an uncertain ability to associate sounds and symbols (the likely result of a long history of ear infections that had reached the critical stage between the ages of four and six). In addition, she was exceptionally unreliable in her recognition of high-frequency sight words. Finally, neither she nor her teachers could read back the invented spellings she used during writing.

She had been receiving intensive phonics instruction as well as isolated practice on sight vocabulary for over a year. She had also been placed in a controlled vocabulary reader for application and practice. During our first session, Jenny was asked to read one of these simple stories aloud. She had read, haltingly, only a few words when she came to the word *there*. She stopped abruptly, held her head, and said, "That's one of *those* words—the ones I can't remember." Her intensive isolated instructional program had certainly sensitized her. She was exceptionally skilled at locating, if not pronouncing, high-frequency sight words; she had also become convinced that the task was an impossible one. Her two most frequent responses to an encounter with these words were to give up in exasperation and remark on "those" words, or to begin a fairly random run through a short list of high-frequency words, hoping to hit on the correct one. Although it is obviously desirable for Jenny to learn these words, any direct assault on them seemed doomed to failure in the immediate future.

Students like Jenny have some print skills, but they are not controlled and accessible for use. Other students have a much larger repertoire, but have not practiced them sufficiently in coordinated settings involving connected text reading. Still others have print skills that are suitable for some reading settings, but they have not acquired sufficient fluency, speed, and automaticity to direct their attention to the demands of more complex text.

The spelling of students who have some print skills is also often problematic. Students may have some ability to spell sight words and often produce phonemically correct spellings for words. They have not, however, acquired the repertoire of memorized and patterned words that tell them that "kiten" or "slamed" are misspelled.

It is especially important to recognize that many of these students may also appear to be unmotivated. Effective teachers and clinicians will be alert to the possibility that limited print skills have diminished the student's pleasure in reading and writing. If this is the case, motivation will only be increased when reading is supported or skill improved. For this large group of students with some, but inadequate, word recognition, word analysis, and spelling skills, differentiated instruction delivered by a thoughtful teacher is absolutely essential.

Word Recognition and Spelling Instruction for Students Who Need More Advanced Print Skills

There is a third distinctive group of students who present themselves as reading problems somewhat later in school life. These students may have experienced reading difficulties earlier, but often, they were considered adequate or even good readers in the early years. These students generally have reasonably good phonic skills and are able to use phonic principles to decode unfamiliar words. Ryder and Graves (1980) found that even less-skilled seventh-grade students have more sound-symbol knowledge than was previously assumed. Indeed, there was relatively little difference between less-skilled and above-average secondary readers in terms of their ability to identify letter-to-sound relationships.

The problem for these secondary students does not appear to be lack of knowledge. Memory (1986) argues that many of these students do have the requisite knowledge and skill but do not use (apply) it during assigned content area reading tasks.

> Possibly one reason that less-able readers in the secondary grades often do not apply their existing decoding knowledge is that the way they were taught to use that knowledge is not the way skilled readers decode words. Rather than use individual grapheme-phoneme relationships and phonic generalizations to sound out words, good readers pronounce words by putting together the sounds of familiar clusters of letters. (Glass and Burton 1973; Baron 1977, 195)

Students at this stage do appear to lack sufficient knowledge and pattern recognition in the areas of syllable juncture—recognizing where syllables begin and end—and in "derivational constancy"—what Templeton (1995) calls the "spelling-meaning connection." This lack of knowledge results in misspellings that result from lack of sensitivity to the underlying morphemes—that is, a misspelling like "compasition" that could be corrected if the student knew the derivational root, "compose."

Skilled and less-skilled readers in the more advanced stages of reading development differ in other ways. Poor readers, for example, frequently do not read for meaning, and they are notably weak in their ability to read multisyllabic words. Less-skilled secondary students often do not have a solid repertoire of skills that can be used flexibly. These problems may be related to poor meaning vocabulary (see Chapter 14) or weak comprehension abilities (see Chapter 15). In terms of word recognition, students' inability to read "long words" often stands in the way of attempts at wider reading that would, in turn, promote better vocabulary and comprehension.

Many students lack strategies for pronouncing and spelling longer, more complex words. Unfortunately, the evidence regarding the most productive approach to instruction in multisyllabic words is mixed, at best. There remains, for example, considerable controversy over the efficacy of teaching children to syllabicate words as an aid to word identification. Johnson and Baumann (1984) describe assumptions underlying syllabication instruction:

> The rationale for teaching syllabication is based on the belief that if children can segment unknown words into more manageable parts, decoding will be facilitated; that is phonics, phonogram identification, or structural skills can then be effectively applied. This position has been bolstered by the popular opinion that the syllable, not the phoneme, is the basic unit of language.... In addition, there is evidence that children are reasonably facile at identifying the number of syllables in words and that better readers intuitively divide unfamiliar words into syllables. (cf. Schell 1967; Sherwin 1970, 596–597)

Researchers and educators are divided about the utility of teaching dictionary rules for syllabication. Although there is no evidence that traditional syllabication instruction improves vocabulary or comprehension, most of these studies have not demonstrated that students had difficulty in this area. The evidence does suggest an improved ability to pronounce words, precisely the area of need for many less-skilled readers (see Johnson and Baumann 1984). In addition, instruction in both syllabic analysis and dictionary usage is effective in improving *spelling* for students at these levels (Henderson 1990).

What does seem unequivocal is the effectiveness of teaching students some technique for identifying elements and patterns within words. Less traditional approaches to helping students recognize word parts and apply sound-symbol information to them have proven effective in improving a wide range of reading behaviors. This type of approach is described later in the chapter.

GUIDELINES FOR INSTRUCTION FOCUSED ON WORD RECOGNITION, WORD ANALYSIS, AND SPELLING

In thinking about word recognition or spelling instruction, decisions about what and how to teach should be informed by the more complex model we have used throughout the text. In particular, we assume that many of the basic conditions for effective teaching described in Chapter 12 have already been established and that careful assessment has suggested that the student will benefit from instruction focused on word recognition, analysis, and/or spelling. Before considering specific techniques, we offer guidelines that provide general frameworks for thinking about the content and delivery of word identification and spelling instruction.

Do Not Oversimplify the Reading and Writing Processes

The close approximation of skilled reading and writing should be the goal of all literacy activities. This does not mean that students will never receive instruction focused on discrete aspects of reading or writing; and not all students with problems in word identification or spelling can be treated the same way with success. However, wherever possible, teachers should develop instructional approaches that permit students to use several word identification skills/strategies at the same time, using relative strength to support relative weakness. Speed and accuracy in word recognition and word meaning retrieval clearly contribute to reading fluency, but so do familiarity, ability to think with print, and various text attributes. Similarly, while spelling accuracy is highly valued in writing, so are attention to detail, effective language use, and excellent ideas.

For example, young beginning readers might use their knowledge of rhyming and text rhythms to aid word analysis in the context of a highly predictable text. In writing, good ideas and a willingness to take risks and use invented spelling will lead to a good first draft that can be used as the basis for revisions.

The dangers inherent in reducing reading or writing to the acquisition of isolated bits and pieces are abundantly clear. The first danger is that a steady diet of isolated, fragmented instruction distorts the reading/writing process so that some students (and some teachers) find it impossible to remember that the goal is purposeful, self-directed learning and enjoyment.

A second danger in oversimplifying is that we may make reading more difficult and writing impossible. Highly controlled vocabulary does not make reading easier, because students are forced to apply their skills without the benefit of good information for self-checking (see Chapters 5 and 6). Students' well-developed sense of syntax may actually cause them difficulty in highly contrived and controlled text.

Similarly, demanding that students produce accurate spellings in the early stages of writing development can keep students from writing at all. Certainly students need to acquire spelling knowledge and expertise, but the focus for writing needs to be on communication and on functionality. Spelling enhances both of these, but is not the goal.

Focus on the Goal of Increased Ability and Fluency During Reading and Writing

Students must be able to decode and recognize almost all of the words they encounter in text if they are to read with comprehension and enjoyment.

Teachers should be certain that they provide systematic instruction in phonics early in reading development, but they must also remember to teach only high-utility decoding skills (Adams 1990).

In addition to providing ample practice in connected text, teachers need to signal the importance of reading (versus worksheets) and writing (versus spelling lists) in every possible way. This must also involve evaluating students as they apply their knowledge and skill during reading and writing. In particular, teachers need to understand that students do not need to know the labels for phonic elements (blends, diphthongs, etc.), nor do they need to be able to provide an explicit rationale (rule) in order to decode or spell effectively. Indeed, the available evidence suggests that students' ability to decode far outstrips their ability to explain what they are doing. Similarly, the knowledge of spelling patterns that good spellers possess is tacit knowledge that they cannot typically describe.

Tovay (1980) designed a study to examine how well children in Grades 2 through 4 understood common phonic terms like *consonant, syllable, diphthong,* and so on. In addition, she examined the relationship between explicit knowledge of terms and students' ability to apply phonics in decoding words. "The results showed that elementary grade children have a poor grasp of the meaning of phonics terms yet a far better grasp of applied phonics" (431). Some of the results were especially startling. For example, only 24 percent of the students in grades 2 through 4 could define or give an example of a "consonant." Similarly, there were no children who could define "consonant blend," but an average performance score in this area was 86 percent accuracy. These results parallel those reported by Rosso and Emans (1981). Tovay concludes that "it seems reasonable to deemphasize the use of phonics terms in deference to the functions they represent" (437) and recommends a procedure that involves making comparisons with known words.

Teach Students to Examine Words for Familiar Patterns and to Make Analogies

Extremely disabled and beginning readers seem to benefit from direct instruction in analyzing, blending, and decoding unknown words (Williams 1980). However, after a very brief initial stage of acquisition, good readers appear to move to more coordinated strategies: identifying familiar patterns in words, assigning sound relationships to those patterns, and blending elements when necessary. The rapid decay of the need for explicit information about sound-symbol relationships caused Anderson et al. (1985) to conclude:

> The right maxims for phonics are: Do it early. Keep it simple. Except in cases of diagnosed individual need, phonics instruction should have been completed by the end of second grade. (43)

More proficient readers rely quite heavily on spelling patterns and other familiar chunks of letters to rapidly identify words. For example, Glass and Burton (1973) reported that fully 85 percent of the decoding done by second- and fifth-grade students in their study involved analysis of letter *groups*. In addition, as good readers become even more skilled, they decode words by attending to larger and larger groupings of letters (Marsh, Desberg, and Cooper 1977).

Memory (1986) argues that "if poor readers are to become even average readers, they, too, must learn to see the phonetically important groupings of letters in words and take advantage of their existing knowledge of those groupings" (195). The recognition of reliable letter clusters or known phonograms that remind readers of familiar words or sound-symbol patterns has proven to be effective in instruction for many years (Wylie and Durrell 1970), and recent revisions of decoding through analogy with known words has proven equally effective (see below).

The same systematic attention to clusters and patterns seems required in spelling. Students who are struggling need to examine, and attend closely to, the patterns and configurations of words. "Children need to study words so that spelling principles that they have been using intuitively become clarified, brought to the level of consciousness" (Stewig and Nordberg 1995, 354).

Provide Early Intervention

Given the difficulties of remediating reading and writing problems among older students, and given the serious social and emotional price that accompanies early reading failure, it makes good sense to address reading and writing problems as early as possible. Several programs have been developed and tested recently that focus on the very early ages and stages of reading and writing, recognizing that early intervention is likely to be both more successful and more economical than is remediation later on (see Pikulski 1995). These programs share a number of attributes, the most notable of which may be that they are based on the assumption that instructional programs for young "at risk" students should provide extensive reading and writing experiences. We take a closer look at two of these programs and then describe some common features of successful early intervention programs.

Reading Recovery

Reading Recovery is a program that has as its goal "to accelerate the child's learning at a rate faster than the learning in the classroom" (Boehnlein 1987, 36). Reading Recovery is based on research and instructional procedures developed by Clay (1979, 1985). The results from this ongoing research effort (see Boehnlein 1987; Pinnell 1985a, 1988) suggest a remarkable success rate:

> After an average of fifteen to twenty weeks, or thirty to forty hours of instruction, 90 percent of the children whose pretest scores were in the lowest 20 percent of their class catch up to the average of their class or above and *never need remediation again*. (Boehnlein 1987, 33)

Although there are no reports of efforts to single out specific features of the program that account for student progress, there are several critical attributes of Reading Recovery that probably work together.

The first is the extensive amount of reading and writing that students do. This is accomplished, in part, because of the intensive one to one instruction that occurs for thirty minutes every day for each student in the program. In addition, the program is premised on early intervention. Although every lesson conforms to a specific sequence within that framework, students' individual needs are addressed very specifically. Students not only read widely but do so in high-quality materials (many predictable, patterned books) and receive strong oral language support as well. Finally, the program also involves extensive teacher training. Teachers are trained in the techniques that require careful observation of students, recording of information, and adapting of instruction. Teachers are observed repeatedly and both give and receive feedback on their instructional interactions.

The first ten lessons, called "Roaming in the Known," require teachers to support students in reading easy books and writing their own stories. Teachers also read aloud, build students' confidence, and establish a pleasant relationship. Thereafter, lessons conform to the following sequence:

1. Students reread familiar material to build fluency and practice new skills.
2. Students reread the new book that was introduced the day before and the teacher does a Running Record (see Chapter 8).
3. Plastic letters are manipulated and identified.
4. Students write a sentence or story of their own, focusing on analyzing and writing the sounds in words.
5. The teacher copies the sentence or story that has just been composed, cuts it apart, and the student rearranges it.
6. Students experience a new book; they attend to meaning and text while the teacher provides appropriate support and encouragement to use specific skills and strategies.
7. Students try to read the new book independently (Boehnlein 1987).

Although the framework is the same for all students, the interactions are planned using detailed assessment information for each child. Teachers must have highly developed observational skills, because they are expected to collect observational data for each child during reading and writing. In addition, teachers are expected to shape the sessions, "actively interacting moment-by-moment with the child as he or she actually reads" (Pinnell 1985a, 71).

Success for All

Unlike Reading Recovery, Success for All is a whole school intervention (Madden, Slavin, Kareweit, Dolan, and Wasik 1991). Implemented in schools with very low socioeconomic status, the program includes a focus on kindergarten through grade 3. All children are placed in heterogenous regular classrooms except during reading time, a ninety-minute period during which students are grouped by ability across all grades (k–3). In addition, twenty-minute, one-to-one tutoring sessions are provided as needed.

Although the materials used in Success for All include both traditional (basal) and nontraditional (predictable little books), the instructional program overall emphasizes aspects of reading that are similar to Reading Recovery. For example, students receive explicit instruction in phonemic awareness and extensive opportunities to write. In addition, opportunities to read are promoted both in and out of school. Finally, periodic and continuous assessment informs the instruction of teachers in the program.

Obviously, there is a need for school-wide responses to the problem of reading and writing difficulties. While potentially powerful, Reading Recovery's one-on-one tutorial approach in first grade clearly cannot address the needs of some schools who have whole cohorts of children who are performing poorly (see Hiebert 1994). It is not difficult, however, to imagine how students receiving the intensive Reading Recovery instruction from highly competent teachers would flourish. For teachers and schools not trained in the techniques, there are also lessons to be learned. Schools must find ways to provide significant blocks of time to teachers and students for literacy instruction. They must also invest in their teaching staff. We say again that there is no substitute for a knowledgeable, skilled teacher. Finally, students need to read and write daily.

Common Elements for Successful Early Intervention Programs

Although we have summarized just two early intervention programs, others also report promising results (see Hiebert et al. 1992; Taylor et al. 1992). Two characteristics of these programs are especially important to note. First, all these programs increase the amount of time students spend reading and writing. Second, all these programs focus considerable attention on the reading and writing of connected text.

Pikulski (1994, 1995) has reviewed five of these programs and summarized the attributes common to all of these successful programs. The following characteristics are noted by Pikulski as especially important:

- Intervention is frequent and lengthy
- Student-teacher ratios are small (or one-to-one)
- Fluency is an important outcome
- Text difficulty is controlled so students read many easy books
- Instruction focuses on building phonemic awareness and print skills
- Writing is used to promote word recognition and spelling
- There is a well-established pattern for instructional sessions
- Instruction is fast paced
- Assessment is frequent, ongoing, and used to inform instruction
- Communication between home and school is critical
- Teachers receive (sometimes extensive) training

And, finally, the accomplished teachers in these programs hold high standards for students and believe that they will achieve. Certainly many of these characteristics can and should be present in all classrooms and available to all students.

INSTRUCTIONAL TECHNIQUES FOCUSED ON WORD RECOGNITION AND ANALYSIS

In this section, we provide detailed descriptions of instructional techniques designed to focus attention on word recognition and word analysis. The instructional strategies have been categorized according to their utility for use with students in the three developmental phases described above. First, we provide suggestions for working with students who have no print skills. Next, we turn our attention to students who have acquired some knowledge and skill in word recognition, and, finally, we suggest some instructional approaches for working with older, more skilled readers.

Instructional Strategies and Tools: Students with No Print Skills

Some students have virtually no conventional print skills. Because these students may be very diverse (very young, very disabled, bilingual, and so on), the range of techniques that might be employed with this group is also great. Some techniques involve merely tightening the focus on traditional good practice. Other strategies involve much more systematic intervention.

Establishing the Foundational Abilities

Age alone does not determine whether students have acquired the prerequisite knowledge and skill to become a mature reader. Although older readers are hardly ever permitted the time it would take to acquire some of the underpinnings of literacy (see Chapter 7), this is precisely what some need. In addition, most young, poor readers need at least some work on the foundations of literacy.

Developing phonemic awareness. It has become increasingly clear that students must learn to segment speech into constituent parts. Some students have mastered this skill before they enter school; most others develop the ability to isolate individual sounds rapidly as they encounter typical beginning reading instruction. There are some students, however, who do not seem to learn this early and easily. For them, the likelihood of reading failure is quite high (Juel, Griffith, and Gough 1986; Stanovich 1986).

As in other areas of word identification, there is disagreement about the appropriate way to deliver this instruction. The notion that sound analysis and writing may actually precede reading is a difficult idea for most educators to grasp. Traditionally, schools have stressed learning letter names first, moving from letters to sounds. However, research does suggest that children's attempts at analyzing words into component sounds, essential to early writing attempts, likely promotes and develops phonics knowledge and skill.

Clay (1979) argues that the experientially based strategies employed in the Reading Recovery program are effective because an important feature of this program is the extensive writing that occurs, with an emphasis on invented spelling (see Chapter 7). As Clay notes, this "forces children to carry out a splendid sound analysis of the words they want to write—a first to last segmenting of the sounds in the word. They pay attention to the sounds of words and search for a visual way of representing these" (66). The strong encouragement students receive for analyzing words for the constituent sounds is buttressed by activities that help students to identify orally rhyming words, to separate words that rhyme from those that don't, and finally, by activities that provide information about sound-symbol patterns.

Clay contrasts this type of visual and auditory program with the phonemic training programs used for years in Russia (see Elkonin 1963, 1973). In Elkonin's program, children do not interact with print at all until they have mastered certain aspects of phonological segmentation. Markers are used to designate individual phonemes. Students are shown pictures with spaces beneath the picture that represent the total number of phonemes in that word. Students say the word and then they separate the word into discrete phonemes, placing a marker in each space as they say it. Over time, students are expected to do this orally, without markers or pictures.

The ABDs of Reading is a word identification program for learning disabled students designed and evaluated by Williams (1980). It focuses on teaching students to analyze, blend, and decode, using both oral training and contextual support. Williams has demonstrated that this type of program has a significant impact on the decoding abilities of learning-disabled students. Its success is probably rooted in the combination of direct instruction and supported practice. The ABDs of Reading involves the following steps:

1. Direct instruction is provided regarding the concept of word segmentation. Students are taught to identify the syllable as an element.
2. Students receive direct instruction in phoneme analysis. Nine phonemes (seven consonants and two vowels) are used for *auditory* analysis and practice.
3. Students receive instruction in blending phonemes into two- and three-phoneme units.
4. Students are taught letter-sound relationships for the nine phonemes.
5. Students manipulate letters to learn to decode phonograms made from the nine phonemes.
6. Six additional letter-sound relationships (five consonants and one vowel) are introduced and practiced.
7. More complex patterns are introduced involving consonant combinations (for example, CCVC).

Williams is careful to note that "this was a decoding program, not a complete reading program" (4), and emphasizes the need to provide experience with words in context and the need to provide instruction in comprehension as well. This may involve using some aspects of the program launched in Chapter 12 and providing time to focus directly on this aspect during some portion of the day. However, it seems safe to say that the instructional program of students who cannot reliably isolate sounds and blend them together should contain some focus on segmentation and blending.

Using sense and syntax.   In order to take full advantage of any word identification instruction, students must be able to use sense and syntax to test out their graphophonic approximations. Students who have limited language proficiency or have had few experiences with book print should be read to extensively. Teachers, peers, older students, and parent volunteers should all be enlisted to aid in this effort.

In addition, daily oral language experiences (shared books, chants, chart stories, etc.) and opportunities to speak should also be provided. From time to time, students should also be encouraged to create dictated stories using the frameworks or language of some read-aloud books. Remember that in general, the focus of these instructional efforts should be to promote oral comprehension and the ability to predict upcoming words and ideas using the semantic and syntactic cueing systems of books.

Developing Sight Word Recognition

One of the major accomplishments of skilled reading involves recognizing instantly *at sight* large numbers of words. Some of these words have become old friends—sight words—because they occur so frequently in print that the well-read student has encountered them many times. Others have been acquired as instantly recognizable words because they have very high value (high-potency words) for the reader.

In the very early stages of formal, or conventional, reading development, there are two ways that teachers can help students recognize words at sight: embed the new word(s) in a highly familiar/strongly supported print context, or provide direct instruction of the new word(s). Both methods are described below, because effective instruction typically involves each at different times. Since the embedding method will require the least adaptation from the types of instruction started in Chapter 12, we address those procedures first.

Embedded exposure: Shared book experiences.   Traditional sight word instruction has generally involved hefty amounts of skill and drill practice, often in isolation. More recently, educators and researchers have questioned the value of games and isolated drill in promoting word recognition development in most children. Rather:

> Automatic recognition of a word from its graphic form is a consequence of extensive experience seeing that word in context and building up a complete linguistic identity around it. (Ehri 1987, 15)

Using as a model the types of heavily supported print encounters provided by parents in literate environments, Holdaway (1979) described a cycle of activity that has been dubbed the "shared book experience." Shared reading in the classroom often involves enlarged print books, called *"big books."* Big books allow teachers and students in a group environment to read a piece of text together in a manner that mimics the intimacy and give-and-take of home lap reading, but also makes the print display available to students. As Holdaway has noted, "Reading to a group of children in school has little instructional value simply because the print cannot be seen, shared, and discussed" (64).

Skilled teachers can develop all of the concepts of print using big books. They model directionality by moving their hand across the pages; they demonstrate speech-print match and concept of word by pointing; and they begin to introduce the relationship of sound-symbol by careful voice pointing across words of different length (McCracken and McCracken 1986; Slaughter 1983). During shared book experiences, the children generally gather around the teacher as he or she uses the following procedures:

1. The teacher focuses children's attention on the cover, helps children to examine other aspects of the book (for example, author, illustrator, and so on) and asks children to predict what might happen in the book.
2. The teacher reads the book aloud for pleasure.
3. Students and teacher discuss what happened in the story, focusing on response and comprehension.
4. In later encounters, the teacher rereads the book, pointing to the words and encouraging students to read along.
5. Students do repeated readings of the text, including taped read-alongs using small copies of the big book.

Some teachers are concerned that students, especially less-able readers, will not receive appropriate instruction if controlled vocabulary texts are not used. In Chapter 9, we described the Bookwords list (Eeds 1985), a list of high-frequency words that had been identified from children's literature books for the early grades. Reading teachers interested in coordinating their remedial program with a literature-based classroom program (or classroom teachers interested in supporting their less-skilled readers within the regular literature program) should find this list helpful. A sampling of the books included in Eeds' analysis is provided in Figure 13.1.

Although it is clearly possible, and potentially beneficial, for remedial students to receive instruction using good literature, most schools and teachers need some assurance that students are acquiring basic sight vocabulary. Teachers can provide some direct instruction using the Bookwords words, coupled with repeated exposure in good books, or use the predictable books technique described next.

Predictable books technique.   Using predictable books and language experience stories, Bridge, Winograd, and Haley (1983) have expanded on the "shared books" approach. They designed a program for teaching the basic sight words to beginning readers and examined its effect on students' recognition of high-frequency sight words. Their results indicate that students reading at a beginning primer level learned more basic sight words through this approach than students using a regular basal with controlled vocabulary.

FIGURE 13.1
Book List

50 Books for a Good Beginning	Total Words	Total Number of Different Words	Percent of Running Words Relative to Bookwords	Percent of Different Words Relative to Bookwords
Bancheck, Linds. *Snake In, Snake Out*	38	8	100	100
Barton, Byron. *Where's Al?*	34	18	82	89
Ginsburg, Mirra. *The Chick and the Duckling*	112	30	75	67
Burningham, John. *The Blanket*	66	33	86	85
Burningham, John. *The Friend*	51	34	86	88
Asch, Frank. *Yellow, Yellow*	97	47	70	62
Burningham, John. *The Dog*	69	48	77	69
Browne, Anthony. *Bear Hunt*	83	52	62	75
Kraus, Robert. *Whose Mouse Are You?*	108	54	77	76
Ets, Marie Hall. *Elephant in a Well*	286	56	71	64
Alexander, Martha. *Blackboard Bear*	128	62	78	70
de Paola, Tomie. *The Knight and the Dragon*	129	65	70	66
Kraus, Robert. *Leo the Late Bloomer*	166	70	68	67
Breinburg, Petronella. *Shawn Goes to School*	132	75	83	77
Mayer, Mercer. *There's a Nightmare in My Closet*	142	76	76	68
Buckley, Helen. *Grandfather and I*	291	79	go	70
Bornstein, Ruth. *Little Gorilla*	173	80	72	63
Brown, Margaret Wise. *The Runaway Bunny*	441	83	81	57
Burningham, John. *Come Away from the Water, Shirley*	129	86	74	65
Asch, Frank. *Rebecka*	203	88	87	80
Asch, Frank. *Elvira Everything*	183	92	81	73
Burningham, John. *Mr Gumpy's Outing*	289	95	73	62
Wells, Rosemary. *Noisy Nora*	206	101	68	55
Hutchins, Pat. *The Surprise Party*	336	101	76	68
Udry, Janice. *Let's Be Enemies*	229	102	73	68
Clifton, Lucille. *Everett Anderson's Goodbye*	200	104	76	64
Brandenburg, Fritz. *I Wish I Was Sick Too*	327	107	68	63
de Paola, Tomie. *Watch Out for Chicken Feet in Your Soup*	254	107	68	63
Alexander, Martha. *Move Over, Twerp*	245	111	78	72
LaFontaine (Wildsmith). *The North Wind and the Sun*	210	113	70	59
Kellogg, Steven. *Pinkerton Behave*	233	116	65	56
Barton, Byron. *Jack and Fred*	263	118	80	72
Flack, Marjorie. *Ask Mr Bear*	632	119	77	66
Asch, Frank. *MacGoose's Grocery*	322	123	76	70
Lionni, Leo. *Little Blue and Little Yellow*	284	123	81	71
Griffith, Helen. *Mine Will Said John*	506	124	70	69

FIGURE 13.1

Book List, Continued

50 Books for a Good Beginning	Total Words	Total Number of Different Words	Percent of Running Words Relative to Bookwords	Percent of Different Words Relative to Bookwords
Boynton, Sandra. *Hester in the Wild*	263	124	75	61
Sendak, Maurice. *Where the Wild Things Are*	350	129	70	57
Allard, Harry. *The Stupids Die*	296	140	55	61
Keats, Ezra Jack. *Goggles*	336	139	66	62
Hoban, Russell. *The Stone Doll of Sister Brute*	494	143	73	65
Sharmat, Marjorie. *I Don't Care*	451	147	74	65
Keats, Ezra Jack. *Whistle for Willie*	391	149	78	69
Asch, Frank. *Sand Cake*	443	153	71	63
Delton, Judy. *New Girl in School*	379	158	80	60
Burningham, John. *Avocado Baby*	373	160	73	60
Allard, Harry. *The Stupids Step Out*	413	176	68	59
Cohen, Miriam. *Will I Have a Friend?*	464	177	74	63
Dauer, Rosamond. *Bullfrog Grows Up*	627	204	75	61
Marshall, James. *George and Martha*	645	210	75	68

From "Bookwords: Using A Beginning Word List of High Frequency Words from Children's Literature K-3" by M. Eeds, *The Reading Teacher*, January 1985, p. 420. International Reading Association. Reprinted by permission.

The instructional strategy designed by Bridge, Winograd, and Haley involves selecting predictable books (see Appendix D) that contain the high-frequency sight words you wish students to learn. Using these materials, the teacher employs the following strategy:

Step 1: Teacher reads the book aloud. Then the teacher rereads the book, encouraging students to join in when they can predict what will come next.

Step 2: The story is transferred to a chart, without pictures to aid the reading. Students reread the story from the chart. Then students match sentence strips from the story to sentences on the chart. Finally, students match individual words to the words in the story.

Step 3: Students engage in choral rereading of the story from the chart. Word cards are presented randomly and the children match them to words in the story.

In addition to these activities, students regularly contributed to group language experience stories (see Chapter 12) that focused on sight word recognition as well as matching.

Like the repeated reading techniques described in Chapter 12, strategies that involve predictable books rely on repeated exposure to high-frequency words to build sight word recognition. Big Books and charts have the additional advantage of providing opportunities to focus on individual words in the context of a whole text. Flaps or *masks* (Holdaway 1979; Salinger 1988) can be used to cover all or part of words so that teachers and students can work instructionally on features of interest (see Figure 13.2). If instruction began using the dictated stories technique described in Chapter 12, it might be adapted in this way to focus on word identification.

Direct instruction. Some students seem to need more explicit instruction focused clearly on the orthographic features of words (Ehri and Wilce 1980). One of the most comprehensive of such approaches is described by McNinch (1981). He devised a framework for providing direct instruction in sight word recognition that includes some key characteristics of effective teaching. Words are introduced in sentences first and are then isolated so that students may examine them more closely. The steps in the *McNinch Procedure* are:

1. The teacher chooses an unknown sight word and uses it orally in the context of discussion, introducing it to or reinforcing it in the students' oral vocabulary.
2. The teacher presents the word in written context, making sure that the new word appears in a sentence with words that are already in the students' sight vocabulary. The teacher reads the sentence and highlights the unknown sight word by underlining, circling, outlining in color, and so on.
3. The new word is isolated from the sentence and read by the teacher, who then asks a series of questions designed to focus students on critical features of the word. For example, students are asked to compare the word to the one in the sentence, to recall how many letters appear in the word, to tell what letter appears in the initial position, and so on.

FIGURE 13.2
Masking Techniques for Word Identification

Reprinted by permission of Merrill, an imprint of Macmillan Publishing Company, from *Language Arts and Literacy for Young Children* by Terry S. Salinger. Copyright © 1988 by Merrill Publishing.

4. Students read the new words in novel sentences that contain no other unknown words. McNinch applies *very* strict criteria at this stage of the process. Teacher guidance and feedback is offered until students can read their sentences with 100 percent accuracy.
5. Students apply and practice by reading other materials containing the word(s) for meaningful purposes.
6. Students are then provided practice on the word in the form of games designed to achieve mastery of the word.

There are students who have such a difficult time learning new words that they require such intensive instructional efforts. The McNinch procedure acknowledges that some students may need extraordinary help and focuses on critical aspects of print (see Step 2). Once students have even a small number of words that can be recognized at sight, the instructional program should include large doses of supported practice in ways like those described in the next section.

Instructional Strategies and Tools: Students with Some Print Skills

As we have already noted, the vast majority of students who are referred with reading difficulties in the area of word recognition fall into this category. The array of teaching strategies is quite varied, since the needs of this group can be diverse.

Building on the Known: Providing Supported Practice
Students with some print skills, no matter how limited, should be supported in using those skills during authentic reading and writing events. This will frequently mean providing extensive scaffolding (see previous chapters). Although some of this can be provided by careful materials selection (see predictable books method above), for the least-skilled readers in the early stages, teachers will need to plan and execute heavily supported reading opportunities. Throughout the assessment-instruction process, we emphasize the need to determine the range of students' abilities—identifying what they can do as well as what is problematic. The instructional program should take this into account.

Heckelman Impress.   The most heavily supported form of reading is the Neurological Impress Method (NIM) described by Heckelman (1966, 1969). The teacher sits slightly behind the student and reads aloud with the student reading along for ten to fifteen minutes. Specific guidelines should be followed carefully:

1. The teacher should maintain a reasonably fluent pace of reading. The point is for the student to match the fluency of the teacher, not vice versa.
2. The teacher runs a finger smoothly along the print as it is being read.
3. The teacher does not launch a discussion of comprehension and does not use this experience to teach word recognition or word analysis strategies.

Although there is somewhat equivocal evidence about the effectiveness of NIM (Kann 1983), it does appear successful in increasing both word recognition and comprehension for some students (Bos 1982). Like Bos, we have found the procedure is most helpful for students who are experiencing extreme reading difficulty. Kemp (1987, 122) details a series of problems that can arise. The list can serve as a helpful troubleshooting list. Problems occur when:

- the amount of print to be read is too great
- the complexity of the story and/or language is too difficult
- the pace set by the teacher is too fast, or too slow, or intonation is lacking
- the activity takes too long
- the child stops using the print and attends only to the teacher's voice
- the session becomes a lesson on word recognition

Henk's (1983) suggestion that NIM might reasonably replace the guided silent reading phase of a directed reading activity may prove helpful to classroom teachers who cannot otherwise accommodate such a high degree of support, and Echo Reading (B. Anderson 1981) might also be accomplished in this fashion. Echo Reading is a variation on the Impress Method. The teacher reads segments of the material followed by student reading (echo) of the material.

Paired reading techniques.

Paired Reading is a procedure described and evaluated by Topping (1987, 1989) that involves parents. Paired Reading is essentially a systematic variation on the NIM. The child and parent read together at the same time from a book that the child has selected. When the child feels ready, he or she reads alone. Topping reports significant gains made by students who have participated in a Paired Reading program, reporting progress three to five times the average on both word recognition and comprehension (Topping 1987). The activity is meant to be done for approximately fifteen minutes every day.

1. Child selects a book to be read.
2. Child and adult read together until the child, using a prearranged signal (for example, a nudge), indicates that he or she is ready to read alone.
3. The child reads independently until an error is made or a word is encountered that is not read correctly in five seconds.
4. The adult immediately rejoins the child in reading together.
5. Reading together continues until the child gives the signal again and the procedure is repeated or the session ends.

Parents are encouraged to praise children for appropriate signalling, self-correcting, fluent reading, decoding difficult words independently, and for thinking about the story while reading.

The advantages to Topping's Paired Reading procedure are several. First, the student receives substantial practice with an important person in a low-risk context. Second, the student self-selects the reading material, so interest should remain reasonably high. Finally, the procedure can accommodate both extensive support and independent practice.

A different type of assistance is generally provided in repeated reading experiences, since students encounter the same words several times and have increased opportunities to add them to their sight vocabulary. The basic procedures described in Chapter 12 can be used, since the evidence suggests that poor readers with decoding problems benefit the most from repeated readings programs (Carver and Hoffman 1981). However, adaptations can also be introduced to add additional practice in word identification or to focus and support students' development in this area. For example, a method proposed by Chomsky (1978) involves the student listening to a tape-recorded version of the text while reading along. Then the student practices until he or she can read it fluently.

Teaching and Extending Word Analysis

As teachers make decisions in the area of word recognition, careful consideration should be given to both what and how to teach. If the prerequisite skills are in place and students can segment the speech flow, blend sounds, and rhyme, they will be in an excellent position to rapidly acquire the necessary word identification skills.

Systematic and carefully planned instruction is important in word analysis. Many students need explicit instruction in substituting initial consonants and consonant clusters as they create rhyming patterns and work with phonograms (see Figure 13.3). However, there is generally no magic in the exact sequence or program. What does seem to be especially potent is a decoding by analogy strategy that has been well documented (see Adams 1990; Cunningham 1975–76; Gaskins et al. 1987). Clearly, mature readers decode unknown words by relating them to spelling patterns in words they do know. For example, skilled readers might think of known words *"paint"* or *"faint"* when encountering the unknown word *"tainted."* As Cunningham (1995) explains:

> Children who learn many common word families also learn something more important—to look carefully at the spelling pattern of a new word and search through the words they already know for words with the same pattern.

As we will see below, this tack also helps students become good spellers.

Students will need to be introduced to word families or phonograms. Lists are available from many sources (see for example, Cunningham 1995), but all include recurrent spelling patterns such as:

bed	rain	cake	kick	boat
red	gain	rake	pick	coat
fed	pain	fake	tick	goat
led	chain	brake	chick	moat

The type of instruction revealed in Figure 13.3 should, of course, be followed closely (or accompanied) by ample opportunities to read and write. Since students generally enjoy the rhyme and rhythm afforded by poetry and nonsense books, these may be good choices.

FIGURE 13.3
Sample Word Analysis Lessons

A Demonstration Lesson on Initial Consonant Clusters

Instructional Steps	Lesson for *cl-cl/*
1. Review the initial sound.	1. Ask the children to identify the initial sound in "can" and "cup."
2. Review the other phoneme.	2. Ask the children to identify the initial sound in "loud" and "lap."
3. Provide auditory experiences having combined consonant phonemes.	3. Ask the children to listen to the combined sound in "cloud," "clam," "close," etc.
4. Provide visual identification.	4. Present the children with the written words "cloud," "clam," "close," etc., and have the youngsters identify graphic similarities.
5. Ask the children to find *cl* words in their word banks.	5. Have the children supply new examples.
6. Present new *cl* words in sentence context.	6. Apply new concepts to new words.

A Demonstration Lesson for Phonograms

Instructional Steps	Lesson for *cl-an*
1. Present known words in a pattern.	1. Remind children that they know the words "pan" and "Dan."
2. Recognize rhyme and graphic similarity.	2. Encourage children to identify two common elements of -an: rhyme and letters.
3. Make a new word.	3. Write "fan"; have the children identify graphic similarity; have them use rhyming and pronounce the word.
4. Supply new and additional words.	4. Let the children suggest another word like "man," and then have them search for more examples from their word banks.
5. Make application to new words.	5. Have each child pronounce new words: for example, "ran" and "tan."

Reprinted by permission of Merrill, an imprint of Macmillan Publishing Company, from *The Development of Language and Literacy in Young Children*, 3/e by Susanna W. Pflaum. Copyright © 1986.

Instructional Strategies and Tools:
Print Skills for More Advanced Readers

Students who are generally skilled in word identification but who have specialized difficulties are often among the most difficult to instruct. Both students and teachers are frequently confused about where to focus attention. Indeed, there are several possible reasons for such difficulties. Students may not have acquired a balanced repertoire of word recognition/word analysis skills, or they may have difficulty using both word analysis and meaning-based strategies together. Alternatively, students may not have gained control over reading, especially reading that involves complex materials with a significant number of multisyllabic words. Of course, students may not have adequate meaning vocabulary, an issue we will take up in the next chapter (see Chapter 14).

Multisyllabic and Content Words

Cunningham (1975–76) designed a compare/contrast strategy that appears to be helpful in promoting word identification of multisyllabic words. By teaching children to make analogies with known words, elementary school children (Grades 2–5) improved their ability to read unfamiliar words, and in addition, to transfer this knowledge to reading two-syllable words. The compare/contrast technique proceeds as follows:

1. Familiar sight words are placed on cards for students to manipulate.
2. Using these word cards, students are taught to compare and contrast known two-syllable words to known one-syllable words that rhyme with individual syllables of the two-syllable words (for example, banter—can, her).
3. Students practice pronouncing the polysyllabic word and the two separate words.
4. Students practice the technique, adding other known sight words to cards for manipulation and matching them to additional two-syllable words.
5. Students receive extensive practice in executing this matching in their heads, without cards.
6. The technique is expanded to three-syllable words.

The great advantage to this technique is that it depends on flexible application of the analogy strategy. Students do not need to learn rules, but rather learn to approximate words, using sound and sense together. Finally, students can learn to identify morphemic units without memorizing long lists of prefixes and suffixes. Although the common practice of "looking for small words" is not warranted, students certainly should be taught to examine words for base words and recurring spelling patterns.

Teaching Strategies for Independence

Some students need to be taught how to approach and analyze multisyllabic words, but others need help in pulling together the skills and strategies they already know. They need to be encouraged to become independent.

Guide for attacking unknown words. Students, even very young ones, should be encouraged to attain some degree of independence and control in using their existing knowledge and skill. Most authors recommend teaching students a general strategy for word recognition and helping them to use it regularly during reading of connected text. The following steps seem reasonable:

1. Ask yourself what would make sense.
   Read ahead.
   Reread.
2. Try to sound it out.
   For one-syllable words: Compare the word to other known words: CVC, CVCe, CVVC.
   For two-syllable words: Identify the parts and compare each syllable to a known word: CVC + CVC.
   For words with more than one morpheme: Identify the root and then add the affixes.
3. Use the sound plus sense. (Get an approximation by sound-symbol and then correct or adapt using the context of the sentence.)
4. Skip it and see if it seems important.
5. If important, ask someone.

As is the case with any aspect of reading competence, independence in word identification takes substantial time and effort to accomplish on the part of both readers and teachers. Sometimes students need a copy of this guide to refer to until the steps become automatic. Teachers should teach this type of independent strategy just as carefully as they teach students the component skills.

Student monitoring and highlighting. Many less-skilled readers have difficulty transferring and coordinating their word analysis skills. In addition (perhaps consequently), they often have trouble attending to the meaningfulness of text. Pflaum and Pascarella (1980) developed a program designed to help students monitor their reading miscues, paying particular attention to those that distort meaning. In addition, these authors taught students to correct these miscues in order to retain meaning.

Reinforcing the developmental nature of some reading abilities, the program improved the reading level of learning disabled students (ages 8–13), but only if they had previously attained a reading level of second grade or higher. Thus, it appears that explicit training in monitoring and repair strategies may depend for its success on a certain level of word identification ability.

Importantly, students were informed about what they were learning. In addition, the teacher discussed when to use the strategy in their own reading. The activities were modeled by the teacher, students received guided practice at each step, and then they received help in applying the strategy to their own reading.

Students received instruction in two phases; half of the lessons focused on helping students to identify miscues that affect meaning and half focused on teaching students to self-correct miscues. During the first set of lessons, students listen to an audiotape of a child who is making miscues. Students are repeatedly advised to think about whether a miscue (substitution) is "serious" (meaning-changing) or not. Specifically:

1. Students listen to ten sentences, underlining the miscue made in each.
2. Students read five short paragraphs, underlining the two miscues in each. They discuss the seriousness of each miscue, using meaning change as the criterion.
3. Students read an instructional selection and record their own performance.
4. Students listen to their tape, underlining their own miscues. They then practice reading and recording additional passages until they reach 70 percent accuracy in noting miscues.
5. Students again listen to five short recorded paragraphs, underlining "serious" miscues twice. Students underline miscues once that do not distort meaning.
6. Students repeat Step 5 using their own recorded reading (underline serious miscues twice and less serious miscues once).

In the second set of lessons, students focus on learning to self-correct miscues that do not make sense. They are taught to use both context and graphophonic cues to self-correct.

1. Students listen to an audiotaped child, marking that child's self-corrections on a worksheet copy of the text.
2. Students discuss the self-corrections noting especially the technique used to self-correct and the reason underlying the self-correction (for example, "that doesn't make sense").
3. Students practice and discuss replacements for blanks in fifteen sentences (use context).
4. Students practice choosing replacement words using initial letter cues, then final letter cues.
5. Students continue practice, first listing possible words for a cloze replacement (using only context), then narrowing the choices using first initial, then finally letter information.
6. Students read their own material, record it, and analyze their own miscues and self-corrections. Students are taught to correct uncorrected miscues as they listen by stopping the tape.

INSTRUCTIONAL TECHNIQUES FOCUSED ON SPELLING

Instructional recommendations for students who are experiencing spelling difficulty parallel those for word recognition in important ways. First, spelling ability is developmental in nature. Second, the specific strategies for developing spelling ability include provisions both for explicit instruction and ample opportunities for practice.

Instructional Focus at Various Developmental Spelling Levels

It will be no surprise to teachers that a great many students who are struggling readers are also having trouble in spelling. Many of the recommendations just suggested for instruction in word recognition will inevitably aid spelling also. Indeed, Templeton (1995) has made a persuasive case for the mutuality of word recognition and spelling instruction:

> Words need to be examined in their own right. The resulting development and understanding of underlying spelling structures will guide rapid and efficient word identification in reading as well as more rapid spelling of words in writing. This is particularly true for struggling readers. (317)

As we have already noted, reading and writing ability and knowledge are closely aligned in the earliest stages and ages of literacy development. As they progress, however, these abilities diverge somewhat. In the struggling reader, however, the underlying phonological and orthographic knowledge required is quite similar. The developmental overlap between word identification and spelling ability is made clear by this progression. In addition, the knowledge (both phonological and orthographic) that students must acquire at various stages clearly fuels both word identification and spelling abilities.

Templeton (1995) recommends that teachers plan their instructional program around a "core list or group of words" and that spelling patterns be identified that relate to the various spelling levels of students. In Figure 13.4, the instructional content of a developmental spelling program is fully described.

In order to be useful, however, teachers must have a clear sense of students' needs. Templeton (1995) has described a progression of spelling, or orthographic knowledge, that provides excellent guidance for spelling assessment (see Chapter 9). Using that information and the content descriptions in Figure 13.4, teachers can plan the appropriate program for struggling students. If students regularly are trying to memorize words that are too difficult for them, they may be successful on the post-test, but they will continue to spell words incorrectly at point of use.

Instructional Strategies and Tools for Spelling

Specialized spelling instruction, like word recognition instruction, should take place within the context of a literacy program that includes effective overall instruction. That means first and foremost that students are encouraged to write continuously for a variety of purposes. It also means that there are explicit conversations that encourage students to note patterns and orthographic regularities.

FIGURE 13.4

Spelling Features That Are Examined at Each Developmental Phase

---

Letter Name

1. Students should be guided to examine and to learn the correct spelling of selected words they are being taught to read.
2. Through activities involving recognition, grouping, substitution, and spelling, beginning consonant elements are examined in the following order: single consonants, common consonant digraphs, and common blends.
3. Short vowel patterns (phonograms) are examined systematically.
4. "Continuant" or nasal consonants that precede other types of consonants are examined (wi*n*ter, ca*m*p).
5. The most common long vowel patterns, or *phonograms*, are examined (m*a*ke, r*i*de). A phonogram is the vowel and what follows within a single syllable.)

Within-Word Pattern

1. Additional common long vowel patterns are examined (/ā/ in b*ai*t, w*ei*ght; /ī/ in l*i*ght; /ē/ in m*ea*t, fr*ee*ze).
2. *R*- and *l*-influenced vowel patterns are studied c*ar*d, f*er*n, f*all*, p*ull*).
3. Common diphthongs are introduced (h*ow*, b*oi*l).
4. Compound words are studied.
5. Through the examination of common homophones, students begin to develop an awareness of the meaning principle in spelling.

Syllable Junction

1. Common and less frequent vowel patterns in stressed syllables continue to be examined.
2. Common inflections and the ways in which they are joined to base words are examined (*-ed, -ing, -ly*).
3. The sound and the meaning of common prefixes and suffixes are analyzed (*un-, re-, -ment, -ness*).
4. The role of stress or accent is introduced in the context of homographs.
5. Unstressed syllables are examined, first in two-syllable words and later in polysyllabic words.
6. More complex prefixes and suffixes are examined.
7. The principle of consonant doubling is examined as it applies to a broader range of vocabulary.

Derivational Patterns: The Spelling-Meaning Connection

1. Silent and sounded consonant patterns are studied (colum*n*/colum*n*ist, resig*n*/resig*n*ation).
2. Considerable attention is given to the different vowel alternation patterns, sequenced for study as follows:
   a. Long-to-short (extr*e*me/extr*e*mity, rev*i*se/rev*i*sion)
   b. Long-to-schwa (infl*a*me/infl*a*mmation, def*i*ne-def*i*nition)
   c. Short-to-schwa (exc*e*l/exc*e*llent, leg*a*l/leg*a*lity)
   d. Predictable sound/spelling alternation (consu*m*e/consu*m*ption, recei*v*e-rece*p*tion)
3. While the vowel-alternation patterns are studied, other accompanying consonant alternation patterns are examined:
   a. Sound change/spelling stable (musi*c*/musi*c*ian, constit*u*te/constit*u*tion)
   b. Predictable sound/spelling alternation (explo*d*e/explo*s*ion, absen*t*/absen*c*e, permi*t*/permi*ss*ion)
4. The role of Greek and Latin forms in spelling and in meaning is explored.
5. "Absorbed" or "assimilated" prefixes are examined (*ad* + tract = *at*tract; *in* + luminate = *il*luminate).

Source: From *Teaching the Integrated Language Arts*, by S. Templeton, 1991. Boston: Houghton Mifflin.
Copyright 1991 by Houghton Mifflin. Reprinted by permission.

Spelling and Writing

In the context of a rich writing community, there will be many opportunities to use invented spelling, where appropriate, *and* to attend more closely to conventional spellings as work is edited and revised for publication. At least some of the spelling words that struggling writers are learning should be drawn from their own writing, although few teachers find that they can plan their entire spelling program using this individualized approach.

Spelling instruction can become more visible during writing in the following ways:

1. Create charts and/or lists of commonly misspelled words in a central place for students to refer to. Alternatively, have students create a "Word Wall" on which they place words they use often and others would find helpful.
2. Use mini-lessons to highlight specific spelling difficulties, particularly when they revolve around various patterns (that is, phonograms at the earliest levels and rules for adding affixes at the upper levels).
3. When students request a spelling for a word, do not provide it out loud. Instead, either write it down (requiring the student to compare/contrast as she rewrites it) or encourage use of the dictionary, when appropriate.
4. Encourage students to write first and worry about spelling later. But, later, be sure to offer good support for editing.
5. Encourage students to use what they know. This means spelling by analogy with known words and it also means writing two or three versions of the word to see which one "looks right." There is evidence to suggest that both strategies improve spelling (Tenney 1980; Templeton 1995).

Even with a strong writing program, many students need additional attention to spelling. As Henderson (1990) has noted, "writing provides sound exercise of spelling knowledge but only modest information for a memorized spelling vocabulary" (92).

Word Sorts

The Word Sort strategy (described in Chapter 8) has already been suggested for assessment. It can also have powerful instructional value. Of course, when used for spelling, instruction will focus on the orthographic structure of the words and on recurrent spelling patterns. Most researchers agree that struggling spellers do not attend closely enough to the print display and, as a result, do not acquire the sensitivity to patterns that good spellers have.

Both the words selected and the directions for sorting will, of course, vary by developmental level (see Bear, Invernizzi, and Templeton 1995; Schlagal 1995). For example, as students move into the "within-word pattern" stage of spelling development, word sorts might include words like *make, train, state, paint*, etc. Such words will encourage students to distinguish the spelling (orthographic) pattern from the sound (phonological) appearance of the words.

Spelling Lists

There are a number of lists from which teachers might choose a master spelling list. Indeed, the words in most commercial programs are selected from such reasonable sources as high frequency lists and/or lists of common elements (Henderson 1990). A relatively small number of words (5000) accounts for 95 percent of all the words that adults use in writing, so, of course, it makes sense to encourage children to acquire these spellings.

There are two critical issues that should guide a teacher's use of spelling lists. First, students must be able to read the words. If they cannot, they will not retain their spellings even if they do well on weekly tests. Similarly, the list should contain words that relate to the relative spelling knowledge (stage of development) that has most currency for that child. Second, there is considerable evidence that students should correct their own pretest spellings using a compare/contrast method (Henderson 1990). This dramatically improves the likelihood that the spelling will be retained.

A Final Note

In summary, what teachers must do is help students develop the ability to tell when a word "looks right" (see Cunningham 1995). Both experience and direct instruction will probably be required for students with reading and writing difficulties to accomplish this.

Classroom teachers and clinical teachers must be especially careful to provide coherent word recognition, word analysis, and spelling instruction to children who are struggling to master print skills. These students are most likely to receive fragmented instruction with a heavy emphasis on isolated skills. Indeed, many of the specialized commercial programs on the market are designed to provide instruction in the components of sound-symbol correspondence to the exclusion of meaningful practice. Although some of these programs and materials may be useful tools in the hands of a knowledgeable teacher, they certainly should not be mistaken for a total reading/literacy program.

Classroom teachers need to guard against the temptation to believe that all children can/should learn using the same materials and methods, while specialized reading personnel need to guard against the notion that all students who are poor readers need strange and unusual instructional approaches. What is most often needed is a coherent approach that increases students' opportunities to learn. In order to accomplish this, classroom teachers will need to find many ways to focus on print during the normal course of the school day. Clinical or special teachers should attempt to use their instructional time to enhance the program that is already being offered.

When special programs are advanced as appropriate for students, all concerned should be very clear about how the special program will be an improvement over methods and materials that have already been tried and how the new interventions are going to support the struggling reader in his or her work with meaningful texts.

CHAPTER SUMMARY

In this chapter, we reexamined the components of word recognition and spelling ability and discussed several issues related to teaching word level instruction. In particular, we described the debate surrounding the appropriate way to help students acquire effective word analysis strategies, noting that views have tended to be polarized. Some educators argue that word identification strategies will not be acquired without direct instruction, while others argue that they cannot be taught at all unless students are helped to learn them as they engage in extensive reading and writing in meaningful settings. Similar, though less strident, arguments have surrounded spelling instruction. Recent advances in knowledge and expertise permit a balanced perspective that acknowledges the importance of both positions. Importantly, there are at least three stages in the acquisition of word identification and spelling competence, and instructional approaches will be most beneficial if teachers differentiate among students who have no conventional print skills, students who have some ability to recognize words, and students with more advanced knowledge and skill in this area.

In the next major section of the chapter, we provided guidelines for teaching word level skills to students. We emphasized the importance of providing instruction in service of meaningful activity, reminding teachers that the goal of instruction should be improved fluency during reading and writing, not better knowledge and skill of phonics or spelling. In addition, we pointed out that instruction should help students to recognize familiar patterns in words, since it appears that this is a particularly effective approach to teaching both word analysis and spelling. In this section we also advocated early intervention, reviewing the growing number of programs such as Reading Recovery that are designed to promote students' early acquisition of word level abilities. Finally, we emphasized once again the importance of providing many practice opportunities.

In the final portion of the chapter, we provided instructional techniques and strategies for word recognition and then for spelling. The word recognition strategies were divided into three categories, paralleling the three developmental stages of word recognition described earlier. We described techniques for embedding word analysis instruction in meaningful book experiences and we also described two direct instruction models for teaching word identification. For students with some print skills, we again described ways to support students as they interact with print, and, as well, we described instructional frames for teaching students to focus on familiar and reliable patterns. For students with more advanced skills, we described some ways to help them become more facile in attacking multisyllabic words and also described ways to teach students to be somewhat more independent in their word reading abilities.

Finally, in a section of instructional strategies for spelling, we reviewed the developmental nature of spelling, suggested content for each level, and described several strategies that have proved effective in addressing the spelling difficulties of some students.

CHAPTER 14

Adapting Instruction to Focus on Vocabulary

INTRODUCTION

Words help us organize life experiences because they represent ideas or concepts in the environment and the interrelationships among those concepts (Searfoss and Readence 1989). As such, words facilitate our thinking processes. Reading and writing are thinking processes; therefore, it is not surprising that vocabulary is a prime contributor to effective reading and writing. Text cannot be understood unless the meanings of most of the words are known, nor can it be created without a large store of vocabulary knowledge.

A wealth of research has demonstrated the strong relationship between vocabulary and reading comprehension. For example, Davis (1968) found that word knowledge was the single most important factor that accounted for variability in comprehension. Similarly, the proportion of difficult words in a text has been found to be the single most powerful predictor of text difficulty, and a reader's general vocabulary knowledge is one of the best predictors of how well that reader can understand text (Anderson and Freebody 1981; Nagy 1988).

As Nagy (1988) points out, the lack of adequate vocabulary knowledge is already a serious obstacle to literacy for many students, and the numbers can be expected to rise as an increasing proportion of students fall into categories considered educationally at risk. For example, there is some evidence that the reading difficulties of limited-English-proficient students in the United States may be related directly to vocabulary knowledge (Garcia 1991, 1993). At the same time, advances in knowledge are creating an ever-larger pool of concepts and words that a person must master to be literate and employable. As a result, considerable attention to vocabulary and teaching students to derive word meanings and attach personal associations to them is vital to instruction at all levels and to success in reading, writing, and learning.

The first half of this chapter discusses the issues surrounding the controversy about when, how, and if vocabulary should be taught. In addition, goals and guidelines for vocabulary instruction are presented. The second half of the chapter describes instructional techniques that correspond to these established goals and guidelines. First, we present basic strategies for independent vocabulary learning during reading and methods for teaching the techniques needed to support these strategies. Second, we describe techniques for providing direct instruction of key terms related to students' assigned reading. Finally, we discuss methods for promoting general vocabulary development and building interest in vocabulary learning that have relevance for success in both reading and writing.

UNDERSTANDING VOCABULARY INSTRUCTION

This section of the chapter discusses the issues surrounding the controversy about when, how, and if vocabulary should be taught and presents goals and guidelines for vocabulary instruction.

Issues

Although there is widespread consensus that vocabulary knowledge is fundamental to comprehension and composition, there is a good deal of controversy about when, how, and if vocabulary should be taught. The issues surrounding this controversy are summarized in the following discussion.

Direct Instruction versus Incidental Learning

The debate about the best way to develop students' vocabulary focuses on the question of the degree to which learners develop vocabulary through incidental learning as they are exposed to unfamiliar words in context, as opposed to direct instruction. Nagy, Herman, and Anderson (1985) have argued that direct instruction in specific words is a slow and inefficient method of vocabulary development. They have shown that readers do use context to learn the meanings of unfamiliar words. In fact, they have argued that this is the primary means of vocabulary development and that wide reading experience is probably the best means of developing students' reading vocabulary.

In contrast, others have argued that direct instruction in vocabulary is essential for good vocabulary growth. For example, a review by Stahl and Fairbanks (1986) concluded that, over the long term, students taught word meanings significantly outperformed students not given instruction, indicating that sustained attention to vocabulary may produce better comprehension. According to this view, the process of learning new words incidentally through repeated exposures in context is a slow and difficult means of vocabulary development.

The research cited in support of direct instruction indicates that skilled readers frequently skip over unfamiliar words as they read (Freebody and Anderson 1983) and that intermediate grade students are not very skilled at using context to determine the meanings of unfamiliar words (Carnine, Kameenui, and Coyle 1984). In addition, it has been found that certain unfamiliar words are learned better through direct instruction than through incidental exposures in reading material (Beck, McKeown, and McCaslin 1983; Omanson, Beck, McKeown, and Perfetti 1984).

The case for incidental learning. Nagy (1988) makes the case for incidental learning as follows. Very few people have received the type of intensive and prolonged vocabulary instruction that would guarantee gains in reading comprehension. However, many people have acquired extensive vocabularies. Few vocabulary programs, no matter how ambitious, cover more than several hundred words a year. Yet current research indicates that the vocabularies of school-aged students grow at the rate of 3,000 new words each year (Nagy and Herman 1987). Furthermore, Fielding, Wilson, and Anderson (1986) found that the amount of time spent in free reading was the best predictor of vocabulary growth for students between grades 2 and 5.

Nagy, Anderson, and Herman (1987) reported that students in the third, fifth, and seventh grades who read grade-level texts under fairly natural conditions had about a one in twenty chance of learning the meaning of any particular word from context. It appears that learning from context is not particularly effective, at least in the short term. However, as Nagy (1988) points out, the short term is not the whole picture.

The average fifth-grade student spends about twenty-five minutes a day reading in and out of school, according to Nagy (1988). Given this amount of reading, he estimates that a student encounters about 20,000 unfamiliar words a year. If one in twenty of these is learned from context, this would amount to a gain of about 1,000 words per year. He argues that if teachers added another 25 minutes per day to a student's reading time, an additional 1,000 words could be learned each year.

With regard to the quality of word knowledge gained from context, Nagy (1988) indicates that a single encounter with a word obviously does not provide in-depth knowledge, which is why context is not an especially effective method of instruction. However, he also maintains that extensive reading can supply all of the characteristics of intensive vocabulary instruction.

> Given that many people do develop in-depth knowledge of large numbers of words apart from much vocabulary instruction, wide reading must be able to produce the kind of word knowledge necessary for reading comprehension. Furthermore, given the number of words to be learned and the number of encounters it takes to learn them thoroughly, reading is necessarily the major avenue of large-scale vocabulary growth. (Nagy 1988, 31)

Contradictory conclusions.   Nagy (1988) presents the apparent contradiction regarding the degree of in-depth vocabulary knowledge necessary for comprehension as follows. On the one hand, it appears that comprehension of text depends on more in-depth knowledge than simply knowing the definitions of words. This implies that, in at least some cases, vocabulary instruction must be rich enough to teach students new concepts in depth. An extreme response to this point of view might be to devote large portions of the school day to intensive vocabulary instruction. On the other hand, it appears that comprehension of text does not require in-depth knowledge of every word in the text. Indeed, reading itself is the major avenue of acquiring in-depth knowledge of words. An extreme response to this point of view would be to abandon vocabulary instruction in favor of increased reading time.

According to Nagy (1988), this contradiction is more apparent than real. If students are to achieve both the depth and the breadth of vocabulary knowledge that they need to become proficient adult readers and writers, a balance between direct instruction and incidental learning is clearly necessary. Most growth in vocabulary knowledge must necessarily come through reading, because there is no way that vocabulary instruction alone can provide enough experiences with enough words to produce the necessary depth and breadth of vocabulary knowledge. Increasing the amount of students' reading is the single most important thing a teacher can do to promote large-scale vocabulary growth. However, vocabulary instruction is also necessary in cases where context does not provide essential information and knowledge of specific words is crucial to comprehension.

Teachers should also guide students in the development of strategies that promote independent word learning. There is no doubt that skilled word learners use context and their knowledge of word parts to deal effectively with new words. Independent word learning is enhanced when these techniques are taught as strategies by modeling how the knowledge of context and word parts can be used to determine the meanings of unfamiliar words encountered while reading, and by providing ample opportunity for guided practice in the use of these strategies.

Which Types of Direct Instruction?

Reviews of the literature indicate that not all types of vocabulary instruction result in improved reading comprehension (Mezynski 1983; Stahl and Fairbanks 1986). Nagy (1988) suggests that one reason vocabulary instruction often fails to increase comprehension is that it does not produce in-depth word knowledge. Research suggests that reading comprehension requires a high level of word knowledge, and that only those methods that produce in-depth knowledge reliably increase readers' comprehension of texts containing those words.

At a minimum, in-depth vocabulary knowledge involves at least two types of information about words—definitional and contextual knowledge (Stahl 1986). Definitional information refers to the knowledge of the logical relations between a word and other known words as provided in dictionary definitions.

Contextual information refers to knowledge of the core concept the word represents and how that core concept changes in different contexts (Stahl 1986).

A large proportion of vocabulary instruction involves the use of definitions: some combination of looking them up, writing them down, and memorizing them. Stahl and Fairbanks (1986) report that when these approaches are used alone, they have no significant effect on comprehension. Nagy (1988) suggests that definitional approaches fail because "reading comprehension depends on a wealth of encyclopedic knowledge and not merely on definitional knowledge of the words in the text" (7).

Another commonly used method involves teaching students to infer the meaning of a new word from the context. Again, Stahl and Fairbanks (1986) report that when a word is used only in context without the definition, there are no significant effects on comprehension. The biggest problem with contextual approaches appears to be that although a context may appear to be quite helpful to those who already know what the word means, it rarely supplies adequate information for those who have no other knowledge about the meaning of a word (Nagy 1988).

It appears that neither definitional nor contextual methods, taken by themselves, are especially effective ways to improve reading comprehension (Nagy 1988). Stahl and Fairbanks (1986) report that the strongest effects are found when there is a combined emphasis on definitional and contextual information, or when the balance is tipped toward contextual information. However, Nagy (1988) maintains that supplying both definitions and contexts does not necessarily guarantee gains in reading comprehension.

> It is safe to say that good definitions and contexts are minimal requirements for good instruction, but by no means do they exhaust what can be put into a good vocabulary lesson. Methods of vocabulary instruction that most effectively improve comprehension of text containing the instructed words go far beyond providing definitions and context. Such methods can be referred to as intensive vocabulary instruction. (9)

Thus, the debate continues as to the most effective means of improving reading comprehension through vocabulary instruction.

When Direct Instruction Is Appropriate

Direct vocabulary instruction is needed to produce in-depth word knowledge. However, since only a fraction of the potentially unfamiliar words in a text can be taught directly, we need to determine when this type of instruction is most appropriate.

Direct vocabulary instruction is most appropriate for conceptually complex words that are not likely to be part of the students' everyday experience (Nagy 1988). In addition, direct instruction is most worthwhile when the words to be taught are important to the understanding of the central ideas in the reading selection and to language development in general. Finally, it is beneficial to teach words in groups that have related meanings.

In further discussions of these issues, Nagy (1988) argues that students' familiarity with the words should be considered, but that it should not be a primary criterion for deciding which words to teach. The words in a selection that are least familiar may not be well suited for instruction because, for example, they may be unimportant to the central ideas of the text. Conversely, it may be important to teach certain complex concepts that may be superficially familiar to the students if a deeper knowledge of them is necessary for understanding the text.

Finally, Nagy (1988) suggests that the single most important question for the teacher who is trying to determine when direct instruction is most appropriate is which words are likely to be conceptually difficult for the reader. Furthermore, the conceptual difficulty of the entire text, and not just the individual words, must be taken into account in determining when direct instruction is necessary. Finally, the greater the proportion of unfamiliar words in a text, the more intensive the instruction that is required to improve comprehension.

Goals

Given the evidence regarding what, when, and why vocabulary instruction is desirable, it appears that we need multiple goals for engaging students in activities designed to increase their vocabulary knowledge. The following are three primary goals for vocabulary instruction:

1. *Teach independent vocabulary learning.* Our first goal is to teach students strategies to learn vocabulary independently as they read. We cannot possibly teach students all the unfamiliar words they will encounter in the course of their reading; however, we can provide them with a repertoire of strategies that will enable them to identify and learn the meanings of unfamiliar words as they read.
2. *Teach concepts important for comprehension.* Our second goal is to teach directly those concepts that are essential for comprehending specific written materials. It is important to provide intensive vocabulary instruction when in-depth knowledge of complex concepts is critical to the understanding of reading assignments, because it is unlikely that this level of knowledge can be obtained by the student independently from context.
3. *Create an environment that promotes general vocabulary development.* Our third goal is to promote general vocabulary development by providing a vocabulary-rich environment with frequent opportunities to learn through reading and writing. Since a major factor distinguishing between more- and less-skilled readers and writers is their level of vocabulary knowledge, a primary goal of instruction must be the continual development and expansion of students' vocabulary knowledge.

In short, we need vocabulary instruction that teaches students strategies for acquiring new vocabulary as they read and write, and increases their knowledge of both general vocabulary and vocabulary specific to their reading materials.

Guidelines

To accomplish the goals set forward in the previous section, research suggests that vocabulary instruction must embody the characteristics outlined in the following guidelines.

Guideline 1: Relate the New to the Known

The first property of powerful vocabulary instruction is that it integrates knowledge of instructed words with other, previously acquired knowledge. This emphasis in instruction is an outgrowth of schema theory which has shown us that knowledge is structured into sets of relationships, and we understand new information by relating it to what we already know (Nagy 1988).

Vocabulary instruction is effective when it helps students relate new vocabulary to their previous experience. In the case of limited-English-proficient students, it appears that relating unknown English vocabulary to known Spanish words with obvious orthographic and semantic similarities is likely to overcome problems with English reading vocabulary (Garcia 1993). By relating the new to the known, new vocabulary becomes personally meaningful and students' understanding is enhanced in ways that lead to increased skill in reading and writing. This practice also leads to improved learning and retention of the meanings of new words.

Guideline 2: Promote Active, In-depth Processing

Effective vocabulary instruction involves students in constructing the meanings of new words. This principle can be related to the "depth of processing" framework used in memory research (cf. Craik and Lockhart 1972). This framework suggests that the harder one "works" to process information to be learned, the better one's retention. For example, retention will be better if one works to construct a relationship rather than simply memorizing a stated relationship.

Stahl (1986) identifies three levels of processing for vocabulary instruction. The first level is *association processing*. At this level a student simply learns an association for a word, such as a synonym or a particular context. At the second level, *comprehension processing,* the student applies a learned association to demonstrate understanding of the word. This involves doing something with the association, such as finding an antonym, fitting the word into a sentence, or classifying the word that requires the student to go beyond just giving back the association or something similar. The third level, *generation processing,* involves taking the comprehended association and generating a novel product using it. This product could be a restatement of the definition in one's own words, comparing the definition to one's own experiences, making up a novel sentence that demonstrates the word's meaning clearly, and so on.

These three increasingly deep levels of processing produce increasingly strong effects on comprehension. When students are actively processing information about each word's meaning, their comprehension of texts using those words improves. Generation could involve having students make their own sentence or definitions, developing semantic maps, breaking words down into semantic features, and so forth. What appears to be most important is that learners not only comprehend a word's meaning, but that they take that comprehension one step farther and make the word their own by interacting with it (Stahl 1986).

Guideline 3: Provide Multiple Exposures

Another important factor for vocabulary instruction to affect comprehension is the number of times the student is exposed to a word and what types of information are given each time. According to Stahl (1986), providing the student with multiple repetitions of the same information about each word's meaning, and providing the student with multiple exposures to the word in different contexts or settings, both significantly improve comprehension. Providing only one or two exposures to a word does not have a positive effect on comprehension.

It is also important to recognize that limited or superficial knowledge of word meanings can have a detrimental effect on comprehension (Nagy 1988). Being able to identify or produce a correct definition for a word does not guarantee that one will be able to access its meaning quickly and effortlessly during reading. Vocabulary instruction must therefore ensure not only that readers know what the word means, but also that they have had sufficient practice using it to make its meaning quickly and easily accessible during reading. In short, it appears that both the amount of time and the way time is spent in vocabulary instruction have a measurable effect on reading comprehension.

Guideline 4: Teach Students to Be Strategic

Effective vocabulary instruction teaches students to be strategic in their acquisition of new vocabulary. Students need to understand how to learn the meanings of new words they encounter in oral and written communication. This guideline can be related to the concept of a strategic reader as described by Paris, Lipson, and Wixson (1983). Strategic readers are those who are responsible for their knowledge, cognizant of that responsibility, and motivated to learn. In the context of vocabulary instruction, being strategic includes awareness of a variety of methods to acquire word meanings, ability to monitor one's understanding of new vocabulary, and the capacity to change or modify strategies for understanding new words if comprehension is not forthcoming.

Teachers can help students become more strategic by teaching different methods of vocabulary learning as strategies rather than as isolated activities. This type of instruction involves modeling and explanation of how particular techniques can help students deal with unfamiliar words encountered while reading, and providing ample opportunity for guided practice, using these strategies with authentic materials.

Summary

In this first section of the chapter, we describe several key issues in understanding vocabulary instruction. We conclude that vocabulary instruction requires careful reflection, since neither direct instruction nor incidental learning account for the complex interplay of learning, vocabulary, and comprehension issues. However, it is possible to conclude that wide reading contributes to vocabulary learning in important ways, and that direct instruction in vocabulary can improve students' word knowledge under some circumstances. To be effective, vocabulary instruction must foster independence and focus on conceptually difficult words that are central to understanding the reading selection.

STRATEGIES FOR VOCABULARY INSTRUCTION

This section of the chapter describes instructional techniques that correspond to the three goals of vocabulary instruction presented previously. First, we present basic strategies students can learn to use during reading, and methods for teaching the techniques needed to support these strategies. Second, we describe techniques for providing direct instruction in specific target words related to students' assigned reading. Finally, we discuss methods for promoting general vocabulary development and building interest in vocabulary learning. The various strategies and techniques adhere to the guidelines presented previously. They focus on relating the new to the known, promoting active, in-depth processing, providing repeated exposures, and promoting the acquisition of independent learning strategies.

A General Framework for Independent Vocabulary Learning

Consistent with our first goal for vocabulary instruction, we are concerned here with the ways in which we can provide the student(s) with a general framework or strategy that can be used independently to identify and learn unknown words during reading. This means that we need to teach them how to employ this type of strategy or framework. To this end, we describe here a general framework for independent vocabulary learning, a specific strategy for implementing this framework, and several techniques that can be used to support the development of the students' ability to use this framework.

The framework described below requires intentional effort and is designed to address vocabulary learning explicitly. The use of such a framework is necessary if vocabulary acquisition in new areas of study is to become habituated.

Phases of the Framework
The general framework we recommend has four phases that involve different types of reading/thinking activities.

Phase 1: Reading and identifying unknown vocabulary; activating prior knowledge regarding the words in relation to the reading.

Phase 2: Applying a repertoire of techniques to identify and learn the meanings of the unfamiliar words including the use of context, word parts, and the dictionary.

Phase 3: Relating the meanings of new words to previous knowledge as an aid to learning and memory.

Phase 4: Repeatedly studying and reviewing the meanings of new words in a variety of contexts.

This framework serves as a guide for students in independently identifying and learning unfamiliar words as they read. There are a number of ways that this framework might be implemented, including the Vocabulary Overview Guide described in the next section.

Vocabulary Overview Guide

One strategy that embodies many of the features of the general framework is the Vocabulary Overview Guide developed by Carr (1985) to teach students a series of steps for self-selecting and defining vocabulary terms from natural text. This teaches students to learn unknown words in their reading materials by establishing a network of relationships among words and relating these words to personal experiences. The students gain greater control over their reading and increase motivation to learn. It also can be used with a variety of reading materials.

The Vocabulary Overview Guide is completed by the students as they read a text. It helps them organize terms and indicate the relations among the terms, passage concepts, and their personal experience. The steps in the strategy are designed to encourage the students to self-monitor as a means of becoming independent learners. Initially, however, teacher modeling is essential to ensure mastery of the strategy. The three basic parts of this strategy are: defining the vocabulary through the use of context, completing the guide, and studying the vocabulary.

Defining the vocabulary in context.   The steps involved in defining the vocabulary require the students to do the following:

1. Survey the text (titles, headings) to determine the nature of the material and to consider what they already know about the topic.
2. Skim the materials to identify unknown or confusing vocabulary words and underline them.
3. Read the selection and try to figure out the meaning of the word from the context of the sentences around it combined with personal experience. Check the accuracy of these definitions by asking someone or using a dictionary.
4. Write the definition in the text or on paper so that it will be available during reading.
5. Reread the passage with the defined vocabulary to ensure understanding.

Completing the guide.   After the students have reread the selection, have them fill in the guide for use in studying the selected terms. Demonstrate this procedure by presenting a sample guide, such as the one in Figure 14.1. Instruct the students to:

FIGURE 14.1

Sample of Vocabulary Overview Guide

A Fourteenth-Century Cargo Makes Port at Last

Sea	Ship	Cargo	Person
treacherous	elaborate	artifacts	numbed
icy/accident	composition	Fort Miamis	hands/snow shoveling
dangerous	develop in detail	primitive objects made by humans	no feeling
sediment	vessel	excavated	
wine	Lake Erie	arrowheads	
matter that settles to the bottom	boat	dug up	
murky	configuration	tantalizing	
Crane Creek	giraffe	Bo Derek	
dark	shape	to tease/withhold something	
thwart	foundered	lacquer	
police/criminal	Titanic	pearls	
stop/prevent	to sink	shiny wax covering	

From "The Vocabulary Overview Guide: A Metacognitive Strategy to Improve Vocabulary and Retention" by E. Carr, *Jounal of Reading*, May 1985, pp. 684–689. International Reading Association. Reprinted by permission.

1. Write the title of the passage on the top line.
2. Select categories of words from the text and place them on the second row of lines. Categories should be selected by studying the vocabulary words and the text to determine what the unknown words describe or discuss. The number of categories will vary according to the vocabulary to be learned and what the words describe.
3. Fill in the vocabulary under the appropriate category on the next line.
4. Write a definition and/or synonym underneath each vocabulary word, leaving space to add more synonyms as new words are learned.
5. Add a personal clue in the box below the vocabulary word that relates the word to a personal experience or a quality or trait of someone or something that is familiar. The meaning of the word is thus related to the student's background knowledge and more clearly understood.

Studying the guide.   After the guide has been filled in, the students are ready to study the vocabulary using the following procedures:

1. Read the title to activate background knowledge and recall words associated with the text.
2. Try to recall the meanings of the words in each category with the personal clue and definition of the word covered by a sheet of paper. If the meaning is not recalled, uncover the personal clue to jog the memory. If the meaning still cannot be recalled, uncover the definition for further study.
3. Use the guide to review the words every day until they are well known; then review them once a week as new words are learned.
4. Add synonyms to old vocabulary words as new words are learned, as a way to connect the old and the new and to refine and extend meanings.

The steps in this procedure can be summarized in a chart and given to the students as an aid until the strategy has become automatic. To ensure that the students are able to construct vocabulary overviews independently, it is important to provide frequent opportunities for practicing this strategy with a variety of reading materials. After demonstrating the strategy, complete several additional guides together, providing direction and feedback to the students. After the students understand how to create the guide, they should create several of them independently to ensure that they can monitor the correct use of the strategy.

The Vocabulary Overview Guide is one strategy for implementing the framework for independent vocabulary learning introduced previously. There are a number of other techniques that can be helpful in teaching students how to apply the framework successfully. Several of these supporting techniques are described in the next section.

Supporting Techniques

This section describes several techniques that can be used to help students learn to apply various parts of the general framework independently. These techniques are not intended to be used in isolation from the larger context of the general framework, nor are they intended to be used for extended periods of time. They are intended to be used as initial supports in teaching students how to apply the general framework.

Teaching Students to Use Context

We agree with Searfoss and Readence (1989) that the best way to teach students to use context clues is by talking through how to use these clues to gain meaning of an unknown word. Toward this end, we describe briefly the *Preview in Context* and *Contextual Redefinition* approaches developed by Readence, Bean, and Baldwin (1985), and the *GLURK* technique developed by Kendall and Mason (1980) .

Preview in context.   This technique uses the students' experiences and teacher questioning to discover the meaning of unknown vocabulary in context. It is a very informal technique that requires little teacher preparation and lends itself to normal classroom interaction. The four steps in this procedure are as follows:

1. Select words from the material to be read that are both important to central ideas in the text and that may present difficulties for the students as they read.
2. Direct the students to the words in context. Read the material aloud as the students follow along in their own texts. Then ask the students to read the material silently.
3. Use questioning and discussion to "talk" the students toward a probable meaning for each word in its immediate context.
4. When the students have an understanding of a word's meaning in its immediate context, extend their understanding through discussion of alternative contexts, synonyms and antonyms, and the like. Encourage the students to use a dictionary or thesaurus to expand their understanding of each word. Word cards or a personal dictionary can be used as a permanent place to put words for later study and review.

Instruction of this type will have a significant cumulative effect. If students are shown how to use contextual analysis for only two words per week over the course of the school year, they will have eighty experiences with the process. This leads the student(s) to develop a habit of trying to discover the meanings of words through their own experiences and knowledge gained from the context.

Contextual redefinition.   This technique was developed by Readence, Bean, and Baldwin (1985) to assist students in learning how to use context as an aid to understanding unfamiliar words. This procedure involves the following steps:

1. Select words from the assigned reading that are necessary to understand the important ideas in the text and that are likely to be unfamiliar to the students.
2. Provide a written context for each word that includes appropriate clues to the word's meaning. Sentences from the text can be used if they provide such a context.

3. Present the words in isolation and ask the students to provide a meaning for each word. The students defend their guesses and come to consensus on the best definition.

4. Present the words in context, using the sentences developed previously. Once again, the students should be asked to offer their best guesses as to the meaning of each word and to defend their definitions. Borrowing from a technique developed by Gipe (1978–79), we would suggest adding to this step the posing of a question that requires the student to relate the word to their own experience. For example, if the word is *surplus*, the question might be, "What do you or your family have a surplus of in your house?"

5. Verify the meaning of the words using a dictionary.

GLURK.   Many words have multiple meanings, so we need to help students have a flexible attitude toward word meanings in order to enable them to recognize the appropriate meanings of words in context. Kendall and Mason (1980) developed a technique called GLURK to help students attend to context, so that they will select the proper meaning of polysemous words. As a first step, the teacher constructs sentences that use the less common meanings of polysemous words. After the sentences have been constructed, the polysemous word is replaced by the word GLURK (for example, John's knees GLURKED from carrying the heavy weight. The music had a clear GLURK.).

After writing the GLURK sentences on paper or a chalkboard, the students are asked what GLURK might mean in each sentence, as well as what it could not mean. For example, they might say that John's knees "hurt," or that the music had a clear "sound." The teacher then replaces GLURK with the target word and the students discuss the intended meaning of the polysemous word (*buckled* and *beat* in our examples). This should lead to a discussion of how words can have more than one meaning and how context can be used to identify and learn new and appropriate meanings.

After the students have worked through a number of GLURK exercises, they should be shown how to apply this technique in actual reading. Using sentences from their reading that contain less common meanings of polysemous words, ask the students to identify the polysemous word and its appropriate meaning from context without first substituting the word GLURK. As a follow-up, the teacher can provide a practice activity consisting of a pair of sentences representing both a primary and a secondary meaning of a polysemous word. The students must then use the sentence context to identify the appropriate meaning for each underlined word. Responses can also be verified using a dictionary.

Teaching Students to Use Word Parts

A word itself provides information about its meaning. Analyzing a word's structure is another tool that students can use to predict meaning. When readers use word parts in combination with context, they have a powerful meaning-getting strategy at their command.

Mason and Au (1990) describe a technique that teaches students to apply their knowledge of familiar roots and affixes to word learning. This technique has the students determine whether a new word is related in meaning to any words they already know. From a knowledge of affixes, root words, and how compound words are formed, the students can have some idea of a word's meaning. They can check their initial hypotheses about it by considering the context provided by the surrounding sentence or passage.

The first step of this technique is to familiarize the students with the concept of the *word family*. Word families consist of words that are so similar that they are closely related in meaning, as in the following lists:

> theory, theorist, theoretical, theorem
> sense, senseless, sensitive, sensation

For instructional purposes, teachers can think of a word family as all those words derived from the same root and related in meaning. The goal, then, is to enable the students to make the connection between root words already known and the obvious variations formed from inflections and affixes. Common prefixes and suffixes can also be introduced as part of this technique using the following steps:

1. Write a short list of familiar words in a column on paper or a chalkboard (for example, *preview, predetermine, predate, premature*).
2. Have the students explain how the words are similar and then add some examples of their own.
3. Have the students think about how the meaning of each word is affected by the prefix and generate a rule that explains how the prefix changes the meaning.
4. Post the list and encourage the students to add to it from their reading.

At some point, the students are likely to come up with words that appear to fit the pattern, but do not (for example, *prefer, preen, present*). These are opportunities to provide the students more information about the kinds of words that do and do not have affixes, and to show that certain affixes have more than one meaning.

After the students have become familiar with a number of prefixes and suffixes, it is important to help them develop a more general understanding of affixes. This can be done by asking the students to review several lists of words with either prefixes or suffixes, and how affixes change the meanings of words. Add one or two new examples for each affix and see if the students can figure out the meanings of these new words. Discuss how knowledge of prefixes and suffixes can be used to determine word meanings. When the students are ready to move on, introduce new words with both prefixes and suffixes. Ask the students to find the root words and identify the affixes, and see if they can figure out the meanings from reading the words in sentences.

A related technique is recommended by Readence, Bean, and Baldwin (1985), in which known parts of familiar words are transferred to parts of unfamiliar words. They recommend the following procedures:

1. Select unfamiliar words that may be troublesome for conceptual understanding of a text and that lend themselves to an analysis of word parts.
2. Identify other words with identical word parts so that the students can associate the new words with known words.
3. Present the unknown words along with the similarly constructed known words in a manner that encourages comparison and provides the basis for predictions about the meaning of the roots or affixes in question.
4. Look up the word in the dictionary to verify predictions about the meanings of the unknown words.

Teaching Students to Use a Dictionary

The use of context and word parts are techniques that usually yield approximate meanings, rather than precise definitions, of unknown words. There are times, however, when context and word parts reveal very little about a word's meaning. At these times, or when a precise definition is needed, a dictionary is a reasonable alternative and a valuable resource for the students.

Knowing when to use a dictionary is just as important as knowing how to use one. One way to make the dictionary a functional resource is to use it to confirm predictions about word meaning arrived at through the use of context and/or word parts. In order to use a dictionary effectively, the students may require some direction. Dictionary skills that may require some assistance include the following:

1. Alphabetizing words
2. Locating words
3. Using the pronunciation key
4. Identifying the correct entry for different word forms
5. Determining which of several definitions is appropriate for a particular context

Teaching Students to Put It Together

After the students have become familiar with the various techniques that can be used to determine the meanings of unfamiliar words in context, it may be helpful to conduct a series of strategy lessons to assist them in deciding when these techniques are most appropriately applied. The procedure described here is an adaptation of the Context-Strategy Lessons presented by Searfoss and Readence (1989), and involves analyzing the text to determine how much help it provides in determining the meanings of unknown words in context.

Strategy lessons teach the students to select an appropriate technique for identifying the meanings of unknown words in a text by analyzing the material to determine the amount of help it provides in understanding the unfamiliar words. The students are taught to look first for direct help in the form of context clues that provide definitions, synonyms, and/or comparisons, as in the following examples.

1. *Context clues of definition.* The *ecologist,* a scientist who studies the environment, is usually quick to attack new sources of air pollution.
2. *Context clues of comparison.* Unlike Len, who was flattering in his actions with people, John was stubbornly flippant.

When no direct help is provided, the students are taught to look for indirect help from familiar root words and/or affixes. Searfoss and Readence (1989) provide an example of such a situation from a text with the sentence "John's mother has *hydrophobia.*" The teacher helps the students recognize that since there is no direct help from the context, they need to look for indirect help from familiar root words and affixes. The teacher then guides the students in breaking down the word and identifying the meanings of its component parts by comparing the parts to other known words and their parts (for example, *phobia, hydroplane, hydroelectric).*

Finally, when the text provides neither direct nor indirect help, the students are taught to consult a dictionary to identify a meaning that is appropriate to the context. Thus, these lessons focus on analyzing the amount of help provided by the text as a means of deciding which techniques should be applied to determine the meanings of unknown words. Naturally, the number and variety of techniques (and therefore the strategy lessons) may be varied according to the needs of the individual student.

Consistent with the gradual release model of instruction described in Chapters 6 and 12, the amount of support provided by the teacher in the use of the techniques described in this section should depend on the students' level of development. Students in the initial stages of acquisition require a great deal of teacher support in the form of modeling and explanation. Students who have acquired some knowledge and skill in vocabulary learning may only require a brief period of guided instruction before they are ready to work independently. Finally, students who have mastered the integrated use of vocabulary learning strategies should be provided opportunities for independent application.

Strategies for Teaching Specific Vocabulary for a Text

Consistent with our second goal for vocabulary instruction, it is important to provide direct vocabulary instruction when in-depth knowledge of complex concepts is critical to the understanding of reading assignments. The following techniques can be used for this purpose.

List-Group-Label
The list-group-label lesson was originally developed by Hilda Taba (1967) to assist students in dealing with the technical vocabulary in subject area reading.

Although the foundation of these procedures is in subject area reading, the concept can be broadened to all areas and levels of vocabulary learning.

To implement the procedure, a one- or two-word topic is selected by the teacher as a stimulus word and written at the top of a chalkboard or large sheet of paper. Topics may be drawn from either literary themes (for example, fear, trust) or subject area content (social studies unit on independence). Although general topics such as events of the school year (Martin Luther King Day, President's Day, etc.) or places (for example, school, home) could be used, we are recommending this procedure primarily for development of specific vocabulary in preparation for reading a particular text.

After the topic is presented, the students are asked to think of related words or expressions. For example, the teacher might ask, "What comes to mind when you think about this topic?" All responses are recorded until a reasonable list has been compiled (that is, between fifteen and twenty-five words). Then the teacher rereads the list orally, or asks the students to do so. The students are then asked to break the larger list into smaller lists of three words or more that have something in common. The students are also asked to give each group of words a label indicating the common characteristics they share. The students must then explain why the words have been grouped in a certain manner. All groupings should be accepted and recorded, although the teacher should point out that meaningful associations are preferable to groupings based on surface-level features such as spelling.

A number of variations of this procedure are possible for students who may need more assistance. For example, the teacher may provide the initial list of words and ask the students to group and label them. Alternatively, the teacher could provide the groups of words and ask the students to label them, or the teacher can supply the list and the label and have the students group the words.

Semantic Mapping

Johnson and Pearson (1984) describe another well-practiced version of the list-group-label strategy called *semantic mapping*. Semantic maps are a graphic representation of text concepts that typically consist of three levels of information about the main topic in a central hub, "spokes" labeled to indicate major ideas or categories, and branches containing specific supporting details. Maps can be used either to organize the students' brainstorming before reading a text or as the basis for summarizing ideas after reading.

To implement this procedure, begin by placing the topic in a central hub and eliciting major category labels related to the topic. Then ask the students either to brainstorm or search the selection for supporting information within each of the categories. After the supporting information has been categorized, the teacher can bring up any important ideas not suggested by the students and ask them to try to place them in an appropriate category. With students who require more structure, a prestructured map with empty slots can be supplied and the students asked to fill these in as the material is discussed. Figure 14.2 presents a semantic map constructed prior to reading an expository selection on wolves.

FIGURE 14.2

Prereading Semantic Map

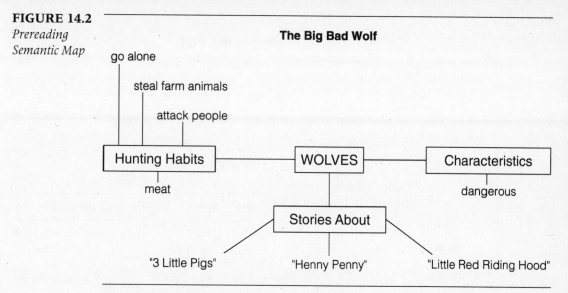

The Big Bad Wolf

go alone

steal farm animals

attack people

| Hunting Habits | WOLVES | Characteristics |

meat

dangerous

Stories About

"3 Little Pigs"   "Henny Penny"   "Little Red Riding Hood"

List-group-label and semantic mapping procedures can also be used as a measure of how well the students have learned the vocabulary from a particular lesson. They can be used at different points in a lesson or unit to determine if the students are beginning to use and categorize the key vocabulary. Each time a list-group-label lesson or semantic map has been completed, the categories can be compared to the previous ones as a means of evaluating progress. Figure 14.3 presents a semantic map for *wolves* created after the students read, embellished, and made corrections as necessary. A comparison between this postreading map and the prereading map reveals increased knowledge about the general attributes and specific characteristics of wolves.

Structured Overview or Graphic Organizer

Structured overviews or graphic organizers are visual representations of the relationships among important vocabulary terms and concepts in a text. They are generally more structured than semantic maps and more tied to the hierarchical structure of the information presented in a text. For this reason, they are particularly well suited for subject area texts.

According to Nelson-Herber (1986), these overviews or organizers have three purposes: to help students expand their knowledge of vocabulary by building from the known to the new, to help students refine their understanding of word meanings and the ways that words interrelate, and to support students

FIGURE 14.3
*Postreading
Semantic Map*

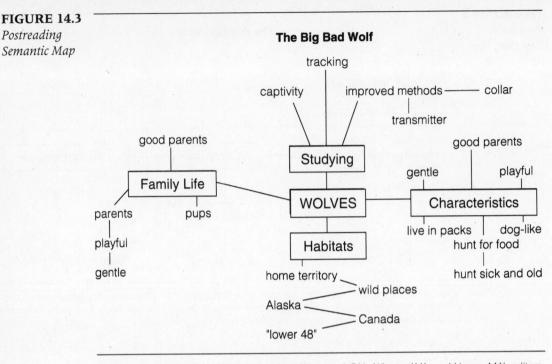

in the use of their word knowledge in reading, writing, and speaking. They are also used to introduce vocabulary in a way that helps students relate new material to what they already know, and to provide an advance organizer for the reading assignment.

The overview or organizer itself is a tree diagram with the most inclusive concepts subsuming subordinate ones. Relationships among the concepts are indicated by the connecting lines between terms (see Figure 14.4). These diagrams can be designed by the teacher prior to instruction or can be developed jointly by the teacher and the students during instruction. As the students work with the text, they refer to the diagram and use it to organize and learn key concepts as presented in their reading.

The following steps are suggested for developing the diagram and introducing it to students (cf. Barron 1969; Herber 1978; Nelson-Herber 1986):

1. Analyze the text and list the major concepts and key terms that are to be stressed in instruction and therefore are important for students to understand.
2. Arrange the list of words into a diagram that shows the interrelationships among the concepts in a manner that relates to and expands on what is

FIGURE 14.4
*Structured
Overview*

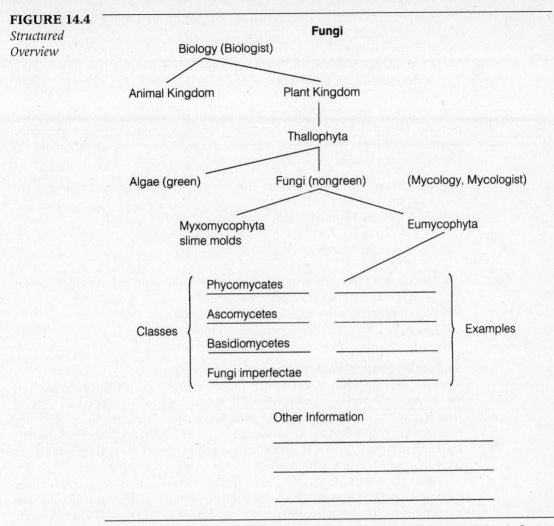

Adapted from "A Structured Overview: Fungi" from "Expanding and Refining Vocabulary in Content Areas" by Joan Nelson-Herber, *Journal of Reading,* April 1986, p. 630.

already known by the students. The arrangement depends on the teacher, the number of concepts to be learned, and the students' prior knowledge of the concepts.

3. Evaluate the overview. Are the major relationships shown clearly? Can the diagram be simplified and still effectively communicate the key ideas? Add to the diagram any vocabulary necessary for students to understand the relationships between the text information and the discipline as a whole.

4. Introduce and talk the students through the diagram. Encourage them to apply previously learned knowledge by adding to the diagram. Engage students in the construction of word meanings from context,

experiences, and reasoning in small group interactive discussions of words and meanings.

5. After discussing the concepts and their interrelationships, leave the diagram in full view of the students as a reference point during reading and/or discussion following reading.

Nelson-Herber (1986) also recommends the use of follow-up activities to provide contexts for students to construct, refine, and reinforce word meanings. Using the concepts from the diagram shown in Figure 14.4, she provides the following sample activities:

I. Directions: Work together to choose the word that best completes the analogy.
  A. Green: chlorophyllous as nongreen:
    1. phyla   2. achlorophyllous   3. mycology
  B. Green: nongreen as algae:
    1. protist   2. mycologist   3. fungi
II. Directions: Circle the word in each set that does not belong and be ready to explain why the other three go together.
  A. fungi, heterotrophic, vascular, achlorophyllous
  B. algae, chlorophyllous, nongreen, autotrophic

Semantic Feature Analysis

Semantic feature analysis (SFA) is a procedure for helping students see how words within a category are alike and different, and to relate the meanings of new words to previous knowledge and experience. The guidelines presented here are recommended by Anders and Bos (1986) as an adaptation of the SFA teaching strategies proposed by Johnson and Pearson (1984). These guidelines were designed and tested for use with subject area reading material.

The first step in the SFA procedure is to read the text thoroughly and make a list of the major ideas that students will encounter. Next, examine the list and determine which ideas represent the superordinate concepts. Then identify words that represent the supporting or subordinate ideas related to the superordinate concepts. This information should then be organized into a relationship chart with the superordinate concepts as column headings across the top and the related vocabulary as row headings down the side (see Figure 14.5).

Each student should receive a copy of the relationship chart before reading the assignment. Then, using a copy of the chart, either on the board or on an overhead projector, the students should be introduced to the topic of the assignment and the meaning of each superordinate word or phrase. Following the discussion of the superordinate concepts, introduce each subordinate concept, giving a simple definition. Students should be encouraged to add their personal experiences or understandings of the terms during these discussions. One key to a successful discussion is to ask students how and why they arrived at a certain relationship rating.

**FIGURE
14.5**
*Sample
Semantic
Feature
Analysis
Relationship
Chart*

The Fourth Amendment					
	Important Ideas				
Important Vocabulary	Citizen's right to privacy versus	Society needs to keep law and order	Police search with a search warrant	Police search without a search warrant	Evidence allowed in court
Search and seizure					
Unreasonable search and seizure					
Probable cause to search					
Your property and possessions					
Absolute privacy					
You give consent					
Hot pursuit					
Moving vehicle					
Stop-and-frisk					
Plain view					
During an arrest					
Evidence					
Exclusionary rule					

From "Semantic Feature Analysis: An Interactive Strategy for Vocabulary Development and Text Comprehension" by P. L. Anders and C. S. Bos. *Journal of Reading*, April 1986, p. 613. International Reading Association. Reprinted by permission.

Next, lead a discussion with the students to determine the relationship between each superordinate term or phrase and each subordinate concept. Fill in the relationship chart using the following symbols to signify the nature of the relationship: a plus sign (+) for a positive relationship, a minus sign (−) for a negative relationship, a zero (0) for no relationship, and a question mark (?) when no consensus can be reached without further information.

After completing the relationship chart, the students read to confirm their predictions and to determine the relationship between the terms for which no agreement could be reached. Following the reading, review with the students the relationship chart, changing any of the relationships if necessary, and reach consensus on the previously unidentified relationships.

A more general, less text-specific application of semantic features analysis uses a group of words that are closely related. These words serve as the headings for the rows, whereas the headings for the columns are the semantic features or phrases describing components of meaning shared by some of the words or that distinguish a word from other meanings. In this way, SFA can be used to promote general vocabulary development in addition to specific vocabulary learning for a particular text.

In concluding this section of the chapter, we would like to reiterate Nagy's (1988) observation that the procedures described above for teaching vocabulary for specific texts serve several purposes. First, they activate appropriate background knowledge, encouraging students to think about experiences in their own lives that relate to the central concepts of the reading. Second, they help students understand the semantic relations and organization of the concepts in their text. Third, they allow the teacher to identify and assess the specific background knowledge of their students. The teacher can then clear up misconceptions and make sure that new concepts and words are related to experiences that are meaningful to those particular students. Finally, these techniques provide a rich basis for further reading, writing, and discussion.

General Vocabulary Development

Consistent with our third goal, it is important to promote general vocabulary development in a variety of ways. One that has been mentioned frequently throughout this chapter is extensive reading, both in and out of school (Nagy 1988). In addition to wide reading, this section presents a well-documented method for teaching general vocabulary, and several suggestions for building interest in and enthusiasm for vocabulary learning as a lifelong process.

Teaching General Vocabulary

Beck and McKeown (1983) describe a vocabulary learning program based on introducing words by semantic categories. This program emphasizes the development of "word consciousness," with the aim of making students more aware of words in general. Grouping the words into meaningful sets helps students learn and remember subtle differences in word meanings.

The program is designed to give students an in-depth knowledge of word meanings through a carefully planned sequence of activities using groups of eight to ten words at a time. For example, a category of words about *moods* would include words such as *cautious, jovial, glum, placid, enthusiastic, envious,* and *impatient.* Words are grouped in this manner to allow the students to build relationships among them.

The students receive a five-day cycle of instruction on each set of words. Each day's lesson lasts about thirty minutes. The first few lessons are designed to be fairly easy, while the later lessons are more demanding. Each cycle covers a range of tasks, including defining, sentence generation, oral production, and games calling for rapid responding. The point of presenting students with a variety of tasks is to help them develop a rich understanding of the words and the ability to use them flexibly.

Beck and McKeown (1983) use a variety of activities for teaching semantically related words. For example, students are asked to compare the features of two new words and consider if the two are mutually exclusive. They are asked questions such as "Could a *virtuoso* be a *rival?*" or "Could a *philanthropist* be a *miser?*" In another activity, a clue word is used to elicit a newly defined word (for example, *crook* is used to elicit *accomplice).* Then the students are required to explain why these two terms should be associated with each other.

In a word-association activity, the teacher says a familiar word, and the students are supposed to respond with a closely related word selected from among those being taught. If the day's words are *virtuoso, accomplice, philanthropist,* and *novice,* the teacher might say *crook.* The students are expected to respond with the word *accomplice* and to be able to defend their choice.

A final activity is completion of sentences containing the target words, for example: "The *accomplice* was worried because … " The use of sentence completion, as opposed to the more open-ended task of "using the word in a sentence," helps steer students in the direction of sentences that really use the meaning of the word, instead of producing stereotyped answers such as "I saw *X* yesterday."

As Nagy (1988) suggests, the exact activity is not the issue, and any of these or similar activities can be adapted for particular classrooms, words, and/or students. What is important is that students be given practice at tasks that require them to *use,* rather than state, the meanings of words they are learning in natural sentence contexts.

Building Interest and Enthusiasm for Vocabulary Learning

In the final analysis, the students who are interested in words are likely to be the most motivated to attend to vocabulary learning. It is important to try and instill in the students a sense of excitement in word learning that will compel them to make vocabulary learning a part of their daily life. A good way for teachers to build students' enthusiasm for words and word learning is to engage them in vocabulary games and other interesting activities.

Creating an environment for word learning.   Students often enjoy sharing with others new words they have learned outside of school (Taylor, Harris, and Pearson 1988). The teacher simply sets aside a few minutes once or twice a week for the students to present and define new words. The students share how they came across the word and the context in which it was used. Students' attention to unfamiliar words often increases if they know they have the opportunity to share them.

As an additional incentive, the students can be responsible for making a bulletin board display to present new words they have encountered outside of school. Bulletin board displays can also be used by the teacher to stimulate interest in key concepts from the students' reading materials through items such as pictures, cartoons, advertisements, and magazine or newspaper articles. Student committees can also be formed to preview reading assignments for new or unusual words and to explain them. An example from Vacca and Vacca (1989) illustrates this type of activity nicely.

> An English class committee called the Word Searchers found this passage from *Flowers for Algernon:* "Sculpture with a living element. Charlie, it's the greatest thing since junkmobiles and tincannia." The Word Searchers introduced the terms *junkmobiles* and *tincannia* to the class. They explained that the two words would not be found in the dictionary. Then the committee challenged the class to come up with definitions that would make sense. To top off the presentation the committee prepared Exhibit A and Exhibit B to demonstrate the words—a mobile made of various assortments of junk and an *objet d'art* made from tin cans, jar lids, and the like. (331)

Playing with words.   There are a variety of ways students can be encouraged to play with words that are likely to enhance their interest and understanding of new vocabulary. For example, crossword puzzles are useful for developing vocabulary and increasing interest in words. In addition to the crossword puzzles that are already available for students to use, many students enjoy constructing their own crossword puzzles for others to complete.

Adapted versions of vocabulary games such as Spill-and-Spell, Scrabble, Bingo, and "Concentration" also can be valuable for increasing students' interest in and learning of new vocabulary. To adapt these games for this purpose, simply include new rules about giving definitions and/or examples of the words that are constructed, identified, or matched as part of each game.

Goldstein (1986) has suggested that cartoons and comics can be used as an inexpensive source for developing interest in and knowledge of vocabulary. Both the teachers and the students locate cartoons and comics that illustrate the use of new vocabulary, or old vocabulary used in new ways. The teacher and the students discuss the meanings of the words and expressions both in and out of the humorous context provided by the cartoon or comic. Then the students keep a record of the vocabulary or expressions in notebooks, journals, or on cards according to categories such as figurative language, colloquial expressions, puns, and palindromes. The students can also use their notes to make humorous constructions of their own.

Word histories.   Brief discussions of word derivations or histories often increase students' interest in words and make the words more memorable. Teachers can collect word origins that have a clear connection to the current meaning of a word and use them as mnemonic devices. Examples provided by Vacca and Vacca (1989) from *Picturesque Word Origins* (1933) include:

> *Muscle.* Metaphorically, the scurrying of a mouse. A Latin word *musculus* means "mouse." The French adapted it because they associated the rippling of a muscle with the movement of a mouse.
> *Calculate.* Originally, the counting stones of the Romans. The Latin word *calx* means "limestone." The ancient Romans used little stones called *calculus* to add and subtract. From this derived the English word *calculate* and its many derivatives.

Vacca and Vacca (1989) suggest that interest and enthusiasm also can be created by discussions of *eponyms* and *acronyms*. Eponyms are words originating from persons or places such as *pasteurize, maverick,* or *chauvinistic.* Acronyms are words formed from the beginning letters or groups of letters that make up phrases. For example, *scuba* is the acronym for *s*elf-*c*ontained *u*nderwater *b*reathing *a*pparatus, and *snafu* stands for *s*ituation *n*ormal *a*ll *f*ouled *u*p. As Vacca and Vacca (1989) note, "interesting words abound. If they appear in a text assignment, don't miss the opportunity to teach them to students" (333).

CHAPTER SUMMARY

This chapter discussed the role of vocabulary and vocabulary instruction in reading comprehension and presented a variety of strategies for teaching vocabulary. Vocabulary knowledge has long been recognized as a significant factor in reading comprehension; however, how this relationship works and what it implies for instruction are still open to debate.

The first half of the chapter discussed the issues surrounding the controversy about when, how, and if vocabulary should be taught and presented goals and guidelines for vocabulary instruction. The major issues addressed were the debate about whether students learn vocabulary best through direct instruction or incidental learning; the debate regarding which types of direct vocabulary instruction (definitional, contextual, or "intensive") are most effective; and the debate regarding when direct vocabulary instruction is most appropriate. These issues were then translated into the following goals and guidelines for vocabulary instruction.

Goals
Teach independent vocabulary learning.
Teach concepts important for comprehension.
Create an environment that promotes general vocabulary development.

Guidelines
Guideline 1: Relate the new to the known.
Guideline 2: Promote active, in-depth processing.
Guideline 3: Provide multiple exposures.
Guideline 4: Teach students to be strategic.

The second half of the chapter described strategies for three different types of vocabulary instruction that correspond to the established goals and guidelines: (1) strategies for teaching independent vocabulary learning during reading; (2) strategies for teaching key vocabulary in preparation for reading specific texts; and (3) strategies for creating an environment that promotes general vocabulary development. A general framework for independent vocabulary learning during reading was presented that consisted of four phases: reading and identifying unknown vocabulary, applying a repertoire of techniques to identify and learn the meanings of the words, relating the meanings of the new words to previous knowledge to aid learning and memory, and reviewing and studying the meanings of the new words in a variety of contexts. This was followed by a description of the Vocabulary Overview Guide, a strategy that embodies the features of the general framework, and of methods for teaching the techniques (for example, using context or word parts) needed to support independent vocabulary learning.

Strategies for teaching vocabulary for specific texts and for general vocabulary development were also presented. The four strategies described for direct instruction of vocabulary related to specific reading assignments were: list-group-label, semantic mapping, structured overviews or graphic organizers, and semantic feature analysis. Finally, methods for using semantic categories to teach general vocabulary and for building interest and enthusiasm for vocabulary learning (for example, word play, word histories) were described.

CHAPTER 15

Adapting Instruction to Focus on Comprehension, Composing, and Studying

INTRODUCTION

The ability to read with comprehension and communicate effectively in writing for age-appropriate purposes is the hallmark of a literate person. In the past, however, prevailing views of reading provided little reason to devote attention to comprehension instruction, since comprehension was assumed to rely exclusively on the ability to pronounce words, coupled with adequate meaning vocabulary. Similarly, until recently, writing instruction was focused more on mechanics and grammar than on creating engaging and effective writing. The view of reading and writing presented throughout this text differs considerably from those earlier, skills-based models.

Readers and writers unquestionably need skills and strategies to attain high levels of ease and efficiency in word level aspects of literacy, but these abilities are the means, not the end itself. Effective readers and writers *use* skills and strategies to comprehend and compose. It is the reader's comprehension and response that are important, not the acquisition of skills and strategies themselves. Similarly, it is the writer's ability to compose and communicate an effective message that is important, not the acquisition of knowledge and skill in spelling, mechanics, grammar, and usage. These facilitate effective writing, but are not themselves the purpose of writing instruction. The challenge is to find instructional approaches and techniques that promote the active use of knowledge and skill to accomplish self-generated and imposed purposes.

The focus of this chapter is on providing instruction that improves students' ability to understand (learn, enjoy, and/or remember) information from different types of texts read under a variety of different conditions and to compose different types of texts for a variety of purposes. First, we describe the nature of comprehension and composition instruction, discussing issues and providing guidelines. Then, we turn to a variety of instructional techniques designed to focus on comprehension and composition. These are divided into techniques for supporting students' comprehension and composing, and techniques for developing students' independence in reading and writing. Finally, we describe instructional techniques for addressing the special case of studying.

FOCUSING INSTRUCTION ON COMPREHENSION, COMPOSITION AND STUDYING

We have described skilled reading and writing in some detail in earlier chapters. We noted, for example, that the success of reading and writing events is dependent on purpose, and we described how perception, memory and prior knowledge interact with other aspects of the reading and writing processes. Reading and writing are functional skills. This means that people engage in reading and writing for a variety of purposes that include enjoyment and the completion of work tasks, both academic and nonacademic. In school settings, students read and write for at least two additional purposes: to improve their reading and to learn about the world and about themselves (DuBois and Stice 1981). Of course, these purposes are not mutually exclusive, but they do often require different reading behaviors.

Some students have difficulty comprehending texts for any purpose. More commonly, students can read and understand some materials, but not all, and can read for some purposes, but not many. This is also true for composition. Students may write acceptable fictional or personal narratives, for example, but be unable to produce persuasive essays or informational pieces. The consequences of this problem become more and more serious as students move through each subsequent grade in school. To succeed in school and work settings, "students must learn to think in such a way that they can tackle, unravel, and understand any author's communication" (Sardy 1985, 216). In the following sections, we discuss some issues surrounding comprehension and comprehension instruction; composition and writing instruction; and provide some guidelines for instruction.

Issues

In the rapidly changing arena of literacy theory and practice, no avenues of instruction have experienced more change than those related to teaching comprehension and writing. Although many classrooms and many teachers continue to work with methods and modes that are indistinguishable from those used thirty years ago, many more have begun to include ways of interacting that are quite different. In this section we review several issues related to our expanded views of reading, writing, and studying.

The Nature of Instruction in Comprehension and Composition

With regard to comprehension instruction, educators have traditionally taken one of two views (see Kameenui and Shannon 1988). Some argue for structured programs involving direct instruction in various comprehension skills (Carnine, Silbert, and Kameenui 1990). In this case, comprehension instruction has often involved teaching fairly discrete skills from a long list, often provided by commercial publishers. Others suggest that students will learn to comprehend without any direct instruction at all (K. Goodman 1989). In this case, students are often expected to generate knowledge and skill through repeated exposure to texts and questions (Durkin 1978–79).

The situation with regard to writing instruction is entirely analogous. Thus, students have generally experienced one of two writing approaches: (1) a skills program involving discrete tasks, assigned topics, and an emphasis on form, or (2) open-ended writing opportunities with little or no teacher direction (often resulting in students not completing many or any written pieces).

Regarding this issue, we argue for balance. Although many students seem to learn to comprehend and compose without apparent effort, the weight of recent research and practice suggests that some students require more thoughtful instruction than has generally been offered in the past (see O'Flahavan and Tierney 1991; Pearson and Gallagher 1983). That some students need only the opportunity to read and write does not relieve us of the responsibility to provide instruction to others who need it. Students need ample opportunities to practice comprehending and composing, but many also require accurate, accessible information about *how to* comprehend or compose a text.

Not all comprehension instruction is effective, however. For example, the available evidence suggests that comprehension instruction focused on discrete components of reading or writing is fruitless. For example, recent research suggests that good decoding skills are no assurance of good comprehension or study strategies (Adams, Carnine, and Gersten 1982).

While underlying skills and strategies may account for many students' inability to comprehend, some young or disabled readers simply do not understand when or why they should use the skills and knowledge they do possess (Paris, Lipson, and Wixson 1983). Without sufficient understanding of the functional value (usefulness) of these skills, students are unlikely to use them during reading. Others do not realize that reading demands attention to meaning. For example, when Susan, a seventh-grade student, was asked to talk about what she had been thinking as she read a portion of text she responded: "Oh, I don't usually think while I read." Clearly, Susan misunderstands that purpose of reading and cannot be successful.

Recent research points to the conclusion that the types of instruction typically offered to disabled readers or writers contribute to the problem (Duffy and

McIntyre 1982). In focusing on understanding specific texts or writing correct sentences, teachers may have inadvertently denied students the instruction they need to learn to be independent and strategic. We discuss this issue next.

Becoming Strategic

Unfortunately, it appears that even when students have acquired some comprehension or composing abilities, they may not make good use of them. There is increasing reason to believe that limited awareness of cognitive activity and limited ability to control it may account for at least some of the problems disabled readers encounter in their attempts to understand text (Torgesen and Licht 1983).

Good readers and writers are planful. They understand and think about their purpose for reading or writing. They preview materials and determine how difficult the task will be. Using their own knowledge and experience, they make predictions and brainstorm ideas and they consider how much time they have.

Then, strategic readers and writers select, from a wide repertoire, the skills and approaches they will use. Sometimes they scan quickly, while at other times they read closely, even highlighting important information. In writing, sometimes they brainstorm many ideas first, sometimes they take painstaking notes from source material before they ever begin to write, and sometimes they quickly begin to write about powerful ideas and experiences that do not need revision because they are for personal use.

Again, the important distinction here is the intentional or planful nature of the activity. Sometimes readers are reasonably successful but it's not because they have behaved strategically. The student who gets a correct answer by chance (for example, circling all the *A's* on a multiple choice test) is lucky, but not strategic. Similarly, the student who writes descriptive sentences at the teacher's direction but cannot or will not use those same techniques during independent writing is compliant, but not strategic (see Paris, Lipson, and Wixson 1983).

Finally, strategic readers and writers change their approach to reading and writing depending on difficulty, purpose, and task. Strategies require using several skills or abilities *in concert*. Individual skills can be very important under some circumstances, but they are generally not, by themselves, sufficient to accomplish the complex jobs required of mature readers and writers. "Strategies are inherently flexible and adaptable" (Dole et al. 1991, 242).

The obvious next questions is "Are there some strategies that really help readers and writers to be more competent; to read and write better?" The answer is clearly "Yes," although the particular list of essential strategies frequently varies slightly from one educator or researcher to another. There *are* two things that most experts agree are essential to understand about strategies. First, the number of these strategies is small—it isn't a long list of discrete abilities. And, second, these strategies, individually, are not as important as a "strategic approach." As Dole et al. (1991) has argued, "The goal of instruction would be to develop [in students] a sense of conscious control, or metacognitive awareness, over *a set of strategies* that they can adapt to any text they read" (emphasis added, 242).

Effective readers and writers *activate existing knowledge* prior to reading or writing. During reading, they make predictions about text content based on the title and other available clues and they fill in the gaps and connect information in text by *making inferences*. In writing, they brainstorm and plan their writing, thinking about both the content and organization of the work.

Skilled readers and writers also *monitor* to check the sensibleness of the text. They ask themselves if there is any portion of text that does not make sense. Poor readers and weak writers, on the other hand, rarely reflect on the meaning of the text. More often they believe that the goal is simply to "say the words" (Paris and Myers 1981) and they focus their revisions on proofreading, not meaning (Graham and Harris 1994). Similarly, effective readers check to see if their initial (and interim) predictions were accurate or their topic was maintained. Finally, they attempt to accommodate new information by checking to see if it is necessary to change the meaning they have constructed. Poor readers often fail to monitor their reading efforts, and therefore are typically insensitive to their comprehension failures (Kennedy and Miller 1976).

Successful comprehension and composition requires students to *evaluate* new (text) information, and also to *integrate* information from several parts of text to form a coherent whole. Younger and less-skilled readers often fail to use textual information to acquire new information or change their minds (see Lipson 1983) and may also fail to evaluate their own writing for meaningfulness (Graham and Harris 1994).

Finally, effective readers *ask themselves questions* about the text. Self-questioning can help promote active involvement and establish purposes for reading and writing, help students to determine the most important information in a selection, encourage students to monitor their own reading (or writing progress), and prompt students to engage in self-evaluation.

Self-questioning can be directed at the content of the reading (for example, "Who was Matthew Henson and what did he do?") or it can focus on reading or writing processes ("Did I use humor effectively in this part?"). Students appear to require careful instruction in question-asking if they are to be successful with it. With good teaching, however, students can use this strategy to improve comprehension (Palincsar and Brown 1984, and see Pearson and Fielding 1991 for review). In addition, students who pose their *own* questions show more improvement in comprehension than students who answer *teachers'* questions (Singer and Donlan 1982). Similarly, students who engage in self-questioning during composition produce both more and better wiring (Graham and Harris 1994). As one student remarked, "[In writing] I had to get my thoughts and opinions together on the subject and also try to find out how much I knew about it" (O'Flahavan and Tierney 1991, 47).

As students read the text they and others create, they reread portions of text, as necessary, to clarify ideas and relationships. People who read with good comprehension and write effectively use a variety of skills and strategies. But they don't really recruit these strategies individually—making them appear like so many rabbits out of a hat. Instead, they use a *strategic approach* to reading and writing, often using several strategies at one time. The hallmark of truly effective readers and writers is that they are able to use their strategic knowledge flexibly, coordinating and adapting the various skills and strategies to fit a particular reading or writing task and purpose (Duffy 1993; Dole et al. 1991; Paris, Lipson, and Wixson 1983).

> Being strategic is much more than knowing individual strategies ... A good strategy user uses sets of strategies, coordinates those strategies, and shifts strategies when appropriate. If one thing does not work, good strategy users try something else ... One must also have an overall idea of what it means to be strategic, that is, how to adapt and combine individual strategies within an overall plan." (Duffy 1993, 232)

The thoughtful reader or writer needs to understand *when* and *why* to use a repertoire of more sophisticated approaches—strategies that are not running on automatic pilot like skills do (Paris, Lipson, and Wixson 1983). Without a clear understanding that strategies can make the job of reading or writing easier and their performance more successful, students may not be motivated to use the strategies they are taught.

The Relationship Between Comprehending and Composing

Current thinking suggests that reading and writing are actually two facets of the same process, and that they emerge simultaneously in terms of literacy development (Kucer 1985; Squire 1983). Researchers have almost unanimously concluded that reading and writing should be developed together from an early age and based on their review of relevant research, O'Flahavan and Tierney (1991) concluded that "The results suggest that reading and writing in combination are more likely to promote critical thinking than when reading is separated from writing" (47). There appear to be many ways in which these relationships fuel each other:

> Children borrow ideas from reading stories and incorporate them into their own stories. Through reading, they build a richer store of meanings from which to write. Reading their own writing provides practice in reading. Writing helps children to see how written and oral language are related and expands their understanding of the parts of print: phonics, spelling, syntax, and semantics. As they write, children begin to think of themselves as writers just as they think of themselves as readers when they read. (Jewell and Zintz 1990, 102)

Despite these realizations, it is still much more common for reading and writing to be taught in separate blocks of time and as completely separate and unrelated activities.

Additionally, many schools and teachers have continued the traditional practice of teaching the mechanics and study of language to young children without providing students with adequate understanding of the reasons for doing so. Just as readers need to acquire word recognition abilities, writers need to acquire the mechanics of writing. But, like word recognition, the mechanics (spelling, grammar, punctuation) are tools for effective communication; they do not have much importance by themselves. Unless students have ample opportunities to write for a wide range of purposes, the mechanics will remain unintegrated and students will fail to apply these skills spontaneously.

Reading and Writing for Different Purposes

Aesthetic and efferent reading.   Effective comprehension instruction also seems to require careful consideration of the various purposes for reading. Rosenblatt (1982) has argued that readers adopt one of two possible approaches during any "reading event" the *efferent stance* or the *aesthetic stance*. There are special reading demands in efferent, or informational, reading:

> In efferent reading, what is important is not the reading experience itself but what the reader can take away from the text. The term *efferent* comes from a Latin word meaning to carry away. We are reading to carry something away from the text when we read for specific information; for example, we read a biography to learn about Harry Truman or a manual to learn how to use a new software program. (Au, Mason, and Scheu 1995, 78).

In both school and work settings, individuals generally read for efferent purposes.
Rosenblatt's descriptions of reading for aesthetic purposes, on the other hand, focus on personal attitudes, responses, and feelings.

> In aesthetic reading, we respond to the very story or poem that we are evoking during the transaction with the text. In order to shape the work, we draw on our reservoir of past experience with people and the world, our past inner linkage of words and things, our past encounters with spoken or written texts.... We participate in the story, we identify with the characters, we share their conflicts and their feelings. (Rosenblatt 1982, 270)

It is fair to say that teachers have generally not encouraged such personal responses, and in fact may undermine the personal response to literature by asking closed questions with discrete answers. Readers' prior knowledge affects the types of response they experience in reading literature, and certain pieces of literature have special or personal meaning for individual readers (Purves 1985). However, it is also possible for this work to have a meaning that is shared by many readers, even if their responses are not identical.

Individual reader response is patterned by certain recurrent factors. For example, reader response appears to vary as a function of development. Younger readers have different kinds of involvement with stories than older readers, often fusing fiction and nonfiction (Applebee 1978). Bleich (1975, 1980) argues that readers interact with text in three ways:

> *Reconstructing the text.* Readers try to summarize the text as the author wrote it, "telling the story in your words."
> *Text association.* Readers make connections between the text (events, characters, etc.) and their own personal experiences.

Value judgments. Readers make judgments about the merit of the selection, at both the emotional and literary level.

In working with students in classrooms, Bleich suggests that students learn to retell, make associations, and render judgments. Teachers who promote and support a diversity of responses help students acquire the range of reading abilities required outside of school settings. In order to encourage strategic reading for a wide range of purposes, teachers will need to encourage responses that are richer and more complex than past practice has dictated. Discussions can often be prompted by the right question (see Figure 15.1). Personal response allows for a range of responses, and there is no one correct answer (see Parsons 1990). There is evidence that literature discussions that rely on student response have great potential for developing the comprehending abilities of a wide range of students, including those with learning disabilities or limited English proficiency (see Goatley, Brock, and Raphael 1995). Both teachers and students will need to develop discussion skills that promote exploration of divergent interpretations. Finally, both teachers and students should be able to make clear distinctions between these stances and shift their approach appropriately for reading and writing different tasks and texts.

Writing to communicate and writing to learn.   Just as people read for a variety of purposes, we write for a variety of purposes.

> Writing is basic to thinking about, and learning, knowledge in all fields as well as to communicating that knowledge. (Fulwiler 1987a, 1)

Most teachers are comfortable with writing that is focused on the generation of a product, whether narrative or exposition. Students may write original narrative stories to entertain themselves and others; they may write poetry to share thoughts and feelings; or they may write research reports to tell others about what they have learned about a topic. Indeed, most of the writing that elementary students do is designed to communicate with others, and an explicit rationale for using the writing process with young students involves the focus on audience and revision for others.

More recently, though, educators in a variety of disciplines have been exploring the use of writing as a tool for learning and thinking. Interestingly, children who are offered many opportunities to write seem aware of this potential. Nine-year-old Naomi was voluntarily writing on the weekend, creating a paper called "Should Women be Allowed to Fight in War?" When asked why she would write such a piece on a sunny Sunday, she explained:

> Well, on TV some people were arguing about whether women should be allowed to fight in war and I knew that if I *wrote* about it, I'd know what *I* thought.

Many teachers have begun to capitalize on the promise of writing as a tool for thinking and learning (see Atwell 1990; Fulwiler 1987b; Young and Fulwiler 1986). Frequently, the writing is spontaneous and unedited, as when teachers ask students to do free-writes to activate prior knowledge or jot down reflec-

FIGURE 15.1
*Sample
Questions*

Prompting Personal Response

- As you think ahead to your next day's reading, what possible directions might the story take? How do you hope the story will unfold?
- What surprised you about the section you read today? How does this change affect what might happen next in the story?
- As you read today, what feelings did you experience in response to events or characters (e.g., irritation, wonder, disbelief, recognition, dislike), and why do you think you responded this way?
- What questions do you hope to have answered as you read more of this story?
- What startling/unusual/effective words, phrases, expressions, or images did you come across in your reading today that you would like to have explained or clarified? Which ones would you like to use in your own writing?
- If the setting and characters were changed to reflect your own neighborhood and friends and acquaintances, how would the events of the story also have to change and why would that be so?
- Have you ever had a dream or daydream that seemed similar to an event or theme in this book? Try to describe the dream or daydream and trace the parallels.

- After reading this far, what more do you hope to learn about what these characters plan to do, what they think, feel, believe, or what happens to them?
- Do you ever wish that your own life or the people you know were more like the ones in the story you're reading? In what ways would you like the real world to be more like the world of your book?
- With what characters do you identify most closely or feel the most sympathy? What is it about these characters that makes you feel this way?
- How much do you personally agree or disagree with the way various characters think and act and the kinds of beliefs and values they hold? Where do you differ and why?
- What issues in this story are similar to real-life issues that you've thought about or had some kind of experience with? How has the story clarified or confused or changed your views on any of these issues?
- What characters and situations in the story remind you of people and situations in your own life? How are they similar and how do they differ?
- How did the characters or events in this book remind you of characters or events in other books you've read or movies or television shows you've seen? Do you prefer one of these treatments over the others? If so, why?

From *Response Journals* by Les Parsons. Copyright © 1990 Pembroke Publishers Limited. Reprinted by permission.

tions as they discuss ideas in a cooperative group. Tchudi (1994) lists several of the reasons why teachers should use writing to advance content goals:

1. Writing about a subject helps students learn better.
2. Writing about content helps students acquire skills they will need in real-world contexts.

3. Nonfiction writing supports unmotivated writers since they may be more interested in writing about content although they have no interest in writing narrative fiction.
4. Teaching writing teaches thinking.

Studying. Students receive little direct information about how to read stories and little encouragement to respond aesthetically to them, and it is even less common for them to acquire knowledge about how to study from, learn about, or manage informational materials. Students are often asked questions, frequently take tests, and are commonly responsible for learning information defined by the teacher for school-based tasks, but they are not helped to acquire expertise in these tasks.

Teachers who do not provide instruction for students in how to accomplish school-imposed tasks are obviously shortchanging their students and are failing to prepare them for their future school lives. Perhaps even more serious is the failure of schools to provide quality instruction in the types of activities students will need once they leave school. Students rarely have opportunities to determine purposes and match materials and strategies to self-imposed needs. Yet the world outside of schools places a high premium on the ability to determine a goal, marshal the resources needed to meet that goal, and communicate with others about it.

Guidelines for Instruction Focused on Comprehension and Composition

Effective instruction does not happen spontaneously. It requires thoughtful preparation, careful execution, and continuous monitoring and adjustment. Just as isolated practice in word identification and vocabulary seem inadequate, isolated comprehension activities completed with small, fragmented texts do not seem to result in improved ability to read real books, poems, newspapers, or brochures for authentic purposes. Neither do writing exercises involving unrelated sentences and paragraphs appear to improve students' ability to write narratives, reports, speeches, etc. Thus, before turning our attention to specific instructional practices, in this section we will review and expand upon some guiding principles for comprehension and composition instruction.

Provide Information (Explicit Instruction)

As we have already noted, the issue of direct or explicit instruction is presently the source of substantial debate. Our position is that many students, in order to reach high levels of performance, need information about reading, writing, and the reading-writing processes. In Chapters 5 and 6 we provided a lengthy discussion of direct, explicit instruction and planned release of responsibility, and a review of those chapters may be helpful.

Fortunately, it is clear that students' writing, comprehension, *and* comprehension ability can be improved. The key aspects of direct instruction appear to be clear, specific teacher explanation; conveying information about when and why to use the skills; feedback on the utility of the action; and scaffolded instruction with dialogue. Teacher provision of this type of information and structure appears to aid comprehension and composition.

Explicit instruction provides poor readers and/or writers with information about skills and strategies in terms of how these would be helpful during authentic literacy tasks. Because strategies are more complicated cognitive activities, they take time and (often) explicit instruction for students to acquire (Duffy 1993; Harris and Pressley 1991). This explicit instruction should make clear to students the value of using a particular strategy(ies) and should model for students appropriate mental processes. Then, teachers should let students know when to use these strategies during reading and writing tasks (Paris, Lipson, and Wixson 1983; Raphael, Englert, and Kirschner 1989). Teachers need to be sure that students receive reinforcement for the right kind of reading and writing behaviors as well as the right answers or acceptable products.

Develop Independence and Self-Control

Research paints a picture of the learning disabled child as an inactive learner (Torgesen and Licht 1983). Students in remedial settings often seem willing to be compliant, but not responsible, readers or writers of text. They often appear willing to do what we ask, but they do not demonstrate any independent ability to apply skills in transfer settings. Often these children seem to use skills and strategies (in both reading and writing) only when they are explicitly directed to do so (see Wong, Wong, and Blenkisop 1989). Lipson and Wickizer (1989, 29) provide the following example of this type of disabled reader:

Tutor: So, you didn't really understand that part (of the text)?
Student: No.
Tutor: Well, do you think it would be helpful to go back and reread that part to see if you can understand it?
Student: I don't know. You tell me. You're the teacher!

Some possible reasons for this failure to perform mastered skill in context are suggested by research. Attention has focused on students' ability to evaluate tasks before reading, monitor (pay attention to meaning) during reading, and self-regulate throughout (Brown 1980; Flavell 1977; Englert 1990). The lack of metacognitive awareness seems to limit adaptive (flexible) reading behaviors among young and disabled children. Students must develop the ability to adapt to the demands of varying texts in reading and writing.

Two related factors appear to contribute to students' inability to efficiently use available resources when they are needed: lack of knowledge about how to control existing skills and strategies and limited understanding of the usefulness of these skills and strategies. Research suggests that effective comprehension and composing instruction must address both factors. In the techniques sections, we describe some instructional strategies that demonstrate how these might be addressed.

Provide Support (Make Reading and Writing as Easy as Possible)

Although students should receive clear, direct information, this will be most effective when teachers view the information (both content and delivery) as a means of supporting students' performance. When teachers provide information that is not needed or for which students are not ready, no learning occurs (Duckworth 1979). The hallmark of effective teaching is thus for teachers to listen and observe carefully so that they identify what information and guidance students might use to become more proficient and strategic.

It is attractive to imagine an area that prescribes the content, difficulty, and pace of instruction appropriate for a given student. The Russian psychologist Vygotsky advanced the idea that students' readiness might be described as *the zone of proximal development* (Vygotsky 1978; Campione, Brown, Ferrara, and Bryant 1984). This zone is thought to be the distance between a student's unaided performance and his or her performance when supported and guided by someone with greater knowledge and expertise. When there is little difference between these two, the child is not likely to take advantage of the proffered support and guidance. On the other hand, the distance is sometimes much greater. "Here, the implication is that with proper input, she could be expected to perform much more capably than her current level would indicate" (Campione et al. 1984, 265).

The notions of scaffolded instruction, dialogue, and release of responsibility were described in earlier chapters. It is important for teachers to acquire a strong sense of the importance of supportive teaching, both in the environment and in their interactions with students. Vygotsky strongly believed that learning occurs as a collaborative effort between adults and children, with competence acquired gradually.

> What a child can do in cooperation today he can do alone tomorrow. Therefore, the only good kind of instruction is that which marches ahead of development and leads it. (Vygotsky 1962, 104)

In classrooms, this means that students are not left at a level of lesser performance. Instead, as they become able to read and write some things for some purposes, they are asked to perform increasingly challenging tasks and are supported in doing so.

This type of instruction cannot be scripted, and it relies heavily on the judgments of knowledgeable teachers. However, the past two decades have produced several specific instructional techniques that conform in important ways to this type of teaching. The Reciprocal Teaching technique introduced in Chapter 12 is one such approach. We will describe others later in this chapter.

Create Extensive Opportunities for Practice and Personal Response

In Chapters 5 and 6 we described the characteristics of classrooms that promote literacy. From Morrow's extensive research (for example, Morrow 1989), we know that a print-rich environment, active student involvement with reading, and adult-child interactions focused on literature contribute to students' comprehension of text. Similarly, student-centered writing programs that focus on creating and revising authentic texts contribute to students' composing abilities (Englert 1992).

No matter how skillful the instruction, students probably cannot become mature, competent comprehenders, skillful at studying and effective at written communication, unless they have extensive opportunities for practice in connected text. Teachers must expand students' reading/writing repertoire, and teaching should always include instructional activities that approximate real literacy events and invite a rich array of responses. Students should have opportunities to retell, judge, and write a wide range of materials. Discussions and projects that promote a personal relationship with characters and/or books are essential.

Teachers also need to take responsibility for directing students to texts and setting tasks that will ensure experiences with a wide range of materials, read or written for a variety of purposes. Similarly, the literacy program must include a wide range of writing tasks and materials. Although they are often engaging, student narratives on self-selected topics are only one type of writing for one purpose. The use of writing as a vehicle for expression, persuasion, and learning is essential to the acquisition of written language competence. In both reading and writing, practice and skill in one type of mode or purpose does not ensure success and expertise in other types.

Integrate Reading and Writing
The research results of the past two decades leave little room to question the desirability of providing more unified experiences in reading and writing. Whereas reading and writing had been defined as opposite processes, current thinking suggests that competence in reading and writing are acquired in an interrelated fashion.

Teachers must help struggling readers to integrate their abilities with continuous instructional support. When the reading material warrants substantial consideration, students should be encouraged to respond in writing to it, from either an aesthetic or efferent stance. Similarly, students should also be encouraged to do free-writing as a prereading activity to stimulate prior knowledge and interest (see Fulwiler 1987b).

These activities vary from traditional ones only in their focus on student knowledge and response. Other aspects of an integrated approach to reading and writing are more subtle and require more pervasive changes in the environment. The suggestions in Chapter 12 regarding the creation of a literate environment and recommendations for using dialogue journals should be reviewed. The adoption of a process approach to writing instruction enhances the likelihood that a reading-writing connection will be made (see Graves 1983; Hansen 1987).

> Through writing and talking about writing, they learn to view published written materials through the eyes of the author as well as from the perspective of the reader. (Raphael and Englert 1989, 237–238)

In addition to this general promotion of the relationships between reading and writing, various researchers and educators have developed specific suggestions for improving students' abilities in these areas. We discuss some of these in the following sections.

INSTRUCTIONAL TECHNIQUES FOCUSED ON COMPREHENSION AND COMPOSING

Students who are having difficulty comprehending and composing generally need support in two areas. They need help completing reading and writing tasks for school and recreational purposes, and they need to learn to comprehend these and other materials. Reading professionals need to know how to adapt the instructional context, and they need skill in teaching students strategies for reading and learning. Consequently, they are almost always engaged in a balancing act, trying to respond to the sometimes competing demands of these two needs.

Providing Support

The teacher's job is not to move students through some set curriculum or to teach and assess, in isolation, some set of comprehension or writing skills. Rather, teachers must introduce texts and tasks that will challenge their students, and then provide the support to help them respond to the text and/or acquire needed information from it. In this section, we describe first some strategies for supporting comprehension and then make similar suggestions for supported writing.

Lesson Frameworks that Support Comprehension

There is certainly nothing new in the idea that good teachers help students comprehend and learn from their reading materials (see Graves and Graves 1994). For over 40 years, teachers have been trained to use standard lesson frames that provide extensive support for understanding texts. Over the years the basic pattern of the Directed Reading Activity (DRA) described in Chapter 5 has been altered and changed to meet new challenges or to provide different kinds of teacher guidance (Spiegel 1981). We describe several of these below, and we also provide some suggestions for other ways to help students understand specific reading materials. Finally, we describe some specific aids to learning and studying that teachers can use to help students with specific texts and tasks.

Directed-Reading-Thinking Activity.   The Directed-Reading-Thinking Activity (DRTA), developed by Stauffer (1969, 1980), is designed to promote students' ability to set purposes for reading and to help them monitor their comprehension. One of the major contributions of the DRTA is its focus on actively involving students in their reading, through prediction. The following steps are generally followed when using the DRTA:

1. *Elicit student predictions* about the outcomes (for fiction) or topic (for nonfiction) of the selection. If students have not done this sort of activity before, they may need help in surveying the title, pictures, and other print clues that can help in making focused predictions.
2. *Students read silently to* confirm, alter, or reject predictions. This may involve reading the whole, or any part of, the selection, depending on student skill and text difficulty.
3. *The cycle of predict-read-monitor predictions* continues, with the teacher helping as little as possible.
4. *After-reading activities* include student summarization, student-teacher discussion, evaluation of the DRTA process, and involvement in any vocabulary or skills work that the teacher deems important.

According to Stauffer (1969), the teacher's role in Steps 1–3 above should be to direct students' reading and thinking. In Step 4, skill instruction or reader response may be included.

Although the DRTA was originally designed as a lesson framework to be used with group instruction, it is possible to adapt the DRTA so that students are working even more independently. For many years we have used prediction sheets with students. As students read, they record the page number and their prediction; after each page (or section), they indicate whether the events they predicted have happened, still might happen, or won't ever happen.

Most suitable for younger students and for fiction, these prediction guides can even be used as a listening activity, as long as the teacher is willing to record the predictions and the prediction checks. We have also used more focused prediction guides with success. The guide in Figure 15.2, for example, supplements a basal lesson and was designed to focus specifically on story structure elements.

Several authors have devised prediction guides that work well with expository material. A sample of one of these, the Extended Anticipation Guide (Dufflemeyer, Baum, and Merkley 1987) is displayed in Figure 15.3. The teacher prepares an anticipation guide ahead of time by listing statements about the selection to be read. Some of the statements accurately state information conveyed in the selection; some are misleading, wrong, or simply not supported by the text. Before reading, students predict the topics/content that they think will appear in their reading. During and after reading, students complete the section portion of the guide which requires them to read the text carefully to support or refute ideas.

The DRTA and prediction guides help students to realize that they already have some ideas about the topic to be considered. Both also provide help and support during reading, so that students are encouraged to monitor and check their comprehension. Prediction guides especially can be useful for students who require quite structured support. They work best when students' ideas about the text are reasonably congruent with the text

FIGURE 15.2
Basal Lesson Prediction Guide

NAME: _____ STORY: Amelia and the Bear	NAME: _____ STORY: Amelia and the Bear
Day I **My predictions are:**	**Day 2** **My predictions are:**

1. Prediction Question #1:
   What do you think life was like for Amelia's family?

   _____

   _____ YES   NO

   _____

2. Prediction Question #2:
   What do you think the bear has to do with the story?

   _____

   _____ YES   NO

   _____

3. Prediction Question #3:
   How do you think Amelia feels about bears?

   _____

   _____ YES   NO

   _____

1. Prediction Question #I:
   What do you think Amelia will do?

   _____

   _____ YES   NO

   _____

2. Prediction Question #2:
   How do you think Amelia's actions will affect the bear?

   _____

   _____ YES   NO

   _____

3. Prediction Question #3:
   How do you think the story will end for Amelia and her family?

   _____

   _____ YES   NO

   _____

information and when students have sufficient prior knowledge to facilitate reading (Spiegel 1981).

Some students will require even more help in the area of prior knowledge. Some may benefit from additional instruction in the area of vocabulary (see Chapter 14). Others may benefit from instructional support that focuses on combining the areas just described. The Vocabulary-Language-Prediction (VLP) and Experience-Text-Relationship (ETR) are two other variations on the directed reading activity that warrant a closer look.

Vocabulary-Language-Prediction (VLP). The VLP provides support for students in several ways (Wood and Robinson 1983). There is extensive pre-reading support, and the activity combines vocabulary and oral language development with prediction and monitoring. The VLP is especially attractive because it can be easily embedded in typical reading lesson frameworks. It requires some preparation by the teacher; indeed, Steps 1–3 have to do with selecting and preparing the vocabulary:

FIGURE 15.3
Extended Anticipation Guide

Extended Anticipation Guide

Directions: Read each statement in Part 1. If you believe that a statement is *true*, place a check in the Agree column. If you believe that a statement is *false*, place a check in the Disagree column. Be ready to explain your choices.

Part 1

Agree | Disagree
[√] | _____ | 1. Worms die when they are cut in half.
[√] | _____ | 2. Some living things don't need sunlight.
_____ | [√] | 3. Some animals can grow a new body part after it has been cut off.
_____ | _____ | 4. Animals that don't have noses can't smell.
_____ | _____ | 5. Laying eggs and giving live birth are the only ways that animals can reproduce.
_____ | _____ | 6. All worms have round bodies.

Directions: Now you will read information related to each of the statements in Part 1. If the information you read supports your choices above, place a check in the Support column in Part 2. If the information does *not* support your choices above, place a check in the No support column and write what the selection says in your own words.

Part 2

	Support	No support	In your own words
1.	_____	[√]	[*Some flatworms split apart and become two flatworms.*]
2.	[√]	_____	
3.	_____	[√]	[*If you cut off a flatworm's head, it will grow a new one.*]
4.	_____	_____	
5.	_____	_____	
6.	_____	_____	

Source: Duffelmeyer, F. A., Baum, D. D., & Merkley, D. J. (1987). Maximizing reader-text confrontation with an Extended Anticipation Guide. *Journal of Reading*, 31, 146–150. International Reading Association. Reprinted by permission.

Vocabulary

Steps 1–3: Select vocabulary, determining which words are important and will cause students difficulty (see Chapter 14). Decide what skill(s) will be addressed in this lesson and how vocabulary is related to the skill(s). The words are then written on individual cards with the page number from the story on them.

Step 4: The words are displayed for the students; students are told they will see these words in the selection and that they will do some activities with the words.

Students can point to or pick up the cards that contain the correct word during the following steps.

Oral language

Step 5: The teacher asks questions about the structural and conceptual features of the words. Other activities may include discussions of categories, context, synonyms, and so on.

Prediction

Step 6: The teacher directs children to use these words to predict what the story will be about and predictions are written on the board. Wood and Robinson suggest the following as possible prediction questions (394): Characterization: "Which words probably tell you about the main character?" Setting: "Which words tell where she/he lives?" Events/Outcomes: "Which words give clues about events in the story?"

Step 7: Children are asked to confirm, reject, or modify their predictions during reading.

Because of the focus on vocabulary and prereading preparation, the VLP can be used with Limited English Proficiency (LEP) students as well as students reading highly unfamiliar material. In addition, the link between story vocabulary and prediction helps students to see other ways to generate hypotheses about the text besides using the title and pictures. Finally, the focus on monitoring in Step 7 helps students to connect the prereading instruction and the postreading discussion—an important feature of the next framework.

Experience-Text-Relationship (ETR). When students' prior knowledge is a significant factor, other adaptations may be needed, and the experience-text-relationship (ETR) variation was developed for these circumstances (Au 1979). In ETR, teachers take an active role in discussing the text and text-related ideas with students and they model skilled reading for students, helping them to build a concept of reading as a meaningful activity. Thus, before reading, the teacher must preview the reading material and identify concepts or themes that might be especially interesting or relevant for students. Before reading as well, teachers should identify places where silent reading can be stopped for students who need to read in smaller segments. ETR itself consists of the following steps:

1. The *Experience or E phase* occurs before reading. The teacher evaluates students' prior knowledge of the themes, concepts, or ideas central to reading the selection. The teacher guides the discussion in two ways: leading discussion toward the selection by showing pictures or using ideas, and helping students to see the relationships between their knowledge and the text. Then, students make predictions about the selection.
2. The *Text or T phase* is like a combination of guided reading (DRA) and the reading-thinking step of the DRTA. Students read, pause, and discuss their predictions, receive help from the teacher, and generate new predictions

as they work their way through segments of text. This phase may take more than one day, depending on the text and the students.

3. The *Relationship or R phase* begins once the text has been completed. The teacher asks questions and leads discussions intended to help students make connections between the selection and their knowledge and experience. Teachers can ask students whether they have had a similar problem, or they can help students to see that although the events might be somewhat different, the underlying motivations are similar to their own.

This focus on connecting past experience and knowledge with text information needs to be done quite explicitly for some students. Teachers should be aware of these connections as well and should actively seek ways to focus students on the important ideas in text. The *underlying* relationships describing how people feel when they do not get the help or cooperation they desire do not require such specific prior knowledge.

Providing Support for Writing

Programs that promote a process (versus product) view of writing have great potential for enhancing students' reading as well as writing abilities. Ours is an admittedly slim review of the issues and techniques. This text is designed to help teachers consider specialized practices designed for struggling students and to identify ways to adapt practice. Ideally, the specialized program is being designed to complement a preexisting developmental program of high quality. Interested readers are referred to one of the many fine books on this topic for more information (for example, Calkins 1991; Graves 1983, 1995; Hansen 1987; Newkirk and Atwell 1988).

Generically called "process writing programs," these approaches to teaching writing have grown out of a clearer understanding of writing and writers. We have already detailed phases of the writing process (see Chapter 2) and described features of effective writing instruction (Chapter 5). As well, we provided guidance for implementing a Writer's Workshop (see Chapter 6). Below, we suggest some ways to help support students as writers and ways to manage writing and reading activities in the classroom so that writing will be sustained as an important *daily* activity. Then, we describe one approach designed to provide extra support for the struggling writer.

Suggestions for process support.   Many students experience considerable difficulty in writing. After reviewing the available research, Graham and Harris (1994) concluded:

> In addition to the low quality of their writing, many poor writers, especially students with learning or behavioral problems, are not especially productive. The papers they produce are often impoverished in their detail and inordinately short. They further have difficulty completing writing assignments and may resist well-intentioned efforts to get them to write regularly. (Graham and Harris 1994, 209)

These extensive difficulties are especially troubling because of the reciprocal nature of the reading-writing processes. Students who have had opportunities to write continuously and to confer with others about their work bring the knowledge they acquire about writing, structure, and communication to their reading (Hansen 1987). Having struggled with various ways to convey meaning themselves, they are likely to recognize and use this knowledge to aid comprehension. Students' writing often begins to reflect some aspects from their reading: ideas, language use, and genre, for example (Paley 1981). In order to complete the work expected of them, many struggling students need considerable support. There are several suggestions for supporting students as they write and read.

Support the classroom writing program.   Many special teachers do not have the types of schedules that allow for a full-blown writing workshop approach. Thus, it is often better to try to support students in the classroom during the regularly scheduled writing time. If the classroom is not using these approaches, your job as a language arts professional may be to help organize and initiate such an approach. Then, support (that is, flexible grouping for skills or extra support for revision) can be planned within this framework.

There are also ways in which the classroom context can be adapted to support many different students. Block (1993), for example, describes a cooperative strategy that would be useful in helping students to "get started" and also provides a fun way to experience different writing styles. The strategy uses a "progressive dinner format" and involves students in each phase of the writing process. Students are grouped and placed at tables. On each table is the same small set of objects (for example, a food item, a ball, a map, an item of clothing) and five sheets of chart paper (for the first five steps of the activity). Other ways to prompt writing may be used. One person in each group serves as a recorder.

Step 1 (Prewriting): Students brainstorm ideas about the objects on the table. Then they move to the next table.

Step 2 (Writing): Each group uses the ideas from the previous group to write a story draft. After twenty minutes, they move to the next table.

Step 3 (Revising): The group revises the previous group's story by adding, deleting, or reorganizing content. After ten minutes, the group moves to the next table.

Step 4 (Editing): The group edits the story as it was left by the previous group. They have seven minutes to attend to grammar, usage, and mechanics. They move to the next table.

Step 5 (Final draft): The group creates a final draft of the edited story. After seven minutes, they return to their writing (Step 2), where they read the final version of their story, paying particular attention to the changes that were made. The group writes a title for the story.

Step 6 (Sharing).

Maintain writing folders.   Students (and teachers) should understand that not all pieces of writing will proceed smoothly from prewriting to publication. Many good ideas will go dry after writing has begun; others will be derailed by a more pressing topic. Still others require more time to develop. Thus, students should keep a folder, not only for their current writing, but as a place to keep other story ideas, notes on topics to be pursued, and early drafts of some project that has not been completed. Teachers and students together should cull this folder periodically for ideas and decide on pieces that should really be brought to completion. These folders can also be used by support personnel to identify areas of need or places where extra support is required and to plan instruction.

Help students select topics. Encourage students to write about things that interest them. Try to ensure that students have more than one topic idea so that they can turn to a different one if the first doesn't seem to be working. Atwell (1987) suggests the following ways to help students in topic selection. Students should interview each other and keep a list of "My Ideas for Writing." Be sure that students know that they can ask for a conference to discuss ideas for generating and selecting topics, and be ready to provide stimulus questions such as: What is special about you? or Who's your best friend? What's special about him/her? Teachers who are unhappy with the topics of students' writing need to take responsibility for helping students choose more wisely.

Develop and teach conference skills. In order for students to advance in a writers' workshop or process writing approach, teachers must confer regularly with students. This may require that teachers develop some new skills or refine dormant ones. Florio-Ruane (1991) worked with novice teachers as they engaged in teacher-student conferences and has remarked:

> Many beginning teachers assume a vision of knowledge as a commodity to be transferred. Clearly the theory of cognitive development underlying dialogic approaches to teaching assumes, in contrast, a view of knowledge development as a continuing process of negotiation and transformation. This difference has profound implications for teaching by conference ... Showing, telling, and evaluating are transformed into diagnostic listening, asking, and responding. (381)

Florio-Ruane (382) goes on to suggest several "maxims" that teachers should use as they engage in conferences with young or struggling writers:

- Assume competence
- Know the learner
- Follow the learner
- Capitalize on uncertainty

These ways of interacting may seem especially alien to many reading teachers and special educators. For a very long time, the skills model has encouraged the older view and the idea that disabled learners would negotiate and discuss their work is not a common one. In order to capitalize on uncertainty, both students and teachers will need to believe that it is all right not to be sure about something and then use these as opportunities for learning.

Students, even primary-age children, can and should be taught to have productive conferences with their peers. In order to conduct effective and fruitful writing conferences, students need to know what is expected and how to behave. General guidelines for how the conference should proceed include:

1. The author should have a clear goal in mind: seeking advice about the title, requesting help on a difficult section, or soliciting overall reaction to the ideas in a piece.
2. Meaning discussions should *always* precede mechanics discussion, although mechanical difficulties may account for difficulties in conveying meaning.
3. First, the author reads his or her draft aloud to the conference partner. During this read aloud, the author is likely to find areas that require revision.

Students need clear guidelines for responding, and many teachers find it helpful to provide a conference guide that is either placed in the students' folder or posted on the wall of the writing center (see Figure 15.4).

Some teachers have found it helpful to make a videotape that demonstrates effective conferencing so that students can see others working through the process. Not only will teachers find it easier to maintain process writing programs if they invest in conference training with their students, these students will benefit from the opportunity to think about other students' writing, and provide feedback to them.

Provide opportunities for sharing.   Students should not be expected to share all pieces of writing. However, there is no clearer motivation for taking writing and revising seriously than to make sure that authors have opportunities to share their work. This may involve bookmaking activities or word processing and desk-top publishing. Some children's magazines regularly publish written work of young people, and these may be interesting for some teachers and students (see Chapter 12).

Teachers should find ways to celebrate students' writing outside of the classroom. However, these activities can become quite elaborate projects, and for struggling writers, specialized teachers should make sure that there is ample time for writing. There are less involved and, in some cases, equally gratifying, ways to share writing. For example, many teachers have long known the power of having older students read to younger ones. This can be extended to having students read their own stories and descriptions to younger students. Many teachers and students have been attracted to the idea of an "author's chair" (Graves and Hansen 1983). This special chair provides a place for authors to sit as they read their work to the class. Teachers may also sit there to read trade books for the purpose of author discussion. These less formal forums for sharing can be powerful social forces for literacy acquisition. They also provide additional models for students who need topic ideas or suggestions for new ways to express themselves.

Quite often struggling students find writing both difficult and painful. Even for these students, though, writing can occasionally provide the key to reading.

FIGURE 15.4
*Writing
Conference
Guidelines*

INITIATING CONFERENCES

So you want to have a conference! There are ways of making sure that your conference is useful and that you gain the help you require with your writing.

- Be ready for the conference: have a pencil, paper, etc.
- Be certain about the person you wish to talk to.
- Decide what kind of feedback you want from her—i.e., do you want her to check spelling, sequencing of ideas, the introduction or conclusion, the clarity and logic of what you have written, etc.?
- Do you want to discuss what you will do next?
- Do you want to find out about how someone else is presenting her information?
- Are you seeking inspiration from the questions others ask you?

As in any interview situation, you have control over the purpose and nature of the conference session. If you make sure that your conference is well organized and if you feel that your ideas have been clarifed or confirmed, then it is likely that your exchange of ideas has been a valuable learning experience!

PEER CONFERENCES

A conference is a discussion in which we share ideas and comments about our writing. The aim of a conference is to allow the individual to focus on her work in a positive and helpful way. She can give and receive feedback on what has been written and can be inspired to reflect on future developments!

If you are talking with another student, there are strategies you can use to make your conference effective. You may find the following useful.

- Find out what is the purpose of the conference. For instance, is it to hear what has been written? Or to check spelling? Or to follow the organization of ideas?

- Ask questions, e.g.
  How can I help you?
  What are you doing? Could you summarize the main points?
  How do you feel about what you've written so far?
  What are you going to do next?

Remember to listen carefully to what is said. Be prepared to comment on what you have liked about:

- her ideas
- her way of explaining/describing ideas, places, events, etc.
- her introduction or ending
- presentation, accuracy or anything else you think is significant.

Be ready to reflect on the following issues as well.

- Is there anything you require more information on?
- Is anything unclear or inaccurate?
- What still needs to be done?

From Ronan, P. (1991). Writing conferences in a secondary classroom, In L. Badger, P. Cormack, & J. Hancock (Eds.), *Success stories from the classoroom* (page 137. Rozelle, Australia: Primary English Teaching Association).

For example, Justin came to a university reading clinic several years ago. At ten years old, he was an extremely reluctant and unskilled reader, who neverthe-less discovered that he loved to write. His own explanation for this is interest-ing: "I like to make my own ideas for what will happen … I don't like reading because you have to get the ideas *they* wrote." The dialogue journal that had been started early took shape as a prewriting idea log. In addition, he avidly lis-tened as his tutor read *Dear Mr. Henshaw* (Cleary 1983), about a young boy who wanted to be an author. Over time, he found that there were things he liked to read as well, and although still struggling, he is no longer stalled.

Provide opportunities for doing different types of writing.   Many struggling writ-ers lack skill but they also lack a sense of the functional value of writing. Teachers should remember the many writing forms and formats that people use everyday and encourage students to explore as many of these as seems reasonable (see Fig-ure 15.5). Many of these forms will seem easier for a struggling student and will also provide the authenticity that many conventional writing tasks lack.

Cognitive Strategy Instruction in Writing (CSIW).   In a well-designed series of studies, Raphael and Englert (Englert 1992; Raphael and Englert 1990) have demonstrated how the writing of both regular and special educa-tion students can be improved by using specific supports. The program is designed to help students as they are engaged in creating whole texts versus sentence writing and worksheets (see Englert 1992). Scaffolding is provided in the CSIW program through a series of "think sheets." "One think sheet was developed to guide thinking during each phase of writing: planning, drafting, reflecting on the first draft and preparing to edit it, editing, revising, and sec-ond or final drafts" (Raphael, Englert, and Kirschner 1989, 269).

In Figure 15.6 you see one of these think sheets, this one focused on the planning phase of the writing process. These researchers report that stu-dents who had used these supports made significant gains in free writing and that they outperformed students in a more conventional language arts/writing program.

Techniques for Using Text Structure and/or Identifying Patterns

Although the use of lesson frameworks is the most common way to support students' understanding of specific texts, it is not the only way. In recent years, there has been a proliferation of ideas designed to guide and support students in reading specific texts (or types of texts). It turns out that using text patterns and identifying text structure are helpful in improving students' writing of specific text forms as well.

Text mapping.   We have already discussed in some detail the elements of narrative and exposition and the issue of mapping to reveal important ideas and themes in text (see Chapters 5 and 8). A good map will help children to see the relationships between the events in a story or informational piece. Students are guided to understand the selection because the map directs their attention. In

FIGURE 15.5

Discourse Forms for Content Area Writing

Journals and diaries
  (real or imaginary)
Biographical sketches
Anecdotes and stories:
  from experience
  as told by others
Thumbnail sketches:
  of famous people
  of places
  of content ideas
  of historical events
Guess who/what descriptions
Letters:
  personal reactions
  observations
  public/informational
  persuasive:
    to the editor
    to public officials
  to imaginary people
  from imaginary places
Requests
Applications
Memos
Resumés and summaries
Poems
Plays
Stories
Fantasy
Adventure
Science fiction
Historical stories
Dialogues and conversations
Children's books
Telegrams
Editorials

Commentaries
Responses and rebuttals
Newspaper "fillers"
Fact books or fact sheets
School newspaper stories
Stories or essays for local
  papers
Proposals
Case studies:
  school problems
  local issues
  national concerns
  historical problems
  scientific issues
Songs and ballads
Demonstrations
Poster displays
Reviews:
  books (including textbooks)
  films
  outside reading
  television programs
  documentaries
Historical "you are there" scenes
Science notes:
  observations
  science notebook
  reading reports
  lab reports
Math:
  story problems
  solutions to problems
  record books
  notes and observations
Responses to literature
Utopian proposals

Practical proposals
Interviews:
  actual
  imaginary
Directions:
  how-to
  school or neighborhood
  guide
  survival manual
Dictionaries and lexicons
Technical reports
Future options, notes on:
  careers, employment
  school and training
  military/public service
Written debates
Taking a stand:
  school issues
  family problems
  state or national issues
  moral questions
Books and booklets
Informational monographs
Radio scripts
TV scenarios and scripts
Dramatic scripts
Notes for improvised drama
Cartoons and cartoon strips
Slide show scripts
Puzzles and word searches
Prophecy and predictions
Photos and captions
Collage, montage, mobile,
  sculpture

From *Teaching Writing in the Content Areas: Elementary School* by Stephen N. Tchudi and Susan J. Tchudi. Copyright © 1983 National Education Association of the United States. Reprinted by permission.

**FIGURE
15.6**
*Think Sheet
for Planning*

PLAN THINK SHEET

Name: _____ Date: _____

Topic: _____

WHO: Who am I writing for?

_____

_____

WHY: Why am I writing this?

_____

_____

WHAT: What do I know? (Brainstorm)

1. _____

2. _____

3. _____

4. _____

5. _____

6. _____

7. _____

8. _____

_____

_____

From Englert, C. S. (1992, March). Writing Instruction From a Sociocultural Perspective: The Holistic, Dialogic, and Social Enterprise of Writing. *Journal of Learning Disabilities*, 25 (3), p. 156. Used by permission.

addition, students generally find it easier to recall information when it has been organized coherently, and maps help here as well. The techniques for mapping stories described earlier in the text should be used to create frameworks that can be used by students who need help perceiving the organization of ideas in stories (See Figure 15.7).

A close relative to story maps are *pattern guides,* designed to help students identify important ideas and see how concepts are related in informational text. McNeil (1992) described steps for generating expository guides that we believe are useful in generating all types of maps:

1. Identify the key idea or generalization to be gained from reading the material.
2. Identify the predominant pattern used in the material—cause and effect, comparison and contrast, or other.
3. Illustrate the pattern and tell the class how you identified it.
4. Make clear to the students that their task is to place relevant information from the text within the pattern. If, for example, you have identified a comparison and contrast pattern, students should know what is to be compared and contrasted (the central idea) and then look for information that can be used in making the comparison.
5. Provide the pattern guide consisting of key concept or generalization pattern to be used and directions. The directions should indicate the kind of information to be placed within the pattern.

FIGURE 15.7

Sample Text Map

Time Ladder Map

It was already dark by the time Beth and Mary left the library. They immediately started walking as quickly as possible to the bus stop. Unfortunately, the bus had already left when they got there. They had to telephone Mary's mother for a ride home.

From "The Time Ladder Map" Practical Ideas by Marion B. Schmidt, *The Reading Teacher,* October 1986, pp. 113–117.

Maps can be used to accommodate a wide range of student abilities by altering the degree of prereading and during-reading support that is provided. For example, students can be provided with a blank but fully structured story map so that their task is to read for the purpose of completing the network. For some children, this will provide the right degree of support. For others who have comprehension abilities that are even less well developed, or who are reading especially difficult material, portions of the map can be filled in, leaving only a few blanks to be completed.

As useful as maps can be, it is important to remember that they are intended to help students comprehend specific materials. As soon as students have control over the various structures and can use them to help them understand difficult or unfamiliar text, then the maps should be abandoned in favor of more usual school or work-response modes.

Textframes.   Creating text-specific maps is a great deal of work, and many classroom teachers will not be able to find the time to do this. Fowler (1982) suggests a somewhat more generic technique for supporting students in text. He developed the idea of story frames, featuring the common characteristics of stories that could be used with elementary students (see Figure 15.8). "Once a frame is constructed it can be used with new passages so long as the passage can support the line of thought or argument implied with the frame" (176).

Fowler suggests using story frames after reading, in place of questions. Students can be guided to complete the frames, and the frames themselves can be shaped to focus on particular elements. Fowler provides copies of frames for focusing on plot, setting, character, and character comparison. He also suggests that students work together to clarify and complete their early frames. We have found that some students with very weak comprehension abilities benefit from being introduced to the frames *before* reading so that they can use the frames to guide them through text.

As Fowler notes, the same story frames can be used with students of widely varying abilities, since they permit open-ended responses. In addition, they are generic enough so that they provide routine structure and students can do new

FIGURE 15.8

Sample Story Frame

Story Summary with One Character Included
Our story is about _____
_____. _____ is an important character in our story. _____
tried to _____
The story ends when _____
_____
Figure 1, "Developing Comprehension Skills in Primary Students Through the Use of Story Frames" by Gerald Fowler, The Reading Teacher, November 1982, p. 177

stories without new instructions. This is especially helpful in working with young or less-skilled readers. The idea of frames evolved, however, from earlier work by Nichols (1980), who examined recurrent types of paragraph structures and used a similar technique with high-school students reading narrative texts.

There are also well-tested frames for helping students to read exposition. Armbruster, Anderson, and Ostertag (1989) have demonstrated that students' comprehension and writing improved when they were instructed in the use of text structure and taught to write summaries using these frames. They have developed quite sophisticated frames to be used with middle-grade students (see Figure 15.9). Using these frames, students are taught the general frame (for example, compare/contrast pattern), to recognize and summarize text that exemplify these structures. Interestingly, the CSIW program described above also employed think sheets related to specific expository forms and found that the writing of students using them showed greater improvement than students engaged in conventional writing programs.

Developing Independence

It is extremely important for teachers to help students comprehend the specific texts they must read. However important these supporting tasks, permanent maintenance is not desirable. Students need to learn how to read and how to learn so that they can do so across many settings over a lifetime. To accomplish this often requires different types of instructional activity. In this section we describe techniques that can be used to help students "learn to learn" (Brown, Campione, and Day 1981).

A General Plan to Teach for Independence

A recurrent finding among researchers and educators over the past two decades is that students need explicit instruction to acquire reading competence (Paris, Cross, and Lipson 1984; Pearson 1984). In addition, teachers need to be sure that they provide for a release of responsibility if they hope that students will transfer and apply newly acquired skills and strategies (Pearson and Gallagher 1983). Using research evidence from several research efforts, Palincsar (1986) concluded that effective comprehension instruction should include *metascripts*, or action plans, that involve general suggestions for instruction but also allow teachers to be responsive to the students' behaviors during teaching.

The metascripts suggested by Palincsar involve several stages in instruction and it seems reasonable to suggest that teachers' long-term planning should include three instructional phases: Heavy Coaching, Supported Reading (Working Together), and Independent Application (On Your Own).

Heavy coaching.   When students are learning brand new skills and strategies or transferring newly acquired skills to difficult material, they need teachers to guide their reading and provide significant coaching. During this phase of instruction, teachers have responsibility for much of the reading/learning event (see Palincsar 1986, for examples). Teachers should:

FIGURE 15.9

Frame for Expository Text

Compare/Contrast Frame

Example [contrast]:

Marsupials are either meat eaters or plant eaters. Generally speaking, one can tell what type of food a marsupial eats by looking at its teeth. Meat-eating marsupials have a great many small sharp teeth designed to tear flesh. In contrast, the front teeth of the plant eating marsupials are large and designed for nipping and cutting. The feet of meat-eating marsupials also differ from those of plant-eating marsupials. The meat eaters have feet that look rather like a dog's or cat's foot. The plant eater's feet are quite different. The second and third toes on the hind feet are joined together and the big toe is opposed to the other toes, just as a person's thumb is to their fingers.

General frame:

	Concept A	Concept B
Feature 1		
Feature 2		
. . .	. . .	. . .
Feature *n*		

Frame for example:

	Meat-eating marsupials	Plant-eating marsupials
Teeth	Many small sharp teeth	Large front teeth, designed for nipping and cutting
Feet	Look like dog's or cat's foot	Second and third toes joined; big toe opposed

Summary pattern:

A. Comparison

_____ and _____ are similar in several ways. Both _____ and _____ _____, _____ and _____ have similar _____. Finally, both _____ and _____ _____.

B. Contrast

_____ and _____ are different in several ways. First of all, _____, while _____. Secondly, _____ but _____. In addition, while _____, _____. Finally, _____ _____, while _____.

From "Teaching Text Structure to Improve Reading and Writing" by B. B. Armbruster, T. H. Anderson, and J. Ostertag, *The Reading Teacher*, 43, November 1989, p. 134. International Reading Association. Reprinted by permission.

- make explicit statements of lesson focus and content
- model the skill or strategy (Teacher Talk Thru)
- support students' contributions
- use students' ideas and link them to new knowledge
- maintain focus and direction

Supported reading (working together).   As students become increasingly competent, they should begin to gain more control over the knowledge and skill they are acquiring. During this phase, teachers should encourage students to take responsibility, but would provide guidance and maintenance functions to support successful reading and learning. Teachers should take primary responsibility for maintaining the focus and direction of the reading/studying event. In other respects, however, there is a shared responsibility:

- students (with teacher support) state the lesson focus
- students (with teacher support) model the skill or strategy (Student Talk Thru)
- students and teacher support students' contribution
- students and teacher use each others ideas and link them to new knowledge

Independent application (on your own).   Student independence is the goal of the reading instructional program. Success in this area results from careful and supportive instruction that includes an explicit self-control component (Brown, Campione, and Day, 1981; Paris, Newman, and McVey 1982; Dewitz, Carr, and Patberg, 1987). In this phase, students are encouraged to generalize their learning to unstructured settings. In addition, students and teachers "troubleshoot" so that the various components work in concert for the desired purposes.

Teaching Students Comprehension Processes

Instruction should not be limited to those periods when reading is being taught directly. The first step in empowering students and helping them gain control over their reading is to help them use and control their skills as they read in a variety of contexts. Because poor readers often do not understand when and why to use their skills and strategies, teachers need to teach students about the functional value of these behaviors during all reading events.

Supported think aloud during reading (STAR).   STAR is an instructional strategy designed to focus students on the *processes* of effective comprehension whenever they are reading (Lipson and Wickizer 1989; Lipson et al. 1987). STAR is a technique that involves student-teacher dialogues about a reading selection. The purpose of these dialogues is to encourage students to actively use the skills and strategies they have available but often do not use. The key to STAR is the teacher's ability to elicit student talk about reading and then to respond with supportive remarks about the value of the student's approach. To do this, students are stopped periodically as they read and they are encouraged to talk about what they had been *doing* and *thinking* as they read each portion of text.

These interruptions open dialogues that provide teachers with instructional opportunities. These exchanges are guided by a checklist that summarizes the comprehending behaviors used by skilled readers (see Figure 15.10). Teachers ask questions that focus on the process versus the products of reading in order to lead students toward self-control and encourage them to take increased responsibility for their own learning.

The specific guidelines below should be considered.

1. *Keep instruction focused.* Many students must first become aware of the reading behaviors that are likely to improve comprehension. When students do not use a range of appropriate reading strategies, teachers can prompt them to become more active in one of the component areas: pause and reflect, hypothesize, monitor, integrate, and clarify (see Figure 15.10).
2. *Provide appropriate feedback.* Because many teachers are not accustomed to teaching with extensive dialogue, Lipson and Wickizer (1989) found that most needed some guidance about how to conduct these teacher-student exchanges. When using STAR in the early stages of instruction:

Listen carefully to what the child is saying.
Attend to what the child is *doing* as well as to the accuracy of the response.
Acknowledge (by naming) the strategy used to understand the text.
Affirm its use with praise or feedback (p. 30).

Often students' statements suggest, but do not explicitly name, a strategy, and it appears that they are relatively unaware that they have employed a useful approach to the task. Under these circumstances, it is even more important that the teacher use acknowledgement and affirmation. For example, in the exchange below, the student does not name the strategy himself and must be informed of its use:

Student: I didn't get that. I couldn't understand it because of that word there.
Teacher: Okay. It's really helpful to try to make sense out of what you're reading. It's important to ask yourself if it makes sense or not and I'm glad you're doing that. Okay, Mitchell, when that happened what did you do?

This teacher is helping Mitchell to become aware of his reading strategies and to see which ones are productive. These patterns of interaction are essential for many older and disabled readers. It appears that middle-school students, even very disabled ones, can benefit from these procedures, improving their comprehension during teacher-supported reading activities but also during silent unsupported reading (see Lipson et al. 1987).

Some students, of course, will need explicit instruction in how to manage one or more of these comprehension strategies/processes. In the case of both question-generation and summarizing, teacher-directed instruction seems critical (see next section).

FIGURE 15.10

Supported Think-Aloud Checklist

Prompts	Stop 1	Stop 2	Stop 3	Stop 4	Stop 5
Pause and Reflect 1. Does this part make sense?	✓	✓	✓	✓	✓
2. Do the words and sentences in this section make sense together?		✓	✓	✓	✓
Hypothesize 3. What do you think will be presented next? (or what will the next part talk about?)				✓	✓
4. What do you think this story is going to be about?	✓				
Monitor 5. Is there any part you didn't understand?			✓		✓
6. Did this part talk about what you predicted (expected)?		✓		✓	✓
7. Did you change your mind about anything?		✓		✓	
Integrate 8. Does the information in this part fit with what you knew before reading?		✓			
9. Does the information in this part fit with the information presented earlier in the text?			✓	✓	
10. What's the most important thing(s) in this part? (or what is the main idea of this part?)				✓	✓
11. Did you get any pictures in your head about this part?			✓		✓
Clarify 12. Did you ask yourself questions about this part?		✓		✓	
13. Do you need to go back in the text to clarify anything? (or do you need to reread anything?)			✓	✓	✓
14. What did you do when you didn't understand a word, a sentence, or a part of a sentence?			✓		✓

Teaching Students to Ask and Answer Questions

As we have already noted, asking and answering questions is perhaps the most persuasive activity in formal school settings. We have also seen that the quantity, quality, and placement of questions all influence students' performance and learning. Although teachers often receive vast amounts of advice about how to become better at asking questions (see Chapters 5 and 9), relatively little attention has traditionally been directed at ways to help students become better at answering them.

Students need to gain control over answering the types of questions often asked in schools, and teachers need to help them learn this skill. In addition, if students are to grow into competent adults, they must become highly skilled at asking their own questions and knowing how to answer them, using one or more sources of printed material.

Question-Answer Relationships (QARs). Using Pearson and Johnson's (1978) taxonomy, Raphael (1982, 1986) developed a training program that has proven effective in improving students' abilities to answer comprehension questions (see Chapters 5 and 8). As with other effective teaching strategies, Raphael suggests using effective instructional features such as feedback, gradual release of responsibility and increasing independence, and movement toward longer and more complex texts. In addition, the QAR training program suggests structuring lessons in the following way.

Lesson 1. Introduce QARs using a chart or transparency to help students focus their attention (see Figure 15.11). Particular attention should be paid to helping students understand how QAR knowledge will help them answer questions more effectively. Following this lesson, in which each type of question is clearly described, students engage in practice activities that increase in complexity. First students receive two- or three-sentence passages that are accompanied by questions, answers, and QARs. Teacher and students discuss and provide a rationale for each of the QARs. The next practice session involves using the same short passages plus questions and answers, but the students must identify the QAR. Finally, students practice with short passages and questions, answering the questions and identifying the QAR.

Lesson 2. Students receive passages of 75–150 words with questions representing each of the types of relationships. The students read the passage(s), answer the questions, and assign a QAR to it. Students must be able to defend their choices, although responses may vary. In this part of the training, teachers should be prepared to help students correct wrong decisions about question-answer-relationships. However, they must also respond to incorrect answers.

Lesson 3. Students work with a basal-length passage that has been divided into at least four segments, with six questions for each segment (two of each type). The first segments should be done as a group, while later sections can be done independently if students seem able.

Lesson 4. The QAR training is applied to normal reading material as used in the classroom. Students identify the QARs and then answer the questions.

Maintenance. For young children (Grades 4 and below), Raphael suggests periodic sessions with shorter passages.

FIGURE 15.11
Illustrations to Explain QARs to Students

In the Book QARs	**In My Head QARs**

Right There
The answer is in the text, usually easy to find. The words used to make up the question and words used to answer the question are Right There in the same sentence.

Author and You
The answer is *not* in the story. You need to think about what you already know, what the author tells you in the text, and how it fits together.

Think and Search
(Putting It Together)
The answer is in the story, but you need to put together different story parts to find it. Words for the question and words for the answer are not found in the same sentence. They come from different parts of the text.

On My Own
The anwer is not in the story. You can even answer the question without reading the story. You need to use your own experience.

From "Teaching Question-Answer Relationships, Revisited" by T. E. Raphael, *The Reading Teacher*, 39, February 1986, pp. 516–522. International Reading Association. Reprinted by permission.

Teachers should use QAR training cautiously. Although many students will benefit from the types of discussion that can occur in this program, the training is not explicitly designed to assure correct question-answering results. Of course, students who know where to look for an answer are at least part of the way toward success. Vacca and Vacca (1989) have demonstrated the use of QAR training for content area teaching-learning, and it is easy to see how this type of activity could enhance work with a three-level study guide as well (see page 619).

Reciprocal Questioning (ReQuest).   Developed by Manzo (1969), ReQuest addresses a different aspect of skilled reading: the ability to formulate and pursue reasonable questions and purposes for reading. ReQuest is often used in regular classrooms as an adaptation to the DRA, but it was originally designed for use in clinical, remedial settings and it is ideally suited for work with inactive readers who comprehend poorly. It can be used with any instructional materials being read by the students, but teachers should be sure that the text is appropriate for the students. As with any new activity, careful introduction is essential. Manzo (1969) suggests that students are told:

> The purpose of this lesson is to improve your understanding of what you read. We will each read silently the first sentence. Then we will take turns asking questions about the sentence and what it means. You will ask questions first, then I will ask questions. Try to ask the kind of questions a teacher might ask, in the way a teacher might ask them. You may ask me as many questions as you wish. When you are asking me questions, I will close my book. When I ask questions, you close your book. (124)

Both students and the teacher read the material silently; then the students begin questioning the teacher. The teacher responds to *all* questions to the best of his/her ability. Teachers should not pretend a level of ignorance or fail to answer a question because they wish a student to answer it.

Similarly, when the roles are reversed and the students are questioned, they are not permitted to respond with "I don't know." Instead, they can provide an explanation for their inability to answer or ask for additional information to respond. Question clarification and/or reworking are permissible if either the teacher or the student does not understand the question itself. Finally, when answering questions, individuals should refer to their source of information (the text or their own experience) as a way to justify answers. Clearly, many students will initially have a difficult time with this, but teachers are participating, providing models, and responding to questions (see also Reciprocal Teaching, Chapter 11, if students have many comprehension problems).

Teaching Students How to Write

Just as strategies have been devised to help students gain control over their comprehending abilities, some educators have developed approaches to help students develop and regulate their writing abilities. The most well-documented of these is a program called Cognitive Strategy Instruction in Writing (CSIW), developed by Raphael and Englert (1989, 1990; Raphael, Kirschner, and Englert 1988). We described some features of this strategy earlier (see above), but the program was later expanded to focus much more fully on student self-regulation and independence (Englert 1992). As they explain it, "the CSIW program combines principles of process writing with principles underlying the teaching of cognitive strategies such as those used during reading and writing" (Raphael and Englert 1989, 242).

CSIW relies heavily on helping students to cope with text organization. Students use a variety of think sheets to help them plan, draft, monitor, and revise their texts. For example, students use one think sheet to get started on the first phases of prewriting and planning. They are directed to ask themselves questions such as Why am I writing this? What do I already know about my topic? Then, students are introduced to another think sheet that helps them to plan how they will organize their ideas. The think sheets in this second stage reflect the various types of text structure and are similar to pattern guides described earlier in the chapter.

Components that were added to CSIW to support a greater focus on independence involved more student engagement and a more dialogic approach. The program calls for teachers to model the writing process, and think sheets are provided to guide writing and editing (see Figure 15.12). It should be appar-

FIGURE 15.12

Think Sheet for Editing Comparison/ Contrast

Writing Conference Guides			
Author's Name _____ Editor's Name _____			

Read to check information

What is the paper mainly about?

What do you like best? Put a * next to the part you liked best and tell here why you like it: What parts are not clear? Put a ? next to the unclear parts, and tell what made the part unclear to you:

Is the paper interesting? Tell why or why not:

Question yourself to check organization

Did the author:

Tell what two things are compared and contrasted?	YES	SORT OF	NO
Tell the things that they are being compared to and contrasted with?	YES	SORT OF	NO
Tell how they are alike?	YES	SORT OF	NO
Tell how they are different?	YES	SORT OF	NO
Use key words clearly?	YES	SORT OF	NO

Plan revision

What two parts do you think should be changed or revised? (For anything marked "sort of" or "no," tell whether the author should add to, take out, or reorder.)

1. _____

_____

2. _____

_____

What could help make the paper more interesting?

Talk

Talk to the author of the paper. Talk about your comments on this think sheet. Share ideas for revising the paper.

ent that though the process is similar to the process writing procedures described above, the focus for this writing is content and structure. Thus, students' attention is drawn to the specialized features of expository writing. In addition, however, students are then encouraged to take control themselves (see Figure 15.13). During revision, students are clearly expected to make judgments and decide what will shape their writing and how. Such explicit instruction in writing exposition apparently provides substantial benefits for reading it as well and improves students' attitudes toward writing (Raphael, Kirschner, and Englert 1988).

When students have opportunities to write with the guidance of others, they appear to learn to write but they also often learn a great deal about reading. General comprehension abilities and specialized study skills, as well as writing, can be improved when students write on a regular basis and receive focused information about writing from skilled teachers.

FIGURE 15.13

Think-Sheet for Revision

Think-Sheet for Revision

Author's Name _____

List suggestions from your Editor.

List all the suggestions your editor has given you:

a. _____

b. _____

c. _____

d. _____

e. _____

Decide on the suggestions to use.

Put a * next to all the suggestions that you will use in revising your paper.

Think about making your paper more interesting.

List ideas for making your paper more interesting to your reader.

_____

_____

_____

Return to your first draft.

On your first draft, make all changes that you think will improve your paper. Use ideas from the lists you have made on this think-sheet.

From "Acquisition of expository writing skills" by T. Raphael, C. S. Englert, & B. Kirschner. In *Reading and Writing Connections*, J. Mason (ed.), P. 280. Copyright © 1989 Allyn and Bacon. Reprinted by permission.

STUDYING: A SPECIALIZED CASE OF READING AND WRITING

Supported Studying

Students must learn to set their own purposes and decide what they want or need to know from specific materials. However, educators must acknowledge that studying places very specific demands on students, demands that are not always consistent with the student's own goals. Studying (usually) requires students to identify or recognize an external purpose. Learning in school texts often demands that students know not only what to read but what the associated tasks are or will be.

Since teachers often set purposes for students in school settings and decide what tasks must be accomplished with the information acquired, it would be helpful if they supported students' content study. Teachers can help all students to learn the information they have identified as important by employing techniques like those described below.

Lesson Frameworks in Content Text

Using a before, during, and after approach to reading specific texts will often help students learn the content of informational texts. Before reading, teachers should take care to introduce any content-specific words or to note cases where vocabulary usage varies from everyday meanings. Structured overviews (see Chapter 14) and other prereading activities can also help students focus and prepare. In addition, teachers can either set a purpose for reading, or they can elicit purpose-setting ideas from the group, thereby assessing students' ability to identify appropriate purposes.

During reading, students can be provided with guided reading questions (either orally or in writing) that many find helpful as an aid to comprehension. These can, of course, be used later as a study guide. After reading, students can be helped to revisit the text to organize information or gather ideas that were missed on an initial read through of the text.

When working with students who need additional guidance and conceptual support, teachers may wish to employ the modifications suggested by the *concept-text-application* (CTA) approach developed by Wong and Au (1985). The CTA, like the ETR, is a variation on the traditional DRA that places particular emphasis on students' prior knowledge. During the concept (C) phase, teachers assess students' knowledge of the major concepts to be encountered in text. Where appropriate and necessary, unfamiliar vocabulary or concepts are pretaught. Students read predetermined segments silently during the text (T) phase, and teachers lead discussions that help students build background knowledge and/or fit new information to older concepts.

It may seem obvious that this teacher-guided lesson framework would be useful in reading the types of dense, unfamiliar texts often encountered for study. Unfortunately, many teachers, even those who use a DRA during reading instruction, do not apply the principles of this plan during the reading of other texts (see Alvermann 1989). As a result, reading teachers and other support personnel may need to help students acquire important content. Creating study aids such as study guides is one option, but so is helping regular teachers to adapt their reading expectations. Both techniques are described next.

Study guides. Studying from content area textbooks is challenging for even the most able school-aged students. It requires students to recognize important information and to locate it in dense, often poorly written text (see Chapter 6). Even when studying from considerate text, students must be able to make use of complex text structures, using these to help identify major ideas and supporting details. One of the most well-documented techniques for helping students maintain their focus in text is the study, or reading, guide (see Wood, Lapp, and Flood 1992 for a review of these).

> Study guides—or reading guides, as they are sometimes called—are teacher-developed devices for helping students understand instructional reading material ... Research and experience show that study guides can help students understand their content area texts by focusing their attention on the major areas of importance within a given chapter or chapter segment." (Wood, Lapp, and Flood 1992, 2–3)

These guides generally involve segmenting text into smaller pieces and interspersing checkpoints throughout that are designed to help students check their comprehension or monitor their progress. This level of support has generally proved helpful for readers of all abilities (Armstrong, Patberg, and Dewitz 1988).

There are presently a wide array of study guide models available to teachers. Herber's (1970) *three-level guide* focuses students' attention on different levels of meaning. Herber contended that there are three levels of comprehension required of students in content area reading: literal, interpretive, and applied. Therefore, he designed the three-level guide to help students interact with the text in three fairly distinct stages. The three questions students are guided to answer in a three-level guide are:

- What does the author say?
- What does the author mean?
- How does this relate to your own life/How can you use this information?

Preparation is obviously very important (see sample guide Figure 15.14). It proceeds in the following way for both three-level and pattern guides (Herber 1978; Ruddell 1993):

1. Analyze the text. Identify the major text organization pattern and specify the relationships between ideas. Decide what inferences or conclusions can be made from the ideas presented in the text.
2. Make decisions. Decide what knowledge and abilities your students have and what your objectives are.

**FIGURE
15.14**

*Levels-of-
Comprehension
Guide
(science—middle
level)*

Food Chains and Food Webs

I. *Literal Level*

As you read "Food Chains and Food Webs," decide which of the statements below are clearly stated in the text. Mark each statement that is clearly stated in the text and be prepared to support your choices.

_____ 1. When a mouse eats a grain, energy is passed from the grain to the mouse.

_____ 2. A food chain is the transfer of energy, in food form, from one organism to another.

_____ 3. The sun is an important source of light.

II. *Interpretive Level*

Read the following statements. Mark each statement that expresses an idea that can be supported with information in the text section you have just read. Be prepared to discuss the supporting evidence.

_____ 1. Owls eat mice, snakes, and rabbits; this makes them all part of a food web.

_____ 2. Only some consumers are part of a food web.

_____ 3. When mice eat grain, they are receiving energy from the sun.

III. *Applied Level*

Read the following statements. Mark each statement that you think is reasonable and that can be supported with information from the text combined with what you already know.

_____ 1. Humans are major consumers in a food chain.

_____ 2. We could live without energy from the sun.

_____ 3. The early bird gets the worm.

Source: Wood, K. D., Lapp, D., & Flood, J. (1992). *Guiding readers through text: A review of study guides*, p. 28. Copyright © 1992 International Reading Association. Used by permission.

3. Decide what quantity and quality of comprehension you require for this reading assignment.

Once these steps have been completed, teachers create a guide. This is done by writing statements for each level of the guide. According to Ruddell (1993), "It is better to have too few rather than too many statements ... A few well-chosen statements will serve to launch the interesting, animated small-group discussions you're attempting to stimulate ..." (150).

The three-level guide, like the pattern guide (see Figure 15.9), requires significant amounts of teacher time and effort, and although these are intended to help students acquire independence in studying, they are heavily teacher-directed.

Task Slicing

There are, of course, times when even the most skillful teacher management of lessons and study guides will not provide sufficient support for students as they interact with assigned reading. Assigning fewer papers, less reading, and so on, are unsatisfactory responses in most cases, because students will only slip further and further behind in terms of the conceptual demands of the content. In such cases, teachers may try "task slicing" (Readence and Moore 1980), in which minor changes in task assignment allow students to work with the same texts as others in the class. "Slicing refers to reexamining the tasks required of students in text assignments and then recasting them to ease their demands" (112).

There are several ways that tasks can be adapted, depending on a reader's skill and knowledge. For example, teachers might limit the scope of the information search. Readers can often cope with difficult text as long as they are not held accountable for all the ideas, concepts, or events. To accommodate such difficulties:

> The number of concepts for which students are responsible can be varied by adding or deleting the number of assigned tasks on their study guides or end-of-chapter questions. Some students may be responsible for fifteen concepts while others may deal with only five. These concepts may or may not be exclusive of each other. Whatever the case, whole-class discussion should follow the directed reading so that all students are exposed to the desired information. (113)

When you adapt the scope of the information search, you do not alter the amount of material to be read, only the degree to which students are expected to understand the material.

The power of this type of slicing is that it helps to focus students' attention on important information and, for those who need it, limits their focus so that they do not have to make as many judgments about what is important and what should be learned. Another way to accomplish this is to *create an information index*. This method of supported studying helps students to locate information by providing interspersed questions throughout the selection and then keying questions to the place in text (page, paragraph, sentence) where the information to answer the question can be found. According to Readence and Moore (1980), "the degree of question interspersing and information indexing may be varied according to the importance of the concept reflected in the questions, the level of thinking required, and students' reading ability" (114).

Teaching Students to Study

Teachers generally believe that students who understand will perform well on their tests, problems, and projects. Although this is often true, there is a sizeable group of students who do not know how to respond to the demands of teachers or tasks and therefore do not demonstrate the knowledge and skill they possess. A much larger group of students do not understand the content, but could if they were provided with tools for learning and remembering important information.

There are some troubling trends in this regard. Although many content area teachers recognize their students' inability to read and comprehend their textbooks, they often respond by circumventing the books altogether.

> Limited as it is, the research on the use of textbooks in helping students learn from text has several implications. First, it suggests that students will not read their content-area textbooks if teachers fail to expect them to learn from text. Second, the research suggests that teachers rarely spend time teaching students how to use their content area texts. (Alvermann 1989, 257)

SQ3R

The grandfather of study strategies, SQ3R (Survey, Question, Read, Recite, Review), was developed by Robinson in 1946. SQ3R is meant to be taught to students as an organized method for dealing with study and learning tasks in assigned textbook reading. Students are taught to approach their textbook reading/studying using the following procedures.

Survey. Students are told to preview the material to get a general overview of the chapter. This step will be most helpful if students are provided with information about how to preview a text effectively. For example, they should be taught to ask themselves questions such as: What appears to be the main topic of this chapter? How has the author organized the information? In addition, students should be taught to survey any maps, figures, captions, and so on for useful information about the topics.

Question. The information students have gained by surveying the text is used to generate questions to guide their reading. Students are specifically directed to restate boldface headings as questions. For example, when using this step of the technique to study the present chapter, a reader might pose the question, "What is SQ3R?"

Read. Using the questions and purposes established in the first steps to guide them, students read the assigned material.

Recite. Students are expected to pause periodically and "recite," or think about their reading (see STAR, page 611). Students are encouraged to try to provide answers to their questions given the reading they have done.

Review. When students have completed the assigned reading, they are expected to stop, review the material, and summarize or take notes on the important information. There are many variations of SQ3R that have been proposed, some designed for study in specific content areas. SQ3R is still widely taught and appears to be an effective technique for students who use it. The biggest concern expressed by critics involves the relatively low incidence of student use (Adams, Carnine, and Gersten 1982). This is probably related to the failure of teachers to provide explicitly for careful instruction in how or why to employ the technique. The next strategy addresses this concern.

SMART

A Self-Monitoring Approach to Reading (SMART) is comprised of a series of steps that students are taught to use. Developed by Vaughan and Estes (1986), the strategy is especially helpful for students who need help attending to meaning in reading.

Step 1: Students are taught to keep track of their comprehension by putting a ≈ or a ? in the margins as they read. The ≈ indicates understanding, the ? confusion.

Step 2: Students self-check, explaining in their own words the concepts or ideas they have understood.

Step 3: Students are taught to deal with comprehension failures: reread, identify the problem (for example, word? relationships? etc.), generate possible solutions, review the text, and so on.

Step 4: Students continue using Steps 1–3 as a cycle of activity to read long passages. Then they self-check and review.

It should be apparent that none of these specific activities is new. All are often suggested to students. What is different is that the students would be taught these steps as a systematic approach to the problem of reading and understanding. In addition, students are encouraged to think about solutions to their problems and to use the skills and strategies they possess. According to Irvin (1990):

> Successful study skills training programs have three main components: (1) training and practice in the use of task-specific strategies (knowing *what* to apply); (2) instruction in the monitoring of these skills (knowing when and how to apply strategies; and (3) information concerning the significance and outcomes of these activities and their range of utility (knowing why we apply strategies) (Paris, Newman, and McVey 1982). (140)

Underlining, Notetaking, and Outlining

Although both notetaking and outlining are generally perceived to be helpful for studying, few students in grades 1–8 are skilled enough in these areas to use the techniques effectively. Because these activities are useful in studying, they should be taught as tools for independence. The evidence suggests, however, that though students are often told to use these strategies, they seldom receive instruction in them (Irvin 1990) and when they do it may not be helpful.

For example, a well-executed outline is a helpful study tool (Anderson and Armbruster 1984b), but only if the content of the outline is reasonable. Outlining is often taught structurally. That is, students are taught the mechanics of outlining; where to put Roman numerals, letters, and so on. Students rarely receive help in the difficult tasks of identifying important ideas, recognizing supporting details, and generating large themes or main ideas. These same problems and criticisms apply to summarization and note-taking activities in most schools.

Effective notetaking and underlining, like outlining, both require that students be able to distinguish important from unimportant information.

Most students, of course, will require some instruction and discussion in these areas before they will be able to manage successfully. Yet one researcher reports that only 17 percent of college students ever received any instruction in how to take notes!

If students merely copy information verbatim from the text, as many research results suggest they typically do (Bretzing and Kulhavy 1981), then the benefits of note taking may be quite weak. Indeed, it is possible that students who simply reread or effectively underline will do at least as well under those circumstances. They could spend more time thinking about the material since a read-rereading strategy takes less time than recording information that they may recall anyway:

> Research has shown that people tend to remember the most important information anyway.... Therefore, note takers may be learning main ideas very well, but at the expense of learning other information. On the other hand, subjects who use less time-consuming studying techniques (for example, read-reread and underline) are able to distribute their attention and effort more evenly over the passage. (Anderson and Armbruster 1984b, 668)

It is possible to teach one of the available systems of notetaking such as the Cornell Notetaking Method (Pauk 1974) or the Notetaking System for Learning (Palmatier 1973). The format of the notetaking system and the specifics are less important than the guidance students receive in learning to note important information and use notes to study. Irvin (1990) suggests the following guidelines be applied when teaching notetaking:

1. Students should be asked to preview the chapter before beginning, attending especially to the structure of the material.
2. Textbooks with clear headings and subheadings should be used during initial instruction.
3. Practice with shorter texts should precede work with longer assignments.
4. Students should be provided with examples and feedback, and their initial attempts at notetaking should be reviewed.
5. Students should receive instruction and practice in using notes to accomplish other tasks; for example, to write a summary, make outlines, etc.
6. Finally, students' notes should be used to study for a test.

In reviewing students' notes with them and helping them to use them for study, teachers should be asking the following questions (Tierney, Readence, and Dishner 1985, 203):

- Has this student noted the essential concepts and supporting detail emphasized in the unit?
- Is the material organized in a way that will lead to successful study of the material for testing purposes?

When students are having difficulty with either of these aspects of notetaking, additional instruction will be needed. It is also possible that students will benefit from instruction designed to focus them more clearly on the central information in texts (see previous sections) or in summarizing (see below).

Summarization

To summarize means to eliminate extraneous information so that only the main points remain. As a study strategy, summarizing is useful only under some circumstances. First, students must be well-equipped to engage in summarization. This often (always with poor readers) involves specific instruction in how to write a summary. A second condition is that the subsequent tasks students are required to do demand the kind of information and thinking that is represented in a summary. Clearly, writing a good summary is not likely to enhance performance on a short-answer/multiple-choice objective test.

In order to summarize effectively, students need to learn how to identify the prevailing text structure, how to recognize or generate important ideas and connections, and how to produce an overarching statement of topic. Fortunately, several effective instructional programs have been designed to teach students how to summarize information in texts. For example, Brown, Campione, and Day (1981) taught students five rules for generating summaries:

1. Delete irrelevant or trivial information.
2. Delete redundant information.
3. Select topic sentences.
4. Substitute a superordinate term or event for a list of terms or actions.
5. Invent topic sentences when none are provided by the author.

Using rules very much like these, and feedback and practice with modeling, Hare and Borchardt (1984) successfully taught high-school students to summarize texts. Similarly, sixth-grade students who were taught rules for summarizing and learned to use them effectively showed improvement in comprehension (Bean and Steenwyk 1984).

Taylor (1982, 1986) has developed a somewhat more sophisticated strategy that has been found effective with middle-school students: the Hierarchical Summary Procedure. It is intended to improve students' ability to summarize using the structure and organization of text. The steps in this procedure are somewhat involved, and it is helpful to see a completed example before you begin (see Figure 15.15).

> *Step 1: Preview.* Students survey a segment of text (three to five pages) and examine the headings, subheadings, and so on. Teacher and students generate an outline framework that reflects each of the major sections. Thus, a Roman numeral is recorded for each major section (but not filled in) and a capital letter is used to designate every major subsection. Spaces are left to enter details at a later point.
> *Step 2: Read.* Students read each segment of the text, noting the important information as they read.
> *Step 3: Outline.* Students summarize using the outline. This can be done as students read or may be conducted in a revisiting of the text. They write

FIGURE 15.15

Hierarchical Summary for Text Selection Containing One Heading and Six Subheadings

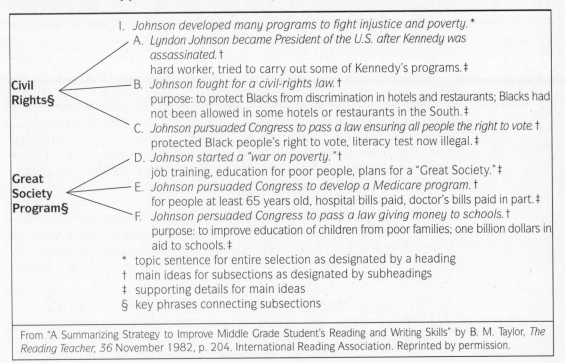

I. *Johnson developed many programs to fight injustice and poverty.* *

   A. *Lyndon Johnson became President of the U.S. after Kennedy was assassinated.* †
     hard worker, tried to carry out some of Kennedy's programs. ‡

Civil Rights§

   B. *Johnson fought for a civil-rights law.* †
     purpose: to protect Blacks from discrimination in hotels and restaurants; Blacks had not been allowed in some hotels or restaurants in the South. ‡

   C. *Johnson pursuaded Congress to pass a law ensuring all people the right to vote.* †
     protected Black people's right to vote, literacy test now illegal. ‡

   D. *Johnson started a "war on poverty."* †
     job training, education for poor people, plans for a "Great Society." ‡

Great Society Program§

   E. *Johnson pursuaded Congress to develop a Medicare program.* †
     for people at least 65 years old, hospital bills paid, doctor's bills paid in part. ‡

   F. *Johnson persuaded Congress to pass a law giving money to schools.* †
     purpose: to improve education of children from poor families; one billion dollars in aid to schools. ‡

* topic sentence for entire selection as designated by a heading
† main ideas for subsections as designated by subheadings
‡ supporting details for main ideas
§ key phrases connecting subsections

From "A Summarizing Strategy to Improve Middle Grade Student's Reading and Writing Skills" by B. M. Taylor, *The Reading Teacher, 36* November 1982, p. 204. International Reading Association. Reprinted by permission.

a topic sentence next to each of the Roman numerals and details under each of the capitals.

> *Step 4: Study.* Students then connect related ideas by using some superordinate term.

The value of Hierarchical Summaries is that students receive substantial amounts of practice in identifying important ideas and additional experience displaying ideas in relation to each other (major and supporting details, for example). With explicit instruction, Taylor reports that middle-grade students can complete hierarchical summaries independently after five or six sessions.

Needed: A Functional, Integrated Approach to Study Skills Instruction

Teachers have always bemoaned the apparent absence of study skills on the part of their students. Until recently, however, only a meager array of tools and strategies were passed along, and students were more often admonished to engage in them than they were taught to employ them (Palmatier and Bennett 1974). The situation has begun to change quite rapidly in recent years, as educators have demonstrated that study strategies and studying approaches could be taught and, more importantly, transferred to other settings.

The wide array of available techniques does not, however, assure that students will use them appropriately or voluntarily. The increasing interest in this area has revealed what earlier examinations of comprehension in general did: that studying is a complex cognitive activity that involves knowledge, skills, and motivation in at least equal parts (see Weinstein, Goetz, and Alexander 1988). If students are going to become effective studiers, they will need an integrated and well-conceived repertoire of knowledge and skills.

The only comprehensive approach to this problem at the moment appears to be the Learning Strategies Curriculum (Schumaker, Deshler, Alley, and Warner 1983). Three large strands comprise the set of instructional materials. Almost all important strategies for studying are included in this set of materials. Unfortunately, the organization of the strands and the mixture of strategies doesn't always promote the idea that these strategies are part of an interconnected whole. Strategies like Multi-Pass (a strategy for working with textbook chapters in a study condition), coupled with strategies like Self-Questioning might be organized to provide students with a coherent studying plan.

Paris (1988) has summarized the characteristics of successful strategy instruction. Not surprisingly, many of these parallel the characteristics of effective comprehension instruction, including the need for explicit instruction and transfer of responsibility from teachers to students. He notes several other characteristics that seem especially important in the promotion of independent study behaviors:

1. Students must believe in the utility and necessity of using the strategies.
2. Teachers must provide a demonstration of how the strategies can be used and when and why they are valuable.
3. The strategies must be appropriate for the student in terms of his/her abilities and willingness to expend effort.
4. Strategy instruction should result in improved student confidence and belief in their own competence.

The ability to study effectively is merely a specialized type of reading and writing ability. As with all aspects of comprehension and composition ability, studying ability emerges over time and in response to need and instruction. It is clear that teachers must provide much more intentional, focused, and continuous instruction in studying if students are going to become independent in this area.

READING, WRITING, AND STUDYING ACROSS THE CURRICULUM

Every developmental or remedial reading teacher and special educator knows that transfer from one setting to another is painfully difficult unless there is a close approximation of the classroom texts and tasks. Students and teachers need to learn and use strategies at the point of need. Students will probably never acquire good, independent comprehending, composing, or studying strategies if they do not receive at least some encouragement and direction from content teachers.

Similarly, classroom teachers must concern themselves with providing appropriate adaptations and supports for students so that they can read and/or study the materials they are using in their classrooms. Teachers may find it especially helpful to review the general guidelines for comprehension instruction and then to become quite comfortable with a range of the strategies provided in the Supporting Students' Comprehension and Studying sections of this chapter. The lesson frames, in particular, are easily adapted to most classrooms.

On the other hand, clinical teachers must be absolutely concerned that they are providing students with instruction aimed at improving their ability to comprehend, compose, and study. The array of techniques provided in this chapter should be helpful here. However, specialized language arts personnel should also consider carefully the implications of the "general plan to teach for independence." The intentional planning for self-controlled learning is of the utmost importance and will be difficult to achieve in an isolated clinical setting. Specialized teachers and classroom teachers must find ways to collaborate to advance this primary goal.

CHAPTER SUMMARY

After a brief introduction, we reviewed several issues related to literacy instruction. Specifically, we noted that research has provided persuasive evidence of the interrelationships between reading and writing and had also resulted in considerable knowledge about effective teaching and productive learning. We argued that teachers should strike a balance, providing rich literacy contexts as well as good explicit instruction regarding the reading and writing processes. Next, we described one particularly important issue related to literacy instruction; the continuum linking teacher support and student independence. We noted that students must achieve the generalized knowledge and skill necessary to comprehend and compose many texts. Third, we devoted a section to discussing the varying purposes for which people read and write. Here, we described recent distinctions between "aesthetic" and "efferent" purposes, noting that readers' responses differ depending on their approach to the text/task. Similarly, we contrasted personal writing with writing to learn and academic writing. Finally, five key guidelines were provided to shape teachers' thinking about instruction, including a strong suggestion that reading and writing instruction need to be more closely aligned.

In the next major section of this chapter, we provided detailed descriptions of instructional techniques for focusing on comprehension and composing. These were divided into two classes of technique: those designed to support students as they read and write particular texts, and those designed to teach students to become independent readers and writers. Strategies such as DRTA, text mapping, and lesson frames were described in the first group. In the second group, we described a general plan for teaching students to become independent, and then described several specific techniques such as QAR training,

ReQuest, and CSIW. In the final section of the chapter, we discussed studying as a specialized purpose for reading and writing. Again, this was approached in terms of strategies that support students in studying particular texts (for example, lesson frames and study guides) and those approaches designed to help students learn how to study (SQ3R and summarizing, for example). Finally, guidelines for developing a more integrated approach to reading and writing in the curriculum were provided.

Professional Roles and Responsibilities

TEACHERS WHO CONDUCT EFFECTIVE assessment and thoughtful, well-designed instruction may feel that they have completed their responsibilities. However, work in assessment and instruction always requires accountability to a wide array of groups and individuals (such as administrators, other teaching professionals, parents, and community members). Consequently, the final step in the assessment-instruction process emphasizes the need to effectively communicate with others about the students and the curriculum (see the figure on the following page).

The single chapter in this section contains a focus on the responsibilities of English language arts professionals that extend beyond working with an individual student or client. We discuss the importance of skillful communication with parents and the need for accurate reporting procedures. Teachers will be guided with samples of exemplary written reports. Finally, we discuss the ethics and responsibilities of literacy professionals.

STEP 1
Getting Started with Assessment (Ch. 4)

STEP 2
Evaluating the Context (Chs. 5 & 6)

STEP 3
Evaluating the Learner (Chs. 7–10)

STEP 4
Evaluating the Match Between Learner and Context

STEP 5
Reflection, Decision Making, and Planning

Ch. 11

STEP 6
Identifying a Better Match: Diagnostic Teaching

STEP 7
Adapting Instruction: Continuous Monitoring and Modification (Chs. 12–15)

STEP 8
Reporting (Ch. 16)

CHAPTER 16

Professional Roles and Responsibilities

INTRODUCTION

In this text we have focused on some specific roles important to literacy leaders, roles involving assessment and instruction. However, most language arts professionals are actually expected to fulfill many roles. Certainly they are expected to be preeminently knowledgeable in reading and writing instruction (Mack, 1991; Radencich 1995), but there are many other expectations of literacy professionals as well, including consulting, supervising, grant-writing, and providing in-service functions.

Skillful communication with parents and community is absolutely essential to the assessment-instruction process. Sophisticated assessment and well-designed instruction must be accompanied by clear and accurate reporting procedures. Otherwise, it is possible for lay people, as well as other professionals, to be confused or to misunderstand the implications of the work done with students or clients.

Throughout the text, we advocated an approach to assessment that valued multiple sources of information collected fairly continuously. Converting the instructionally useful information that is gathered in a portfolio into information suitable for communicating with others is one issue facing teachers, especially classroom teachers. Similarly, it can be challenging to communicate the results of diagnostic teaching and other innovative approaches to assessment and instruction. Finally, teachers must also be able to convey the results of standardized tests in a clear and concise manner.

In this chapter, we describe the range of functions and responsibilities that may be associated with the various roles of literacy leaders. A listing of competencies helpful for professionals in the English language arts is provided.

Among the most important of these is the ability to communicate effectively. Consequently, we provide a major section on reporting to others that includes some general guidelines and some suggestions for organizing and reporting on the contents of portfolios. In addition, teachers are guided through the process of writing formal reports and are also provided with samples of exemplary written reports. We describe how different types of reports may be appropriate for different purposes and discuss conferences as well as written reporting. In the final section of this chapter, we describe the professional and ethical responsibilities associated with providing literacy assessment and support to students and clients.

THE ROLE(S) OF THE ENGLISH LANGUAGE ARTS PROFESSIONAL

There is a rather wide range of ideas about the appropriate roles and functions of reading and writing teachers. For example, Bean (1979) reports that classroom teachers valued in-service and conferring activities considerably more highly than they did either group or individual diagnosis. However, Pikulski and Ross (1979) report that whereas teachers do expect reading and writing specialists to be well-informed about literacy and to provide some consultative service, they clearly preferred that reading personnel spend most of their time delivering reading instruction to individual students. More recently, other roles, including administrative ones, have been added. Mack (1991), for example, reports that English language arts professionals are expected to be knowledgeable about the most recent research and practice, but they are also often asked to supervise (other) reading personnel, coordinate (and evaluate) federal and district-wide programs, and supervise the implementation of reading programs by classroom teachers.

Confusion over the appropriate functions led the International Reading Association (1986) to identify roles and responsibilities of various reading professionals. The list includes the following three categories: Category I, Classroom Teachers; Category II, Reading Specialists; and Category III, Allied Professions. Category II is the largest category, encompassing all roles involving consulting, coordinating reading programs, and delivering diagnostic-remedial services. The Allied Professions category includes special educators, administrators, and others such as counselors and psychologists.

Within each of the broad categories, specific roles are identified and defined. For example, Role 3 (within Category II) is Diagnostic-Remedial Specialist. This role includes such functions as assessing reading and planning instructional programs. In addition, it designates coordinating services for individual students. Role 5, Reading Consultant/Reading Resource Teacher, lists somewhat different functions, including organizing and administering school reading programs, providing staff development, and coordinating reading specialist/other specialist activity. In many school situations, however, the reading professional is expected to perform a variety of functions spanning several roles. Indeed, the situation is made even more complex by the existence of various mandated special education programs, as well as the wide variety in literacy programs. Sometimes special education programs employ individuals who are expected to assess reading and writing and to deliver literacy instruction, but who are not well-versed in reading or writing themselves. Other situations exist where both the special education and the compensatory programs are run by the same persons.

Whatever the formally designated role, there is a need for school-level leadership surrounding literacy and reading-writing disabilities. No matter what the title, professionals who are well-versed in literacy and literacy instruction will have a responsibility to function as an educational leader in the school or school district. Although somewhat dated, the competencies described by Garry as most highly valued by reading professionals in 1974 are generally desirable today as well (see Figure 16.1). What many of these have in common is an emphasis on effective communication.

REPORTING TO OTHERS

English language arts professionals are often expected to report to a wide range of people regarding the literacy abilities and progress of students. There are a number of ways professionals communicate with others. Reporting may be as

FIGURE 16.1
Desirable Competencies for Literacy Professionals

Ability and Skill in:
1. Working with teachers to plan appropriate instruction for students who need special support, in the classroom, and in special programs.
2. Working with small instructional groups of disabled readers or writers.
3. Helping teachers to interpret test results.
4. Helping classroom teachers to assess the strengths and weaknesses of students in their classroom.
5. Providing expertise in diagnosing students with extreme reading or writing difficulties and in suggesting instructional programs for them.
6. Referring students to appropriate specialized service personnel.
7. Determining the degree of reading and/or writing difficulty.
8. Identifying students for special services and programs.
9. Helping teachers to document progress in reading and writing.
10. Recommending and modeling the use of instructional techniques and materials.
11. Using and generating tools and techniques for improving students' "higher level" thinking skills.
12. Supporting teachers as they develop additional strategies for teaching reading and/or writing.

Adapted from "Desirable Competencies of Reading Personnel" from "Competencies That Count Among Reading Specialists" by V. V. Garry, *Journal of Reading*, May 1974, pp. 608–613.

informal as a chat in the teachers' lounge, as routine as a parent-teacher conference, or as formal as a complete case report. Its purpose should always be to communicate or solicit information about an individual student.

In this section we provide some guidelines for effective reporting, describe some ways to use the portfolio in reporting to others, and discuss several types of written reports. Finally, specific procedures for writing formal reports are detailed.

General Guidelines

No matter what form the reporting takes, there are some guidelines that should be considered:

1. *Provide a clear summary* of what has been done in both assessment and instruction. The tools, strategies, and techniques should be clear, and the results should be understandable, apparent, and reasonable. Effective reports provide detailed descriptions so that others can understand the learner and the instructional context with little chance of confusion.
2. *Include only relevant information.* No matter how interesting, information should not be included unless there appears to be a close link to reading, writing, or overall academic performance. When sensitive personal information is discussed, this should be treated as discreetly as possible.
3. *Highlight the most important information* about the learner and the context. Always make sure that the student's most salient strengths and obvious difficulties are described as priorities. Similarly, critical positive supports in the instructional context should be noted along with suggestions for instruction that is likely to be effective for the student. Less central information should be discussed later in the reporting session or at the end of any written report. It is not necessary or desirable to report the same information about all individuals; the report should reflect the particular needs and abilities of the learner.
4. *Use language and format appropriate for the audience.* When reporting to parents, it is important to keep discussions free of jargon and as straightforward as possible. When specialized terms seem necessary to use, be sure to define them. If there is any reason at all to suspect the literacy skills of parents or guardians, all information should be communicated orally. On the other hand, when reporting to teachers, schools, or other agencies, the form and language should be professional and technical terms should be used to ensure precision.

In deciding on the form of reporting, it is important to consider the needs of the audience as well as the purposes for communicating. Too often, professionals believe that reporting must always involve transmitting and interpreting formal test data. Yet, parents often would prefer periodic meetings that inform them about their children's general progress. This is where assessment portfolios are particularly powerful tools in reporting.

Reporting Via Diagnostic Portfolio Summaries

Throughout this text we have described how diagnostic portfolios may be created and maintained. A diagnostic portfolio, unlike some others, probably should contain *all* types of available information about an individual student. It will include *at least* three types of information:

1. formal, standardized test information, where available (see Chapter 10);
2. the results of intentionally planned assessments of reading/writing ability such as retellings (see Chapters 8 and 9);
3. work samples collected as representative of the activities and abilities of that student/classroom.

These pieces of evidence are themselves relatively uninformative, however. They are essentially raw data unless a knowledgeable teacher organizes the information and interprets its significance.

When preparing to report the contents of portfolios to others, it is helpful to organize the information in some way so that it takes on meaning for others who are less well-informed. Even a simple cover sheet stapled to a folder can systematize the information (see Figure 16.2).

Listing the pieces of information in the portfolio and the dates collected can help the teacher and any others to see the range of information available. If, in addition, the teacher writes a narrative periodically (for example, at conference time), then the information can be even more accessible to others.

FIGURE 16.2
Portfolio Cover Sheet

| Name _____ | Teacher(s) _____ |
| Grade _____ | Birthdate _____ |

COMMENTS	DATE
1. _____	
2. _____	
3. _____	
4. _____	
5. _____	
6. _____	
7. _____	
8. _____	

COMMENTS	DATE

For the purposes of reporting to others, it may be important to organize the information and the patterns of literacy behavior to an even greater extent. In such cases, teachers can use a Portfolio Analysis Sheet (see Figure 16.3). The example provided is only suggestive, since teachers should use an analysis system that parallels the types of assessment and instruction that are most central to their program.

It is important that the portfolio analysis offer systematic evaluation of the contents of the portfolio—analysis that could be replicated by others who are interested in this student's performance. While the contents may be helpful to classroom teachers as they work with students, they are unlikely to be informative to others (or considered valid and reliable) unless some additional effort is made to interpret and formalize the results. If this effort is made, however, both parents and administrators are likely to be pleased with the specificity of information and the depth of knowledge available. In Chapters 8 and 9 we described a variety of ways to strengthen organizational aspects of gathering informal data (see also Valencia, Hiebert, and Afflerbach 1994).

There are times, of course, when the information about students must be interpreted and summarized for other purposes or in other ways. Written reports vary in both type and purpose and are discussed in the next section.

Report Writing: Different Types for Different Purposes

Writing reports is an essential part of the job of most English language arts professionals. However, these may vary from very brief reports to extensive formal case reports. Parents generally want to know what is happening in the clinical or classroom setting, especially when the student is receiving specialized help for an identified problem. Brief reports about the student's program and progress can and should be sent periodically to parents and other involved professionals. This kind of report can alert parents and teachers to special accomplishments that have occurred or to problems that have been identified. At other times, this report may be used to enlist the help of parents and classroom teachers (see Figure 16.4).

It is also important for classroom teachers and specialized personnel to communicate with each other. Issues of congruence discussed earlier (see Chapters 5 and 6) have obvious implications for reporting. As Shake (1989) has noted:

> It seems safe to say that remedial teachers cannot provide instruction that either introduces or reinforces the classroom literacy curriculum if they do not know what that curriculum contains. Both classroom and remedial teachers report concern regarding the lack of time for communication about programs and target students. (Allington and Shake 1986; Johnston, Allington, and Afflerbach 1985, 74)

Clearly, the type of reporting called for in this situation is somewhat different, though no less important. Shake suggests that teachers and specialists keep a record form (see Chapter 5) that travels with the student. This type of documentation can diminish the need for extensive formal reporting at a later date and also increases the likelihood that instruction will have some coherence

**FIGURE
16.3**
*Portfolio
Analysis Sheet*

Observations of Reading and Writing	
Date	**Student Interview**
	Summarize results of
	Observations
	Record observations of student's development in reading/writing

Reading Materials/Tasks	
Date	
	Books/selections read (assigned)
	Books/selections read (self-selected)
	Book/reading-related written work completed
	Group activities

Reading Performance (Note materials, task, level of support)	
Date	
	Word recognition ability
	Oral reading fluency
	Comprehension: Question answering
	Comprehension: Retelling
	Strategy use
	Studying strategies

**FIGURE
16.3**
(Continued)

Writing Development	
Date	
	Describe writing samples (include all drafts)
	Note types of writing represented
	Summarize writer's development of written mechanics (spelling and writing conventions)
	Student-selected "best piece" (describe)
	Evaluate writing development (progress over time and in terms of age-appropriateness)
Summary	
Date	
	Student's reading development
	Student's writing development

**FIGURE
16.4**
*Parents/
Teacher
Report Form*

Student _____   Date _____
Teacher _____
Summary of the following instructional periods (dates/times of sessions):
_____
Summary of reading/writing abilities: _____
_____
_____
Summary of instructional program (materials, activities): _____
_____
_____
Summary of progress: _____
_____
_____
Comments: _____
_____
_____

across settings. Of course, if a portfolio system is being employed, then the student as well as all teachers can and should contribute samples, observations, and evaluations.

Just as the audience and format for reporting may vary, so may the content. For example, all of the specially funded programs for reading, writing, and related difficulties require some sort of reporting procedures. These programs often require the teacher only to report program data; extensive individual reporting is not necessary. Even when formal individual case reports are expected, they may vary depending on the audience and the program. For many school-based purposes, the literacy report format outlined in Figure 16.5 would be appropriate. Teachers and specialists alike should think about using this fairly streamlined approach that focuses on important literacy goals and outcomes (See Figure 16.5)

Sometimes it is important to write much more comprehensive case reports that include summaries of all available standardized test information and interpretations of the results for specific uses. A written report of a student's reading and writing ability generally includes all or some of the following: background information, summary of assessment information, summary of factors influencing performance, and implications for instruction or future placement (or summary of instructional progress).

Formal reports about individual students in public school settings are used most often when the student has been referred for special services or for a determination of eligibility for special education (see Chapter 1). These often

FIGURE 16.5
Literacy Report Format

Development
Reading Strategies Response to Literature Comprehension of Content Area Text Writing: Content, organization, voice, coherence, range Writing: Grammar, usage, mechanics
Attitudes and Motivation
Ownership/Engagement Self-Reflection Work Habits Effort
Text Levels
Individual Goals
Teacher Comments Parent Comments or Questions Student Comments
Next Steps

make recommendations regarding the student's eligibility for services, but are less helpful regarding the specific implications for instructional programs.

As we have seen, literacy leaders may be asked or required to perform in a variety of contexts and may need to be responsive to different people and their needs. Perhaps the most frequent responsibility, however, involves the need to pull together an array of assessment information and use it to plan an instructional program. This type of reporting, something we call the *case report*, is described in much greater detail in the next section.

Procedures for Writing Diagnostic Case Reports

Fully executed case reports are very time-consuming to write, and few settings require such extensive documentation. Although it is not the most frequent format for reporting and communicating about students, it is the format that professionals often use as the vehicle for *learning how to report.* A formal, written report requires discipline in organizing information, ability to interpret results, and well-developed writing skills. It demands careful examination of all information regarding a student, and involves learning to communicate that information to others in a much more public forum than many teachers typically experience.

Choosing and using a fairly standard format for writing case reports saves time. There are a wide array of formats used. Several factors need to be considered in selecting a format. First, it should accommodate and support reporting of the types of information that you wish to communicate. Second, it should be flexible enough so that it can be shaped to take the focus appropriate to the particular individual and purpose. Third, it should offer a format that is convenient for the consumer of the report—considerate both in terms of what is expected and familiar and clearly organized for ease of reading. Finally, there is a political consideration as well. Although the situation is rapidly changing, the educational community still has a bias toward data gathered from standardized, norm-referenced tools. Since we include large amounts of nontraditional information in our reports, we are particularly sensitive to the ways in which we display these data.

The format described in this section has an overall appearance that is similar to traditional case reports and provides for formally reporting all existing assessment information. We want consumers to take the information seriously and to consider it as reliable and valid as the more familiar test scores (see Figure 16.6). The format also offers flexibility in accommodating the types of information we have advocated throughout this text. If the Thumbnail Sketch was done earlier (see Chapter 11), this information will be very useful in preparing the case report.

The case of "Marvin," discussed periodically throughout this text, is now used to illustrate the sections in a diagnostic case report (a second full case report is presented in Appendix A). Each of the procedures described below parallels a major component of the diagnostic case report (see Figure 16.7).

Display the Assessment Information

The cover sheet should contain a concise, yet complete, description of the assessment information. To the extent possible, all available information about the reader should be displayed on a cover sheet (see Figure 15.6). This includes identifying information such as name, age, school, and so on. It should also clearly indicate the date of the report, who has prepared the report, and who administered the tests (if this was different). The date and source of the report should be easy to find. Remember, these reports end up in files, and often follow students for some time. It can be both irritating and confusing to find a report in a file and be unable to tell when the results were generated.

Previous results may be included on the cover sheet when they are recent and the data are useful in the total report (for example, a recent psychological report, an existing IEP, etc.; see Appendix A). In such cases, both the examiner

**FIGURE
16.6**
Cover Sheet

Confidential Diagnostic Report

NAME <u>Marvin B.</u>   DATE <u>December 27, 1988</u>

EXAMINER <u>Marjorie Y. Lipson, Ph.D.</u>

NAME OF PARENT/GUARDIAN <u>Joan and Phillip B.</u>

ADDRESS   <u>15 East View</u>   PHONE <u>923-6570</u>

          <u>Lakeville, VT</u>   BIRTHDATE _____

SCHOOL   <u>Apple Elementary School</u>   AGE <u>11</u>   GRADE <u>5</u>

       <u>Lakeville, Vermont</u>

Previous Test Information

<u>WISC-R</u> (Administered 4/88 by M. Hawkins, Psychologist):

   Verbal: 109   Performance: 114   Full scale: 112

<u>Metropolitan Achievement Tests</u> (Administered 4/88, 4th grade)

   Total Reading: 37th percentile (4th stanine)

   Word Identification: 23rd percentile (3rd stanine)

   Comprehension: 45th percentile (5th stanine)

Summary of Assessment Results

Woodcock Reading Mastery (Form B)	Relative Mastery	Percentile Rank
Letter Identification	93%	58
Word Identification	7%	10
Word Attack	32%	9
Word Comprehension	55%	15
Passage Comprehension	29%	8

Analytic Reading Inventory	Independent Reading Level	Instructional Reading Level	Frustrational Reading Level
Word Recognition	2	3	5–6
Oral Comprehension	2 & 3	4 & 5	6
Silent Comprehension	2–4	5	6
Classroom Reading Inventory			
Word Recognition	NA	1	2–6
Oral Comprehension	1–4 & 6	5	7
Silent Comprehension	2, 3, & 5	4	6
Burns and Roe, Informal Reading Inventory			
Word Recognition	NA	2	3–5
Oral Comprehension	NA	2	3–5
Silent Comprehension	NA	2 & 3	4 & 5

Summary

Comprehension Scores:

   Highest Instructional/Independent Level: (7-Ind. Silent)

   Lowest Instructional: 1 (Oral and Silent)

   Lowest Frustrational: 2 (Oral)

Listening Comprehension: (Analytic Reading Inventory)

   Independent: Grades 2–6; Instructional: Grade 7

Relevant Instruction Information

   Grades K-1:   Conrad Elementary, Lakeville Public Schools Readiness and Primer
                 levels of Ginn 360 (1982)

   Grades 2–4:   St. Mary's School, Lakeville Vermont
                 Basal books for Grades 2–4, synthetic phonics series

   Currently: Fifth grade, recently placed in Apple School, Lakeville Public Schools.
               Literature-based individualized reading program.

FIGURE 16.7

Diagnostic Case Report Format

Cover Sheet(s)
  Identifying information for student
  Name of reporter and date of report
  Summary of assessment results
Background Information
  Reason for referral
  Distinctive developmental history
  School history
  Results of initial student, parent,
  teacher interviews
Summary of Assessment Results
  Reader factors (areas discussed as
  appropriate for individual):
      Emergent literacy development
      Word recognition
      Vocabulary
      Comprehension
      Studying
      Writing
      Integrated discussion of results
  Instructional factors
      Results of classroom/other
        observation
      Analysis of text and task
        demands

Diagnostic Teaching
  Strategies
  Results
Diagnostic Statement
  Summarize major findings
  Summarize learner's strengths/
    weaknesses
  Note factors that influence
    performance (peaks/valleys)
Suggestions for Instruction
  Content of instruction
  Delivery of instruction
  Materials
  Level of support
Other Suggestions/Recommendations
  Home involvement
  Additional assessment
  Special placement

and the date of testing should be clearly labeled. School achievement test data can be provided as well, when they demonstrate a pattern or are relevant to the referral or the summary.

The remainder of the cover sheet involves presenting both formal and informal data in brief numerical or descriptive form. This serves two purposes. First, the report reader can get an overview of what has been done and what pattern of results is emerging without reading the entire report. Second, it eliminates the need to include extensive numerical data in the body of the report, thus focusing attention on the interpretation of these results.

Describe Background Information

This section should open with a clear statement about who referred the student for special evaluation and instruction, and the reason for this referral. The content of the remainder of this section of the report will vary. For some students, it is important to describe rather extensive amounts of relevant background information. Critical aspects of health history, notable school factors, or particularly disruptive emotional incidents need to be included. There are other students for whom this section is brief, since there are no factors that seem related to the reading/writing difficulties. In these cases, simply noting that the student's development appears normal and the school history uneventful should be sufficient.

It is also helpful to convey in this background section both the student's and the family's attitude toward reading/writing activities and toward the student's particular problems. Information gleaned from interviews and from observations should be summarized here and used to support any statements made about attitudes, motivation, or the influence of correlational factors (see Figure 16.8).

Summarize the Assessment Information

The section called Summary of Assessment Results is designed to convey critical aspects of student performance as clearly as possible. There are a number of ways to do this, and the emphasis and focus should reflect the *particular* reader being described. In some cases, the reader will be the focus of the summary and analysis; in other cases, instructional factors will loom large.

Summarize the instructional factors. This portion is the least common in traditional reports. In some cases, it would make more sense to include observations and information about the instructional factors in the Background Section (see p. 646). In others, the information is included as a part of the discussion regarding the test results. In still other cases, it is important only to state that the instructional context has included appropriate instruction and literacy experiences for the student. However, there are times when the information collected in the assessment-instruction process warrants separate commentary.

In Marvin's case, there seemed to be little point in conducting a classroom observation, since he had only just transferred to the school/classroom. Critical information about instructional history was placed here in the Background Section (see Figure 16.8). It was important to note that he had received no individualized instruction in his program and that the methodologies were quite sparse. Specific information about texts and tasks that influence Marvin's performance was placed in the Summary of Assessment Results section (see Figure 16.9).

Information about the reader. This section is not designed to reiterate tests scores that have already been summarized, although these can be used when needed for clarity. Rather, it is designed to interpret and pull into clear view the overall performance patterns of the reader. As the various components of reading and writing are discussed, all pieces of evidence about that component are described (see Figure 16.7). When the test or some aspect of the assessment task contributes strongly to the results, they should also be discussed and interpreted. In Marvin's case, this type of description was offered to help interpret the results of the various IRIs (see Figure 16.9).

It is important to point out again that the reports of specific students may vary considerably from this. Effective reporting describes the reader and focuses attention on important aspects of his or her performance. In some cases, this may be done more effectively by using subheads that parallel the various components

FIGURE 16.8

*Case Report:
Background
Information
Section*

Reason for Referral

Marvin has just returned to a public school settng, having been enrolled in a private parochial school for three years. Concerns about Marvin's reading abilities, expressed by both school and parents, led to a referral for reading assessment.

Observation and Interview Information

Neither Marvin's mother nor the available records suggest any remarkable health or development problems. Throughout the current series of assessment activities, Marvin appeared to be an engaging, friendly, and open fifth-grade boy. His manner was quite easy-going and he appeared to have excellent self-confidence. He approached each task with vigor, never tired of the activities, and always appeared ready for the next one. He smiles easily and does not appear ruffled by even the most difficult tasks. Marvin has extraordinary stamina for reading activities, especially given his slow pace and rate.

These observations are somewhat at odds with Marvin's case history (see Confidential Psychological Report in files). Marvin's mother reports that the family has experienced significant disruption for the past two years as a result of a separation and impending divorce between Marvin's parents. A psychologist's report suggests that Marvin's reading difficulties may result from his inability to attend to school tasks and from high levels of anxiety related to these family problems. At the present time, the family appears to have settled into a more regular routine and Marvin regularly visits with his father and he reports enjoying these visits.

When asked to reflect on reading in general and his own abilities in particular, Marvin offered very little. He could neither think of anything to say about how he viewed reading nor describe what a good reader was like. With regard to his own reading ability he believes he is a "medium" reader and that his biggest problem is "understanding what I read." On the other hand, Marvin believes that people read "to learn and to get away from things." He suggests that he reads because "it's fun—but, not all the time."

Marvin exhibits enthusiastic curiosity about a wide range of topics and he brings this interest to bear on his reading. He becomes actively involved with reading, stopping to comment and/or chuckle over parts of the text. He indicated an interest in reading books with a high degree of action and humor and also said he likes to read books about his hobbies and about machines and the outdoors. He is not, however, interested in reading about American heroes, biographies, or sports. Marvin builds model cars as a hobby and he says he generally likes to "take stuff apart."

School/Instructional History

Due to family moves, Marvin attended two different schools during kindergarten and first grade. During these early years, Marvin was reported to be struggling with reading. Because his parents were concerned about his limited reading abilities after first grade, they decided to send him to a private parochial school for second grade. He remained there throughout the second, third, and fourth grades. During Marvin's fourth-grade year, his teacher reported that Marvin was experiencing serious difficulties in reading: precipitating a psychological evaluation (see file). At least partly because this private school does not have any remedial services, Marvin's parents decided to return him to the public school in their neighborhood and he was referred for reading assessment at that time.

FIGURE 16.8
Continued

Marvin has received reading instruction with a basal reading program since kindergarten. In Grades K-1, the program was an eclectic one published in the early 1980s and he progressed as a member of the lowest reading group. From Grades 2 through 4, he was placed in the phonics-oriented basal used in his new school. No grouping or special support was employed in this school, so he progressed through the materials at the pace determined appropriate for the whole class. The reading methods of the school appear to revolve around daily oral reading of assigned basal selections followed by independent completion of assigned workbook pages. Neither silent reading time nor process writing activities were provided on a regular basis. Starting in fourth grade, the school used textbooks for science and social studies, although it is not clear how often students received reading assignments in these materials.

Marvin has only just been placed in the fifth grade of a public school. Although the classroom program is a literature-based individualized one, with individual work folders assigned to each student, the least-able readers are often placed in a dated basal series. The teacher is anxious to receive information about Marvin's reading abilities in order to make some instructional decisions. Oral reading occurs in this classroom during one-to-one conferences with the teacher and generally involves student-selected and prepared excerpts from books of stories. Silent reading is a daily activity although writing activities are more irregular and generally involve writing book reports and research reports.

In summary, Marvin presents himself as a vigorous, active, and undaunted boy who is remarkably at ease in new settings.

of reading and writing that are posing problems for that student. For example, there might appear within the Summary of Results section a subsection on Emergent Literacy Development, another on Vocabulary, and another on Word Recognition, but no separate heads for Studying or Writing, if those were less critical areas for the student.

On the other hand, the reports for other students seem to be more straightforward and coherent when the various tests are discussed and the results interpreted. This format is likely to be most helpful when the tests themselves contribute to a student's performance and a discussion of the test or assessment strategy is needed. This organization can be helpful when there are important anecdotal aspects to the student's interactions.

Describe and Report the Results of Diagnostic Teaching

In this section, specific manipulations of the literacy event should be described. Since diagnostic teaching is not included in most traditional assessment plans, it is important to describe briefly the purpose of such activity. The reader should understand both what was done and why this was attempted. In addition, the section should conclude with a summary that interprets the results.

In Marvin's case (see Figure 16.10), the specific procedures were developed using a framework like that described earlier (see Chapter 11) . The evaluation was conducted by someone other than school personnel, and for very specific

FIGURE 16.9
Case Report: Summary and Interpretation of Results

Summary of Assessment Results

The pattern of Marvin's performance is quite stable. An examination of the pattern of results for the various informal reading inventories (IRIs) demonstrates that his word recognition scores are consistently poor and he reaches frustrational level on word recognition at Level 3 on all three IRIs (see Cover Sheet). On the other hand, his comprehension scores are consistently higher than his word recognition scores and, on two IRIs, he does not reach frustrational level in comprehension until Grade 6 or 7.

Marvin's performance on the word analysis subtest reflects his limited ability to decode non-meaningful words out-of-context. He does, however, demonstrate adequate knowledge of the basic phonic relationships. There are two possible phonic components that may also require additional instruction: (1) consonant blends and digraphs, and (2) complex vowel combinations like "ea," "ou," and "oi." Marvin's miscues on these ("tragic" for "task," "find" for "friend," etc., and a persistent problem with "ea" words) suggest that he has not yet mastered these phonic elements. It should be noted, however, that his phonics skills *overall* appear to be adequate except as he fails to apply these skills to multisyllabic words.

An analysis of Marvin's miscues (see Chapter 5) demonstrates the large number of word recognition difficulties he experiences during reading. Many of these miscues appear on high-frequency sight words ("the" for "our," "and" for "the," "the" for "her," etc.). Thus, it would appear that Marvin needs continued opportunities to practice these high-frequency words. Many of Marvin's remaining miscues involve word endings—inflectional endings and suffixes (for example: "safe" for "safer," "means" for "meant," "quick" for "quickly," etc.) Marvin consistently deletes such endings, and occasionally adds endings not present. There is also evidence that Marvin has underdeveloped syllabication skills ("enginical" for "energetic," "detoof" for "develop," etc.) and it would appear that direct instruction in structural analysis as a word recognition strategy would be helpful to Marvin.

The disparity between his word recognition and comprehension performance is substantial. Marvin demonstrated good to excellent comprehension of most materials read. He was able to answer questions following both oral and silent reading with ease and he appears capable of answering a broad range of question types. Analysis of his rate of self-correction and the proportion of meaningful miscues (see Chapter 5) provide additional evidence of Marvin's substantial comprehension abilities. His rate of self-correction is extremely high (especially at lower levels), suggesting that he actively monitors his reading progress and attempts to construct meaning from text. Indeed, when his rate of self-correction is coupled with the percentage of meaningful miscues (i.e., the "error" does not affect the meaning of the text), it becomes apparent how impressive Marvin's efforts to understand really are. He rarely produces nonsensical substitutions or "wild guesses" and, often, his substitutions could go undetected since they do not significantly affect the meaning of the selection.

Though Marvin's comprehension abilities are quite robust (note the overall pattern of performance), he also demonstrates differential ability across the texts and tasks. (Note both his "peak"—silent reading on the CRI (instructional at Grade 7) and his "valley" [frustrational comprehension at Grade 3 on the oral reading Burns and Roe]. It is obvious that the Burns and Roe passages were more difficult for him than any others. In fact, if only the Burns and Roe IRI had been administered, it would have appeared that limited power and automaticity in decoding skills was the sole source of his comprehension problems, so that as decoding accuracy decreased, so did comprehension.

This explanation obviously cannot account for Marvin's performance at other times. His performance on the other two IRIs in fact suggests exactly the opposite—that comprehension ability drives his reading efforts and that he is likely to perform poorly overall only when the reading process cannot be driven from a position of understanding. Marvin's weakest performance occurred while reading several rather ambiguous texts in the Burns and Roe IRI. Two are set in a foreign country and are guided almost entirely by a type of lyrical internal response structure. All three are fragments from longer texts and none have a very strong story structure. While Marvin often understood all the relevant explicit information in these texts, he did not always make the inferences necessary to answer the question. Thus, while neither the type of text (exposition versus narrative) nor the type and number of questions significantly affect Marvin's performance, other factors such as coherence and conformity to expected story structures did. The diagnostic teaching pursued with Marvin supports this conclusion and this segment of the assessment is described in the next section.

purposes. The descriptions of diagnostic teaching may be a much more substantial part of some reports. This is especially true when the reports are written after significant instructional contact (see Progress Reports, p. 651).

Provide a Diagnostic Summary Statement

This section provides a brief, coherent statement of the student's strengths and weaknesses (see Figure 16.11). In a straightforward way, the report reader is reminded of the ground that has been covered and helped to see the big picture.

FIGURE 16.10

Case Report: Diagnostic Teaching

Diagnostic Teaching

In order to clarify Marvin's problem, diagnostic teaching was attempted with him. Diagnostic teaching involves manipulating the assessment process in any of a number of ways. The purpose of manipulating the assessment process is twofold: to collect additional information to clarify and test the hypotheses about Marvin's reading problems, and to try out potential methods of instruction.

Marvin clearly needs additional decoding skills and a great deal of attention directed toward increasing his automaticity. Marvin's strength is comprehension. However, his performance in comprehension was not universally strong and it was in this area that more information might be useful.

Because he had performed poorly on the Burns and Roe IRI, these selections were used in the diagnostic teaching. Marvin had reached the frustration level on a selection without a title that dealt with a young boy's concern about a test. The main idea of this selection was subtle and Marvin constructed a different main theme for the selection. Marvin also asked several questions related to the main theme. It seemed likely that Marvin might be able to understand challenging material if some organizational support were provided. Therefore, he was asked to reread the selection, this time imagining that the story was entitled, "Peter Worries About a Test." Given that much support, Marvin answered all the questions posed correctly and was able, in addition, to provide a coherent and accurate summary of the selection. The exercise was repeated with two other selections and each time Marvin was totally successful in his comprehension efforts. Given a general idea of the topic, Marvin has no difficulty linking ideas, locating information, or supporting inferential conclusions.

It is clear that Marvin's forte involves responding to questions after reading coherent or well-structured text (even when his percentage of miscues is extremely high). However, Marvin also will need to be able to comprehend text on his own. Thus, a final activity was employed. Marvin was asked to silently read a very lengthy (5-page) narrative story written at the high third/low fourth-grade readability and to do a retelling of the story. Marvin appeared very interested in the selection and launched into the retelling with enthusiasm. Despite this obvious interest, Marvin's reconstruction of the story left out vital events and concepts and his recount involved no sound sequence. In addition, his recount failed to name the important characters, to identify their problem in the story, or to accurately identify the final solution to the problem. On the other hand, when Marvin was asked specific questions about the selection, he was able to demonstrate a far clearer understanding of the text or, perhaps more accurately, he was able to use the questions asked to *re*-organize his understanding of the story.

**FIGURE
16.11**
*Case Report:
Diagnostic
Summary*

Diagnostic Summary

Marvin has a great many strengths, not the least of which is his interest in reading and his obvious enjoyment of it. Marvin makes an excellent showing in silent reading comprehension, especially as measured by ability to answer questions. In addition, Marvin has good to excellent memory skills which he uses to aid his understanding. He uses all pre-reading information (introductory statements, for example) to the greatest possible extent to drive his reading efforts. In addition, Marvin actively attends to his reading. He self-corrects frequently, does not produce "wild guesses," and is able to respond effectively to what he reads. He uses context very effectively to aid his word recognition and to derive meaning from text.

Marvin has serious word recognition difficulties, including limited sight-word recognition. He also has difficulty reading multisyllabic words and has not acquired a strategy for coping with words that require structural analysis (including syllabication). He also demonstrates limited ability to apply knowledge of consonant blends and digraphs and vowel digraphs and dipthongs. He will need to improve his word recognition skills if he is not to be overwhelmed by lengthy reading assignments, since his lack of automaticity slows him down.

While comprehension is generally a strength for Marvin, his ability to impose structure and meaning on longer, denser, or less-considerate text is limited. He seems to lack experience reading different types of materials. In addition he has had limited opportunities to read for a variety of purposes or for different tasks.

Marvin is capable of handling much of the material at his grade level, although he will not sound fluent in oral reading situations. His performance is improved significantly when relevant pre-reading supports are provided. Narrative selections are easier for Marvin to read than expository ones. In addition, dense, poorly organized texts of all types are more difficult for him to read and should be avoided wherever possible.

Because no assessment data are specifically cited here, it is especially important that there be no surprises. This is not the time to introduce new information. In addition, what is concluded in this section should be clearly related to the earlier data that were described.

The diagnostic statement should synthesize information across the various assessment and instructional contexts. The results of the diagnostic teaching are embedded to inform the conclusions drawn. The summary statement should contain enough information to function as an overview of the entire report so that individuals who cannot read or reread the whole document can read an accurate statement that captures the reading or writing process for that student/client.

Describe Recommendations for Instruction

In this section, the specific implications for instruction are described. Again, there should be no surprises here. Suggestions for improving word identification cannot be offered when no evidence for a problem in this area was provided earlier. There should be a clear link between the assessment portions of the report and these instructional suggestions.

There are several types of instructional advice that can be offered in this section, both of which are evident in Marvin's report (see Figure 16.12). Suggestions often include ideas for shaping literacy instruction and/or offering instructional support (Recommendations 1, 3, and 4). Of course, instructional recommendations should also specify the component areas to be emphasized in instruction (Recommendations 2 and 3).

Other suggestions for instruction may involve naming particular instructional strategies or techniques (Recommendation 3). In these cases, it is important to make sure that teachers reading the report are familiar with the techniques. If there is any doubt about the familiarity of the method, strategy, or text suggested, the information should be provided as a part of the report. This can be done in the body of the report for brief recommendations. For instructional techniques that require greater additional explanation, an appendix works best.

Note Any Additional Suggestions and/or Recommendations (Optional)
There are times when the literacy professional completes an assessment and is aware that there is more to be done. Often, it would be desirable to collect information from other professional sources. For example, medical services

**FIGURE
16.12**
*Case Report:
Recommen-
dation for
Instruction*

Recommendations
Marvin is a very able, hard-working, eager boy who should progress in reading if offered the opportunity. It is entirely possible that his history (see Confidential Psychological Report in school files) has slowed his progress in reading and that he is currently in a position to take advantage of some remedial help.

1. Marvin needs to have his reading assignments structured for him. Wherever possible, pre-reading questions will help Marvin significantly. In addition, visual story "maps," structured overviews, etc. would be very helpful to Marvin, and he should be able to learn to construct them for himself in a very short time.

2. Some direct instruction in structural analysis skills (specifically, syllabication and recognizing suffixes) is essential. This instruction should be coupled with a reminder to Marvin that he can employ his rather good phonics skills after he has analyzed the structure of the words (thus, this provides the opportunity for review in phonics as well). Since Marvin enjoys "taking things apart," he should be able to employ these skills to good effect once he understands how this will aid his reading.

3. Marvin could benefit from a holistic approach to his word recognition problems. I would recommend two strategies for Marvin (as opposed to more isolated work in phonics or word recognition): [a] Repeated Readings Approach, or its variation, the Talking Dictionary; and [b] taped read-alongs requiring Marvin to read in a book along with an oral rendition that has been taped for him. Several commercial companies produce good tape-book combinations. The Neurological Impress (NIM) might also be a good approach to use with Marvin in a tutorial or other one-on-one setting.

4. Every effort should be made to sustain Marvin's positive attitude and cooperation in any remedial program. At the moment he has an excellent approach to reading and school and he should be encouraged to develop his substantial strengths.

may be needed to explore health, vision, or auditory contributions to the reading or writing difficulties. Alternatively, it might be concluded that a psychologist and/or special educator should become involved to determine eligibility for special services. Referrals to other professionals should be done generally; specific recommendations should be avoided.

The reporter may also wish to recommend that the student receive additional support services. Again, the nature and/or duration of the support should be described, but the report should avoid recommending specific sources of service. The obvious exception is the case where the person reporting is also responsible for delivering the type of service recommended, although in that case, the reporter may wish to summarize the planned services so that everyone is clear about what will happen next (see Figure 16.13).

Finally, it is often desirable to specify what types of activities would be appropriate in the home environment (see Figure 16.14). It is not possible to ensure home involvement and support, but parents often welcome specific suggestions for helping their children. We often attach some parent information to each report, since many parents are unaware of the importance of some simple ways they can help. Tips about reading to children, ideas for writing at home, local sources of good books, guidelines for controlling TV watching, and directions for supporting students with specific techniques are generally welcomed.

Progress Reports

The procedures described above are appropriate for an initial and complete diagnostic assessment. Students often become involved in special programs or receive special instructional services as the result of such reports. In such cases, periodic reports may be very desirable, but there is no need to write such a comprehensive diagnostic report. The format for progress reports is somewhat different, with a focus on instruction rather than assessment (see Figure 16.15).

The first two sections of a Progress Report are almost identical to a Diagnostic Report. Only minor variations in the cover sheet and background information components are obvious. For example, the Cover Sheet may include both test and retest information. Since the Progress Report is written after some period of instructional intervention, it is important to date and note this information carefully. Similarly, the Background Information component may contain information that has been gathered over a considerable period of time. Thus, it is important to note if an observation was made early in the program or was made more recently.

In a Progress Report, one of the most important components is the Diagnostic Summary. This section should be written carefully, because it essentially provides the rationale for the instructional program that is described. This brief, accurate, and focused statement is usually not more than a page in length. It may refer to earlier assessments (by date and examiner) but should not be viewed as a complete diagnostic report.

FIGURE 16.13   **Special Services Scheduling Survey**

Student _____ _____ Teacher_____ Date _____

	Reading	Math	Writing
1. Student will fully participate in regular classroom without any Special Services support (specially designed instruction).			
2. Student will fully participate in regular classroom with direct Special Services support (Specialist staff in regular classroom).			
3. A combination of 2 and 4 (student may receive support in classroom some of the time and receive services out of the classroom sometimes).			
4. Student will fully participate in regular classroom with supplementary support outside of classroom (student brings regular classroom materials).			
5. Student will work at a program similar to that in the regular classroom, but conducted entirely out of classroom by Special Services staff.			

Specific areas of concern:

_____ YES   If there were a mixed-grade Writer's Workshop in the Resource Room,

_____ NO   would this student be a good candidate for that group?

Check any Special Services currently received by the student:

_____ Developmental K _____ Chapter 1 _____ ESL _____ Resource Room _____ Highly Capable

What is your "best guess" as to the times these subjects will fit into your classroom schedule for this student? (e.g. from 10:00 to 10:45)

Reading _____

Math _____

Writing _____

_____ YES   Would you be willing to have within your class a small group of students who require similar Special Services, if a member of the appropriate Special

_____ NO   Services staff was scheduled to be in your room for the part of each day when students would need support?

From Hill, D.C., and Ruptic, C. (1994). *Practical Aspects of Authentic Assessement.* © 1994 Christopher-Gordon Publishers, Inc.

FIGURE 16.14
Case Report: General Recommendations

Additional Recommendations

Marvin could benefit from additional individualized or small group instruction. A tutorial or clinical setting would be beneficial to him. Additional testing does not, however, seem necessary at this time.

At home, Marvin should set aside a short period each day for silent reading. Marvin's mother reads regularly herself and might consider setting aside a "family reading time" each evening. It might be helpful if Marvin were encouraged to read aloud (after practice) to his younger brother and sister as well.

Marvin could also benefit from doing the Talking Dictionary at home several times a week. This should be a relaxed, enjoyable time for both Marvin and whomever he is reading with. Family participation in word and memory games could be helpful to Marvin. Games such as Scrabble and Memory could increase Marvin's word analysis skills.

Finally, Marvin should be encouraged to write as often as possible. Letters and notes to family and friends should be actively encouraged. He might also be charged with making lists of activities and notes to remind family members of special events.

_____   _____
Marjorie Y. Lipson, Ph.D.   Date

FIGURE 16.15
Progress Report Format

Cover Sheet(s)
  Identifying information for student
  Name of reporter and date of report
  Summary of existing assessment
    information
  Summary of new or retest information

Background Information
  Summary of relevant referral
    information
  Summary of continuing observation
    or interview data

Diagnostic Summary
  Brief summary of relevant
    assessment information
  Conclusions re: major instructional
    implications

Summary of Instructional Program
  Description of instructional goals
  Description of instructional
    activities/program

Summary of Progress
  Description of areas of
    improvement (with evidence)
  Description of areas that
    remain problematic

Recommendations
  Further intervention and
    instructional programs
  Parental support

The Summary of the Instructional Program is also a critical component of the Progress Report. It should describe exactly what was done and why. The excerpt in Figure 16.16 demonstrates how instructional goals are linked to specific activities. These activities are either described in the body of the report or descriptions can be provided in an appendix. If there were changes in the instructional program, these should be noted also. It is obviously quite common

FIGURE 16.16
Excerpt from Summary of Instructional Program

Much of Jason's instruction this term has focused on two main areas: foundation skills, designed to help him see the purposes of reading, and comprehension. Comprehension activities were designed to help Jason see reading as a process of getting meaning from text and to help him acquire strategies for understanding.

The Think Aloud activity has been used several times with Jason to encourage more active comprehension. The first time he did this activity, it was clear that word recognition greatly affected his performance. He offered very little in response to the initial prompt of, "What were you doing and thinking as you read that part?" Jason's main concern centered around how well he was going to read. Since then, Jason's responses to prompts have been more focused on comprehension. He prefaces his responses with, "Well, I was thinking about . . ." or, "That makes sense." Recently, during a Think Aloud selection, when he was asked what he had been doing or thinking as he read, Jason responded: "I wasn't thinking about nothing, but I made a picture in my mind about a cave with stone pictures." When he was asked if he had to think to make a picture in his mind, Jason paused and said, "Yeah—I guess I do think!"

for student progress to occur that results in refocusing the program or changing the activities. The rationale for program decisions should be carefully described.

The Summary of Progress section should contain a description of the student's performance at the current time. Quantitative and/or qualitative evidence should be provided regarding areas of improvement. In addition, there should be clear descriptions of the types of texts, tasks, or skills that require continued attention. Finally, the report should contain recommendations about changes in instructional focus, the desirability of continued support services, and the need for continued support at home.

Conferences

Conferences are a common format for reporting to others. They differ somewhat from other forms of reporting because they are generally less formal. The skills and strategies for conducting interviews (see Chapter 4) are helpful in conducting conferences. Whereas the purpose of an interview is to gather information, the purpose of a conference is to report or clarify information.

As in all forms of reporting, there are a variety of reasons why conferences are conducted. For example, professionals are frequently expected to confer with classroom teachers, administrators, and other specialized professionals about the abilities or progress of individual students. English language arts professionals are also often expected to participate in formal conferences like those conducted for IEP hearings. And, of course, there are usually regularly scheduled conferences for parents.

The different types of conferences are likely to be focused on slightly different issues, and often require slightly different skills. A conference with a classroom teacher sometimes involves specific issues about which there has been ongoing communication prior to the conference. Perhaps, for example, the classroom teacher and the English language arts teacher have been keeping an eye on the progress of one young girl, Krista. They have set a conference time to examine all the pieces of information they have about her and to review her progress and performance in the classroom. As a result, they may decide to continue observing, or they may decide that Krista should be evaluated more fully by the literacy professional.

Conferences can also focus on solving problems or sharing perceptions. The classroom teacher may report, for example, that Jay is having trouble with some task in the classroom. The conference may involve:

- evaluating the appropriateness of that task for the child
- examining the task itself
- other evidence that the child has problems in a particular area
- developing ways to work on this problem in the support program
- developing ways to address the problem in the regular classroom

In some parts of the country, these "pre-referral" conferences have become a formal part of the process to be used in responding to students with special needs. The school designates Student Support Teams (SSTs) that meet to discuss students when teachers are concerned. The format presented in Figure 6.17 is used by one school district to guide the work of the SST. Only after the teacher and support personnel have tried a variety of options discussed and described during the "staffing" can children be referred for further evaluation or eligibility determination.

Parents are not generally part of an SST conference, but if it is decided that further assessment is needed they would, of course, be consulted (see Chapters 1 and 4). Particular care must be taken when conferring with parents. Parents can react emotionally to information about their children, and this may prevent them from receiving the information as you intended. It is important to help parents understand the significance of what you are saying. In addition, you should always be sensitive to different cultural modes of interacting. Every effort should be made to communicate in the language most comfortable to the parents and to use interactional styles appropriate to them. If that is not possible, then it will be important to maintain contact and to follow up on any requests for parental action.

It is important to provide clear, concise information during a conference. It is also important to listen carefully and attend to the other individual(s). Be especially alert to the possibility that the parent or teacher has not clearly understood what you are saying. Also be sure to request new or additional information about the student or the situation. Finally, be sure to enlist the support of these individuals. Be as specific as possible about the ways that they can help.

**FIGURE
16.17**
*Pre-conference
Questionnaires
and SST
Report Form*

I. Student Support Team Questionnaire
*Please consider these questions prior to the STT meeting.
Bring work samples to the meeting.*

What materials are you using with this student?

Do you think other materials could be more effective?

What are some instructional strategies that you've found effective with this student.

What doesn't work?

What are this student's areas of strength?

Could you use these strengths to increase learning?

What methods have you used to reach the above conclusions?

How do you prepare the student for a lesson?
    Do you use preteaching methods?
    Do you consider prior knowledge?

Does the student work well with a group?

Does the student work well independently?

Does the student complete work in the time allowed?

What services are presently provided for this student?

What is your most important learning goal for this student?

What information/ideas can the S.S.T. help you with?

II. Student Support Team Minutes and Plan for Intervention

Student's name _____

Date of meeting _____

Present at meeting _____

_____

_____

_____

Reason for referral:

Ideas for Intervention:

With thanks to Mrs. Anne Browne, Principal of Orchard Elementary School. South Burlington, VT.

ETHICAL RESPONSIBILITIES

Like all those who work with people, literacy professionals must be careful to attend to their ethical responsibilities. Since they often work with young or vulnerable people, these responsibilities must be taken particularly seriously. The International Reading Association Code of Ethics (see Figure 16.18) should be given careful consideration by all English language arts professionals. The portion regarding ethical standards in reading services has critical implications for teachers and clinicians who work with disabled readers or writers.

This statement conveys most of what we believe to be important professional conduct, but there are two other responsibilities that we believe literacy professionals should shoulder. First, they should be advocates for students and their families. This means ensuring that parents and clients understand forms they must sign, and that those who cannot read are provided with information to make informed decisions about their programs and options.

Being an advocate involves much more, of course. It means insisting that inadequate programs are revised, that misleading test results be reconsidered, and that instructional programs respond to students' needs. It means being concerned with issues of equity, funding, and politics. Clearly, this is not easy, and an in-depth discussion is beyond the scope of this text. However, disabled readers often need strong voices, and the families of poor readers frequently need an advocate as well. Institutions are not always responsive to the needs of individuals; literacy professionals must be, to the fullest extent possible.

A second responsibility that English language arts professionals should accept is the responsibility to remain current regarding developments and research in the field. They must make a commitment to read and communicate about the important advances and techniques available. In doing so, they should advance high standards in assessment and instruction for all students. We opened this book with a section entitled Why Theory? We close with an admonishment to continue in the areas of professional growth and development, since there is every reason to believe that the field will remain dynamic for several years to come. New information, better practice, and fresh approaches are all likely to emerge. The effective professional must take as an ethical responsibility the responsibility to be informed.

FIGURE 16.18

IRA Code of Ethics

The members of the International Reading Association who are concerned with the teaching of reading form a group of professional persons obligated to society and devoted to the service and welfare of individuals through teaching, clinical services, research, and publication. The members of this group are committed to values which are the foundation of a democratic society—freedom to teach, write, and study in an atmosphere conducive to the best interests of the profession. The welfare of the public, the profession, and the individuals concerned should be of primary consideration in recommending candidates for degrees, positions, advancements, the recognition of professional activity, and for certification in those areas where certification exists.

Ethical Standards in Professional Relationships

1. It is the obligation of all members of the International Reading Association to observe the Code of Ethics of the organization and to act accordingly so as to advance the status and prestige of the Association and of the profession as a whole. Members should assist in establishing the highest professional standards for reading programs and services, and should enlist support for these through dissemination of pertinent information to the public.
2. It is the obligation of all members to maintain relationships with other professional persons, striving for harmony, avoiding personal controversy, encouraging cooperative effort, and making known the obligations and services rendered by professionals in reading.
3. It is the obligation of members to report results of research and other developments in reading.
4. Members should not claim nor advertise affiliation with the International Reading Association as evidence of their competence in reading.

Ethical Standards in Reading Services

1. Professionals in reading must possess suitable qualifications for engaging in consulting, clinical, or remedial work. Unqualified persons should not engage in such activities except under the direct supervision of one who is properly qualified. Professional intent and the welfare of the person seeking services should govern all consulting or clinical activities such as counseling, administering diagnostic tests, or providing remediation. It is the duty of the professional in reading to keep relationships with clients and interested persons on a professional level.
2. Information derived from consulting and/or clinical services should be regarded as confidential. Expressed consent of persons involved should be secured before releasing information to outside agencies.
3. Professionals in reading should recognize the boundaries of their competence and should not offer services which fail to meet professional standards established by other disciplines. They should be free, however, to give assistance in other areas in which they are qualified.
4. Referral should be made to specialists in allied fields as needed. When such referral is made, pertinent information should be made available to consulting specialists.
5. Reading clinics and/or reading professionals offering services should refrain from guaranteeing easy solutions or favorable outcomes as a result of their work, and their advertising should be consistent with that of allied professions. They should not accept for remediation any persons who are unlikely to benefit from their instruction, and they should work to accomplish the greatest possible improvement in the shortest time. Fees, if charged, should be agreed on in advance and should be charged in accordance with an established set of rates commensurate with that of other professions.

Breaches of the Code of Ethics should be reported to IRA Headquarters for referral to the Committee on Professional Standards and Ethics for an impartial investigation.

IRA Code of Ethics, *The Reading Teacher,* November 1987, p. 143. Reprinted by permission of the International Reading Association.

CHAPTER SUMMARY

In the first section of this chapter we described the various roles that literacy professionals are expected to perform. These range from direct instructional contact with students to consultative roles with teachers. We noted that these critical roles all share a common requirement for effective communication. We argued that literacy leaders must be able to interact with a wide array of people, sharing information and advocating effective assessment and instructional practices.

We described several modes for reporting including summaries of portfolios and the most formal type of communication, case reports. We detailed the contents of a formal case report, using the case of Marvin (see earlier chapters) to exemplify each section. These sections include descriptions of background information, summaries of assessment information, descriptions and reports of the results of diagnostic teaching, a diagnostic summary statement, and recommendations for instruction. In addition to formal case reports, we described progress reports, noting the similarities and differences between various reporting forms. Finally, we described the role of conferences in the reporting process.

In the final portion of this chapter, we presented the International Reading Association Code of Ethics. Several aspects of this code were elaborated to focus on issues of particular importance to professionals who work with disabled students.

Sample Case Report: Seth

COLLEGE OF EDUCATION READING CLINIC PROGRESS REPORT

Name: Seth C. *Date of Report*: May 19, 1986

Address: Route 390
            Pleasantville, Vermont

Phone: 624–0111

Birthdate: 6/26/76

Age: 9 years *Grade*: 3 (R1) *School Name*: Pleasantville Elementary

School Address: Pleasantville, Vermont

Parent's/Guardian's Name: Mr. & Mrs. C.

Tutor: W. Jorgan

Attendance for Tutoring

A. *Times present*: 12
B. *Times absent*: 12
C. *Reasons for absences*: NA
D. *Attitude toward tutoring*: Seth appears highly motivated to work hard in those areas where he feels he is competent and/or where he is succeeding. Seth appears tired much of the time. He yawned several times during the classroom observation and yawns and rubs his eyes three to five times during each clinic session. Seth is an open and friendly child who smiles often, is animated in discussions, makes eye contact when working with the examiner, and likes to laugh.

SUMMARY OF ASSESSMENT RESULTS

Dolch Word List (2–27–86)
    Post Test (4–24–86) — *Recognized 192/220*
     — *Recognized 196/220*

Peabody Picture Vocabulary
    Test (form M) — *Standard Score Equivalent: 95*
    Date of Testing: 2–13–86 — *Percentile Rank: 37*
    Age: 9 years, 8 months — *Age Equivalent: 8 years, 11 months*

El Paso Phonics Survey — *Frustrational level errors: 2.9*
    Date of Testing: 2–20–86 — *Level 1.9 errors: 19/30*
    Post Test (4–24–86) — *Retest of skills taught at grade 1.9: 22/30 correct*

Analytical Reading Inventory
    by Mary Lynn Woods and
    Alden J. Moe — *Instructional: primer–1*
    Date of Testing: 2–6–86 — *Frustrational: 2*
     — *Hearing Capacity: 2*

Durrell Analysis of Reading Difficulty:
    Visual Memory of Words Subtest
    Date of Testing: 2–20–86 — *Low second grade*

Auditory Discrimination of Pairs (Bader)
    Date of Testing: 2–13–86 — *29/30 items correct (competent)*

Hearing Letter Names in Sounds (Bader)
    Date of Testing: 2–13–86 — *9/12 items correct (competent)*

Woodcock Reading Mastery Tests (Form B)

	Relative Mastery	*Percentile Rank*
Letter Identification	93%	58
Word Identification	7%	10
Word Attack	32%	9
Word Comprehension	55%	15
Passage Comprehension	29%	8

Specified Areas of Reading Difficulty: Despite a reading expectancy of 4.1, Seth demonstrates difficulty in skills taught as early as first grade. Specific areas needing attention are vowels, reversals, visual discrimination, blending, sight words, fluency in oral reading, the graphemes *g, ch, sch, sp, str, squ, spl, qu,* and *s,* ending consonant sounds, and comprehension strategies.

BACKGROUND INFORMATION

Reason for Referral

Seth's reading level is considerably below his grade placement. The Chapter 1 reading teacher in Seth's school requested that Seth be tested for further data and insight.

Family and Medical History

Seth lives at home with both parents, who are farmers. When asked to tell the examiner something about himself, the first thing Seth mentioned was that he lived on a farm. At the beginning of nearly every clinic session, when asked how he's been doing, Seth invariably tells a story about something that has happened on the farm. Seth's primary interest beyond the farm is his four-wheeler; the friend he plays with most is a 12-year-old from down the road with whom he rides his four-wheeler. Seth has mentioned special days he has spent in the fields and woods as well.

Seth says that he doesn't like television that much; he says that he doesn't like "being cooped up" and would rather play outside. He watches television about 1/2 hour after school and 1 to 1-1/2 hours in the evenings—usually movies on his VCR.

Seth indicated that no one in his family reads and that only occasionally does either his mother or his sister read to him. Despite this, there is obvious concern about Seth's reading difficulties on the part of the family, and the commitment that they have made to drive him the considerable distance to the clinic each week is indicative of this. In addition, the interview with Seth's mother and sister revealed that despite Seth's contention that he does not read at home, he has been reading as part of a Pizza Hut promotion, his family is aware of his favorite kind of book, he does read a farm journal occasionally, and he receives *Humpty-Dumpty* magazine.

Seth was 11-1/2 pounds at birth and several weeks late. Forceps were used as a result of a difficult delivery, pinching nerves in his left arm. It is shorter than the right arm, and because of a lack of mobility, he receives physical therapy. Beyond this, Seth's health has been normal except for a series of ear infections suffered during his first year in the first grade. Tubes were inserted to rectify his problems.

Seth goes to bed between 8:00 and 8:30 on weeknights and gets up at 7:00. He goes to sleep with the radio playing.

School History and Teacher Comments

Seth is in a third-grade classroom with Mrs. Garvey, an experienced teacher who replaced Seth's regular teacher when the latter went on maternity leave in February. Seth repeated first grade after a difficult year of health and academic problems. Mr. Williams, the Chapter 1 reading teacher with whom Seth works, feels that the phonetic approach used by Seth's teacher that first year was inappropriate, given Seth's ear problems. Presently, Seth receives help from Mr. Williams in reading and math.

Mrs. Garvey reports that Seth seems much younger than the other children in the class and that he sometimes asks questions or makes comments that are "babyish"; she says at times even the other children react negatively to his immaturity. She feels that Seth acts "cute" when he can't do something or wants help. Seth is required to complete all assigned tasks before going out to recess. Mrs. Garvey reports that he really likes recess and doesn't like to miss it.

SUMMARY OF ASSESSMENT RESULTS

Reader Factors

On the Metropolitan Achievement Tests (most recently administered in Seth's school in the fall of 1985), Seth scored in the first percentile in reading comprehension. No other subtest scores were available.

Seth underwent an extensive psychoeducational evaluation in November, 1985, at the request of the Special Educator at his school. The results of the Weschler Intelligence Scale for Children—Revised (WISC-R) indicate a Full Scale score of 88. Results of the Bender Visual Motor Gestalt Test and the Visual Aural Digit Span Test appear to demonstrate a preference for visual processing; however, his score on the former reflects a slightly more than one-year delay, and his scores on visual processing subtests of the latter placed him in the 25th to 50th percentile.

Seth's standard score equivalent on the Peabody Picture Vocabulary Test (PPVT) was 95, and, consistent with the WISC-R results, his score places Seth in the low-average to average range of ability.

Observations made by the examiner during the administration of the Analytic Reading Inventory indicate that Seth only sporadically attempts to construct meaning from the text. On a primer-level selection, Seth omitted the word "I" at the beginning of three different sentences, rendering them semantically and syntactically incorrect. Other miscues as early as the primer level reflect an inattention to meaning; for example, "I can run as fast as a turn (train)."

Some miscues, however, do reflect an effort on Seth's part to construct meaning from the passage. This was particularly evident on a passage about a boy's dog being hit by a car. "Hit" was misread as "hurt" twice, "pup lying" became "puppy laying," and "badly hurt" was misread as "belly hurt." On this selection, Seth's miscues (16) rendered a score of frustrational level. However, he had only two comprehension errors, both of which may be construed as logical, based on Seth's experience. When asked how the child felt seeing his pet hurt, Seth answered "sad" (the correct answer being "scared"). In answer to the question "What does the child say to make you think he loved the dog?" Seth answered, "I'll hurry right home" (to get help for the dog). The writers of the inventory consider the answer to be "Shep is my best friend."

The nature of many of Seth's miscues on this story and his level of comprehension appear to be a result of the structure and content of the story. Both primer-level selections and one of the first-grade passages appear to begin in the middle of stories; they lack a strong structure and interesting plot. The story about the dog getting hit by a car (Level 2) had no clear resolution, but elements of the story (i.e., the subject, the clear statement of a problem, Seth's ability to relate to a child with a hurt pet) may have encouraged him to construct meaning from it. Seth's other strong comprehension performance was on a Level 1 passage with a clear story line (about a child who brings home stray animals) and a conclusion (his mother puts a halt to it). Not only did Seth answer four out of six questions competently, he retold the story in detail and made a well-formulated statement of the main idea.

Despite Seth's performance on the second-grade passage about the hurt dog, the examiner weighed the large number of miscues (16) as well as his comprehension on a second-grade passage that he read silently (42%) to determine this level as frustrational. Seth's listening level was determined by weighing his answers to traditional postreading questions and the quality of his retellings. Seth was tested at the third-grade level twice. In both cases, he answered a percentage of questions correctly, which placed this level on the instructional/frustrational border for him. However, his retellings in both cases lacked organization and missed the main ideas. Based on this, the examiner determined Seth's instructional listening level to be second-grade.

Analysis of Seth's miscues reveals strong attention to initial letters, i.e., *hit-hurt* (with any pair of words or phrases listed in this case report, the first word or phrase will represent the text and the second will represent Seth's word calling). Other miscues demonstrate use of both beginning and ending sounds (*drop-drip, thud-tried, anyway-always*). Seth also appears to rearrange letters in the medial portions of words to create new words (*felt-flat, still-sitting, train-turn*). Miscues on the Word Identification subtest of the Woodcock Reading Mastery Tests (WRMT) reflect these patterns as well (*grow-grew, happen-hope, heart-hurt*).

Except for the Letter Identification subtest, all of the other subtests of the WRMT indicate that Seth is far below the norm in these tasks. Seth's Word comprehension score reveals this as an area of some strength. Seth's only errors prior to reaching a ceiling level were with analogies in which Seth could not read one or more of the words. For diagnostic purposes, the examiner gave Seth those words. In all cases, Seth was able to complete the analogies. The results of the Passage Comprehension subtest confirm observations made by the examiner during clinic sessions. The cloze exercise requiring Seth to use context to determine the meanings of words is especially difficult for him.

Word analysis skills were tested with two different instruments. The results of both the Word Attack subtest of the WRMT and the El Paso Phonics Survey indicate difficulties in a number of decoding skills. The validity of tests requiring children to read nonsense words has been questioned, and indeed, Seth did miscall a number of the nonsense words as legitimate words. A second weakness of the testing situation—the tendency for Seth's eyes to wander to letters above and below the word which he was reading—was eliminated when the El Paso Phonics Survey was readministered with the words written on cards.

Despite the drawbacks of these kinds of tests, the skill difficulties that surfaced consistently are worth noting. Although Seth is capable of reading the phonograms *up, in,* and *am,* in four out of twenty-two cases he had difficulty blending one of these with an initial consonant. Vowels, both long and short, surfaced as an area of weakness for Seth on the Word Attack subtest of the WRMT. Other error patterns include adding an *m* before a final *p* (*shup-shump*), changing the initial sound entirely despite a correct pronunciation of it prior to word analysis (*quam-cume*), adding ending consonants (*blin-blant*), and separating the letters of blends (*plip-pilip*). It should be noted, however, that Seth performed accurately on 26/32 blends taught as late as Grade 3.5.

The Visual memory subtest of the Durrell Analysis of Reading Difficult (DARD) reveals a weakness in visual memory and discrimination (level attained: low second-grade). This weakness is evident in other areas of Seth's reading. The reading inventory miscues noted earlier which appear to be a rearrangement of letters (*felt-flat*), as well as several on the Dolch Word List (*could-cloud*), may be evidence of a visual memory problem, as are miscues such as *plip-pilip*. Seth says he prefers to read with his finger underlining the words; he missed entire lines on the reading inventories, thus adding additional support to the suggestion that he has difficulty with visual discrimination and tracking.

The Bader auditory tests were administered because of Seth's history of ear problems. No deficiencies in discrimination surfaced.

A second testing of the Dolch Word List demonstrated that Seth lacks automaticity on many of the words which he read correctly on the first testing. Although he had only twenty-four errors on the second testing, eighteen of these were not repeat errors.

Instructional Factors

Seth receives instruction both in a regular classroom and in a Chapter I reading program outside the classroom. Seth is not part of a regular reading group within the classroom, although workbook tasks are assigned frequently. He is rarely expected to read full-length texts in either setting. In the Chapter I classroom, his reading instruction has focused largely on word analysis and work is assigned from a program that emphasized visual and auditory perception of letter clusters in words. The method of instruction used by this particular program emphasized the analysis of words into their constituent parts.

The classroom teacher indicated Seth was responsible for the same assigned work required of all other children in the class, and that there was no differentiation of tasks among students. The language arts, spelling, and social studies books used in Seth's classroom are standard third-grade texts with readability estimates ranging from a 2.5 to a 5.0 grade level. Seth is expected to complete all classroom assignments before going to recess. The teacher reported that Seth really likes recess and does not like to miss it, although he frequently does because his work is incomplete.

The examiner observed Seth in his classroom for approximately one hour on April 7, 1986. At the beginning of the observation period, Mrs. Garvey was phasing children into a painting project. Seth was one of the first students done with his project. While the majority of the class continued to paint, Seth washed his hands and returned to his desk.

Throughout the period during which Seth painted, as well as during the work period, no other children initiated an interaction with him. Seth appears to enjoy the other children, often responding and laughing at general comments made by others to the group as a whole.

Only occasionally did Seth look up from his work after returning to his desk. Six children were coloring on the floor near him, two children were painting at the table behind him, and except for three other children working, the rest of the class was engaging in one of these activities around the room. Despite the noise level and the proximity of two groups of children chatting, Seth seemed undistracted.

Although Seth appears to work well independently, he is very reliant on his teacher. He asks questions frequently, requiring her help on nearly every individual task on which the examiner observed him working.

DIAGNOSTIC TEACHING

Using three different approaches to instruction and three groups of five words, Seth was systematically taught to recognize the words instantly. The instructional sequence was timed to determine how long it took under each set of instructional circumstances for him to learn the five words in each set. He was retested on these words after 1-1/2 hours to see how many he had retained from each sequence. Thus, both effectiveness and efficiency were evaluated. Finally, Seth was asked to tell which method he thought had been most effective for him.

At delayed retesting, Seth knew all 15 new words at sight (2-second flash). Thus, all three instructional approaches were equally effective. However, using one approach he learned the five new words in 1-1/2 minutes, whereas, using a different approach, it took ten minutes for him to learn the words! In terms of efficiency, Seth is likely to benefit from a phonics program that blends parts into wholes, as opposed to a phonics program that breaks the whole into component parts. It should be noted, however, that he learned the words with equal ease when they were presented as sight words. The approach that was least efficient for Seth was the whole-to-part phonics approach, similar to his current instructional program. Seth's perception confirmed these conclusions. He felt he had learned the words most easily in the part-to-whole phonics approach.

In order to clarify issues related to approach and content, we initiated a language experience activity designed to allow Seth to read and write about topics of interest to him. During the first diagnostic teaching segment we were chagrined to find that, while Seth was enthusiastic about discussing a personal encounter with a "coydog" (half dog, half coyote), the story he dictated was sparse and incoherent. Subsequent work with a conference partner did nothing to improve the quality of the product. Two additional trials, yielding similar results, led to the conclusion that this was not the most effective method for improving Seth's word recognition or comprehension skills at the present time.

DIAGNOSTIC STATEMENTS
AND SUGGESTIONS FOR INSTRUCTION

Structuring concepts for Seth will be valuable in all remedial activities. Evidence indicates that he is not grasping the "whole" and that "parts-to-whole" instruction may be helpful in improving comprehension as well. Seth needs to acquire a *story schema*, including a knowledge of story grammar. By focusing Seth's attention on the elements of story structure with prereading and postreading questions and activities, he will begin to acquire a sense of the parts of a well-written story. Given Seth's limited independent reading, it is suggested that this be done initially with books read aloud by the teacher.

Another vehicle for structuring reading selections for Seth is concept mapping. This spatial visualization task may fit his learning style, given his preference for visual processing as indicated on the psychoeducational report. A variety of models exist. For story structure, a map can be constructed to show the flow of the problem/resolution pattern, completed initially with teacher direction. Other models can be specifically used to map expository writing. Mapping can also be used to help Seth structure his own writing. As with expository maps, he could begin with his superordinate concept and extend his map with subordinate details.

To further expand instruction in the concept of the whole as a sum of its parts, *writing* can be taught through conventional parts of a piece of writing. In the clinic Seth has generated ideas for a piece of writing through discussion with the examiner. After Seth has written what he believes is a finished product, the examiner rewrites it with an introduction, episode, and conclusion. It is read to Seth and the parts of a strong piece of writing are discussed, as is the importance of writing for an audience. One of the examiner-written parts is then excluded and Seth composes that part. This process is continued until Seth has rewritten the entire piece within this framework. Thus far, it has been a successful technique, although repetition and reinforcement are indicated. Seth's revisions have become more detailed, but his initial drafts are still only two or three sentences about the episode.

Of extreme importance are instructional programs that would teach Seth to think about what he is reading. By attending to the meaning of what he is reading, Seth will correct miscues that are not appropriate to the text. A number of strategies can be employed to improve Seth's *thinking/reading skills*. Think-Aloud, a program which requires the reader to discuss what s/he is thinking about while reading, has been used, as have teacher-directed cloze activities. Cloze exercises that are guided and directed by the teacher will encourage Seth to look for contextual cues for a word that he doesn't know, improve his understanding of the structure of language, inform the teacher of his instructional needs, and allow the teacher to provide activities that are specifically designed to fill those needs.

In addition to monitoring his reading comprehension, Seth needs to attend to the word display. An analysis of Seth's errors on the El Paso Phonics Survey indicated that at times he retrieves letters from lines above and below where he is reading. Specific decoding exercises that require that Seth attend to the symbols and sounds will provide less opportunity for his eyes to wander. Although such procedures defy common views of reading as holistic, Seth's lack of progress and his demonstrated difficulties with the whole (both words and concepts) indicate that a parts-to-whole approach may be appropriate.

Seth's concept of reading and of himself as a reader would improve with more *fluency* in his oral reading. In addition, fluency and phrasing facilitates comprehension by redirecting the child's focus from the individual words to the flow of writing as "talk written down." Neurological impress is a method for improving fluency with which Seth has met success in the clinic. He is anxious to try reading the practice passage himself and likes to bring it home to read to his parents. Also appended is an article describing ways to improve comprehension by using this technique.

As the test results indicate, Seth has specific areas of instructional need. His *sight vocabulary* is adequate, but the results of the posttest indicate a lack of automaticity on at least eighteen words (read correctly on the pretest but incorrectly on the posttest) in addition to the twenty-eight he missed on the pretest. It is critical in this, and in all of Seth's instruction, that a variety of techniques be employed. Initial presentation of each word should be in a variety of modes; Seth should say the word, write it, hear it said and used in a sentence, and use it himself. Suggesting that he note configuration and providing opportunities for him to experience the word kinesthetically (such as tracing or building the word) would also be helpful. Of particular value in the clinic has been the use of VAKT, a technique that will capitalize on Seth's preference for visual processing and help him to focus on the display of the word.

There are other methods which can encourage Seth to attend to all parts of the word. Because of the wide range of vowel errors, it is suggested that *vowel instruction* include all vowel sounds and be concurrent with instruction in *phonograms*. Activities should require Seth to say, hear, write, read, and feel the vowels and phonograms taught.

Seth's tendency to rearrange letters in the medial portions of words and add letters near the end suggests a need for instruction in structural analysis. Initially, instruction in this area needs to focus on the parts of simple words. Instruction could build on vowel and phonogram instruction with the teacher asking Seth to identify in what part of a word he hears a sound (i.e., when teaching the long *o* have him hold up a card with the word *middle* on it to demonstrate that he heard the *o* in the middle of the word *boat*). Written exercises can be designed on this same premise.

Seth's miscues indicate that he lacks skill in *blending*. While teaching any of the skill areas, the teacher could include activities that provide practice in blending the sound taught to produce a word. Many enjoyable and productive oral and kinesthetic activities can be employed to aid Seth in learning to blend all parts of a word. The teacher can point to each part of a word, having Seth say and hold the sound represented until the teacher moves his/her finger to the next word part. Letters could be placed on the floor and Seth could "skate" from one phoneme of a word to the next while saying the word aloud. These and other activities would be especially beneficial when teaching Seth vowels and *ending consonant sounds* that testing identified as weak.

A technique that may be of benefit to Seth in seeing the whole and its parts is that of using one book in all reading exercises in a given day. There is added power in doing this. It will be easier for him to operate within a familiar and consistent context, and to be working on varying skills toward one purpose: to complete and understand the story.

SUGGESTIONS AND RECOMMENDATIONS

The above are specific skill areas in which Seth needs instruction. Other strategies can be employed both in school and at home to improve his reading.

1. The lack of self-reliance that Seth demonstrated in the classroom indicates a need to provide assignments and tasks on which he can become self-directed. Seth must fulfill the high standards set for him; however, he will benefit from a quantity of work that he can complete and a level of work at which he can succeed.
2. An accompanying shift of responsibility to Seth at home may benefit him. Perhaps he could do more chores in the barn or around the house to help build an image of himself as a mature and helpful member of the family.
3. Goal-setting is a technique that might be employed to encourage responsibility for himself and his work at both school and home. If Seth is exhibiting difficulty in completing tasks, he can set a goal for himself (i.e., finishing a number of math problems before recess).
4. Seth should be encouraged to use a marker when reading, to limit the distraction of extraneous print.
5. As noted above, Seth will benefit tremendously from using one book in all reading exercises in a given day.
6. Seth needs help choosing books that are appropriate for his reading ability and interests. His performance on the passage about a dog who gets hit by a car indicates an interest in exciting stories that he can relate to personally. In conversations with the examiner Seth had indicated an interest in horse stories as well. These interests are one of Seth's strengths in reading, a major part of what he brings to the process, and it will be to his benefit to capitalize on them.
7. Seth needs more exposure to reading and language. At home this could be accomplished by trips to the library, a family "reading time," and a time during which Seth is read to daily. It is recommended that Seth be read to daily at school as well. Only with repeated exposure to story structure will Seth utilize it as a comprehension strategy.

8. Seth's parents may employ the Talking Dictionary approach to oral reading. Seth enjoyed his success in this activity at the clinic and loved to graph his progress.

9. It is recommended that Seth go to bed earlier. He seemed very tired in school and at the clinic. It is also recommended that Seth receive complete physical and eye examinations. Some of his fatigue may be due to health problems.

10. It is recommended that objectives be stated for Seth. He will benefit from clear direction in instruction.

Seth brings to the reading process specific interests and a positive attitude toward most tasks asked of him. The examiner believes that with opportunities to succeed, more exposure to literature that meets his interests, and most importantly, a unified instruction plan across all of Seth's academics, his reading will improve.

_____   _____
Clinician   Date

Award-Winning Books for Children and Youth

CALDECOTT MEDAL WINNERS (1961–1995)

The Caldecott Medal has been awarded since 1938 by the American Library Association. It is awarded to the most distinguished picture book for children and honors the illustrators of these books.

1995   *Smoky Night*. David Diaz. San Diego: Harcourt, 1994.

1994   *Grandfather's Journey*. Allen Say. Boston: Houghton Mifflin, 1993.

1993   *Mirette on the High Wire*. Arnold McCulty. New York: Putnam, 1992.

1992   *Tuesday*. David Wiesner. New York: Clarion. 1991.

1991   *Black and White*. David Macaulay. Boston: Houghton Mifflin, 1990.

1990   *Lon Po Po: A Red Riding Hood Story from China*. Ed Young. New York: Philomel, 1989.

1989   *Song and Dance Man*. Karen Ackerman. Illus. by Stephen Gammell. New York: Knopf, 1988.

1988   *Owl Moon*. Jane Yolen. Illus. by John Schoenherr. New York: Philomel, 1987.

1987   *Hey, Al*. Arthur Yorinks. Illus. by Richard Egielski. New York: Farrar, Straus and Giroux, 1986.

1986   *The Polar Express*. Chris Van Allsburg. Boston: Houghton Mifflin, 1985.

1985   *Saint George and the Dragon*. Retold by Margaret Hodges. Illus. by Tina Schart Hyman. Boston: Little, Brown, 1984.

1984   *The Glorious Flight: Across the Channel with Louis Bleriot*. Alice and Martin Provensen. New York: Viking, 1983.

1983   *Shadow*. Blaise Cendrars. Illus. by Marcia Brown. New York: Scribner's, 1982.

1982   *Jumanji*. Chris Van Allsburg. Boston: Houghton Mifflin, 1981.

1981   *Fables*. Arnold Lobel. New York: Harper & Row, 1980.

1980   *Ox-Cart Man.* Donald Hall. Illus. by Barbara Cooney. New York: Viking, 1979.

1979   *The Girl Who Loved Wild Horses.* Paul Goble. New York: Bradbury, 1978.

1978   *Noah's Ark.* Peter Spier. New York: Doubleday. 1977.

1977   *Ashanti to Zulu.* Margaret Musgrove. Illus. by Leo and Diane Dillon. New York: Dial, 1976.

1976   *Why Mosquitoes Buzz in People's Ears.* Verna Aardema. Illus. by Leo and Diane Dillon. New York: Dial, 1975.

1975   *Arrow to the Sun.* Gerald McDermott. New York: Viking, 1974.

1974   *Duffy and the Devil.* Retold by Harve Zemach. Illus. by Margot Zemach. New York: Farrar, Straus and Giroux, 1973.

1973   *The Funny Little Woman.* Retold by Arlene Mosel. Illus. by Blair Lent. New York: Dutton, 1972.

1972   *One Fine Day.* Nonny Hogrogian. New York: Macmillan, 1971.

1971   *A Story A Story.* Gail Haley. New York: Atheneum, 1970.

1970   *Sylvester and the Magic Pebble.* William Steig. New York: Windmill Books, 1969.

1969   *The Fool of the World and the Flying Ship.* Retold by Arthur Ransome. Illus. by Uri Shulevitz. New York: Farrar, Straus and Giroux, 1968.

1968   *Drummer Hoff.* Adapted by Barbara Emberley. Illus. by Ed Emberley. Englewood Cliffs, N.J.: Prentice-Hall, 1967.

1967   *Sam, Bangs, and Moonshine.* Evaline Ness. New York: Holt, Rinehart and Winston, 1966.

1966   *Always Room for One More.* Sorche Nic Leodhas. Illus. by Nonny Hogrogian. New York: Holt, Rinehart and Winston, 1965.

1965   *May I Bring a Friend?* Beatrice Schenk de Regniers. Illus. by Beni Montresor. New York: Atheneum, 1964.

1964   *Where the Wild Things Are.* Maurice Sendak. New York: Harper & Row, 1963.

1963   *The Snowy Day.* Ezra Jack Keats. New York: Viking, 1962.

1962   *Once a Mouse.* Marcia Brown. New York: Scribner's, 1961.

1961   *Baboushka and the Three Kings.* Ruth Robbins. Illus. by Nicholas Sidjakov. Orleans, Mass.: Parnassus, 1960.

NEWBERY MEDAL WINNERS (1961–1995)

The Newbery Medal is awarded each year by the American Library Association. Since 1922 this medal has been awarded to honor the author of the book that is deemed to be the most distinguished contribution to children's literature.

1995   *Walk Two Moons.* Sharon Creech. New York: Harper Collins, 1994.

1994   *The Giver.* Lois Lowry. Boston: Houghton Mifflin, 1993.

1993   *Missing May.* Cynthia Rylant. New York: Orchard, 1992.

1992   *Shiloh.* Phyllis Reynolds Naylor. New York: Atheneum, 1991.

1991   *Maniac Magee*. Jerry Spinelli. Boston: Little, Brown, 1990.

1990   *Number the Stars*. Lois Lowry. Boston: Houghton Mifflin, 1989.

1989   *Joyful Noise: Poems for Two Voices*. Paul Fleischman. New York: Harper & Row, 1988.

1988   *Lincoln: A Photobiography*. Russell Freedman. Boston: Houghton Mifflin, 1987.

1987   *The Whipping Boy*. Sid Fleischman. New York: Greenwillow, 1986.

1986   *Sarah, Plain and Tall*. Patricia MacLachlan. New York: Harper & Row, 1985.

1985   *The Hero and the Crown*. Robin McKinley. New York: Greenwillow, 1984.

1984   *Dear Mr. Henshaw*. Beverly Cleary. New York: William Morrow, 1983.

1983   *Dicey's Song*. Cynthia Voigt. New York: Atheneum, 1982.

1982   *A Visit to William Blake's Inn: Poems for Innocent and Experienced Travelers*. Nancy Willard. New York: Harcourt Brace Jovanovich, 1981.

1981   *Jacob Have I Loved*. Katherine Paterson. New York: Crowell, 1980.

1980   *A Gathering of Days*. Joan Blos. New York: Scribner's, 1979.

1979   *The Westing Game*. Ellen Raskin. New York: Dutton, 1978.

1978   *Bridge to Terabithia*. Katherine Paterson. New York: Crowell, 1977.

1977   *Roll of Thunder, Hear My Cry*. Mildred D. Taylor. New York: Dial, 1976.

1976   *The Grey King*. Susan Cooper. New York: Atheneum, 1975.

1975   *M. C. Higgins, the Great*. Virginia Hamilton. New York: Macmillan, 1974.

1974   *The Slave Dancer*. Paula Fox. New York: Bradbury, 1973.

1973   *Julie of the Wolves*. Jean Craighead George. New York: Harper & Row, 1972.

1972   *Mrs. Frisby and the Rats of NIMH*. Robert O'Brien. New York: Atheneum, 1971.

1971   *Summer of the Swans*. Betsy Byars. New York: Viking, 1970.

1970   *Sounder*. William H. Armstrong. New York: Harper & Row, 1969.

1969   *The High King*. Lloyd Alexander. New York: Holt, Rinehart and Winston, 1968.

1968   *From the Mixed-up Files of Mrs. Basil E. Frankweiler*. E. L. Konigsburg. New York: Atheneum. 1967.

1967   *Up a Road Slowly*. Irene Hunt. Chicago: Follett, 1966.

1966   *I, Juan de Pareja*. Elizabeth Borton de Trevino. New York: Farrar, Straus and Giroux, 1965.

1965   *Shadow of a Bull*. Maia Wojciechowska. New York: Atheneum, 1964.

1964   *It's Like This, Cat*. Emily Neville. New York: Harper & Row, 1963.

1963   *A Wrinkle in Time*. Madeleine L'Engle. New York: Farrar, Straus and Giroux, 1962.

1962   *The Bronze Bow*. Elizabeth George Speare. Boston: Houghton Mifflin, 1961.

1961   *Island of the Blue Dolphins*. Scott O'Dell. Boston: Houghton Mifflin, 1960.

CORETTA SCOTT KING AWARD (1970–1995)

This award was established in 1969 "to commemorate the life and works of the late Dr. Martin Luther King, Jr; to honor Mrs. King for her courage to continue to fight for peace and world brotherhood; to encourage creative artists and authors to promote the cause of brotherhood through their work; and to inspire children and youth to dedicate their talents and energies to help achieve these goals." The award is presented annually. Since 1979, an additional award has been presented for illustration.

1970   *Martin Luther King, Jr.: Man of Peace*. Lillie Patterson. Illus. by Victor Mays.

1971   *Black Troubadour: Langston Hughes*. Charlemane Rollins.

1972   *Seventeen Black Artists*. Elton Clay Fax. Illus. with photographs.

1973   *I Never Had It Made*. Jackie Robinson as told to Alfred Duckett.

1974   *Ray Charles*. Sharon Bell Mathis. Illus. by George Ford.

1975   *The Legend of Africania*. Dorothy Robinson. Illus. by Herbert Temple.

1976   *Duey's Tale*. Pearl Bailey. Photographs by Arnold Skolnick and Gary Azon.

1977   *The Story of Stevie Wonder*. James Haskins. Illus. with photographs.

1978   *African Dream*. Eloise Greenfield. Illus. by Carole Byard.

1979   *Escape to Freedom: A Play About Young Frederick Douglass*. Ossie Davis.

1979   Special Award for Illustration
      Something on My Mind. Nikki Grimes. Illus. by Tom Feelings.

1980   Author
      The Young Landlords. Walter Dean Myers.

1980   Illustration
      Cornrows. Camille Yarbrough. Illus. by Carole Byard.

1981   Author
      This Life. Sidney Poitier.

1981   Illustration
      Beat the Story-drum, Pum-pum. Written and illus. by Ashley Bryan.

1982   Author
      Sweet Whispers, Brother Rush. Virginia Hamilton.

1982   Author Honorable Mention
      This Strange New Feeling. Julius Lester.

1982   Illustration
      Black Child. Written and photographed by Peter Magubane.

1983   Author
      Let the Circle Be Unbroken. Mildred D. Taylor.

1983   Illustration
      Mother Crocodile—Maman-Caiman. Birango Diop. Trans. and adapted by Rosa Guy. Illus. by John Steptoe.

1984   Author
      Everett Anderson's Goodbye. Lucille Clifton. Illus. by Ann Grifalconi.

1984   Illustration
My Mama Needs Me. Mildred Pitts Walter. Illus. by Pat Cummings.

1984   Honorable Mention
Because We Are. Mildred Pitts Walter.
Bright Shadow. Joyce Carol Thomas.
Lena Horne. James Haskins. Illus. with photographs.
The Magical Adventures of Pretty Pearl. Virginia Hamilton.

1984   Special Citation
The Words of Martin Luther King, Jr. Selected by Coretta Scott King.

1985   Literature
Motown and Didi. Walter Dean Myers.

1985   Literature Honorable Mention
Little Love. Virginia Hamilton.
The Circle of Gold. Candy Dawson Boyd.

1985   Illustration
No Award.

1986   Literature
The People Could Fly. Virginia Hamilton. Illus. by Leo and Diane Dillon.

1986   Literature Honorable Mention
Junius Over Far. Virginia Hamilton.
Trouble's Child. Mildred Pitts Walter.

1986   Illustration
The Patchwork Quilt. Valerie Fluornoy. Illus. by Jerry Pinkney.

1986   Illustration Honorable Mention
The People Could Fly. Virginia Hamilton. Illus. by Leo and Diane Dillon.

1987   Literature
Justin and the Best Biscuits in the World. Mildred Pitts Walter. Illus. by Catherine Stock.

1987   Literature Honorable Mention
Which Way Freedom? Joyce Hansen.
The Lion and the Ostrich Chicks. Written and illus. by Ashley Bryan.

1987   Illustration
Half a Moon and One Whole Star. Crescent Dragonwagon. Illus. by Jerry Pinkney.

1987   Illustration Honorable Mention
C.L.O.U.D.S. Written and illus. by Pat Cummings.

1988   Literature
The Friendship. Mildred Taylor. Illus. by Max Ginsburg.

1988   Illustration
Mufaro's Beautiful Daughters. Written and illus. by John Steptoe.

1989   Literature
Fallen Angels. Walter Dean Myers.

1989   Illustration
Mirandy and Brother Wind. Patricia McKissack. Illus. by Jerry Pinkney.

1990 Literature
A Long Hard Journey. Patricia and Frederick McKissack.

1990 Illustration
Nathaniel Talking. Eloise Greenfield. Illus. by Jan Gilchrist.

1991 Literature
The Road to Memphis. Mildred D. Taylor.

1991 Illustration
Aida. Illus. by Leo and Diane Dillon.

1992 Literature
Now Is Your Time! The African American Struggle for Freedom. Walter Dean Myers.

1992 Illustration
Tar Beach. Faith Ringgold

1993 Literature
The Dark-Thirty. Patricia McKissack.

1993 Illustration
The Origin of Life on Earth. Illus. by Kathleen Atkins Wilson (retold by D. Anderson).

1994 Literature
Toning the Sweep. Angela Johnson.

1994 Illustration
Soul Looks Back in Wonder. Illus. by Tom Feelings.

1995 Literature
Christmas in the Big House, Christmas in the Quarters. Patricia C. and Frederick L. McKissack.

1995 Illustration
The Creation. Illus. by James E. Ransome (written by Weldon Johnson).

JANE ADDAMS CHILDREN'S BOOK AWARD WINNERS (1953–1994)

This award is presented annually for the book that "best promotes peace, dignity, and equality for all people, as well as social justice." The award was created in 1953 by the U.S. section of the Women's International League for Peace and Freedom to honor Jane Addams.

1953 *People Are Important*. Eva Knox Evans. Illus. by Vana Earle.

1954 *Stick-in-the-Mud: A Tale of a Village, a Custom and a Little Boy*. Jean Ketchum. Illus. by Fred Ketchum.

1955 *Rainbow Around the World: A Story of UNICEF*. Elizabeth Yates. Illus. by Betty Alden and Dirk Gringhuis.

1956 *Story of the Negro*. Arna Wendell Bontemps. Illus. by Raymond Lufkin.

1957 *Blue Mystery*. Margaret Benary Isbert. Trans. by Clara and Richard Winston. Illus. by Enrico Arno.

1958   *The Perilous Road.* William O. Steele. Illus. by Paul Galdone.

1959   No Award.

1960   *Champions of Peace: Winners of the Nobel Peace Prize.* Edith Patterson Meyer. Illus. by Eric von Schmidt.

1961   *What Then, Raman?* Shirlee Lease Arora. Illus. by Hans Guggenheim.

1962   *The Road to Agra.* Aimee Sommerfelt. Illus. by Ulf Aas.

1963   *The Monkey and the Wild, Wild Wind.* Ryerson Johnson. Illus. by Lois Lignell.

1964   *Profiles in Courage.* John F. Kennedy. Illus. by Emil Weiss.

1965   No Award.

1966   *Berries Goodman.* Emily Cheney Neville.

1967   *Queenie Peavy.* Robert Burch. Illus. by Jerry Lazare.

1968   *The Little Fishes.* Eric Christian Haugaard. Illus. by Milton Johnson.

1969   *The Endless Steppe: Growing Up in Siberia.* Esther Hautzig.

1970   No Award.

1971   *Jane Addams: Pioneer for Social Justice, a Biography.* Cornelia L. Meigs. Illus. with photographs.

1972   *The Tamarack Tree.* Mary Betty Underwood. Illus. by Bea Holmes.

1973   *The Riddle of Racism.* S. Carl Hirsch.

1973   Honor

        The Upstairs Room. Johanna Reiss.

1974   *Nilda.* Written and illus. by Nicholasa Mohr.

1974   Honor

        A Hero Ain't Nothing But a Sandwich. Alice Childress.
        Men Against War. Barbara Habenstreit.
        A Pocket Full of Seeds. Marilyn Sachs.

1975   *The Princess and the Admiral.* Charlotte Pomerantz. Illus. by Tony Chen.

1975   Honor

        My Brother Sam Is Dead. James Lincoln Collier and Christopher Collier.
        Viva La Raza! The Struggle of the Mexican-American People. Elizabeth Sunderland Martinez and Enriqueta Martinez.
        The Eye of Conscience. Milton Meltzer and Bernard Cole.

1976   *Paul Robeson.* Eloise Greenfield. Illus. by George Ford.

1976   Honor

        Song of the Trees. Mildred D. Taylor. Illus. by Jerry Pinkney.
        Dragonwings. Laurence Yep.
        Z for Zachariah. Robert C. O'Brien.

1977   *Never to Forget: The Jews of the Holocaust.* Milton Meltzer.

1977   Honor

        Roll of Thunder, Hear My Cry. Mildred D. Taylor. Illus. by Jerry Pinkney.

1978   *Child of the Owl.* Laurence Yep.

1978   Honor

        Mischling, Second Degree: My Childhood in Nazi Germany. Ilse Koehn.
        Alan and Naomi. Myron Levoy.

1978   Special Recognition
        Amifka. Lucille Clifton. Illus. by Thomas DeGrazia.
        The Wheel of King Asoka. Written and illus. by Ashok Davar.
1979   *Many Smokes, Many Moons: A Chronology of American Indian History Through Indian Art*. Jamake Highwater. Illus. with photographs.
1979   Honor
        Escape to Freedom: A Play About Young Frederick Douglass. Ossie Davis.
        The Great Gilly Hopkins. Katherine Paterson.
1980   *The Road from Home: The Story of an Armenian Girl*. David Kherdian.
1980   West Coast Honor Book
        Woman from Hiroshima. Toshio Mori.
1980   Special Recognition
        Natural History. Written and illus. by M.B. Goffstein.
1981   *First Woman in Congress: Jeanette Rankin*. Florence Meiman White.
1981   Honor
        Chase Me, Catch Nobody! Erik C. Haugaard.
        Doing Time: A Look at Crime and Prisons. Phyllis E. Clark and Robert Lehrman.
        We Are Mesquakie, We Are One. Hadley Irwin. Illus. with maps.
1982   *A Spirit to Ride the Whirlwind*. Athena V. Lord.
1982   Honor
        Lupita Manana. Patricia Beatty.
        Let the Circle Be Unbroken. Mildred D. Taylor.
1983   *Hiroshima No Pika*. Written and illus. by Toshi Maruki.
1983   Honor
        The Bomb. Sidney Lens. Illus. with photographs.
        If I Had a Paka: Poems in Eleven Languages. Charlotte Pomerantz. Illus by Nancy Tafuri.
1983   West Coast Honor Book
        All the Colors of the Race: Poems. Arnold Adoff. Illus. by John Steptoe.
        Children as Teachers of Peace, by our children. Ed. by Gerald G. Jampolsky. Forward by Hugh Prather.
1984   *Rain of Fire*. Marion Dane Bauer.
1985   *The Short Life of Sophie Scholl*. Hermann Vinke. Trans. by Hedwig Pachter.
1985   Honor
        The Island on Bird Street. Uri Orlev. Trans. by Hillel Halkin.
        Music, Music for Everyone. Written and illus. by Vera B. Williams.
1986   *Ain't Gonna Study War No More: The Story of America's Peace Seekers*. Milton Meltzer.
1986   Honor
        Journey to the Soviet Union. Samantha Smith. Illus. with photographs.
1987   *Nobody Wants a Nuclear War*. Written and illus. by Judith Vigna.
1987   Honor
        All in a Day. Written and illus. by Mitsumasa Anno.
        Children of the Maya: A Guatemalan Indian Odyssey. Brent Ashabranner. Photographs by Paul Conklin.

1988   *Waiting for the Rain: A Novel of South Africa*. Sheila Gordon.
1989   *Anthony Burns: The Defeat and Triumph of a Fugitive Slave*. Virginia Hamilton.
1989.   Honor
         Looking Out. Victoria Boutis.
1990   *Long Hard Journey: The Story of the Pullman Porter*. Patricia and Frederick McKissack.
1991   *The Big Book for Peace*. Ann Durell and Marilyn Sachs.
1992   *Journey of the Sparrows*. Fran Leeper Buss.
1993   *A Taste of Salt: A Story of Modern Haiti*. Frances Temple.
1994   *Kids at Work: Lewis Hine and the Crusade Against Child Labor*. Russell Freedman.

Resources for Multicultural Literature and Teaching

Anderson, V. (1994). *Native Americans in fiction: A guide to 765 books for librarians and teachers, K–9*. Jefferson, NC: MacFarland & Co., Inc.

Au, K. H. (1993). *Literacy instruction in multicultural settings*. Fort Worth, TX: Harcourt Brace Jovanovich.

Austin, M. C., & Jenkins, E. C. (1987). *Literature for children about Asians and Asian Americans*. New York: Greenwood Press.

Baker, G. C. (1994). *Planning and organizing for multicultural instruction* (2nd edition). Menlo Park, CA: Addison-Wesley.

Banks, J. A. (1994). *An introduction to multicultural education*. Needham Heights, MA: Allyn and Bacon.

Banks, J. A. (1991). *Teaching strategies for ethnic studies* (4th ed.). Needham Heights, MA: Allyn and Bacon.

Barrera, R. B. (1992). The Cultural gap in literature-based literacy instruction. *Education and Urban Society, 24*, 227–234.

Bennett, C. I. (1995). *Multicultural education: Theory and practice* (3rd edition). Boston: Allyn & Bacon.

Bielke, P. F., & Sciara, F. J. (1986). *Selecting materials for and about Hispanic and East Asian children and young people*. Hamden, CT. Library Professional Services.

Bishop, R. S. (1990). Walk tall in the world: African American literature for today's children. *Journal of Negro Education, 59* (4), 556–565.

Caldwell-Wood, N., & Mitten, A. (1991). *Selective Bibliography and Guide for "I" is not for Indian: The portrayal of Native Americans in books for young people*. Program of the ALA/OLOS Subcommittee for Library Services to American Indian People. Chicago: American Indian Library Association.

Cooperative Children's Book Center. (1991). Multicultural literature for children and young adults (3rd ed.). Madison: University of Wisconsin.

Crawford, L. W. (1993). *Language and literacy learning in multicultural classrooms*. Boston: Allyn & Bacon.

Diamond, B. J., & Moore, M. A. (1995). *Multicultural literacy: Mirroring the reality of the classroom*. White Plains, NY: Longman.

Garcia, J., Hadaway, N. L., & Beal, G. (1988). Cultural pluralism in recent nonfiction tradebooks for children. *The Social Studies, 79*, 252–255.

Grant, C. A. (Ed.) (1995). *Educating for diversity*. Boston: Allyn & Bacon.

Grant, C. A. (1991). *Reading in a pluralistic society: Concepts, models, strategies*. New York: Harper Collins.

Greenfield, E. (1985). Writing for children—A joy and responsibility. In D. MacCann & G. Woodard (Eds.), *The black American in books for children: Readings in racism* (2nd Ed.). Metchen, NJ: Scarecrow Press.

Harris, V. J. (1992). *Teaching multicultural literature in grades K–8*. Norwood, MA: Christopher Gordon.

Heath, S. B., & Mangiola, L. (1991). *Children of promise: Literate activity in linguistically and culturally diverse classrooms*. NEA.

Jenkins, E. C., & Austin, M. C. (1987). *Literature for children about Asians and Asian Americans*. New York: Greenwood Press.

Kiupers. B. J. (1995). *American Indians reference and resource books for children and young adults* (2nd ed.). Englewood, CO: Libraries Unlimited, Inc.

Lindgren, M. (Ed.) (1991). *The multicolored mirror: Cultural substance in literature for children and young adults*. Fort Atkinson, WI.

Loughlin, C., & Martin, M. (1987). *Supporting literacy*. Teachers College Press, 1987.

Martinez, J. A., & Lomeli, F. (Eds.). (1985). *Chicano literature: A reference guide*. Westport, CT: Greenwood Press.

Moore, R. B., & Hirschfelder, A. B. (1982). Feathers, tomahawks and tipis: A study of stereotyped "Indian" imagery in children's picture books. In A. B. Hirschfelder (Ed.), *American Indian stereotypes in the world of children: A reader and bibliography*. Metuchen, NJ: Scarecrow Press.

Multicultural Education, a quarterly magazine. Published by Caddo Gap Press, 3145 Geary Blvd., Ste. 275, San Francisco, CA 94118.

Myers, W. D. (1991).   *Now is your time! The African-American struggle for freedom*. New York: Harper Trophy.

Nieto, S. (1985). Children's literature on Puerto Rican themes. *Bulletin of the Council on Interracial Books for Children, 14* (1 & 2), 10–16.

Nieto, S. (1987). Self-affirmation or self-destruction? The image of Puerto Ricans in children's literature written in English. In A. Rodriguez de Lagun (Ed.), *Images and identities: The Puerto Rican in two world contexts*. New Jersey: Transaction Books.

Ogbu, J. U. (1992). Understanding cultural diversity and learning. *Educational Researcher,* (November), 5–14, 24.

Pang, V. O., Colvin, C., Tran, M., & Barba, R. H. (1992). Beyond chopsticks and dragons: Selecting Asian-American literature for children. *The Reading Teacher, 46*, 216–224.

Peterson, S. B., & Lach, M. A. (1990). Gender stereotypes in children's books: Their prevalence and influence on cognitive and affective development. *Gender and Education, 2*(2), 185–197.

Reimer, K. M. (1992). Multiethnic literature: Hold fast to dreams. *Language Arts, 69*, 14–21.

Roney, R. C. (1986). Multiethnicity in children's fiction. *Social Education, 50*, 464–466.

Rudman, M. K. (1984). *Children's literature: An issues approach* (2nd ed.). Lexington, MA: D. C. Heath.

Schon, I. (1989). Recent children's books about Hispanics. *Journal of Youth Services in Libraries, 2*(2), 157–162.

Shannon, P. (1986). Hidden within the pages: A study of social perspective in young children's favorite books. *The Reading Teacher, 39*, 656–663.

Simonson, R., & Walker, S. (Eds.) (1988). *The Graywolf annual five: Multicultural literacy*. St. Paul, MN: Graywolf Press.

Sims, R. (1982). *Shadow and substance: Afro-American experience in contemporary children's books*. Urbana, IL: NCTE.

Slapin, B., & Seale, D. (Eds.) (1992). *Through Indian eyes: The native experience in books for children*. Philadelphia: New Society Publishers.

Slapin, B., Seale, D., & Gonzales, R. (1989). *How to tell the difference: A checklist for evaluating Native American children's books*. Berkeley, CA: Oyate.

Smith, H. M. (1994). *The Coretta Scott King Awards Book: From vision to reality*. Chicago: American Library Association.

Smith, N. J., Greenlaw, M. J., & Scott, C. J. (1987). Making the literate environment equitable. *The Reading Teacher, 40,* 400–407.

Stoll, D. R. (Ed.)(1990). *Magazines for Children*. Educational Press Association of America and the International Reading Association.

Takaki, R. (1989). *Strangers from a different shore: A history of Asian Americans*. New York: Penguin.

Taxel, J. (1986). The black experience in children's fiction: Controversies surrounding award winning books. *Curriculum Inquiry, 16*(3), 245–281.

Taxel, J. (1988). Children's literature: Ideology and response. *Curriculum Inquiry, 18,* 217–229.

Teaching Tolerance, a twice-yearly magazine published by the nonprofit Southern Poverty Law Center. Teaching Tolerance, 400 Washington Ave., Montgomery, Alabama.

Tiedt, P. A., & Tiedt, I. M. (1995). *Multicultural teaching: A handbook of activities, information, and resources* (4th Ed.). Boston: Allyn & Bacon.

Yokota, J. (1993). Issues in selecting multicultural literature. *Language Arts, 70,* 156–167.

Zarillo, J. (1995). *Multicultural literature, multicultural teaching: Units for the elementary grades*. New York: Harcourt Brace.

Listing of Predictable Books

PREDICTABLE BOOKS

Books with a repetitive pattern in which a certain phrase or sentence is repeated throughout the story.

Ahlberg, Janet & Allan. *Peek-a-boo.* Viking Press, 1981.

Allen, Roach Van. *I Love Ladybugs.* DLM Teaching Resources, 1985.

Balina, Lorna. *Mother's Mother's Day.* Abingdon Press, 1982.

Barrett, Judi. *Animals Should Definitely Not Act Like People.* Atheneum, 1980.

Barrett, Judi. *Animals Should Definitely Not Wear Clothes.* Atheneum, 1981.

Barrett, Judi. *A Snake Is Totally Tail.* Atheneum, 1983.

Barton, Byron. *Harry Is a Scaredy-Cat.* Macmillan, 1974.

Berenstain, Stan & Jan. *Old Hat New Hat.* Random House, 1970.

Brooke, Leslie. *Johnny Crow's Garden.* F. Warne & Co., 1941.

Brooke, Leslie. *Johnny Crow's New Garden.* F. Warne & Co., 1938.

Brown, Margaret Wise. *Goodnight Moon.* Harper & Row, 1947.

Brown, Margaret Wise. *The Friendly Book.* Western Publishing, 1954.

Brown, Margaret Wise. *The Important Book.* Harper & Row, 1949.

Brown, Margaret Wise. *Where Have You Been?* Hastings House, 1952.

Brown, Ruth. *A Dark Dark Tale.* Dial Press. 1981.

Caldwell, Mary. *Henry's Busy Day.* Viking Press, 1984.

Carle, Eric. *The Grouchy Ladybug.* Thomas Y. Crowell Co., 1977.

Crews, Donald. *Light.* Greenwillow Books, 1981.

Degen, Bruce. *Jamberry.* Harper & Row, 1983.

deRegniers, Beatrice Schenk. *Going for a Walk.* Harper & Row, 1961.

Domanska, Janina. *If All the Seas Were One Sea.* Macmillan, 1971.

Eastman, P.D. *Go, Dog, Go!* Random House, 1961.

Galdone, Paul. *The Teeny-Tiny Woman.* Clarion Books, 1984.

Ginsburg, Mirra. *The Chick and the Duckling.* Macmillan, 1972.

Hamsa, Bobbie. *Dirty Larry.* Children's Press. 1983.

Harper, Anita. *How We Work.* Harper & Row, 1977.

Harper, Anita & Roche, Christine. *How We Live.* Harper & Row, 1977.

Hutchins, Pat. *Goodnight Owl.* Macmillan, 1972.

Isadora, Rachel. *I See.* Greenwillow Books. 1985.

Kraus, Robert. *I'm a Monkey.* Windmill Books, 1975.

Krauss, Ruth. *A Hole is to Dig.* Harper & Row, 1952.

Krauss, Ruth. *I Write It.* Harper & Row, 1970.

Krauss, Ruth. *The Happy Day.* Harper & Row, 1949.

Langstaff, John M. *Oh, A-Hunting We Will Go.* Atheneum, 1977.

Malloy, Judy. *Bad Thad.* E. P. Dutton, 1980.

Martin, Bill. *Brown Bear, Brown Bear.* Holt, Rinehart & Winston, 1970.

Martin, Bill. *King of the Mountain.* Holt, Rinehart & Winston, 1970.

Martin, Bill. *Silly Goose and the Holidays.* Holt, Rinehart & Winston, 1970.

Martin, Bill. *The Haunted House.* Holt, Rinehart & Winston, 1970.

Martin, Bill. *Up and Down the Escalator.* Holt, Rinehart & Winston, 1970.

Mosel, Arlene. *Tikki Tikki Tembo.* Holt, Rinehart & Winston, 1968.

Muntean, Michaela. *I Like School.* Golden Press, 1980.

Paterson, Diane. *If I Were a Toad.* Dial Press, 1977.

Peek, Merle. *Mary Wore Her Red Dress.* Clarion Books, 1985.

Preston, Edna Mitchell. *Where Did My Mother Go?* Four Winds Press, 1978.

Quackenbush, Robert. *Skip to My Lou.* J. B. Lippincott, 1975.

Rockwell, Anne. *Thump Thump Thump!* E. P. Dutton, 1981.

Scheer, Julian. *Rain Makes Applesauce.* Holiday House, 1964.

Seuss, Dr. *The Foot Book.* Random House, 1968.

Shaw, Charles G. *It Looked Like Spilt Milk.* Harper & Row, 1947.

Simon, Norma. *I Know What I Like.* Whitman, 1971.

Titherington, Jeanne. *Big World, Small World.* Greenwillow Books, 1985.

Udry, Janice May. *A Tree Is Nice.* Harper & Row, 1956.

Watanabe, Shigeo. *I Can Ride It!* Philomel Books, 1981.

Watanabe, Shigeo. *Where's My Daddy?* Philomel Books, 1979.

Williams, Barbara. *Never Hit a Porcupine.* E. P. Dutton & Co., 1977.

Books with predictable plots in which the events occur in such as way as to enable the reader to predict future events.

Aliki. *At Mary Bloom's.* Greenwillow Books, 1976.

Allard, Harry. *I Will Not Go to Market Today.* Dial Press. 1979.

Aylesworth, Jim. *Hush Up!* Holt, Rinehart & Winston, 1980.

Balian, Lorna. *Where in the World is Henry?* Abingdon, 1972.

Barton, Byron. *Buzz, Buzz, Buzz.* Puffin Books, 1979.

Brown, Margaret Wise. *The Runaway Bunny.* Harper & Row, 1972.

Burningham, John. *Mr. Gumpy's Outing.* Scholastic, 1974.

Charlip, Remy. *Fortunately.* Four Winds Press, 1964.

Emberley, Ed. *Klippity Klop.* Little, Brown and Co., 1974.

Fregosi, Claudia. *Are There Spooks in the Dark?* Four Winds Press, 1977.

Galdone, Paul. *The Three Bears.* Scholastic, 1972.

Galdone, Paul. *The Three Billy Goats Gruff.* Scholastic, 1963.

Galdone, Paul. *The Three Little Pigs.* Seabury Press, 1970.

Ginsburg, Mirra. *Where Does the Sun Go at Night?* Greenwillow Books, 1981.

Joslin, Sesyle. *What Do You Do, Dear?* Young Scott Books, 1961.

Klein, Leonore. *Brave Daniel.* Scholastic, 1958.

Lobel, Arnold. *A Treeful of Pigs.* Greenwillow Books, 1979.

Mayer, Mercer. *Just for You.* Golden Press, 1975.

Nodset, Joan. *Who Took the Farmer's Hat?* Scholastic, 1963.

Silverstein, Shel. *Who Wants a Cheap Rhinoceros?* Macmillan, 1983.

Stevenson, James. *Could Be Worse!* Greenwillow Books. 1977.

Tobias, Tobi. *A Day Off.* G. P. Putnam's Sons, 1973.

Zolotow, Charlotte. *Do You Know What I'll Do?* Harper & Row, 1958.

Books with a repetitive-cumulative pattern in which a word, phrase, or sentence is repeated in each succeeding episode and with each episode adding a new word, phrase, or sentence to the sequence.

Aardema, Verna. *Bringing the Rain to Kapiti Plain.* Dial Press, 1981.

Aardema, Verna. *Why Mosquitoes Buzz in People's Ears.* Scholastic, 1975.

Berenstain, Stan & Jan. *The B Book.* Random House, 1971.

Berenstain, Stan & Jan. *C is for Clown.* Random House, 1972.

Berenstain, Stan & Jan. *Inside Outside Upside Down.* Random House, 1968.

Bonne, Rose. *I Know an Old Lady.* Scholastic, 1961.

Brenner, Barbara. *The Snow Parade.* Crown Publishers, 1984.

Dodd, Lynley. *Hairy Maclary from Donaldson's Dairy.* Gareth Stevens, Inc., 1983.

Emberly, Barbara. *Drummer Hoff.* Prentice-Hall, Inc. 1967.

Ets, Marie Hall. *Elephant in a Well.* Viking, 1972.

Galdone, Paul. *Chicken Little.* Seabury Press, 1968.

Galdone, Paul. *The Greedy Old Fat Man.* Clarion Books, 1983.

Galdone, Paul. *The Old Woman and Her Pig.* MacGraw-Hill, 1960.

Granowsky, Alvin. *Pat's Date and Plate.* D. C. Heath & Co., 1975.

Guilfoile, Elizabeth. *Nobody Listens to Andrew.* Scholastic, 1957.

Hogrogian, Nonny. *One Fine Day.* Collier Books, 1971.

Hoguet, Susan R. *I Unpacked My Grandmother's Trunk.* E. P. Dutton, 1983.

Kalan, Robert. *Jump, Frog, Jump.* Greenwillow Books, 1981.

Kent, Jack. *Jack Kent's Twelve Days of Christmas.* Scholastic, 1973.

Kent, Jack. *The Fat Cat.* Scholastic, 1971.

Lobel, Arnold. *The Rose in My Garden.* Greenwillow Books, 1984.

Parnall, Peter. *The Mountain.* Doubleday, 1971.

Patrick, Gloria. *A Bug in a Jug and other Funny Rhymes.* Scholastic, 1970.

Peppe, Rodney. *The House That Jack Built.* Delacorte Press, 1970.

Quackenbush, Robert. *No Mouse for Me.* Franklin Watts, 1981.

Sadler, Marilyn. *It's Not Easy Being a Bunny.* Random House, 1983.

Seuss, Dr. *Green Eggs and Ham.* Random House, 1960.

Shoemaker, Kathryn. *Children, Go Where I Send Thee.* Winston Press, 1980.

Silverstein, Shel. *A Giraffe and a Half.* Harper & Row, 1964.
Tolstoy, Alexi. *The Great Bit Enormous Turnip.* Franklin Watts, 1968.
Wood, Audrey. *The Napping House.* Harcourt Brace Jovanovich. 1984.

Books with a repetitive refrain in which a certain phrase or sentence is repeated at various points in the story.

Aardema, Verna. *The Vinganese and the Tree Toad.* Frederick Warne & Co., 1983.
Aardema, Verna. *Who's in Rabbit's House?* Dial Press, 1969.
Bang, Betsy. *The Old Woman and the Rice Thief.* Greenwillow Books, 1978.
Brown, Margaret Wise. *Home for a Bunny.* Golden Press, 1980.
Brown, Margaret Wise. *Wait Till the Moon Is Full.* Harper & Row, 1948.
daPaola, Tomie. *Marianna May and Nursey.* Holiday House, 1983.
Gag, Wanda. *Millions of Cats.* Coward, McCann & Geoghegan, 1977.
Littledale, Freya. *The Magic Fish.* Scholastic, 1967.
Shannon, George. *The Piney Woods Peddler.* Greenwillow Books, 1981.

Books with rhyming patterns, many of which have rhyme combined with repetition and cumulative-repetition.

Aliki. *Hush Little Baby.* Prentice-Hall, 1968.
Battaglia, Aurelius. *Old Mother Hubbard.* Golden Press, 1972.
Cameron, Polly. *"I Can't" Said the Ant.* Scholastic, 1961.
Cranstoun, Margaret. *1, 2, Buckle My Shoe.* Holt, Rinehart & Winston, 1967.
Einsel, Walter, *Did You Ever See?* Scholastic, 1962.
Hawkins, Colin & Jacqui. *Pat the Cat.* G. P. Putnam's Sons. 1983.
Kessler, Leonard. *Hey Diddle Diddle.* Garrard Publishing, 1980.
Krauss, Ruth. *Bears.* Harper & Row, 1948.
Petersham, Maud & Miska. *The Rooster Crows: A Book of American Rhymes and Jingles.* Macmillan, 1971.
Schermer, Judith. *Mouse in a House.* Houghton Mifflin, 1979.
Sendak, Maurice. *Pierre.* Harper & Row, 1962.
Seuss, Dr. *I Can Read with My Eyes Shut!* Random House, 1978.
Seuss, Dr. *The Cat in the Hat.* Random House, 1957.
Spier, Peter. *London Bridge Is Falling Down.* Doubleday & Co., 1967.
Stadler, John. *Cat at Bat.* E. P. Dutton, 1979.
Withers, Carl. *Favorite Rhymes from a Rocket in My Pocket.* Scholastic, 1967.
Zolotow, Charlotte. *Some Things Go Together.* Thomas Y. Crowell, 1969.
Zuromskis, Diane. *The Farmer in the Dell.* Little, Brown & Co., 1978.

Books with a wordplay pattern in which pictures illustrate characteristics of words.

Gwynne, Fred. *The King Who Rained.* Windmill Books, 1970.
Hanson, Joan. *Antonyms.* Lerner Publishing Co., 1972.
Hanson, Joan. *Homographic Homophones.* Lerner Publishing Co., 1973.

Sequenced Books

Books with patterns based on familiar cultural sequences (cardinal and ordinal numbers, alphabet, months of the year, days of the week, seasons and colors).

Numbers

Anno, Mitsumasa. *Anno's Counting Book.* Thomas Y. Crowell Co., 1975.
Anno, Masaichiro & Mitsumasa. *Anno's Mysterious Multiplying Jar.* Philomel Books, 1983.
Bang, Molly. *Ten, Nine, Eight.* Greenwillow Books, 1983.
Berenstain, Stan & Jan. *Bears on Wheels.* Random House, 1969.
Bruna, Dick. *I Can Count.* Methuen Children's Books, 1968.
Carle, Eric. *1, 2, 3 to the Zoo.* Philomel Books, 1968.
Cleveland, David. *The April Rabbits.* Coward, McCann & Geoghegan.
Duvoisin, Roger. *Two Lonely Ducks.* Alfred A. Knopf, 1955.
Emberley, Barbara. *One Wide River to Cross.* Scholastic, 1966.
Feelings, Muriel. *Moja Means One: Swahili Counting Book.* Dial Press, 1971.
Ginsburg, Mirra. *Kitten from One to Ten.* Crown Publishers, Inc., 1980.
Hoberman, Mary Ann. *The Looking Book.* Alfred A. Knopf, 1973.
Hopkins, Lee Bennett. *Small Circus.* Macmillan, 1975.
Hughes, Shirley. *When We Went to the Park.* Lothrop, Lee & Shepard Books, 1985.
Hutchins, Pat. *I Hunter.* Greenwillow Books, 1982.
Keats, Ezra Jack. *Over in the Meadow.* Scholastic, 1971.
Kredenser, Gail & Mack, Stanley. *I One Dancing Drum.* S. G. Phillips, 1971.
LeSieg, Theo. *I Can Write!* Random House, 1971.
Lewin, Betsy. *Cat Count.* Dodd, Mead & Co., 1981.
Martin, Bill. *Ten Little Squirrels.* Holt, Rinehart & Winston, 1970.
McLeod, Emilie Warren. *One Snail and Me.* Little, Brown & Co., 1961.
Nedobeck, Don. *Nedobeck's Numbers Book.* Ideal Publishing Co., 1981.
Peek, Merle. *Roll Over! A Counting Song.* Clarion Books, 1981.
Scarry, Richard. *The Best Counting Book Ever.* Random House, 1975.
Schertle, Alice. *Goodnight, Hattie, My Dearie, My Dove.* Lothrop, Lee & Shepard Books, 1985.
Smollin, Michael J. *I Can Count to 100 ... Can You?* Random House, 1979.

Alphabet

Anno, Mitsumasa. *Anno's Alphabet.* Thomas Y. Crowell Co., 1974.
Arnosky, Jim. *Mouse Writing.* Harcourt Brace Jovanovich, 1983.
Attwell, Lucie. *Lucie Attwell's ABC 123 Pop-up Book.* Deans International Publishers, 1984.
Baskin, Leonard. *Hosie's Alphabet.* Viking Press, 1972.
Bridwell, Norman. *Clifford's ABC.* Scholastic, 1983.
Brown, Marcia. *All Butterflies—an ABC.* Charles Scribner's Sons, 1974.

Carle, Eric. *All About Arthur (An Absolutely Absurd Ape)*. Franklin Watts.

Duke, Kate. *The Guinea Pig ABC*. E. P. Dutton, 1983.

Duvoisin, Roger. *A for the Ark*. Lothrop, Lee & Shepard Co., 1952.

Eastman, P. D. *The Alphabet Book*. Random House, 1974.

Eichenberg, Fritz. *Ape in a Cape—An Alphabet of Odd Animals*. Harcourt Brace & World, 1952.

Elting, Mary & Folsom, Michael. *Q is for Duck*. Clarion Books, 1980.

Emberley, Ed. *Ed Emberley's ABC*. Little, Brown & Co., 1978.

Gretz, Susanna. *Teddy Bears ABC*. Follett, 1977.

Hoban, Tana. *A. B. See!* Greenwillow Books, 1982.

Isadora, Rachel. *City Seen from A to Z*. Greenwillow Books, 1983.

Kitchen, Bert. *Animal Alphabet*. Dial Books, 1984.

Miller, Elizabeth, & Cohen, Jane. *Cat and Dog and the ABCs*. Watts Publishing Co., 1981.

Munari, Bruno. *Bruno Munari's ABC*. Collins/World Publishing Company, Inc., 1960.

Ruben, Patricia. *Apples to Zippers*. Doubleday, 1976.

Schmiderer, Dorothy. *The Alphabeast Book*. Holt, Rinehart & Winston, 1971.

Sendak, Maurice. *Alligators All Around*. Harper & Row, 1962.

Seuss, Dr. *ABC*. Random House, 1963.

Stevenson, James. *Grandpa's Great City Tour*. Greenwillow Books, 1983.

Tallon, Robert. *Rotten Kidphabets*. Holt, Rinehart & Winston, 1975.

Warren, Cathy. *Victoria's ABC Adventure*. Lothrop, Lee & Shepard, 1984.

Wildsmith, Brian. *Brian Wildsmith's ABC*. Franklin Watts, 1962.

Yolen, Jane. *All in the Woodland*. Collins, 1979.

Colors

Miller, J. P., & Howard, Katherine. *Do You Know Colors?* Random House, 1978.

O'Neill, Mary. *Hailstones and Halibut Bones*. Doubleday & Co., 1961.

Rossetti, Christina G. *What Is Pink?* Macmillan, 1971.

Days

Carle, Eric. *The Very Hungry Caterpillar*. Philomel Books, 1983.

Clifton, Lucille. *Some of the Days of Everett Anderson*. Holt, Rinehart & Winston, 1970.

Domanska, Janina. *Busy Monday Morning*. Greenwillow Books, 1985.

Elliott, Alan C. *On Sunday the Wind Came*. William Morrow & Co., 1980.

Hooper, Meredith. *Seven Eggs*. Harper & Row, 1985.

Quackenbush, Robert. *Too Many Lollipops*. Scholastic, 1975.

Sharmat, Mitchell. *The Seven Sloppy Days of Phineas Pig*. Harcourt Brace Jovanovich, 1983.

Yolen, Jane. *No Bath Tonight*. Thomas Y. Crowell, 1978.

Months and Seasons

Clifton, Lucille. *Everett Anderson's Year.* Holt, Rinehart & Winston, 1974.
Lionni, Leo. *Mouse Days.* Pantheon Books, 1981.
Sendak, Maurice. *Chicken Soup with Rice.* Scholastic, 1962.
Wolff, Ashley. *A Year of Birds.* Dodd, Mead & Co., 1984.
Zolotow, Charlotte. *Summer Is ...* Abelard-Schuman, 1967.

Bibliography

Abrahamson, R. F., & Carter, B. (1991). Nonfiction: The missing piece in the middle. *English Journal, 80,* 52–57.

Adams, A., Carnine D., & Gersten, R. (1982). Instructional strategies for studying content area texts in the intermediate grades. *Reading Research Quarterly, 18,* 27–55.

Adelman, H., & Taylor, L. (1977). Two steps toward improving learning for students with (and without) "learning problems." *Journal of Learning Disabilities, 10,* 455–461.

Agnew, A.T. (1982). Using children's dictated stories to assess code consciousness. *The Reading Teacher, 35,* 450–454.

Allen, R.V. 1976). *Language experience in communication.* Boston: Houghton Mifflin.

Allington, R. L. (1975). Sustained approaches to reading and writing. *Language Arts, 52,* 813–815.

Allington, R. L. (1977). If they don't read much how they ever gonna get good? *Journal of Reading, 21,* 57–61.

Allington, R. L. (1980). Teacher interruption behaviors during primary grade oral reading. *Journal of Educational Psychology, 72,* 371–377.

Allington, R. L. (1983a). The reading instruction provided readers of differing reading abilities. *Elementary School Journal, 83,* 548–558.

Allington, R. L. (1983b). Fluency: The neglected reading goal. *The Reading Teacher, 36,* 556–561.

Allington, R. L. (1984). Content coverage and contextual reading in reading groups. *Journal of Reading Behavior, 16,* 85–96.

Allington, R. L. (1991). The legacy of "slow it down and make it more concrete." In J. Zutell & S. McCormick (Eds.), *Learner factors/teacher factors: Issues in literacy research and instruction* (pp. 19–30). Chicago: National Reading Conference.

Allington, R. L. (1994). Critical issues: What's special about special programs for children who find learning to read difficult? *Journal of Reading Behavior, 26,* 95–115.

Allington, R. L., Chodos, L., Domaracki, J., & Truex, S. (1977). Passage dependency: Four diagnostic oral reading tests. *The Reading Teacher, 30,* 369–375.

Allington, R. L., & Johnston, P. (1989). Coordination, collaboration, and consistency: The redesign of compensatory and special education intervention. In R. Slavin, M. Madden, & N. Karweit (Eds.), *Preventing school failure: Effective programs for students at risk* (pp. 320–354). Boston: Allyn and Bacon.

Allington, R. L., & McGill-Franzen, A. (1980). Word identification errors in isolation and in context: Apples vs. oranges. *The Reading Teacher, 33,* 795–800.

Allington, R. L., & McGill-Franzen, A. (1989). Different programs, indifferent instruction. In D. Lipsky & A. Gartner (Eds.), *Beyond separate education: Quality education for all* (pp. 75–98). Baltimore, MD: Brookes.

Allington, R. L., Stuetzel, H., Shake, M., & Lamarche, S. (1986). What is remedial reading? A descriptive study. *Reading Research and Instruction, 26,* 15–30.

Altwerger, B., Diehl-Faxon, J., & Dockstader-Anderson, K. (1985). Read-aloud events as meaning construction. *Language Arts, 62,* 476–484.

Alvermann, D. E. (1984). Second graders' strategic preferences while reading basal stories. *Journal of Educational Research, 77,* 184–189.

Alvermann, D. E. (1989). Creating the bridge to content-area reading. In P. Winograd, K. Wixson, & M.Y. Lipson (Eds.), *Improving basal reading instruction* (pp. 256–270). New York: Teachers College Press.

Alvermann, D. E., Dillon, D. R., & O'Brien, D. G. (1987). *Using discussion to promote reading comprehension.* Newark, DE: International Reading Association.

American Educational Research Association (AERA) (1985). *Standards for educational and psychological testing.* Washington, DC: American Psychological Association.

Anders, P. L., & Bos, C.S. (1986). Semantic feature analysis: An interactive strategy for vocabulary development and text comprehension. *Journal of Reading, 29,* 610–616.

Anderson, B. (1981). The missing ingredient: Fluent oral reading. *Elementary School Journal, 81* 173–177.

Anderson, L. M., Brubaker, N. L., Alleman-Brooks, J., & Duffy, G.G. (1985). A qualitative study of seat-work in first-grade classrooms. *Elementary School Journal, 86,* 132–140.

Anderson, R. C., & Freebody, P. (1981). Vocabulary knowledge. In J.T. Guthrie (Ed.), *Comprehension and teaching: Research perspectives* (pp. 71–117). Newark, DE: International Reading Association.

Anderson, R.C., Hiebert, E. H., Scott, J. A., & Wilkinson, I. G. (1985). *Becoming a nation of readers: The report of the Commission on Reading.* Washington, DC: The National Institute of Education.

Anderson, R. C., Wilson, P. T., & Fielding, L. G. (1988). Growth in reading and how children spend their time outside of school. *Reading Research Quarterly, 23,* 285–303.

Anderson, T. H., & Armbruster, B. B. (1984a). Content area textbooks. In R. C. Anderson, J. Osborn, & R. J. Tierney (Eds.), *Learning to read in American schools: Basal readers and content texts* (pp. 193–226). Hillsdale, NJ: Lawrence Erlbaum.

Anderson, T. H., & Armbruster, B. B. (1984b). Studying. In P. D. Pearson, R. Barr, M. Kamil, & P. Mosenthal (Eds.), *Handbook of reading research* (pp. 657–679). New York: Longman.

Anthony, R. J., Johnson, T. D., Mickelson, N. I., & Preece, A. (1991). *Evaluating literacy: A perspective for change.* Portsmouth, NH: Heinemann.

Applebee, A. (1974). *Tradition and reform in the teaching of English: A history.* Urbana, IL: National Council of Teachers of English.

Applebee, A. (1981). *Writing in the secondary school: English and the content areas.* Urbana, IL: National Council of Teachers of English.

Applebee, A. N. (1978). *A child's concept of story.* Chicago: University of Chicago Press.

Applebee, A. N., Langer, J. A., Mullis, I.V.S., & Jenkins, L. B. (1990) *The writing report card, 1984–1988.*
Report No. 19-W-01: Princeton, NJ: Educational Testing Services

Argiro, M. (1987). The development of written language awareness in Black preschool children. *Journal of Reading Behavior, 19,* 49–67.

Armbruster. B. B. (1984). The problem of "inconsiderate text." In G.G. Duffy, L. R. Roehler, & J. Mason (Eds.), *Comprehension instruction* (pp. 202–217). New York: Longman.

Armbruster, B. B., & Anderson, T.H. (1981). Research synthesis on study skills. *Educational Leadership, 39,* 154–156.

Armbruster, B.B., Anderson, T.H., & Ostertag, J. (1989). Teaching text structure to improve reading and writing. *The Reading Teacher, 43,* 130–137.

Armstrong, D. P., Patberg, J., & Dewitz, P. (1988). Reading guides— Helping students understand. *Journal of Reading, 31,* 532–541.

Ash, B. H. (1990). Reading assigned literature in a reading workshop.. *English Journal, 79,* 77–79.

Asher, S. (1980). Topic interest and children's reading comprehension. In R. J. Spiro, B. C. Bruce, & W. F. Brewer (Eds.), *Theoretical issues in reading comprehension* (pp. 525–534). Hillsdale, NJ: Lawrence Erlbaum.

Ashton-Warner, S. (1963). *Teacher.* New York: Simon and Schuster.

Atwell, N. (1987). *In the middle.* Portsmouth, NH: Boynton/Cook.

Atwell, N. (1990). *Coming to know: Writing to learn in the intermediate grades.* Portsmouth, NH: Heinemann.

Au, K. H. (1979). Using the experience-text-relationship method with minority children. *The Reading Teacher, 32,* 677–679.

Au, K. H. (1980). Participation structures in a reading lesson with Hawaiian children: Analysis of a culturally appropriate instructional event. *Anthropology and Education Quarterly, 11,* 91–115.

Au, K. H. (1993). *Literacy instruction in multicultural settings.* Fort Worth, TX: Harcourt Brace.

Au, K. H. (1994). Portfolio assessment: Experiences at the Kamehameha Elementary Education Program. In S. W. Valencia, E. H. Hiebert, & P. P. Afflerbach (Eds.), *Authentic reading assessment: Practices and possibilities* (pp. 103–133).

Au, K. H., & Kawakami, A. J. (1986). The influence of the social organization of instruction on children's text comprehension ability: A Vygotskian perspective. In T. E. Raphael (Ed.), *The contexts of school-based literacy* (pp. 63–77). New York: Random House.

Au, K. H., Mason, J. M., & Scheu, J. A. (1995). *Literacy instruction for today.* New York: HarperCollins.

Aulls, M. W. (1982). *Developing readers in today's elementary school.* Boston: Allyn & Bacon.

Bader, L. A. (1980). *Reading diagnosis and remediation in classroom and clinic.* New York: Macmillan.

Baker, L., & Brown, A. L. (1984). Metacognitive skills and reading. In P. D. Pearson, R. Barr, M. Kamil, & P. Mosenthal (Eds.), *Handbook of reading research* (pp. 353–394). New York: Longman.

Baker, T. A., Torgesen, J. K., & Wagner, R. K. (1992). The role of orthographic processing skills on five different tasks. *Reading Research Quarterly, 27,* 335–345.

Ballard, R. (1978). *Talking dictionary.* Ann Arbor, MI: Ulrich's Books.

Barr, R., & Sadow, M.W. (1989). Influence of basal programs on fourth-grade reading instruction. *Reading Research Quarterly, 24,* 44–71.

Barrett, T. C. (1976). Taxonomy of reading comprehension. In R. Smith & T. C. Barrett (Eds.), *Teaching reading in the middle grades* (pp. 53–58). Reading, MA: Addison-Wesley.

Barron, R. (1969). The use of vocabulary as an advance organizer. In H. L. Herber & P. L. Sanders (Eds.), *Research in reading in the content areas: First report* (pp. 29–39). Syracuse, NY: Syracuse University Reading and Language Arts Center.

Baumann, J. F. (1986). Effect of rewritten content textbook passages on middle grade students' comprehension of main ideas: Making the inconsiderate considerate. *Journal of Reading Behavior, 28,* 1–21.

Baumann, J. F. (1988). *Reading assessment: An instructional decision-making perspective.* Columbus, OH: Charles E. Merrill.

Bean, T. W., & Steenwyk, F. L. (1984). The effect of three forms of summarization instruction on sixth graders' summary writing and comprehension. *Journal of Reading Behavior, 16,* 297–306.

Beck, I. L., & McKeown, M. G. (1981). Developing questions that promote comprehension: The story map. *Language Arts, 58,* 913–918.

Beck, I. L., & McKeown, M.G. (1983). Learning words well—A program to enhance vocabulary and comprehension. *The Reading Teacher, 36,* 622–625.

Beck, I. L., McKeown, M. G., & McCaslin, E. S. (1981). Does reading make sense? Problems of early readers. *The Reading Teacher, 34,* 780–785.

Beck, I. L., McKeown, M. G., & McCaslin, E. S. (1983). Vocabulary development: All contexts are not created equal. *Elementary School Journal, 83,* 177–181.

Beers, J., & Henderson, E. H. (1977). A study of developing orthographic concepts among first graders. *Research in the Teaching of English, 11,* 133–148.

Bembridge, T. (1994). A multi-layered assessment package. In S. W. Valencia, E. H. Hiebert, & P. P. Afflerbach (Eds.), *Authentic reading assessment: Practices and possibilities* (pp. 167–196).

Bender, L. (1938). *A visual-motor gestalt test and its clinical use.* New York: American Orthopsychiatric Association.

Betts, E. A. (1946). *Foundations of reading instruction.* New York: American Books.

Bialystok, E., & Ryan, E. (1985). A metacognitive framework for the development of first and second language skills. In D. L. Forrest-Pressley, G. E. MacKinnon, & T. G. Waller (Eds.), *Metacognition, cognition, and human performance* (pp. 207–252). New York: Academic Press.

Binkley, M. R. (1988). New ways of assessing text difficulty. In B. L. Zakaluk & S. J. Samuels (Eds.), *Readability: Its past, present, and future* (pp. 98–120). Newark, DE: International Reading Association.

Bleich, D. (1975). *Readings and feelings.* Urbana, IL: National Council of Teachers of English.

Bleich, D. (1980). *Subjective criticism.* Bloomington: Indiana University Press.

Block, C. C. (1993). *Teaching the language arts: Expanding thinking through student-centered instruction.* Boston: Allyn & Bacon.

Bloom, B. S. (Ed.). (1956). *Taxonomy of educational objectives. Handbook I: Cognitive domain.* New York: David McKay.

Blumenfeld, P. C., Hamilton, V. L., Bossert, S. T., Wessels, K., & Meece, J. (1983). Teacher talk and student thought: Socialization into the student role. In J. Levine & M. Wang (Eds.), *Teacher and student perceptions: Implications for learning* (pp. 143–192). Hillsdale, NJ: Lawrence Erlbaum.

Blumenfeld, P. C., Mergendoller, J. R., & Swarthout, S.W. (1987). Task as a heuristic for understanding student learning and motivation. *Journal of Curriculum Studies, 19,* 135–148.

Boehm, A. E. (1986). *Boehm Test of Basic Concepts—Revised.* San Antonio, TX: The Psychological Corporation.

Boggs, S. T. (1985). *Speaking, relating and learning: A study of Hawaiian children at home and at school.* Norwood, NJ: Ablex.

Bormuth, J. R. (1968). Cloze test readability: Criterion scores. *Journal of Educational Measurement, 5,* 189–196.

Bossert, S.T. (1979). *Tasks and social relationships in classrooms.* New York: Cambridge University Press.

Botel, M. (1982). New informal approaches to evaluating word recognition and comprehension. In J. J. Pikulski & T. Shanahan (Eds.), *Approaches to the informal evaluation of reading* (pp. 30–41). Newark, DE: International Reading Association.

Bowey, J. A., & Frances, J. (1991). Phonological analysis as a function of age and exposure to reading instruction. *Applied Psycholinguistics, 12,* 91–121.

Bowles, S., & Gintis, H. (1976). *Schooling in capitalist America.* New York: Basic Books.

Bradley, J. M., & Ames, W. S. (1977). Readability parameters of basal readers. *Journal of Reading Behavior, 9,* 175–183.

Bransford, J. D., Goldman, S. R., & Vye, N. J. (1991). Making a difference in people's abilities to think: Reflections on a decade of work and some hopes for the future. In L. Okagaki & R. J. Sternberg (Eds.), *Directors of development: Influences on the development of children's thinking* (pp. 147–180.) Hillsdale, NJ: Lawrence Erlbaum.

Bransford, J. D., & Johnson, M. K. (1972). Contextual prerequisites for understanding: Some investigations of comprehension and recall. *Journal of Verbal Learning and Verbal Behavior, 11,* 717–726.

Bratcher, S. (1994). *Evaluating children's writing.* NY: St. Martin's Press.

Brecht, R. D. (1977). Testing format and instructional level with the informal reading inventory. *The Reading Teacher, 31,* 57–59.

Brennan, A. D., Bridge, C. A., & Winograd, P.N. (1986). The effects of structural variation on children's recall of basal reader stories. *Reading Research Quarterly, 21,* 91–104.

Bretzing, B. B., & Kulhavy, R.W. (1981). Note-taking and passage style. *Journal of Educational Psychology, 73,* 242–250.

Bricker, D. D. (1986). *Early education of at-risk and handicapped infants, toddlers, and preschool children.* Glenview, IL: Scott, Foresman.

Bridge, C., & Hiebert, E. H. (1985). A comparison of classroom writing practices, teachers' perceptions of their writing instruction, and textbook recommendations on writing practices. *The Elementary School Journal, 86,* 155–172.

Bridge, C. A. (1989). Beyond the basal in beginning reading. In P. Winograd, K. Wixson, & M. Lipson (Eds.), *Improving basal reading instruction* (pp. 177–209). New York: Teachers College Press.

Bridge, C. A., Belmore, S., Moskow, S., Cohen, S., & Matthews, P. (1984). Topicalization and memory for main ideas in prose. *Journal of Reading Behavior, 16,* 27–40.

Bridge, C. A., & Burton, B. (1982). Teaching sight vocabulary through patterned language materials. In J. A. Niles & L. A. Harris (Eds.), *New inquiries in reading research and instruction*

(31st Yearbook of The National Reading Conference, pp. 119–123). Washington, DC: National Reading Conference.

Bridge, C. A., & Winograd, P. N. (1982). Readers' awareness of cohesive relationships during cloze comprehension. *Journal of Reading Behavior, 14,* 299–312.

Bridge, C. A., Winograd, P. N., & Haley, D. (1983). Using predictable materials vs. preprimers to teach beginning sight words. *The Reading Teacher, 36,* 884–891.

Brigance, A. H. (1976) *BRIGANCE® Diagnostic Inventories.* North Billerica, MA: Curriculum Associates.

Brophy, J. E. (1983a). Conceptualizing student motivation. *Educational Psychologist, 18,* 200–215.

Brophy, J. E. (1983b). Research on the self-fulfilling prophecy and teacher expectations. *Journal of Educational Psychology, 75,* 631–661.

Brophy, J. E., & Good, T.L. (1974). *Teacher-student relationships: Causes and consequences.* New York: Holt, Rinehart & Winston.

Brown, A. L. (1978). Knowing when, where, and how to remember: A problem of metacognition. In R. Glaser (Ed.), *Advances in instructional psychology 1* (pp. 77–165). Hillsdale, NJ: Lawrence Erlbaum.

Brown, A. L. (1980). Metacognitive development and reading. In R. Spiro, B. Bruce, & W. Brewer (Eds.), *Theoretical issues in reading comprehension* (pp. 453–481). Hillsdale, NJ: Lawrence Erlbaum.

Brown, A. L., Armbruster, B. B., & Baker, L. (1986). The role of metacognition in reading and studying. In J. Orasanu (Ed.), *A decade of reading research: Implications for practice* (pp. 49–75). Hillsdale, NJ: Lawrence Erlbaum.

Brown, A. L., & Campione, J. C. (1986). Psychological theory and the study of learning disabilities. *American Psychologist, 14,* 1059–1068.

Brown, A. L., Campione, J. C., & Day, J. D. (1981). Learning to learn: On training students to learn from texts. *Educational Researcher, 10,* 14–21.

Brown, J. S., Collins, A., & Duguid, P. (1989). Situated cognition and the culture of learning. *Educational Researcher, 18,* 32–42.

Brown, V. L., Hammill, D. D., & Wiederholt, J. L. (1995). *Test of Reading Comprehension, 3rd Ed.* Austin, TX: PRO-ED.

Bruce, B. (1984). A new point of view on children's stories. In R.C. Anderson, J. Osborn, & R. J. Tierney (Eds.), *Learning to read in American schools: Basal readers and content texts* (pp. 153–174). Hillsdale, NJ: Lawrence Erlbaum.

Bruner, J. S. (1964). The course of cognitive growth. *American Psychologist, 19,* 1–15.

Bryant, P. E., MacLean, M., Bradley, L. L., & Crossland, J. (1990). Rhyme and alliteration, phoneme detection, and learning to read. *Developmental Psychology, 26,* 429–438.

Burns, P. C., & Roe, B. D. (1985). *Informal reading inventory* (2nd ed.). Boston: Houghton Mifflin.

Butkowsky, I. S., & Willows, D. M. (1980). Cognitive-motivational characteristics of children varying in reading ability: Evidence for learned helplessness in poor readers. *Journal of Educational Psychology, 72,* 408–422.

Calfee, R. C. (1987). The design of comprehensible text. In J. R. Squire (Ed.), *The dynamics of language learning.* Urbana, IL: ERIC Clearinghouse on Reading and Communication Skills and the National Conference on Research in English (NCRE).

Calfee, R. C., & Drum, P.A. (1979). *Teaching reading in compensatory classes.* Newark, DE: International Reading Association.

Calfee, R., Lindamood, P., & Lindamood, C. (1973). Acoustic-phonetic skills and reading: Kindergarten through twelfth grade. *Journal of Educational Psychology, 64,* 293–298.

Calkins, L. (1991). *Living between the lines.* Portsmouth, NH: Heinemann.

Calkins, L. M. (1983). *Lessons from a child.* Exeter, NH: Heinemann.

Campione, J. C., & Brown, A. L. (1987). Linking dynamic assessment with school achievement. In C.S. Lidz (Ed.), *Dynamic assessment* (pp. 82–109). New York: Guilford.

Campione, J. C., Brown, A. L., Ferrara, R. A. (1982). Mental retardation and intellignece. In R. J. Sternberg (Ed.), *Handbook of human intelligence.* New York: Cambridge University Press.

Campione, J. C., Brown, A. L., Ferrara, R. A., & Bryant, N.R. (1984). The zone of proximal development: Implications for individual differences and learning. In B. Rogoff & J. Wertsch (Eds.), *New directions for child development: Children's learning in the "zone of proximal development"* (Vol. 23, pp. 265–294). San Francisco: Jossey-Bass.

Carew, J. V., & Lightfoot, S. L. (1979). Beyond bias: Perspectives on classroom. Cambridge, MA: Harvard University Press.

Carnine, D., Silbert, J., & Kameenui, E.J. (1990). *Direct instruction reading* (2nd ed.). Columbus, OH: Charles E. Merrill.

Carnine, D. W., Kameenui, E. J., & Coyle, G. (1984). Utilization of contextual information in determining the meaning of unfamiliar words. *Reading Research Quarterly, 19,* 188–204.

Carr, E. (1985). The vocabulary overview guide: A metacognitive strategy to improve vocabulary and retention. *Journal of Reading, 28,* 684–689.

Carr, E., & Ogle, D. (1987). K-W-L Plus: A strategy for comprehension and summarization. *Journal of Reading, 30,* 626–631.

Cazden, C. B. (1986). Classroom discourse. In M.C. Wittrock (Ed.), *Handbook of research on teaching* (3rd ed., pp. 432–463). New York: Macmillan.

Chall, J. S. (1984). Readability and prose comprehension: Continuities and discontinuities. In J. Flood (Ed.), *Understanding reading comprehension* (pp. 233–246). Newark, DE: International Reading Association.

Chall, J. S., & Curtis, M. E. (1987). What clinical diagnosis tells us about children's reading. *The Reading Teacher, 40,* 784–789.

Chittenden, E. (1991). Authentic assessment, evaluation, and documentation of student performance. In V. Perrone (Ed.), *Expanding student assessment.* Alexandria, VA: Association for Supervision and Curriculum Development.

Chomsky, C. (1978). When you still can't read in third grade: After decoding, what? In S. J. Samuels (Ed.), *What research has to say about reading instruction* (pp. 13–30). Newark, DE: International Reading Association.

Chomsky, C. (1981). Write now, read later. *Childhood Education, 47,* 296–299.

Cioffi, G., & Carney, J. J. (1983). Dynamic assessment of reading disabilities. *The Reading Teacher, 36,* 764–768.

Clark, C. H. (1993). *Personal communication.*

Clark, C. H. (1982). Assessing free recall. *The Reading Teacher, 35,* 434–439.

Clark, C. M. (1984). Teacher planning and reading comprehension. In G. G. Duffy, L. R. Roehler, & J. Mason (Eds.), *Comprehension instruction* (pp. 58–70). New York: Longman.

Clay, M. M. (1979). *Reading: The patterning of complex behavior* (2nd ed.). Auckland/Exeter, NH: Heinemann.

Clay, M. M. (1985). *The early detection of reading difficulties* (3rd ed.). Auckland, New Zealand: Heinemann.

Cleary, B. (1983). *Dear Mr. Henshaw.* New York: Bantam Doubleday Dell Publishing, Inc.

Clifford, G. (1984). Buch und lesen: Historical perspectives on literacy and schooling. *Review of Educational Research, 54,* 472–500.

Clifford, G. (1989). A Sisyphean task: Historical perspectives on writing and reading instruction. In A. Dyson (Ed.), *Collaboration through writing and reading.* Urbana, IL: National Council of Teachers of English.

Clifford, M. M. (1991). Risk taking: Theoretical, empirical and educational considerations. *Educational Psychologist, 26,* 263–297.

Cline, R. L., & Kretke, G. L. (1980). An evaluation of long-term SSR in the junior high school. *Journal of Reading, 23,* 503–506.

Cockrum, W. A., & Castillo, M. (1991). Whole language assessment and evaluation strategies. In B. Harp (Ed.), *Assessment and evaluation in whole language programs* (pp. 73–86). Norwood, MA: Christopher Gordon.

Cole, M. (1990). Cultural psychology: A once and future discipline? In J. Berman (Ed.), *Nebraska's symposium on motivation: Cross cultural perspectives, 37.* Lincoln: University of Nebraska Press.

Coles, G. S. (1978). The learning disabilities test battery: Empirical and social issues. *Harvard Educational Review, 48,* 313–340.

Coles, G. S. (1987). *The learning mystique.* New York: Pantheon.

Commins, N. L., & Miramontes, O. B. (1989). A descriptive study of the linguistic abilities of a selected group of low achieving Hispanic bilingual students. *American Educational Research Journal, 26,* 443–472.

Conrad, S. S. (1984). *On readability and readability formula scores* (Ginn Occasional Papers No. 17). Columbus, OH: Ginn and Co.

Cooley, W. W., & Leinhardt, G. (1980). The instructional dimensions study. *Educational Evaluation and Policy Analysis, 2,* 7–25.

Cooper, J. D. (1993). *Literacy.* Boston: Houghton-Mifflin.

Cooper, J. L. (1952). *The effect of adjustment of basal reading materials on reading achievement.* Unpublished doctoral dissertation, Boston University, Boston.

Covington, M. V., & Omelich, C. L. (1979). Effort: The double-edged sword in school achievement. *Journal of Educational Psychology, 71,* 169–182.

Craik, F., & Lockhart, R. (1972). Levels of processing: A framework for memory research. *Journal of Verbal Learning and Verbal Behavior, 11,* 671–684.

Cramer, R. L. (1982). Informal approaches to evaluating children's writing. In J. J. Pikulski & T. Shanahan (Eds.), *Approaches to the informal evaluation of reading* (pp. 80–93). Newark, DE: International Reading Association.

Cremin, L. (1989). *Popular education and its discontents.* New York: Harper & Row.

Critchley, M. (1975). Specific developmental dyslexia. In E. H. Lenneberg & E. Lenneberg (Eds.), *Foundations of language development* (Vol. 2, pp. 361–366). New York: Academic Press.

Cullinan, B., & Fitzgerald, S. (1984). *Statement on readability.* Joint statement by the Presidents of the International Reading Association and the National Council of Teachers of English.

Cunningham, A. E. (1990). Explicit vs. implicit instruction in phonemic awareness. *Journal of Experimental Child Psychology, 50.*

Cunningham, P. M. (1975–76). Investigating a synthesized theory of mediated word identification. *Reading Research Quarterly, 11,* 127–143.

Cunningham, P. M. (1984). What would make workbooks worthwhile? In R. C. Anderson, J. Osborn, & R. T. Tierney (Eds.), *Learning to read in American Schools* (pp. 113—120). Hillsdale, NJ: Lawrence Erlbaum.

Cunningham, P. M., & Cunningham, J. W. (1992). Making words: Enhancing the invented spelling-decoding connection. *The Reading Teacher, 46.* 106–113.

Cunningham, P. M., Moore, S. A., Cunningham, J. W., & Moore, D.W. (1989). *Reading in elementary classrooms* (2nd ed.). New York: Longman.

Curry, L. (1993). *Educating professionals: Responding to new expectations for competence and accountability.* San Francisco: Jossey-Bass.

Dale, E., & Chall, J. (1948). A formula for predicting readability. *Educational Research Bulletin, 27,* 11–20, 37–54.

D'Amato, J. (1987). The belly of the beast: On cultural differences, castelike status, and the politics of school. *Anthropology and Education Quarterly, 18,* 357–361.

D'Amato, J. (1988). "Acting": Hawaiian children's resistance to teachers. *Elementary School Journal, 88,* 529–544.

Dansereau, D. F. (1985). Learning strategy research. In J. Segal, S. Chipman, & R. Glaser (Eds.), *Thinking and learning skills: Relating instruction to basic research* (Vol. 1, pp. 209–240). Hillsdale, NJ: Lawrence Erlbaum.

Darling-Hammond, L., Ancess, J., & Falk, B. (1995). *Authentic assessment in action.* New York: Teachers College Press.

Davison, A. (1984). Readability—Appraising text difficulty. In R. C. Anderson, J. Osborn, & R. T. Tierney (Eds.), *Learning to read in American schools: Basal readers and content texts* (pp. 121–140). Hillsdale, NJ: Lawrence Erlbaum.

Davison, A., & Kantor, R. N. (1982). On the failure of readability formulas to define readable texts: A case study from adaptations. *Reading Research Quarterly, 17,* 187–209.

Day, J. D. (1992). *Population projections of the United States by age, sex, race, and Hispanic origin: 1992–2050.* Washington, DC: Bureau of Census.

Day, J. D., & Cordon, L. A. (1993). Static and dynamic measures of ability: An experimental comparison. *Journal of Educational Psychology, 85,* 75–82.

Day, K. C., & Day, H. D. (1986). Tests of metalinguistic awareness. In D. B. Yaden & S. Templeton (Eds.), *Metalinguistic awareness and beginning literacy: Conceptualizing what it means to read and write* (pp. 187–198). Portsmouth, NH: Heinemann.

Dechant, E. V. (1970). *Improving the teaching of reading* (2nd ed.). Englewood Cliffs, NJ: Prentice-Hall.

DeFord, D. (1991). Using reading and writing to support the reader. In D. E. DeFord, C. A. Lyons, & G. S. Pinnell, *Bridges to literacy* (pp. 77–95). Portsmouth, NH: Heinemann.

DeFord, D. E. (1980). Young children and their writing. *Theory into Practice, 19,* 157–162.

DeFord, D.E. (1986). Classroom contexts for literacy learning. In T. E. Raphael (Ed.), *The contexts of school-based literacy* (pp. 163–180). New York: Longman.

Dewitz, P., Carr, E. M., & Patberg, J. P. (1987). Effects of inference training on comprehension and comprehension monitoring. *Reading Research Quarterly, 22,* 542–546.

Dickinson, D., & McCabe, A. (1991). A social interactionist account of language and literacy development. In J. Kavanaugh (Ed.), *The language continuum,* Parkton, MD: The York Press.

Dillon, J. T. (1988). *Questioning and teaching: A manual of practice.* New York: Teachers College Press.

Doctorow, M., Wittrock, M. C., & Marks, C. (1978). Generative processes in reading comprehension. *Journal of Educational Psychology, 70,* 109–118.

Dolch, E. W. (1942). *Basic sight word test.* Champaign, IL: Garrard.

Dolch, E. W. (1942). *Better spelling.* Champaign, IL: Garrard Press.

Dole, J. A., Duffy, G. G., Roehler, L. R., & Pearson, P. D. (1991). Moving from the old to the new: Research on reading comprehension instruction. *Review of Educational Research, 61,* 239–264.

Downing, J. (1970). Children's concepts of language in learning to read. *Educational Research, 12,* 106–112.

Downing, J. (1978). Linguistic awareness, English orthography and reading instruction. *Journal of Reading Behavior, 10,* 103–114.

Downing, J., Ayers, D., & Schaefer, B. (1983). *Linguistic Awareness in Reading Readiness (LARR) Test.* Slough, England: NFER-Nelson.

Downing, J., & Leong, C. K. (1982). *Psychology of reading.* New York: Macmillan.

Doyle, W. (1983). Academic work. *Review of Educational Research, 53,* 159–199.

Doyle, W. (1986). Classroom organization and management. In M.C. Wittrock (Ed.), *Handbook of research on teaching* (3rd ed., pp. 392–431). New York: Macmillan.

Drahozal, E. C., & Hanna, G. S. (1978). Reading comprehension subscores: Pretty bottles for ordinary wine. *Journal of Reading, 21,* 416–420.

Dreeben, R. (1968). The contribution of schooling to the learning of norms. In *Socialization and schools* (Harvard Educational Review Reprint Series No. 1). Cambridge, MA: Harvard University Press.

DuBois, D., & Stice, C. (1981). Comprehension instruction: Let's recall it for repair. *Reading World, 20,* 172–183.

Duckworth, E. (1979). Either we're too early and they can't learn it or we're too late and they know it already: The dilemma of "applying Piaget." *Harvard Educational Review, 49,* 297–312.

Duell, O. K. (1974). Effect of types of objective, level of test questions, and judged importance of texted materials upon posttest performance. *Journal of Educational Psychology, 66,* 225–232.

Dufflemeyer, F. A., Baum, D. D., & Merkley, D. J. (1987). Maximizing reader-text confrontation with an extended anticipation guide. *Journal of Reading, 31,* 146–150.

Duffy, G. G. (1993). Rethinking strategy instruction: Four teachers' development and their low achievers' understandings. *Elementary School Journal, 93,* 231–247.

Duffy, G. G., & McIntyre, L. (1982). A naturalistic study of instructional assistance in primary grade reading. *Elementary School Journal, 83,* 5–23.

Duffy, G. G., & Roehler, L. R. (1989). *Improving classroom reading instruction: A decision making approach* (2nd ed.). New York: Random House.

Duffy, G. G., Roehler, L. R., Meloth, M. S., Vavrus, L. G., Book, C., Putnam, J., & Wesselman, R. (1986). The relationship between explicit verbal explanations during reading skills instruction and student awareness and achievement: A study of reading teacher effects. *Reading Research Quarterly, 21,* 237–252.

Dunn, L. M., & Dunn, L. M. (1981). *Peabody Picture Vocabulary Test—*

Revised. Circle Pines. MN: American Guidance Service.

Durkin, D. (1978). *Teaching them to read* (3rd ed.). Boston: Allyn & Bacon.

Durkin, D. (1978–79). What classroom observations reveal about reading comprehension instruction. *Reading Research Quarterly, 14,* 481–533.

Durkin, D. (1981). Reading comprehension instruction in five basal reader series. *Reading Research Quarterly, 16,* 515–544.

Durkin, D. (1983). *Teaching them to read* (4th ed.). Boston: Allyn & Bacon.

Durkin, D. (1984). Is there a match between what elementary teachers do and what basal reader manuals recommend? *The Reading Teacher, 37,* 734–749.

Durkin, D. (1987). Testing in kindergarten. *The Reading Teacher, 40,* 766–770.

Durr, W. K. (1973). Computer study of high frequency words in popular trade journals. *The Reading Teacher, 27,* 37–42.

Dweck, C. S., & Bempechat, J. (1983). Children's theories of intelligence: Consequences for learning. In S. G. Paris, G. M. Olson, & H. S. Stevenson (Eds.), *Learning and motivation in the classroom* (pp. 239–258). Hillsdale, NJ: Lawrence Erlbaum.

Eckhoff, B. (1983). How reading affects children's writing. *Language Arts, 60,* 607–616.

Edmonds, R. (1980). *A discussion of the literature and issues related to effective schooling.* St. Louis, MO: Cemrel.

Eeds, M. (1985). Bookwords: Using a beginning word list of high frequency words from children's literature K–3. *The Reading Teacher, 38,* 418–423.

Ehri, L. (1979). Linguistic insight: Threshold of reading acquisition. In T. G. Waller & G. E. MacKinnon (Eds.), *Reading research: Advances in theory and practice* (Vol. 1, pp. 63–114). New York: Academic Press.

Ehri, L. (1987). Learning to read and spell words. *Journal of Reading Behavior, 19,* 5–32.

Ehri, L. C. (1989). Movement into word reading and spelling: How spelling contributes to reading. In J. M. Mason (Ed.), *Reading and writing connections* (pp. 65–81). Needham Heights, MA: Allyn & Bacon.

Eisenberg, L. (1975). Psychiatric aspects of language disability. In D. Duane & M. Rawson (Eds.), *Reading, perception, and language* (pp. 215–229). Baltimore: York Press.

Ekwall, E. E. (1979). *Ekwall reading inventory* (1st ed.). Boston: Allyn & Bacon.

Ekwall, E. E., & Shanker, J. L. (1985). *Teaching reading in the elementary school.* Columbus, OH: Charles E. Merrill.

Elley, W. B. (1989). Vocabulary acquisition from listening to stories. *Reading Research Quarterly, 24,* 174–187.

Elley, W. G., & Mangubhai, F. (1983). The impact of reading on second language learning. *Reading Research Quarterly, 19,* 53–67.

Elliot, S. N. (1980). Children's knowledge and uses of organizational patterns of prose in recalling what they read. *Journal of Reading Behavior, 12,* 203–212.

Ellis, A. (1984). *Reading, writing and dyslexia: A cognitive view.* Hillsdale, NJ: Lawrence Erlbaum.

Englert, C. S. (1990). Unraveling the mysteries of writing through strategy instruction. In T. E. Scruggs & B. Y. L. Wong (Eds.), *Intervention research in learning disabilities* (pp. 186–223). New York: Springer-Verlag.

Englert, C. S. (1992). Writing instruction from a sociocultural perspective: The holistic, dialogic, and social enterprise of writing. *Journal of Learning Disabilities, 25,* 153–172.

Englert, C. S., & Palincsar, A. S. (1991). Reconsidering instructional research in literacy from a sociocultural perspective. *Learning Disabilities Research and Practice, 6,* 225–229.

Englert, C. S., Raphael, T. E., Anderson, L. M., Anthony, H. M., & Stevens, D. D. (1991). Making strategies and self-talk visible: Writing instruction in regular and special education classrooms. *American Educational Research Journal, 28,* 337–372.

Englert, C. S., Raphael, T. E., Anderson, L. M., Gregg, S. L., & Anthony, H. M. (1989). Exposition: Reading, writing, and the metacognitive knowledge of learning disabled students. *Learning Disabilities Research, 5,* 5–24.

Entin, E. B., & Klare, G. R. (1985). Relationships of measures of interest, prior knowledge, and readability to comprehension of expository passages. In B. Hutson (Ed.), *Advances in reading/language research* (Vol. 3, pp. 9–38). Greenwich, CT: JAI Press.

Ericsson, K. A., & Simon, H. A. (1980). Verbal reports as data. *Psychological Review, 87,* 215–251.

Estes, T. H., & Vaughan, J.L. (1973). Reading interest and comprehension: Implications. *The Reading Teacher, 27,* 149–153.

Estes, T. H., & Vaughan, J. L. (1978). *Reading and learning in the content classroom.* Boston: Allyn & Bacon.

Fass, W., & Schumacher, G. M. (1978). Effects of motivation, subject activity, and readability on the retention of prose materials. *Journal of Educational Psychology, 70,* 803–808.

Federal Register (29 December 1977). Washington, DC: 65062–65085.

Feitelson, D., Kita, B., & Goldstein, Z. (1986). Effects of listening to series stories on first graders' comprehension and use of language. *Research in the Teaching of English, 20,* 339–356.

Fernald, G. M. (1943). *Remedial techniques in basic school subjects.* New York: McGraw-Hill.

Ferreiro, E. (1978). What is written in a written sentence? A developmental answer. *Journal of Education, 160,* 25–39.

Ferreiro, E. (1980, May). *The relationship between oral and written language: The children's viewpoints.* Paper presented at the 25th Annual Conference of the International Reading Association, St. Louis, MO.

Ferreiro, E., & Teberosky, A. (1979/1982). *Literacy before schooling.* Exeter, NH: Heinemann.

Feuerstein, R., Rand, Y., & Hoffman, M.B. (1979). *The dynamic assessment of retarded performance.*

Baltimore, MD: University Park Press.

Fielding, L.G., Wilson, P.T., & Anderson, R.C. (1986). A new focus on free reading: The role of trade books in reading instruction. In T.E. Raphael (Ed.), *The contexts of school-based literacy* (pp. 149–160). New York: Random House.

Fillion, B., & Brause, R. S. (1987). Research into classroom practices: What have we learned and where are we going? In J. R. Squire (Ed.), *The dynamics of language learning* (pp. 201–225). Urbana, IL: ERIC Clearinghouse on Reading and Communications Skills and the National Conference on Research in English.

Firth, U. (1980). Unexpected spelling problems. In U. Firth (Ed.), *Cognitive processes in learning to spell.* London: Academic Press.

Fisher, C. W., Berliner, D. C., Filby, N., Marliave, R., Cohen, L., Dishaw, M., & Moore, J. (1980). Teaching behaviors, academic learning time, and student achievement: An overview. In C. Denham & A. Lieberman (Eds.), *Time to learn* (pp. 7–32). Washington, DC: National Institute of Education.

Flanders, N. (1975). The use of interaction analysis to study pupil attitudes toward learning. In R. A. Weinberg & F. H. Wood (Eds.), *Observation of pupils and teachers in mainstream and special education settings: Alternative strategies* (pp. 41–74). Minneapolis: The Leadership Training Institute/Special Education, The University of Minnesota.

Flavell, J. H. (1977). *Cognitive development.* Englewood Cliffs, NJ: Prentice-Hall.

Flavell, J. H., & Wellman, H. M. (1977). Metamemory. In R. Kail, Jr., & J. W. Hagen (Eds.), *Perspectives on the development of memory and cognition* (pp. 3–33). Hillsdale, NJ: Lawrence Erlbaum.

Flesch, R. (1948). A new readability yardstick. *Journal of Applied Psychology, 32,* 221–233.

Flood, J., & Lapp, D. (1987). Forms of discourse in basal readers. *The Elementary School Journal, 87,* 299–306.

Flores, B., & Hernandez, E. (1988). A bilingual kindergartener's socio-psychogenesis of literacy and bi-literacy. *Dialogue, 3,* 43–49.

Florio-Ruane, S. (1991). Instructional conversations in learning to write and learning to teach. In L. Idol & B. F. Jones (Eds.), *Educational values and cognitive instruction: Implications for reform* (pp. 365–386). Hillsdale, NJ: Lawrence Erlbaum.

Flower, L., & Hayes, J. (1981). Plans that guide the composing process. In C. H. Frederiksen & J. Dominic (Eds.), *Writing: The nature, development, and teaching of written communication* (pp. 39–58). Hillsdale, NJ: Lawrence Erlbaum.

Fowler, G. L. (1982). Developing comprehension skills in primary students through the use of story frames. *The Reading Teacher, 36,* 176–184.

Fowler, J. W., & Peterson, P. L. (1981). Increasing reading persistence and altering attributional style of learned helpless children.

Journal of Educational Psychology, 73, 251–260.

Fox, B., & Routh, D. K. (1976). Phonemic analysis and severe reading disability in children. *Journal of Psycholinguistic Research, 9*, 115–119.

Fox, C. (1987). Talking like a book: Young children's oral monologues. In M. Meek (Ed.), *Opening moves: Work in progress in the study of children's language development* (Bedford Way Papers 17, pp. 12–25). London, UK: Institute of Education, University of London, Turnaround Distribution Ltd.

Fraatz, J. M. (1987). *The politics of reading: Power, opportunity, and prospects for change in America's public schools.* New York: Teachers College Press.

Francis, H. (1973). Children's experience of reading and notions of units of language. *British Journal of Educational Psychology, 43*, 17–23.

Freebody, P., & Anderson, R.C. (1983). Effects on text comprehension of differing proportions and locations of difficult vocabulary. *Journal of Reading Behavior, 15*, 19–40.

Fry, E. (1968). A readability formula that saves time. *Journal of Reading, 11*, 513–516, 578.

Fry, E. (1980). The new instant word list. *The Reading Teacher, 34*, 284–289.

Fulwiler, T. (1980). Journals across the disciplines. *English Journal, 69*, 14–19.

Fulwiler, T. (1982). The personal connection: Journal writing across the curriculum. In T. Fulwiler &

A. Young (Eds.), *Language connections: Writing and reading across the curriculum* (pp. 15–32). Urbana, IL: National Council of Teachers of English.

Fulwiler, T. (1987a). *Teaching with writing.* Portsmouth, NH: Boynton/Cook.

Fulwiler, T. (Ed.). (1987b). *The journal book.* Portsmouth, NH: Boynton/Cook.

Gage, N. L., & Berliner, D. C. (1988). *Educational psychology.* Boston: Houghton-Mifflin.

Galda, L. (1982). Assessment: Responses to literature. In A. Berger & H. A. Robinson (Eds.), *Secondary school reading: What research reveals for classroom practice* (pp. 111–125). Urbana, IL: National Council of Teachers of English and ERIC Clearinghouse on Reading and Communications Skills.

Gallagher, J. (1984). Policy analysis and program implementation/PL 94–142. *Topics in Early Childhood Special Education, 4 (1)*, 43–53.

Gallego, M., & Hollingsworth, S. (1992). Research directions: Multiple literacies: Teachers' evolving perceptions. *Language Arts, 69*, 206–213.

Gambrell, L. B. (1978). Getting started with sustained silent reading and keeping it going. *The Reading Teacher, 32*, 328–331.

Gambrell, L. B. (1985). Dialogue journals: Reading-writing interaction. *The Reading Teacher, 38*, 512–515.

Garcia, G. E. (1991). Factors influencing the English reading test performance of Spanish-speaking Hispanic children. *Read-*

ing Research Quarterly, 26, 371–392.

Garcia, G. E. (1993). Spanish-English bilingual students' use of cognates in English reading. *Journal of Reading Behavior, 25,* 241–259.

Garcia, G. E., & Pearson, P. D. (1991). The role of assessment in a diverse society. In E. H. Hiebert (Ed.), *Literacy for a diverse society* (pp. 253–278). New York: Teachers College Press.

Garcia, G. E., Pearson, P. D., & Jimenez, R. T. (October, 1994). *The at-risk situation: A synthesis of reading research.* Special Report. Champaign, IL: Center for the Study of Reading, University of Illinois at Urbana-Champaign.

Garcia, M. W., & Verville, K. (1994). Redesigning teaching and learning: The Arizona state assessment program. In S. W. Valencia, F. Hiebert, & P. P. Afflerbach (Eds.), *Authentic reading assessment: Practices and possibilities* (pp. 228–246). Newark, DE: International Reading Association.

Gardner, E. F. (1978). Bias. *Measurement in Education, 9,* 1–4.

Gardner, H. (1983). *Frames of mind.* NY: Basic Books.

Garner, R., & Reis, R. (1981). Monitoring and resolving comprehension obstacles: An investigation of spontaneous text lookbacks among upper-grade good and poor comprehenders. *Reading Research Quarterly, 16,* 569–582.

Gaskins, I. (1987). Helping teachers adapt to the needs of students with learning problems. In S.J. Samuels & P.D. Pearson (Eds.), *Changing school reading programs*

(pp. 143–160). Newark, DE: International Reading Association.

Gates, A. I., McKillop, A. S., & Horowitz, E.C. (1981). *Gates-McKillop-Horowitz reading diagnostic tests* (2nd ed.). New York: Teachers College Press.

Gavelek, J. R., & Palincsar, A.S. (1988). Contextualism as an alternative worldview of learning disabilities: A response to Swanson's "Toward a metatheory of learning disabilities." *Journal of Learning Disabilities, 21,* 278–281.

Gee, J. P. (1989). Commonalities and differences in narrative construction. *Discourse Processes, 12,* 287–307.

Geertz, C. (1983). Blurred genres: The refiguration of social thought. In C. Geertz (Ed.), *Local knowledge: Further essays in interpretive anthropology.* New York: Basic Books.

Genishi, C., & Dyson, A. H. (1984). *Language assessment in the early years.* Norwood, NJ: Ablex.

Gentry, J. R. (1978). Early spelling strategies. *Elementary School Journal, 79,* 88–92.

Gentry, J. R. (1981). Learning to spell developmentally. *The Reading Teacher, 34,* 378–381.

Gentry, J. R. (1982). An analysis of developmental spelling in GYNS AT WORK. *The Reading Teacher, 36,* 192–200.

Gillet, J., & Temple, C. (1982). *Understanding reading problems* (1st ed.). Boston: Little, Brown.

Gillet, J., & Temple, C. (1990). *Understanding reading problems* (3rd ed.). Glenview, IL: Scott, Foresman.

Gipe, J. (1978–79). Investigating techniques for teaching word meanings. *Reading Research Quarterly, 14*, 624–644.

Glazer, S.M., & Searfoss, L. (1988). *Reading diagnosis and instruction: A C-A-L-M approach.* Englewood Cliffs, NJ: Prentice Hall.

Gleason, H. A., Jr. (1965). *Linguistics and English grammar.* NY: Holt, Rinehart & Winston.

Goatley, V. J., Brock, C. H., & Raphael, T. E. (1995). Diverse learners participating in regular education "Book Clubs." *Reading Research Quarterly, 30*, 352–380.

Goetz, E., & Armbruster, B. (1980). Psychological correlates of text structure. In R.J. Spiro, B.C. Bruce, & W.F. Brewer (Eds.), *Theoretical issues in reading comprehension* (pp. 201–220). Hillsdale, NJ: Lawrence Erlbaum.

Goldenberg, C. (1993). Instructional conversations: Promoting comprehension through discussion. *The Reading Teacher, 46*, 316–326.

Goldenburg, C., & Gallimore, R. (1991). Changing teaching takes more than a one-shot workshop. *Educational Leadership, 49*, 69–72.

Goldstein, B. S. (1986). Looking at cartoons and comics in a new way. *Journal of Reading, 29*, 657–661.

Good, T. (1983). Research on classroom teaching. In L. S. Shulman & G. Sykes (Eds.), *Handbook of teaching and policy* (pp. 42–80). New York: Longman.

Good, T. L., & Brophy, J. E. (1987). *Looking in classrooms* (4th ed.). New York: Harper & Row.

Good, T. L., & Marshall, S. (1984). Do students learn more in heterogeneous or homogeneous achievement groups? In P. Peterson, L. Cherry-Wilkinson, & M. Hallinan (Eds.), *The social context for instruction* (pp. 15–38). New York: Academic Press.

Goodman, K. S. (1969). Analysis of oral reading miscues: Applied psycholinguistics. *Reading Research Quarterly, 5*, 9–30.

Goodman, K.S. (1973). Miscues: Windows on the reading process. In K. S. Goodman (Ed.), *Miscue analysis: Applications to reading instruction* (pp. 3–14). Urbana, IL: ERIC Clearinghouse on Reading and Communication Skills and the National Council of Teachers of English.

Goodman, K. S. (1989). Whole language *is* whole: A response to Heymsfeld. *Educational Leadership, 46(6)*, 69–70.

Goodman, K. S., & Goodman, Y. M. (1977). Learning about psycholinguistic processes by analyzing oral reading. *Harvard Educational Review, 47*, 317–333.

Goodman, K. S., Shannon, P., Freeman, Y. S., & Murphy, S. (1988). *Report card on basal readers.* New York: Richard C. Owen.

Goodman, Y. M. (1986). Children coming to know literacy. In W.H. Teale & E. Sulzby (Eds.), *Emergent literacy: Writing and reading* (pp. 1–14). Norwood, NJ: Ablex.

Goodman, Y. M., & Burke, C. L. (1972). *Reading miscue inventory.* New York: Richard C. Owen.

Goodman, Y. M., & Goodman, K. S. (1994). To err is human: Learning about language processes by analyzing miscues. In R. B. Ruddell &

H. Singer (Eds.), *Theoretical models and processes of reading.* Newark, DE: International Reading Association.

Goodman, Y. M., Watson, D. J., & Burke, C. L. (1987). *Reading miscue inventory: Alternative procedures.* New York: Richard C. Owen.

Gordon, C., & Pearson, P. D. (1983). *The effects of instruction in metacomprehension and inferencing on children's comprehension abilities* (Tech. Rep. 269). Urbana, IL: University of Illinois, Center for the Study of Reading.

Goswami, U. (1986). Children's use of analogy in learning to read: A developmental study. *Journal of Experimental Child Psychology, 42,* 73–83.

Gough, P. B. (1972). One second of reading. In J. F. Kavanagh & I. G. Mattingly (Eds.), *Language by ear and by eye* (pp. 331–358). Cambridge, MA: MIT Press.

Graesser, A. C., Golding, J. M., & Long, D. L. (1991). Narrative representation and comprehension. In R. Barr, M.L. Kamil, P. Mosenthal, & P. D. Pearson (Eds.), *Handbook of reading research* (Vol. II, pp. 171–205). New York: Longman.

Graesser, A. C., & Riha, J. R. (1984). An application of multiple regression techniques to sentence reading times. In D. Kieras & M. Just (Eds.), *New methods in comprehension research* (pp. 183–218). Hillsdale, NJ: Lawrence Erlbaum.

Graham, S., & Harris, K. R. (1994). The role and development of self-regulation in the writing process. In D. H. Schunk & B. J. Zimmerman (Eds.), *Self-regulation of learning and performance* (pp. 203–228). Hillsdale, NJ: Lawrence Erlbaum.

Graves, D. H. (1983). *Writing: Teachers and children at work.* Portsmouth, NH: Heinemann.

Graves, D. H. (1994). *A Fresh Look at Writing.* Portsmouth, NH: Heinemann.

Graves, D. H., & Hansen, J. (1983). The author's chair. *Language Arts, 60,* 176–183.

Graves, M., & Graves, B. (1994). *Scaffolding reading experiences.* Norwood, MA: Christopher Gordon.

Graves, M. F., Cooke, C. L., & LaBerge, M. J. (1983). Effects of previewing short stores. *Reading Research Quarterly, 18,* 262–276.

Gray, W. S. (1920). The value of informal tests of reading achievement. *Journal of Educational Research, 1,* 103–111.

Gray, W. S., & Leary, B. E. (1935). *What makes a book readable?* Chicago: University of Chicago Press.

Greaney, V. (1980). Factors related to amount and type of leisure reading. *Reading Research Quarterly, 15,* 337–357.

Green, G. (1984). On the appropriateness of adaptations in primary-level basal readers. In R.C. Anderson, J. Osborn, & R. J. Tierney (Eds.), *Learning to read in American schools: Basal readers and content texts* (pp. 175–191). Hillsdale, NJ: Lawrence Erlbaum.

Green, J., & Bloome, D. (1983). Ethnography and reading: Issues, approaches, criteria, and findings. *Searches for meaning in reading/language processing and instruction*

(32nd Yearbook of The National Reading Conference, pp. 6–30). New York: National Reading Conference.

Grimes, J. E. (1975). *The thread of discourse.* The Hague, Netherlands: Mouton.

Gronlund, N. E. (1981). *Measurement and evaluation in teaching* (4th ed.). New York: Macmillan.

Gronlund, N. E. (1985). *Measurement and evaluation in teaching* (5th ed.). New York: Macmillan.

Gump, P. V. (1969). Intra-setting analysis; The third grade classroom as a special but instructive case. In E. Willems & H. Rausch (Eds.), *Naturalistic viewpoints in psychological research* (pp. 200–220). New York: Holt, Rinehart & Winston.

Guthrie, J. T. (1980). Research reviews: Time in reading programs. *The Reading Teacher, 33,* 500–502.

Hall, N. A. (1976). Children's awareness of segmentation in speech and print. *Reading, 10,* 11–19.

Halliday, M. A. K., & Hasan, R. (1976). *Cohesion in English.* London: Longman.

Hammill, D. D., & Larsen, S. C. (1988). *Test of Written Language—2.* Austin, TX: Pro-Ed.

Hammill, D. D., & Larsen, S. C. (1996). *Test of Written Language–3.* Austin, TX: PRO-ED.

Hansen, J. (1981). The effects of inference training and practice on young children's reading comprehension. *Reading Research Quarterly, 16,* 391–417.

Hansen, J. (1987). *When writers read.* Portsmouth, NH: Heinemann.

Hare, V. C. (1984). What's in a word? A review of young children's difficulties with the construct of "word." *The Reading Teacher, 37,* 360–364.

Hare, V. C., & Borchardt, K. (1984). Direct instruction of summarization skills. *Reading Research Quarterly, 20,* 62–78.

Hare, V. C., Rabinowitz, M., & Schieble, K. M. (1989). Text effects on main idea comprehension. *Reading Research Quarterly, 24,* 72–88.

Harris, A. J. (1977). Ten years of progress in remedial reading. *The Reading Teacher, 31,* 29–35.

Harris, A.J., & Sipay, E.R. (1985). *How to increase reading ability* (8th ed.). New York: Longman.

Harris, A. J., & Sipay, E. R. (1990). *How to increase reading ability* (9th ed.). New York: Longman.

Harris, K. R., & Pressley, M. (1991). The nature of cognitive strategy instruction: Interactive strategy construction. *Exceptional Children, 57,* 392–404.

Harste, J., Woodward, V. A., & Burke, C. (1984). *Language stories and literacy lessons.* Portsmouth, NH: Heinemann.

Haskins, R., Walden, T., & Ramey, C. (1983). Teacher and student behavior in high- and low-ability groups. *Journal of Educational Psychology, 75,* 865–876.

Hayes, B., & Peters, C. W. (1989). The role of reading instruction in the social studies. In D. Lapp, & J. Flood (Eds.), *Handbook of instructional theory and practice* (pp. 152–178). Englewood Cliffs, NJ: Prentice-Hall.

Hayes, J. R., & Flower, L. S. (1980). Identifying the organization of writing processes. In L. W. Gregg & E. R. Steinberg (Eds.), *Cognitive processes in writing* (pp. 3–30). Hillsdale, NJ: Lawrence Erlbaum.

Hazlett, J. A. (1972). *A national assessment of educational progress. Report 8, Writing: National results.* Washington DC: U. S. Government Printing Office.

Heath, S. B. (1981). Questioning at home and at school: A comparative study. In G. Spindler (Ed.), *Doing ethnography: Educational anthropology in action* (pp. 102–131). New York: Holt, Rinehart & Winston.

Heath, S. B. (1983). *Ways with words: Language, life, and work in communities and classrooms.* Cambridge, England: Cambridge University Press.

Heath, S. B. (1991). The sense of being literate. In R. Barr, M. Kamil, P. Mosenthal, & P. D. Pearson (Eds.), *Handbook of reading research* Vol II. White Plains, NY: Longman.

Henderson, E. H. (1980). Developmental concepts of word. In E. H. Henderson & J. W. Beers (Eds.), *Developmental and cognitive aspects of learning to spell: A reflection of word knowledge* (pp. 1–14). Newark, DE: International Reading Association.

Henderson, E. H. (1992). *Teaching spelling* (2nd ed.), Boston: Houghton-Mifflin.

Hendley, B. P. (1986). *Dewey, Russell, Whitehead: Philosophers as educators.* Carbondale, IL: Southern Illinois University Press.

Herber, H. L. (1970). *Teaching reading in the content areas.* Englewood Cliffs, NJ: Prentice-Hall.

Herber, H. L. (1978). *Teaching reading in the content areas* (2nd ed.). Englewood Cliffs, NJ: Prentice-Hall.

Herman, P. A., Anderson, R. C., Pearson, P. D., & Nagy, W. E. (1987). Incidental acquisition of word meaning from expositions with varied text features. *Reading Research Quarterly, 22,* 263–284.

Hiebert, E. H. (1981). Developmental patterns and interrelationships of preschool children's print awareness. *Reading Research Quarterly, 16,* 236–260.

Hiebert, E. H. (1983). An examination of ability grouping for reading instruction. *Reading Research Quarterly, 18,* 231–255.

Hiebert, E. H. (1994). Becoming literate through authentic tasks: Evidence and adaptations. In R. R. Ruddell, M. R. Ruddell, H. Singer (Eds.), *Theoretical models and processes of reading* (4th Ed.). (pp. 391–413). Newark, DE: International Reading Association.

Hiebert, E. H., & Fisher, C. W. (1991). Task and talk structures that foster literacy. In E. H. Hiebert (Ed.), *Literacy for a diverse society.* (pp. 341–156). New York: Teachers College Press.

Hiebert, E. H., Winograd, P. N., & Danner, F. W. (1984). Children's attributions for failure and success in different aspects of reading. *Journal of Educational Psychology, 76,* 1139–1148.

Higgins, K. M., Harris, N. A., & Kuehn, L. L. (1994). Placing assessment into the hands of young children: A study of student-generated criteria and self-assessment. *Educational Assessment, 2,* 309–324.

Hillocks, G. (1986). *Research on written composition: New directions for teaching.* Urbana, IL: National Conference on Research in English.

Hillocks, G., & Smith, M. W. (1991). In J. Flood, D. Lapp & J. Squire (Eds.), *Handbook of research on teaching the English language arts* (pp. 591–603). New York: Macmillan.

Hoffman, J. V., McCarthey, S. J., Abbott, J., Christian, C., Corman, L., Curry, C., Dressman, M., Elliott, B., Matherne, D., & Stahle, D. (1994). So what's new in the new basals? A focus on first grade. *Journal of Reading Behavior, 26,* 47–73.

Holdaway, D. (1979). *Foundations of literacy.* Sydney, Australia: Ashton Scholastic.

Holmes, B. C., & Roser, N.L. (1987). Five ways to assess readers' prior knowledge. *The Reading Teacher, 40,* 646–649.

Hong, L. K. (1981). Modifying SSR for beginning readers. *The Reading Teacher, 34,* 888–891.

Hood, J. (1978). Is miscue analysis practical for teachers? *The Reading Teacher, 32,* 260–266.

Hoskisson, K., & Tompkins, G. E. (1987). *Language arts: Content and teaching strategies.* Columbus, OH: Merrill.

Howell, K. W., & Morehead, M.K. (1987). *Curriculum-based evaluation for special and remedial education.* Columbus, OH: Charles E. Merrill.

Hresko, W. P., Herron, S. R., & Peak, P. K. (1996). *Test of Early Written Language, Second Edition.* Austin, TX: PRO-ED.

Hudelson, S. (1986). ESL children's writing: What we've learned, what we're learning. In P. Rigg, & D. S. Enright (Eds.), *Children and ESL: Integrating perspectives* (pp. 23–54). Washington, DC: Teachers of English to Speakers of Other Languages.

Hudelson, S. (1987). The role of native language literacy in the education of language minority children. *Language Arts, 64,* 827–834.

Huey, E. B. (1908/1968). *The psychology and pedagogy of reading.* Cambridge, MA: MIT Press. (Republished: Cambridge, MA: MIT Press, 1968).

Hunt, J. McV. (1961). *Intelligence and experience.* NY: Ronald.

Hunt, K. W. (1965). *Grammatical structures written at three grade levels: NCTE research report #3.* Urbana, IL: National Council of Teachers of English.

Hunt, L. C. (1970). Effect of self-selection, interest, and motivation upon independent, instructional, and frustrational levels. *The Reading Teacher, 24,* (2), 146–151.

Hynd, C. R., & Alvermann, D. E. (1986). Prior knowledge activation in refutation and non-refutation text. In J. A. Niles & R. Lalik (Eds.), *Solving problems in literacy: Learners, teachers, and researchers.* (Thirty-fifth Yearbook of The National Reading Conference, pp. 55–60). Rochester, NY: National Reading Conference.

Ilg, F. (1982). *Scoring notes: The developmental examination.* New Haven, CT: Gesell Institute of Human Development.

Ilg, F.L., & Ames, L.B. (1965). *Gesell Developmental Tests of School Readiness.* Lumberville, PA: Programs for Education.

IRA/NCTE (1994). *Standards for the assessment of reading and writing.* Newark, DE: IRA-NCTE.

Irvin, J. L. (1990). *Reading and the middle school student.* Boston: Allyn & Bacon.

Irwin, J. W., & Davis, C. (1980). Assessing readability: The checklist approach. *Journal of Reading, 24,* 124–130.

Irwin, P. A., & Mitchell, J. N. (1983). A procedure for assessing the richness of retellings. *Journal of Reading, 26,* 391–396.

Jewell, M. C., & Zintz, M. V. (1990). *Learning to read and write naturally* (2nd ed.). Dubuque, IA: Kendall/Hunt.

Johns, J. J. (1988). *Basic reading inventory* (4th ed.). Dubuque, IA: Kendall/Hunt.

Johnson, D. D. (1971). A basic vocabulary for beginning reading. *The Elementary School Journal, 72,* 29–34.

Johnson, D. D., & Pearson, P. D. (1984). *Teaching reading vocabulary* (2nd ed.). New York: Holt, Rinehart & Winston.

Johnson, D. W., & Johnson, R. T. (1986). *Learning together and alone* (2nd ed). Englewood Cliffs, NJ: Prentice-Hall.

Johnson, M. S., & Kress, R. A. (1965). *Informal reading inventories.* Newark, DE: International Reading Association.

Johnston, P.H. (1985). Teaching students to apply strategies that improve reading comprehension. *Elementary School Journal, 85,* 635–645.

Johnston, P. H. (1987). Teachers as evaluation experts. *The Reading Teacher, 40,* 744–748.

Johnston, P. H. (1992). *Constructive evaluation of literate activity.* New York: Longman.

Johnston, P. H., Allington, R. L., & Afflerbach, P. (1985). The congruence of classroom and remedial reading instruction. *Elementary School Journal, 85,* 465–477.

Johnston, P. H., Allington, R., & Franzen, A. (1985, April). Obstacles to an integrated understanding of reading failure. In M.Y. Lipson (Chair.), *Research on reading disabilities: Theoretical and methodological issues.* Symposium conducted at the meeting of the American Educational Research Association, Chicago, IL.

Jones, B. F. (1983, April). *Integrating learning strategies and text research to teach higher order thinking skills in schools.* Paper presented at the Annual Meeting of the American Educational Research Association, Montreal, Canada.

Jongsma, E. A. (1982). Test review: Peabody Picture Vocabulary Test-Revised (PPVT-R). *Journal of Reading, 20,* 360–364.

Jongsma, K. S., & Jongsma, E. A. (1981). Test review: Commercial informal reading inventories. *The Reading Teacher, 34,* 697–705.

Jordan, C. (1985). Translating culture: From ethnographic information to educational program. *Anthropology and Education Quarterly, 16,* 105–123.

Juel, C. (1988). Learning to read and write: A longitudinal study of fifty-four children from first through fourth grade. *Journal of Educational Psychology, 80,* 437–447.

Juel, C., Griffith, P. L., & Gough, P. B. (1986). Acquisition of literacy: A longitudinal study of children in first and second grade. *Journal of Educational Psychology, 78,* 243–255.

Kalmbach, J. R. (1986). Getting at the point of retellings. *Journal of Reading, 29,* 326–333.

Kameenui, E. J., & Shannon, P. (1988). Point/counterpoint: Direct instruction reconsidered. In J. Readence, R. Baldwin, J. Konopak, & P. O'Keefe, *Dialogues in literacy research* (37th Yearbook of the National Reading Conference, pp. 35–44). Chicago: National Reading Conference.

Kappelman, M., Kaplan, E., & Ganter, R. (1969). A study of learning disorders among disadvantaged children. *Journal of Learning Disabilities, 2,* 262–268.

Karlsen, B., & Gardner, E. (1995). *Stanford Diagnostic Reading Test.* 4th Ed. San Antonio, TX: Harcourt Brace.

Kastler, L. A., Roser, N. L., & Hoffman, J. V. (1987). Understanding the forms and functions of written language: Insights from children and parents. In J. E. Readence & R. S. Baldwin (Eds.), *Research in literacy: Merging perspectives* (36th Yearbook of the National Reading Conference, pp. 85–92). Rochester, NY: National Reading Conference.

Katz, M. (1987). *Reconstructing American education.* Cambridge, MA: Harvard University Press.

Kemp, M. (1987). *Watching children read and write.* Portsmouth, NH: Heinemann.

Kendall, J., & Mason, J. (1980). *Comprehension of polysemous words.* Paper presented at the Annual Meeting of the American Educational Research Association, Boston, MA.

Kennedy, B. A., & Miller, D. J. (1976). Persistent use of verbal rehearsal as a function of information about its value. *Child Development, 47,* 566–569.

Kibby, M.W. (1979). Passage readability affects the oral reading strategies of disabled readers. *The Reading Teacher, 32,* 390–396.

Kilgallon, P. A. (1942). *The study of relationships among certain pupil adjustments in reading situations.* Unpublished doctoral dissertation, Pennsylvania State College, Pennsylvania.

King, L. H. (1983). Pupil classroom perceptions and the expectancy effect. *South Pacific Journal of Teacher Education, 11,* 54–70.

Kintsch, W. & van Dijk, T. (1978). Toward a model of text comprehension and production. *Psychological Review, 85,* 363–394.

Kintsch, W., & Vipond, D. (1979). Reading comprehension and readability in educational practice and psychological theory. In L. G. Nilsson (Ed.), *Perspectives on memory research* (pp. 329–366). Hillsdale, NJ: Lawrence Erlbaum.

Klare, G. (1984). Readability. In P.D. Pearson (Ed.), *Handbook of reading* research (pp. 681–744). New York: Longman.

Klare, G. (1988). The formative years. In B. L. Zakaluk & S. J. Samuels (Eds.), *Readability: Its past, present, and future* (pp. 14–34). Newark, DE: International Reading Association.

Klesius, S. E. (1972). Perceptual motor development and reading— A closer look. In R. C. Aukerman (Ed.), *Some persistent problems in beginning reading* (pp. 151–159). Newark, DE: International Reading Association.

Kobrin, B. (1988). *Eyeopeners.* New York: Penguin Books.

Koppitz, E. M. (1963). *The Bender Gestalt Test for Young Children.* New York: Grune & Stratton.

Koppitz, E. M. (1975). *The Bender Gesalt Test for Young Children: Volume II: Research and application, 1963–1973.* New York: Grune & Stratton.

Kounin, J. S. (1970). *Discipline and group management in classrooms.* New York: Holt, Rinehart & Winston.

Kucer, S. (1985). The making of meaning: Reading and writing as parallel processes. *Written Communication, 2.* 317–336.

LaBerge, D., & Samuels, J. (1974). Toward a theory of automatic information processing in reading. *Cognitive Psychology, 6,* 293–323.

Langer, J. A. (1981). From theory to practice: A prereading plan. *Journal of Reading, 25,* 152–156.

Langer, J. A. (1982). Facilitating text processing: The elaboration of prior knowledge. In J. Langer &

M.T. Smith-Burke (Ed.), *Reader meets author/bridging the gap* (pp. 149–162). Newark, DE: International Reading Association.

Langer, J. A. (1984). Examining background knowledge and text comprehension. *Reading Research Quarterly, 19,* 468–481.

Langer, J. A. (1991). Literacy and schooling: A sociocognitive perspective. In E. H. Hiebert (Ed.), *Literacy for a diverse society* (pp. 9–27). New York: Teachers College Press.

Langer, J. A., & Allington, R. L. (1992). Curriculum research in writing and reading. In P. W. Jackson (Ed.), *Handbook of research on curriculum* (pp. 687–725). New York: Macmillan.

Larsen, S. C., & Hammill, D. D. (1994). *Test of Written Spelling, Third Edition.* Austin, TX: PRO-ED.

Leinhardt, G., Zigmond, N., & Cooley, W. (1981). Reading instruction and its effects. *American Educational Research Journal, 18,* 171–177.

Lesley, L., & Caldwell, J. (1995). *Qualitative Reading Inventory-II.* New York: HarperCollins.

LeTendre, M. J. (1991) The continuing evolution of a federal role in compensatory education. *Educational Evaluation and Policy Analysis, 13,* 328–344.

Liberman, I. Y., & Shankweiler, D. (1979). Speech, the alphabet, and teaching to read. In L. B. Resnick & P. A. Weaver (Eds.), *Theory and practice of early reading* (Vol. 2, pp. 109–134). Hillsdale, NJ: Lawrence Erlbaum.

Lidz, C. S. (1987). Historical perspectives. In C.S. Lidz (Ed.), *Dynamic assessment* (pp. 3–34). New York: Guilford.

Lindfors, J. W. (1980). *Children's language and learning.* Englewood Cliffs, NJ: Prentice-Hall.

Lipson, M. Y. (1982). Learning new information from text: The role of prior knowledge and reading ability. *Journal of Reading Behavior, 14,* 243–262.

Lipson, M. Y. (1983). The influence of religious affiliation on children's memory for text information. *Reading Research Quarterly, 18,* 448–457.

Lipson, M. Y. (1996). Conversations with children and other classroom-based assessment strategies. In L. R. Putnam (Ed.), *How to become a better reading teacher: Strategies for assessment and intervention* (pp. 167–179). Englewood, NJ: Merrill.

Lipson, M.Y., Bigler, M., Poth, L., & Wickizer, B. (1987, December). *Instructional applications of a verbal report methodology.* Paper presented at the 37th Annual Meeting of the National Reading Conference, St. Petersburg, FL.

Lipson, M. Y., & Lang, L. B. (1991). Not as easy as it seems: Some unresolved questions about fluency. *Theory into Practice, 30,* 218–227.

Lipson, M. Y., & Wickizer, E. (1989). Promoting reading independence through instructional dialogue. *Teaching Exceptional Children, 21 (2),* 28–32.

Lipson, M. Y., & Wixson, K. K. (1986). Reading disability research: An interactionist perspective. *Review of Educational Research, 56,* 111–136.

Lipson, M. Y., & Wixson, K. K. (1989). Student evaluation and basal instruction. In P. Winograd, K.K. Wixson, & M.Y. Lipson (Eds.), *Improving basal reading instruction* (pp. 109–139). New York: Teachers College Press.

Lloyd-Jones, R., & Lunsford, A. A. (Eds.) (1989). *The English Coalition Conference: Democracy through language.* Urbana, IL: National Council of Teachers of English and New York: Modern Language Association.

Loban, W. (1976). *Language development: Kindergarten through grade twelve.* Urbana, IL: National Council of Teachers of English.

Lodge, H. C., & Trett, G. L. (1968). *New ways in English.* Englewood Cliffs, NJ: Prentice-Hall.

Lomax, R. G., & McGee, L. M. (1987). Young children's concepts about print and reading: Toward a model of word reading acquisition. *Reading Research Quarterly, 22,* 237–256.

Loughlin, C. E., & Martin, M. D. (1987). *Supporting literacy: Developing effective learning environments.* New York: Teachers College Press.

Lund, N. J., & Duchan, J. F. (1988). *Assessing children's language in naturalistic contexts.* Englewood Cliffs, NJ: Prentice-Hall.

MacGintie, W.H., & MacGinitie, R.K. (1989). *Gates-MacGinitie Reading Tests* (3rd ed.). Chicago, IL: Riverside.

Maier, A. A. (1980). The effect of focusing on the cognitive processes of learning disabled children. *Journal of Learning Disabilities, 13,* 143–147.

Malmstrom, J. (1968). *Introduction to modern English grammar.* Rochelle Park, NJ: Hayden Press.

Mandler, J. M. (1978). A code in the node: The use of story schema in retrieval. *Discourse Processes, 1,* 14–35.

Mandler, J. M., & Johnson, N.S. (1977). Remembrance of things parsed: Story structure and recall. *Cognitive Psychology, 9,* 111–115.

Mangieri, J. N., & Corboy, M. R. (1981). Recreational reading: Do we practice what is preached? *The Reading Teacher, 34,* 923–925.

Manzo, A.V. (1969). The request procedure. *Journal of Reading, 13,* 123–126.

Maria, K. (1986, December). *Refuting misconceptions: Its effect on middle grade children's comprehension.* Paper presented at the 35th Annual Meeting of the National Reading Conference. Austin, TX.

Maria, K. (1990). *Reading comprehension instruction: Issues and strategies.* Parkton, MD: York Press.

Marshall, H. H., & Weinstein, R. S. (1984). Classroom factors affecting students' self-evaluations: An interactional model. *Review of Educational Research, 54,* 301–325.

Marshall, N., & Glock, M. (1978–79). Comprehension of connected discourse: A study into the relationship between the structure of text and information recalled. *Reading Research Quarterly, 14,* 10–56.

Martinez, M., & Roser, N. (1985). Read it again: The value of repeated readings during storytime. *The Reading Teacher, 38,* 782–786.

Marzano, R. J., Pickering, D., & McTighe, J. (1993). *Assessing student outcomes.* Alexandria, VA: ASCD.

Mason, J. (1980). When do children begin to read: An exploration of four-year-old children's letter and word reading competencies. *Reading Research Quarterly, 15,* 203–227.

Mason, J. M., & Au, K. H. (1990). *Reading instruction for today* (2nd ed.). Glenview, IL: Scott, Foresman.

Mason, J., Osborn, J., & Rosenshine, B. (1977). *A consideration of skill hierarchy approaches to the teaching of reading* (Tech. Rep. No. 42). Urbana, IL: University of Illinois, Center for the Study of Reading.

Mason, J., Roehler, L. R., & Duffy, G. G. (1984). A practitioner's model of comprehension instruction. In G. G. Duffy, L. R. Roehler, & J. Mason (Eds.), *Comprehension instruction* (pp. 299–314). New York: Longman.

McAuliffe, S. (1993). Toward understanding one another: Second graders' use of gendered language and story styles. *The Reading Teacher, 47,* 302–310.

McCarthey, S., & Raphael, T. (1992). Alternative perspectives of reading/writing connections. In J. W. Irwin & M. A. Doyle (Eds.), *Reading/writing connections: Learning from research* (pp. 2–30). Newark, DE: International Reading Association.

McCloughlin, (1987). *Parent-teacher conferencing.* Springfield, IL: Charles Thomas Publisher.

McConaughy, S. H. (1982). Developmental changes in story comprehension and levels of questioning. *Language Arts, 59,* 580–589, 600.

McConaughy, S. H. (1985). Good and poor readers' comprehension of story structure across different input and output modalities. *Reading Research Quarterly, 20,* 219–232.

McConnell, C. R. (1982). Readability formulae as applied to college economics textbooks. *Journal of Reading, 26,* 14–17.

McCracken, R. A., & McCracken, M. (1971). Initiating sustained silent reading. *Journal of Reading, 14,* 521–524, 582–583.

McCracken, R. A., & McCracken, M. (1978). Modeling is the key to sustained reading. *The Reading Teacher, 31,* 406–408.

McDermott, R. P. (1977). The ethnography of speaking and reading. In R. W. Shuy (Ed.), *Linguistic theory: What can it say about reading?* (pp. 153–185). Newark, DE: International Reading Association.

McGee. L. A. (1981) Good and poor readers: Ability to distinguish among and recall ideas on different levels of importance. In M. Kamil (Ed.), *Directions in reading: Research and instruction* (30th Yearbook of National Reading Conference, pp. 162–168). Washington, DC: National Reading Conference.

McGee, L. A. (1982). Awareness of text structure: Effects on children's recall of expository text. *Reading Research Quarterly, 17,* 581–590.

McGill-Franzen, A. (1992). Early literacy: What does "developmentally appropriate" mean? *The Reading Teacher, 46,* 56–58.

McKenna, M. C. (1980). *An introduction to the cloze procedure: An annotated bibliography.* Newark, DE: International Reading Association.

McKenna, M. C. (1983). Informal reading inventories: A review of the issues. *The Reading Teacher, 36,* 670–679.

McNeil, J. D. (1992). *Reading comprehension: New directions for classroom practice* (3rd ed.). NY: HarperCollins.

McWilliams, L., & Rakes, T. A. (1979). *Content inventories: English, social studies, science.* Dubuque, IA: Kendall/Hunt.

Meisels, S. (1994). *The WorkSampling System.* Ann Arbor, MI: University of Michigan.

Meltzer, N. S., & Herse, R. (1969). The boundaries of written words as seen by first graders. *Journal of Reading Behavior, 1,* 3–14.

Menyuk, P. (1984). Language development and reading. In J. Flood (Ed.), *Understanding reading comprehension* (pp. 101–121). Newark, DE: International Reading Association.

Messick, S. (1989). Validity. In R. E. Linn (Ed.), *Educational measurement (3rd Ed.).* New York: Macmillan.

Meyer, B. J., Brandt, D. M., & Bluth, G. S. (1980). Use of top-level structure in text: Key for reading comprehension of ninth-grade students. *Reading Research Quarterly, 16,* 72–103.

Meyer, B. J., & Freedle, R. O. (1984). Effects of discourse type on recall. *American Educational Research Journal, 21,* 121–143.

Mezynski, K. (1983). Issues concerning acquisition of knowledge: Effects of vocabulary training on reading comprehension. *Review of Educational Research, 53,* 253–279.

Michaels, S. (1981). "Sharing time": Children's narrative styles and differential access to literacy. *Language in Society, 10,* 423–442.

Mikkelsen, N. (1991). Toward greater equity in literacy education: Storymaking and non-mainstream students. *Language Arts, 67,* pp. 556–566.

Millett, N. C. (1986). *Teaching the writing process: A guide for teachers and supervisors.* Boston: Houghton-Mifflin.

Mills, R. E. (1956). An evaluation of techniques for teaching word recognition. *Elementary School Journal, 56,* 221–225.

Minami, M., & McCabe, A. (in press). Haiku as a discourse regulation device: A stanza analysis of Japanese children's personal narratives. *Language in Society.*

Mitchell, J. V. (1985). *The ninth mental measurements yearbook.* Lincoln, NE: Buros Institute of Mental Measurements.

Moffett, J. (1985). Hidden impediments to improving English teaching. *Phi Delta Kappan, 67,* 50–56.

Moll, L. C., & Diaz, E. (1987). Change as the goal of educational research. *Anthropology and Education Quarterly, 18,* 300–311.

Moll, L. C., & Diaz, S. (1985). Ethnographic pedagogy: Promoting effective bilingual instruction. In E. Garcia & R. V. Padilla (Eds.), *Advances in bilingual education research* (pp. 127–149). Tucson, AZ: University of Arizona Press.

Moll, L. C., Estrada, E., Diaz, E., & Lopes, L. M. (1980). The organization of bilingual lessons: Implications for schooling. *The Quarterly Newsletter of the Laboratory of Comparative Human Cognition, 2,* 53–58.

Moll, L. C., & Gonzalez, N. (1994). Critical Issues: Lessons from research with language-minority children. *Journal of Reading Behavior, 26,* 439–456.

Montague, M., Cleborne, D., Maddux, D., & Dereshiwsky, M. I. (1990). Story grammar and comprehension and production of narrative prose by students with learning disabilities. *Journal of Learning Disabilities, 23,* 190–197.

Morgan, D. P. (1981). *A primer on individualized education programs for exceptional children.* Reston, VA: The Foundation for Exceptional Children.

Mork, T. A. (1972). Sustained silent reading in the classroom. *The Reading Teacher, 25,* 438–441.

Morris, D. (1981). Concept of word: A developmental phenomenon in the beginning reading and writing processes. *Language Arts, 58,* 659–668.

Morrow, L. M. (1983). Home and school correlates of early interest in literature. *Journal of Educational Research, 76,* 221–230.

Morrow, L. M. (1986). Encouraging voluntary reading: The impact of a literature program on children's use of library centers. *Reading Research Quarterly, 21,* 330–346.

Morrow, L. M. (1987). Promoting voluntary reading: Activities represented in basal reader manuals. *Reading Research and Instruction, 26,* 189–202.

Morrow, L. M. (1989). Creating a bridge to children's literature. In P. Winograd, K. Wixson, & M. Lipson (Eds.), *Improving basal reading instruction* (pp. 210–230). New York: Teachers College Press.

Mosenthal, P., & Na, T. (1980). Quality of children's recall under two classroom testing tasks: Towards a socio-psycholinguistic model of reading comprehension. *Reading Research Quarterly, 15* 504–528.

Moss, P. A. (1994). Validity. In R. J. Sternberg (Ed.), *Encyclopedia of human intelligence*, Vol. 2 (pp. 1101–1106). New York: Macmillan.

Mulligan, J. (1974). Using language experience with potential high school dropouts. *Journal of Reading, 18,* 206–211.

Nagy, W. E. (1988). *Teaching vocabulary to improve reading comprehension*. Urbana, IL: ERIC Clearinghouse on Reading and Communication Skills and the National Council of Teachers of English.

Nagy, W. E., & Anderson, R. C. (1984). How many words are there in printed school English? *Reading Research Quarterly, 19,* 304–330.

Nagy, W. E., Anderson, R. C., & Herman, P. (1987). Learning word meanings from context during normal reading. *American Educational Research Journal, 24,* 237–270.

Nagy, W. E., & Herman, P. (1987). Breadth and depth of vocabulary knowledge: Implications for acquisition and instruction. In M.G. McKeown & M.E. Curtis (Eds.), *The nature of vocabulary acquisition* (pp. 19–36). Hillsdale, NJ: Lawrence Erlbaum.

Nagy, W.E., Herman, P. A., & Anderson, R. C. (1985). Learning words from context. *Reading Research Quarterly, 20,* 233–253.

Neill, D. M., & Median, J. (1989). Standardized tests: Harmful to educational health. *Phi Delta Kappan, 70,* 688–697.

Nelson-Herber, J. (1986). Expanding and refining vocabulary in content areas. *Journal of Reading, 29,* 626–633.

Newkirk, T., & Atwell, N. (1988). *Understanding writing: Ways of observing, learning and teaching.* Portsmouth, NH: Heinemann.

Newmann, F. M., & Wehlage, G. G. (1993). Five standards of authentic instruction. *Educational Leadership, 8–12.*

Newton, E. S. (1977). Andragogy: Understanding the adult as learner. *Journal of Reading, 20,* 361–363.

Nicholson, T., Pearson, P. D., & Dykstra, R. (1979). Effects of embedded anomalies and oral reading errors on children's understanding of stories. *Journal of Reading Behavior, 11,* 339–354.

North, S. (1987). *The making of knowledge in composition: Portrait of an emerging field.* Portsmouth, NH: Boynton Cook, Heinemann.

Norton, D. E. (1993). *The effective teaching of language arts* (4th ed.). NY: Merrill/Macmillan.

Nurss, J. R. (1979). Assessment of readiness. In T. G. Waller & G. E. MacKinnon (Eds.), *Reading research: Advances in theory and practice* (Vol. 1, pp. 31–62). New York: Academic Press.

Nurss, J. R., & McGauvran, M.E. (1976/1986). *Metropolitan Readiness Tests (MRT)*. San Antonio, TX: The Psychological Corporation.

Nurss, J. R., & McGauvran, M. E. (1995). *Metropolitan Readiness Test. Sixth Edition*. San Antonio, TX: The Psychological Corporation.

Oberlin, K. J., & Shugarman, S. L. (1989). Implementing the reading workshop with middle school learning-disabled readers. *Journal of Reading, 32,* 682–687.

O'Flahavan, J. F., & Tierney, R. J. (1991). Reading, writing, and critical thinking. In L. Idol, & B. F. Jones (Eds.), *Educational values and cognitive instruction: Implications for reform* (pp. 41–64). Hillsdale, NJ: Lawrence Erlbaum.

Ogle, D. M. (1986). K-W-L: A teaching model that develops active reading of expository text. *The Reading Teacher, 39,* 564–570.

Ogle, D. M. (1989). The know, want to know, learn strategy. In K. D. Muth (Ed.), *Children's comprehension of text: Research into practice* (pp. 205–223). Newark, DE: International Reading Association.

Okagaki, L., & Sternberg, R. J. (1991). Cultural and parental influences on cognitive development. In L. Okagaki and R. J. Sternberg (Eds.), *Directors of development: Influences on the development of children's thinking* (pp. 101–120). Hillsdale, NJ: Lawrence Erlbaum.

Ollila, L. O., & Mayfield, M. I. (1992). Home and school together: Helping beginning readers succeed. In J. Samuels & A. E. Farstrup (Eds.), *What research has to say about reading instruction* (pp. 17–45). Newark, DE: International Reading Association.

Olshavsky, J.E. (1978). Comparison profiles of good and poor readers across materials of increasing difficulty. In P. D. Pearson & J. Hansen (Eds.), *Reading: Disciplined inquiry in process and practice* (27th Yearbook of The National Reading Conference, pp. 73–76). Washington, DC: National Reading Conference.

Olson, M. W. (1985). Text type and reader ability: The effects of paraphrase and text-based inference questions. *Journal of Reading Behavior, 17,* 199–214.

Omanson, R. C., Beck, I. L., McKeown, M. G., & Perfetti, C.A. (1984). Comprehension of texts with unfamiliar versus recently taught words: An assessment of alternative models. *Journal of Educational Psychology, 76,* 1253–1268.

Onosko, J. J., & Newmann, F. M. (1994). Creating more thoughtful learning environments. In J. N. Mangieri & C. C. Block (Eds.), *Creating powerful thinking in teachers and students* (pp. 27–49). Fort Worth, TX: Harcourt Brace.

Osborn, J. H. (1984). The purposes, uses, and contents of workbooks and some guidelines for publishers. In R. C. Anderson, J. Osborn, & R. J. Tierney (Eds.), *Learning to read in American schools: Basal readers and content texts* (pp. 45–112). Hillsdale, NJ: Lawrence Erlbaum.

Osborn, J. H. (1989). Summary: Improving basal reading programs. In P. Winograd, K.

Wixson, & M. Y. Lipson (Eds.), *Improving basal reading instruction* (pp. 203–226). New York: Teachers College Press.

Otto, W., Wolf, A., & Eldridge, R. (1984). Managing instruction. In P. D. Pearson, R. Barr, M. Kamil, & P. Mosenthal (Eds.), *Handbook of reading research* (pp. 799–828). New York: Longman.

Ovando, C. J. (1988). Language diversity and education. In J. A. Banks & C. A. McGee Banks (Eds.), *Multicultural education: Issues and perspectives* (pp. 208–227). Boston, MA: Allyn & Bacon.

Ovando, C. J. (1993). Language diversity and education. In J. A. Banks & C. A. McGee Banks (Eds.), *Multicultural education: Issues and perspectives* (pp. 215–235). Boston: Allyn & Bacon.

Page, W. D., & Pinnell, G. S. (1979). *Teaching reading comprehension: Theory and practice.* Urbana, IL: ERIC Clearinghouse on Reading and Communication Skills and the National Council of Teachers of English.

Paley, V. (1981). *Wally's stories.* Chicago: University of Chicago Press.

Palincsar, A. S. (1986). The quest for the meaning from expository text: A teacher-guided journey. G. Duffy, L. Roehler, & J. Mason (Eds.), *Comprehension instruction: Perspectives and suggestions* (pp. 251–264). White Plains, NY: Longman.

Palincsar, A. S. (1986). The role of dialogue in providing scaffolded instruction. *Educational Psychologist, 21,* 73–98.

Palincsar, A. S., & Brown, A. L. (1984). Reciprocal teaching of comprehension-fostering and monitoring activities. *Cognition and Instruction, 1,* 117–175.

Palmatier, R. A. (1973). A notetaking system for learning. *Journal of Reading, 17,* 36–39.

Palmatier, R. A., & Bennett, J.M. (1974). Notetaking habits of college students. *Journal of reading, 18,* 215–218.

Pany, D., & Jenkins, J. (1978). Learning word meanings: A comparison of instructional procedures and effects on measures of reading comprehension with learning disabled students. *Learning Disabilities Quarterly, 1,* 21–32.

Pappas, C. C., Kiefer, B. Z., & Levstik, L. S. (1995). *An integrated language perspective in the elementary school, 2nd edition.* New York: Longman.

Paratore, J. R., & Indrisano, R. (1987). Intervention assessment of reading comprehension. *The Reading Teacher, 40,* 778–783.

Paris, S. G. (1988). Models and metaphors of learning strategies. In C. Weinstein, E. T. Goetz, & P. A. Alexander (Eds.), *Learning and study strategies: Issues in assessment, instruction, and evaluation* (pp. 299–321). San Diego: Academic Press.

Paris, S. G. (1991). Assessment and remediation of metacognitive aspects of children's reading comprehension. *Topics in Language Disorders, 12,* 32–50.

Paris, S. G., Cross, D. R., & Lipson, M.Y. (1984). Informed strategies for learning: A program to improve children's reading awareness and comprehension. *Journal of Educational Psychology, 76*, 1239–1252.

Paris, S. G., Lipson, M. Y., & Wixson, K.K. (1983). Becoming a strategic reader. *Contemporary Educational Psychology, 8*, 293–316.

Paris, S. G., & Myers, M. (1981). Comprehension monitoring in good and poor readers. *Journal of Reading Behavior, 13*, 5–22.

Paris, S. G., Newman, R. S., & McVey, K. A. (1982). Learning the functional significance of mnemonic actions: A microgenetic study of strategy acquisition. *Journal of Experimental Child Psychology, 34*, 490–509.

Paris, S. G., Olson, G., & Stevenson, H. (Eds.). (1983). *Learning and motivation in the classroom.* Hillsdale, NJ: Lawrence Erlbaum.

Paris, S. G., Wixson, K. K., & Palincsar, A. S. (1986). Instructional approaches to reading comprehension. In E. Rothkopf (Ed.) *Review of research in education* (pp. 91–128). Washington, DC: American Educational Research Association.

Parsons, L. (1990). *Response journals.* Portsmouth, NH: Heinemann.

Pauk, W. (1974). *How to study in college.* Boston: Houghton Mifflin.

Pearson, P. D. (1974–75). The effects of grammatical complexity on children's comprehension, recall, and conception of certain semantic relations. *Reading Research Quarterly, 10*, 155–192.

Pearson, P. D. (1982). *Asking questions about stories* (Ginn Occasional Papers, No. 15). Lexington, MA: Silver Burdett & Ginn.

Pearson, P. D. (1993). Standards for the English language arts: A policy perspective. *Journal of Reading Behavior, 25*, 457–475.

Pearson, P. D., & Fielding, L. (1991). Comprehension instruction. In R. Barr, M. Kamil, P. Mosenthal, & P. D. Pearson (Eds.), *Handbook of reading research*, Vol. 2, (pp. 815–860). New York: Longman.

Pearson, P. D., & Gallagher, M. (1983). The instruction of reading comprehension. *Contemporary Educational Psychology, 8*, 317–344.

Pearson, P. D., Hansen, J., & Gordon, C. (1979). The effect of background knowledge on young children's comprehension of explicit and implicit information. *Journal of Reading Behavior, 11*, 201–209.

Pearson, P. D., & Johnson, D. (1978). *Teaching reading comprehension.* New York: Holt, Rinehart & Winston.

Perfetti, C. A., & Hogaboam, T. (1975). The relationship between single word decoding and reading comprehension skill. *Journal of Educational Psychology, 67*, 461–469.

Peterson, B. (1991). Selecting books for beginning readers. In D. E. DeFord, C. A. Lyons, & G. S. Pinnell (Eds.), *Bridges to literacy: Learning from reading recovery* (pp. 119–138). Portsmouth, NH: Heinemann.

Peterson, J., Greenlaw, M. J., & Tierney, R. J. (1978). Assessing instructional placement with an IRI: The effectiveness of comprehension questions. *Journal of Educational Research, 17*, 247–250.

Philips, S. U. (1982). *The invisible culture: Communication in classroom and community on the Warm Springs Indian Reservation.* New York: Longman.

Piaget, J. (1960). *Language and thought of the child.* London: Routledge & Kegan Paul.

Picturesque word origins (1933). Springfield, MA: Merriam.

Pikulski, J. J. (1994). Preventing reading failure: A review of five effective programs. *The Reading Teacher, 48,* 30–39.

Pikulski, J. J., & Shanahan, T. (1982). Informal reading inventrories: A critical analysis. In J. J. Pikulski & T. Shanahan (Eds.), *Approaches to the informal evaluation of reading* (pp. 94–116). Newark: DE International Reading Association.

Pikulski, J. J., & Tobin, A. W. (1982). The cloze procedure as an informal assessment technique. In J. J. Pikulski & T. Shanahan (Eds.), *Approaches to the informal evaluation of reading* (pp. 42–62). Newark, DE: International Reading Association.

Pinnell, G. S. (1985). Helping teachers help children at risk: Insights from the Reading Recovery Program. *Peabody Journal of Education, 62,* 70–85.

Pinnell, G. S. (1987). Helping teachers see how readers read: Staff development through observation. *Theory into Practice, 26,* 51–58.

Pinnell, G. S. (1991). Interactive assessment: Teachers and children as learners. In J. A. Roderick (Ed.), *Context-responsive approaches to assessing children's language* (pp. 79–96). Urbana, IL: National Conference on Research in English.

Pinnell, G. S., Pikulski, J. J., Wixson, K. K., Campbell, J., R., Gough, P. B., and Beatty, A. S. (1995). *Listening to children read aloud.* Washington, DC: U. S. Department of Education, National Center for Education Statistics.

Polloway, E. A., & Patton, E. A. (1993). *Strategies for teaching learners with special needs* (5th ed.). New York: Merrill.

Popham, W. J. (1978). *Criterion-referenced measurement.* Englewood Cliffs, NJ: Prentice-Hall.

Poplin, M. (1984). Summary rationalizations, apologies and farewell: What we don't know about the learning disabled. *Learning Disabilities quarterly, 7,* 130–134.

Porter, J. (1974). Research report. *Elementary English, 51,* 144–151.

Powell, W. R. (1980). Measuring reading performance informally. *Journal of Children and Youth, 1,* 23–31.

Powell, W. R., & Dunkeld, C. G. (1971). The validity of IRI reading levels. *Elementary English, 48,* 637–642.

Purves, A. C. (1985). That sunny dome: Those caves of ice. In C. R. Cooper (Ed.), *Researching response to literature and the teaching of literature: Points of departure* (pp. 54–59). Norwood, NJ: Ablex.

Rakes, T. A., & Smith, L. (1986). Assessing reading skills in the content areas. In E. K. Dishner, T. W. Bean, J. E. Readence, & D. W. Moore (Eds.), *Reading in the content areas: Improving classroom instruction* (2nd ed., pp.

145–159). Dubuque, IA: Kendall/Hunt.

Raphael, T. E. (1982). Question-answering strategies for children. *The Reading Teacher, 36,* 186–190.

Raphael, T. E. (1986). Teaching question-answer relationships, revisited. *The Reading Teacher, 39,* 516–522.

Raphael, T. E., & Englert, C. S. (1989). Integrating writing and reading instruction. In P. Winograd, K. Wixson, & M. Lipson (Eds.), *Improving basal reading instruction* (pp. 231–255). New York: Teachers College Press.

Raphael, T. E., & Englert, C. S. (1990). Writing and reading: Partners in constructing meaning. *The Reading Teacher, 43,* 388–400.

Raphael, T. E., Englert, C. S., & Kirschner, B. W. (1989). Acquisition of expository writing skills. In J. M. Mason (Ed.), *Reading and writing connections* (pp. 261–290). Boston: Allyn & Bacon.

Raphael, T. E., Winograd, P. & Pearson, P. D. (1980). Strategies children use in answering questions. In M. L. Kamil & A. J. Moe (Eds.), *Perspectives in reading research and instruction* (29th Yearbook of The National Reading Conference, pp. 56–63). Washington, DC: National Reading Conference.

Rasinski, T. V. (1986). Repeated readings–naturally. *The Reading Teacher, 39,* 244–245.

Read, C. (1971). Preschool children's knowledge of English phonology. *Harvard Educational Review, 41,* 1–34.

Read, C. (1975). *Children's categorization of speech sounds in English.*

Urbana, IL: National Council of Teachers of English.

Read, C. (1986). *Children's creative spelling.* London: Routledge & Kegan Paul.

Readence, J. E., Bean, T. W., & Baldwin, R. S. (1985). *Content area reading: An integrated approach* (2nd ed.). Dubuque, IA: Kendall/Hunt.

Readence, J. E., & Moore, D. (1980). Differentiating text assignments in content areas: Slicing the task. *Reading Horizons, 20,* 112–117.

Reid, D. K., Hresko, W. P., & Hammill, D. D. (1989). *The Test of Early Reading Ability (TERA–2).* Austin, TX: Pro-Ed.

Reid, J. F. (1966). Learning to think about reading. *Educational Research, 9,* 56–62.

Resnick, L. B., & Resnick, D. L. (1992). Assessing the thinking curriculum: New tools for educational reform. In B. R. Gifford & M.C. O'Connor (Eds.), *Future assessments: Changing views of aptitude, achievement, and instruction* (pp. 37–75). Boston, MA: Kluwer.

Reutzel, D. R. (1985). Story maps improve comprehension. *The Reading Teacher, 38,* 400–404.

Rey, H. A. (1941). *Curious George.* Boston: Houghton Mifflin.

Rhodes, L. K., & Shanklin, N. (1990). Miscue analysis in the classroom. *The Reading Teacher, 44,* 252–254.

Ringler, L. H., & Weber, C. K. (1984). *A language-thinking approach to reading.* San Diego: Harcourt Brace Jovanovich.

Roberts, P. (1962). *English sentences.* New York: Harcourt Brace Jovanovich.

Robinson, H. M. (1972). Perceptual training–Does it result in reading improvement? In R.C. Aukerman (Ed.), *Some persistent questions in beginning reading* (pp. 135–150). Newark, DE: International Reading Association.

Rogers, D. B. (1984). Assessing study skills. *Journal of Reading, 27,* 346–354.

Rogers, V. R., & Stevenson, C. (1988). How do we know what kids are learning in school? *Educational Leadership, 45 (5),* 68–75.

Rogoff, B. (1990). *Apprenticeship in thinking: Cognitive development in social context.* New York: Oxford University Press.

Rosenbaum, J. E. (1980). Social implications of educational grouping. In D. C. Berliner (Ed.), *Review of Research in Education* (Vol 8, pp. 361–401). Washington, DC: American Educational Research Association.

Rosenblatt, L. (1978). *The reader, the text, and the poem: The transactional theory of literary work.* Carbondale: Southern Illinois University.

Rosenblatt, L. (1982). The literary transaction: Evocation and response. *Theory into Practice, 21,* 268–277.

Rosenshine, B. V. (1979). Content, time, and direct instruction. In P. L. Peterson & H. J. Walberg (Eds.), *Research on teaching: Concepts, findings, and implications* (pp. 28–56). Berkeley, CA: McCutchan.

Rosenshine, B. V., & Stevens, R. (1984). Classroom instruction in reading. In P. D. Pearson, R. Barr, M. Kamil, & P. Mosenthal (Eds), *Handbook of reading research* (pp.

745–798). New York: Longman.

Rowe, M. B. (1974). Wait time and rewards as instructional variables, their influence on language, logic, and fate control: Part one—Wait time. *Journal of Research in Science Teaching 11,* 81–94.

Ruddell, M. R. (1993). *Teaching content reading and writing.* Boston, MA: Allyn & Bacon.

Ruddell, R. B. (1965). Effect of the similarity of oral and written language structure on reading comprehension. *Elementary English, 42,* 403–410.

Rumelhart, D. (1977). Toward an interactive model of reading. In S. Dornic (Ed.), *Attention and performance VI* (pp. 573–603). Hillsdale, NJ: Lawrence Erlbaum.

Rupley, W. H. (1976). Effective reading program. *The Reading Teacher, 29,* 616–623.

Russell, D. (1991). *Writing in the academic disciplines, 1870–1990: A curricular history.* Carbondale, IL: Southern Illinois University Press.

Sadowski, M. (1980). Ten years of uninterrupted sustained silent reading. *Reading Improvement, 17,* 153–156.

Salvia, J., & Ysseldyke, J. E. (1988). *Assessment in special education and remedial education* (4th ed.). Boston: Houghton Mifflin.

Samuels, S. J. (1979). The method of repeated readings. *The Reading Teacher, 32,* 403–408.

Sarason, S. B, & Doris, J. (1979). *Educational handicap, public policy, and social history.* New York: Free Press.

Sardy, S. (1985). Thinking about reading. In T. L. Harris & E. J.

Cooper (Eds.), *Reading, thinking and concept development* (pp. 213–229). New York: College Entrance Examination Board.

Savage, J. F. (1977). *Effective communication.* Chicago: Science Research Association.

Sawyer, D. J. (1987). *Test of Awareness of Language Segments (TALS).* Rockville, MD: Aspen.

Scardamalia, M., Bereiter, C., & Goelman, H. (1982). The role of production factors in writing ability. In M. Nystrand (Ed.), *What writers know: The language process and structure of written discourse* (pp. 173–210). San Diego, CA: Academic Press.

Schell, L. M. & Hanna, G. S. (1981). Can informal reading inventories reveal strengths and weaknesses in comprehension subskills? *The Reading Teacher, 35,* 263–268.

Scheu, J. A., Tanner, D. K., & Au, K. H. (1989). Integrating seatwork with the basal lesson. In P. Winograd, K. K. Wixson, & M. Y. Lipson (Eds.), *Improving basal reading instruction* (pp. 58–73). New York: Teachers College Press.

Schlagal, R. (1995). Teaching disabled spellers. In R. Putnam (Ed.), *How to become a better reading teacher* (pp. 307–316). Englewood Cliffs, NJ: Merrill.

Schmidt, W., Caul, J. Byers, J., & Buchman, M. (1984). Content of basal reading selections: Implications for comprehension instruction. In G. Duffy, L. R. Roehler, & J. Mason (Eds.), *Comprehension instruction* (pp. 144–162). New York: Longman.

Schmuck, R. A. (1980). The school organization. In J. H. McMillan (Ed.), *The social psychology of school learning* (pp. 169–214). New York: Academic Press.

Schumaker, J. B., Deshler, D. D., Alley, G. R., & Warner, M. M. (1983). Toward the development of an intervention model for learning disabled adolescents. *Exceptional Education Quarterly, 3 (4),* 45–50.

Schunk, D. H. (1989). Social cognitive theory and self-regulated learning. In B. J. Zimmerman & D. H. Schunk (Eds.), *Self-regulated learning and academic achievement* (pp. 83–110). New York: Springer-Verlag.

Schuyler, M. R. (1982). A readability program for use on microcomputers. *Journal of Reading, 25,* 560–591.

Scribner, S., & Cole, M. (1981). *The psychology of literacy: A case study among the Vai.* Cambridge, MA: Harvard University Press.

Searfoss, L. W., & Readence, J. E. (1985). *Helping children learn to read* (1st ed.). Englewood Cliffs, NJ: Prentice-Hall.

Searfoss, L. W., & Readence, J. E. (1989). *Helping children learn to read* (2nd ed.). Englewood Cliffs, NJ: Prentice-Hall.

Sendak, M. (1963). *Where the wild things are.* New York: Harper & Rowe.

Shake, M. C. (1989). Grouping and pacing with basal materials. In P. Winograd, K. K. Wixson, & M. Y. Lipson (Eds.), *Improving basal reading instruction* (pp. 62–85). New York: Teachers College Press.

Shanahan, T., & Lomax, R. (1986). An analysis and comparison of theoretical models of the reading-writing relationship. *Journal of Educational Psychology, 78,* 116–123.

Shannon, P. (1983). The use of commercial reading materials in American elementary schools. *Reading Research Quarterly, 19,* 68–85.

Sharp, S. J. (1990). Using content subject matter with LEA in middle school. *Journal of Reading, 33,* 108–112.

Shepard, L. A. (1986, April). *School readiness and kindergarten retention: A policy analysis.* Paper presented at the Annual Meeting of the American Educational Research Association, San Francisco, CA.

Shepard, L. A., & Smith, M. L. (1986). Synthesis of research on school readiness and kindergarten retention. *Educational Leadership, 20,* 78–86.

Shimmerlik, S. (1978). Organization theory and memory for prose: A review of the literature. *Review of Educational Research, 48,* 103–121.

Silvaroli, N. J. (1982). *Classroom reading inventory* (4th ed.). Dubuque, IA: William C. Brown.

Silvaroli, N. J. (1994). *Classroom reading inventory.* (7th ed.), Madison, WI: Wm. C. Brown and Benchmark.

Silvaroli, N. J., Kear, D. J., & McKenna, M. C. (1982). *A classroom guide to reading assessment and instruction.* Dubuque, IA: Kendall/Hunt.

Simmons, W., & Resnick, L. (1993). Assessment as a catalyst of school reform. *Educational Leadership, 50,* 11–15.

Singer, J., & Donlon, D. (1982). Active comprehension: Problem-solving schema with question generation for comprehension of complex short stories. *Reading Research Quarterly, 17,* 166–168.

Sipay, E. R. (1974). *Sipay Word Analysis Tests.* Cambridge, MA: Educators Publishing Service.

Slavin, R. E. (1983). *Cooperative learning.* New York: Longman.

Slavin, R. E. (1989). Students at risk of school failure: The problem and its dimensions. In R. E. Slavin, N. L. Karweit, & N. A. Madden (Eds.), *Effective programs for students at risk* (pp. 3–19). Boston: Allyn and Bacon.

Slavin, R. E., Stevens, R. J., & Madden, N. A. (1988). Accommodating student diversity in reading and writing instruction: A cooperative learning approach. *Reading and Special Education, 9,* 60–66.

Sleeter, C. E. (1985, March). *Why is there learning disabilities? A critical analysis of the birth of the field in its social context.* Paper presented at the Annual Meeting of the American Education Research Association, Chicago, IL.

Slosson, R. L. (1983). *Slosson Oral Reading Test/Slosson Intelligence Test* (2nd ed.). East Aurora, NY: Slosson.

Smith, D. D. (1979). The improvement of children's oral reading though the use of teacher modeling. *Journal of Learning Disabilities, 12,* 39–42.

Smith, T. E., Polloway, E. A., Patton, J. R., & Dowdy, C. A. (1995). *Teaching children with special needs in inclusive settings.* Boston: Allyn and Bacon.

Spector, J. E. (1992). Predicting progress in beginning reading: Dynamic assessment of phonemic awareness. *Journal of Educational Psychology, 84,* 353–363.

Spiegel, D. L. (1981). Six alternatives to the Directed Reading Activity. *The Reading Teacher, 34,* 914–923.

Squire, J. (1983). Composing and comprehending: Two sides of the same basic process. *Language Arts, 60,* 581–589.

Squire, J. (1991). The history of the profession. In J. Flood, J. Jensen, D. Lapp, & J. Squire (Eds), *Handbook of research on teaching the English language arts.* New York: Macmillan.

Stahl, S. A. (1986). Three principles of effective vocabulary instruction. *Journal of Reading, 29,* 662–668.

Stahl, S. A., & Fairbanks, M. (1986). The effects of vocabulary instruction: A model-based meta-analysis. *Review of Educational Research, 56,* 72–110.

Stallings, J., Needels, M., & Sparks, G. M. (1987). Observation for the improvement of classroom learning. In D. C. Berliner & B. V. Rosenshine (Eds.), *Talks to teachers* (pp. 129–158). New York: Random House.

Stanovich, K. E. (1986). Matthew effects in reading: Some consequences of individual differences in the acquisition of literacy. *Reading Research Quarterly, 21,* 360–406.

Staton, J. (1987). The power of responding in dialogue journals. In T. Fulwiler (Ed.), *The journal book* (p. 63). Portsmouth, NH: Heinemann.

Stauffer, R. (1969). *Teaching reading as a thinking process.* New York: Harper & Row.

Stauffer, R. (1980). *Directing the reading-thinking process.* New York: Harper & Row.

Stein, N. L., & Glenn, C. G. (1979). An analysis of story comprehension in elementary school children. In R. O. Freedle (Ed.), *New directions in discourse processing* (Vol. 2, pp. 53–120). Norwood, NJ: Ablex.

Stein, N. L., & Nezworski, M. T. (1978). The effects of organization and instructional set on story memory. *Discourse Processes, 1,* 177–193.

Stein, N. L., & Policastro, M. (1984). The concept of a story: A comparison between children's and teachers' viewpoints. In H. Mandl, N. L. Stein, & T. Trabasso (Eds.), *Learning and comprehension of text* (pp. 113–158). Hillsdale, NJ: Lawrence Erlbaum.

Sternberg, R. J. (1985). *Beyond IQ: Toward a triarchic theory of intelligence.* Cambridge, MA: Cambridge University Press.

Stevens, R. J., Madden, N. A., Slavin, R. E., & Farnish, A. M. (1987). Cooperative integrated reading and composition: Two field experiments. *Reading Research Quarterly, 23,* 433–454.

Stewig, J. W., & Nordberg, B. (1995). *Exploring language arts in the elementary classroom.* Belmont, CA: Wadsworth Publishing Co.

Stoll, D. R. (1990). *Magazines for children.* Newark, DE: International Reading Association.

Stotsky, S. (1983). Research on reading/writing relationship: A synthesis and suggested directions. *Language Arts, 60,* 627–642.

Sulzby, E. (1986a). Children's elicitation and use of metalinguistic knowledge about "word" during literacy interactions. In D. B. Yaden & S. Templeton (Eds.), *Metalinguistic awareness and beginning literacy* (pp. 219–234). Portsmouth, NH: Heinemann.

Sundbye, N. (1987). Text explicitness and inferential questioning: Effects on story understanding and recall. *Reading Research Quarterly, 22,* 82–98.

Swanson, H. L., & Watson, B. L. (1982). *Educational and psychological assessment of exceptional children.* St. Louis: Mosby.

Taba, H. (1967). *Teacher's handbook for elementary social studies.* Reading, MA: Addison-Wesley.

Tancock, S. M. (1994). A literacy lesson framework for children with reading problems. *The Reading Teacher, 48,* 130–140.

Taylor, B. M. (1982). A summarizing strategy to improve middle grade students' reading and writing skills. *The Reading Teacher, 36,* 202–205.

Taylor, B. M. (1986). Teaching middle grade students to summarize content textbook material, In J. F. Baumann (Ed.), *Teaching main idea comprehension* (pp. 195–209). Newark, DE: International Reading Association.

Taylor, B. M., Harris, L. A., & Pearson. P. D. (1988). *Reading difficulties: Instruction and assessment.* New York: Random House.

Taylor, B. M., & Samuels, S. J. (1983). Children's use of text structure in the recall of expository material. *American Educational Research Journal, 20,* 234–237.

Taylor, W. L. (1953). Cloze procedure: A new tool for measuring readability. *Journalism Quarterly, 30,* 415–433.

Tchudi, S. (1994). *Integrated language arts in the elementary school.* Belmont, CA: Wadsworth Publishing Company.

Teale, W. H., Hiebert, E. H., & Chittenden, E. A. (1987). Assessing young children's literacy development. *The Reading Teacher, 40,* 772–777.

Teale, W. H., & Sulzby, E. (Eds.). (1986). *Emergent literacy: Writing and reading.* Norwood, NJ: Ablex.

Temple, C., & Gillet, J. W. (1984). *Language Arts.* Boston: Little, Brown, and Co.

Temple, C., & Gillet, J. W. (1989). *Language arts: Learning processes and teaching practices* (2nd ed.). Glenview, IL: Scott, Foresman.

Temple, C., Nathan, R., Burris, N., & Temple, F. (1988). *The beginnings of writing.* Boston: Allyn & Bacon.

Templeton, S. (1991). *Teaching the integrated language arts.* Boston: Houghton-Mifflin.

Templeton, S. (1995). Spelling: The foundation of word knowledge for the less proficient reader. In M. L. Putnam (Ed.), *How to become a better reading teacher* (pp. 317–329). Englewood Cliffs, NJ: Merrill.

Thorndike, R. L. (1972). *Stanford-Binet Intelligence Scale,* (Third Revision, Form L-M). Boston: Houghton-Mifflin.

Thorndyke, P. W. (1977). Cognitive structures in comprehension and memory of narrative discourse. *Cognitive Psychology, 9,* 77–110.

Tierney, R., Readence, J. E., & Dishner, E. (1985). *Reading strategies and practices: A compendium* (2nd ed.). Boston: Allyn & Bacon.

Tierney, R. J. (1992). Ongoing research and new directions. In J. W. Irwin & M. A. Doyle (Eds.), *Reading/writing connections: Learning from research* (pp. 247–259). Newark, DE: International Reading Association.

Tierney, R. J., Carter, M. A., & Desai, L. E. (1991). *Portfolio assessment in the reading-writing classroom.* Norwood, MA: Christopher Gordon.

Tikunoff, W. J., & Ward, B. A. (1983). Collaborative research on teaching. *Elementary School Journal, 83,* 453–468.

Tinker, M. A., & McCullough, C. M., (1968). *Teaching elementary reading.* (3rd ed.). New York; Appleton-Century-Crofts.

Torgesen, J. K., & Bryant, B. R. (1994). *Test of Phonological Awareness.* Austin, TX: PRO-ED.

Torgesen, J. K., & Licht, B. G. (1983). The learning disabled child as an inactive learner; Retrospect and prospects. In J. McKinney & L. Feagans (Eds.), *Topics in learning disabilities* (Vol. 1, pp. 3–31). Norwood, NJ: Ablex.

Trabasso, T. (1981). On the making of inferences during reading and their assessment. In J. T. Guthrie (Ed.), *Comprehension and teaching: Research reviews* (pp. 56–76). Newark, DE: International Reading Association.

Tunmer, W. E., Herriman, M. L., & Nesdale, A. R. (1988). Metalinguistic abilities and beginning reading. *Reading Research Quarterly, 23,* 134–158.

Turner, J. C. (1995). The influence of classroom contexts on young children's motivation for literacy. *Reading Research Quarterly, 30,* 410–441.

Turner, J., & Paris, S. G. (1995). How literacy tasks influence children's motivation for literacy. *The Reading Teacher, 48,* 662–673.

Vacca, R. T., & Padak, N. D. (1990). Who's at risk in reading? *Journal of Reading, 33,* 486–488.

Vacca, R. T., & Vacca, J. L. (1989). *Content area reading* (3rd ed.). Glenview, IL: Scott, Foresman.

Valencia, S. (1990a). A portfolio approach to classroom assessment; The whys, whats, and hows. *The Reading Teacher, 43,* 338–340.

Valencia, S. (1990b). Portfolio Assessment: Separating the wheat from the chaff. *The Reading Teacher, 44,* 60–61.

Valencia, S.W., & Calfee, R. (1991). The development and use of literacy portfolios for students, classes, and teachers. *Applied Measurement in Education, 4*(4), 333–345.

Valencia, S., McGinley, W., & Pearson, P. D. (1990). Assessing reading and writing: Building a more complete picture. In G. Duffy & P. Anders (Eds.) *Reading in the middle schools* (pp. 124–153). Newark, DE: International Reading Association.

Valencia, S., & Pearson, P. D. (1987). Reading assessment: Time for a change. *The Reading Teacher, 40,* 726–733.

Valencia, S. W., & Place, N. A. (1994). Literacy portfolios for teaching, learning, and accountability: The Bellevue literacy assessment project. In S. W. Valencia, E. H. Hiebert, & P. P. Afflerbach (Eds.), *Authentic reading assessment: Practices and possibilities* (pp. 134–166). Newark, DE: International Association.

Valencia, S., Stallman, A. C., Commeyras, M., Hartman, D.K., Pearson, P. D., & Greer, E. A. (1987, December). *Three methods of assessing prior knowledge: A validation sutdy.* Paper presented at The National Reading Conference, St. Petersburg, FL.

Vaughan, J. L., & Estes, T. H. (1986). *Reading and reasoning beyond the primary grades.* Boston: Allyn & Bacon.

Villa, R. A., & Thousand, J. S. (Eds.) (1995). *Creating an inclusive school.* Alexandria, VA: ASCD.

Villaume, S. K., Worder, T., Williams, S., Hopkins, L., Rosenblatt, C. (1994). Five teachers in search of a discussion. *The Reading Teacher, 47,* 480–487.

Vygotsky, L. S. (1978). *Mind in society: The development of higher psychological process.* Cambridge, MA: Harvard University Press.

Vygotsky, L. S. (1986). *Thought and language.* Cambridge, MA: MIT Press.

Wade, S. E. (1990). Using think alouds to assess comprehension. *The Reading Teacher, 43,* 442–453.

Walp, T. P., & Walmsley, S. A. (1989). Instructional and philosophical congruence: Neglected aspects of coordination. *The Reading Teacher, 42,* 364–368.

Walsh, W. B., & Betz, N. E. (1990). *Tests and assessment* (2nd ed.).

Englewood Cliffs, NJ: Prentice-Hall.

Walters, J., Seidel, S., & Gardner, H. (1994). Children as reflective practitioners. In J. N. Mangieri & C. C. Block (Eds.), *Creating powerful thinking in teachers and students* (pp. 289–303). Fort Worth, TX: Harcourt Brace.

Wang, M. C., Haertel, G. D., & Walberg, H. J. (1994). What helps students learn? *Educational Leadership, 51,* 74–79.

Warncke, E. W., & Shipman, D. A. (1984). *Group assessment in reading: Classroom teacher's handbook.* Englewood Cliffs, NJ: Prentice-Hall.

Weiner, B. (1992). *Human motivation: Metaphors, theories, and research.* Newbury Park, CA: Sage.

Weinstein, C. E., Goetz, E. T., & Alexander, P. A. (1988). *Learning and study strategies: Issues in assessment, instruction, and evaluation.* San Diego: Academic Press.

Weinstein, R. S. (1976). Reading group membership in first grade: Teacher behaviors and pupil experience over time. *Journal of Educational Psychology, 68,* 103–116.

Wells, G. (1982). Story reading and the development of symbolic skills. *Australian Journal of Reading, 5,* 142–152.

Wells, G. (1986). *The meaning makers: Children learning language and using language to learn.* Portsmouth, NH: Heinemann.

Wepner, S. B., & Feeley, J. T. (1993). *Moving forward with literature: Basals, books, and beyond.* New York: Merrill.

Westby, C. (1988). Test Review: Test of Language Development—2.

Primary. *The Reading Teacher, 42,* 236–237.

Wide Range Achievement Test 3 (1993). Wilmington, DE: Wide Range Inc.

Wiederholt, J. L., & Bryant, B. R. (1992). *Gray Oral Reading Test–3.* Austin, TX: PRO-ED.

Wigfield, A., & Asher, S. R. (1984). Social and motivational influences on reading. In P. D. Pearson, R. Barr, M. Kamil, & P. Mosenthal (Eds.), *Handbook of reading research* (pp. 423–452). New York: Longman.

Wiggins, G. (1989). Teaching to the (authentic) test. *Educational Leadership, 46,* 141–147.

Will, M. (1986). *Educating students with learning problems: A shared responsibility.* Washington, DC: Office of Special Education and Rehabilitation Services, U. S. Department of Education.

Williams, J. P., Taylor, M. B., & deCani, J. S. (1984). Constructing macrostructure for expository text. *Journal of Educational Psychology, 76,* 1065–1075.

Wilson, R. M., & Cleland, C. J. (1989). *Diagnostic and remedial reading for classroom and clinic.* Columbus, OH: Charles E. Merrill.

Winograd, P. N., & Johnston, P. (1987). Some considerations for advancing the teaching of reading comprehension. *Educational Psychologist, 22,* 213–230.

Wisconsin Department of Public Instruction. (1989). *Strategic learning in the content areas.* Madison, WI.

Wittrock, M. C., Marks, C., & Doctorow, M. (1975). Reading as a generative process. *Journal of Educational Psychology, 67,* 484–489.

Wixson, K. K. (1979). Miscue analysis: A critical review. *Journal of Reading Behavior, 11,* 163–175.

Wixson, K. K. (1983a). Postreading question-answer interactions and children's learning from text. *Journal of Educational Psychology, 30,* 413–423.

Wixson, K. K. (1983b). Questions about a text: What you ask about is what children learn. *The Reading Teacher, 37,* 287–293.

Wixson, K. K. (1984). Level of importance of postquestions and children's learning from text. *American Educational Research Journal, 21,* 419–434.

Wixson, K. K., & Lipson, M. Y. (1986). Reading (dis)ability: An interactionist perspective. In T.E. Raphael (Ed.), *Contexts of school-based literacy* (pp. 131–148). New York: Random House.

Wixson, K. K., & Peters, C. W. (1989). Teaching the basal selection. In P. Winograd, K. K. Wixson, & M. Y. Lipson (Eds.), *Improving basal reading instruction* (pp. 21–61). New York: Teachers College Press.

Wixson, K. K., Peters, C. W., Weber, E. M., & Roeber, E. D. (1987). New directions in statewide reading assessment. *The Reading Teacher, 40,* 749–755.

Wixson, S. E. (1985). Test review: The Test of Early Reading Ability (TERA). *The Reading Teacher, 38,* 544–547.

Wong, B. Y. L., Wong, R., & Blenkisop, J. (1989). Cognitive and metacognitive aspects of learning-disabled adolescents' composing problems. *Learning Disabilities Quarterly, 12,* 300–323.

Wong, F. L. (1991). Second-language learning in children: A model of language learning in social context. In E. Bialystok (Ed.), *Language processing in bilingual children* (pp. 49–69). Cambridge UK: Cambridge University Press.

Wong, J., & Au, K. H. (1985). The concept-text-application approach: Helping elementary students comprehend expository text. *The Reading Teacher, 38,* 612–618.

Wood, D. J., Burner, J. S., & Ross, G. (1976). The role of tutoring in problem solving. *Journal of Child Psychology and Psychiatry, 17,* 89–100.

Wood, K. D. (1988). Techniques for assessing students' potential for learning. *The Reading Teacher, 41,* 440–447.

Wood, K. D., & Robinson, N. (1983). Vocabulary, language, and prediction: A prereading strategy. *The Reading Teacher, 36,* 392–395.

Wood, K. D., Lapp, D., & Flood, J. (1992). *Guiding readers through text: A review of study guides.* Newark, DE: International Reading Association.

Woodcock, R. (1978). *Woodcock-Johnson Psychoeducational Battery.* Hingham, MA: Teaching Resources Corp.

Woodcock, R. W. (1987). *Woodcock Reading Mastery Test-Revised.* Circle Pines, MN: American Guidance Service.

Woods, M. L., & Moe, A. J. (1985). *Analytical reading inventory* (3rd ed.). Columbus, OH: Charles E. Merrill.

Yopp, H. T. (1988). The validity and reliability of phonemic awareness tests. *Reading Research Quarterly, 23,* 159–177.

Young, A., & Fulwiler, T. (Eds.). (1986). *Writing across the disciplines.* Portsmouth, NH: Boynton/Cook.

Ysseldyke, J. E., & Christenson, S. L. (1987). *The Instructional Environment Scale (TIES).* Austin, TX: Pro-Ed.

Zakaluk, B. L., & Samuels, S. J. (1988). Toward a new approach to predicting text comprehensibility. In B. L. Zakaluk & S. J. Samuels (Eds.), *Readability: Its past, present, and future* (pp. 121–144). Newark, DE: International Reading Association.

Zigmond, N., Vallecorsa, A., & Leinhardt, G. (1980). Reading instruction for students with learning disabilities. *Topics in Language Disorders, 1,* 89–98.

Zins, J. E., Curtis, M. J., Graden, J. L., & Ponti, C. R. (1988). *Helping students succeed in the regular classroom.* San Francisco: Jossey-Bass.

Author Index

Subject Index